AF412556

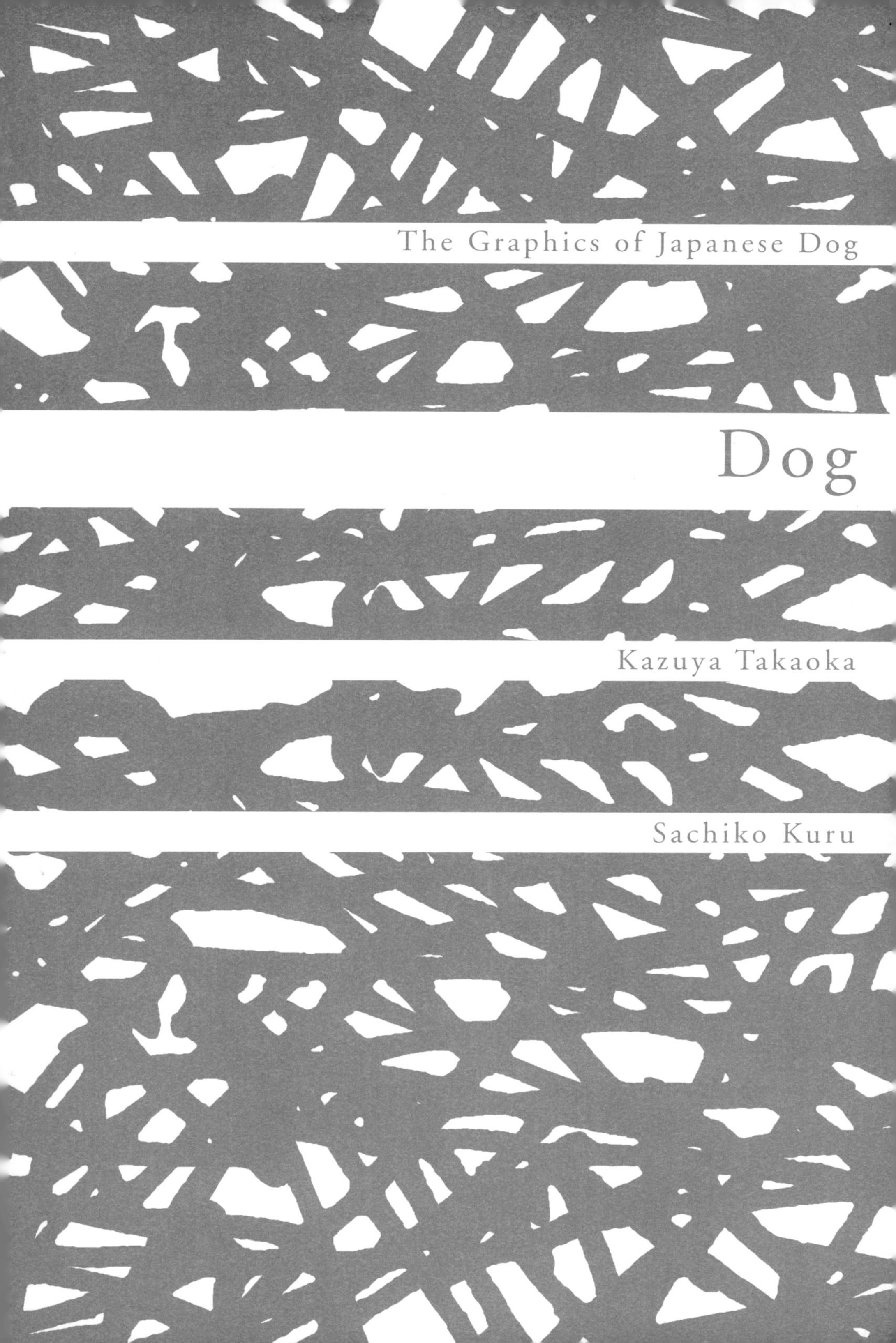

The Graphics of Japanese Dog

Dog

Kazuya Takaoka

Sachiko Kuru

日本の犬

高岡一弥

久留幸子

Dog

Book and cover design © 2005 Kazuya Takaoka
Photographs © 2005 Sachiko Kuru
Published by PIE BOOKS

PIE BOOKS
2-32-4, Minami-Otsuka, Toshima-ku, Tokyo 170-0005 Japan
Tel: +81-3-5395-4811 Fax: +81-3-5395-4812
http://www.piebooks.com
e-mail: editor@piebooks.com e-mail: sales@piebooks.com

ISBN 4-89444-493-3 C0072
Printed in Japan

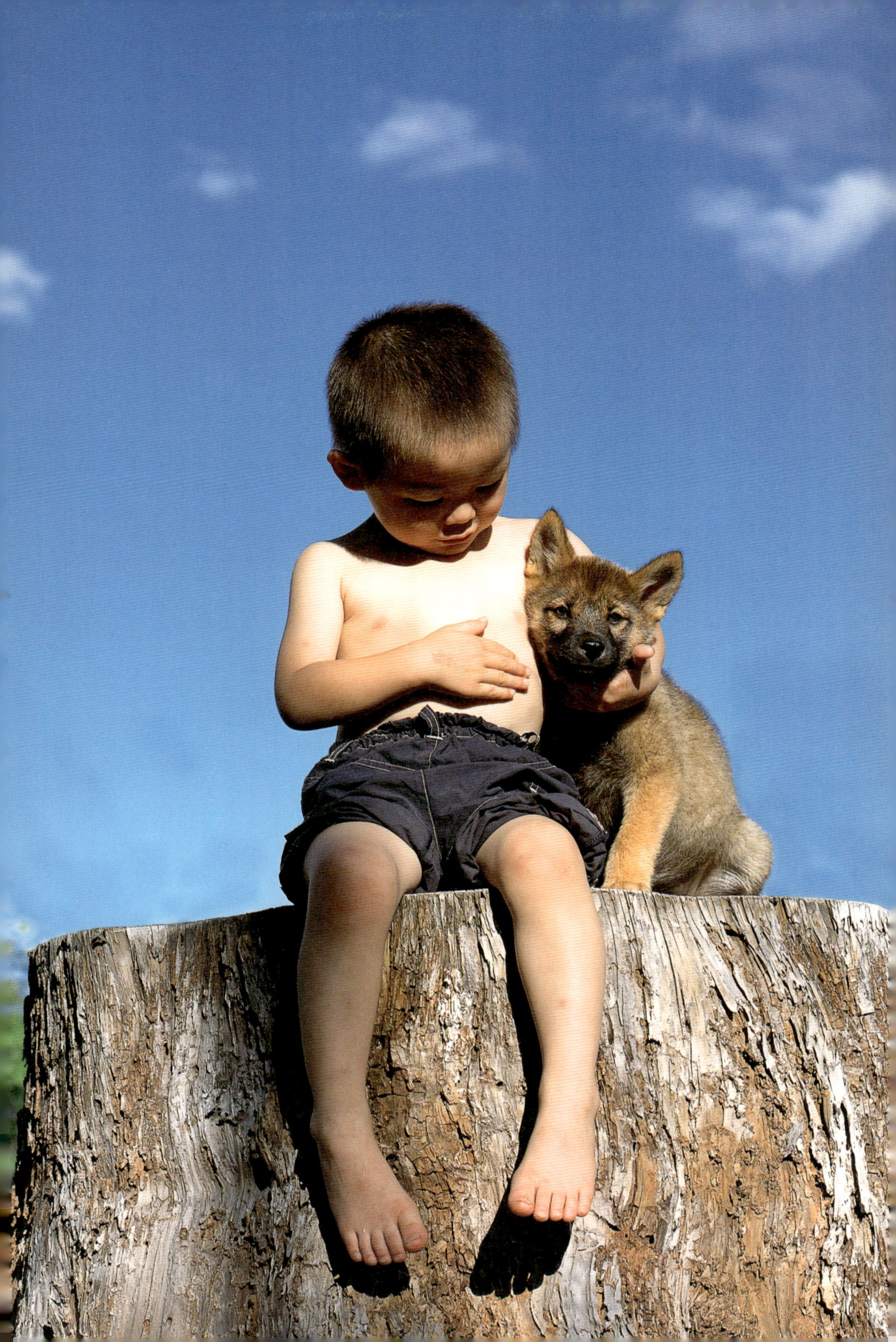

十二支第十一番

戌・イヌ・犬

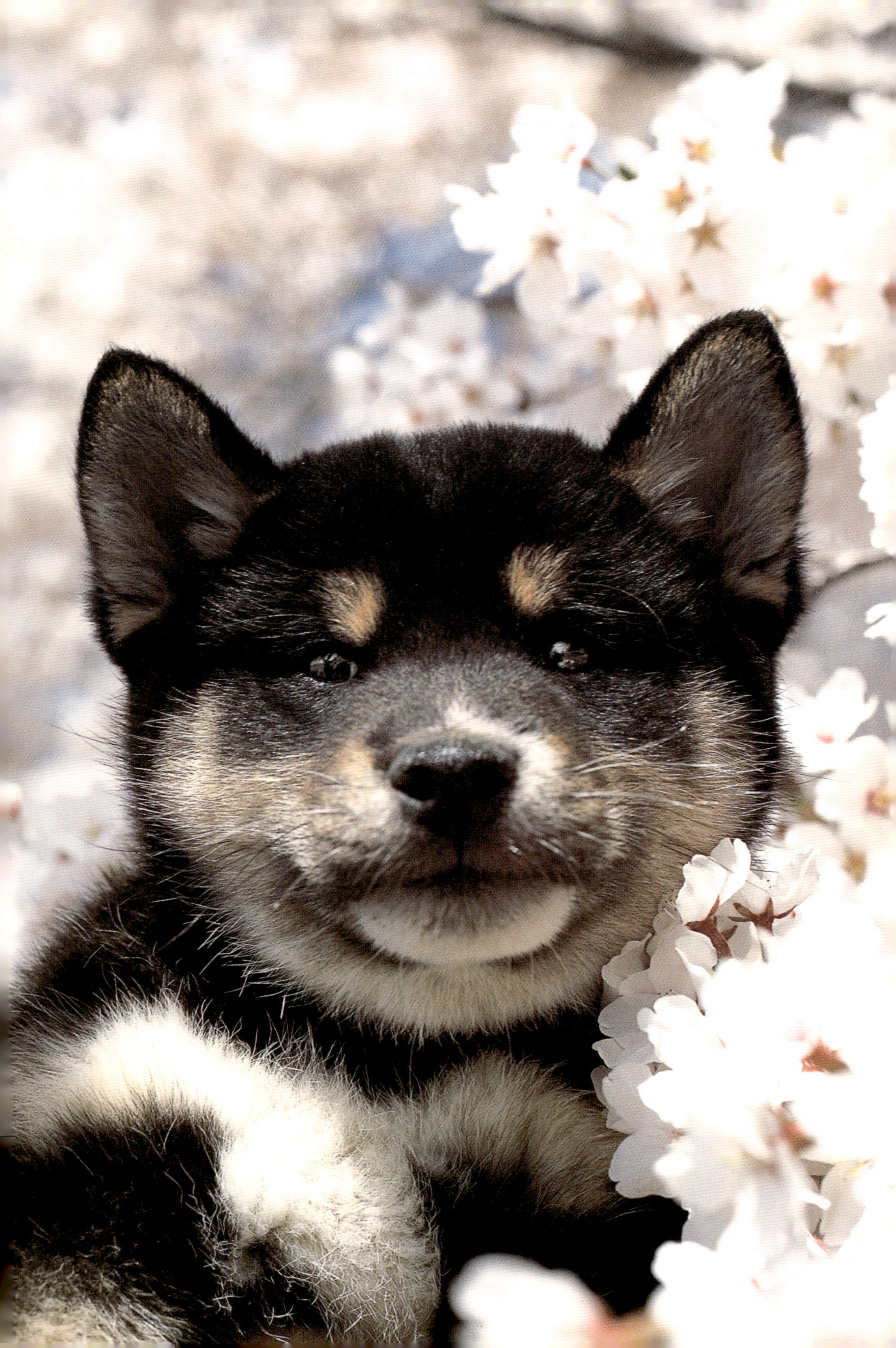

Contents

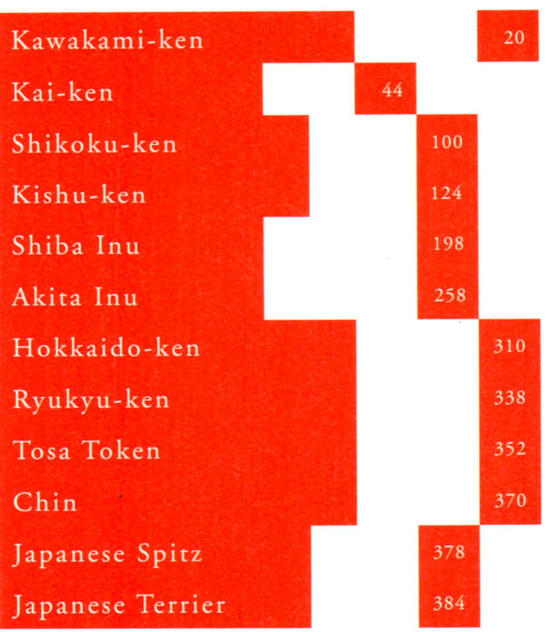

目次

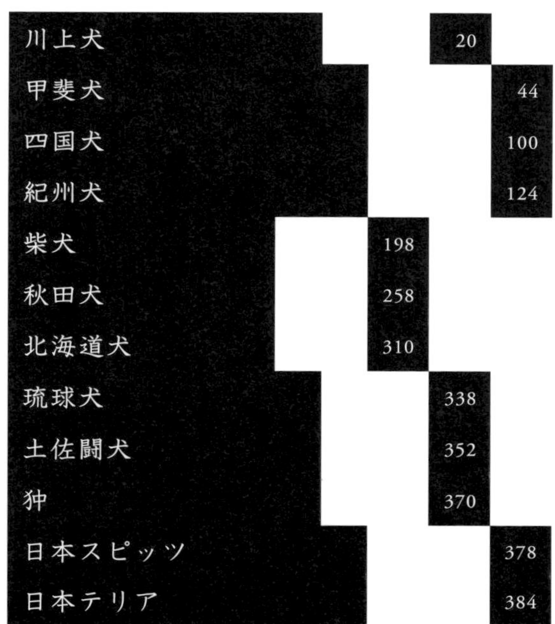

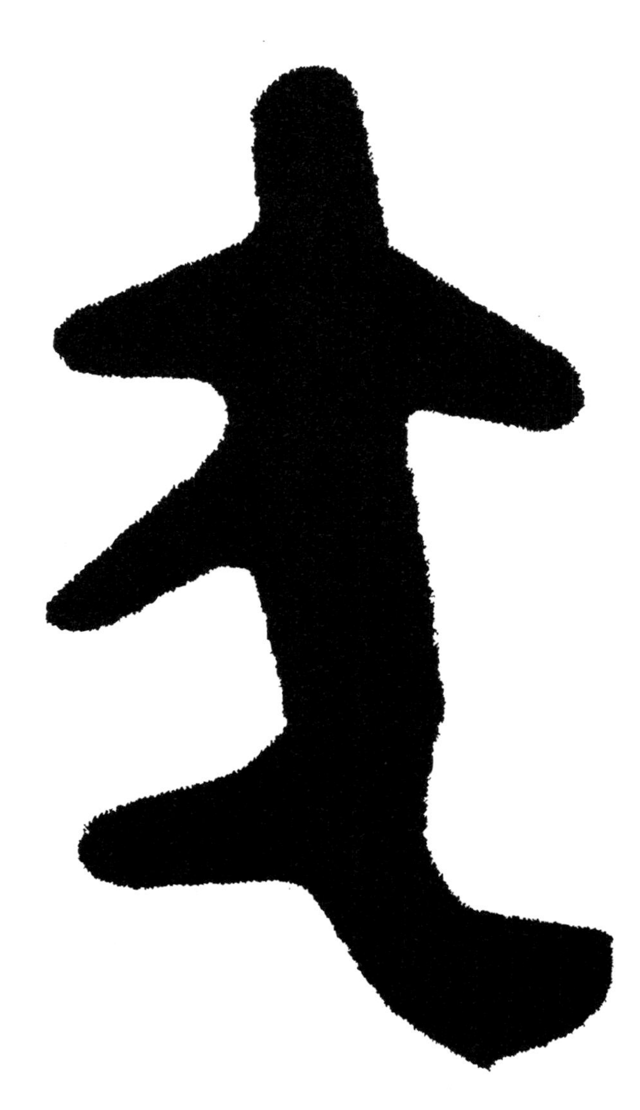

金分 1 – Kinbun Type

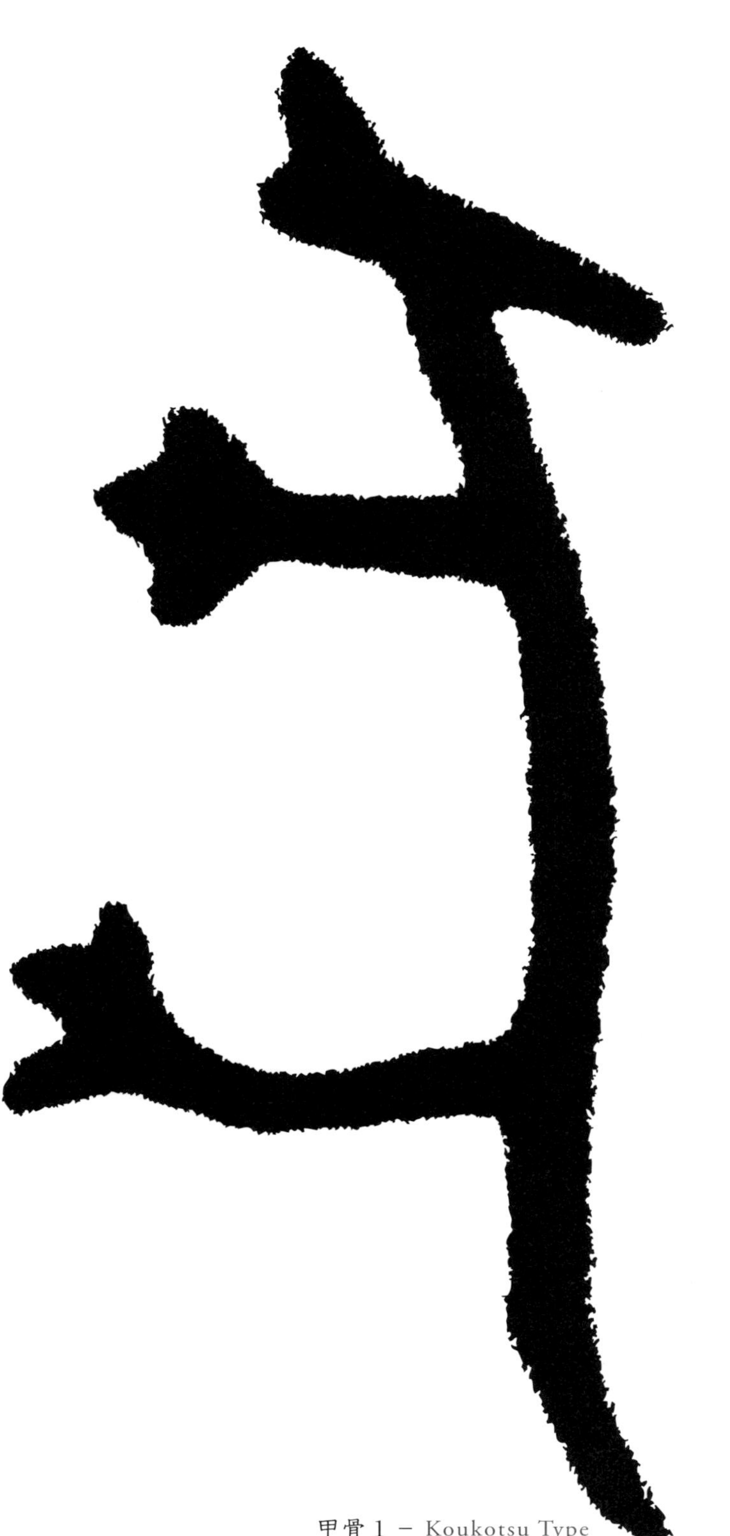

甲骨 1 － Koukotsu Type

犬 【いぬ】 象形。犬の形。「いぬ」をいう。猟犬と

Inu (dog)　　Hieroglyph in the shape of a dog, pronounced "inu". Takes the shape

して使われたらしい逞しい犬の形に書かれている。

Such dogs were interred beneath the coffin or along the wall of the burial chamber in

殷・周代の古い王墓には、王の墓を衞る武人ととも

along with warriors to guard the grave of the king, in a practice known in Japanese as

に棺の下や墓室の壁よりの所に犠牲（いけにえ）

meaning to inter a person and a dog to ward off evil spirits lurking in the ground. In

として埋められていることがあり、これを伏（人と

dogs that seem to have been beloved pets of the king were decked out in gold and

犬とを組み合わせた形）・伏瘞（人と犬とを埋めて

Dogs were especially esteemed as a sacrifice. The practice of worshipping the all-

地中にひそむ悪霊を祓うこと）という。戦国時代

(later referred to as "rui ni tsukuru" i.e. to "make rui"). This involved making an

（紀元前四世紀〜前三世紀）の王墓には、愛犬であっ

sending the smell of the burning beast up into the heavens.　　＞＞

たらしい犬が金銀の飾りをつけて埋葬されている。

of a burly hound of the type that was apparently used for hunting.

ncient royal tombs of the Yin and Zhou dynasties,

uku (combining the characters for person and dog) or fukuei,

he royal tombs of the Warring States period (4000–3000 BC),

ilver finery for burial with their master.

owerful deity in the heavens was known as rui

ffering of grain and burning a sacrificial dog,

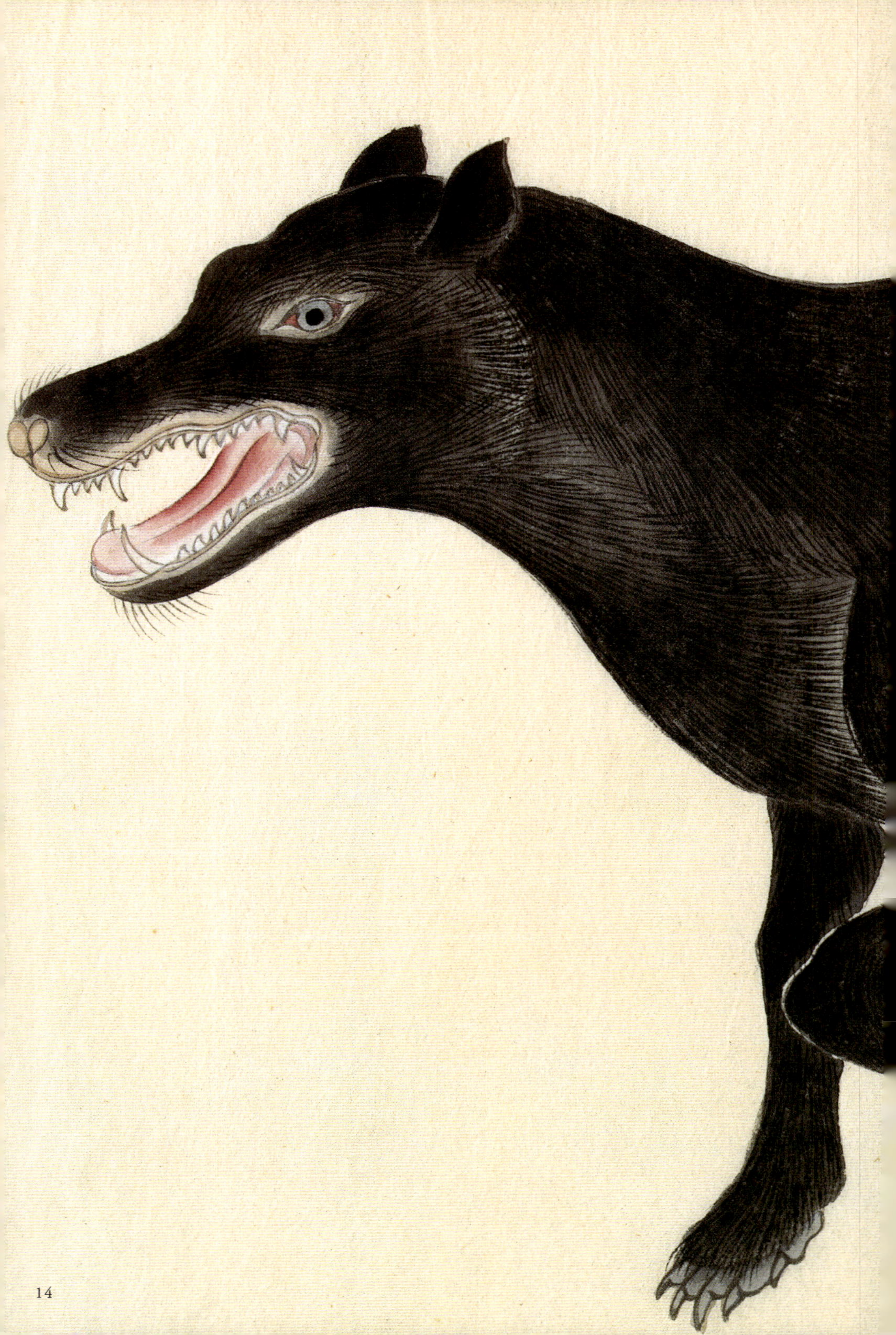

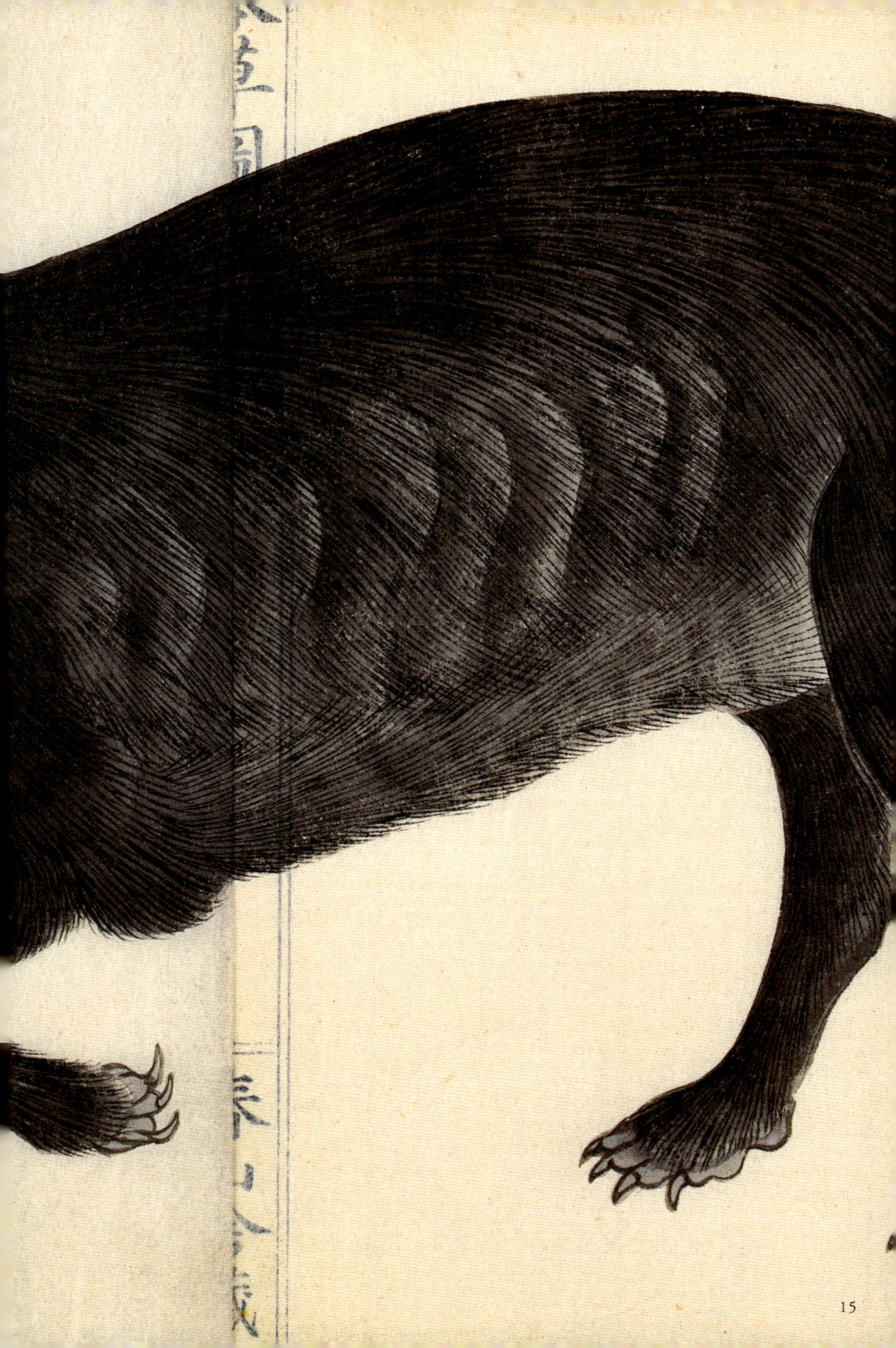

犬は犠牲としては特に貴いものとされ、天にいる上帝

The practice of placing a sacrificial dog alongside well-aged sake (furuzake

を祀ることを類（類。のちには禷に作る）といい、

the gods and ask their will is known as hakarigoto（獷），

穀物を供え、いけにえの犬を焼いてその臭いを天

a combination of the characters for furuzake and dog.

に昇らせて祀っている。神に供える酋（ふるざけ）

A term for a puppy is ku（狗），the radical on the left being a variant of the characte

にいけにえの犬をそえて、神を祀り神意に謀るこ

just as the word for colt is also written as ku（駒），with the character for horse o

とを獣（はかりごと）という。子犬を狗というの

The joyo kanji (list of kanji in common usage)

は、子馬を駒というのと同じ。常用漢字の字形は類・

includes the characters 類（rui: type）　　and 器（utsuwa: vessel）in which

器となっており、犬の部分が大（手足を広げて立っ

the dog（犬）part has been changed to 大（big: a front-on view of a person standin

ている人を正面から見た形）に変えられ、犬牲と

In the process, the important meaning of a canine sacrifice has been lost.

いう重要な意味が失われている。――――― 常用字解

used as an offering to worship

or dog,

he left.

with their arms and legs spread).

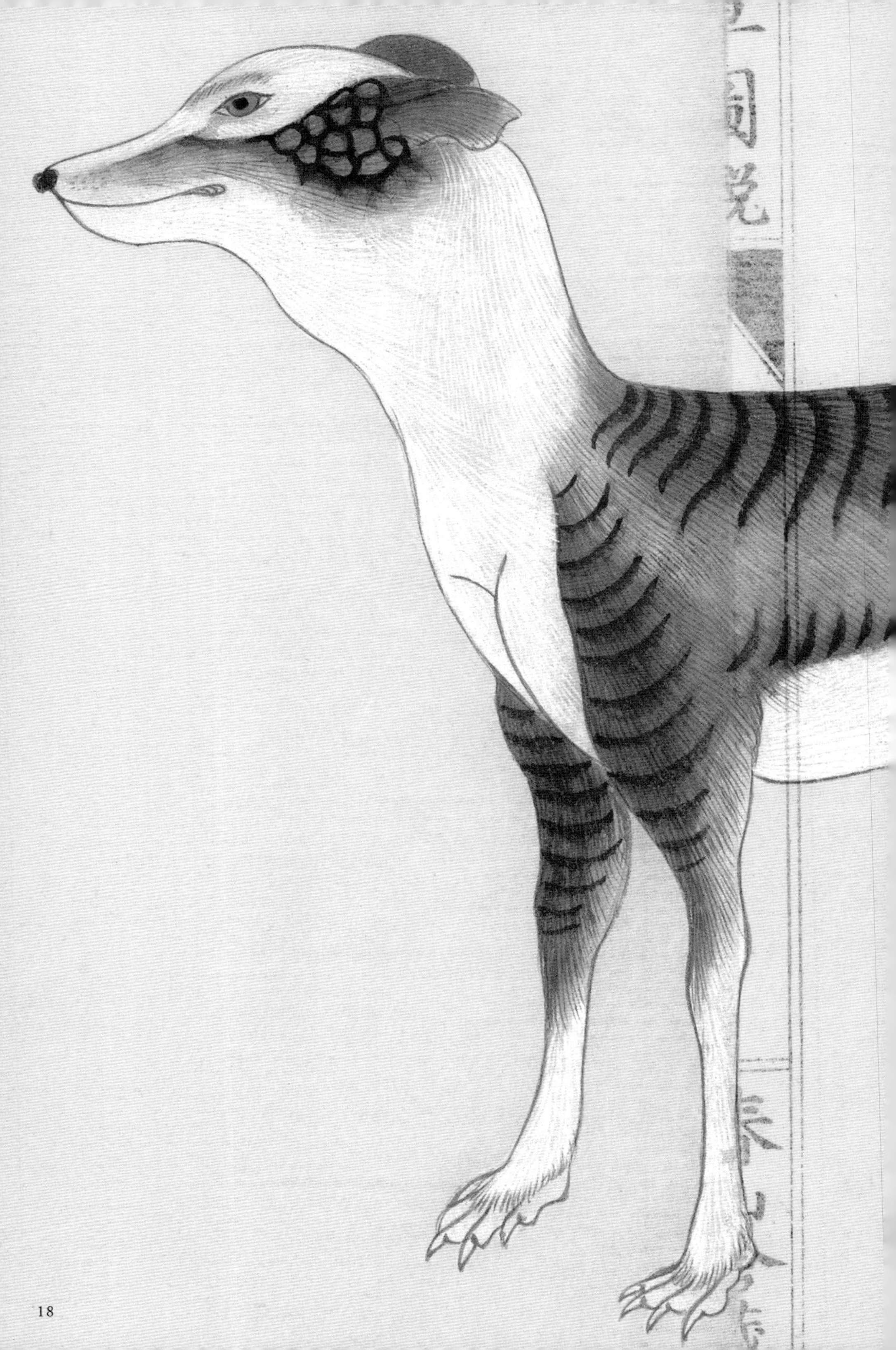

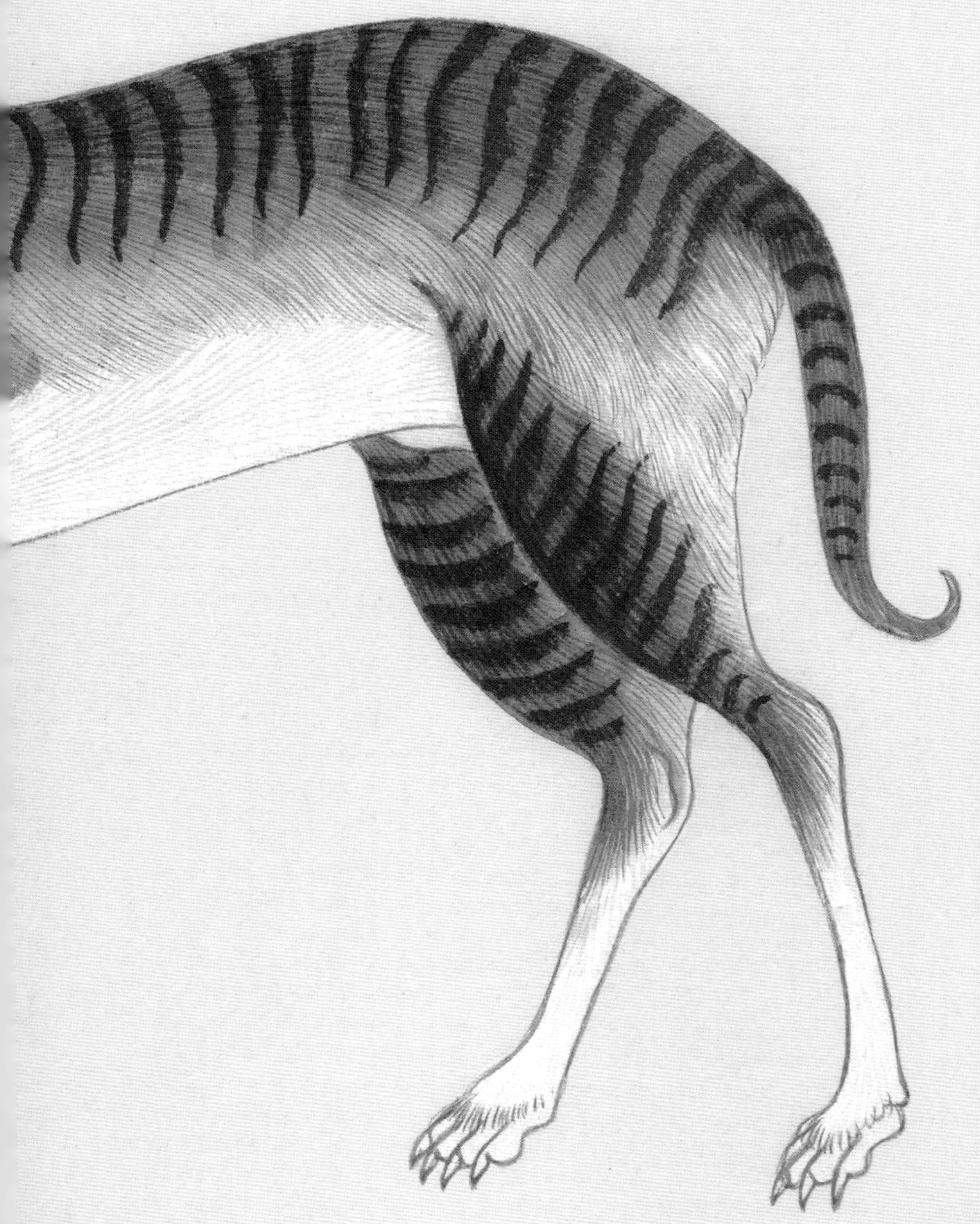

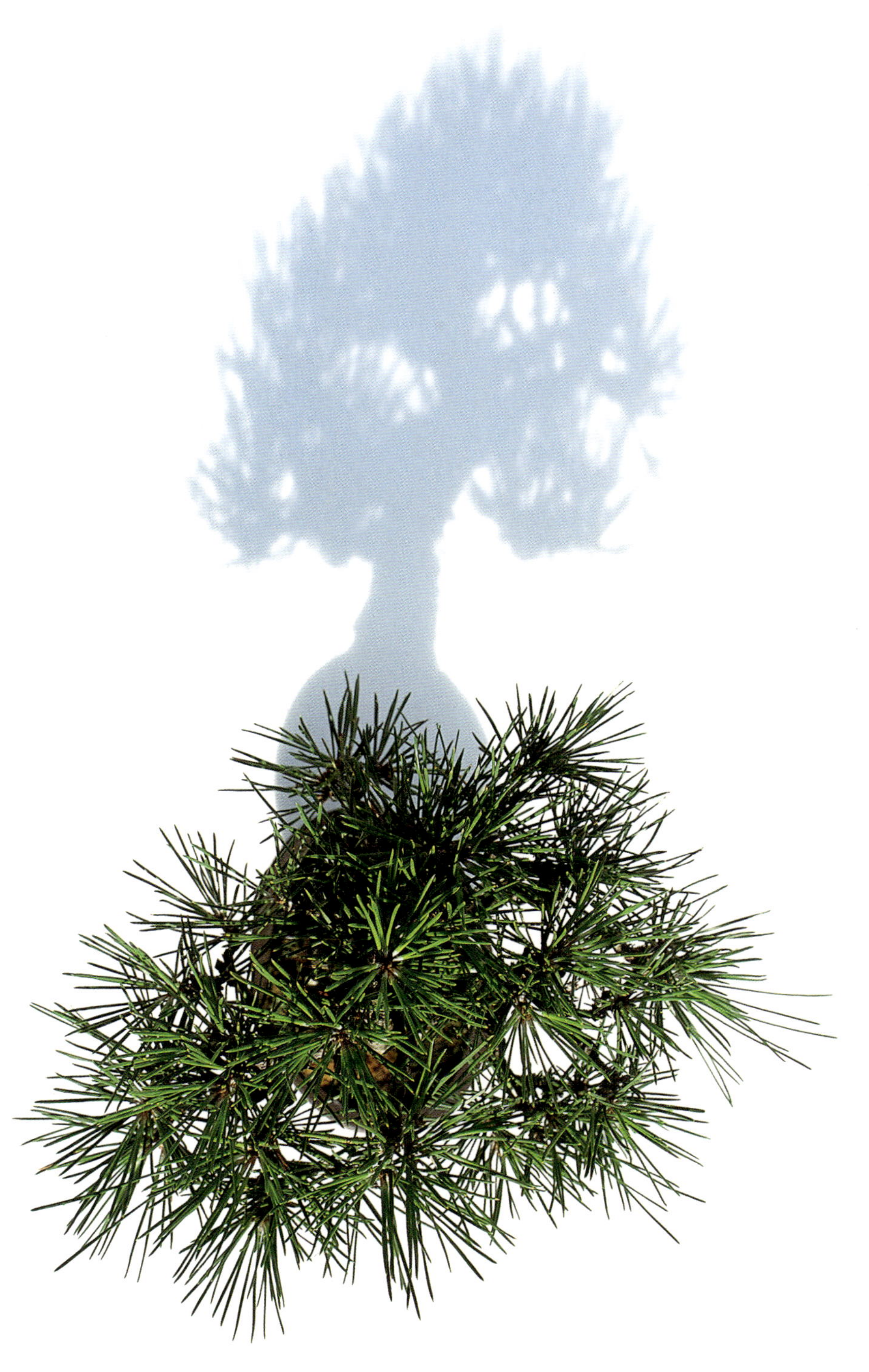

川上犬

Kawakami-ken

A type of Shinshu Shiba,
one of the Shinshu varieties of the Shiba Inu.
In fact, the present-day Shiba Inu was bred from
Kawakami-ken from in and around Nagano Prefecture.
According to legend,
the Kawakami-ken is the descendant of wolves
that once inhabited the Chichibu Mountains
that rise above Yamanashi, Saitama,
Gunma, and Nagano prefectures
that were domesticated by hunters.

信州系の柴犬である信州柴の一種。
現在の柴犬のもとになったのが、
長野県周辺にいた川上犬である。
伝わるところ、もともと川上犬とは、
山梨、埼玉、群馬、長野にまたがる秩父山塊にいた
山犬が猟師によって飼いならされたものだという。
川上犬
かわかみけん

Kawakami-ken

The Kawakami-ken is gentle by nature,
and has an air of dignity and reserve strength.
Its coat comes in a variety of colorings,
including reddish purple, blackish purple,
whitish purple, white, and red.
The distinguishing features of the breed are its eyes,
which are dark with a reddish tinge,
and the size of its head,
which is large in proportion to its body.
It also has a thick, strong tail that extends
almost as far as its hocks.
The Kawakami-ken usually grows to a height of 35-45 cm.

性質は温厚で威厳を漂わせ、底力がある。
毛色は、赤柴、黒柴、白柴、白、赤など。
眼色は紅彩を帯びた濃い色で、
体つきに比べて頭骨が大きいのも特徴だ。
また、太くて力強い尾を持ち、
その長さはほぼ飛節に達するほど。
体長は標準で 35 〜 45 センチ。

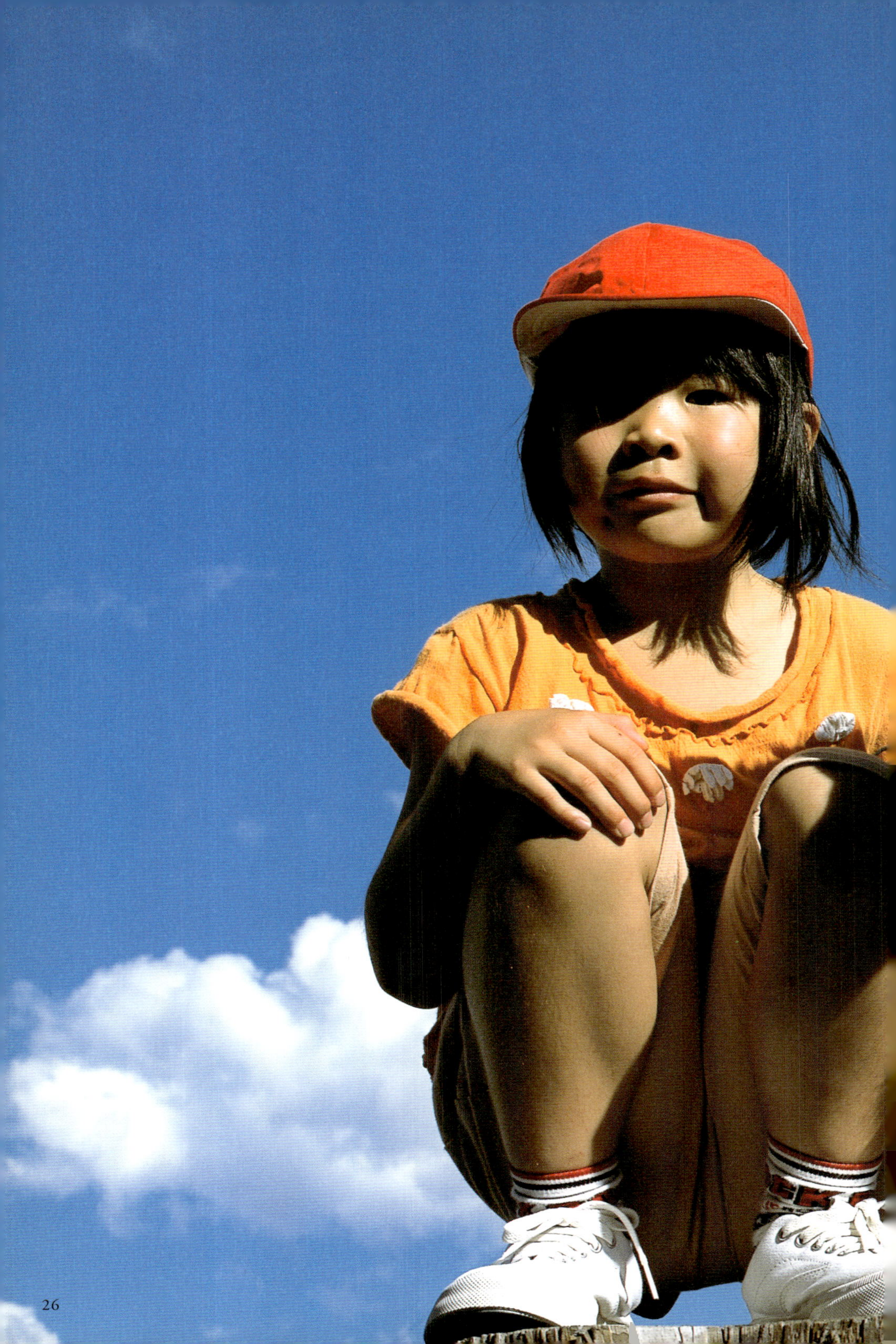

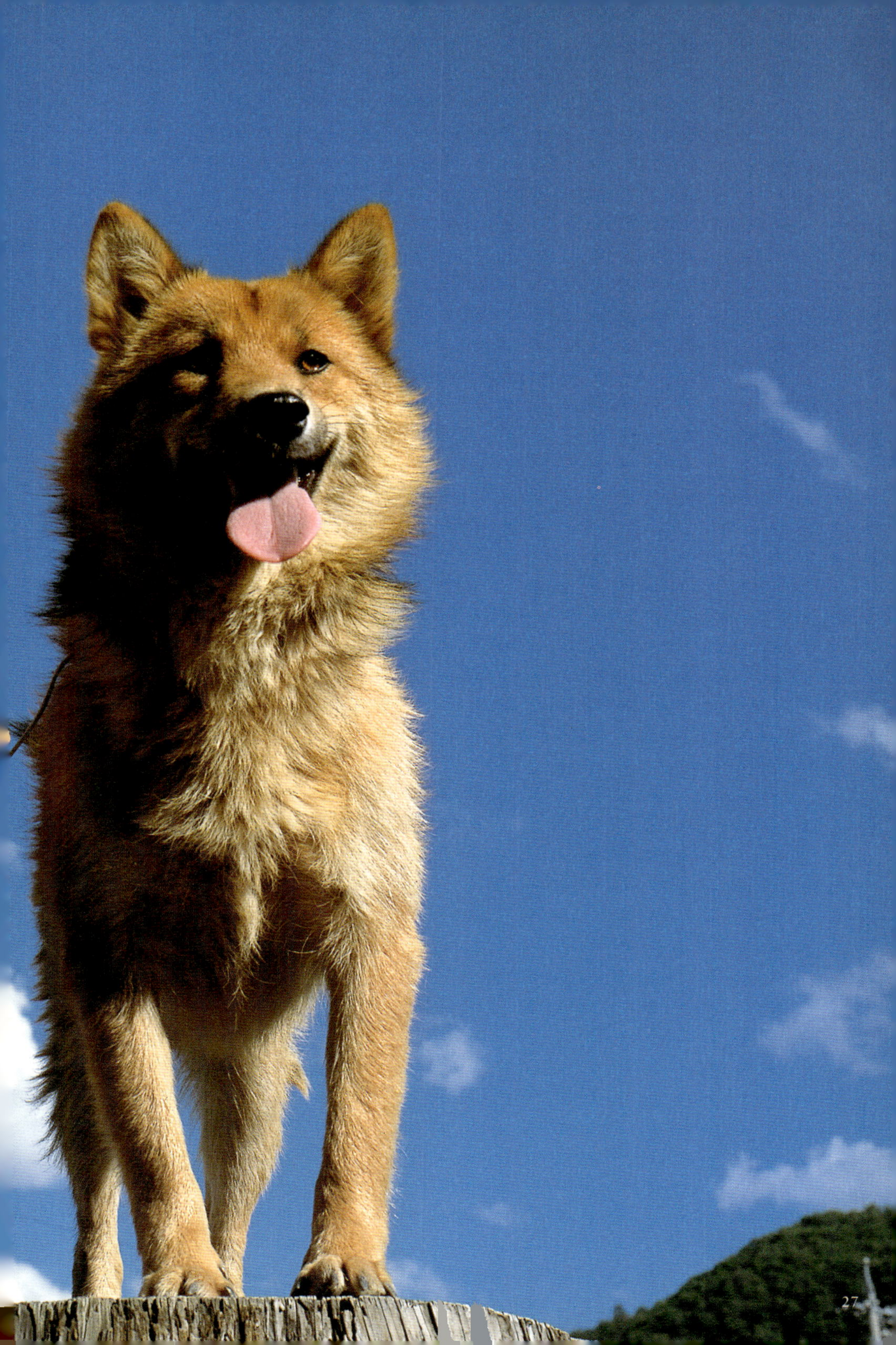

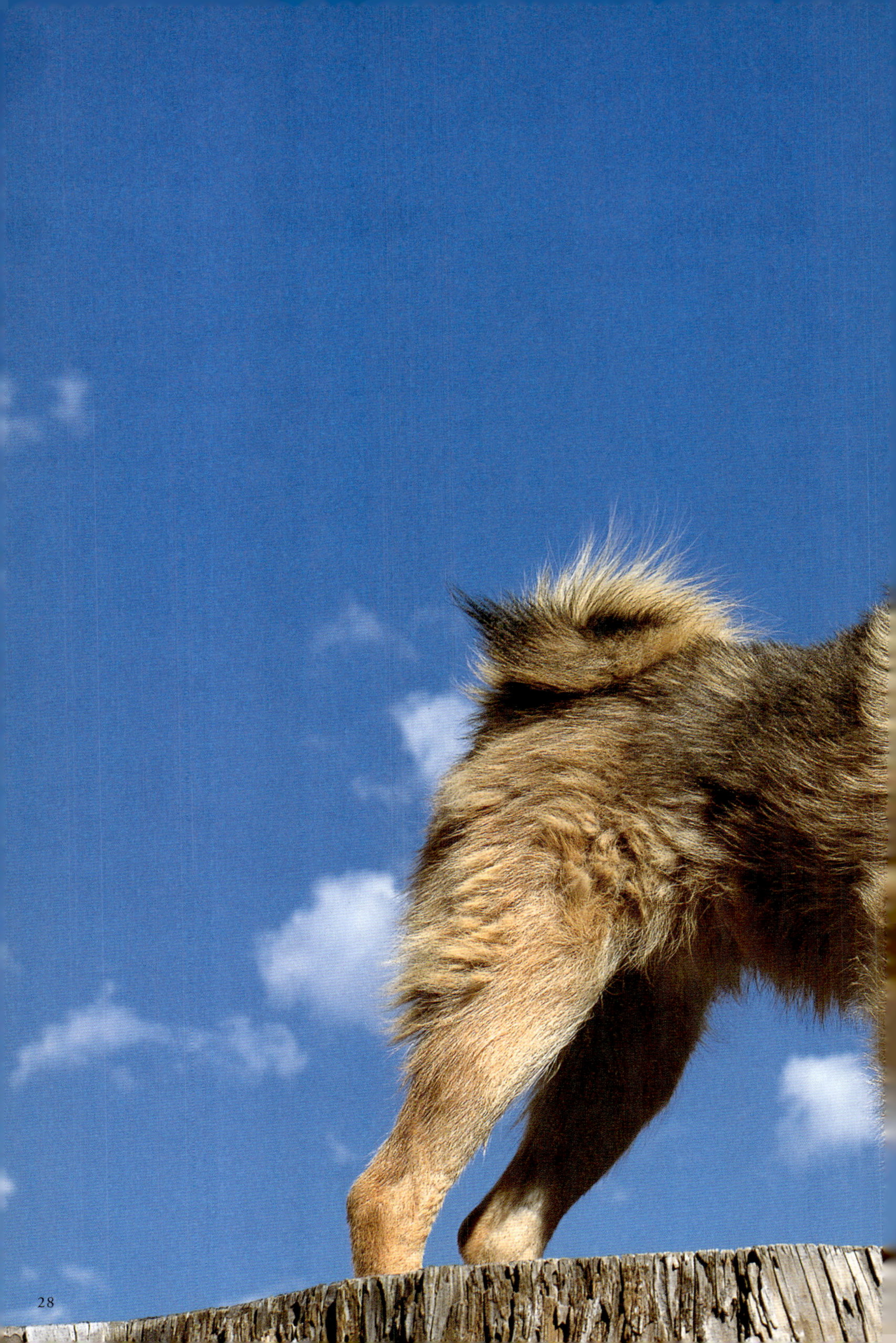

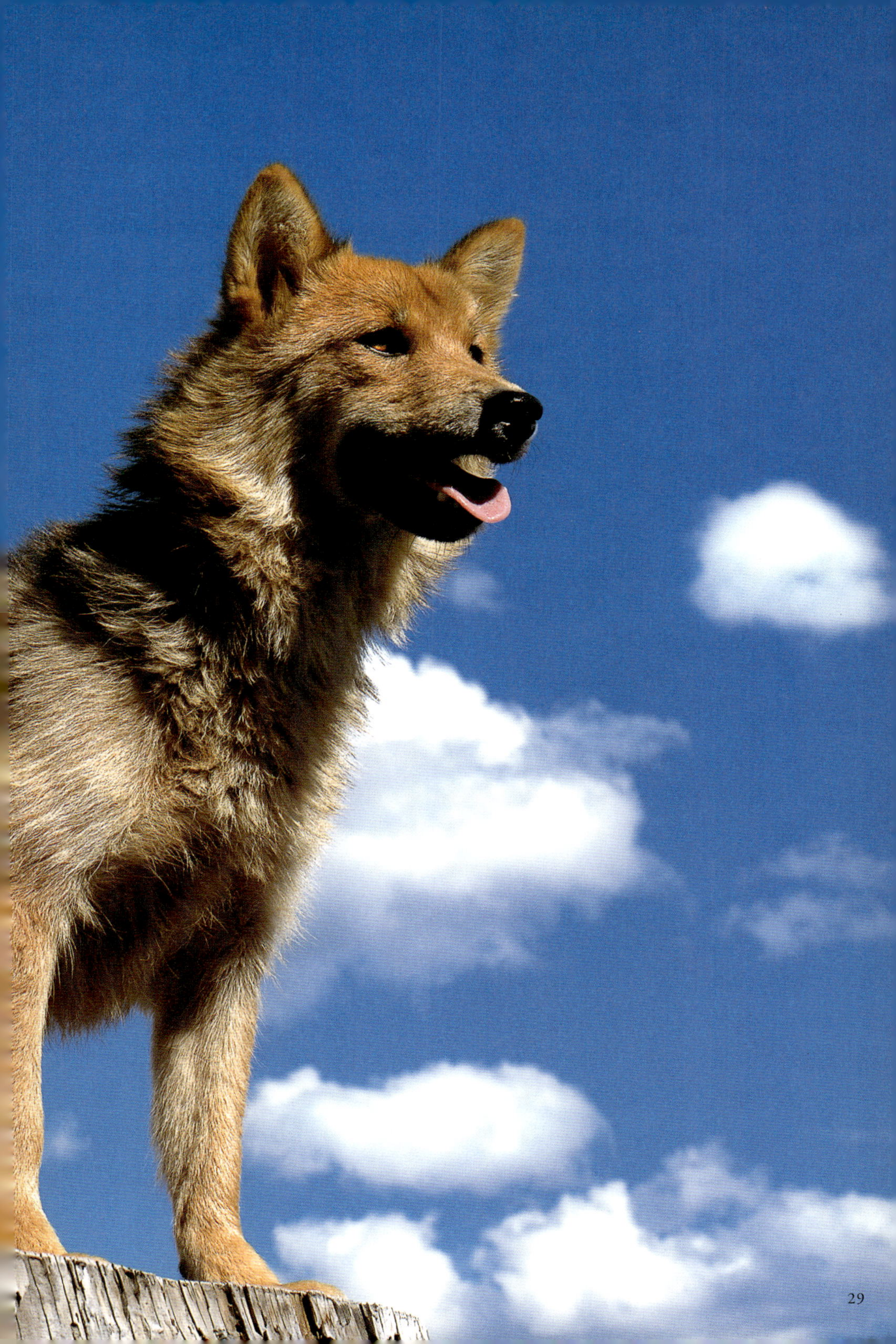

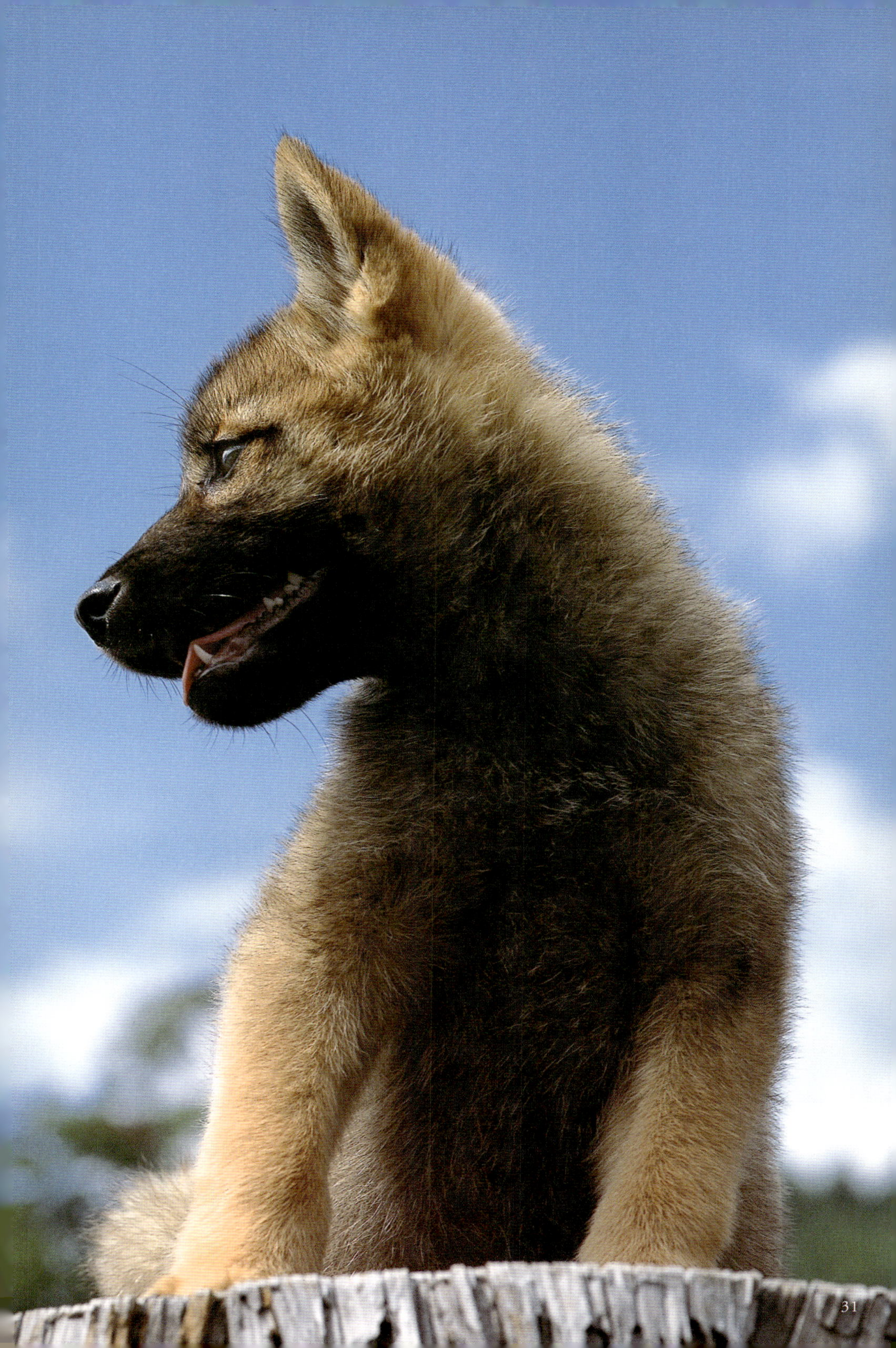

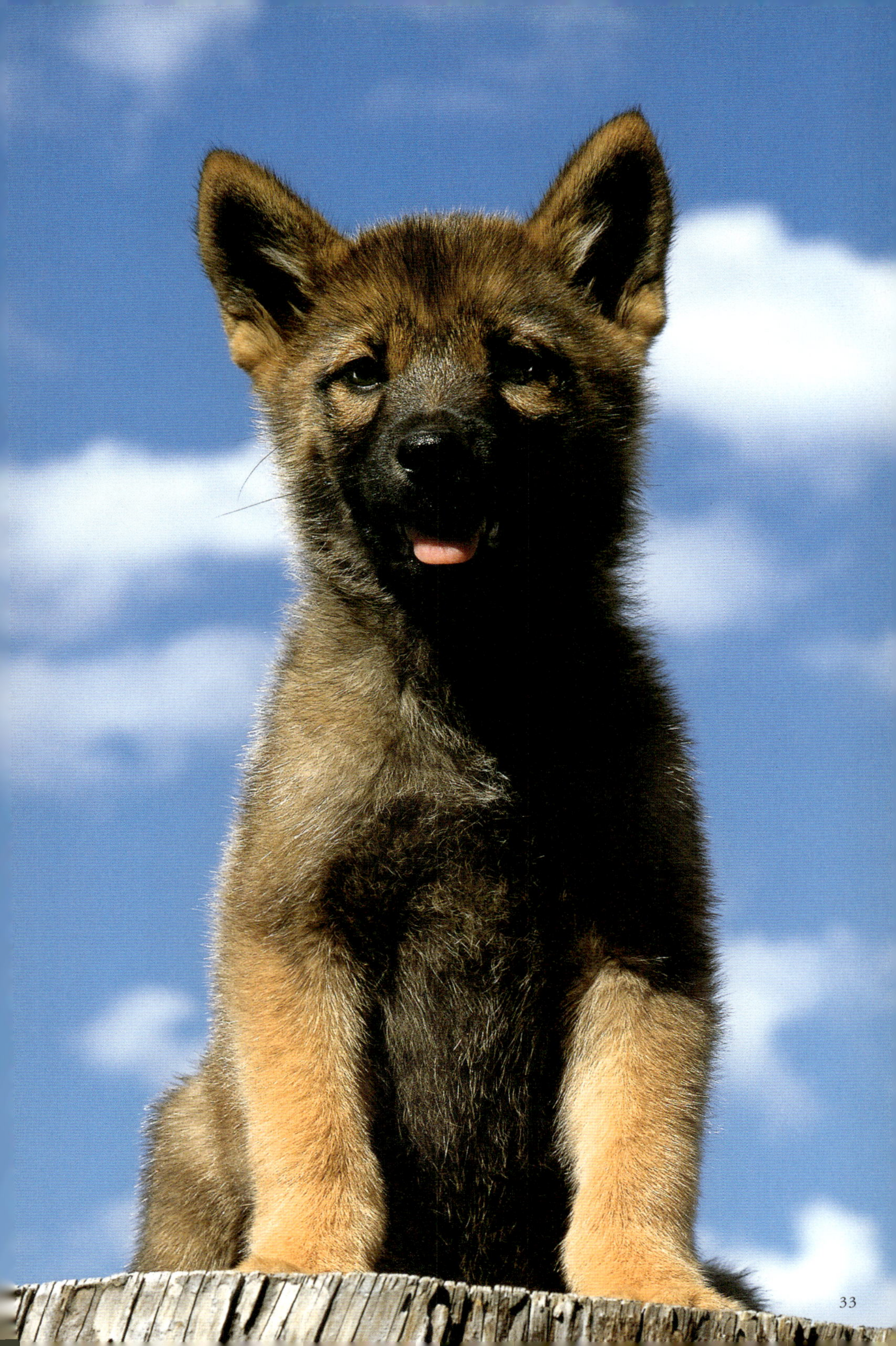

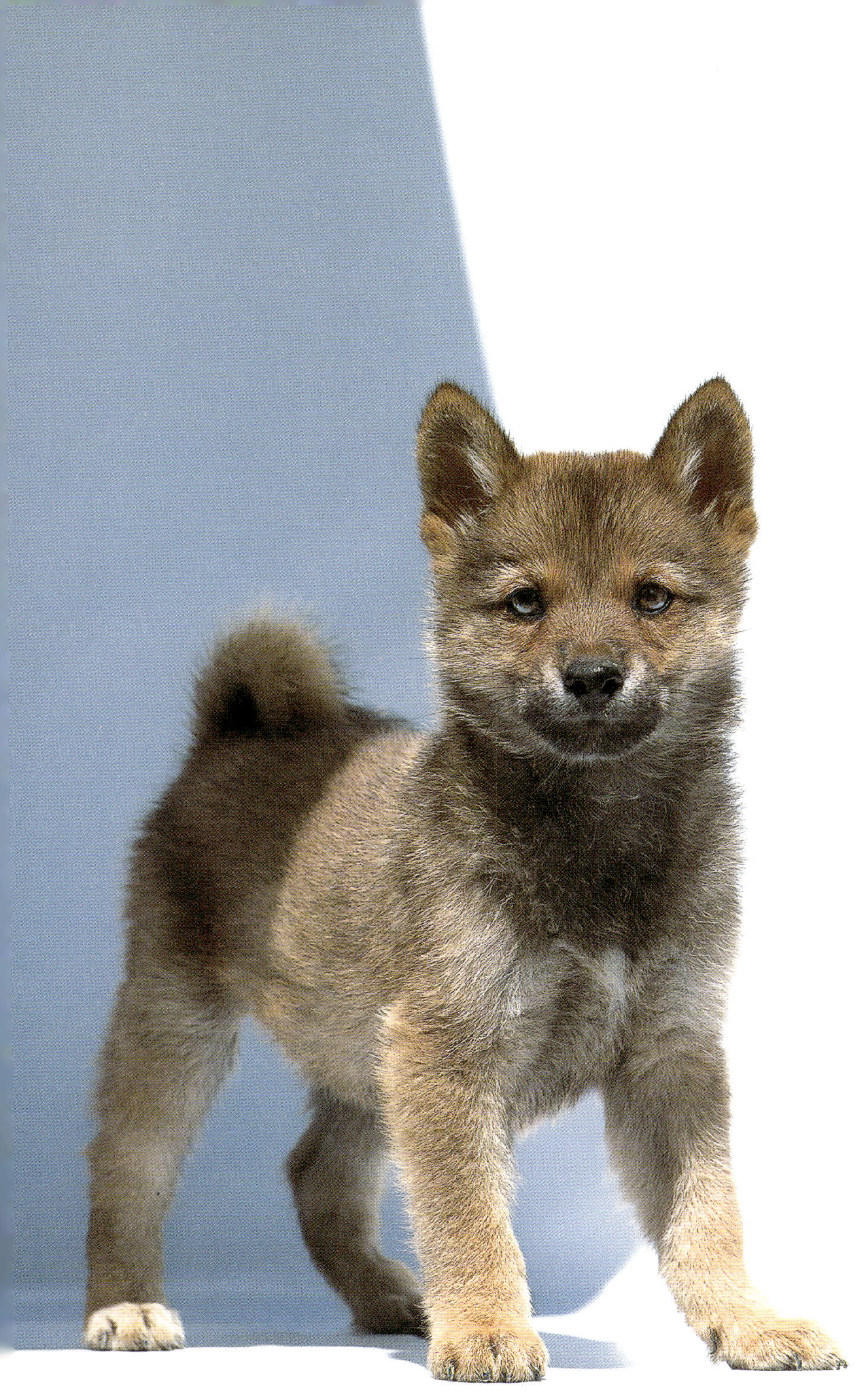

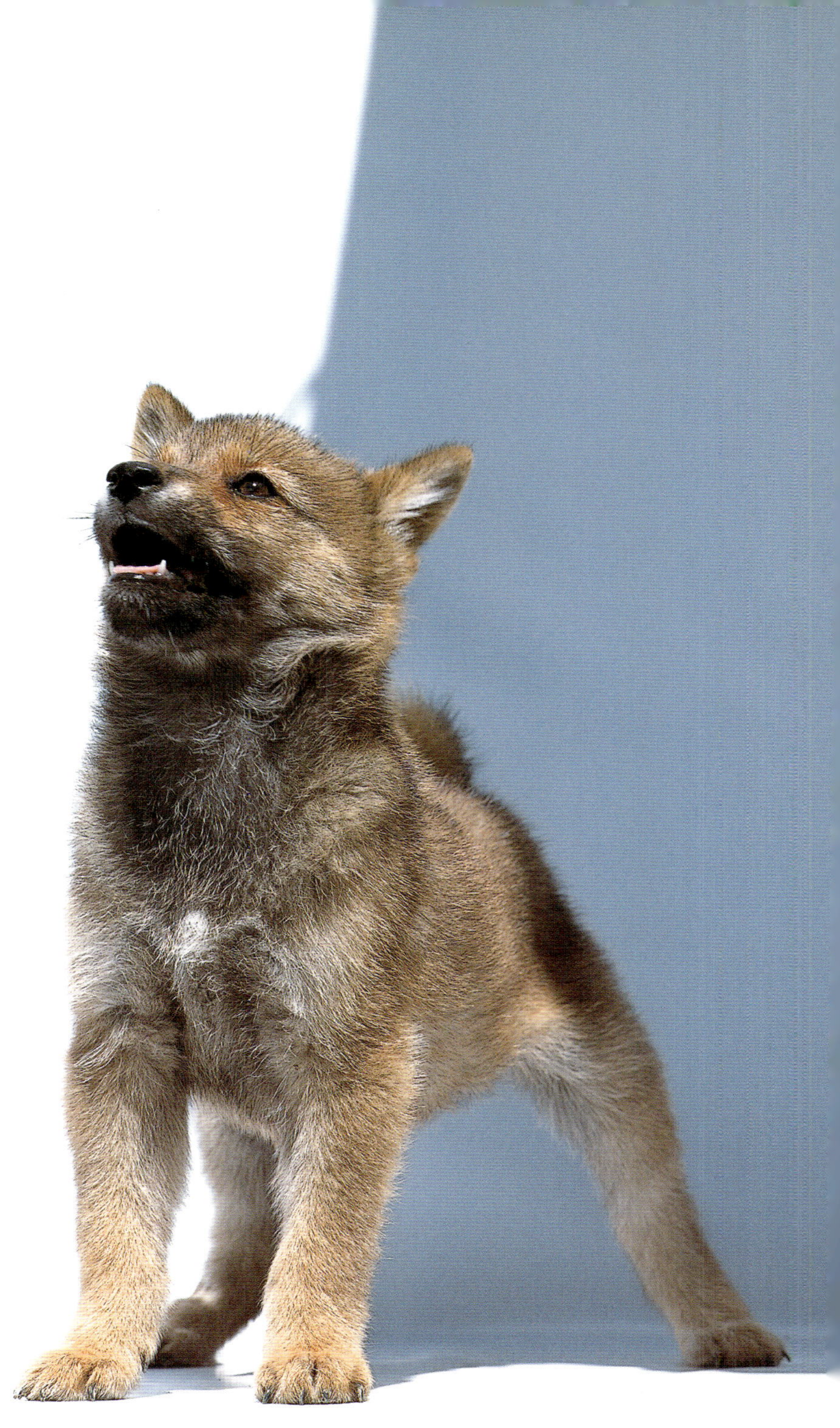

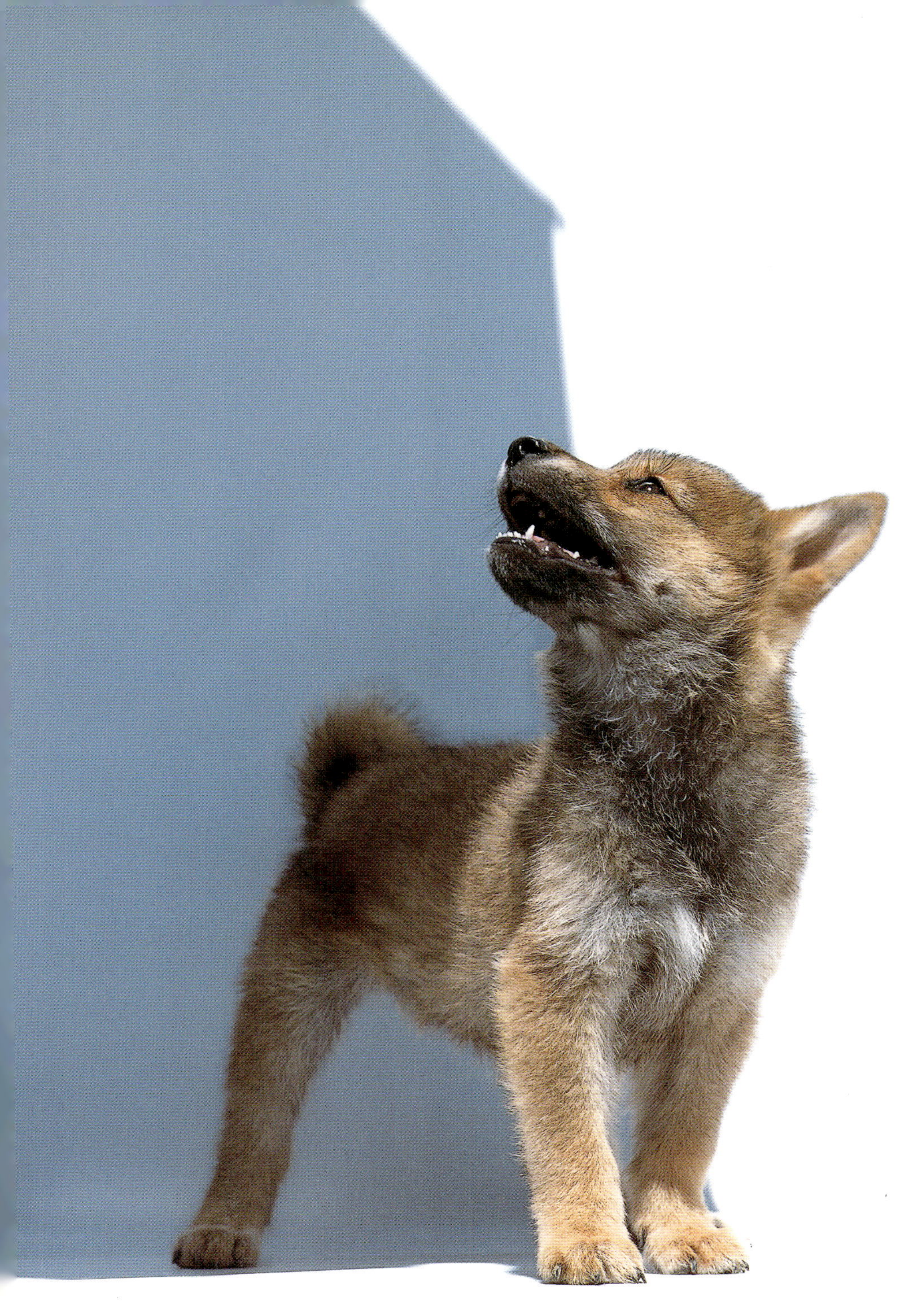

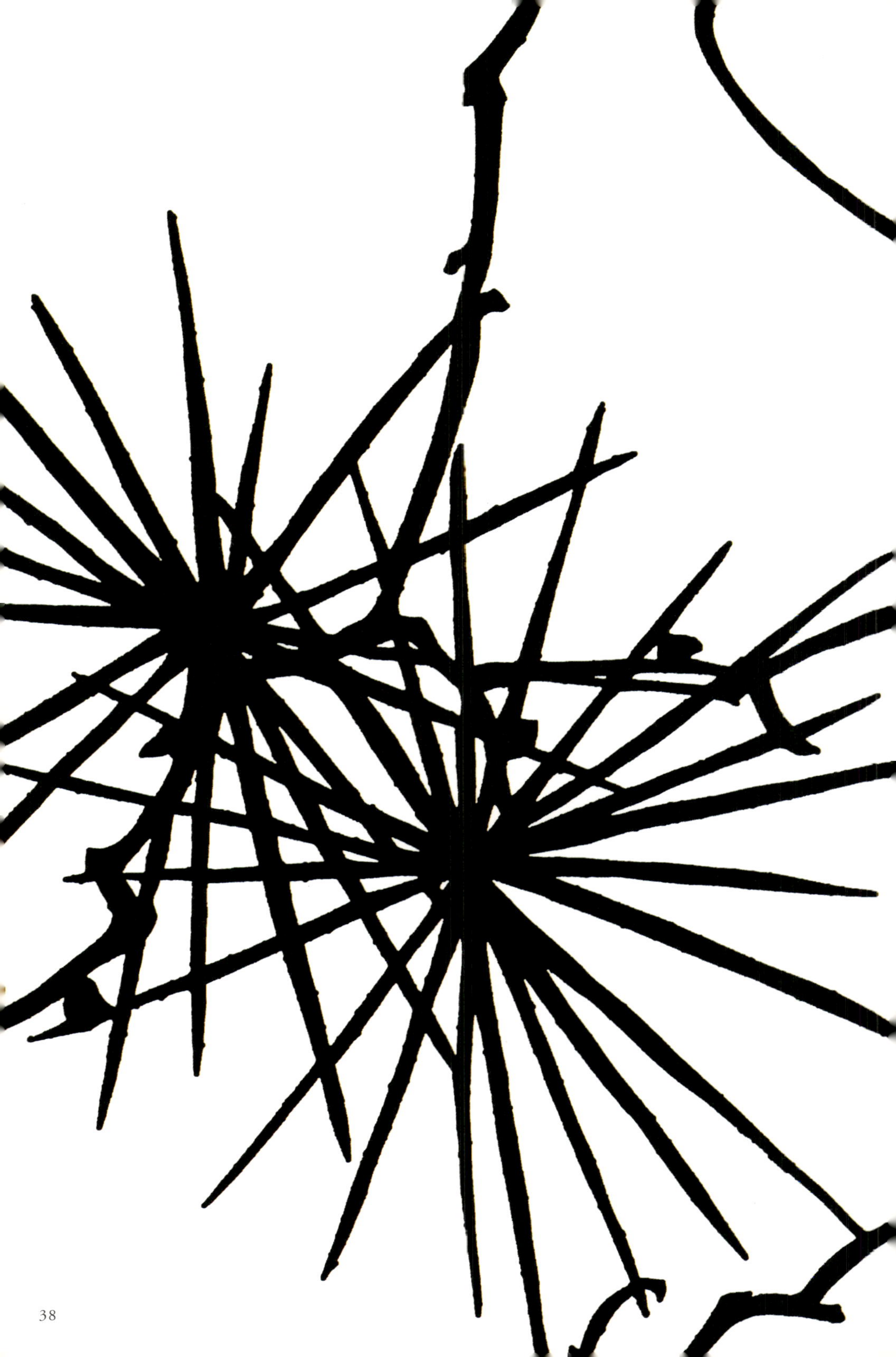

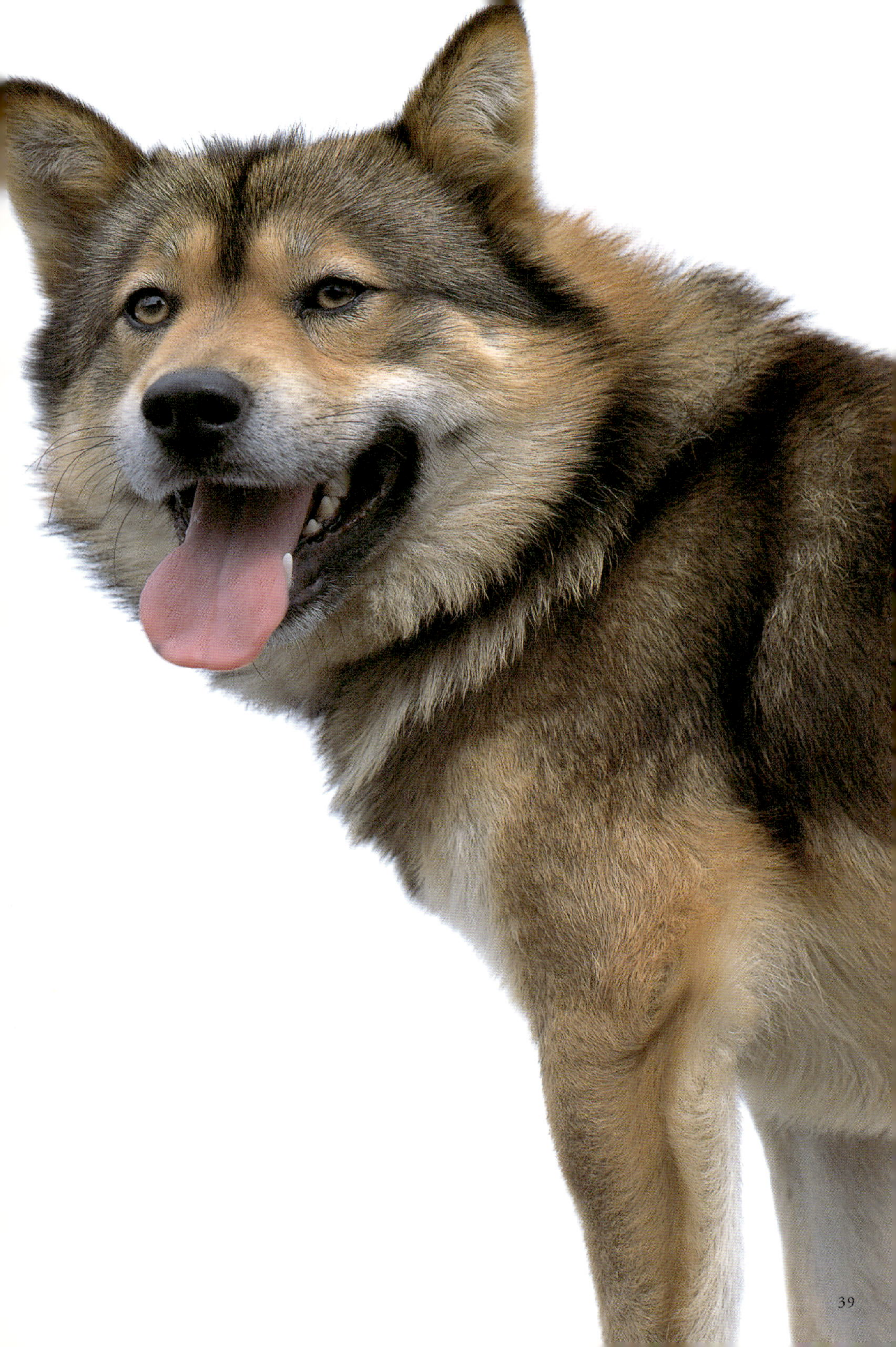

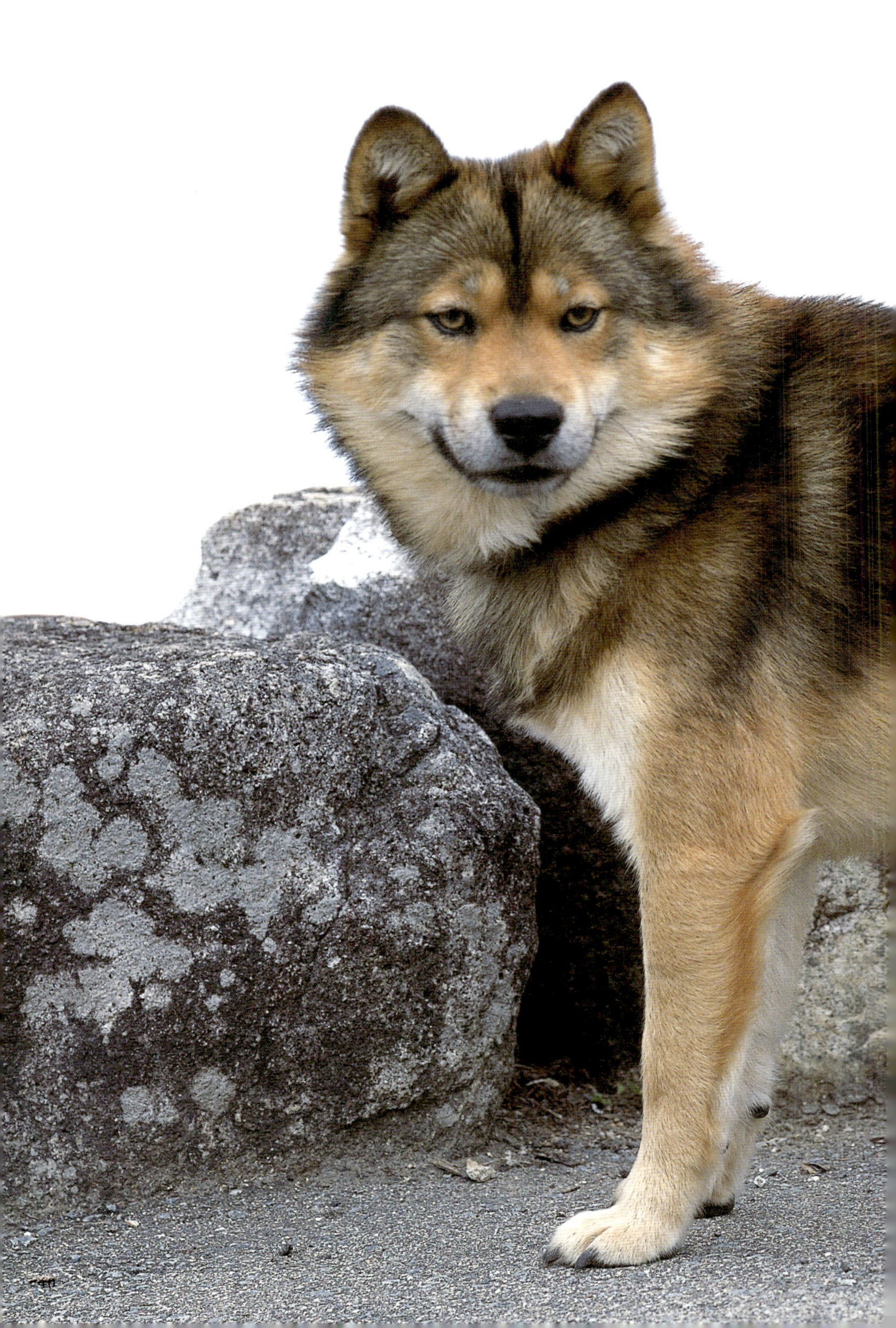

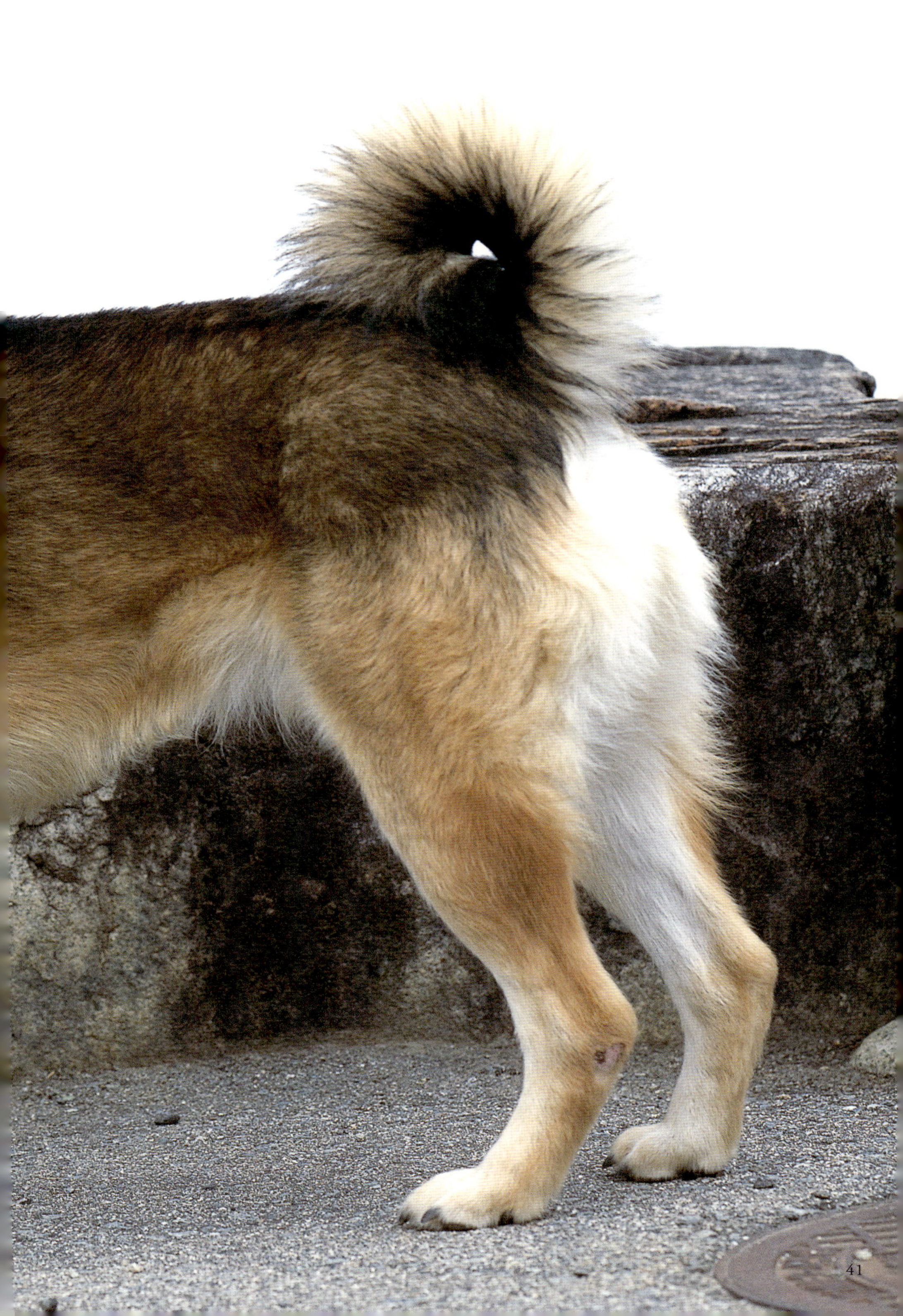

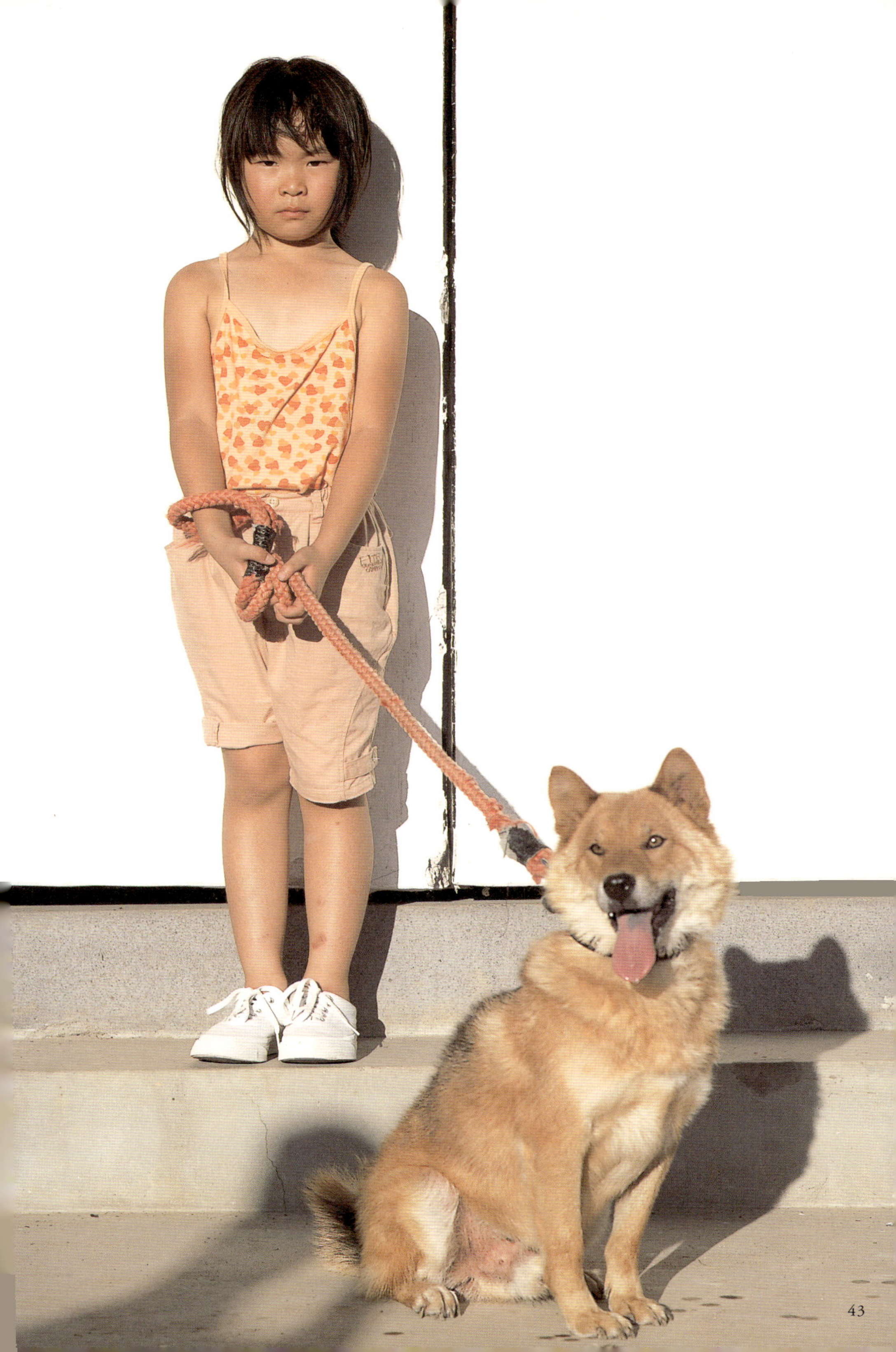

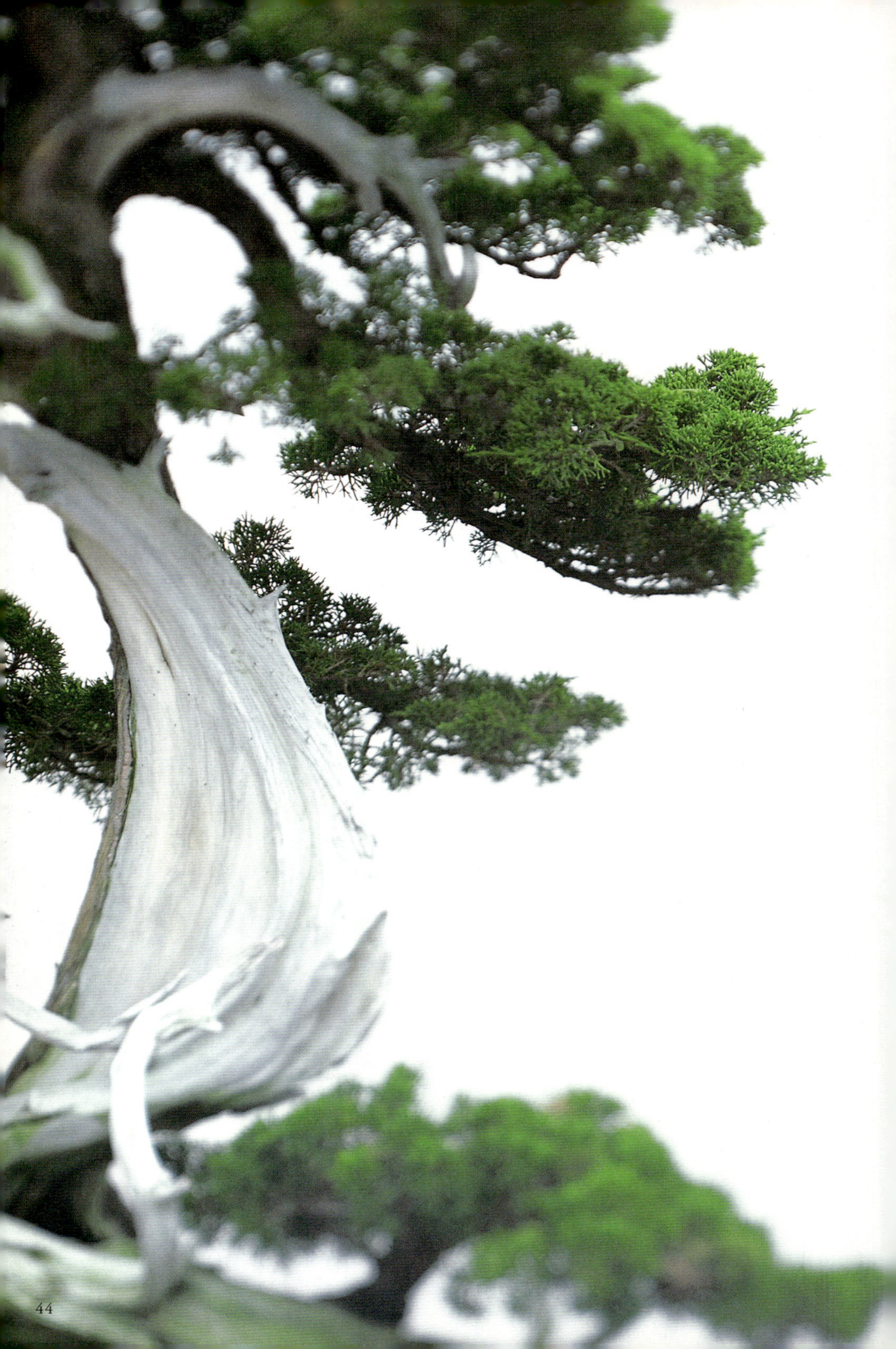

甲
斐
犬

Kai-ken

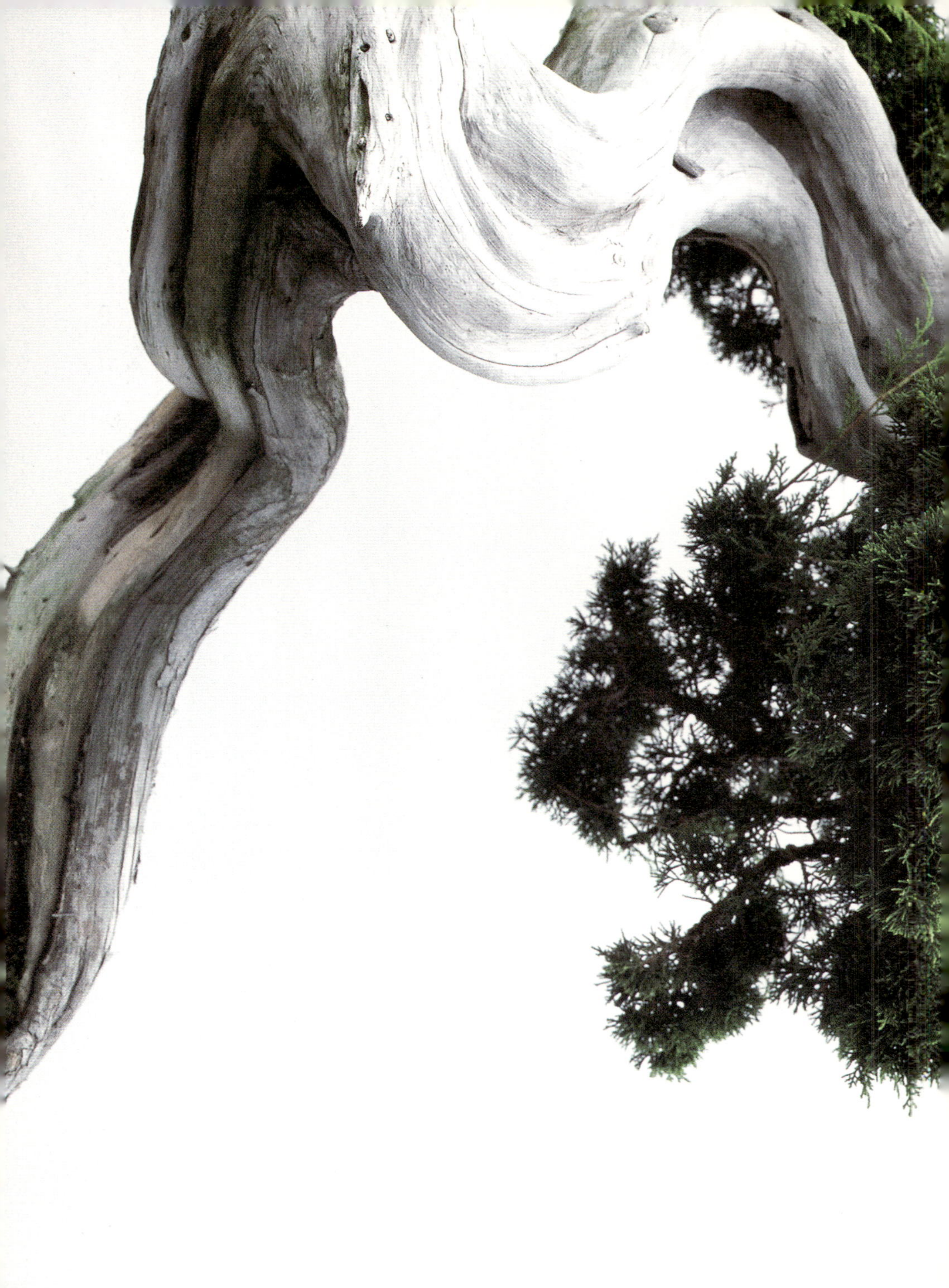

甲斐犬
南アルプス山岳地帯で大型獣の狩りの
パートナーとして飼育されてきた。
黒い縞のある虎毛が特徴で、
そのため甲斐虎（かいとら）の別名をもつ。
幼犬のときには一色でも、
成長に伴って虎毛に変化する。
これが山野で狩りをするときの保護色となる。

Bred in the mountainous Minami Alps region
as a hunting dog for hunting large animals.
A distinguishing feature of the breed is its
brindled coat, from which derives
the alternative name of Kai Tora-ken
("tora" being the Japanese word for tiger).
Puppies are born solid-colored,
with the brindle pattern appearing
as the animals mature,
and serving as camouflage when the dogs are
used for hunting in the fields or mountains.

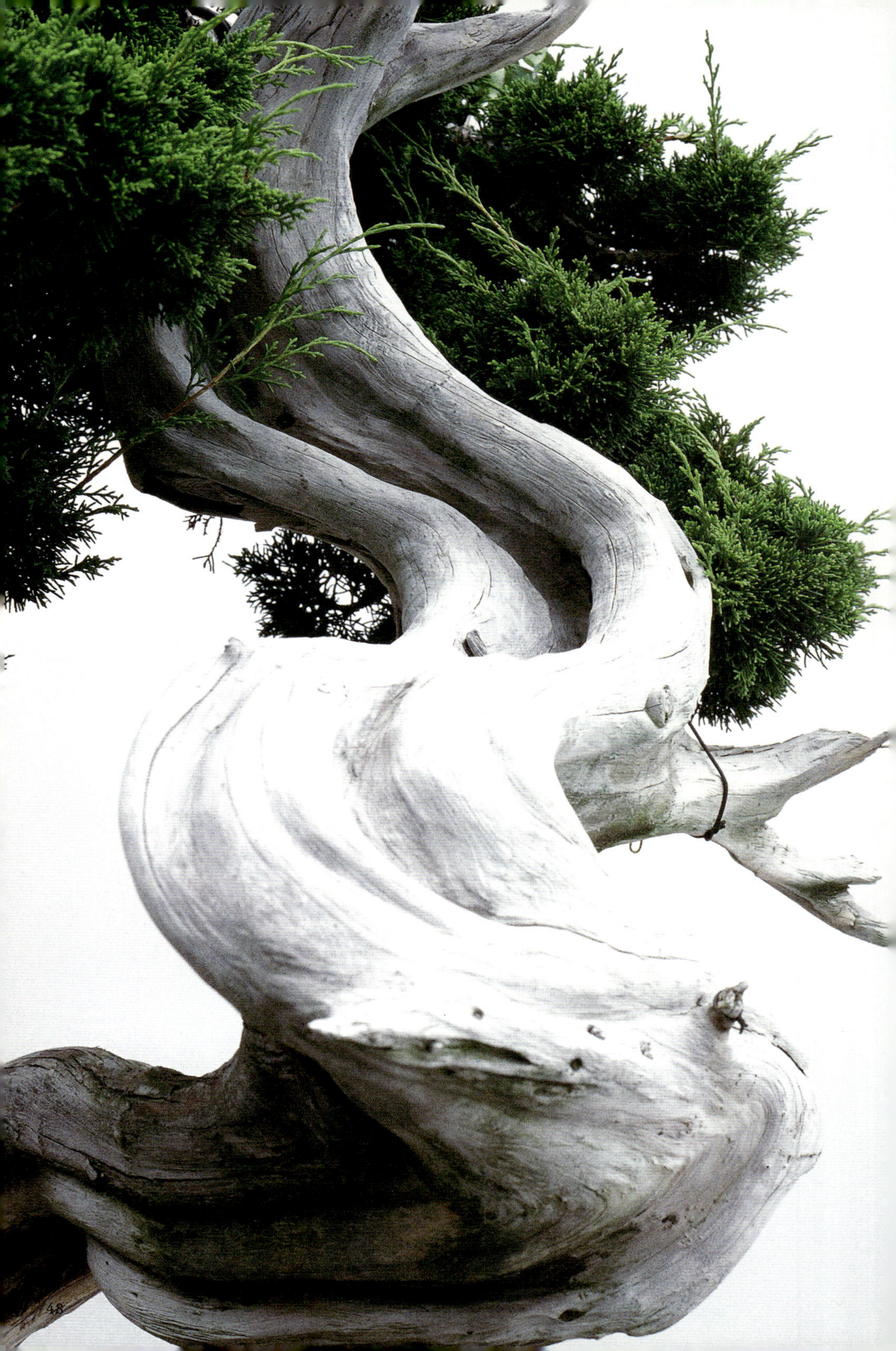

色は黒虎毛、中虎毛、赤虎毛の三種類。
四肢は特に長く、飛節がよく発達している。
抜群の反射神経と跳躍力で、
猟師の間では特に調教しなくても本能的に
猟の上手な犬として重宝がられてきた。
唯一の飼い主に一生忠誠をつくすことから、
一代一主の犬といわれている。
体高は雄 45 センチ、雌 41 センチ。
昭和 9 年、国の天然記念物に指定。

The Kai-ken appears in one of three colors:
black, red-black, or red brindled.
Its limbs are particularly long,
and its hocks are well developed.
It has excellent reflexes and is a strong jumper,
and is prized by hunters as a natural hunting dog
that performs well without any special training.
The Kai-ken is regarded as a one-man dog
due to its tendency to remain loyal to
a single master throughout its lifetime.
Males grow to a height of 45 cm, females to 41 cm.
The Kai-ken was designated
a Natural Monument in 1934.

Kai-ken

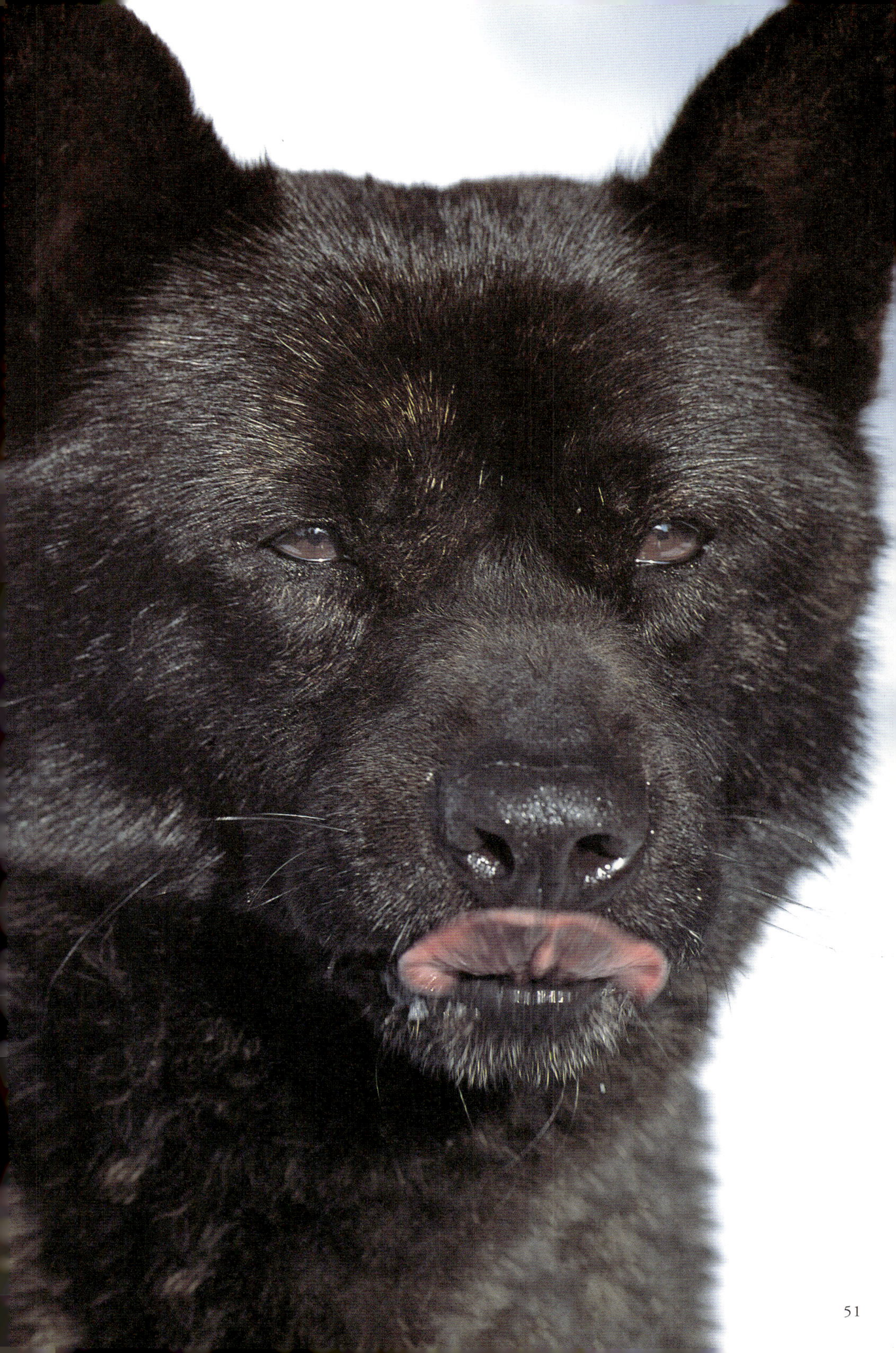

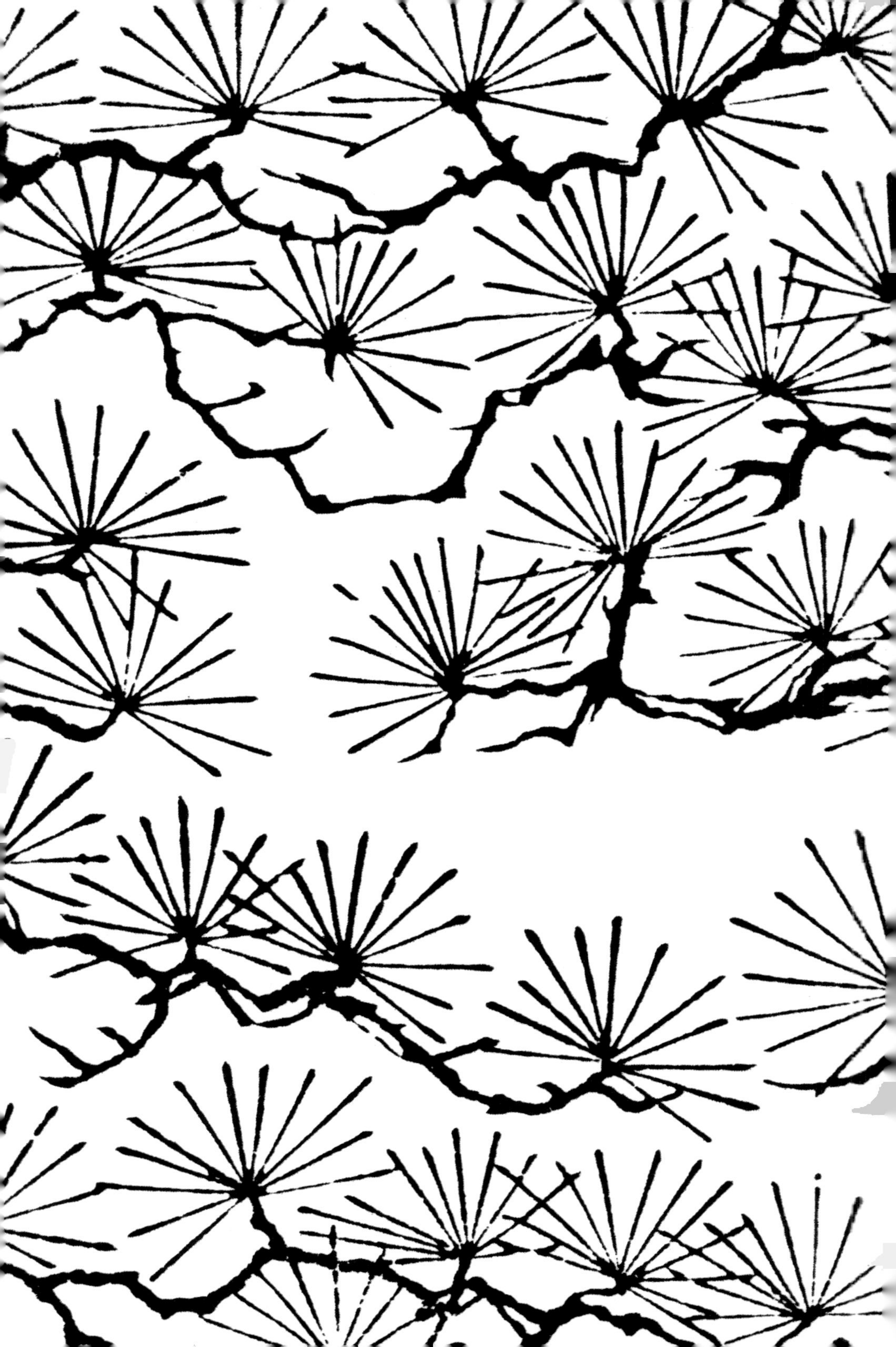

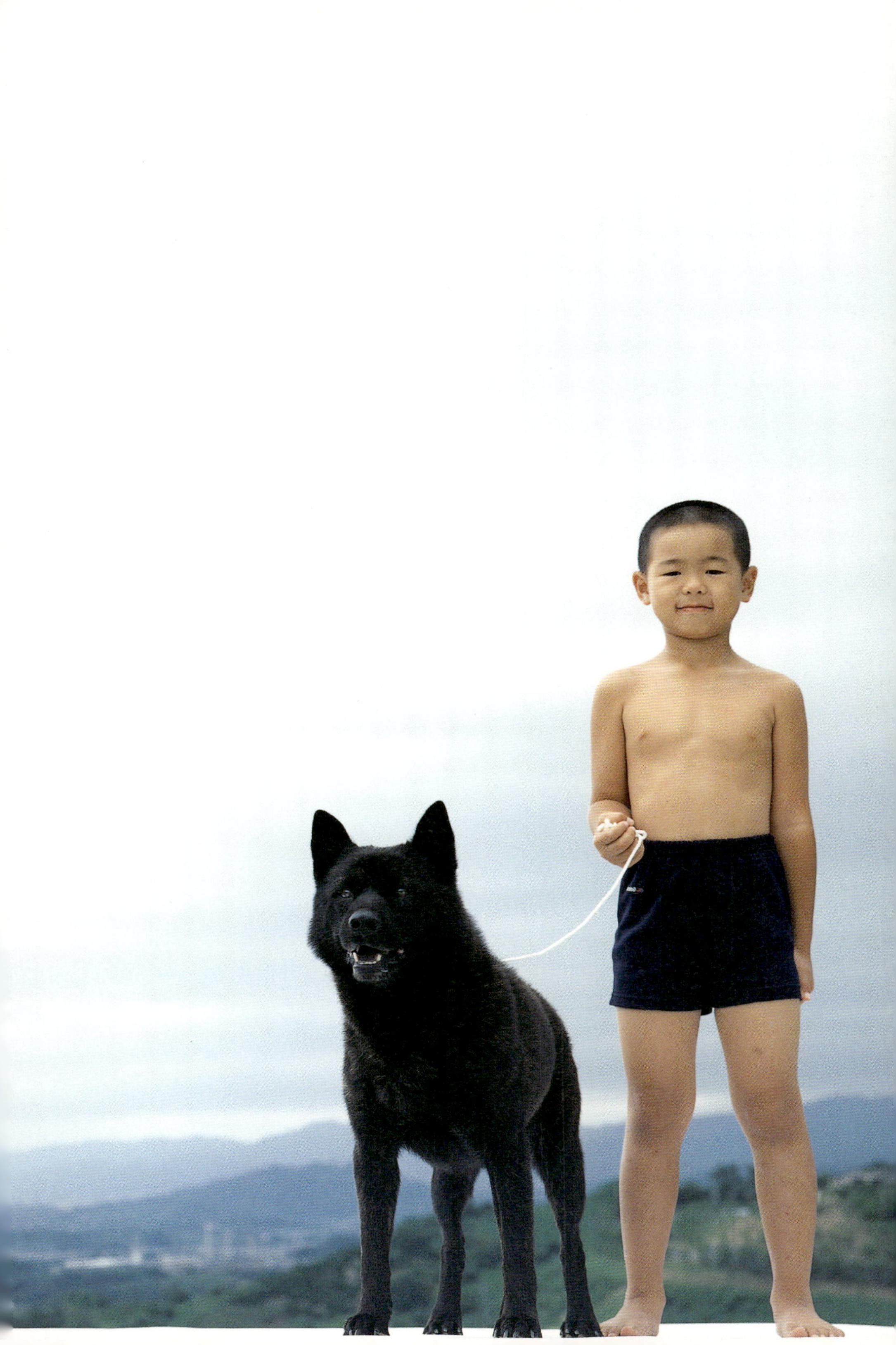

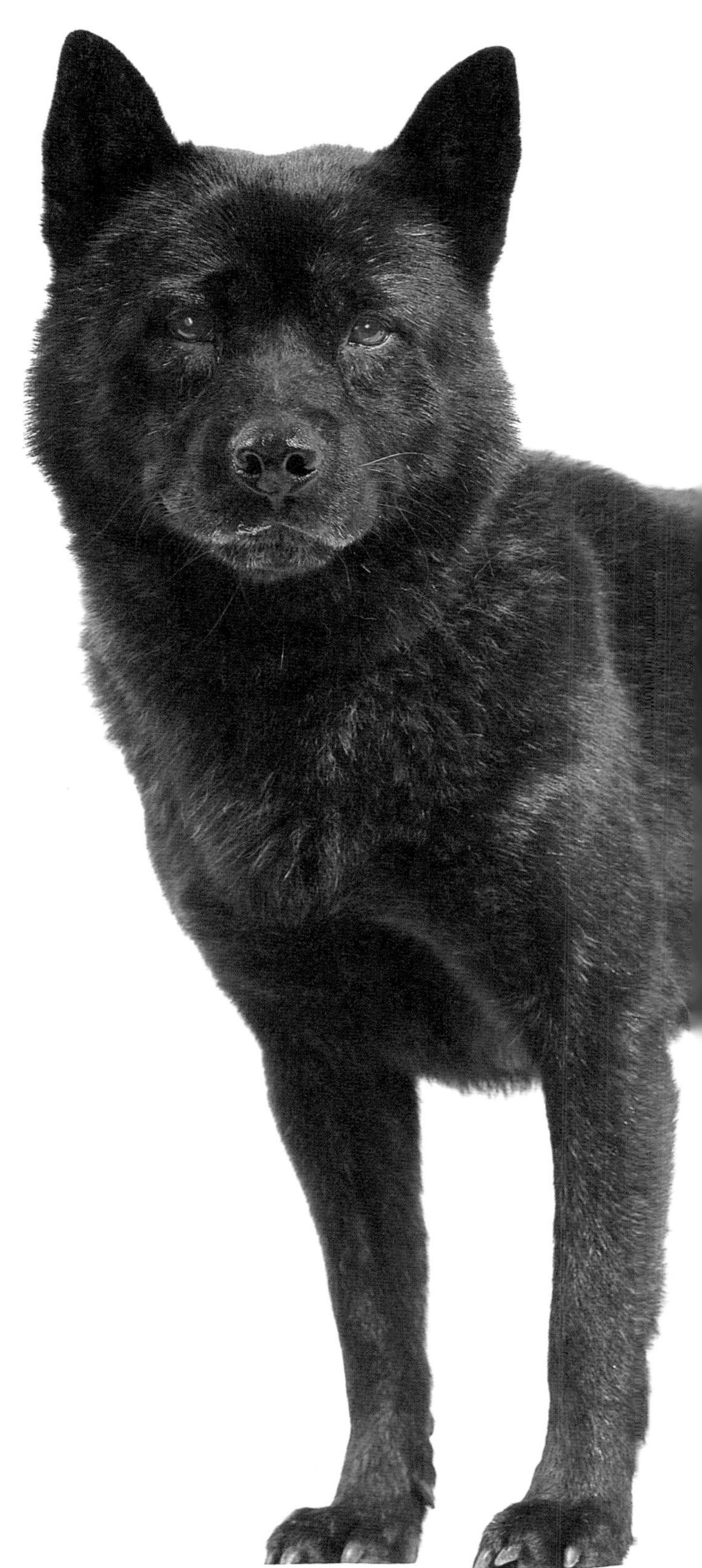

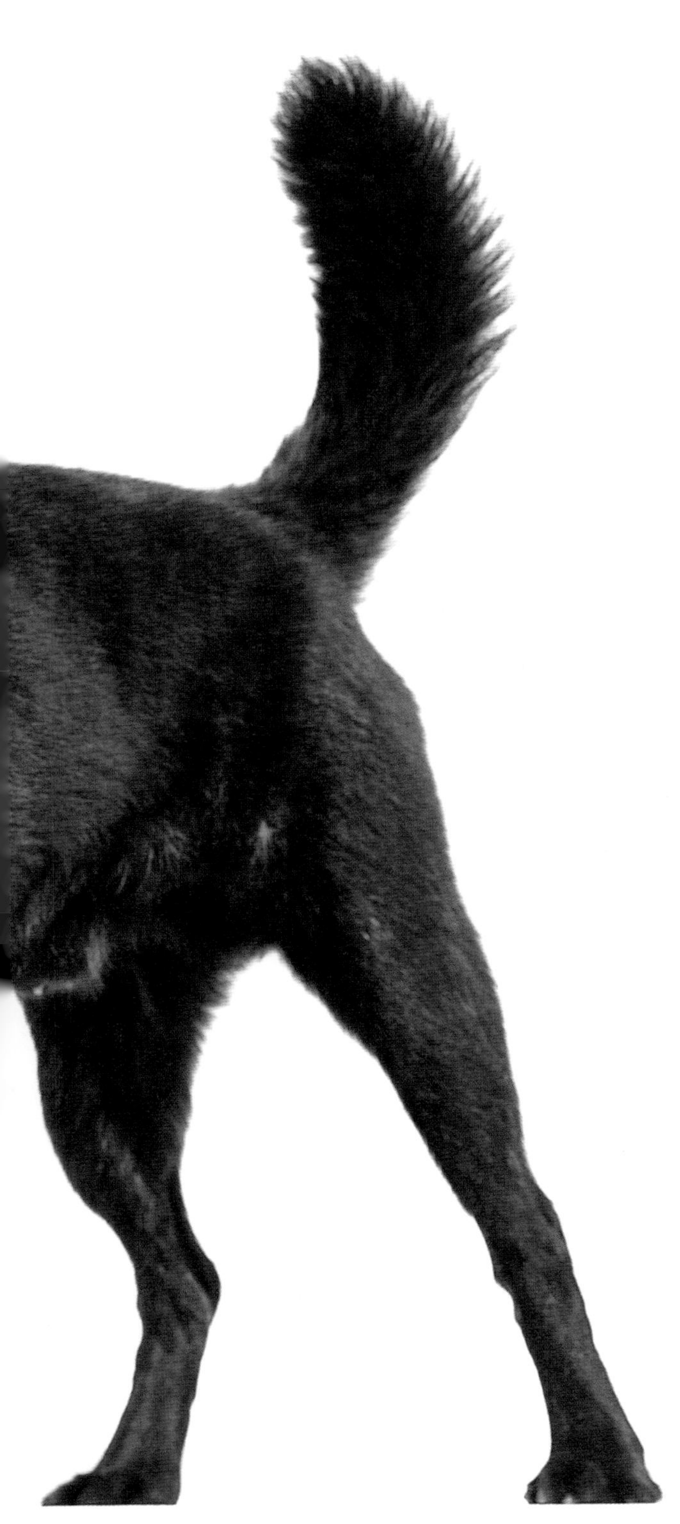

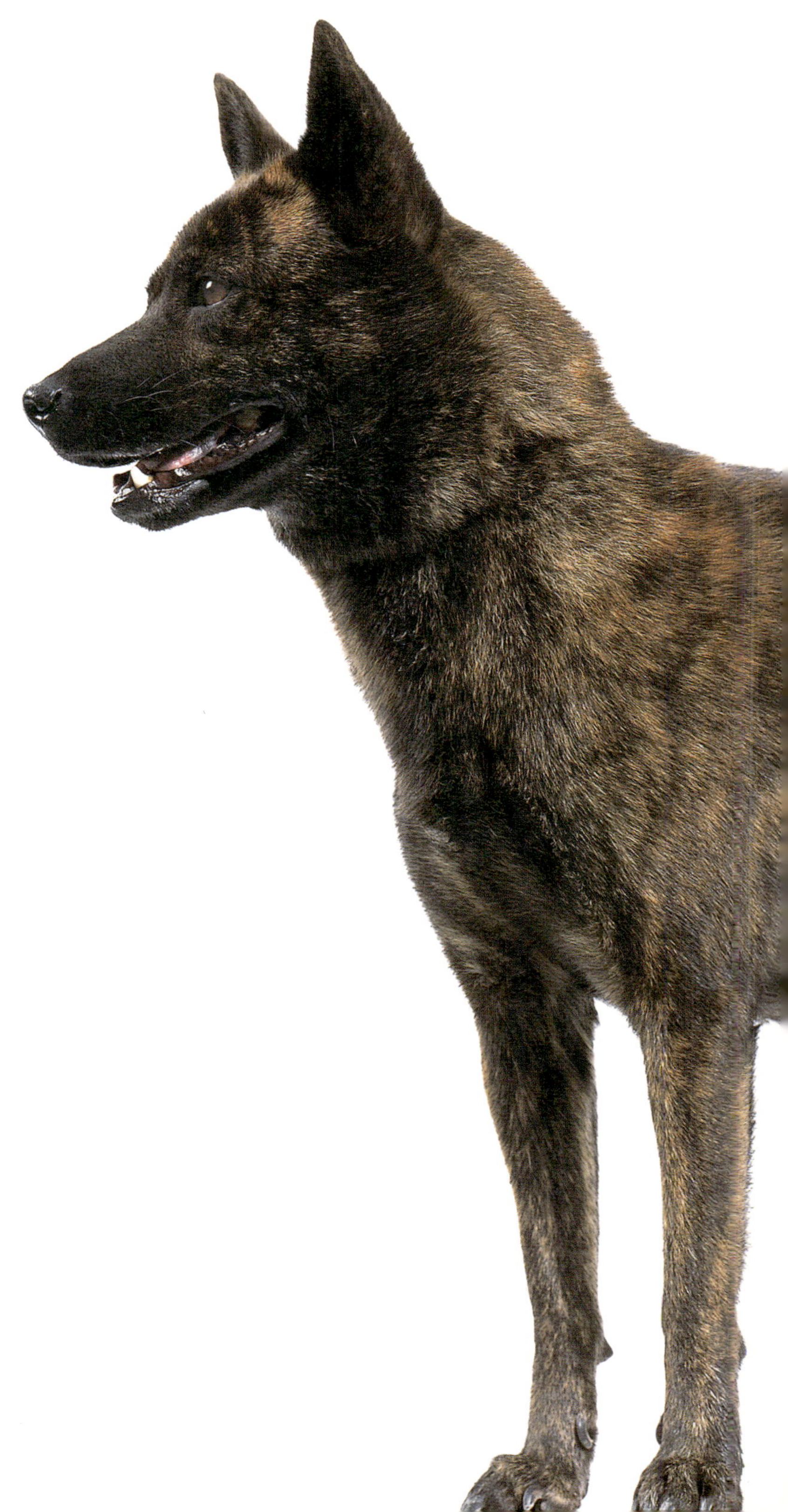

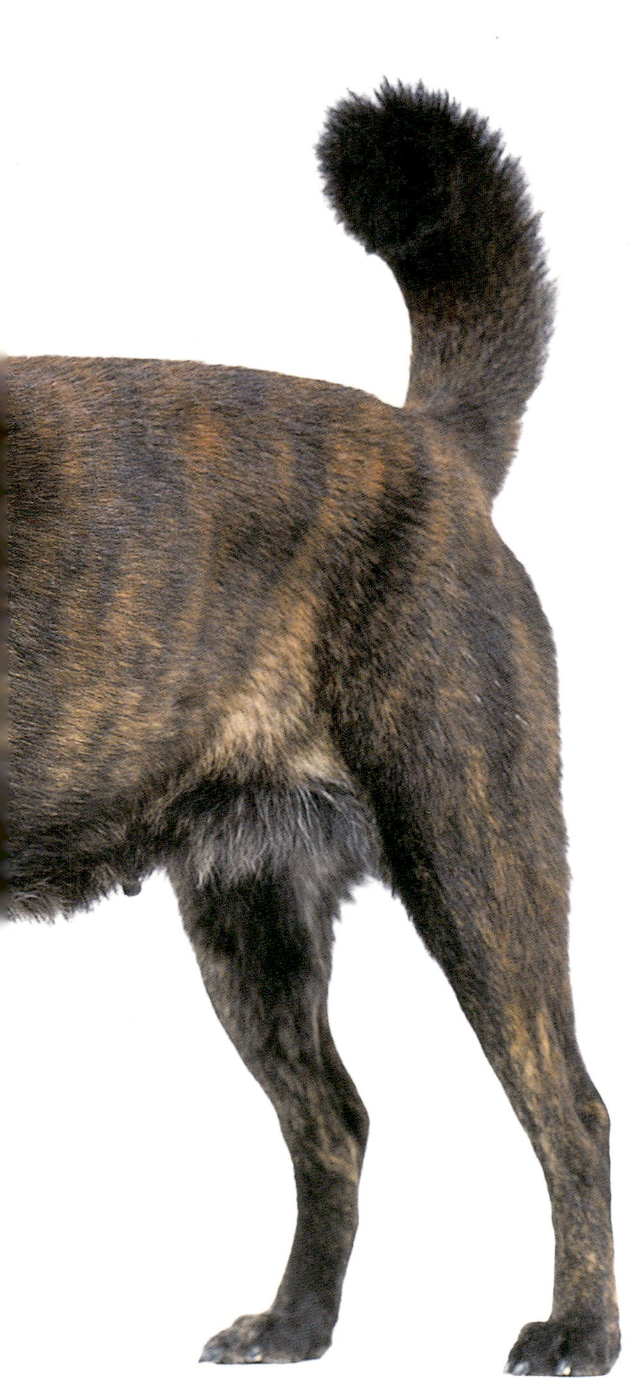

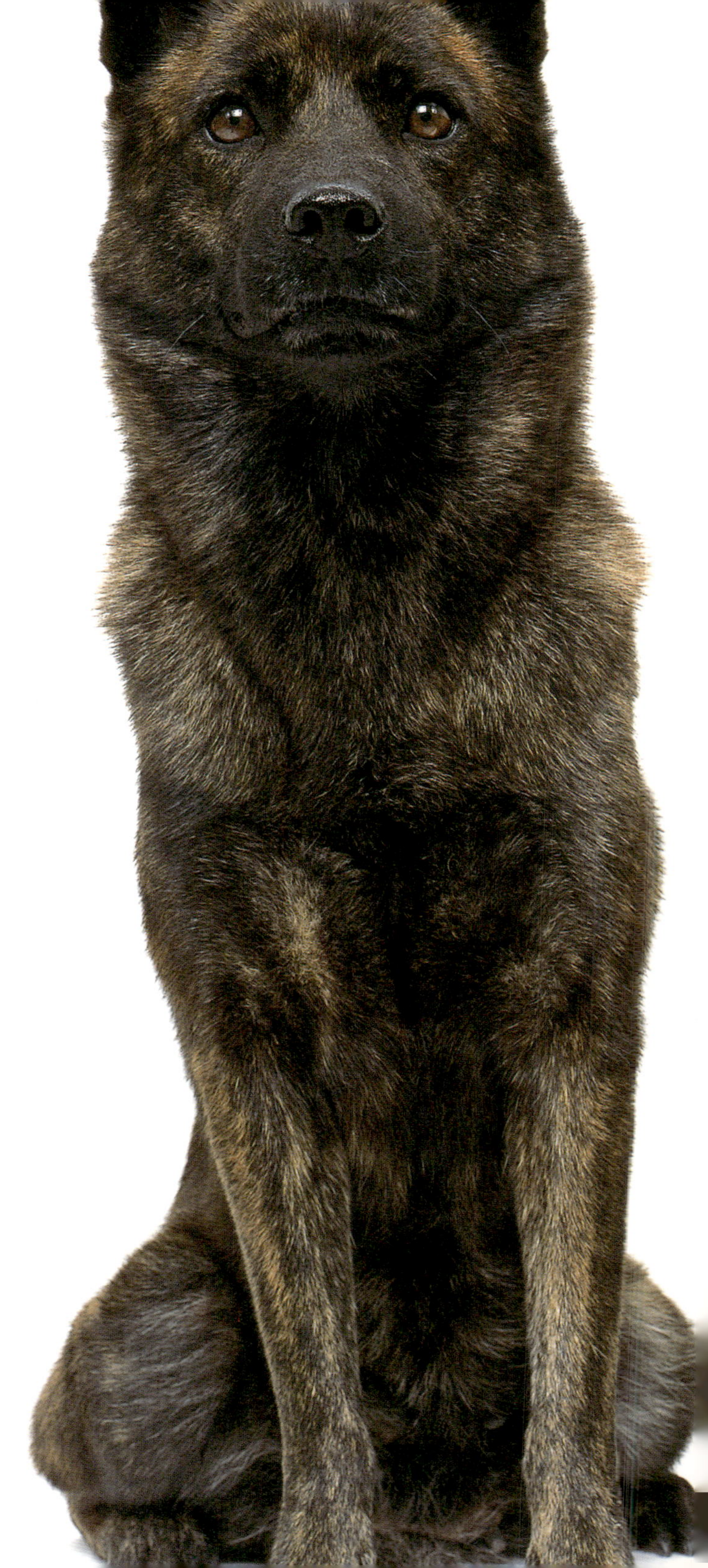

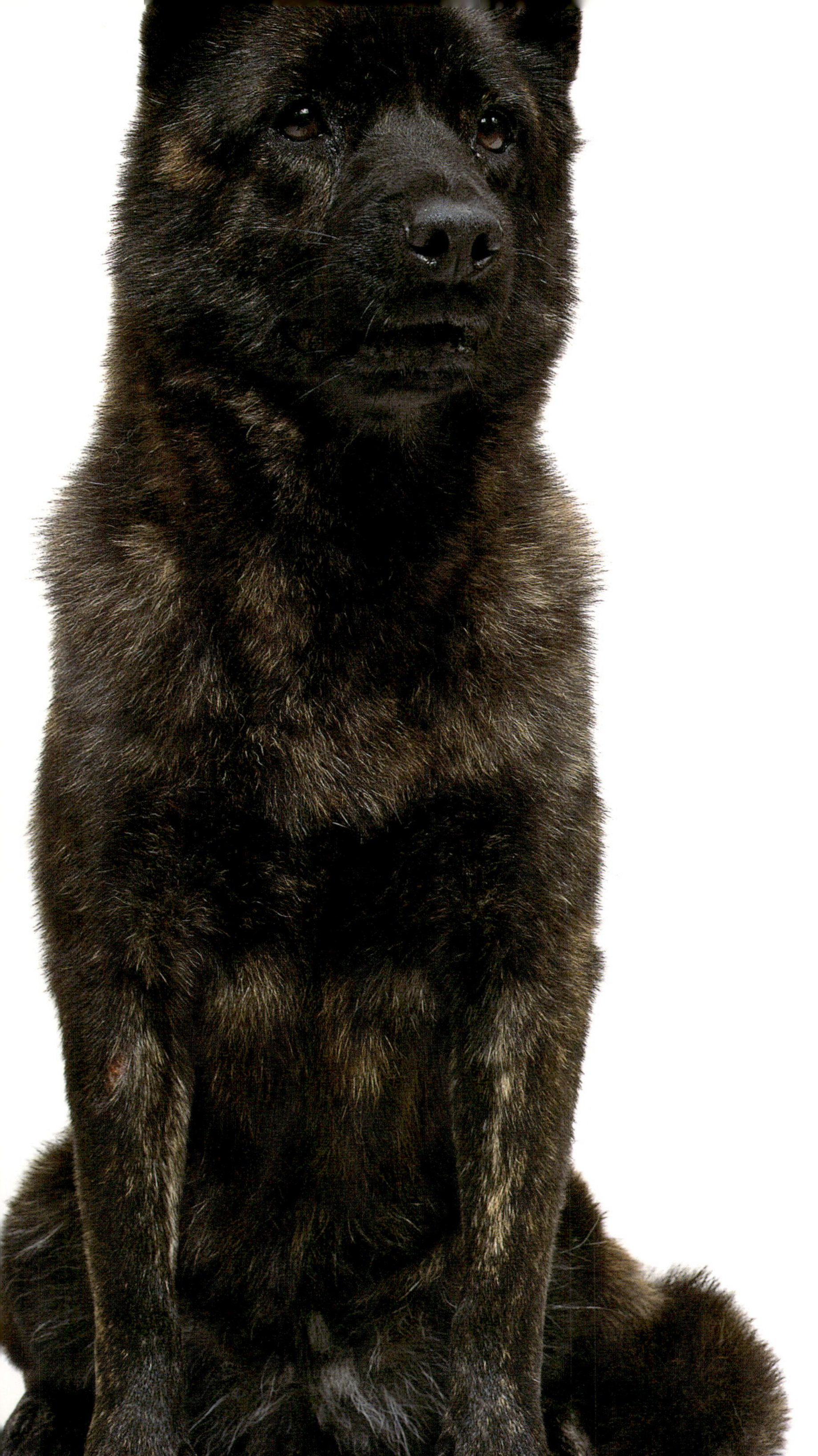

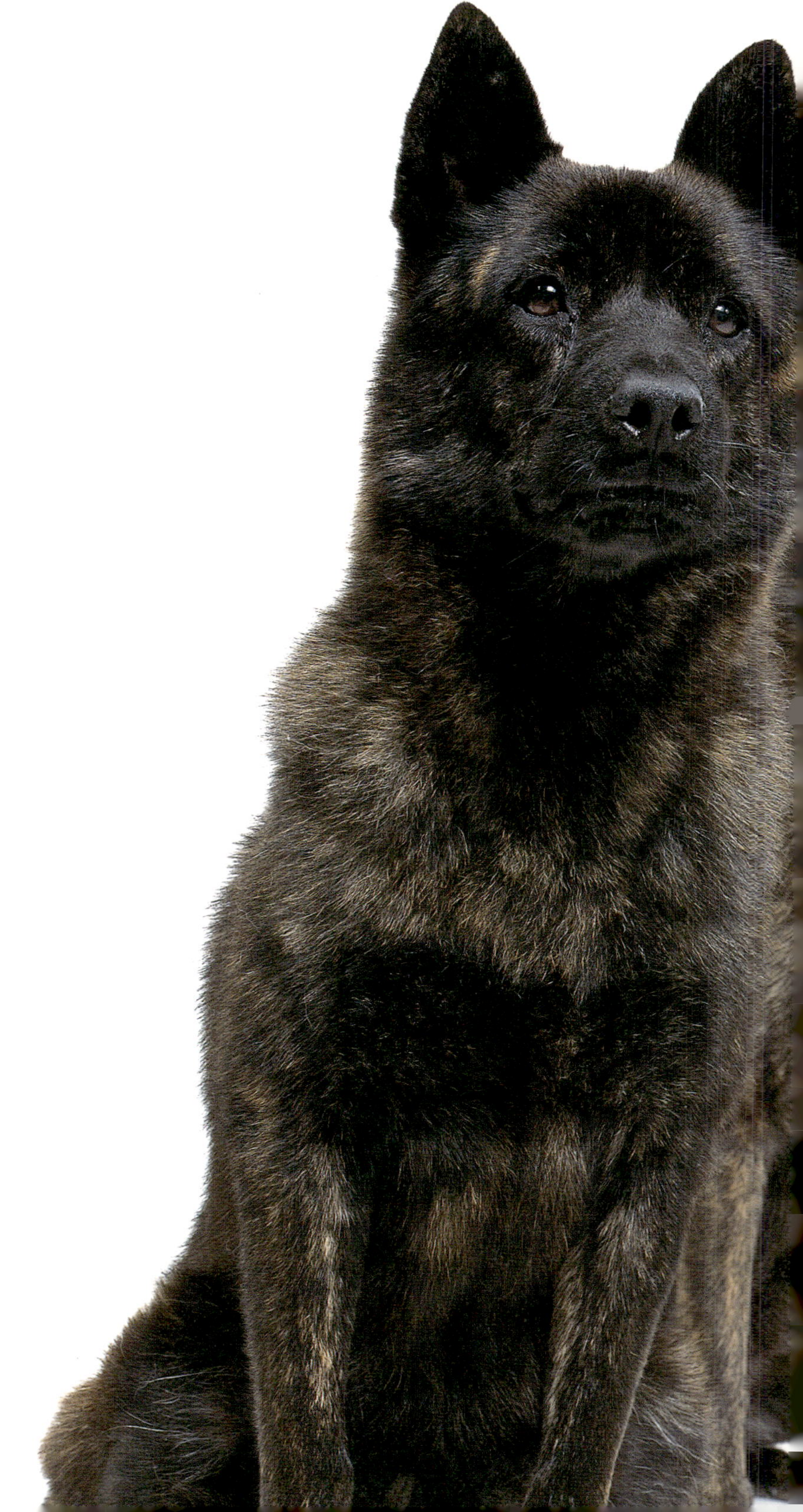

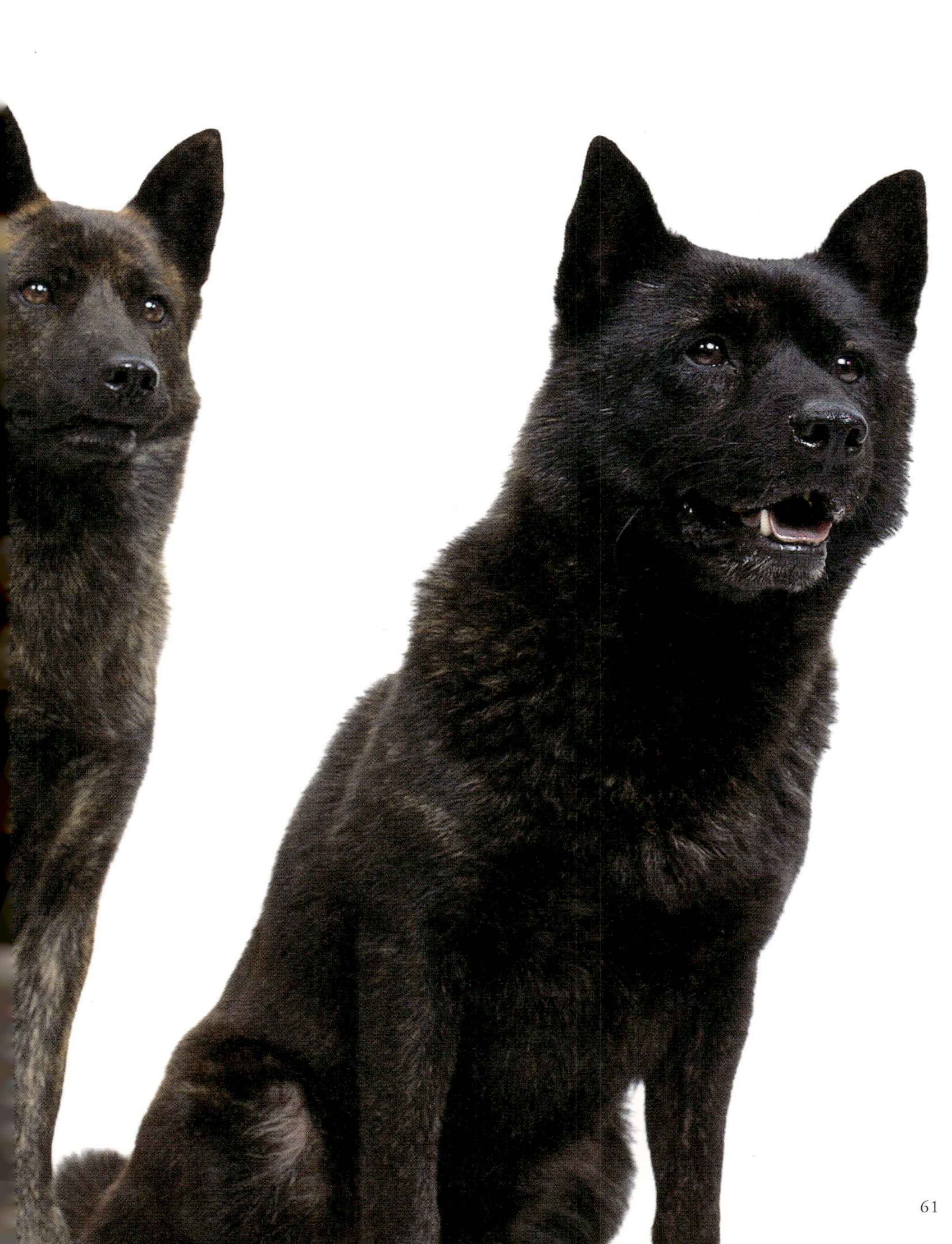

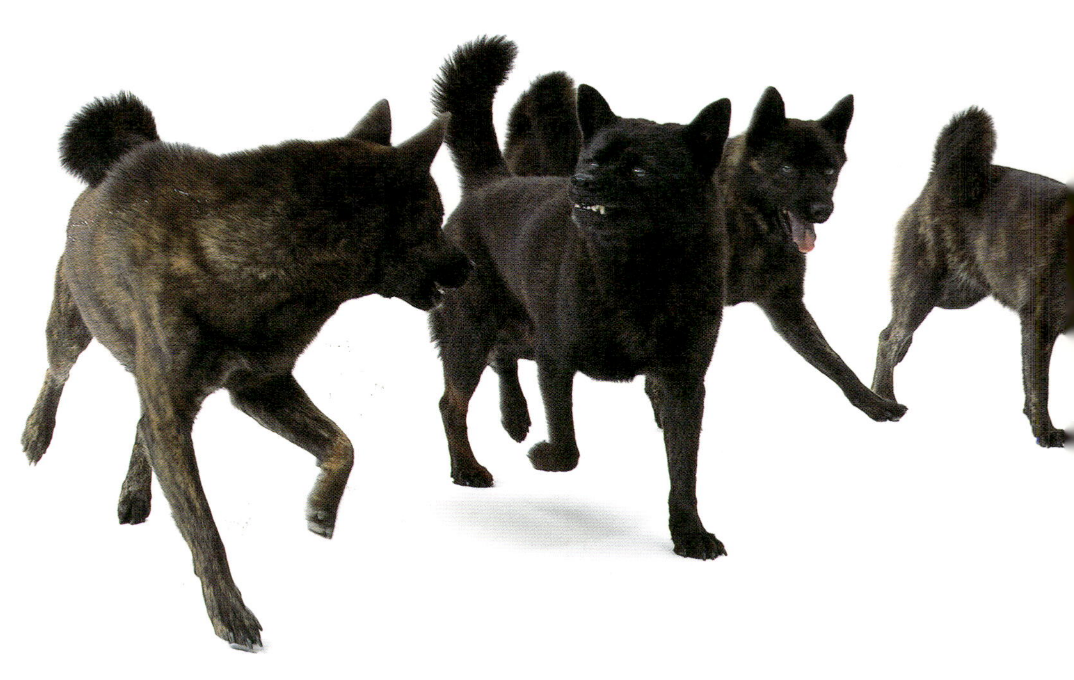

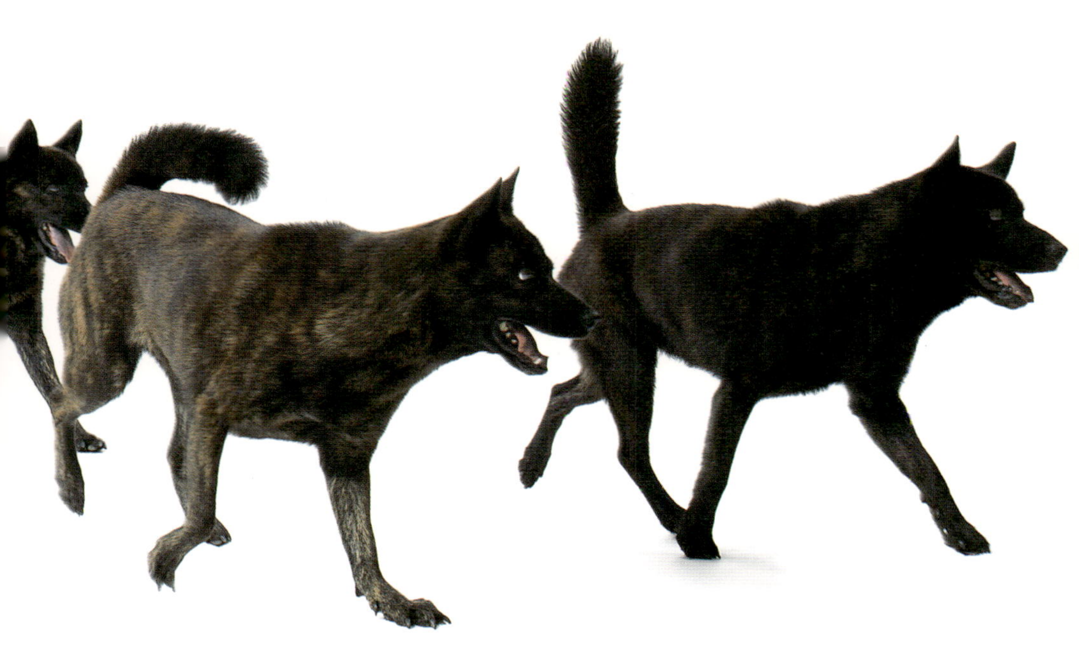

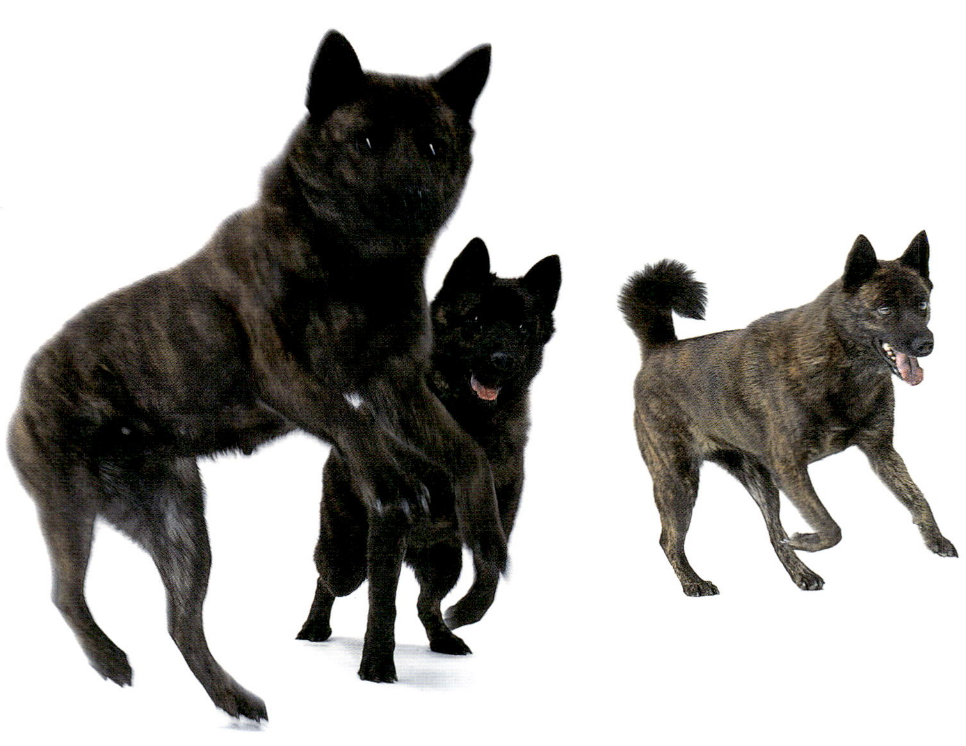

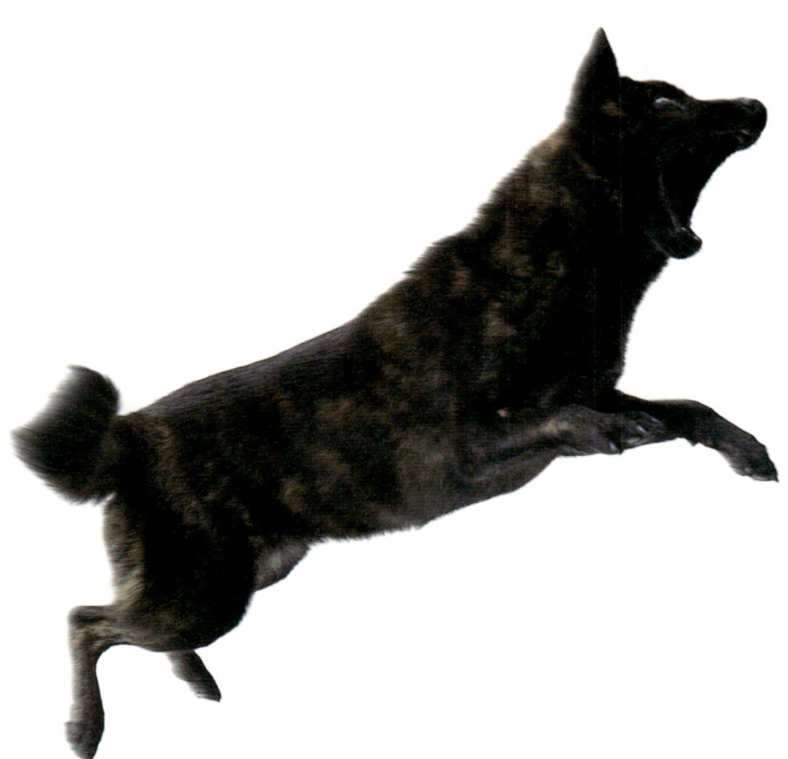

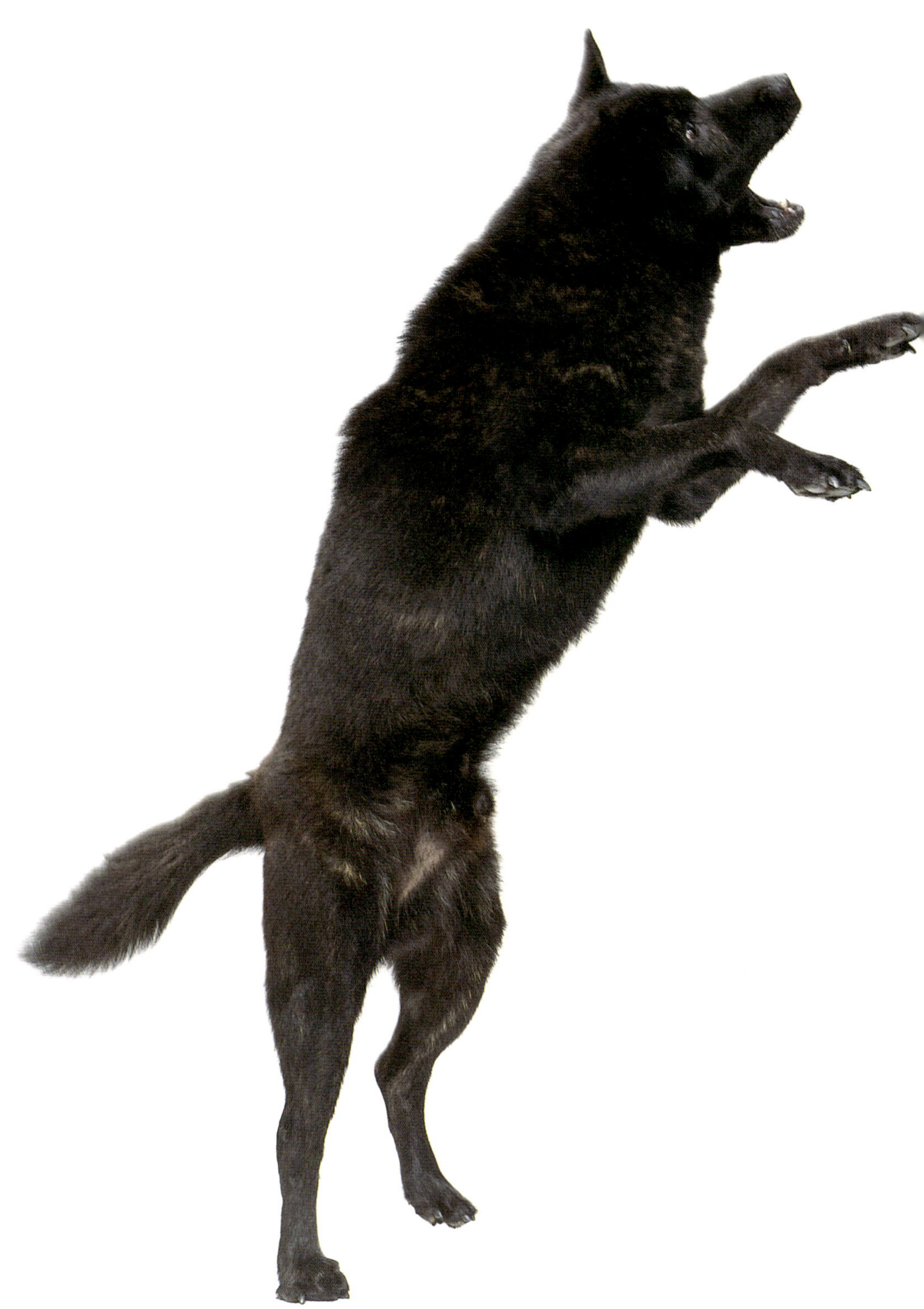

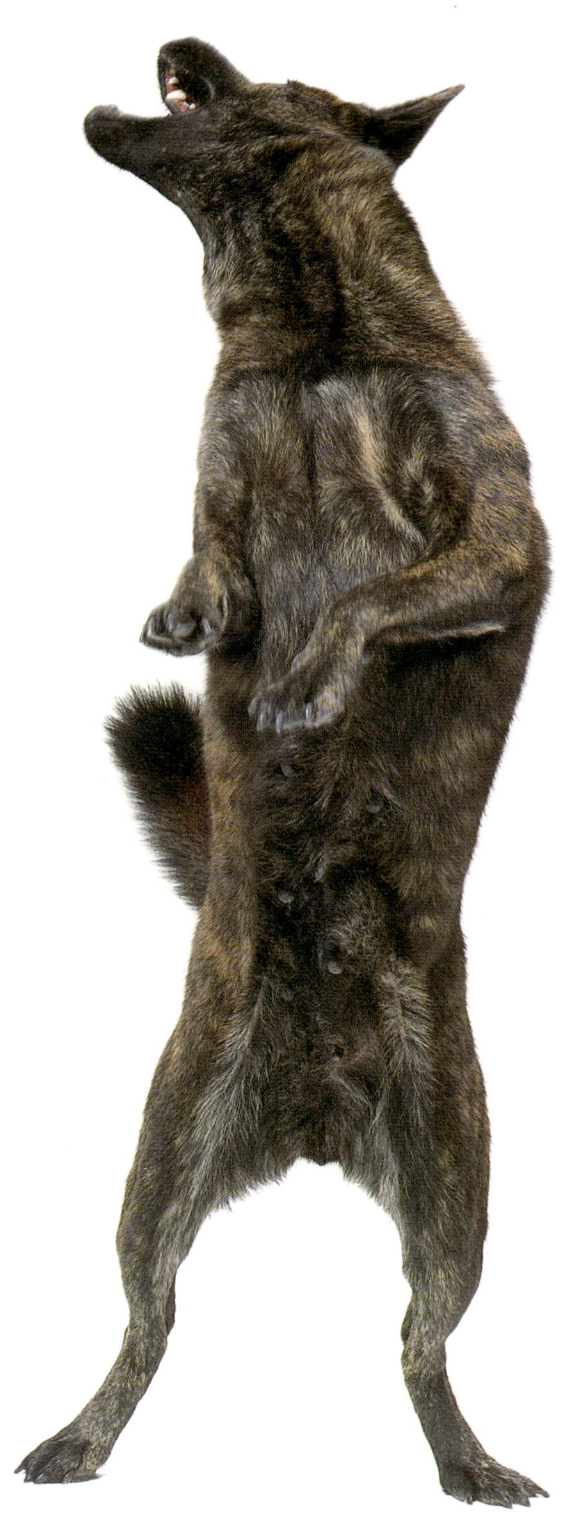

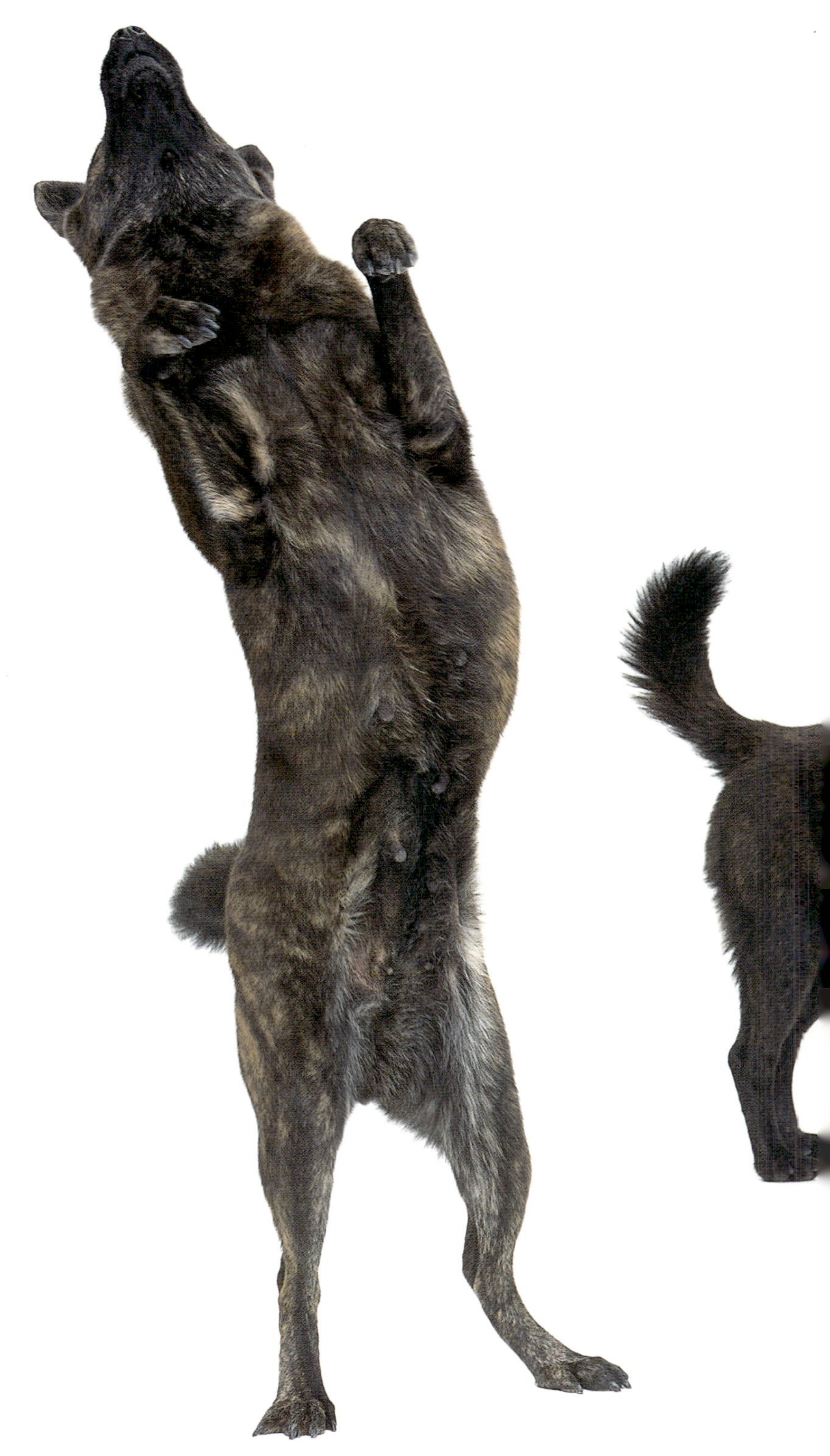

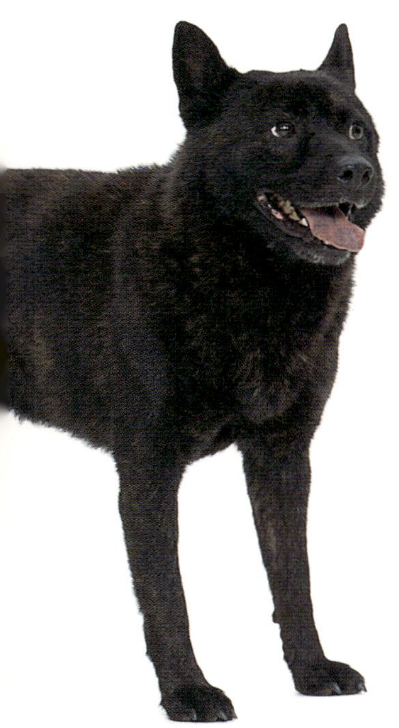

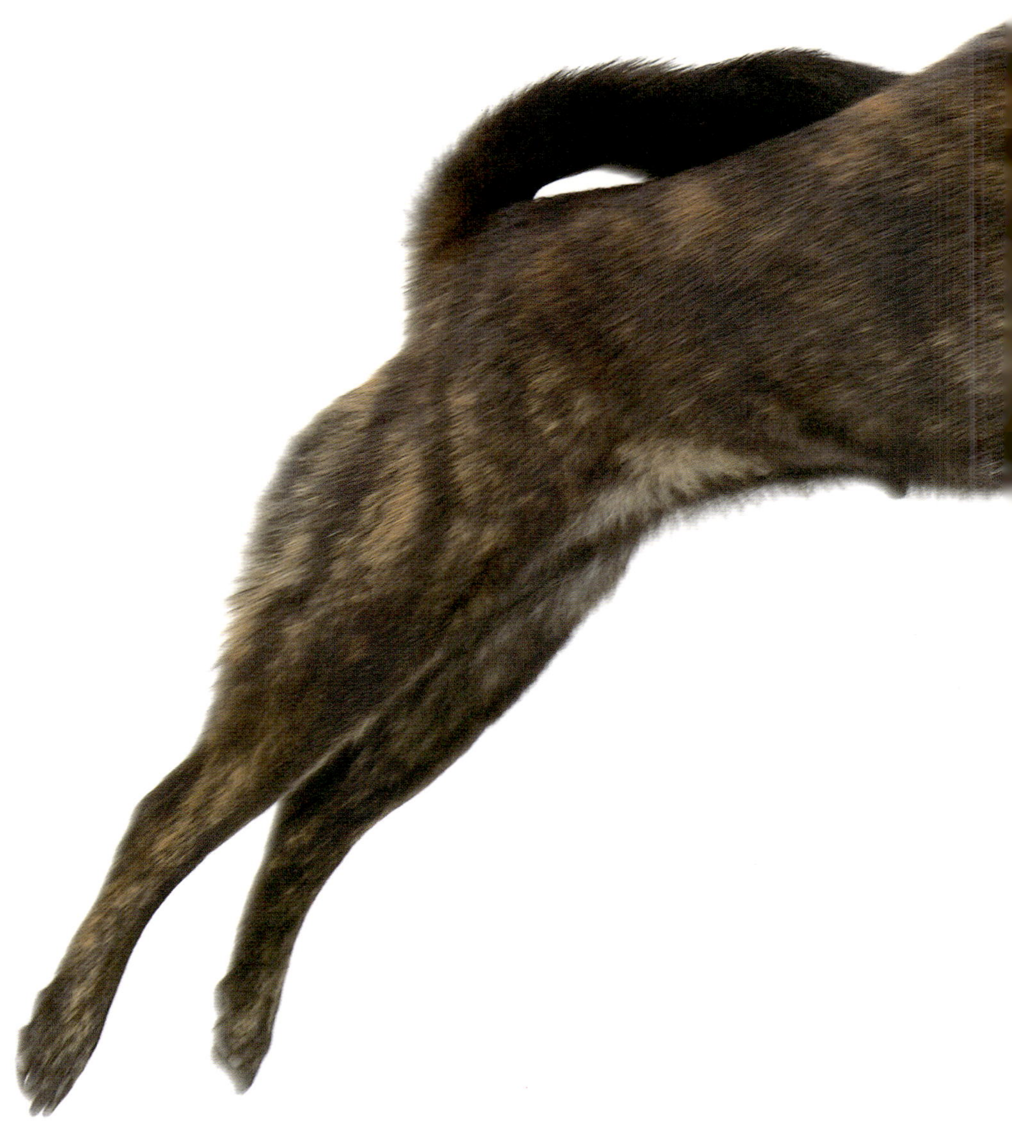

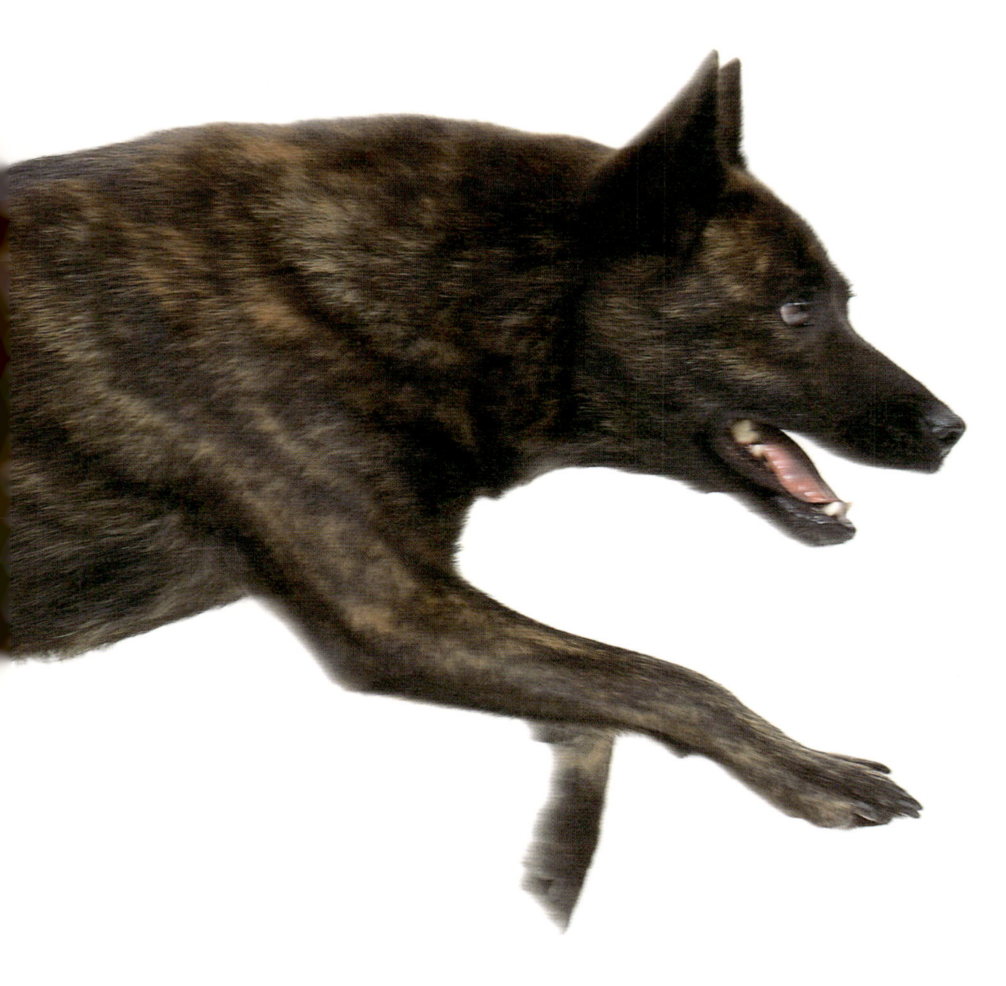

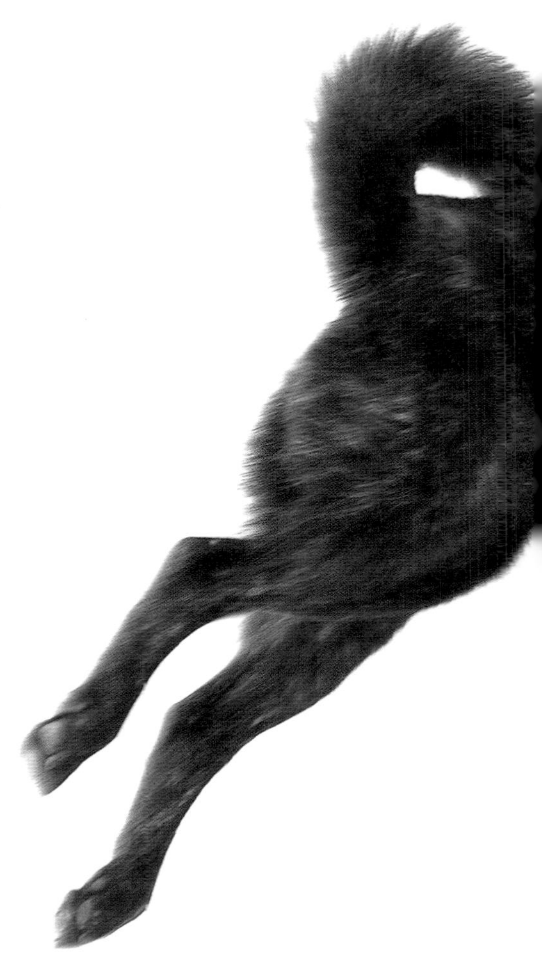

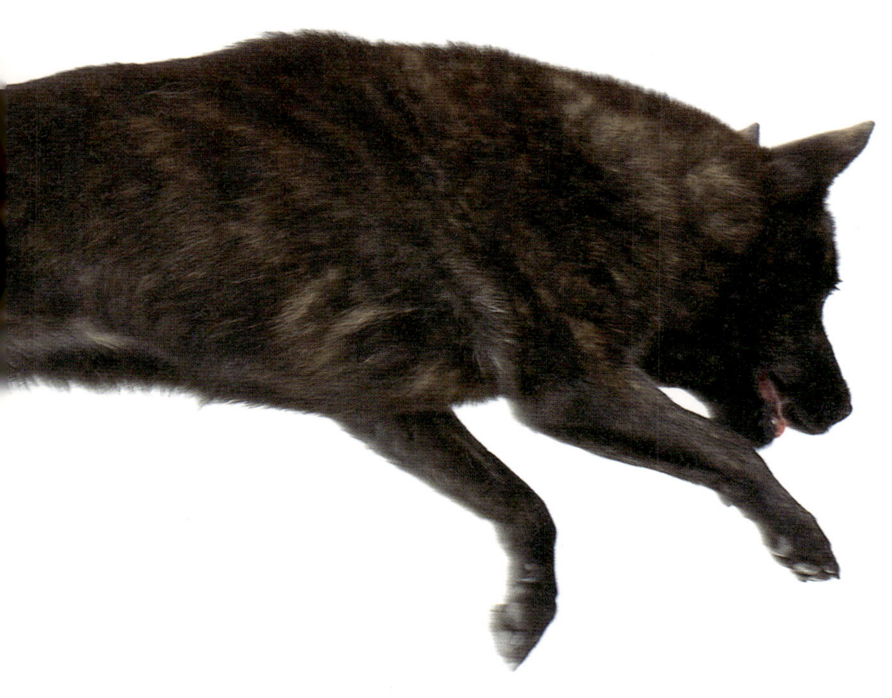

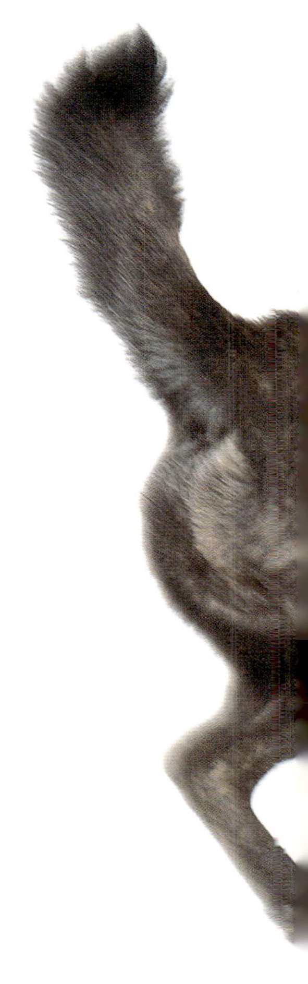

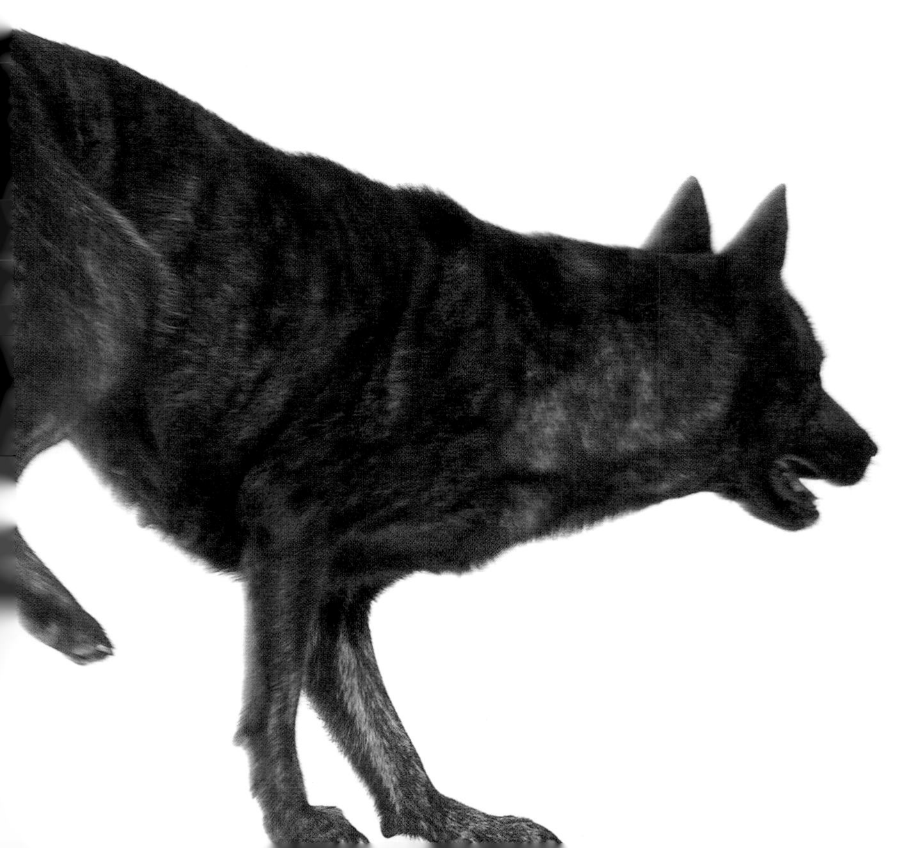

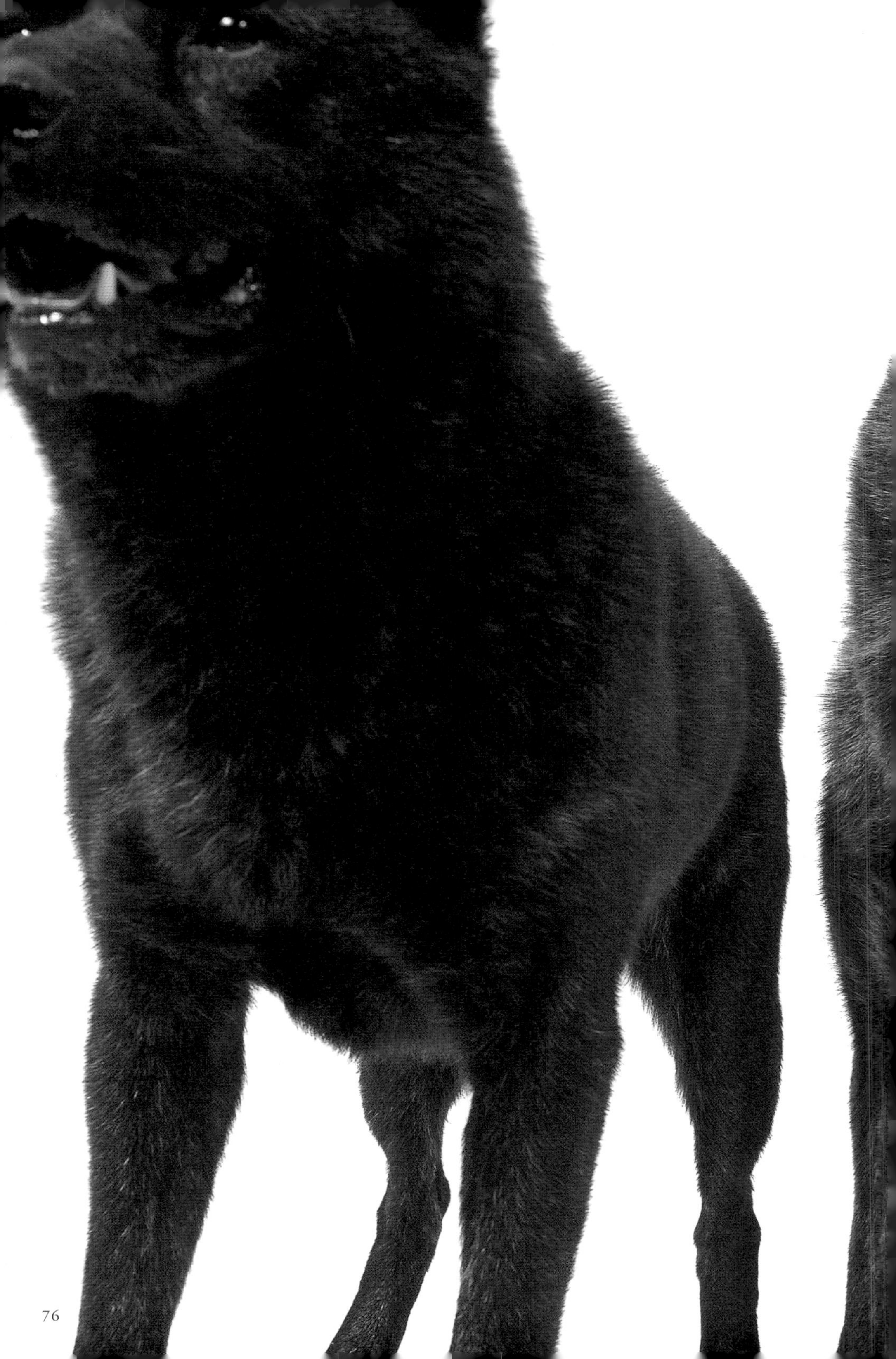

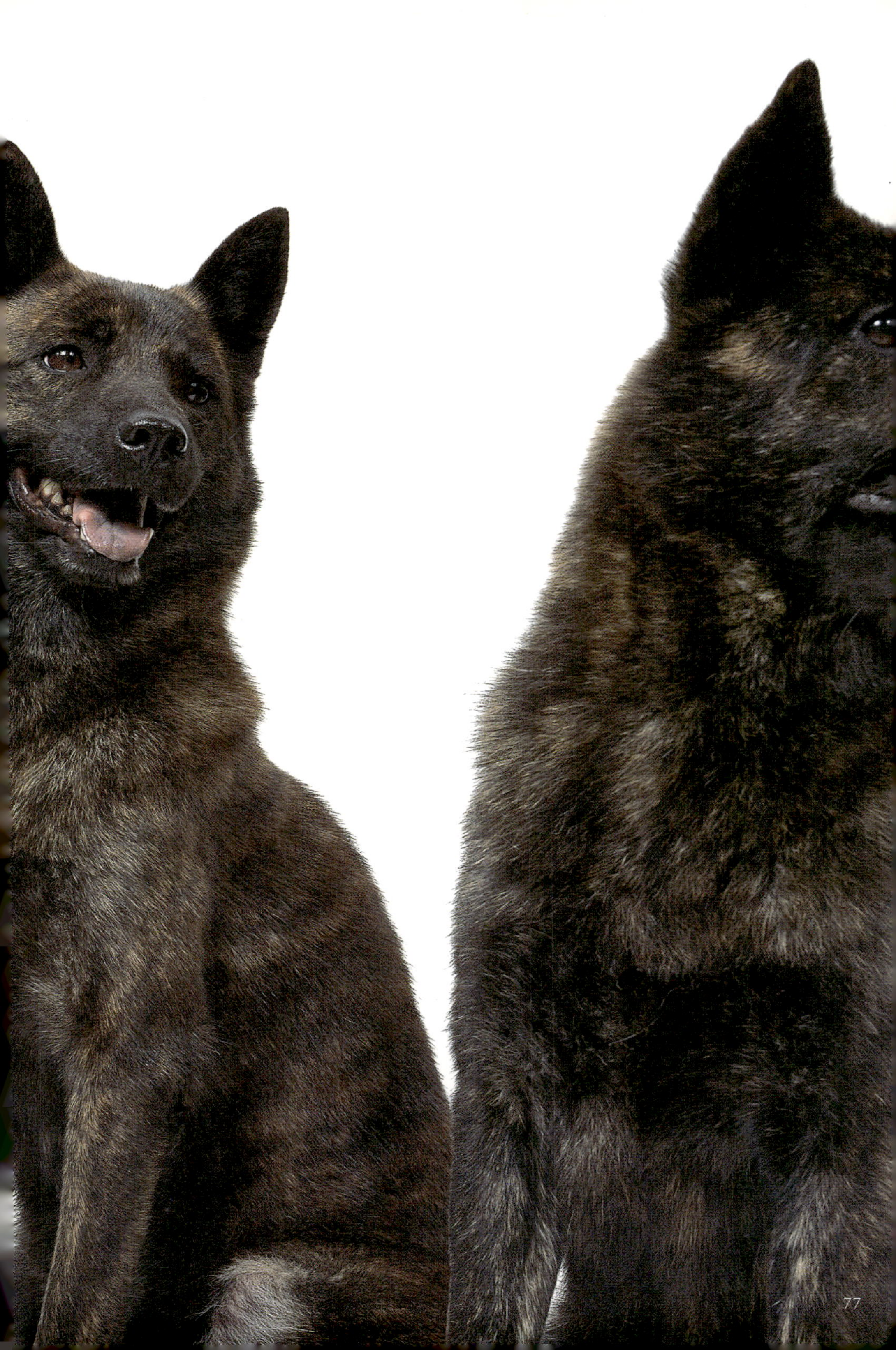

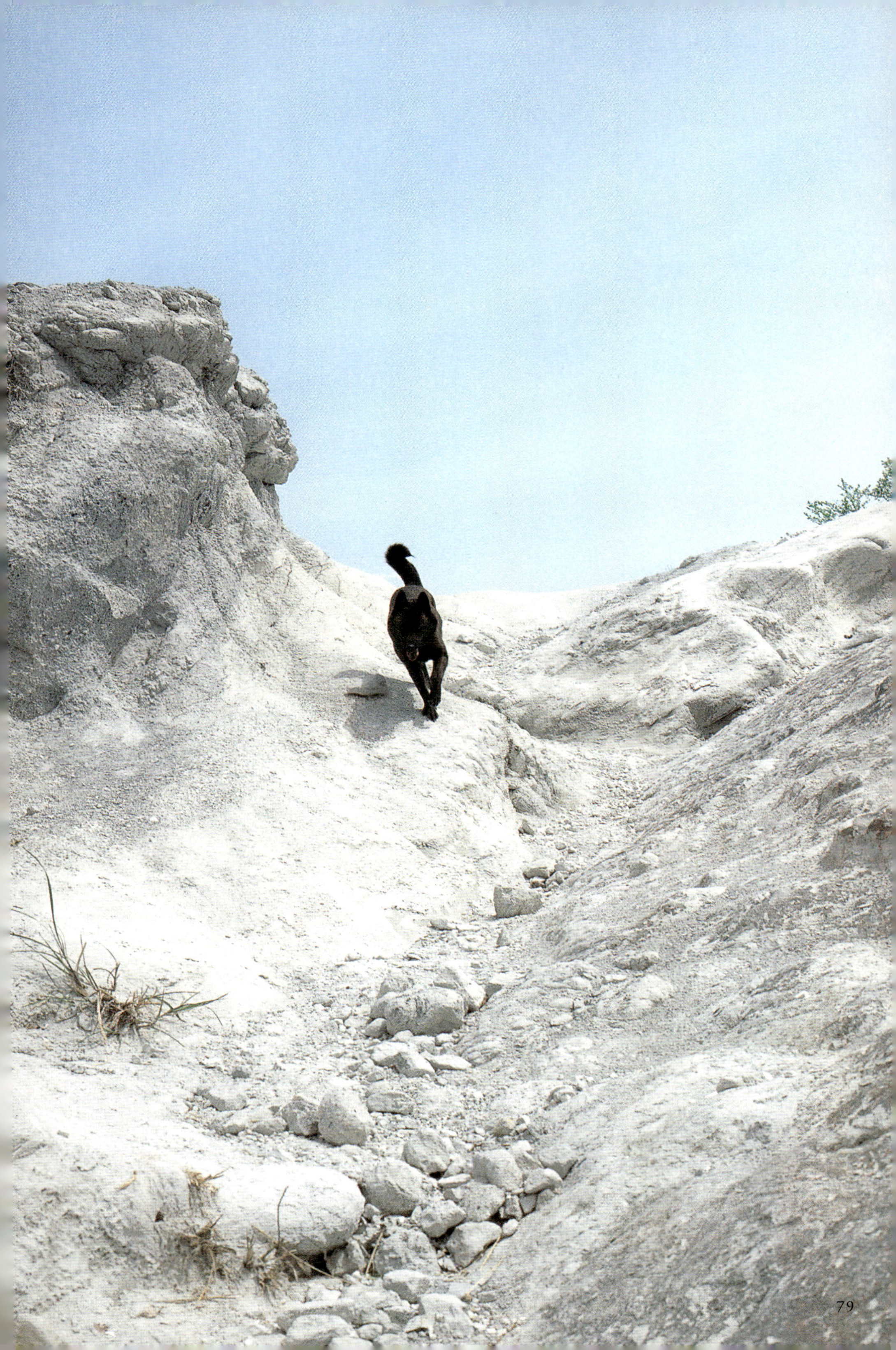

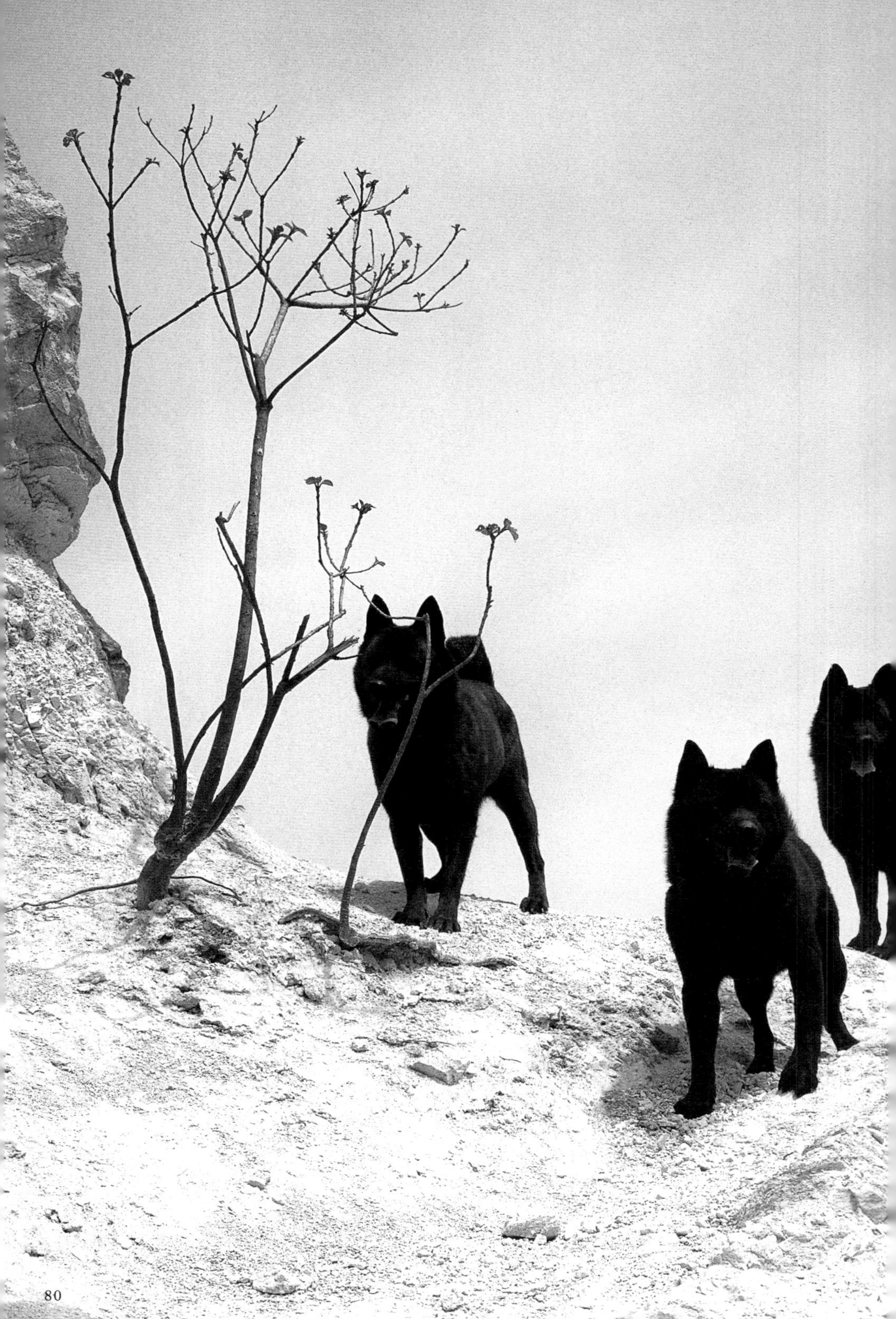

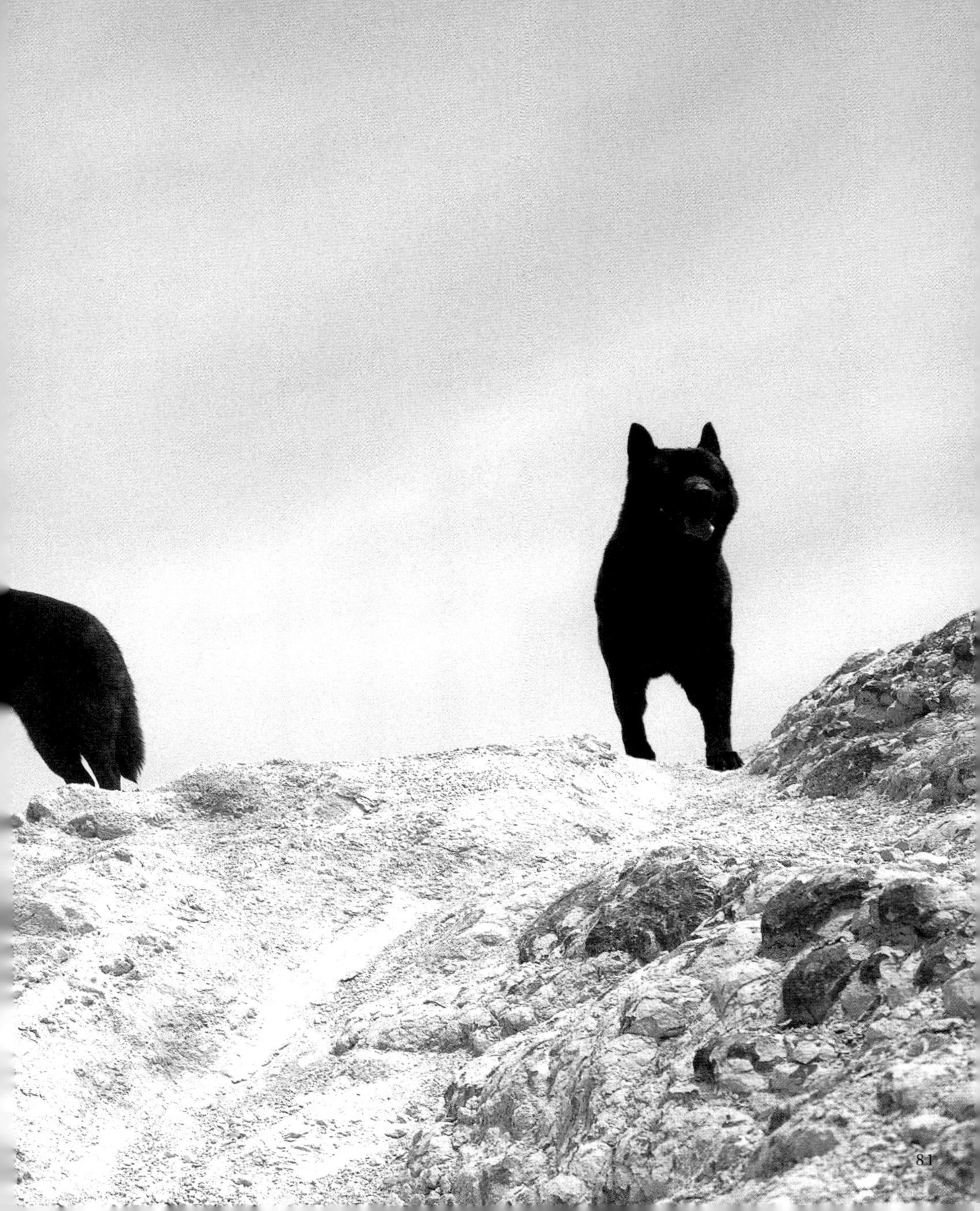

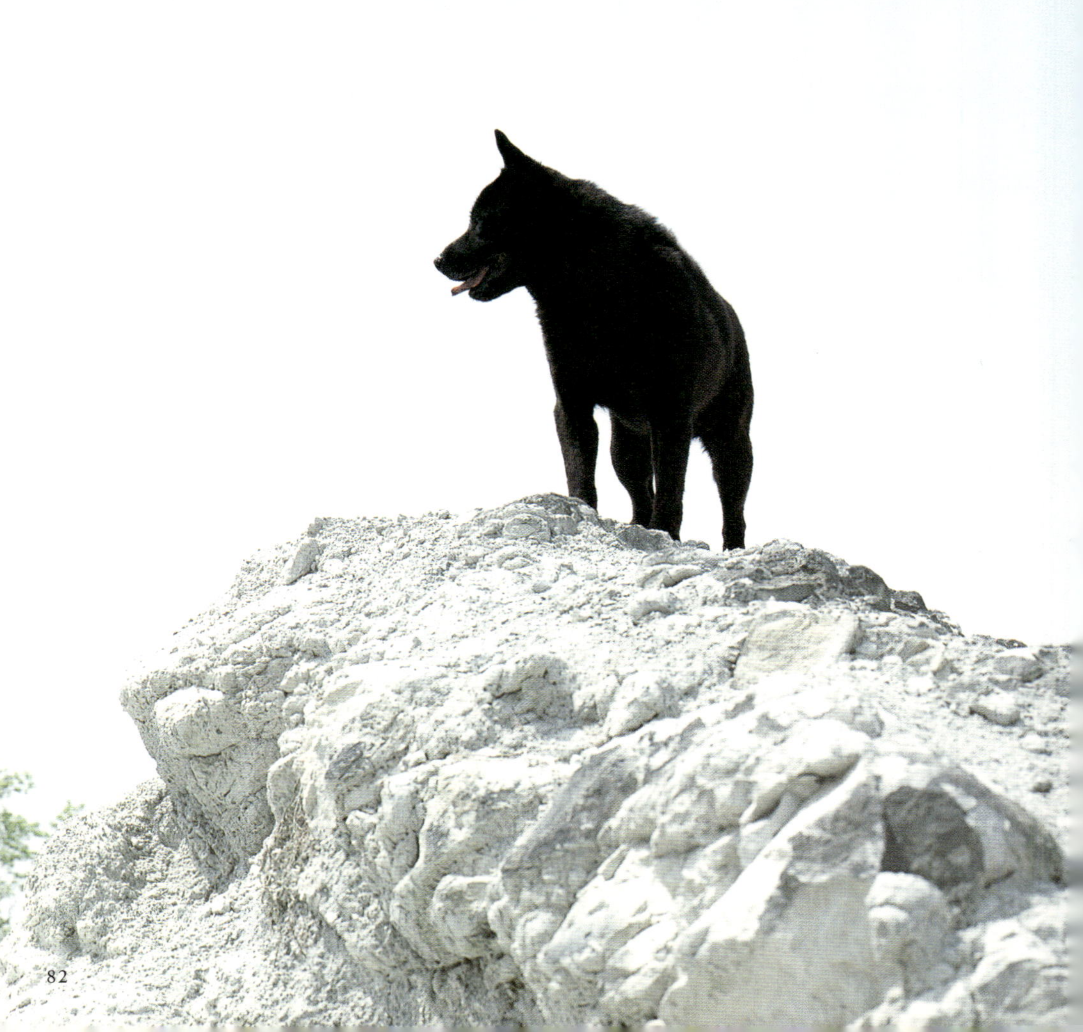

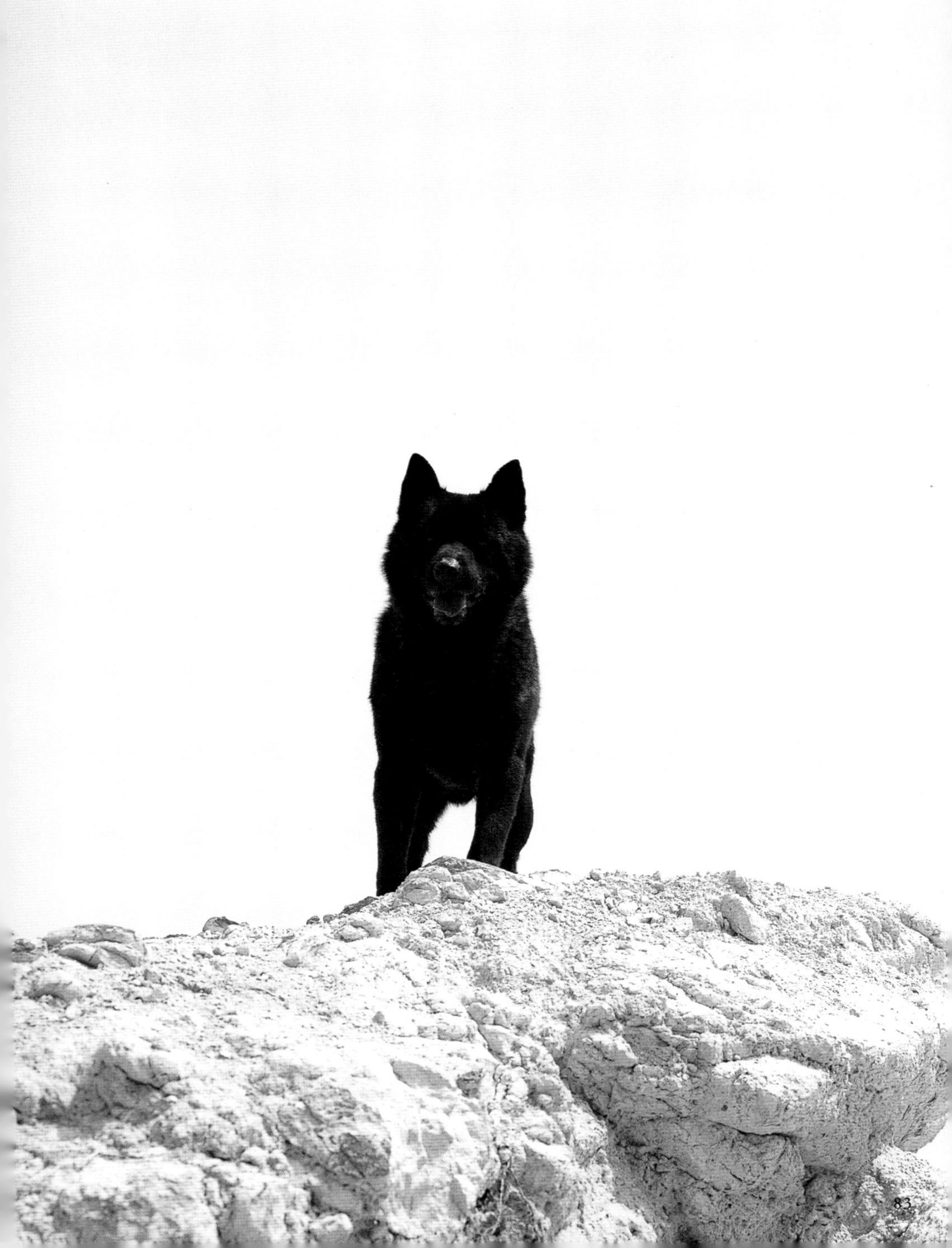

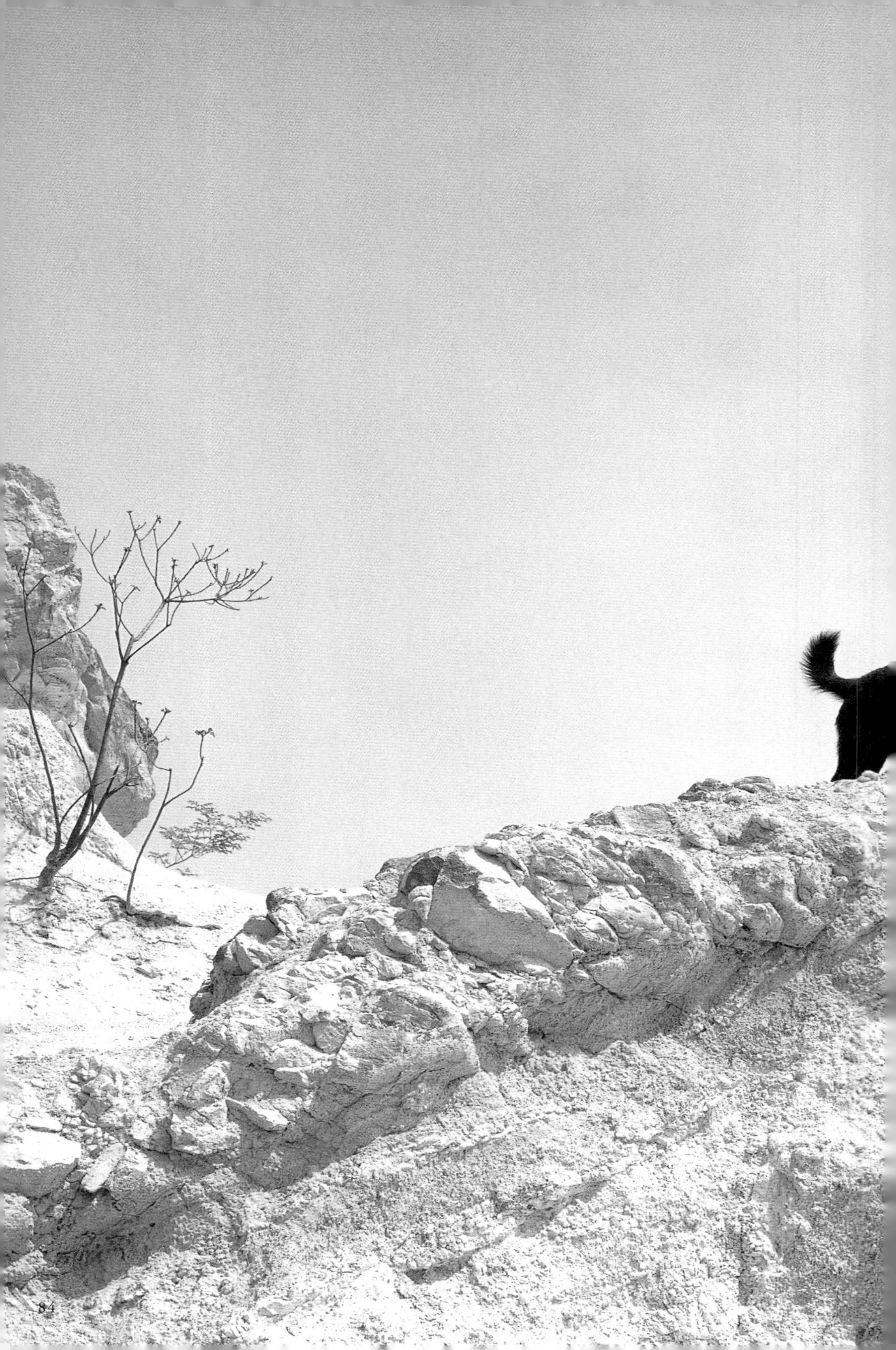

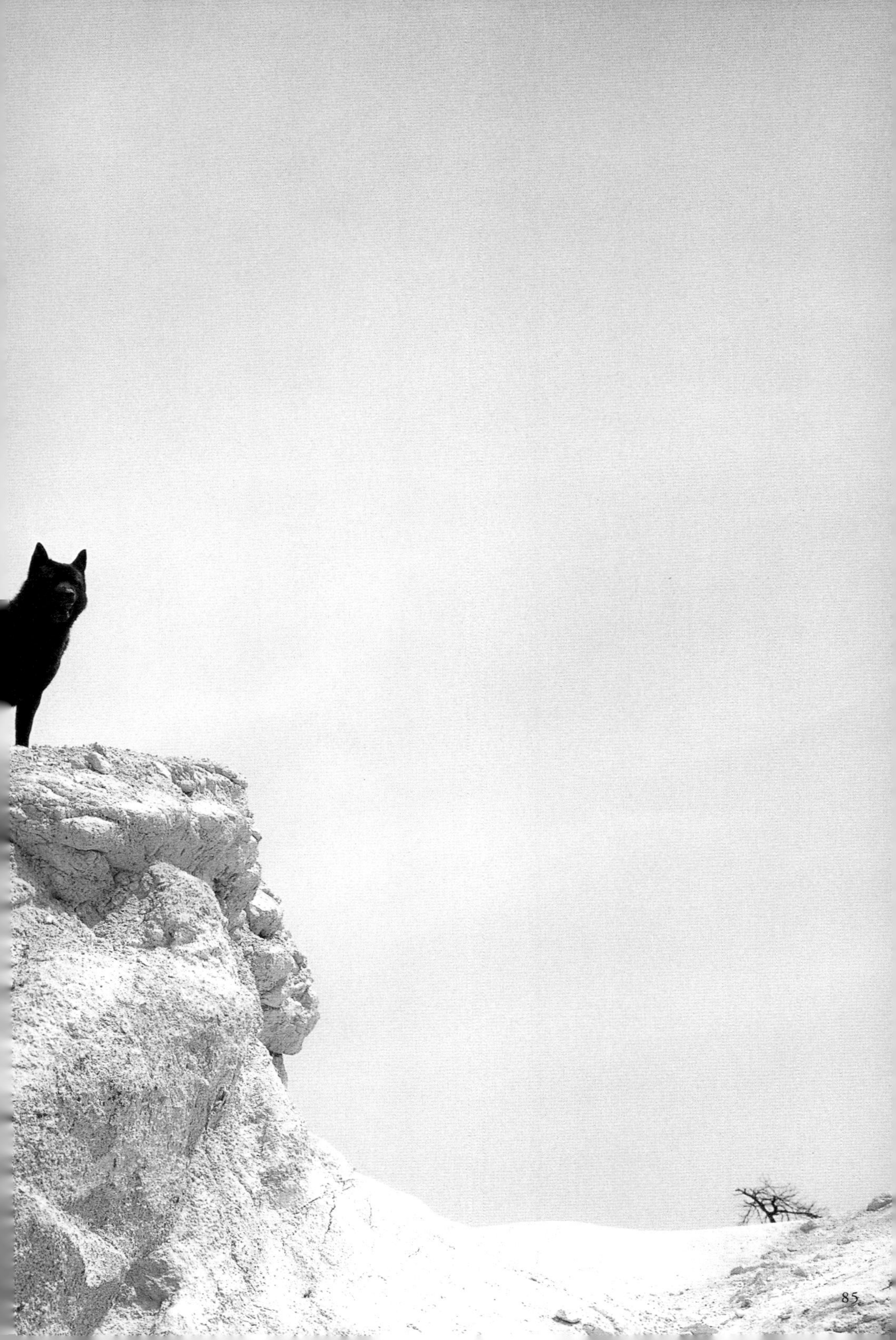

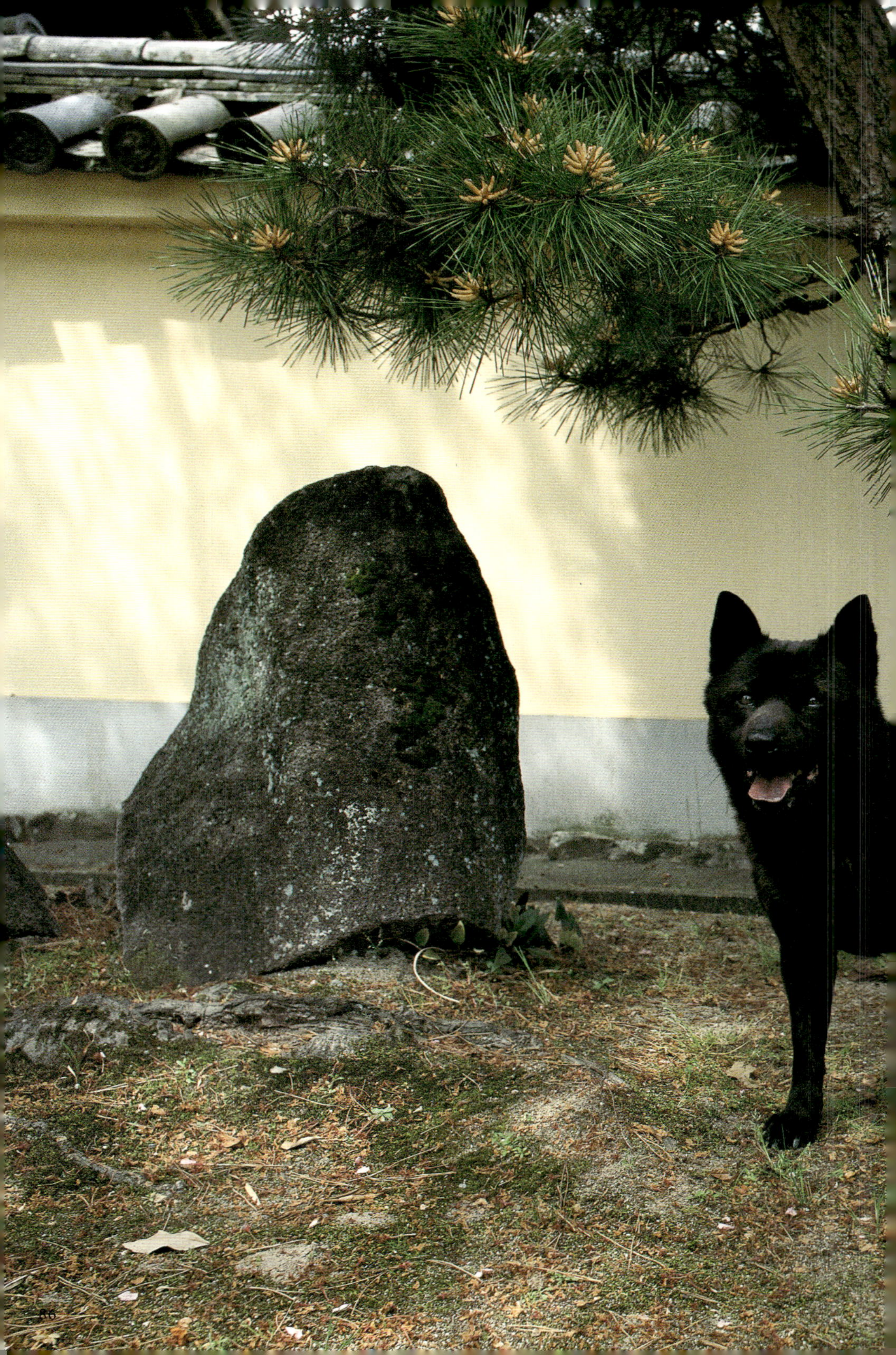

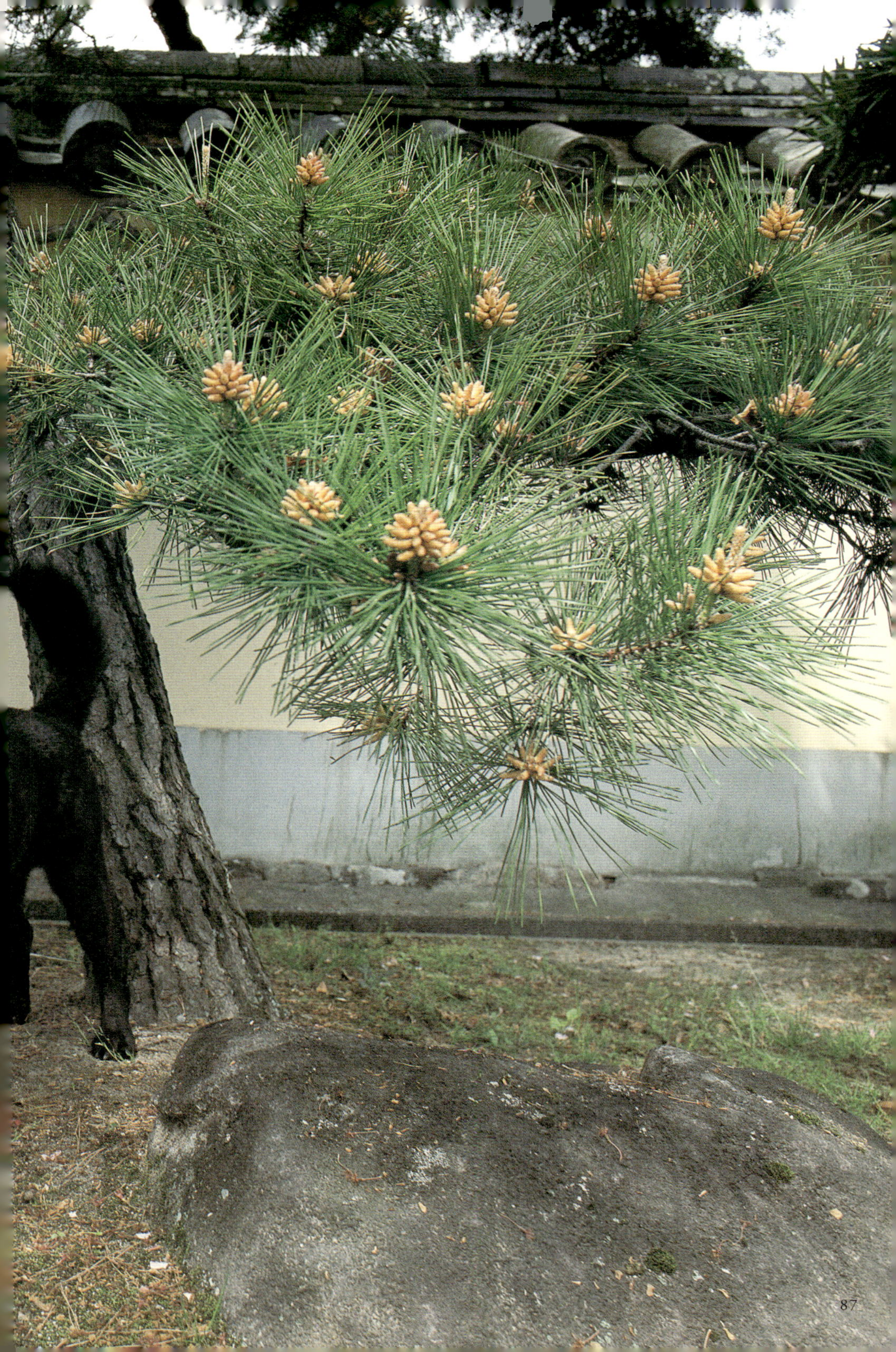

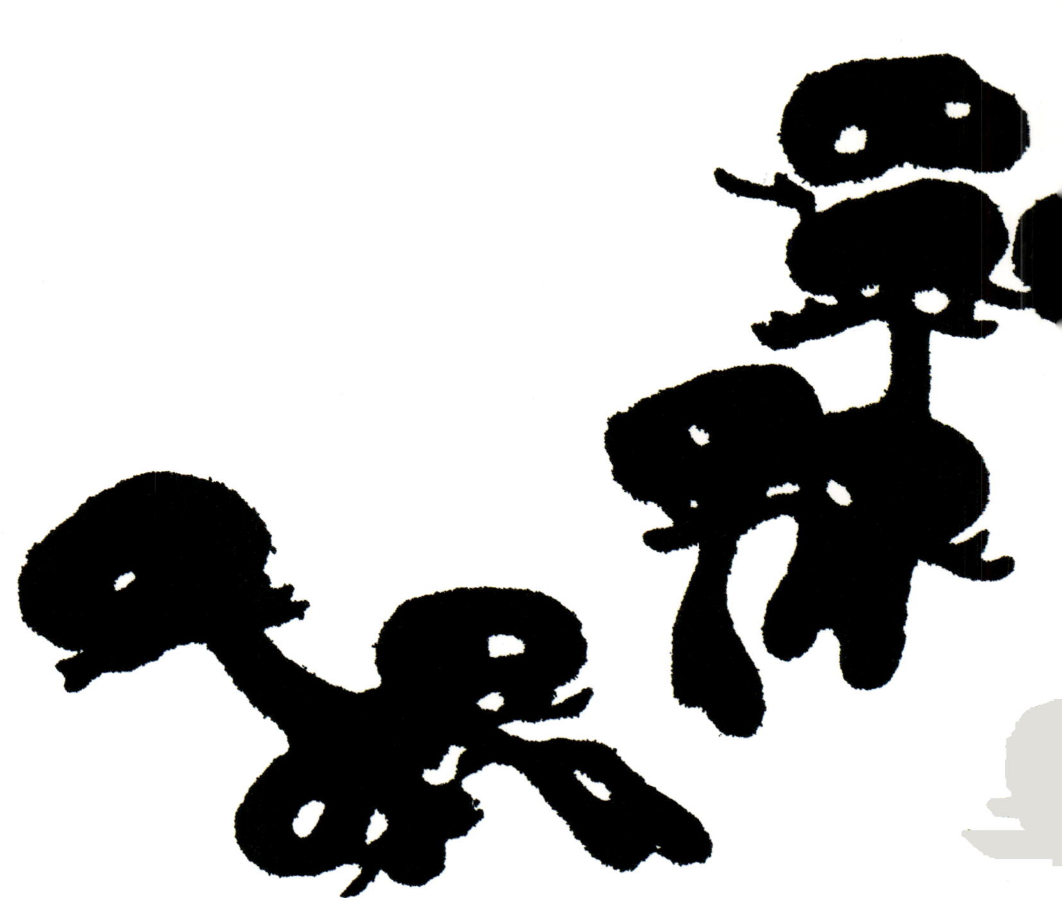

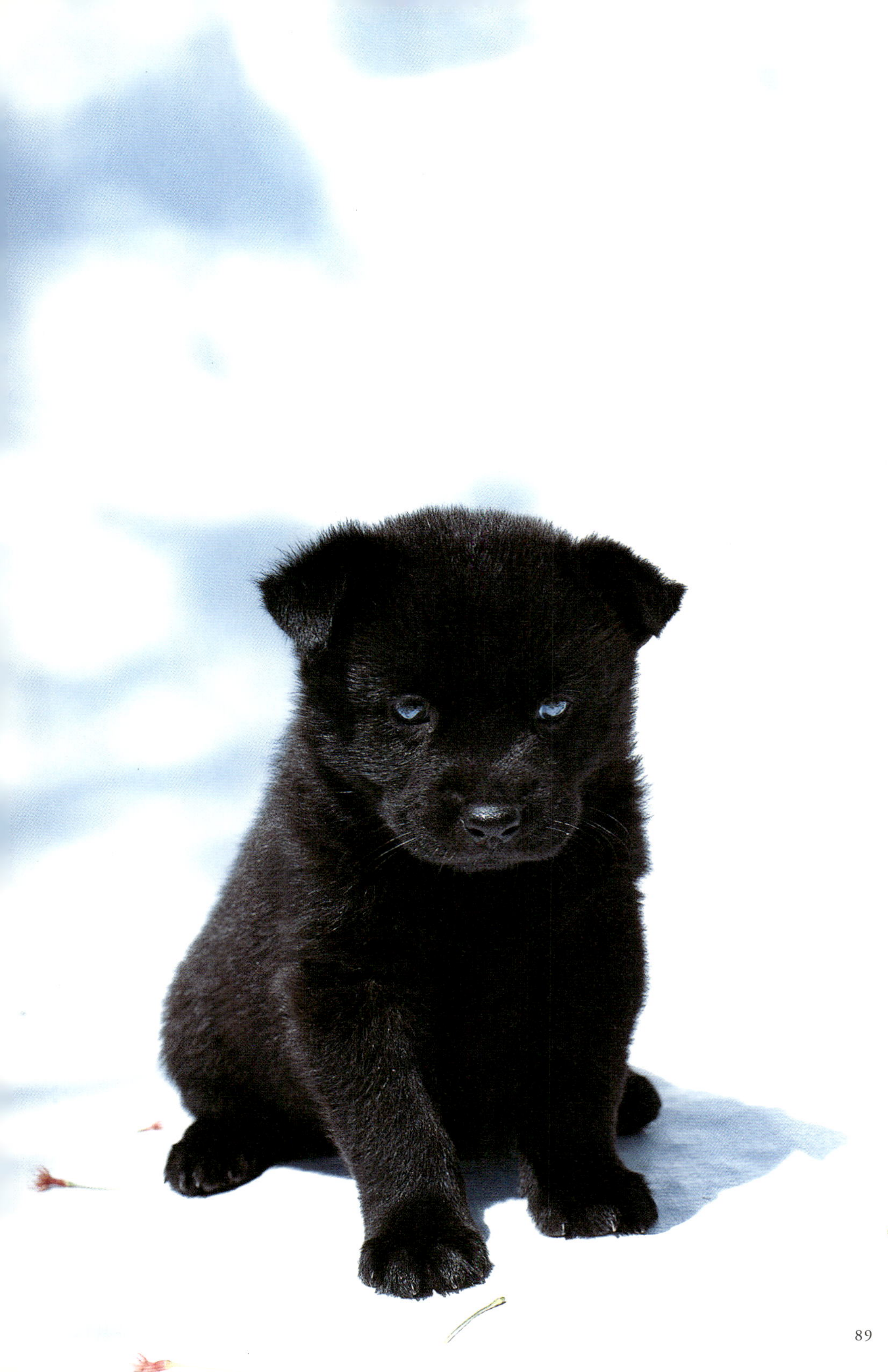

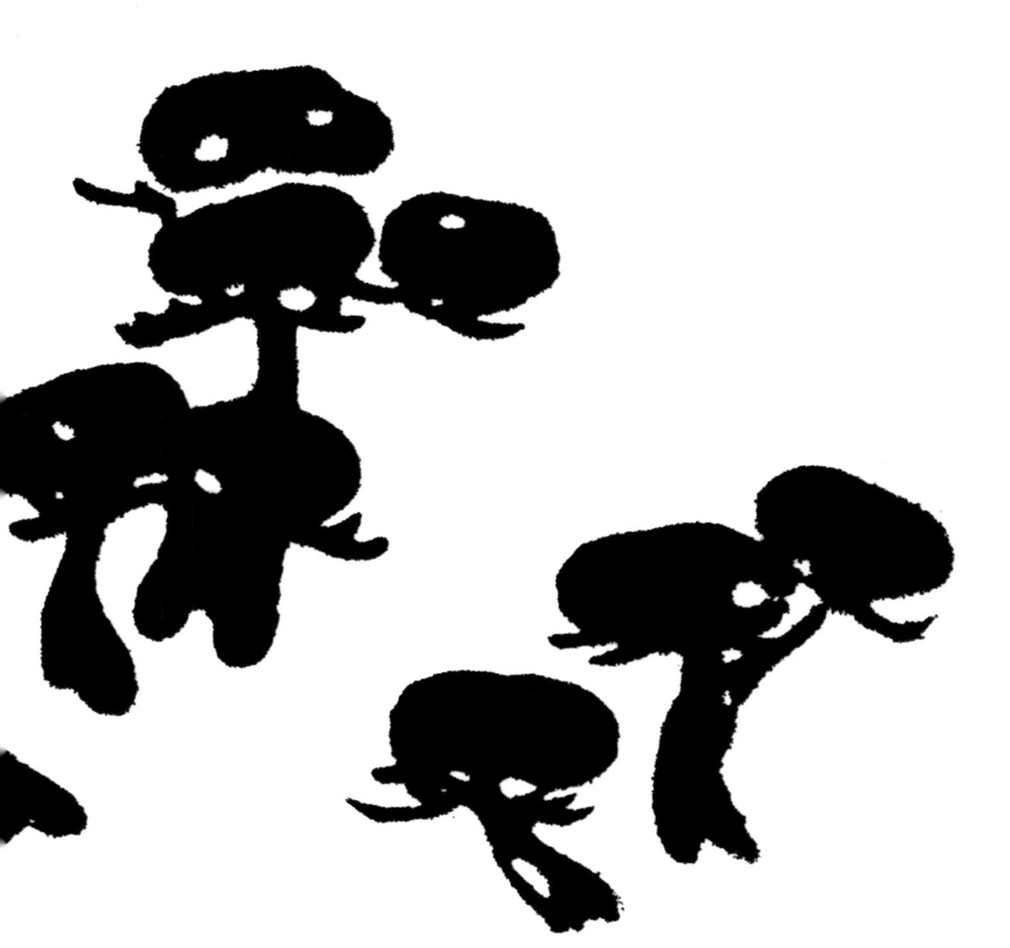

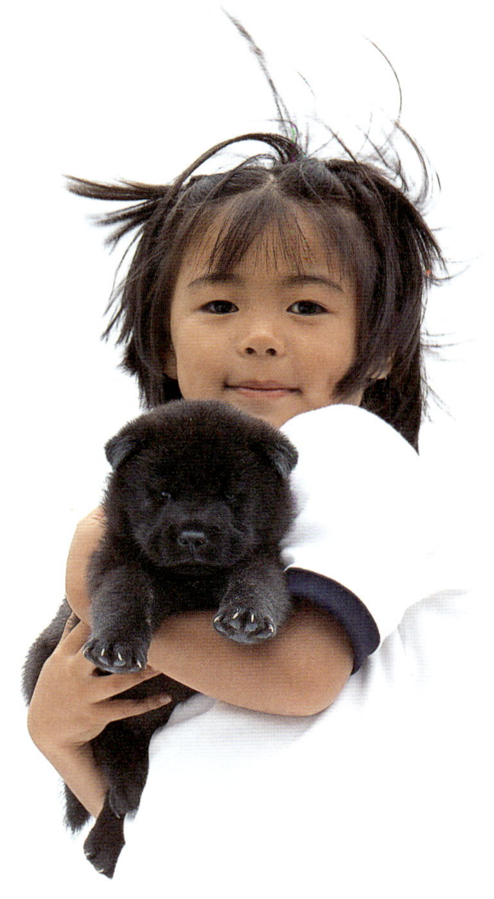
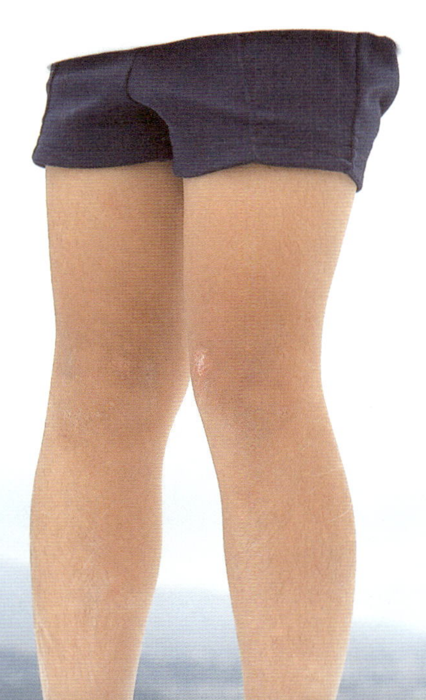

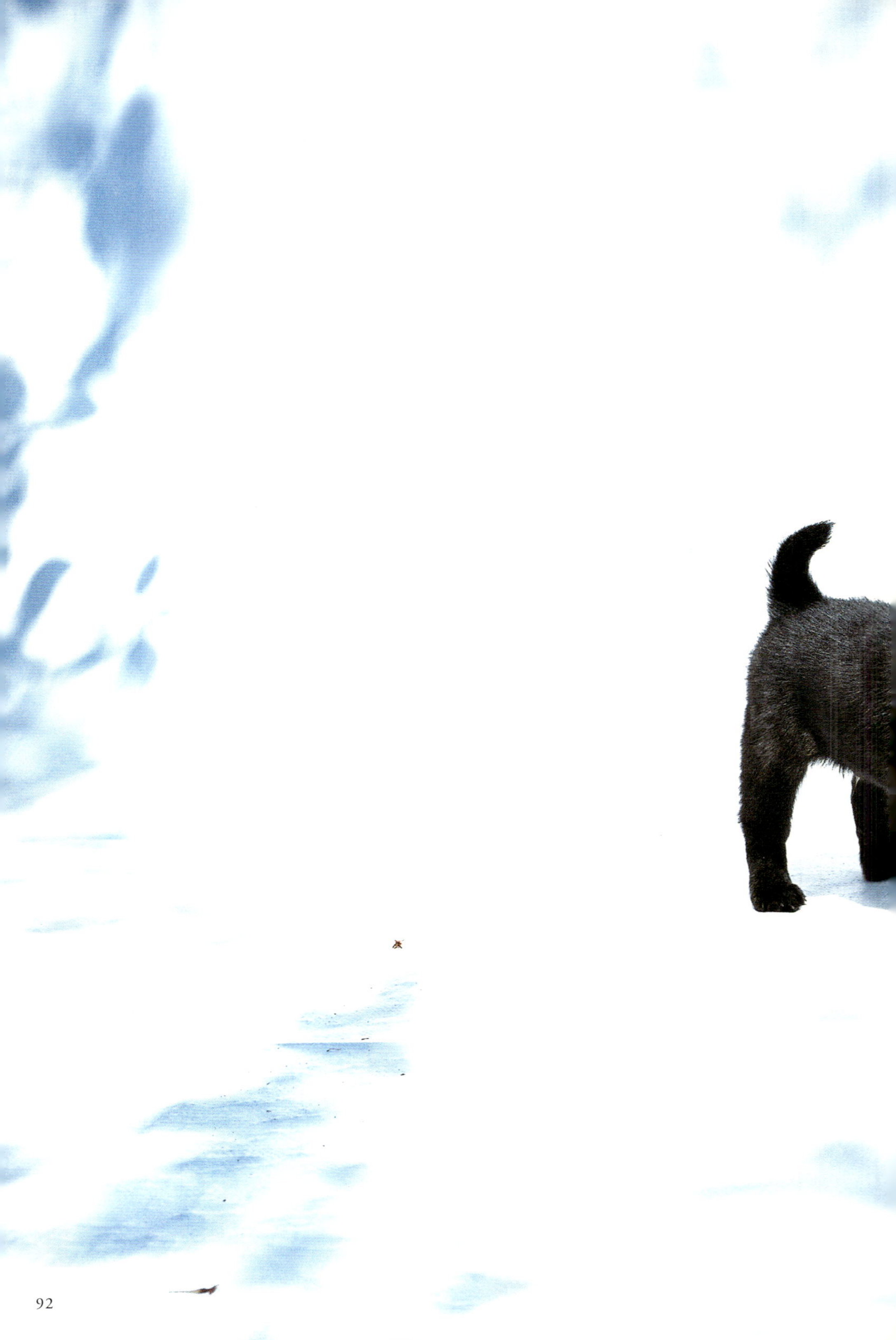

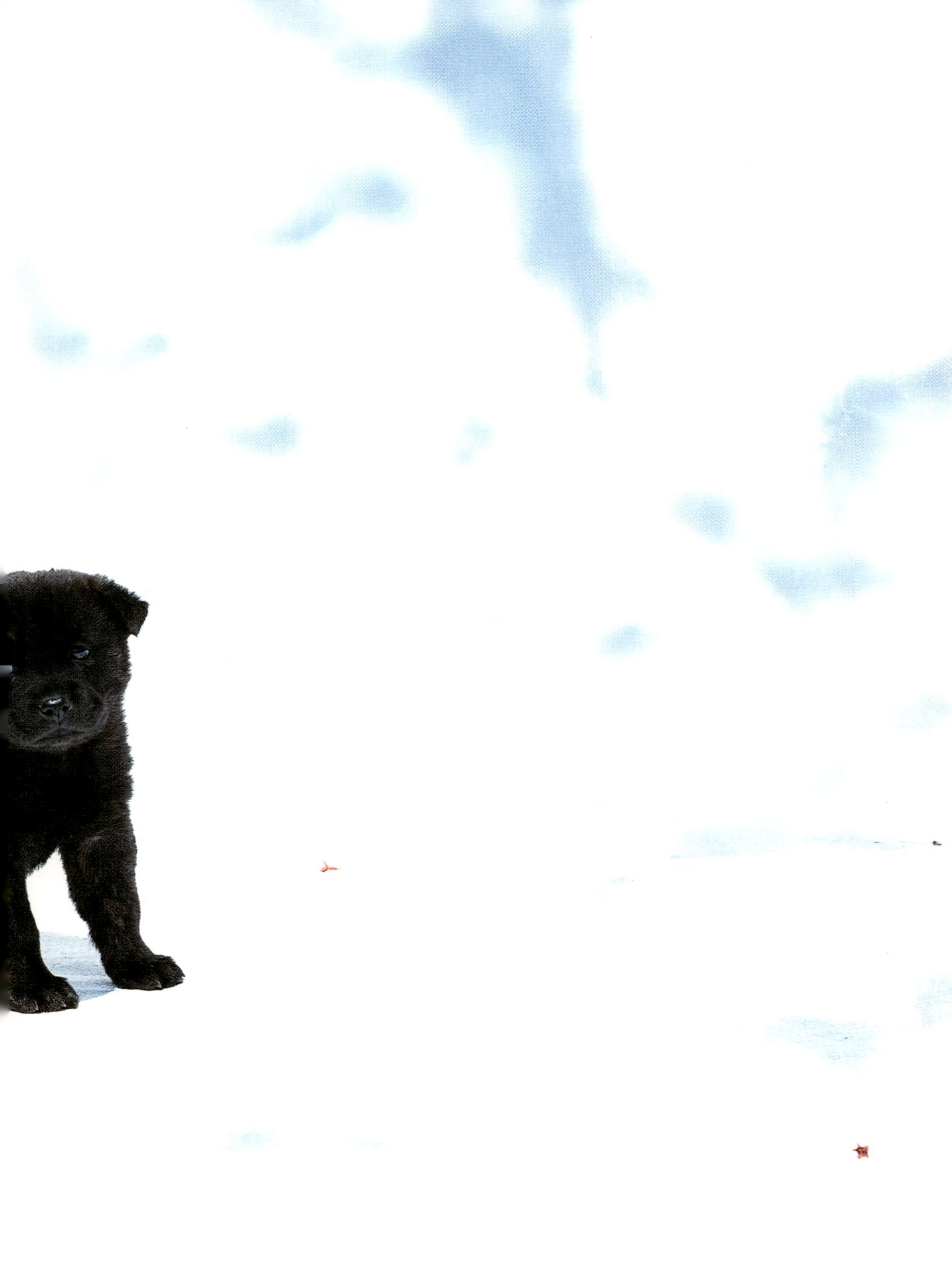

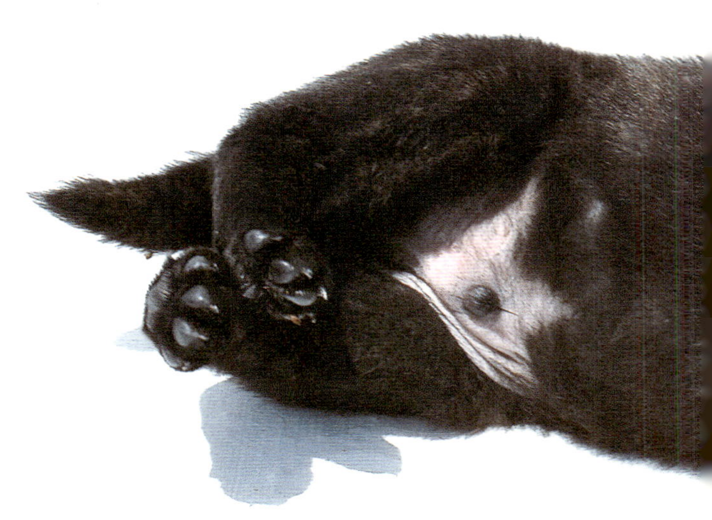

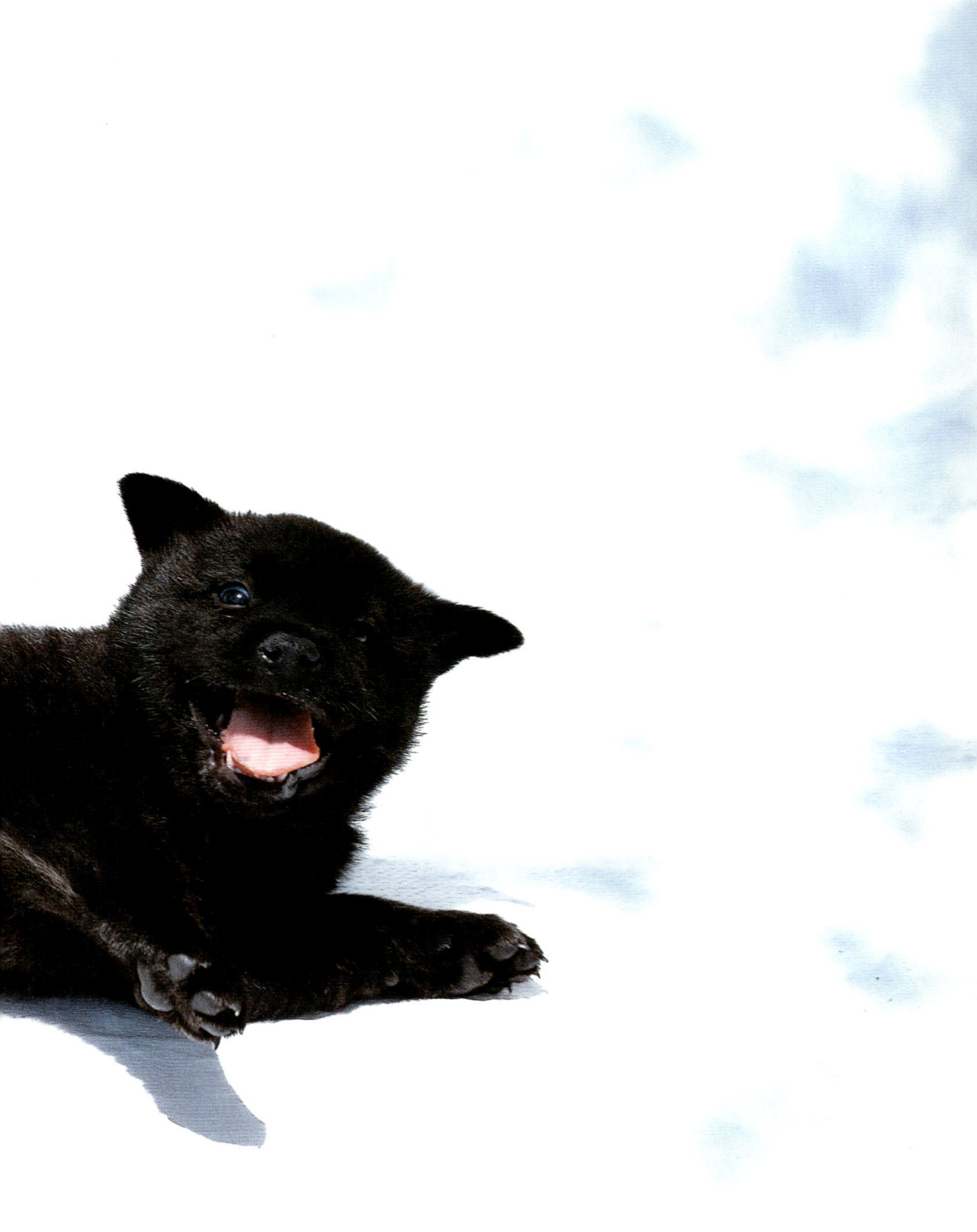

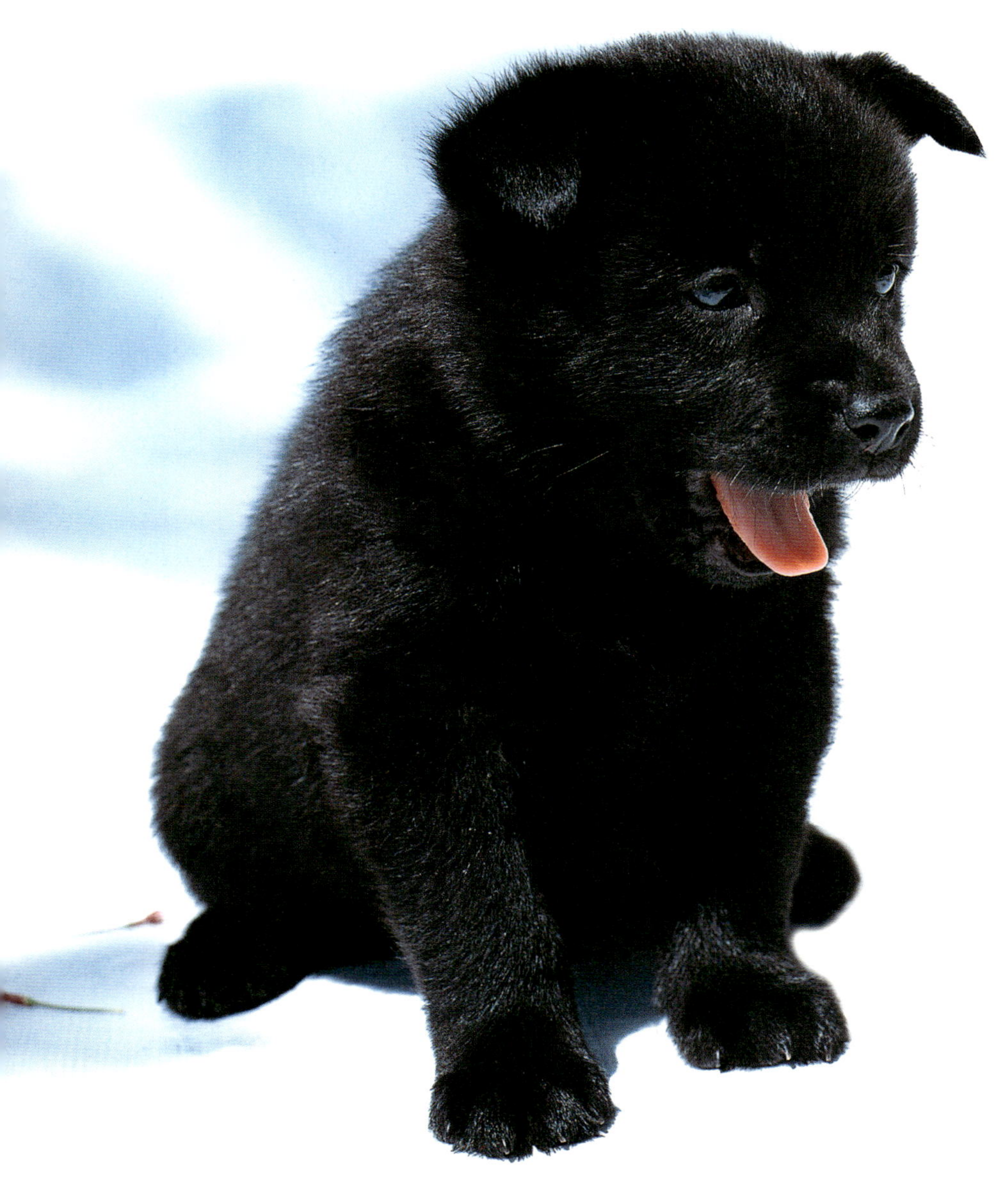

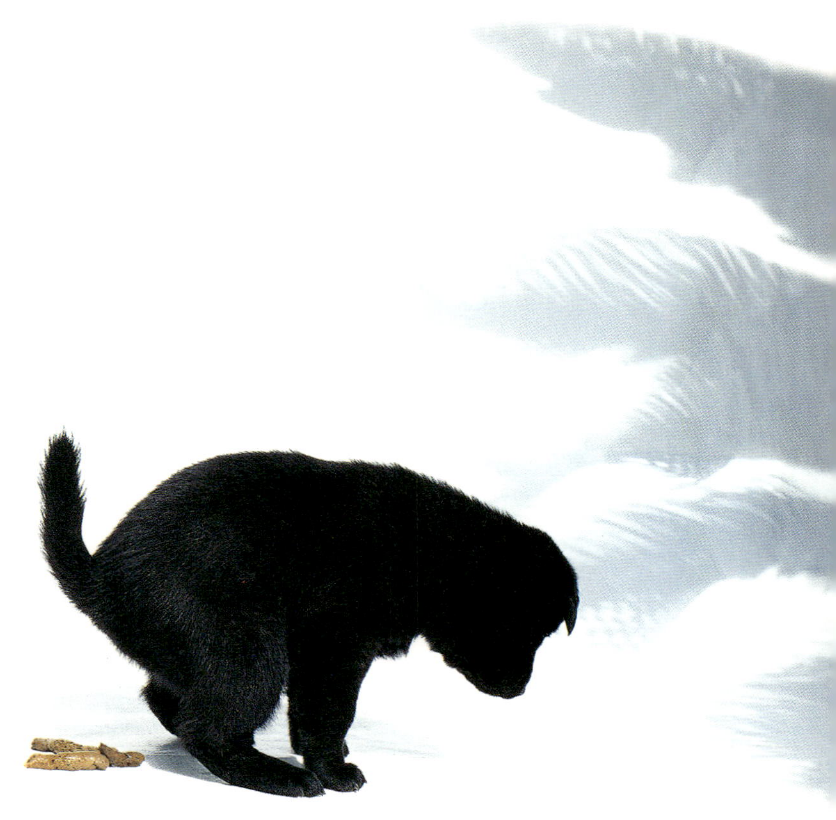

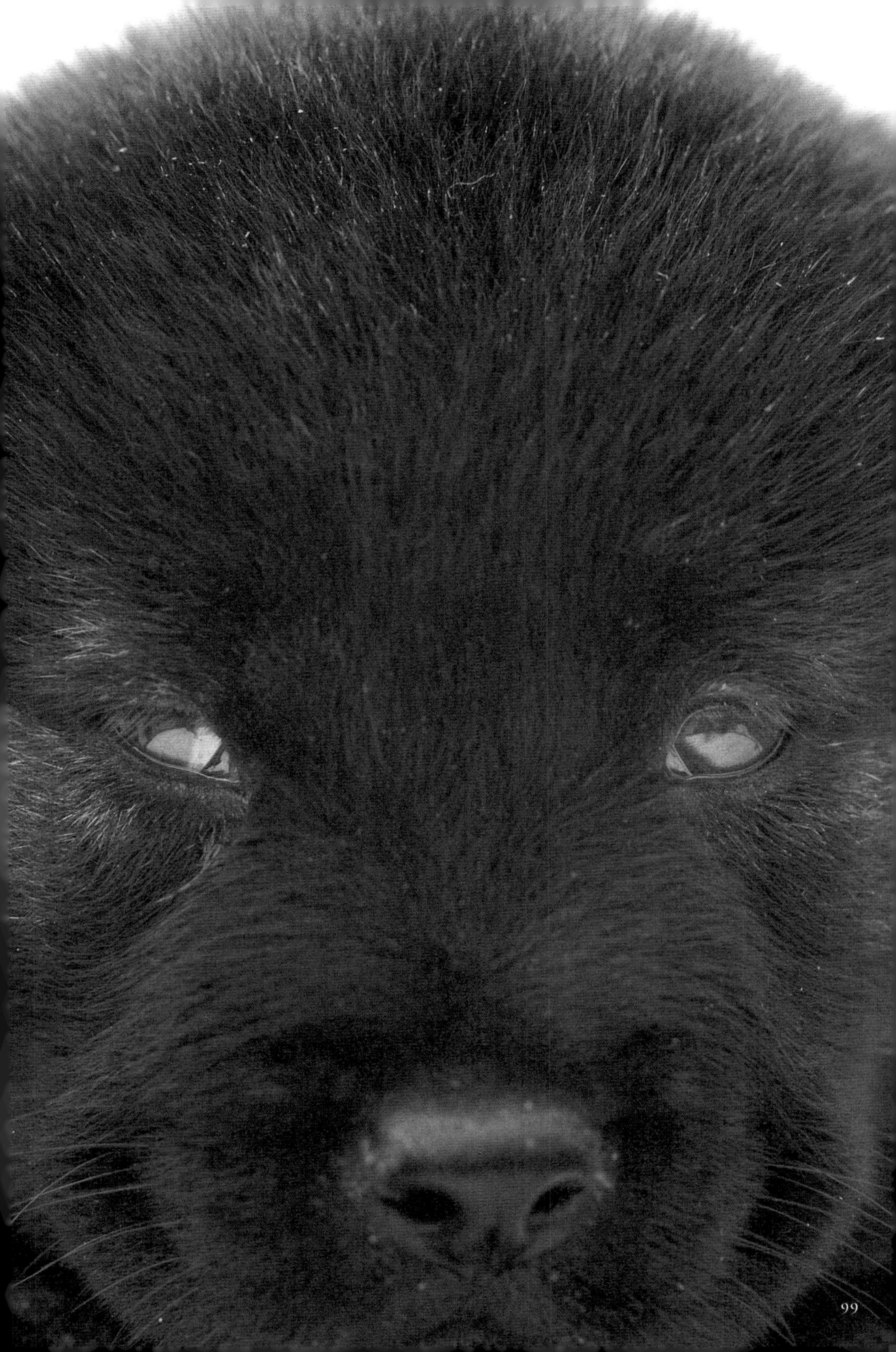

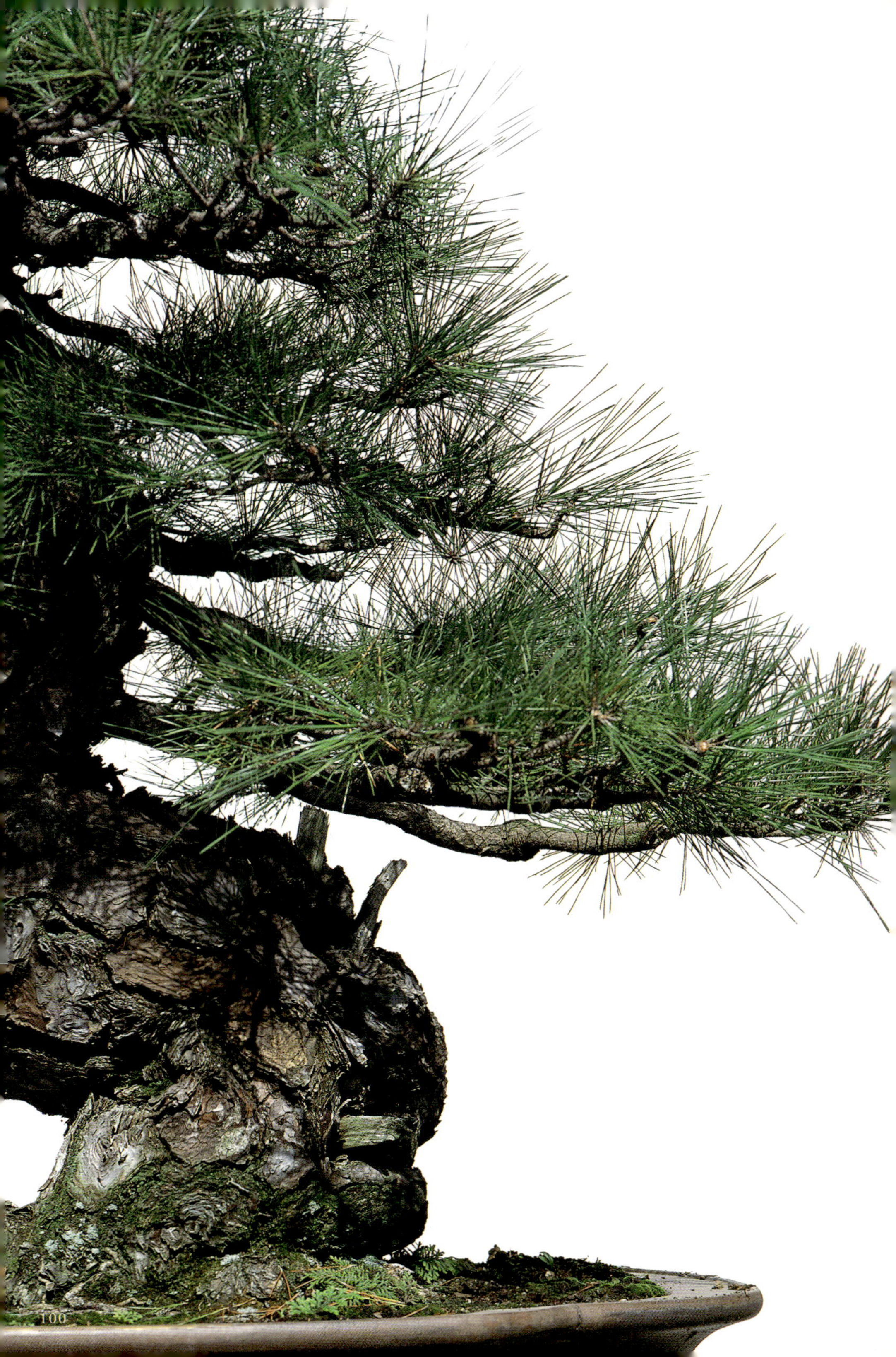

四国犬

Shikoku-ken

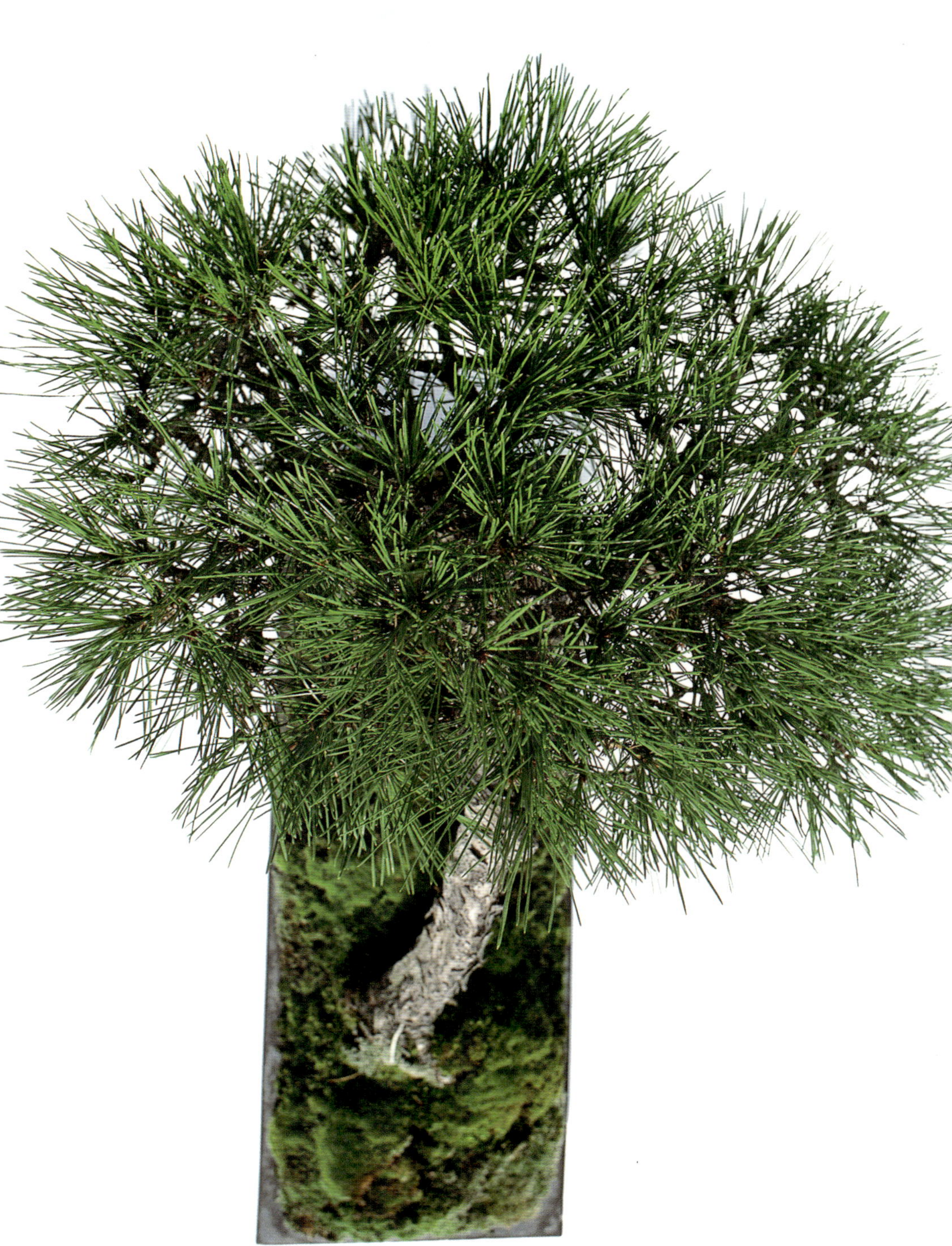

四国犬

四国の剣山から石鎚山を貫く山脈の麓を原産地とする。
別名を高知犬。
持久力に富み、山岳地帯の疾走に適した跳躍力を備えている。
筋骨がたくましく、迫力がある。
目尻が切れ上がり、他の日本犬と比べて顔の表情が鋭いのが特徴だ。
三角形の耳は前傾して立ち、尾は背中に巻き上がる。
柔らかく密生した下毛と硬くまっすぐな上毛のダブルコートで、
毛色は胡麻が多い。
タフで根性があり、闘争心にたけ、
狩猟犬としての性質を強く残している。
体型は中型で、体高は雄52センチ、雌46センチ。
昭和12年、国の天然記念物に指定。

Originally bred in the area around the foot of the
mountain range extending from Mount Tsurugi to
Mount Ishizuchi on the island of Shikoku.
It is also known as the Kochi-ken.
Its superior endurance and jumping ability are
perfect forscampering over mountainous terrain.
It has a sturdy, powerful build.
The outside corners of its eyes are typically raised,
lending the Shikoku-ken an expression
that is keener than the other Japanese dog breeds.
The ears are triangular, pricked, and inclining forward,
and the tail is curled over the back.
The Shikoku-ken has a double coat comprising a soft,
dense undercoat and a hard, straight outer coat,
and is usually sesame colored.
It has a tough, tenacious, pugnacious disposition,
retaining many of the qualities it developed as a hunting dog.
A medium-sized dog, Shikoku-ken males grow to a height of 52 cm,
and females to 46 cm.
It was designated a Natural Monument in 1937.

Shikoku-ken

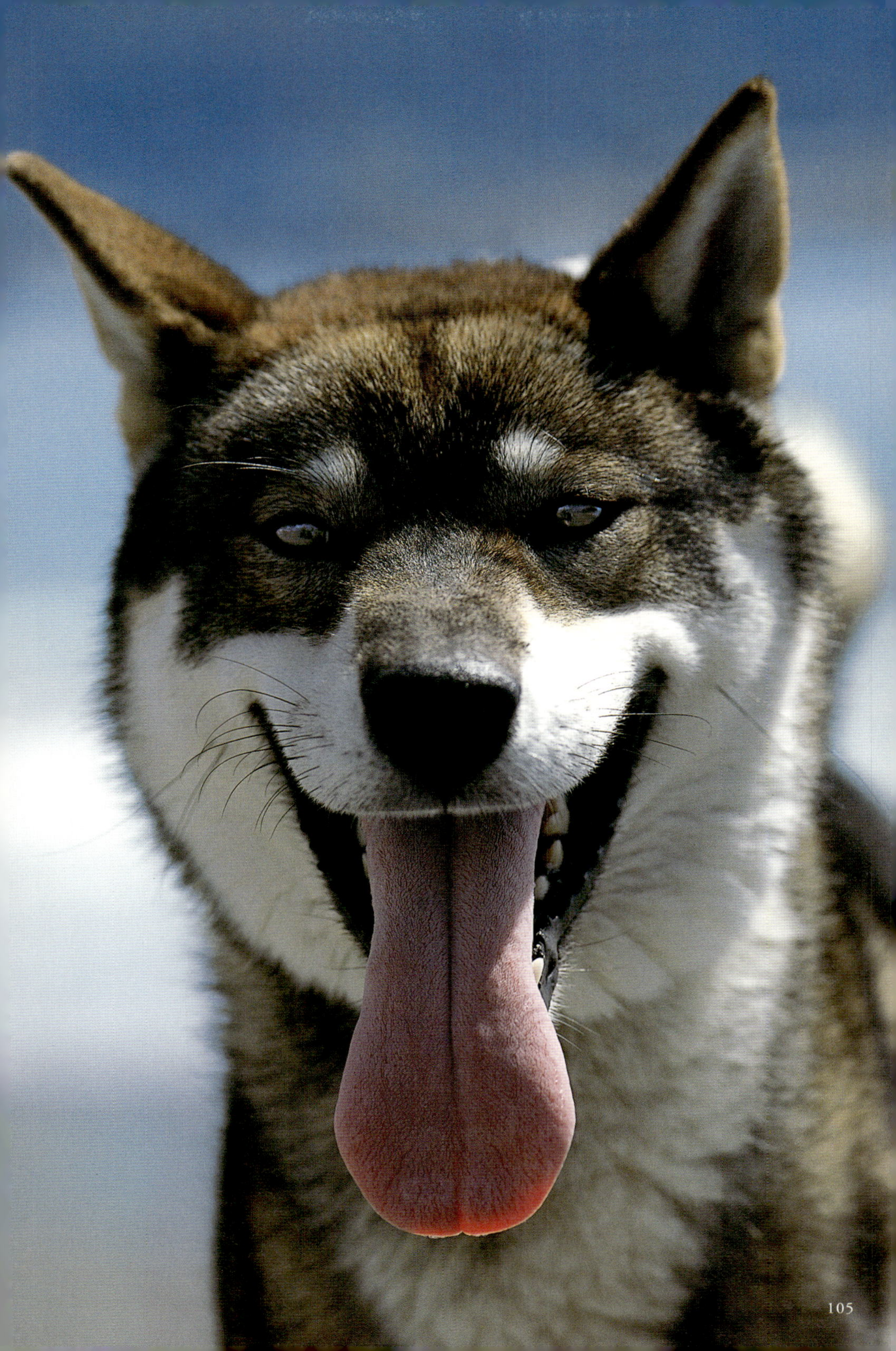

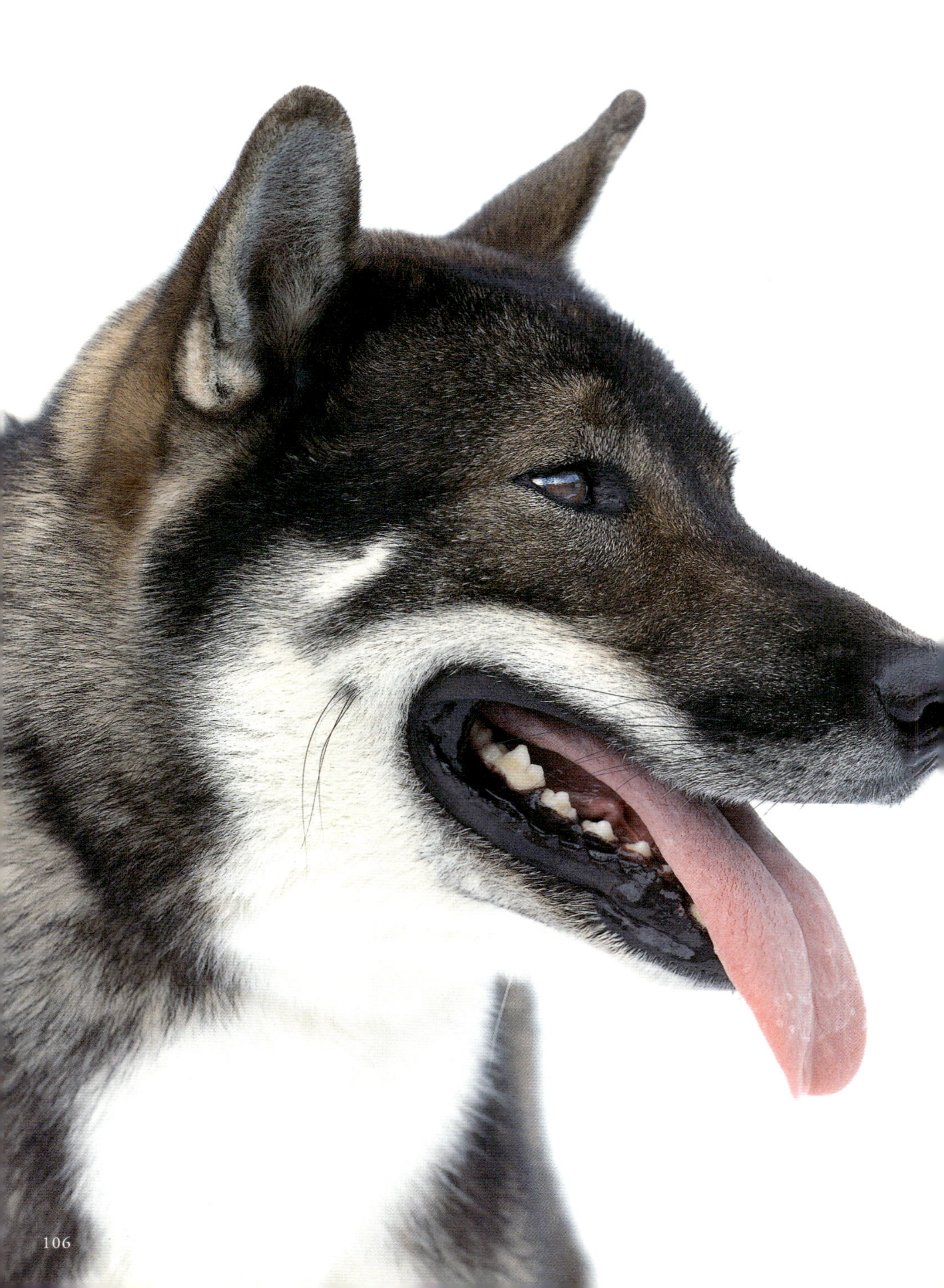

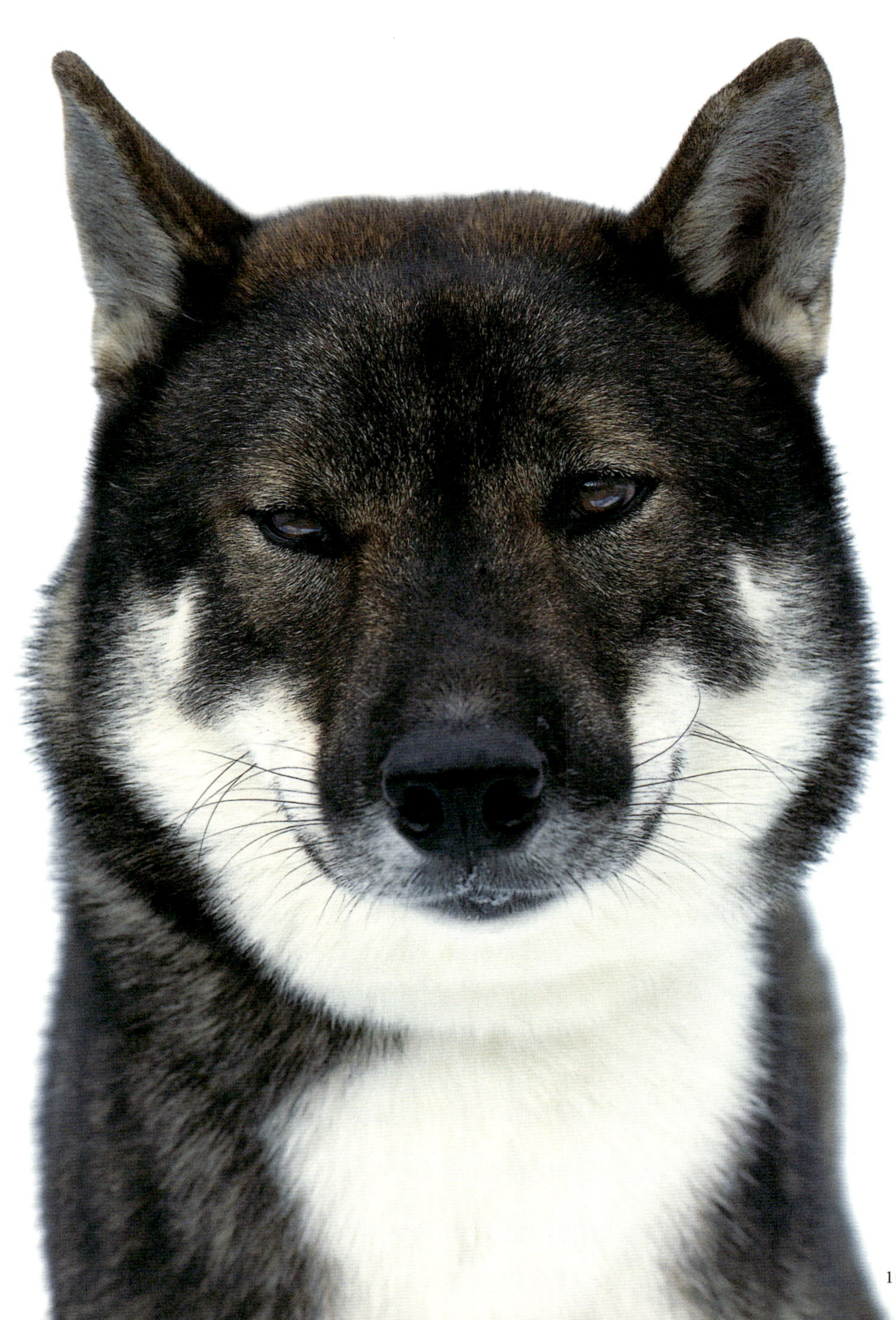

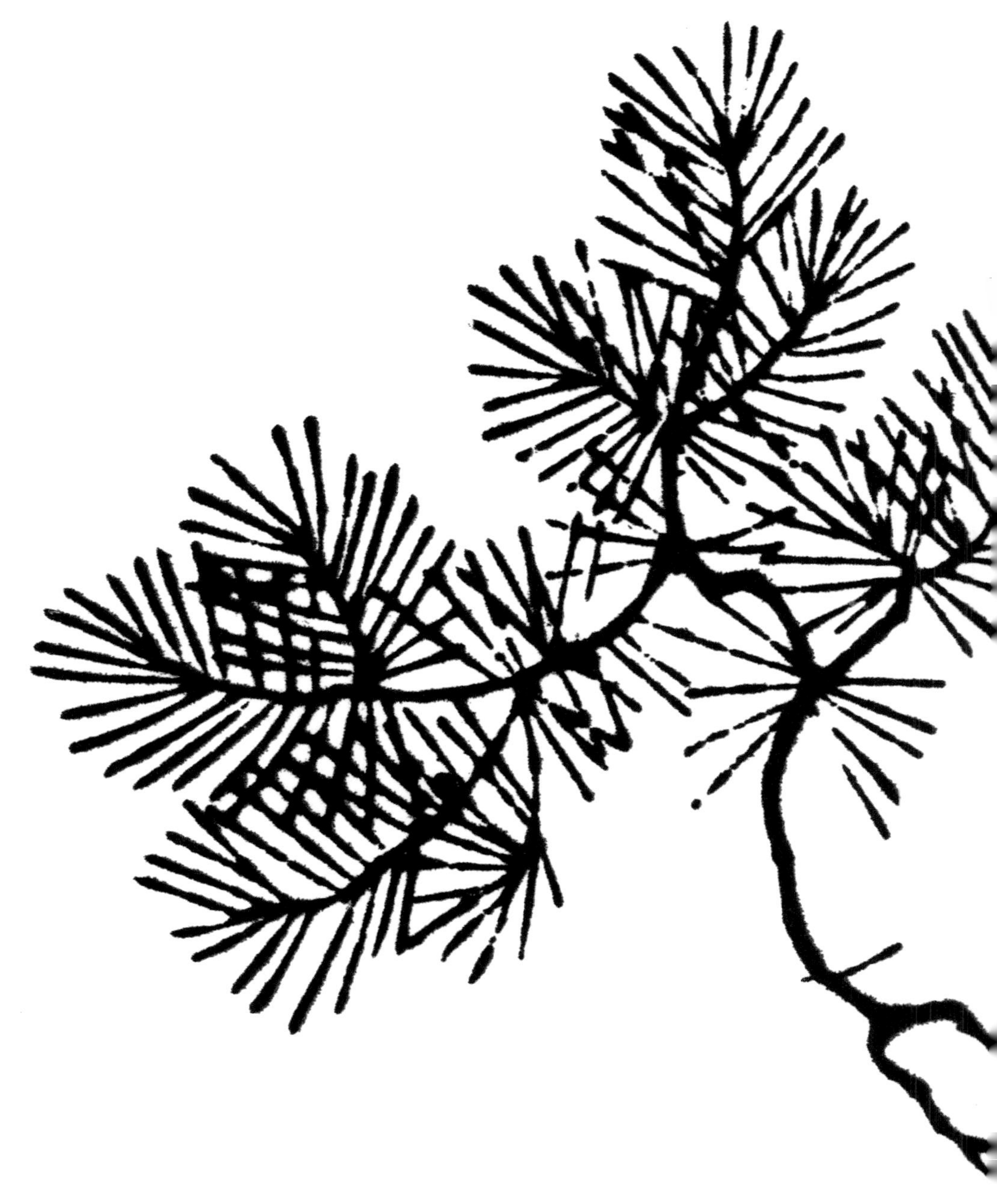

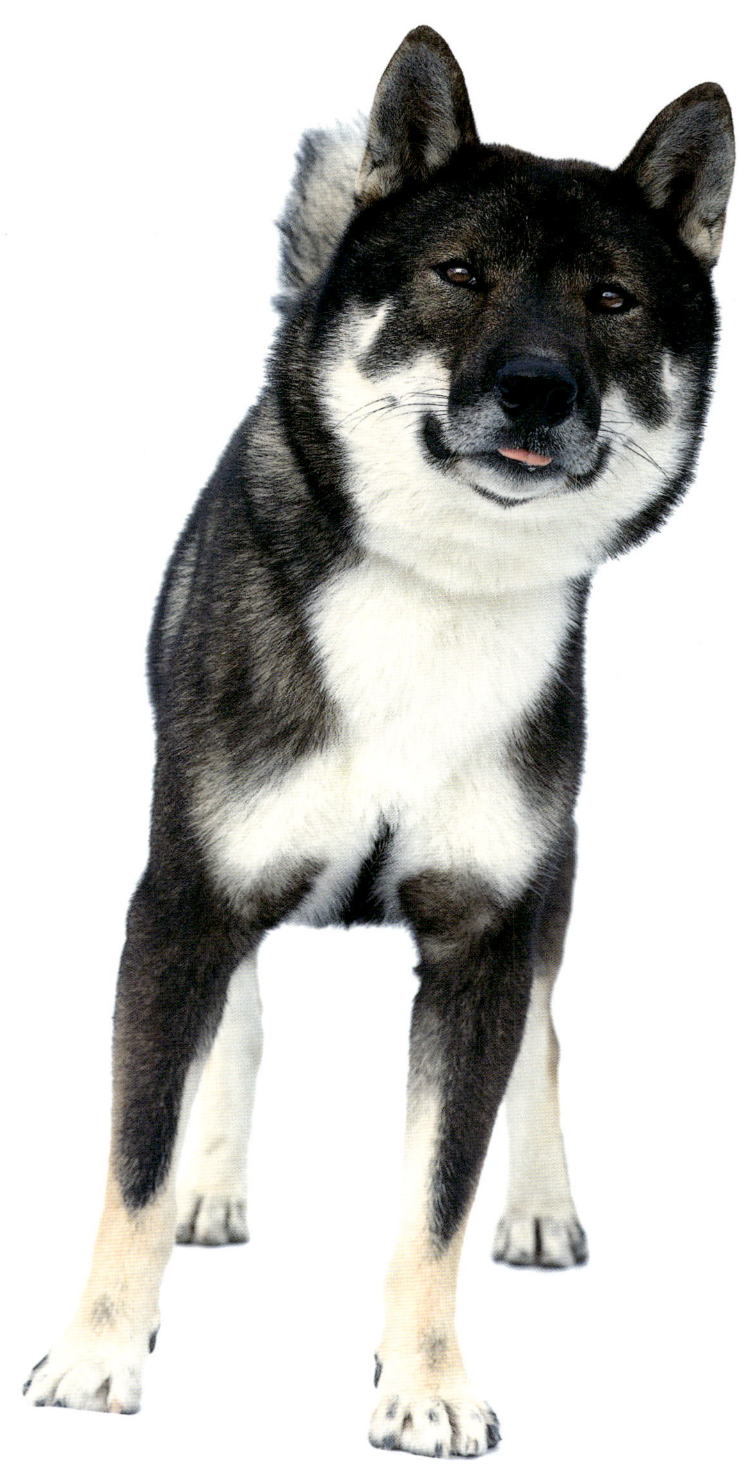

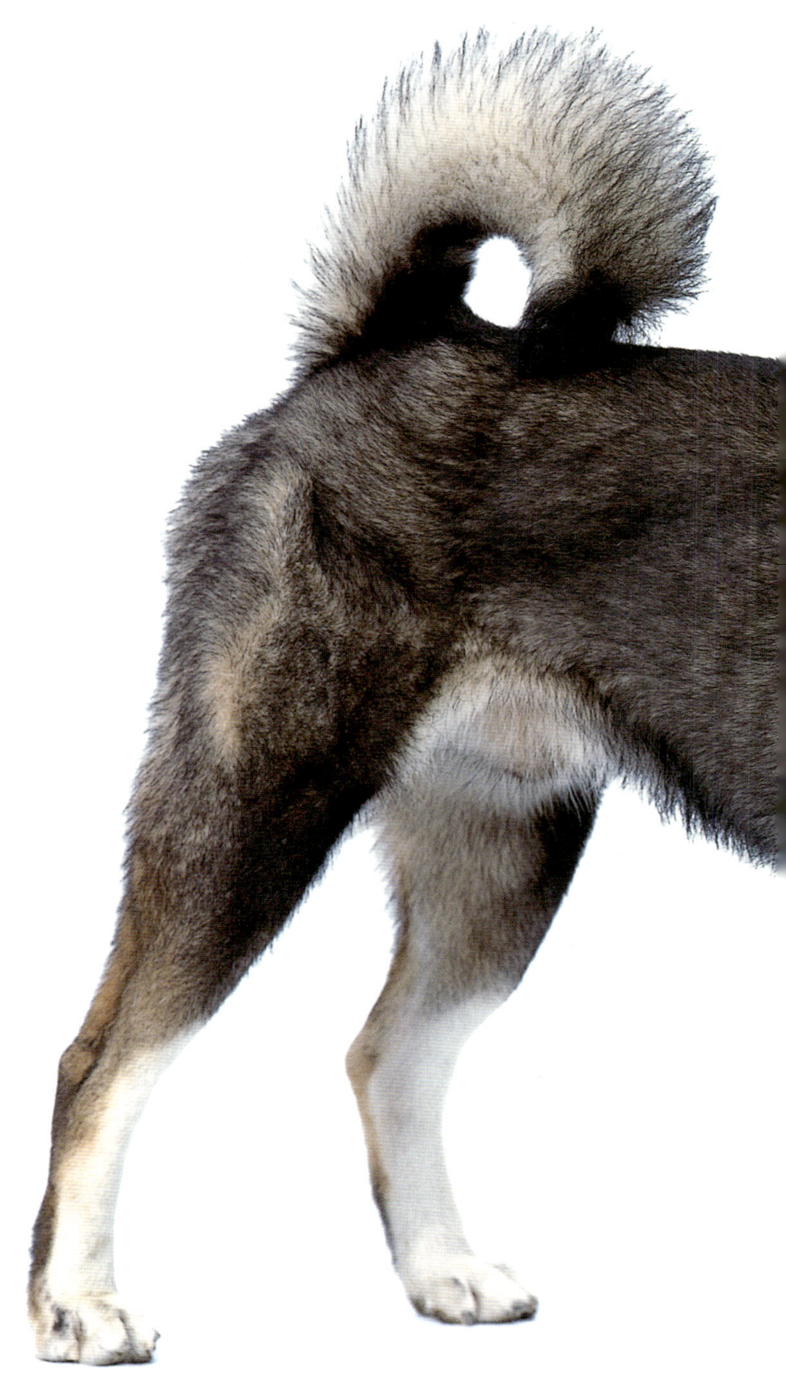

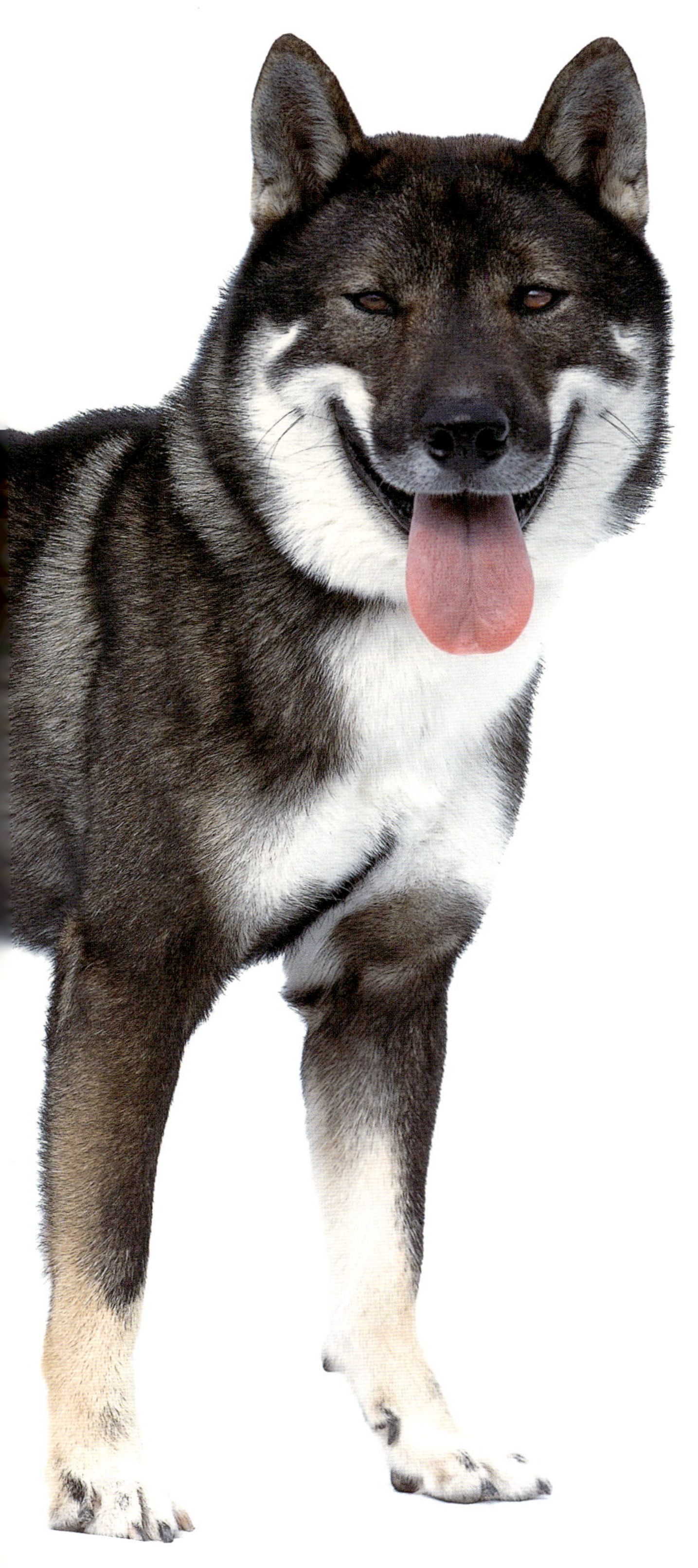

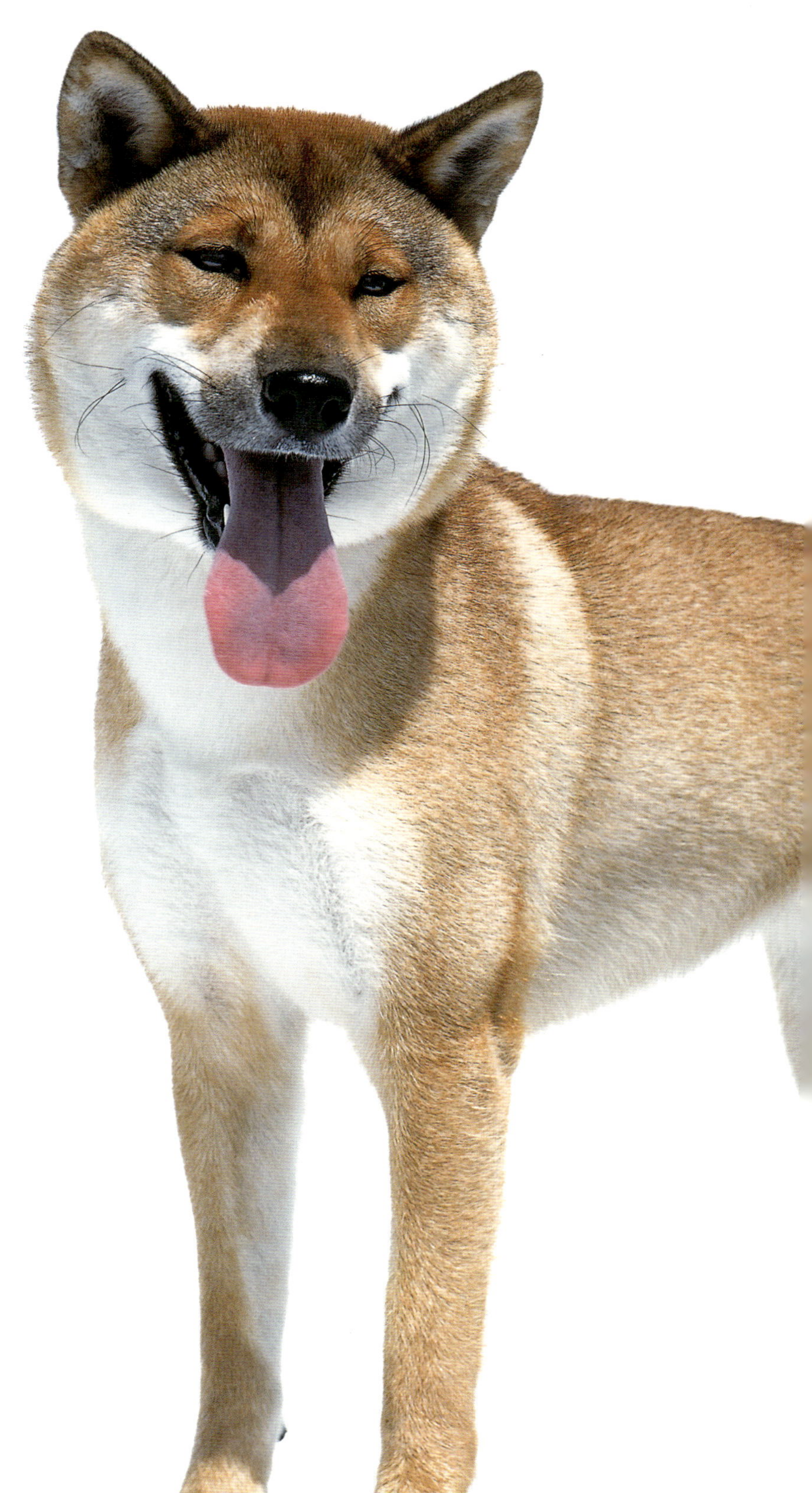

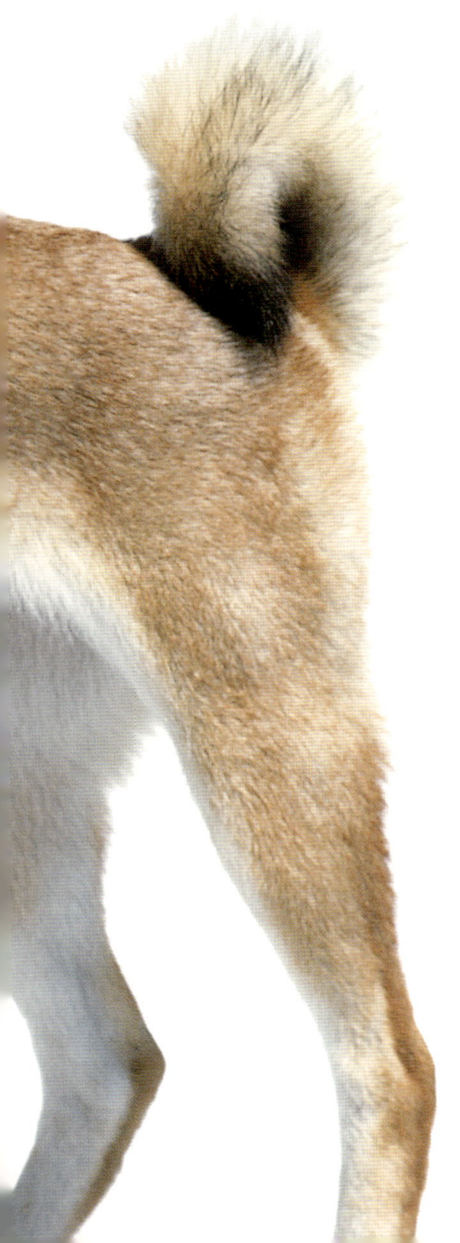

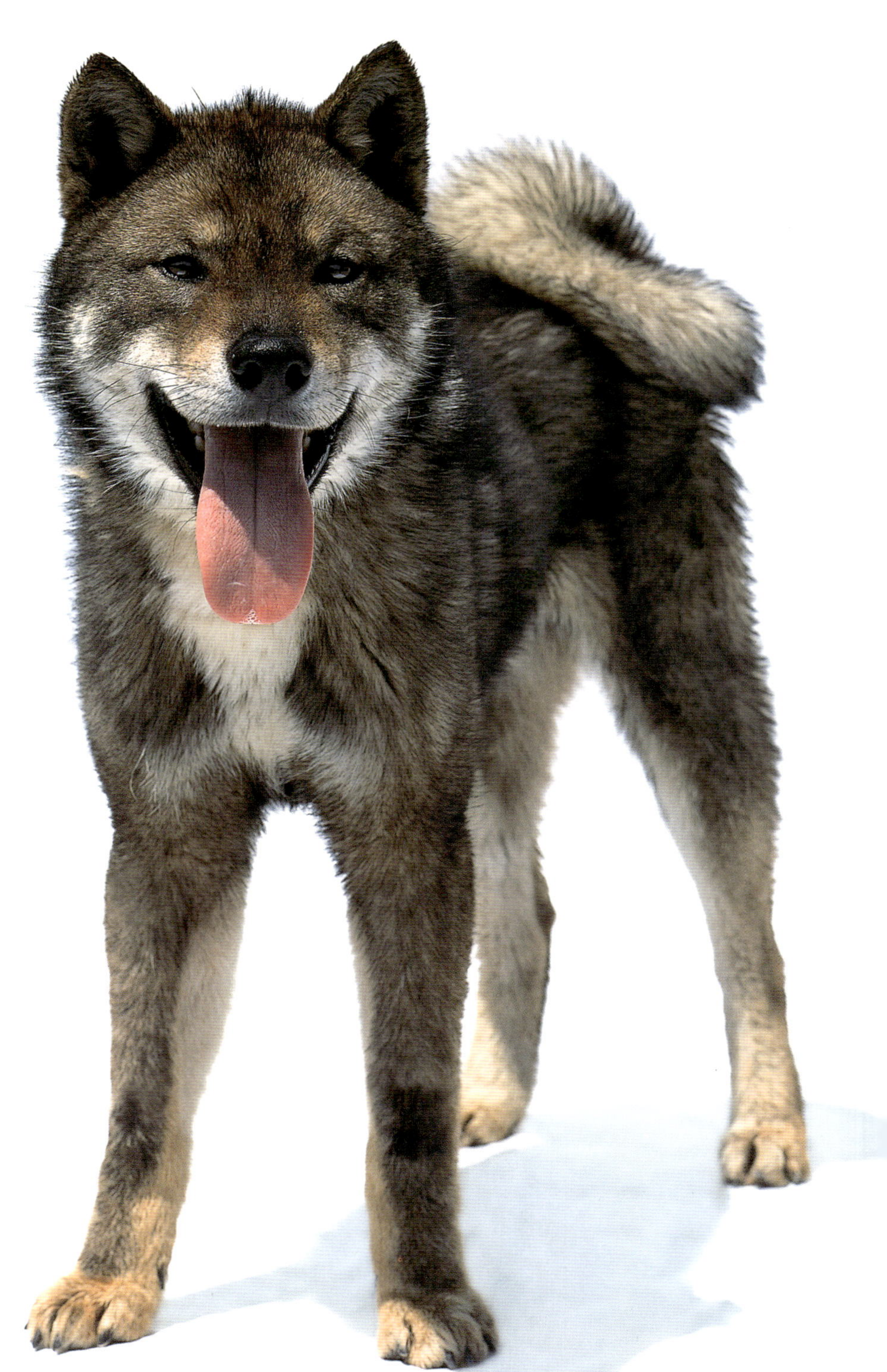

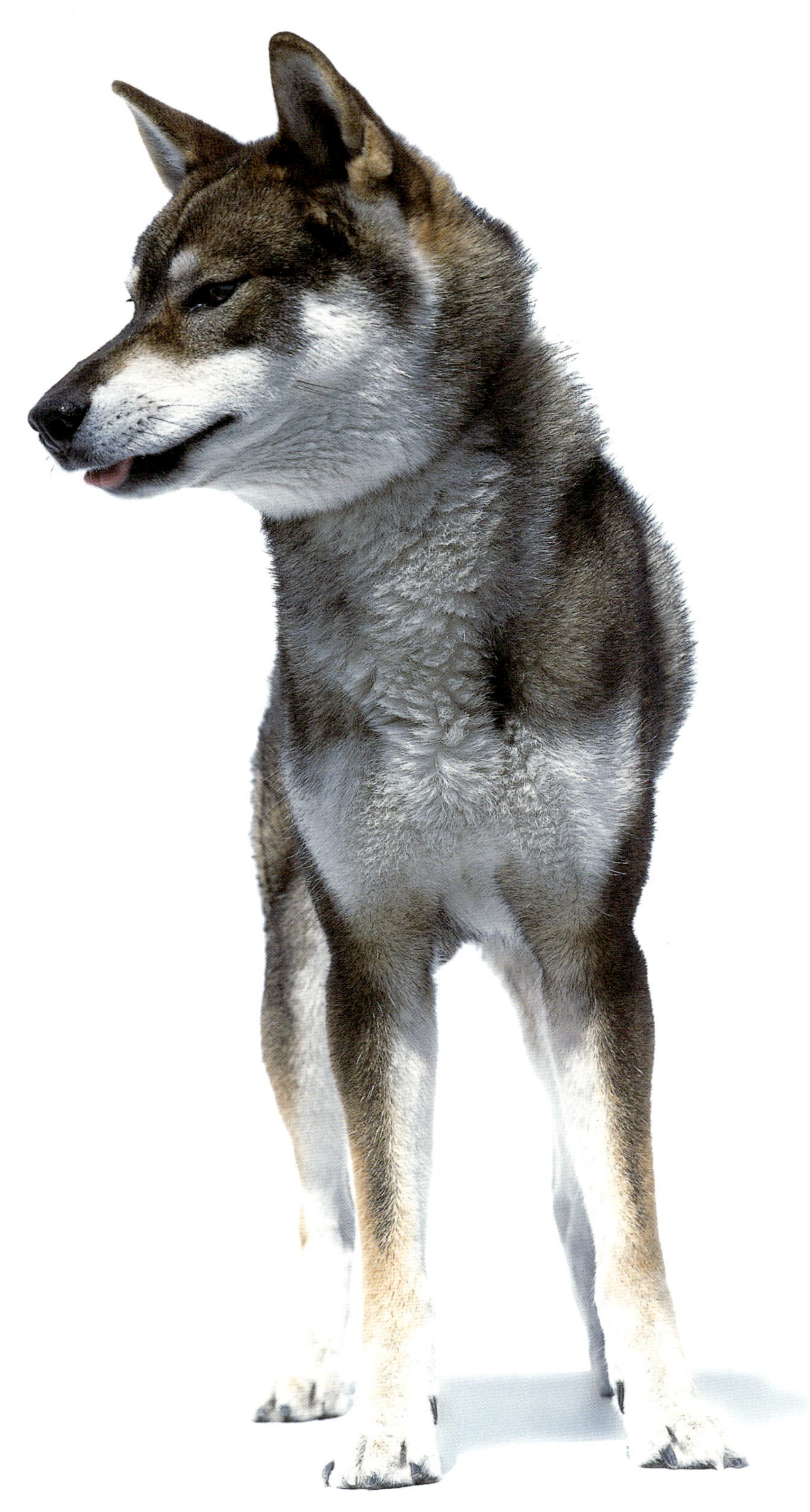

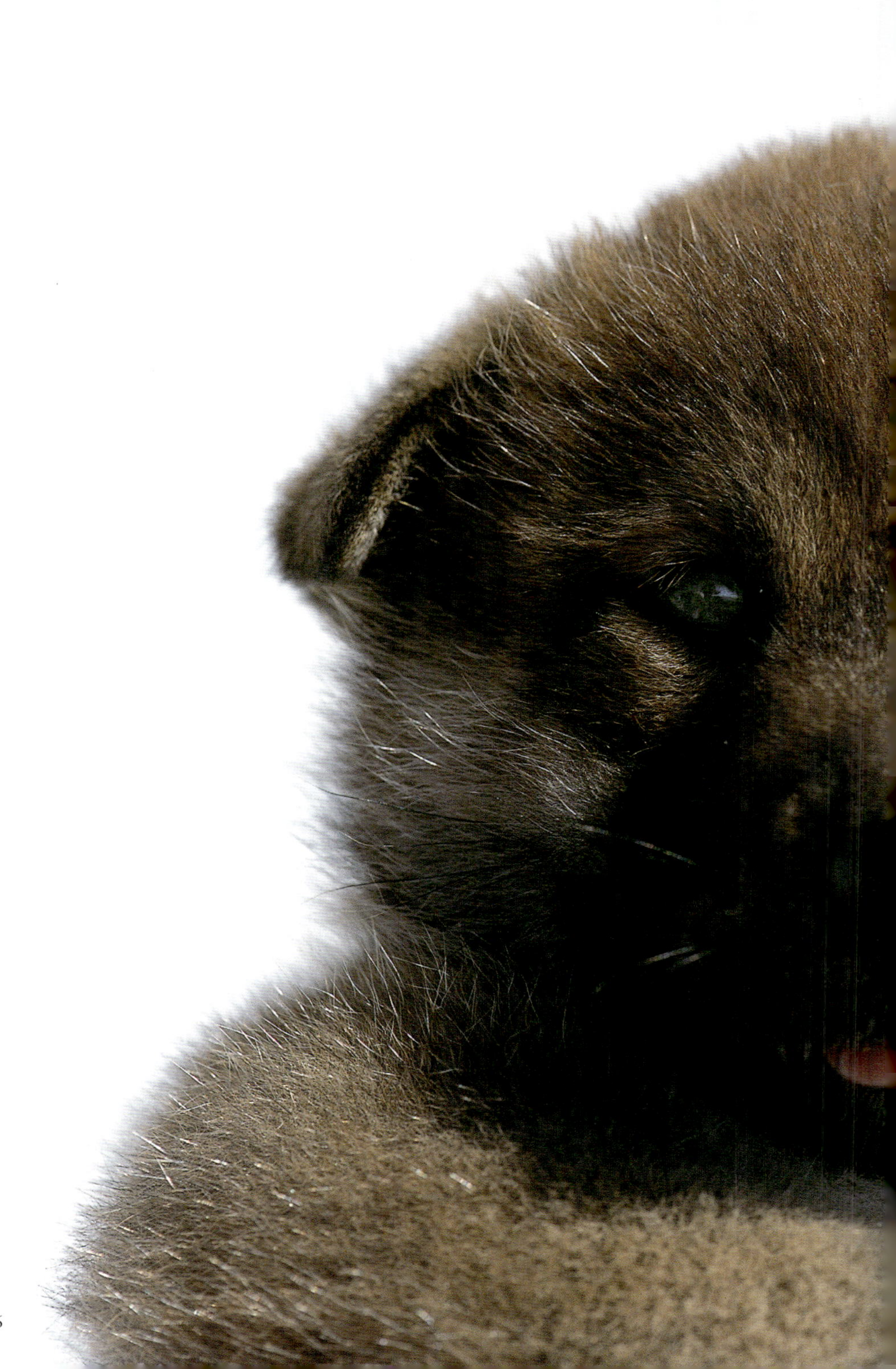

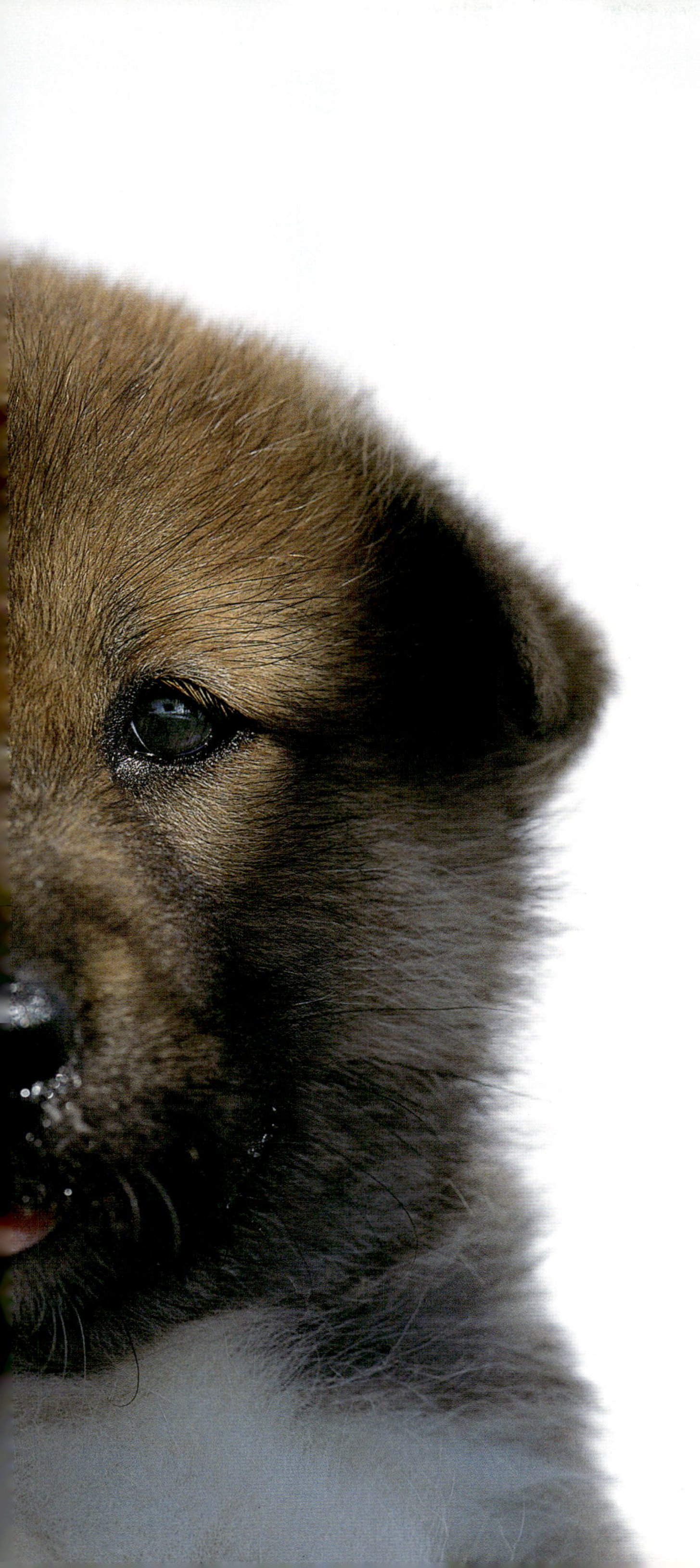

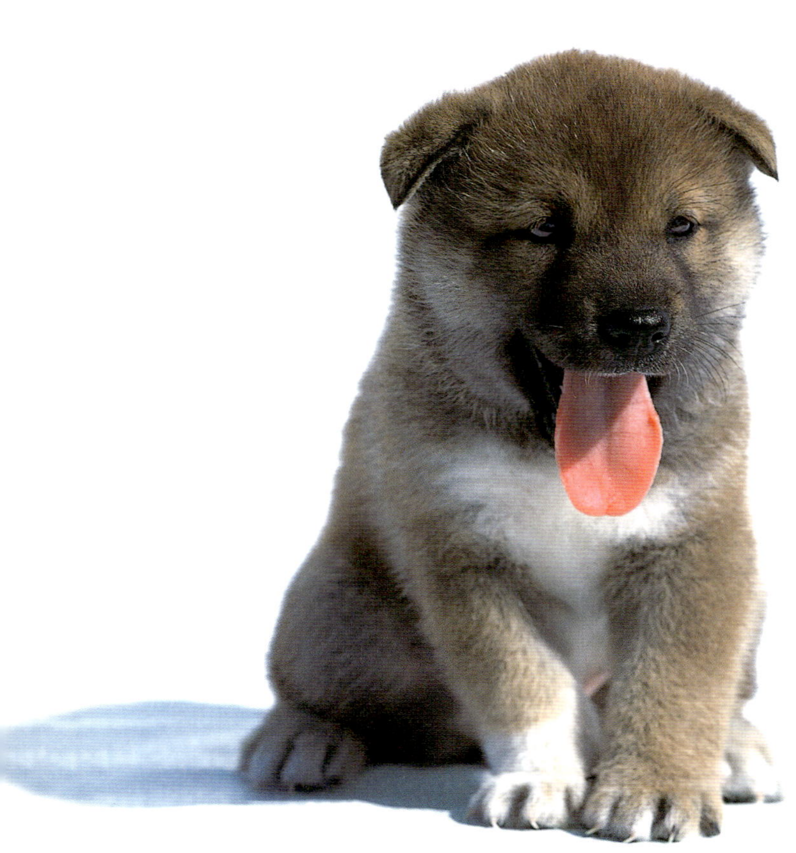

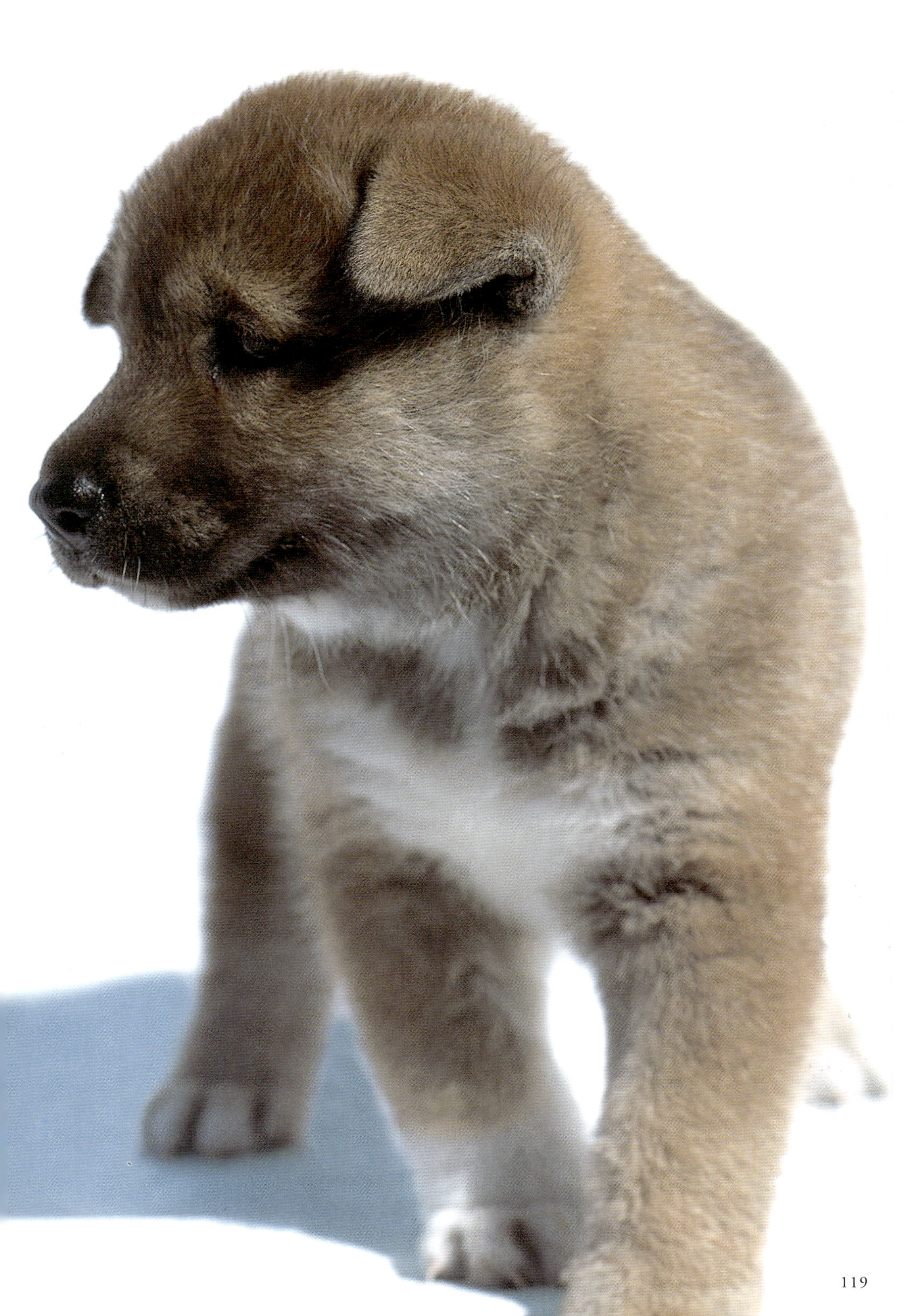

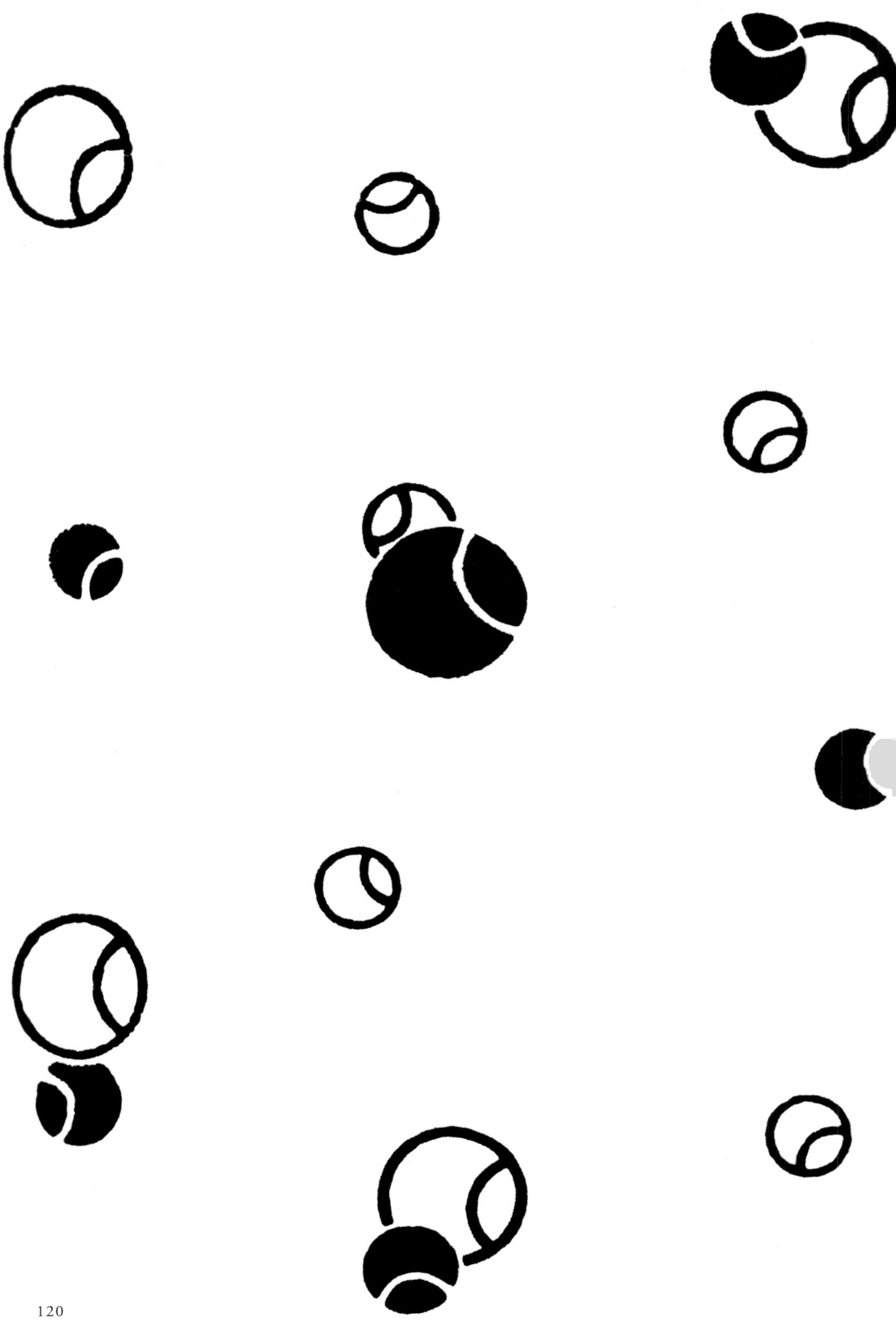

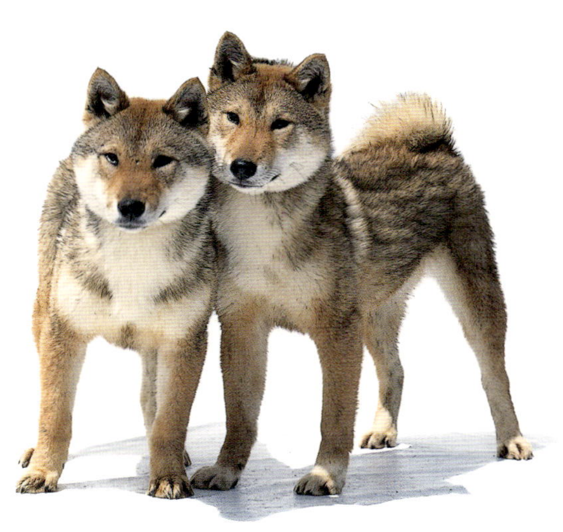

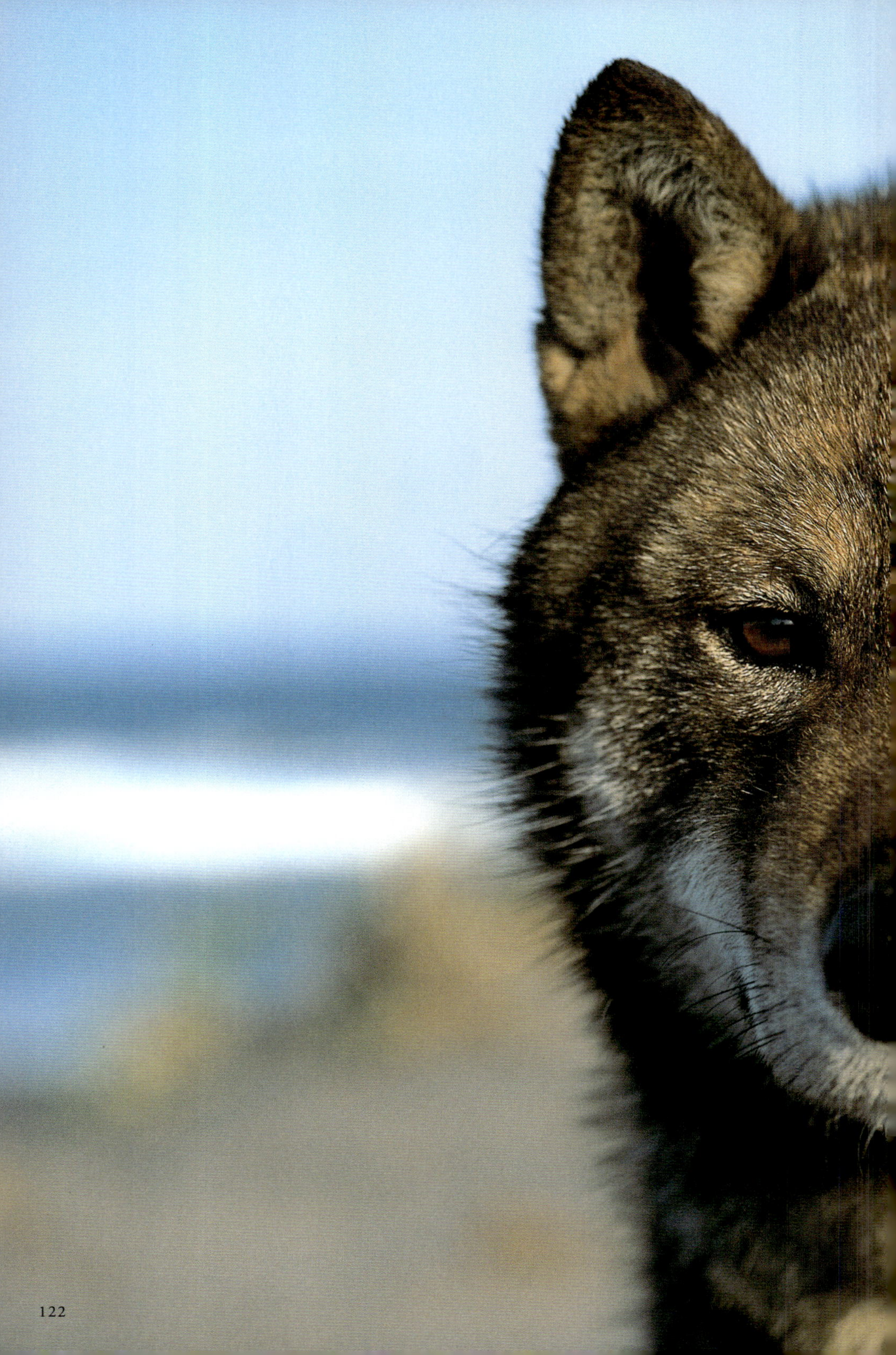

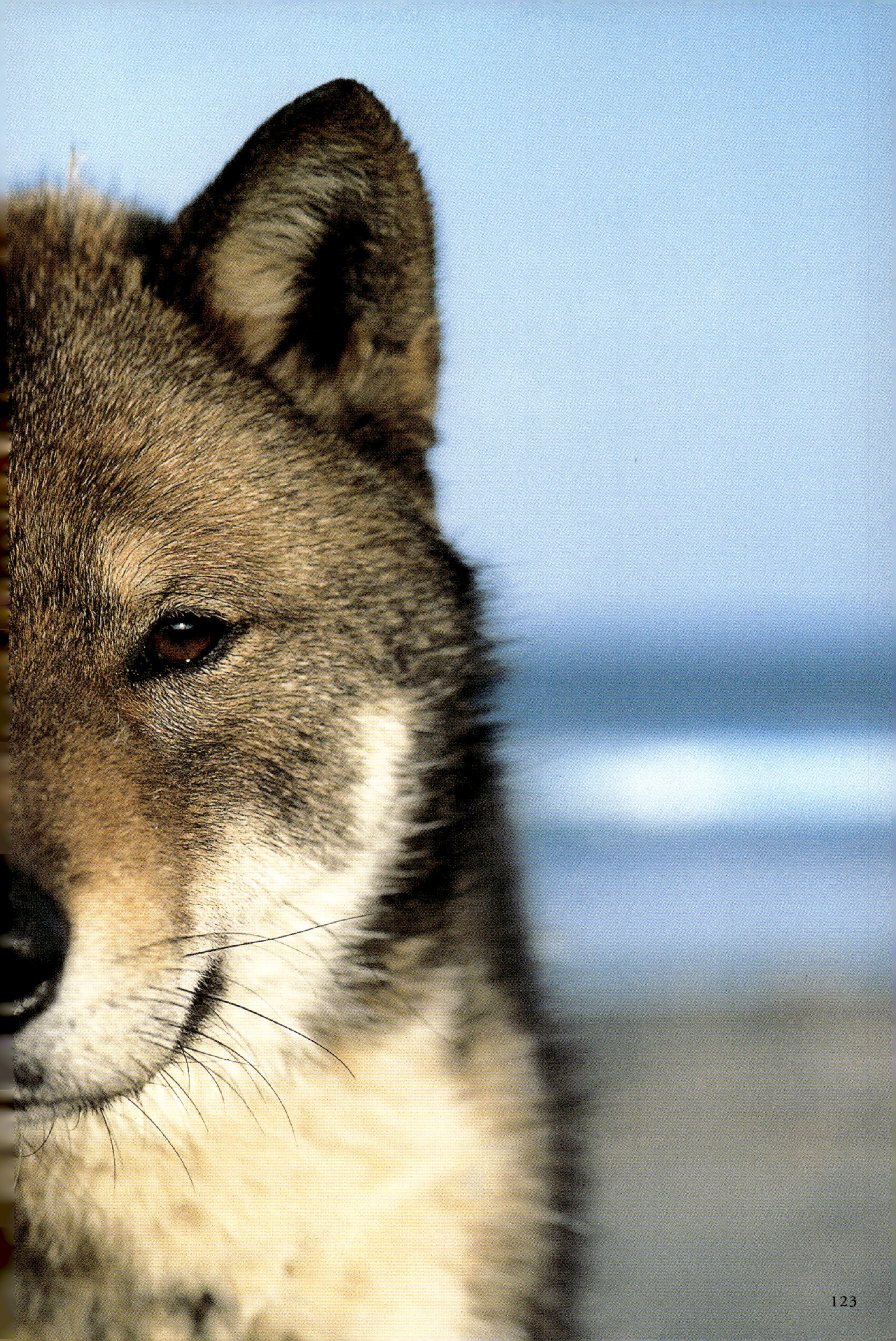

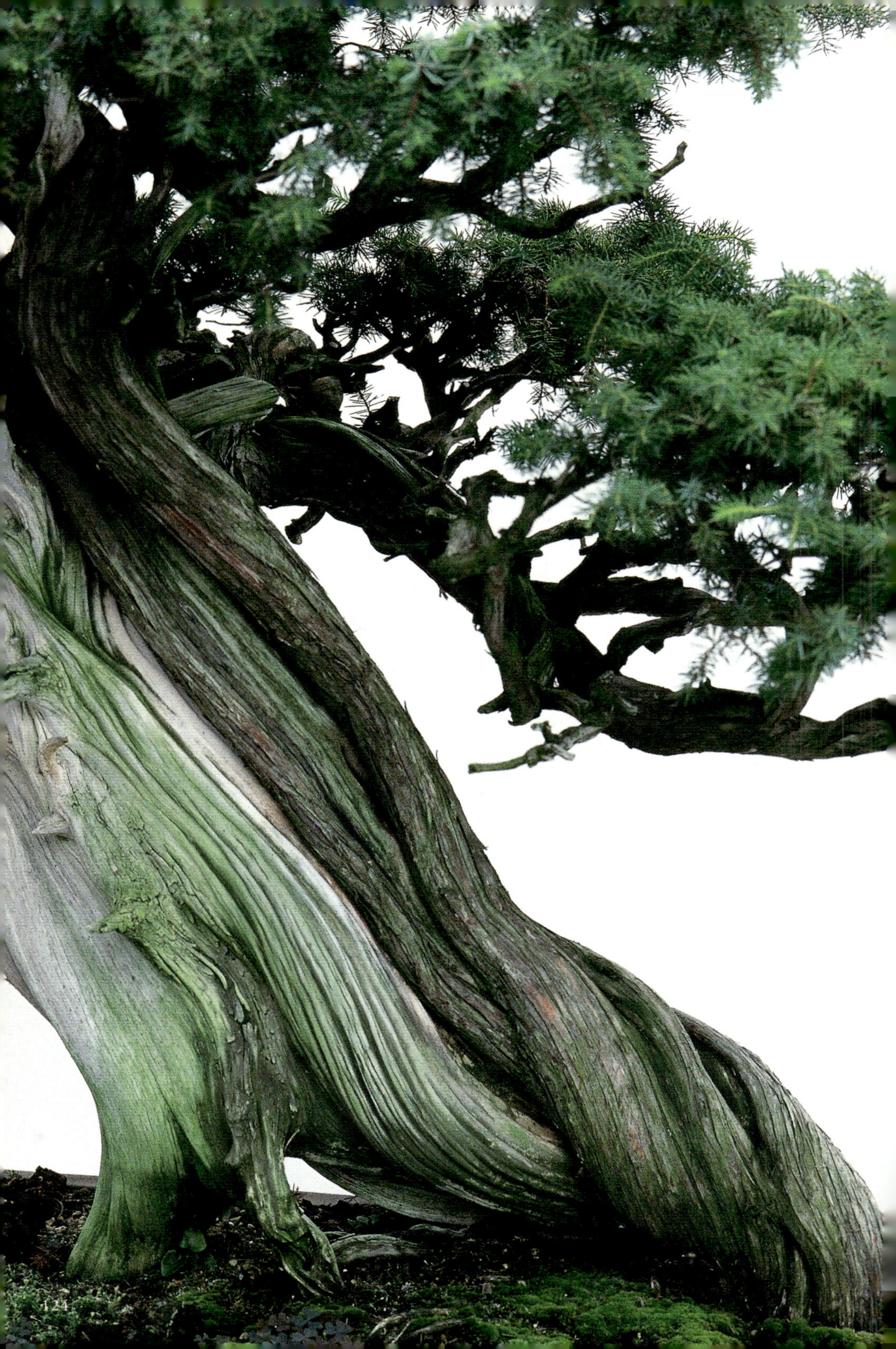

紀州犬

Kishu-ken

紀州犬
和歌山県、三重県など紀伊半島一帯で、
古くからイノシシ、クマ、シカなどの
実猟犬として活躍した。
平安時代の伝説に、二頭の紀州犬が空海を
高野山まで守護して導いたという話も残っている。

Originally used as a hunting dog for hunting wild boar,
bears, and deer in Wakayama and Mie prefectures and
throughout the Ise Peninsula.
According to a Heian Period legend,
two Kishu-ken led the monk Kukai to Mount Koya and
protected him along the way.

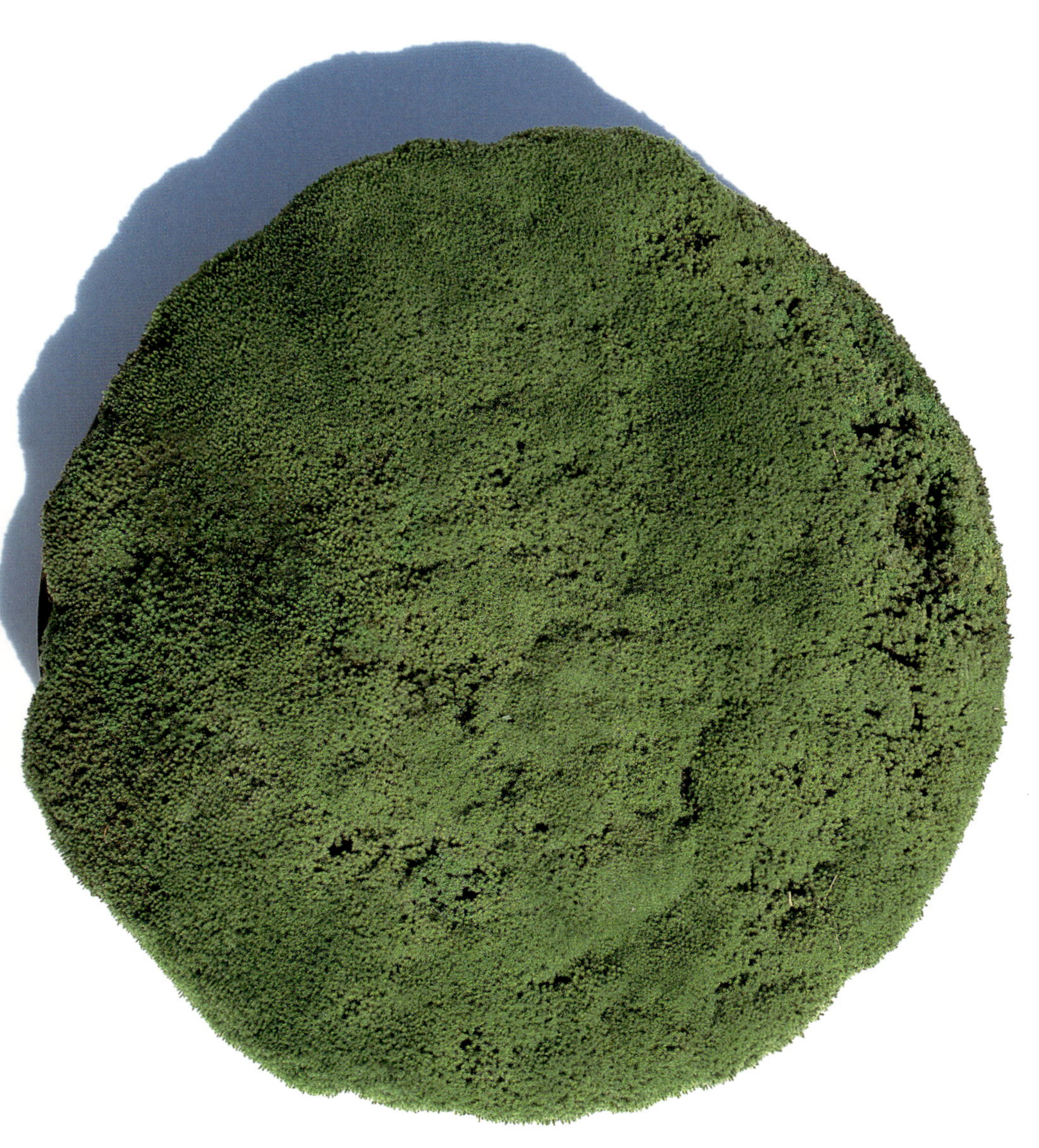

The Kishu-ken has a solid build
that is well balanced with compact muscles.
Many have dewclaws, yet this is not regarded a fault in
the Kishu-ken as it suits walking in mountainous areas.
The vast majority of Kishu-ken have white coats,
although occasionally red or sesame coats are also found.
They have pricked ears and a curly or sickle tail.
The Kishu-ken has an extremely patient,
determined disposition, and usually stands with
an air of perfect composure.
Males grow to a height of 50 cm,
and females to a height of 47 cm.
The Kishu-ken was designated
a Natural Monument in 1934.

Kishu-ken

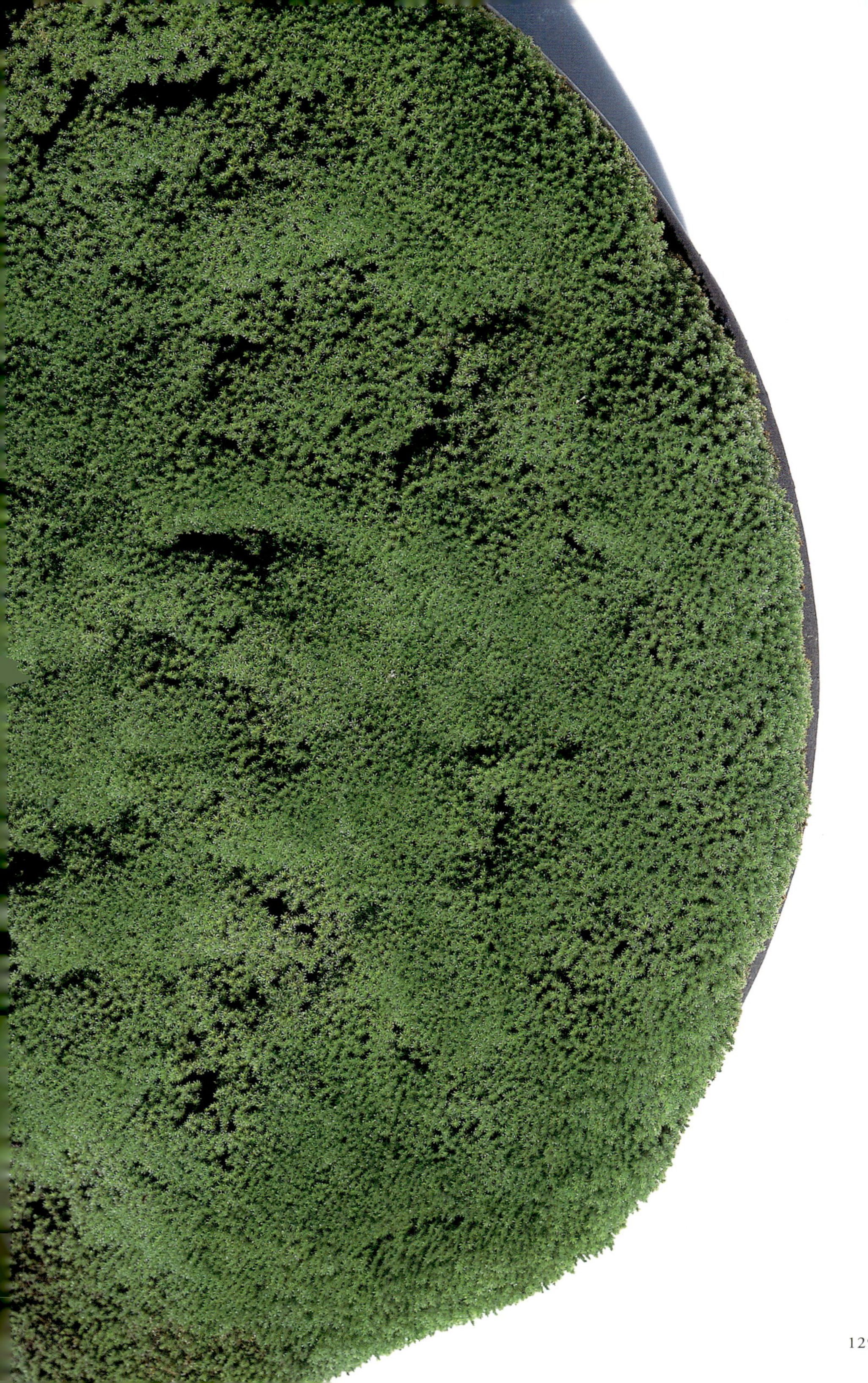

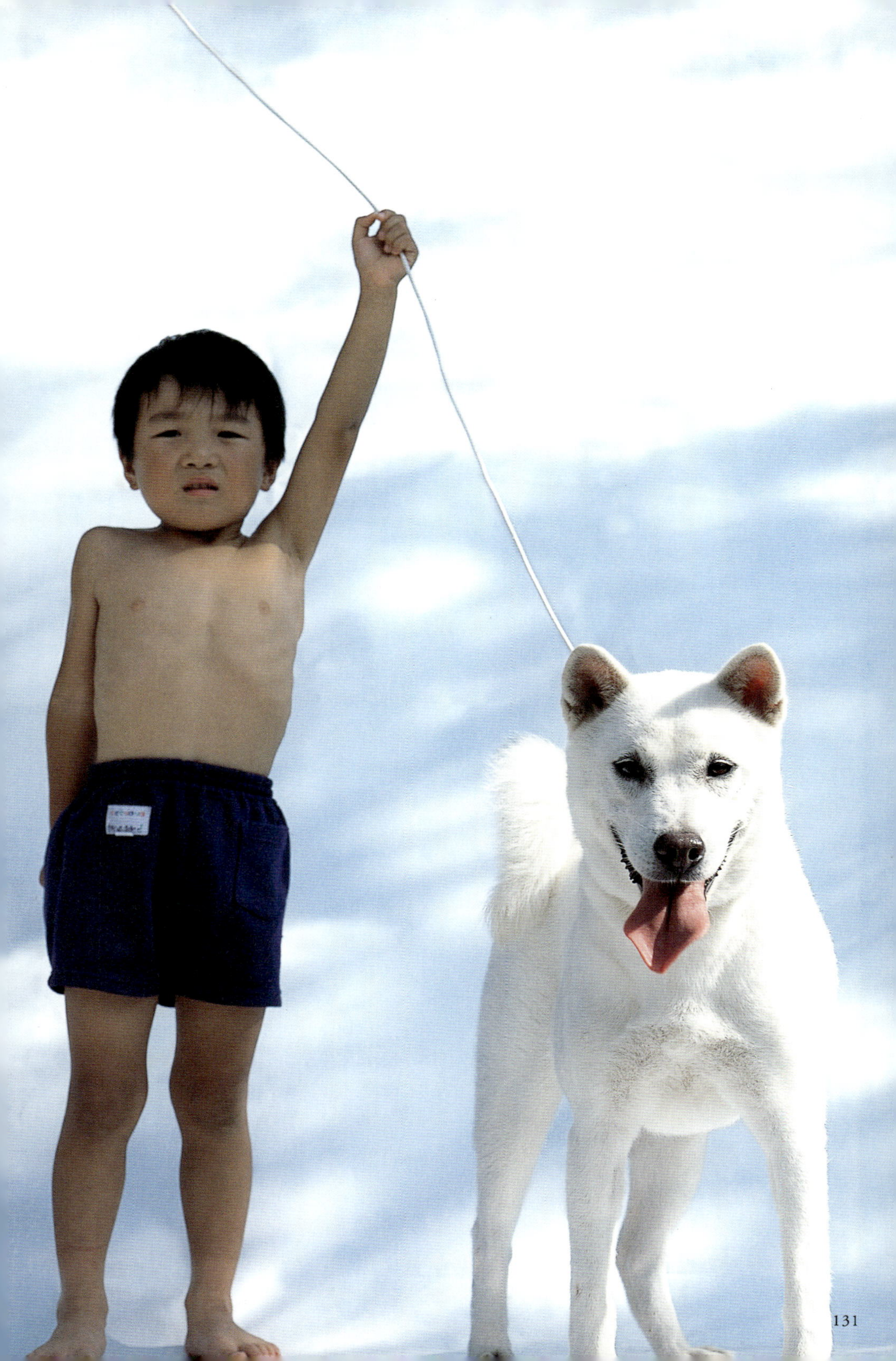

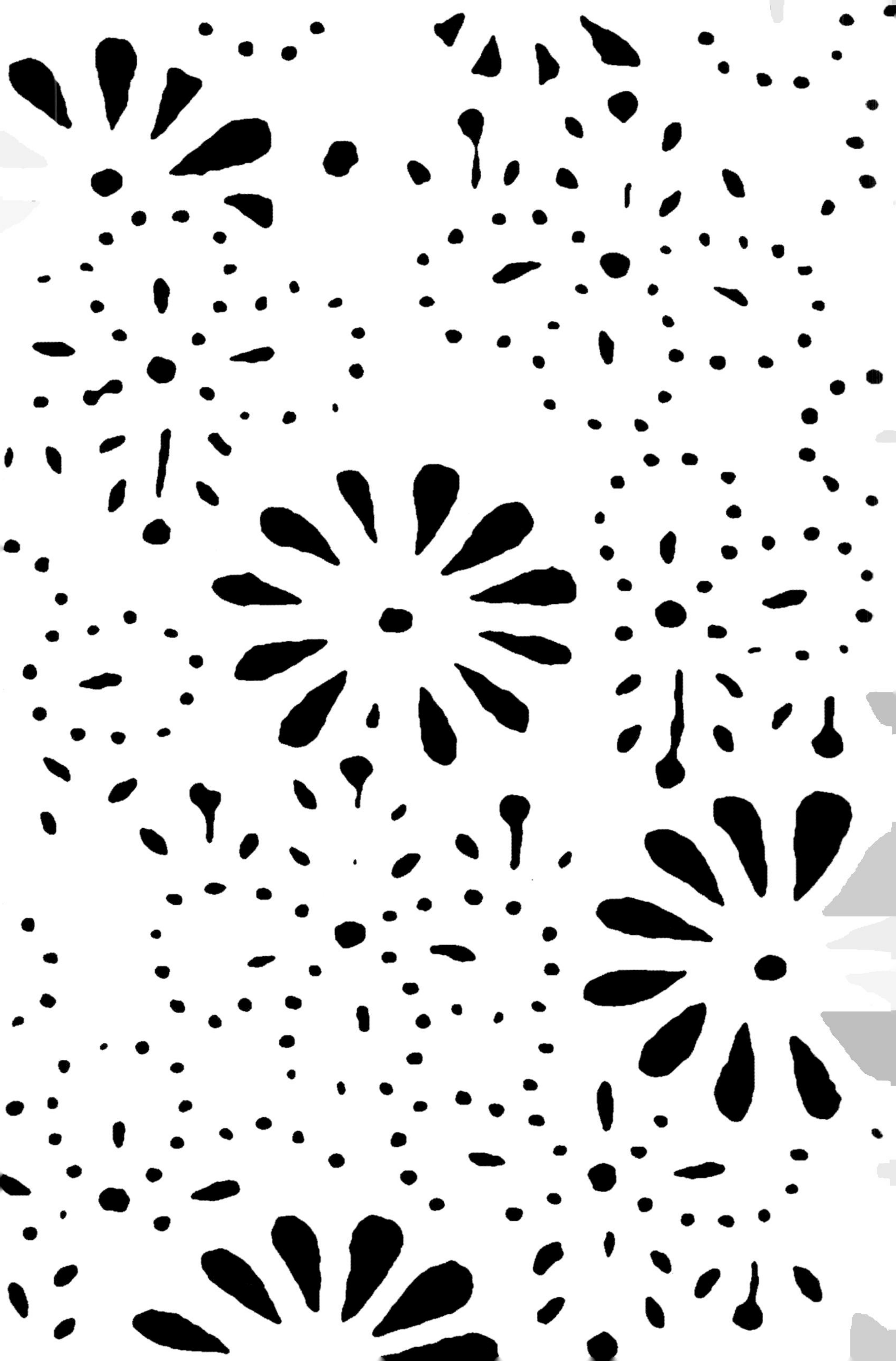

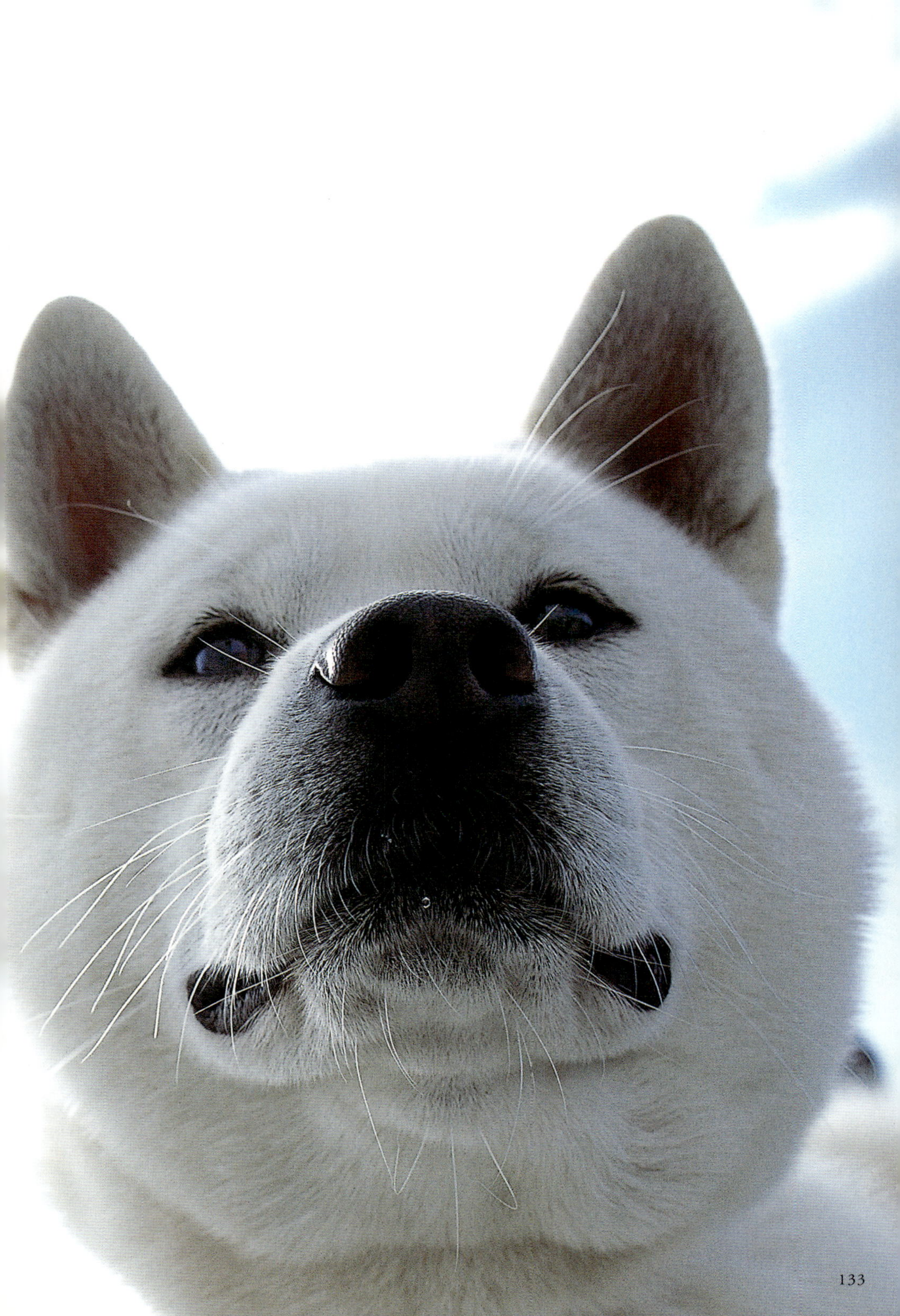

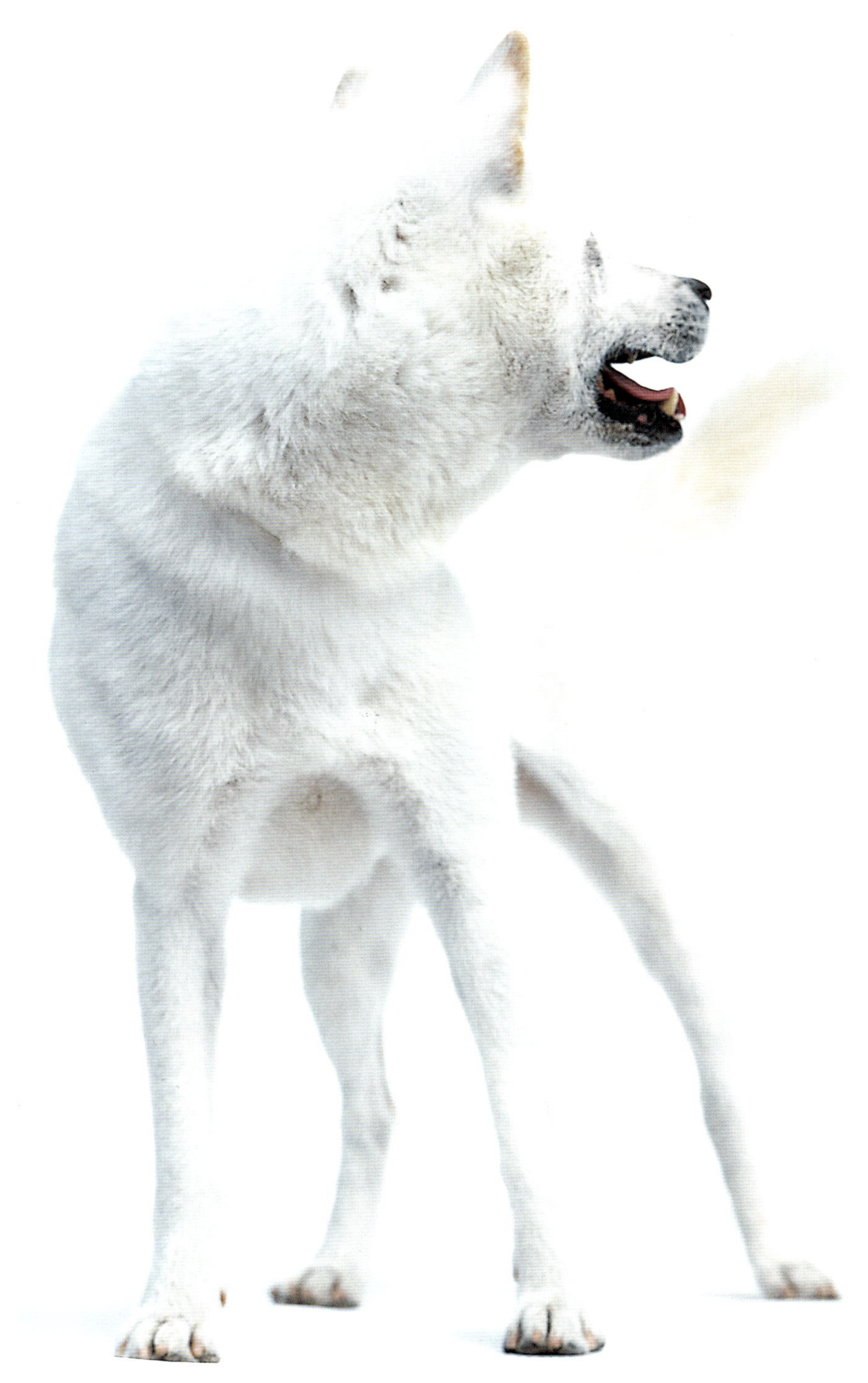

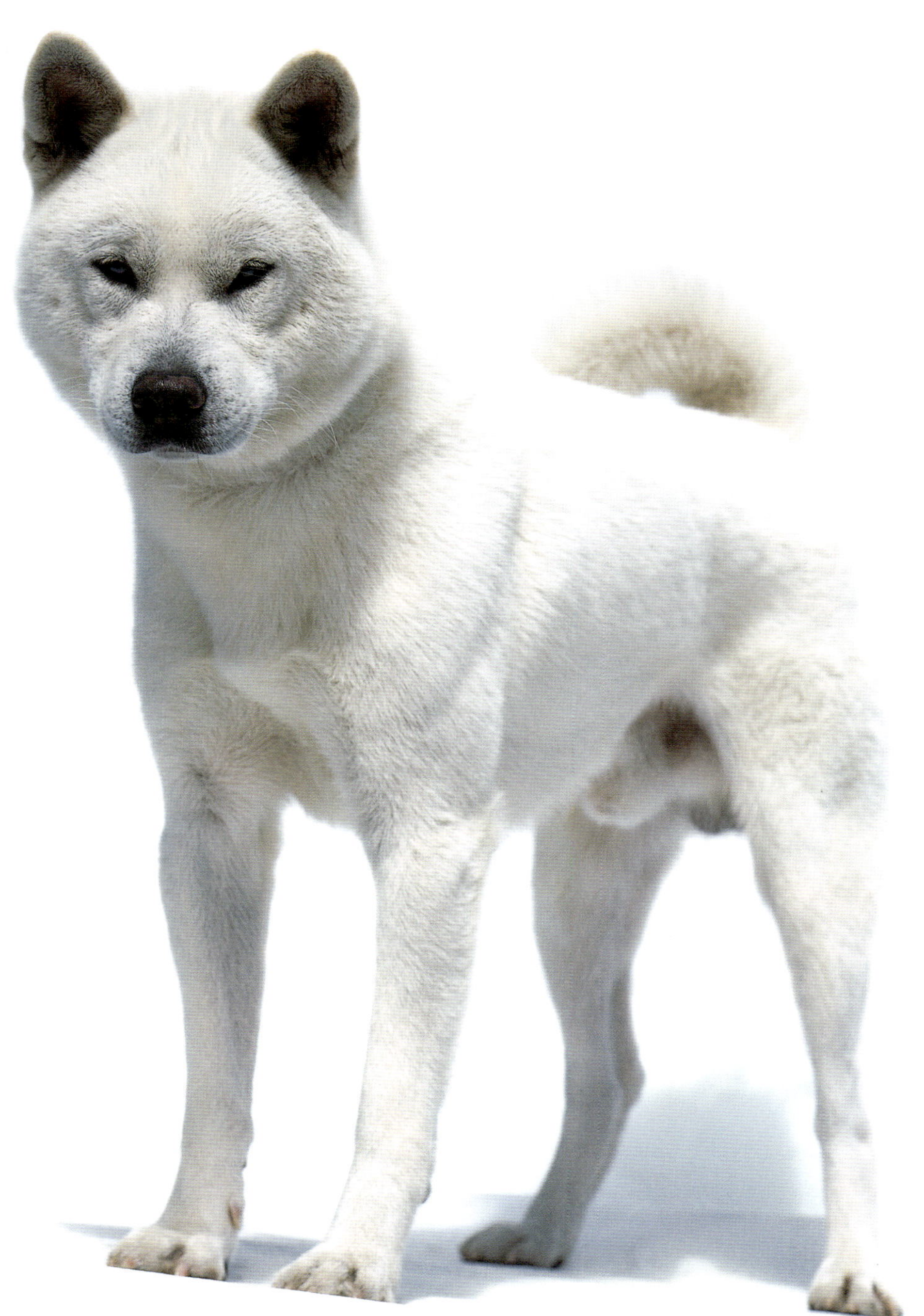

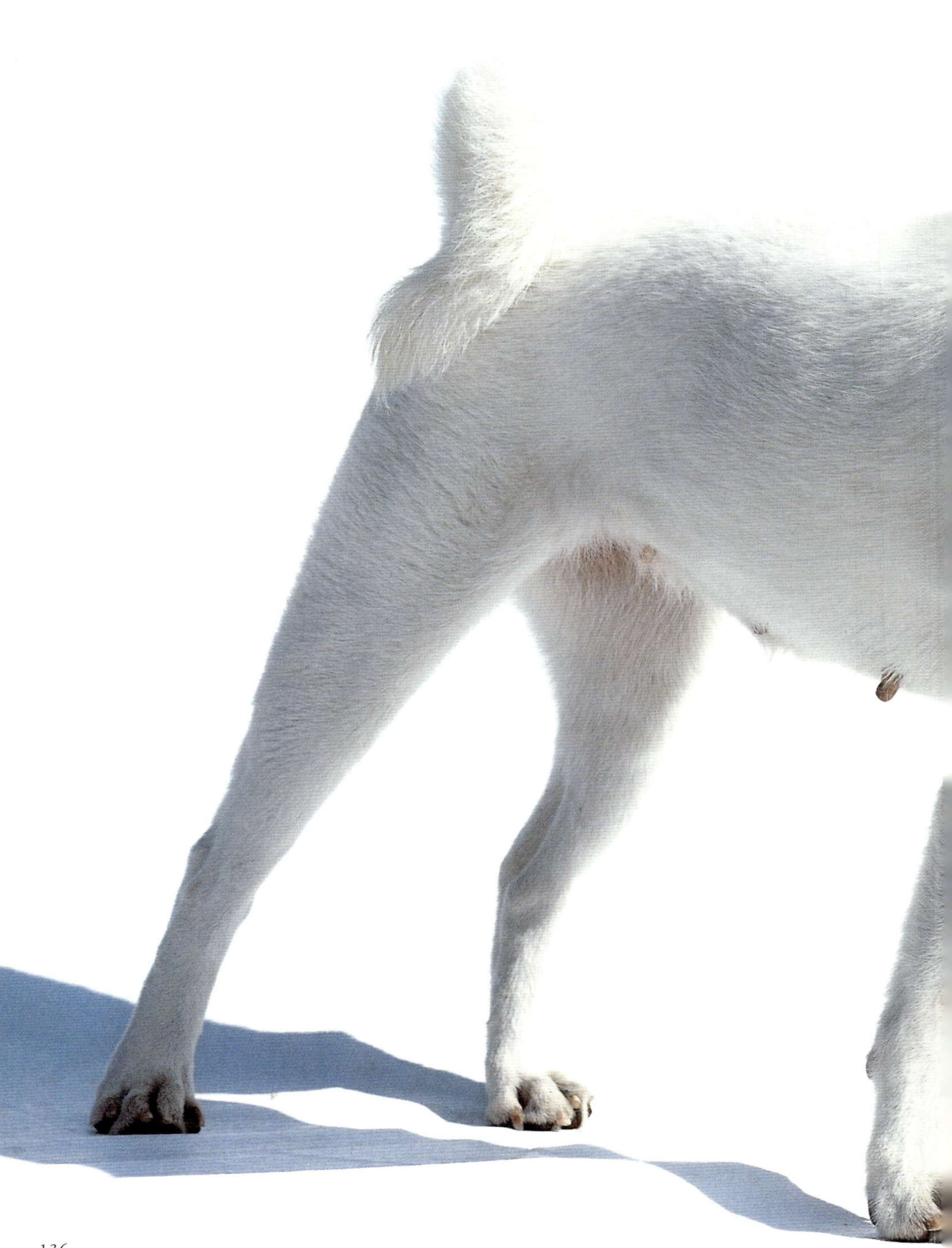

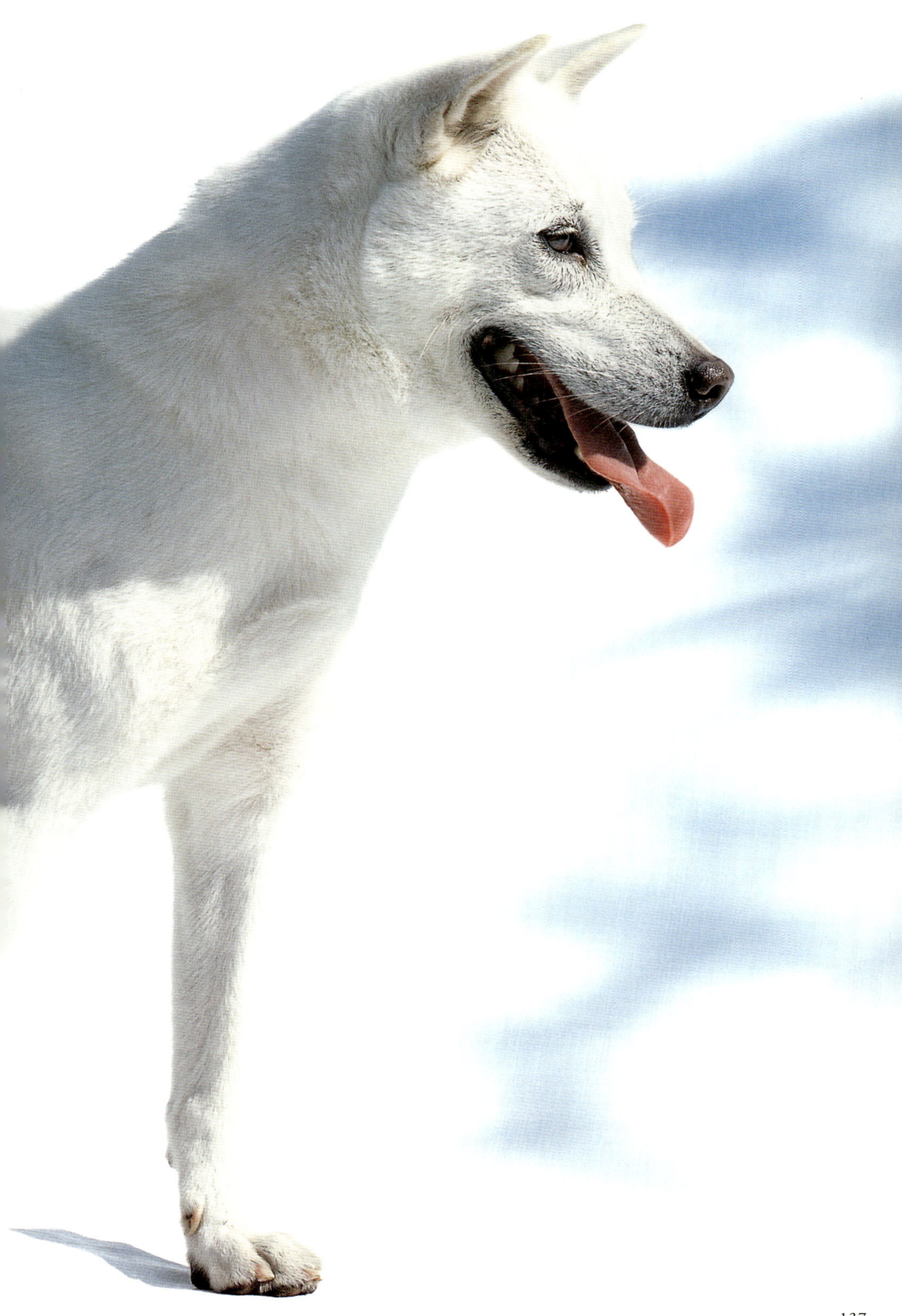

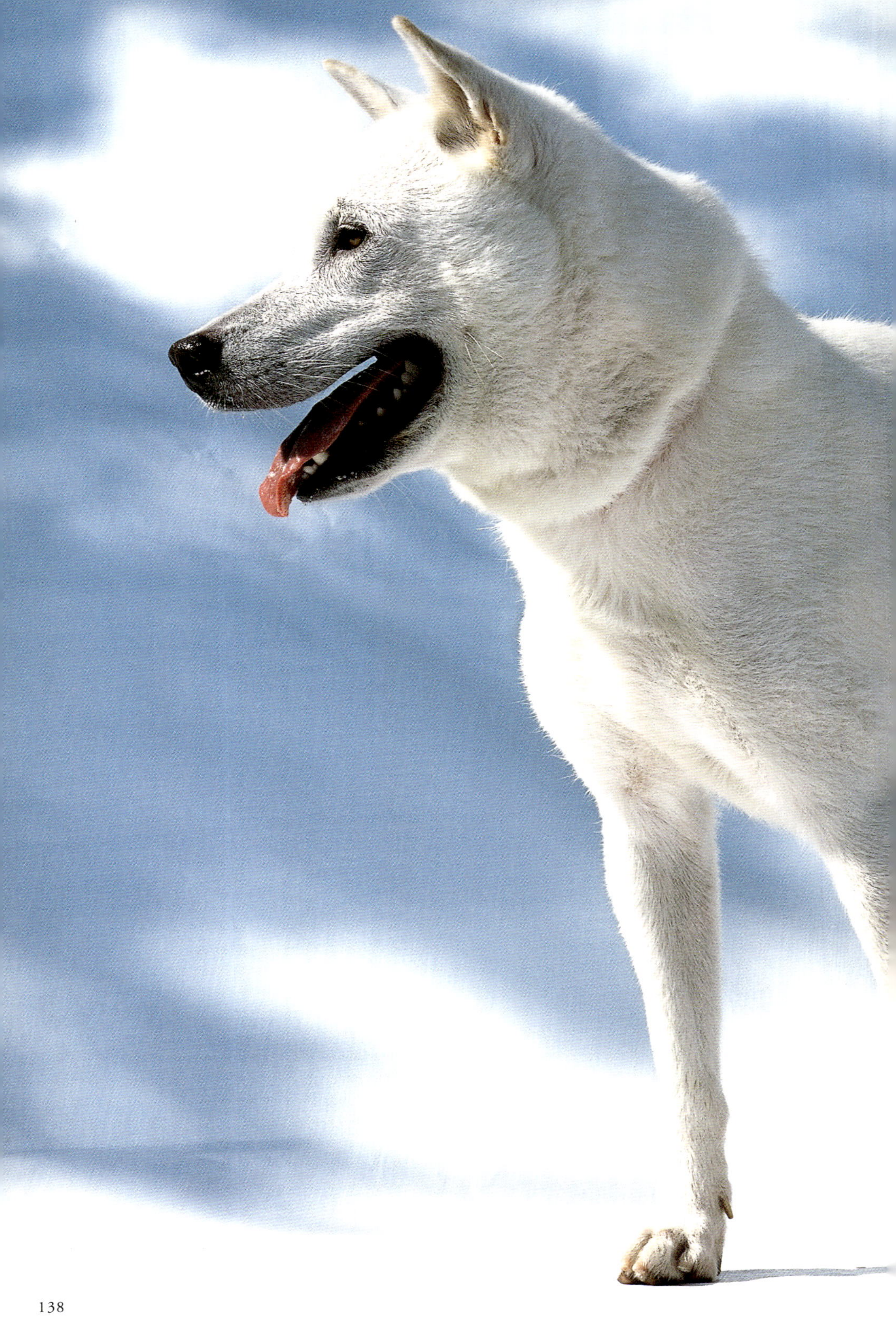

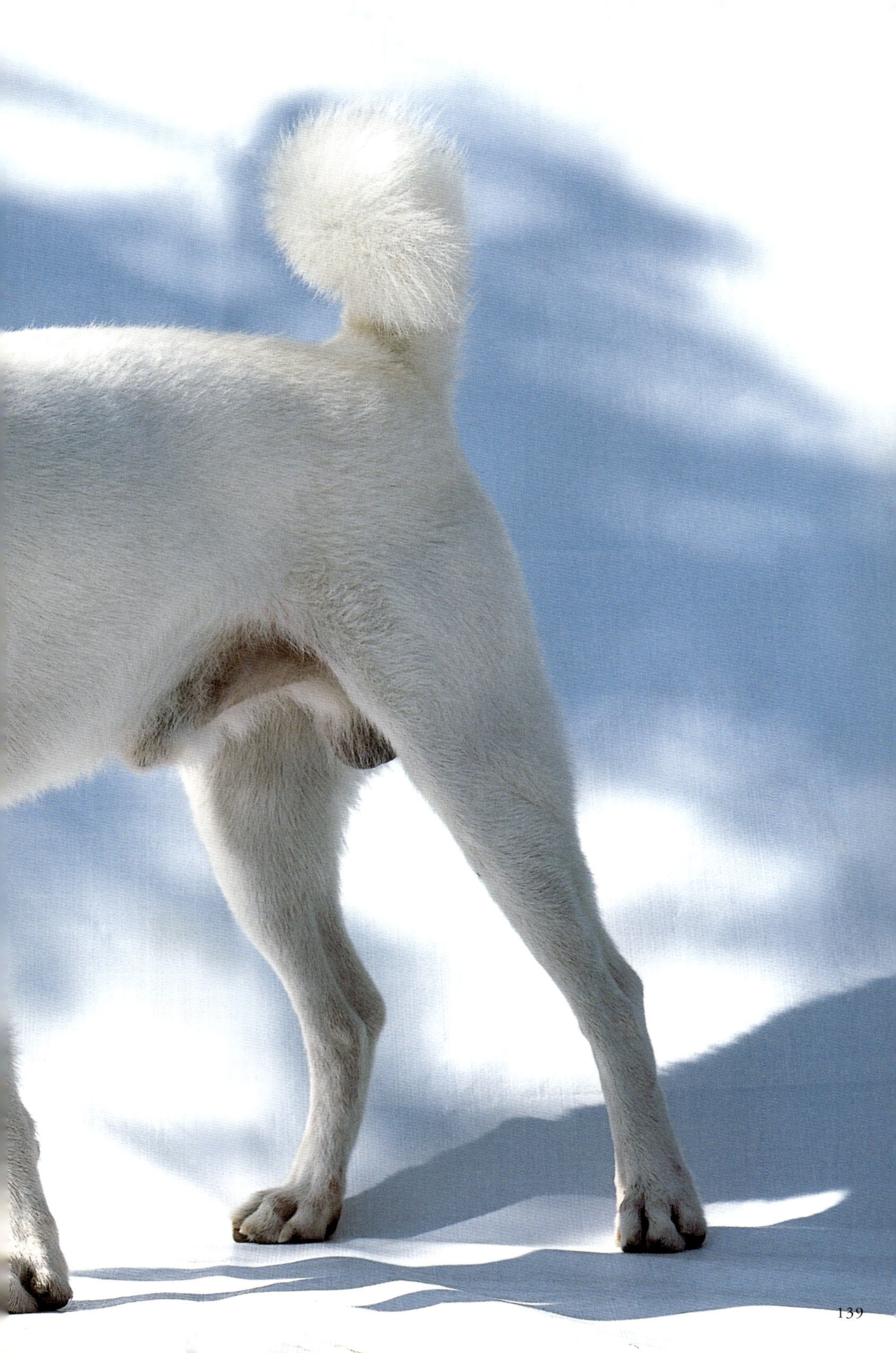

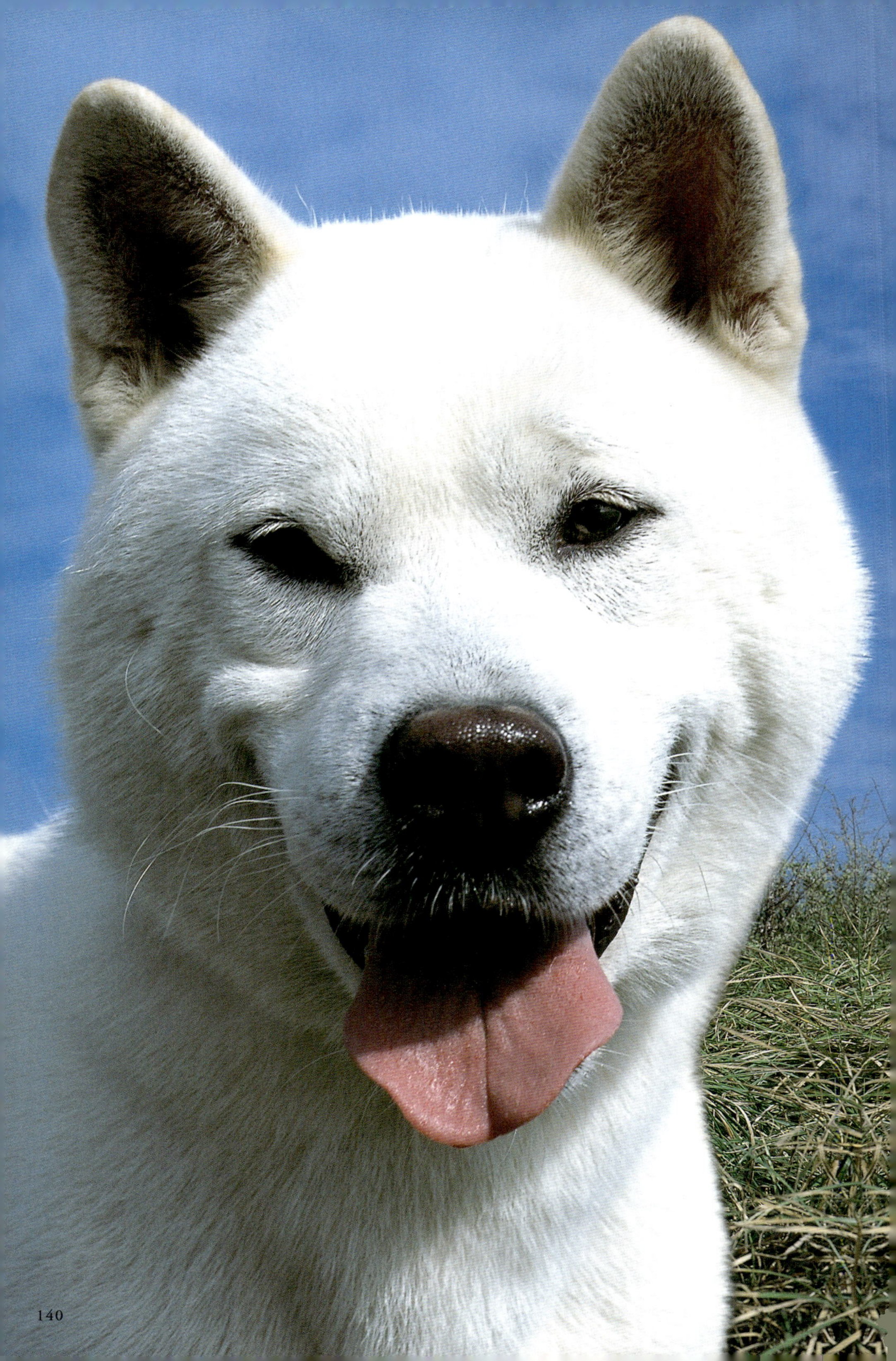

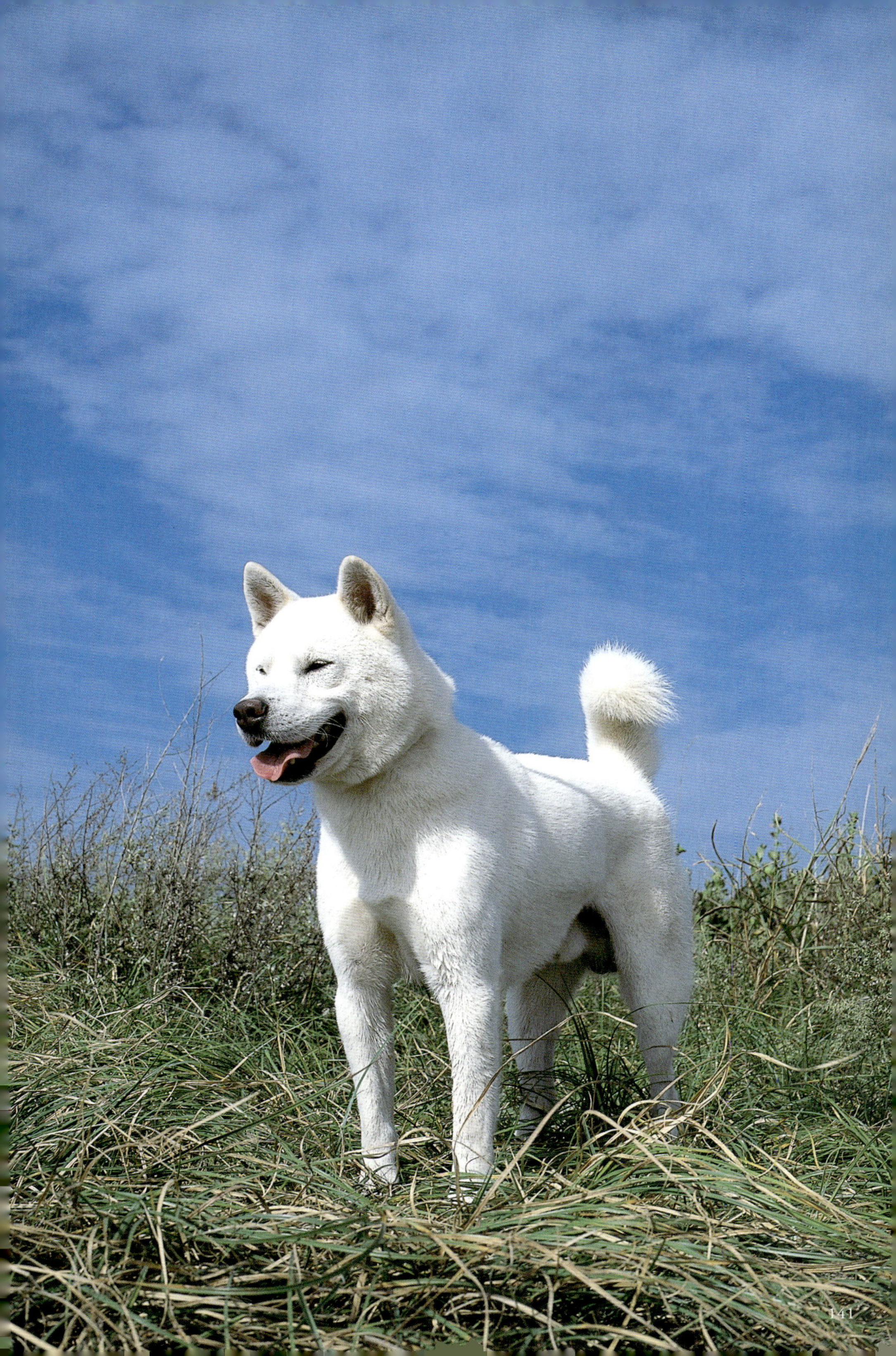

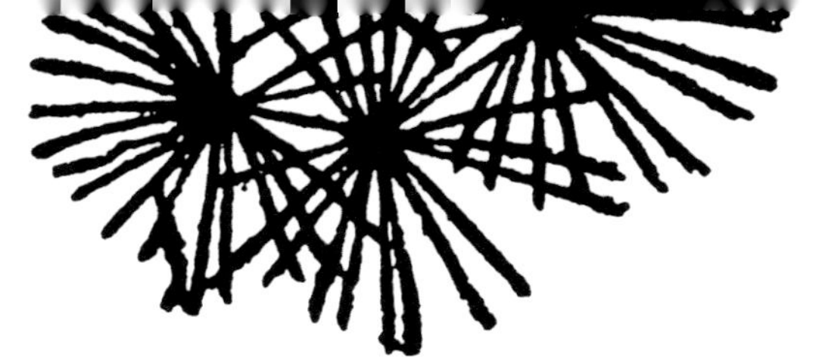

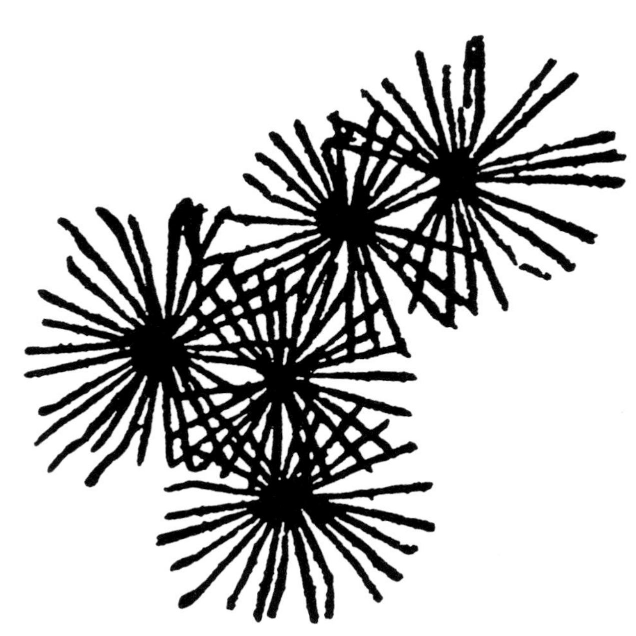

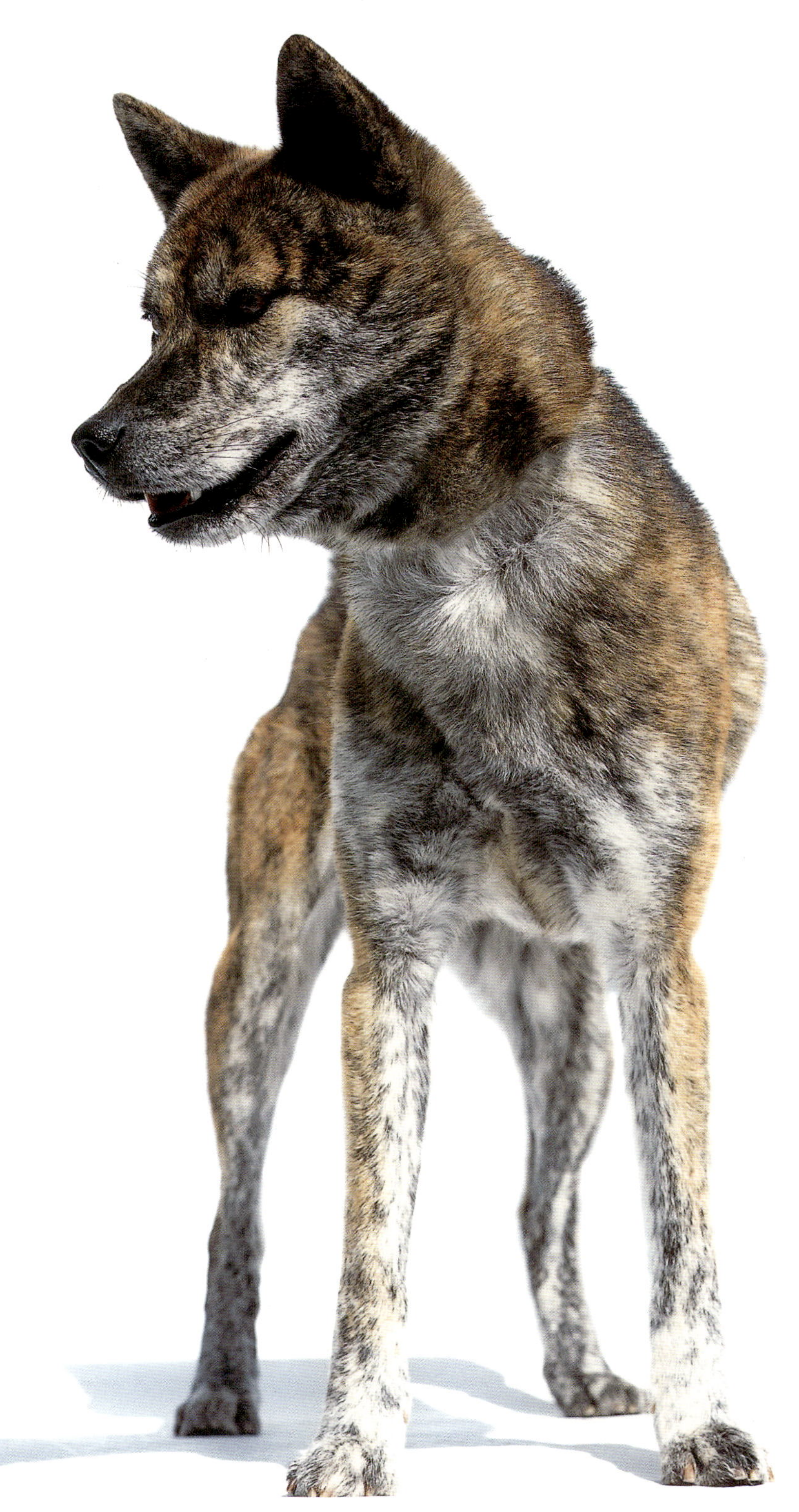

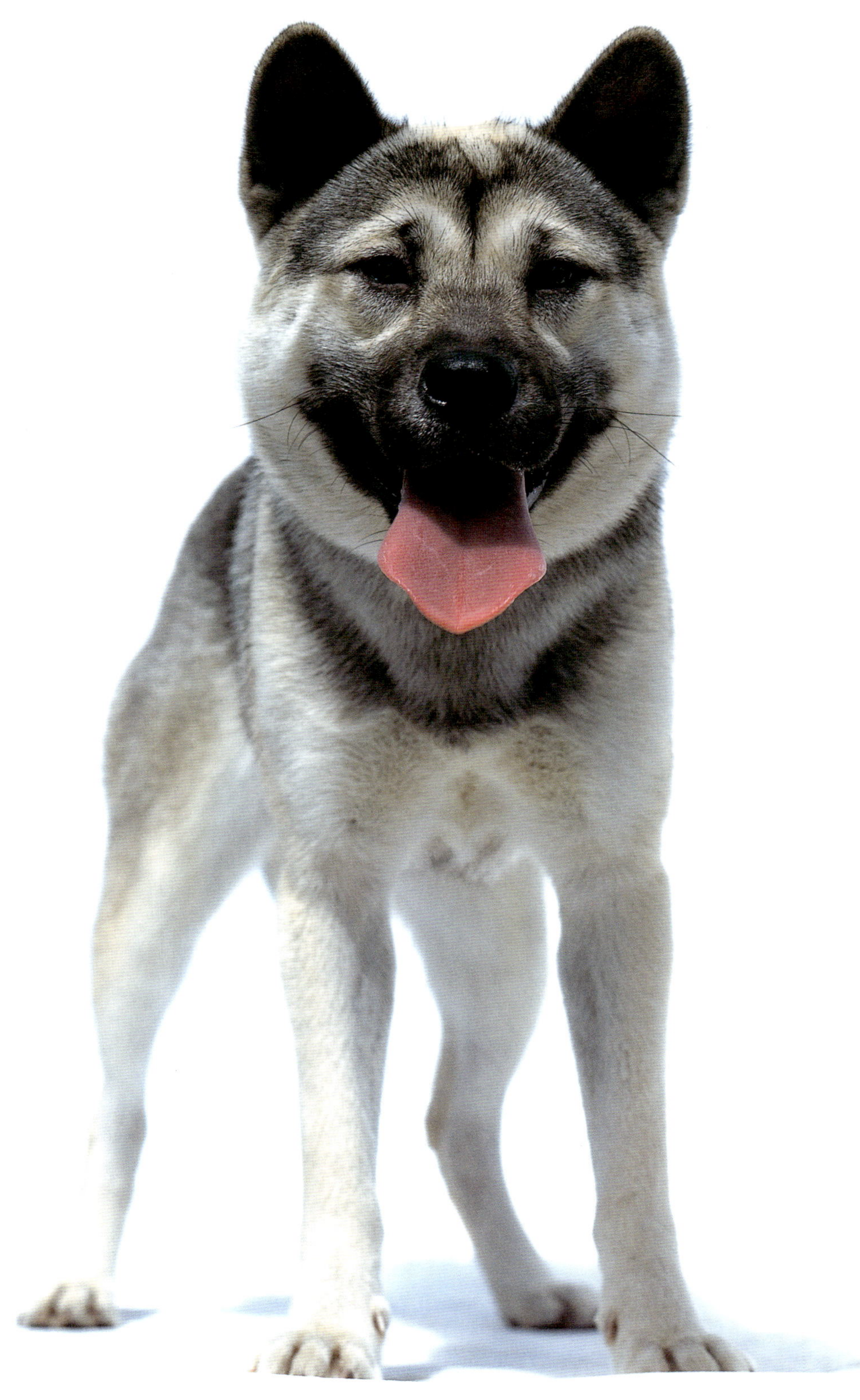

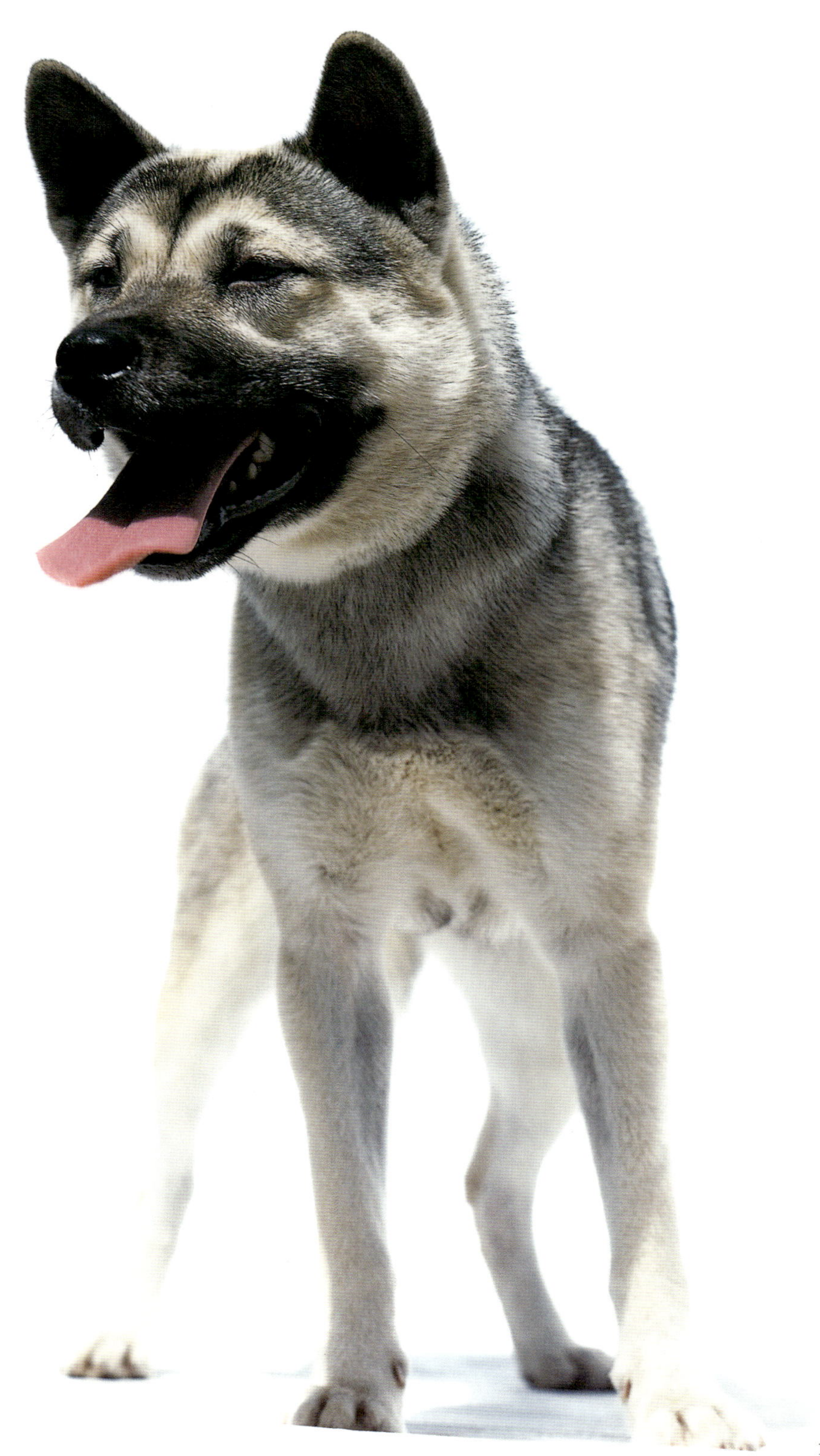

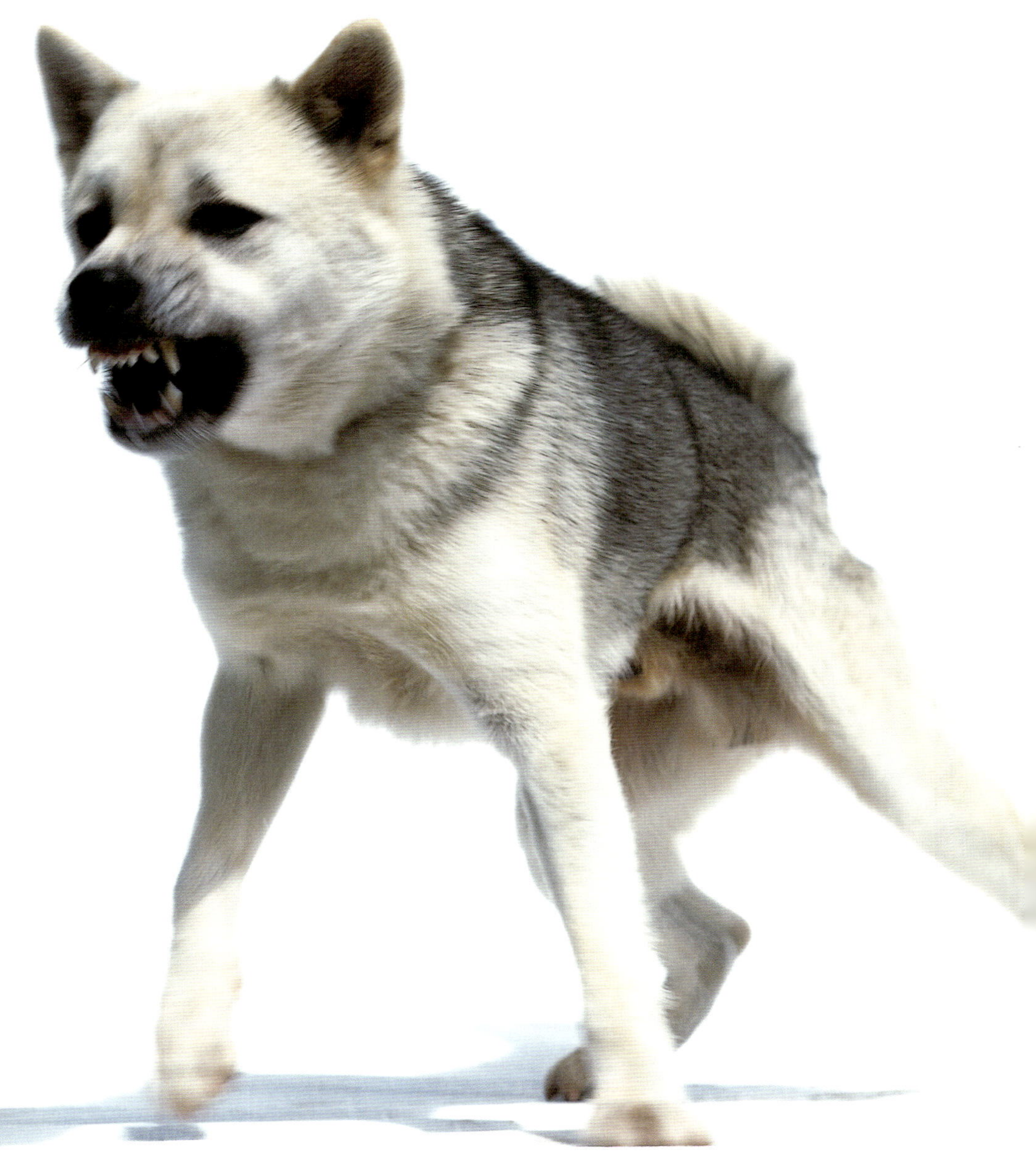

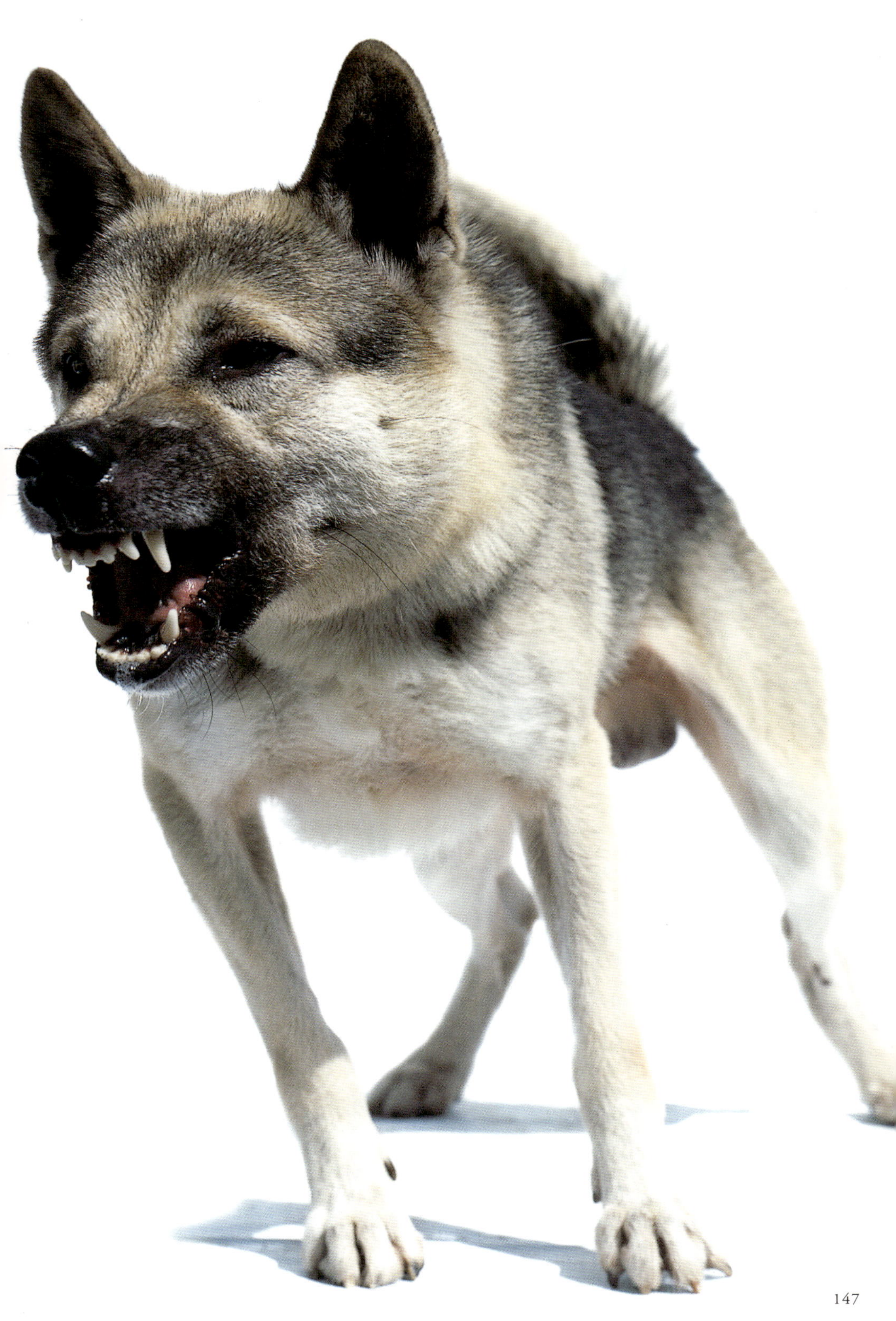

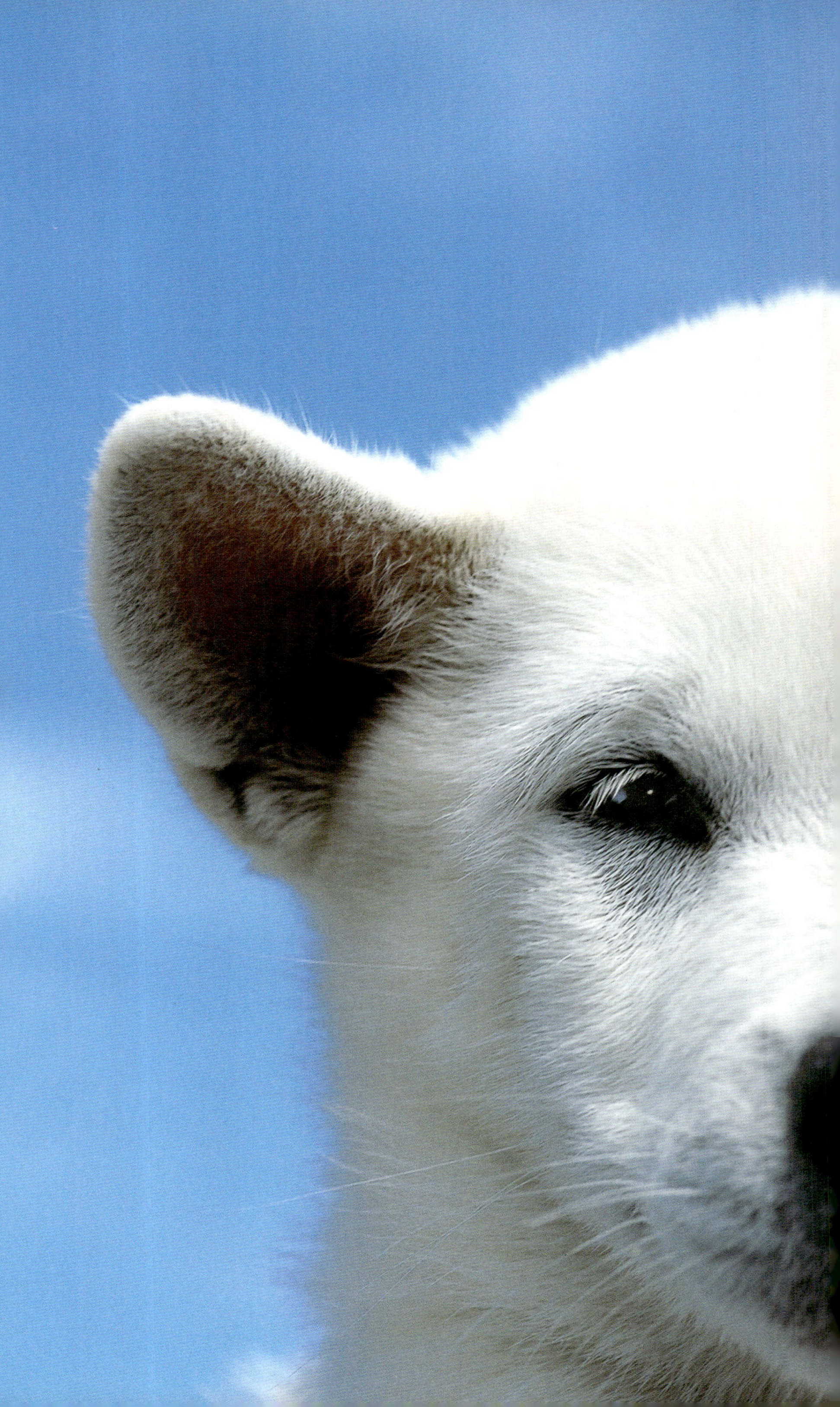

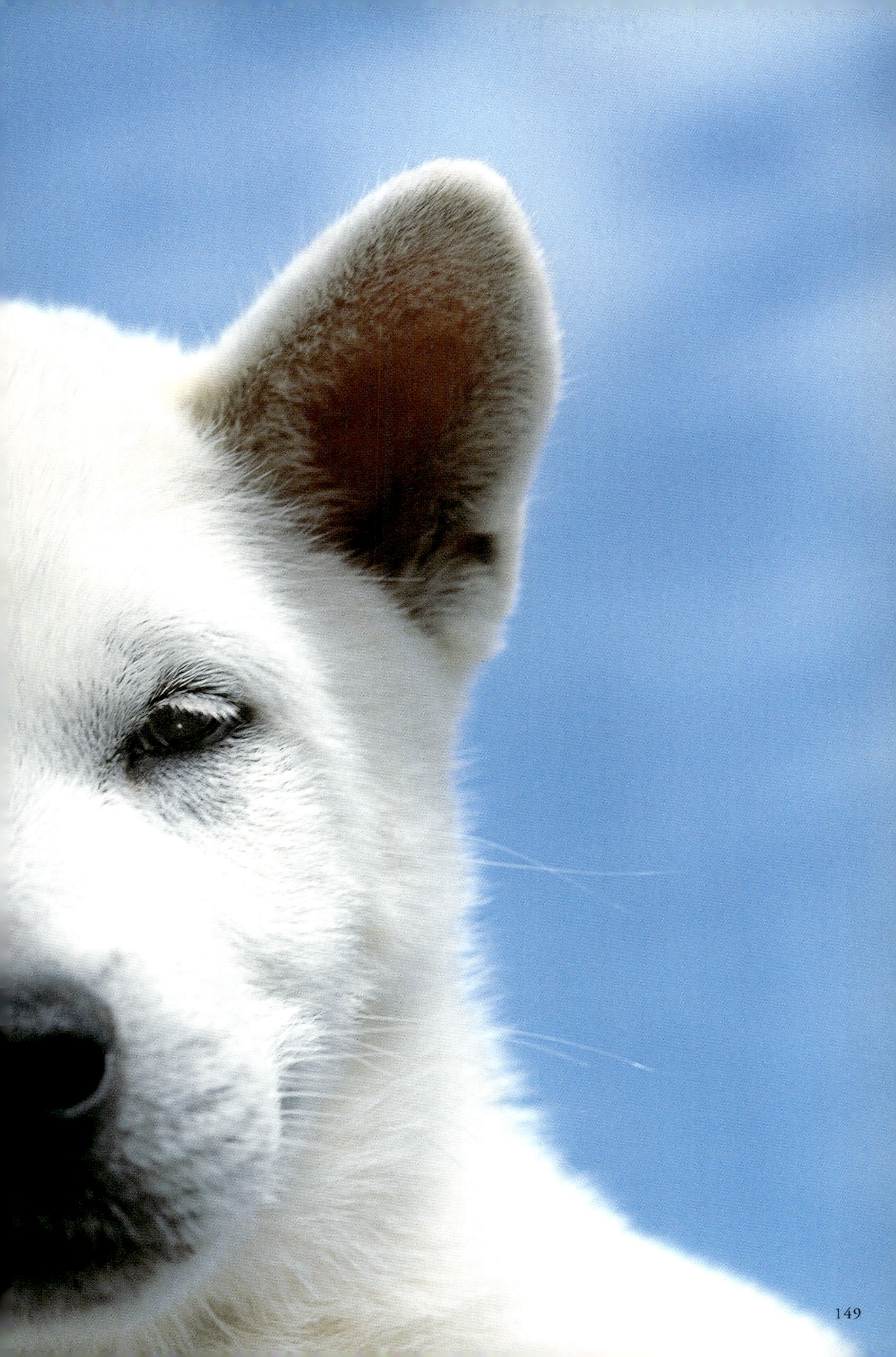

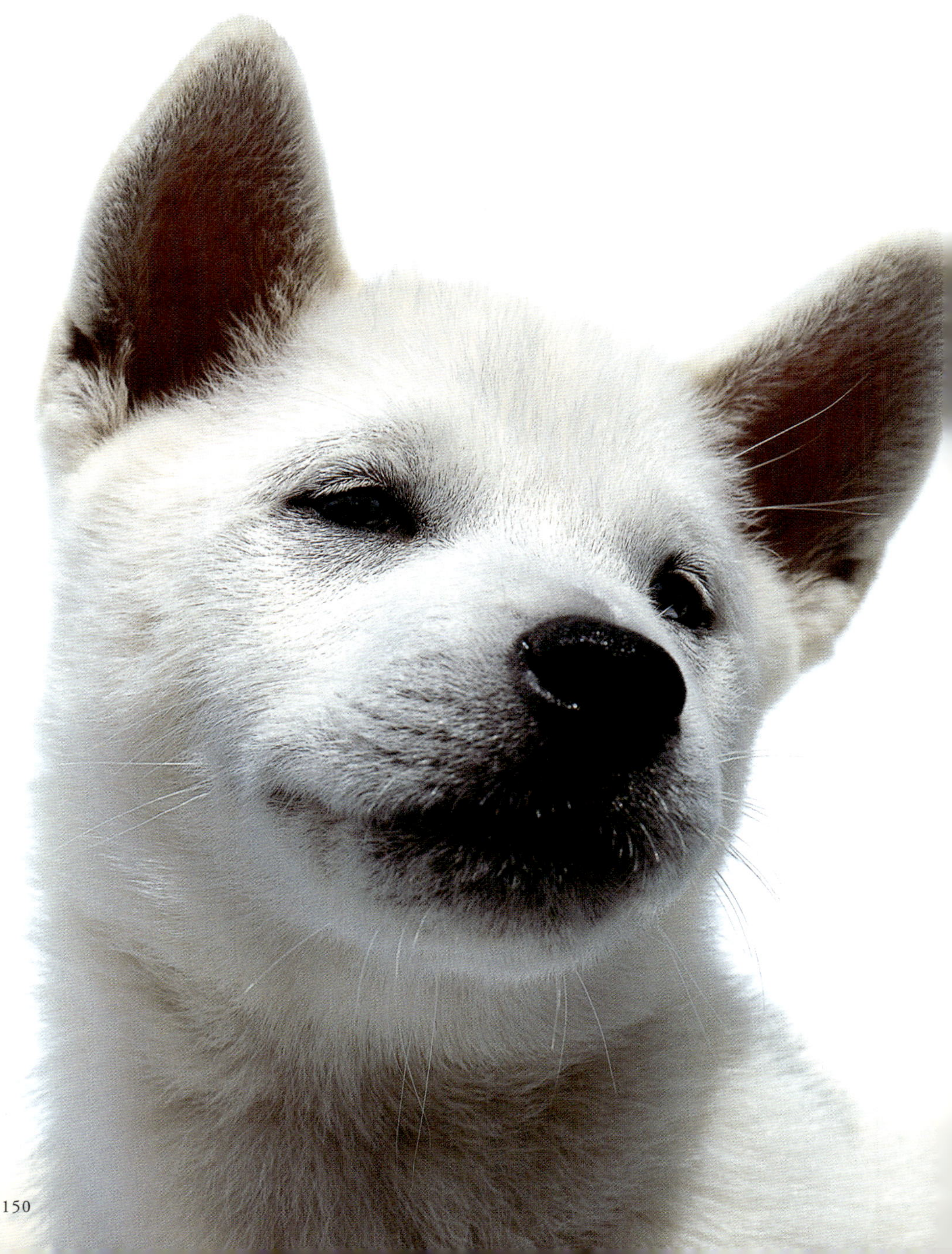

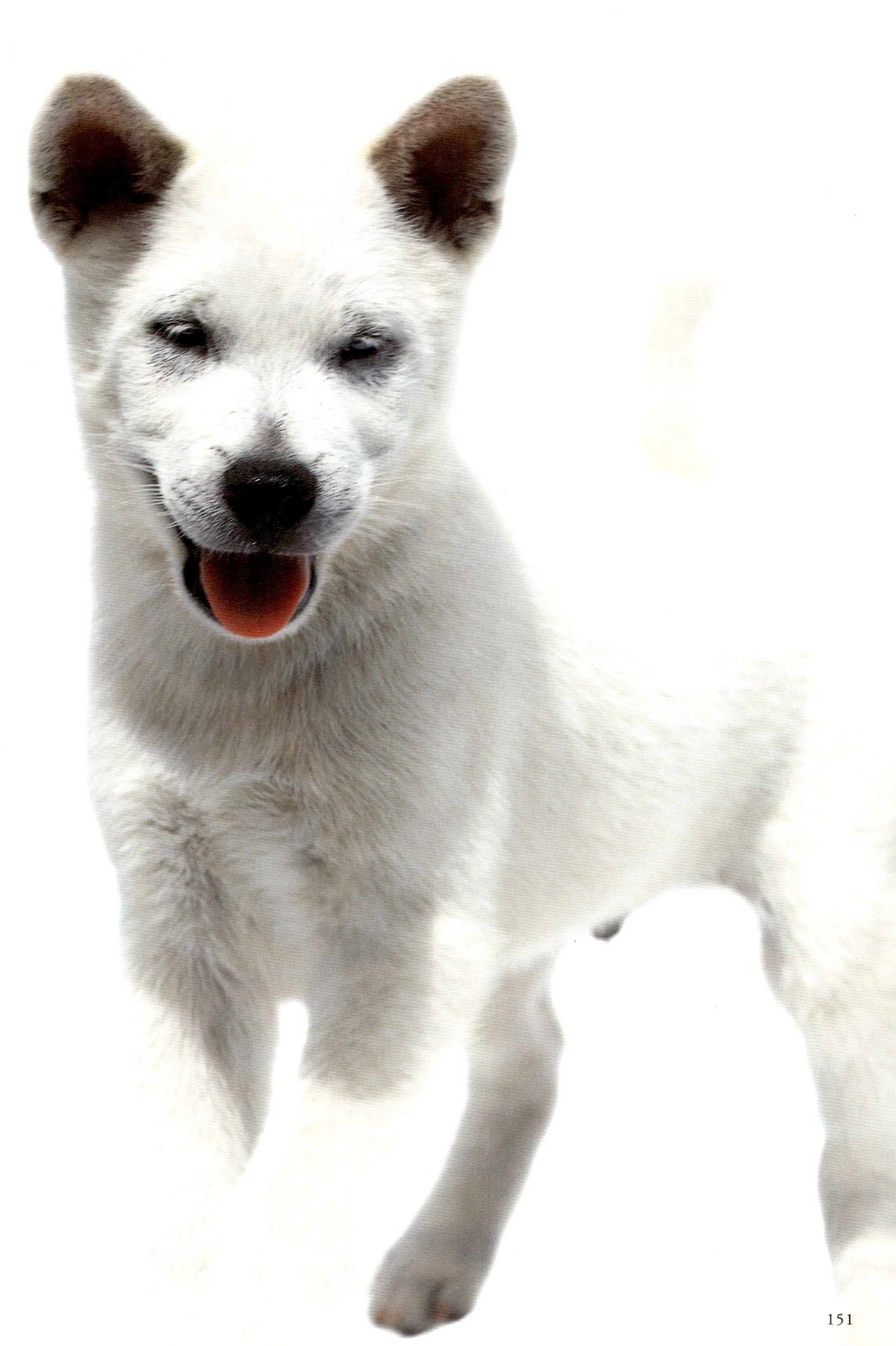

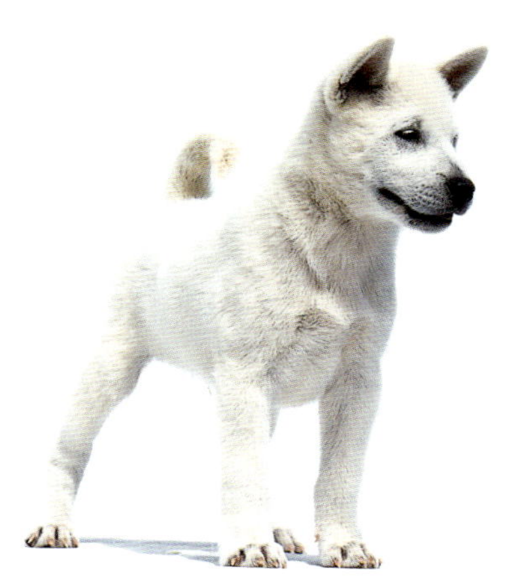

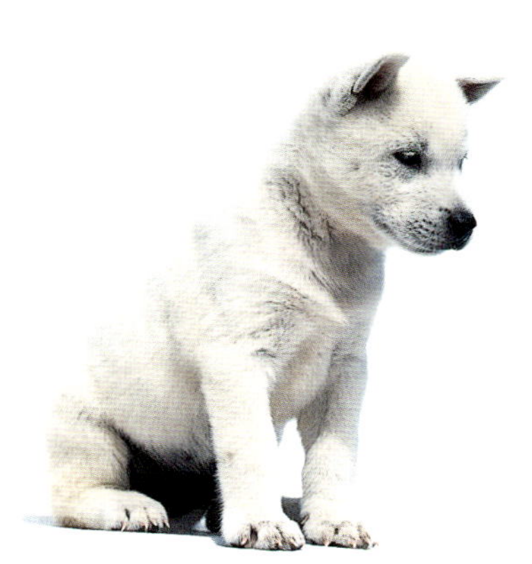

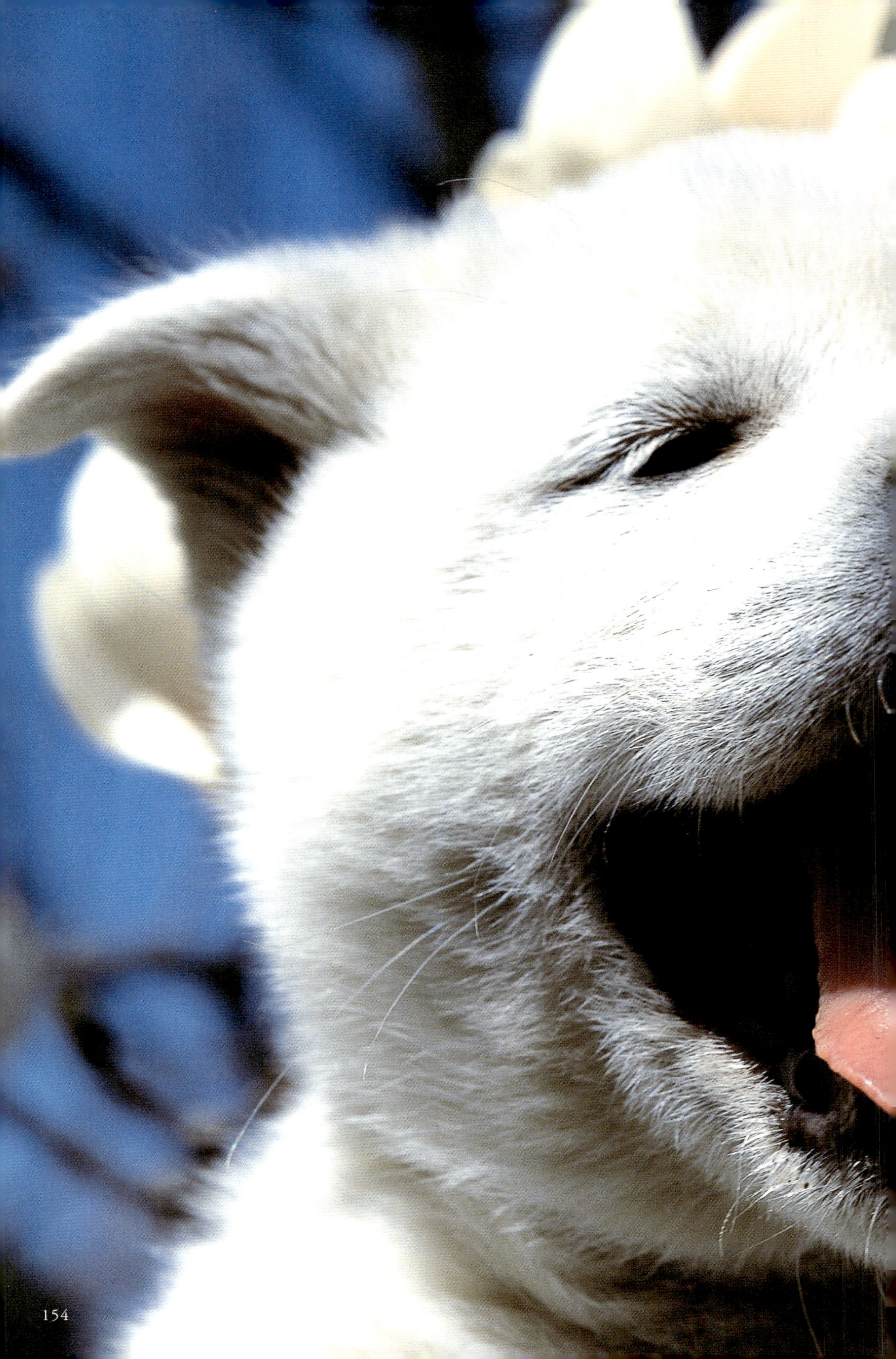

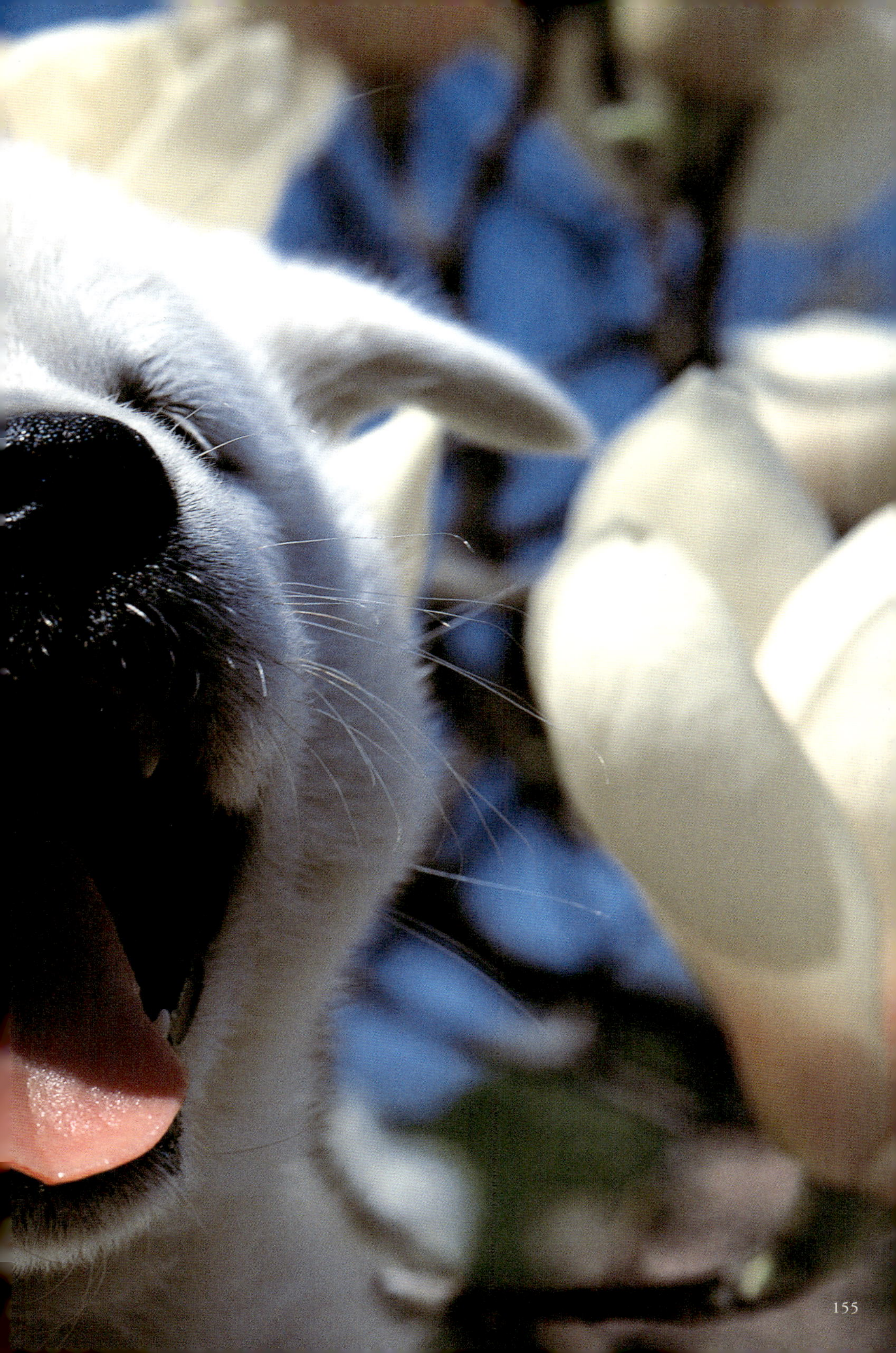

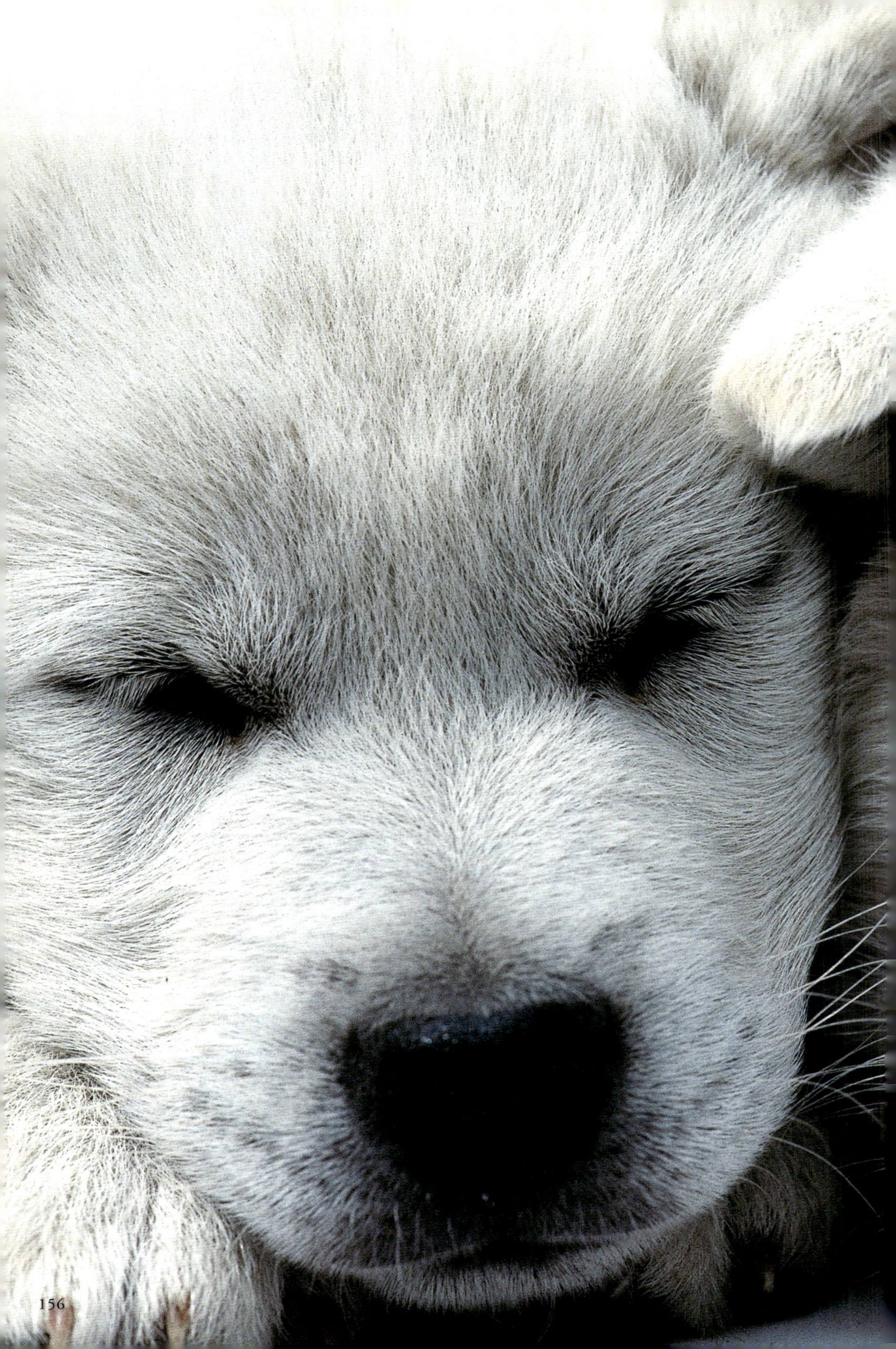

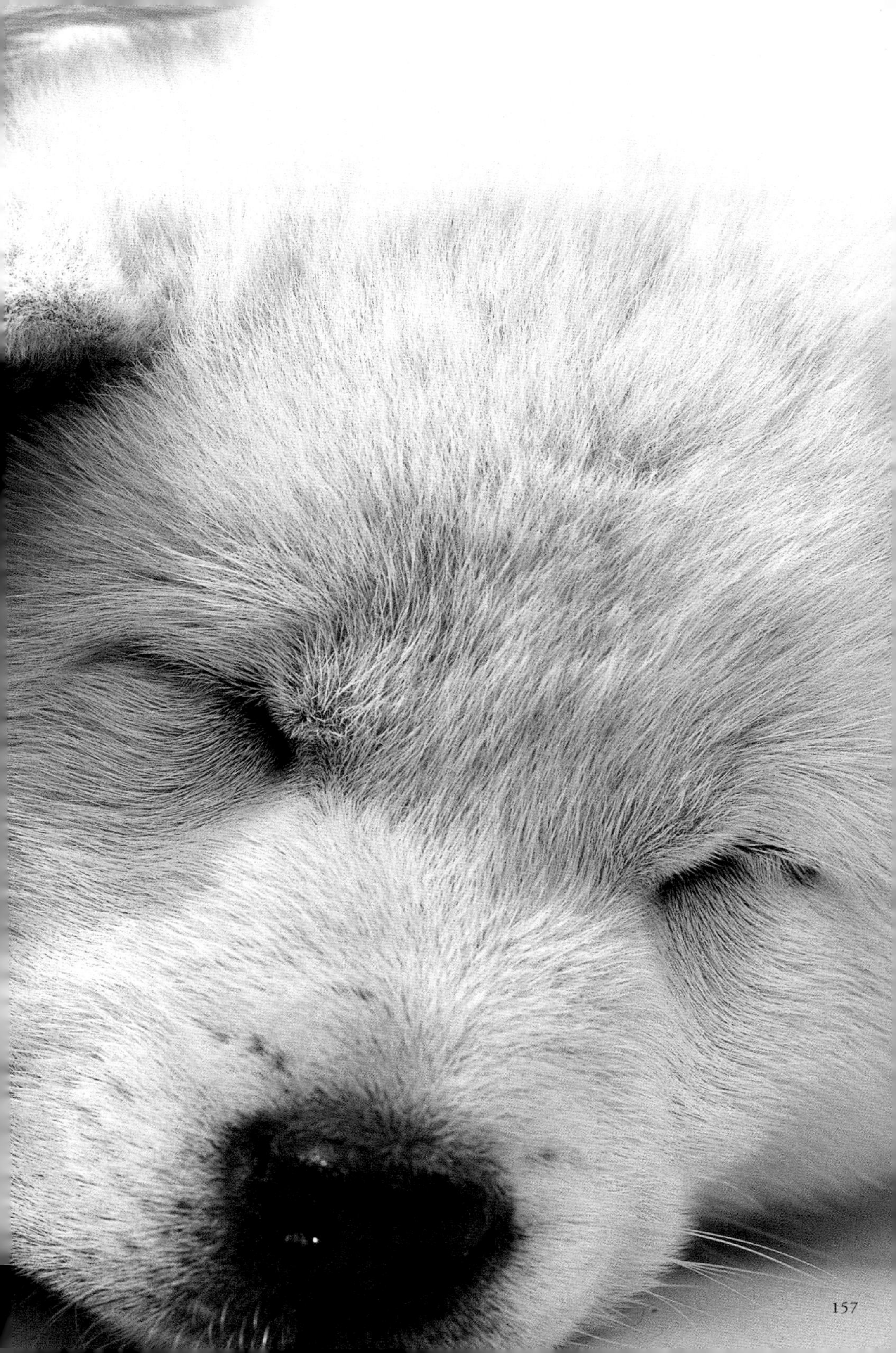

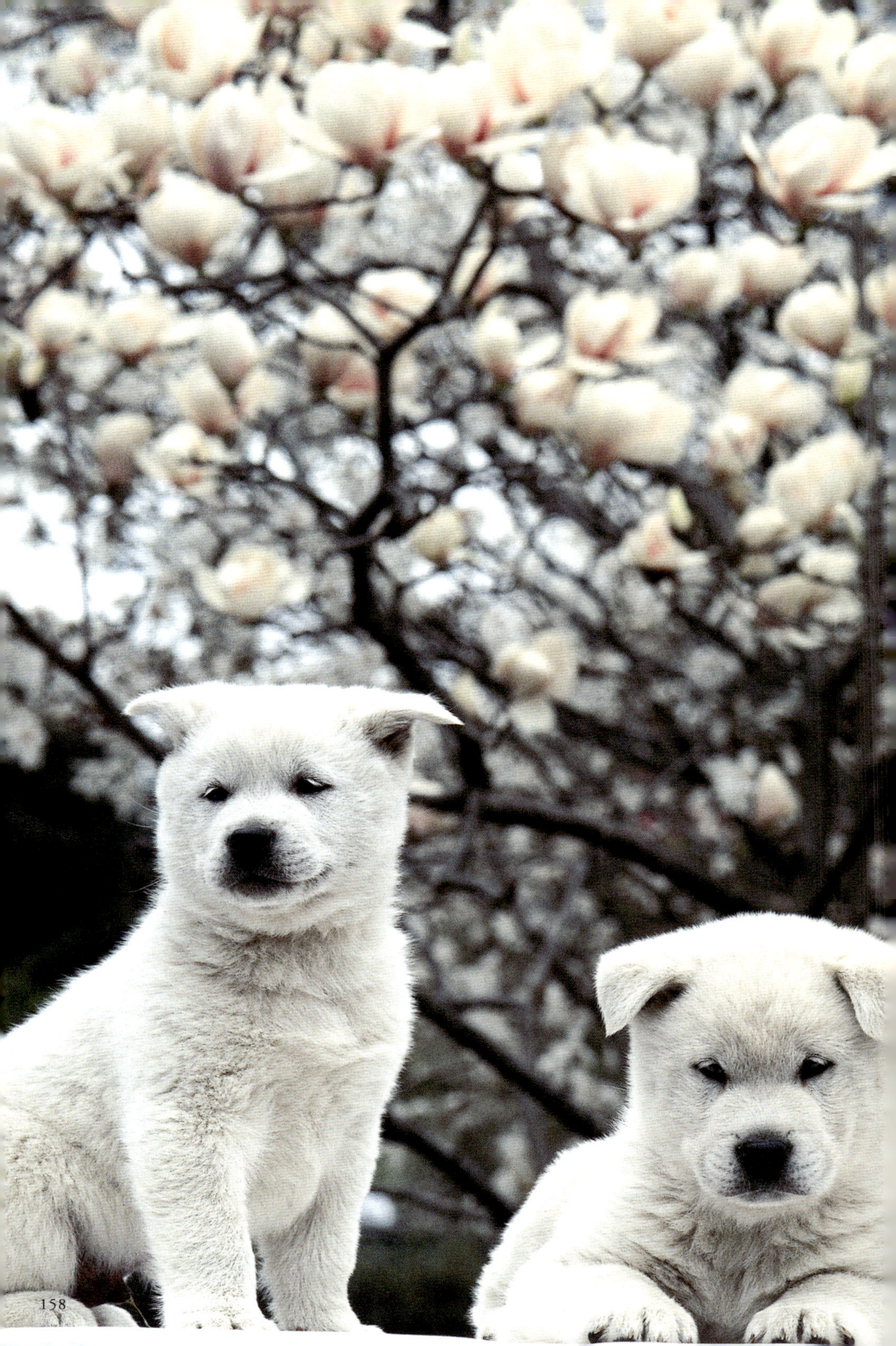

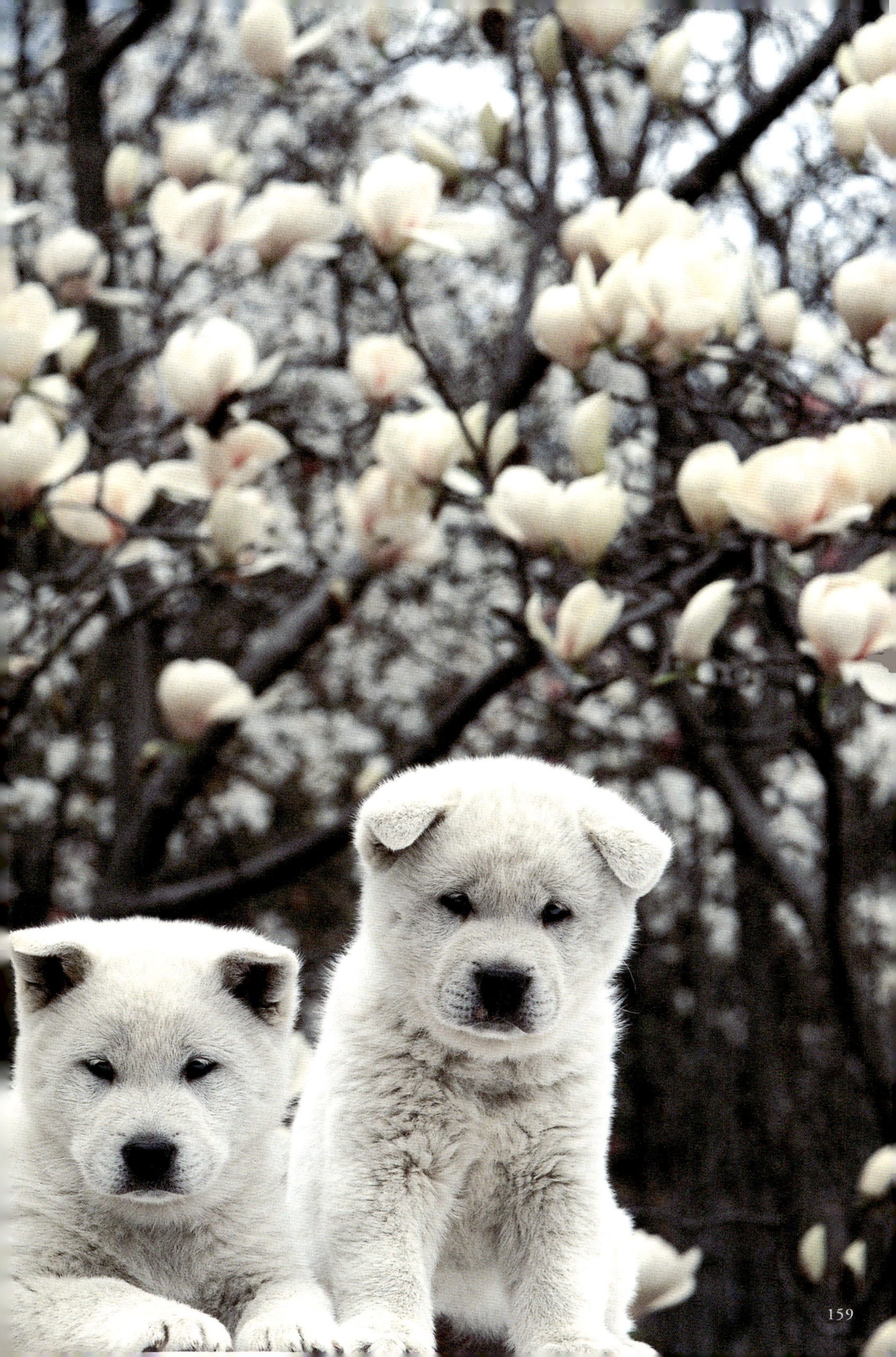

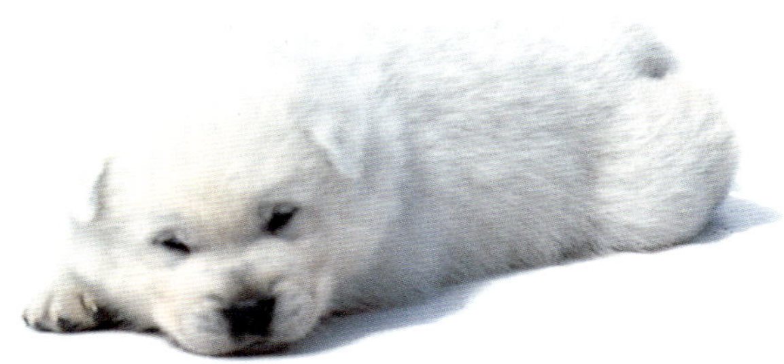

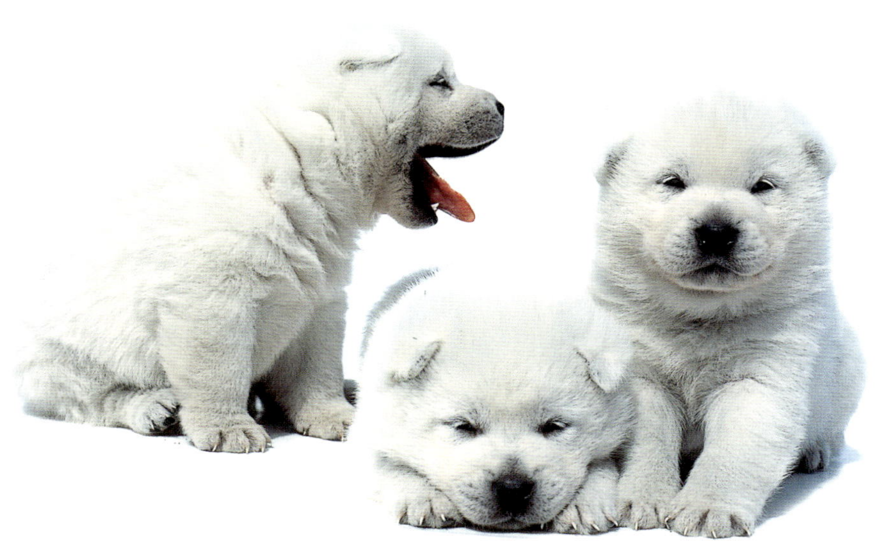

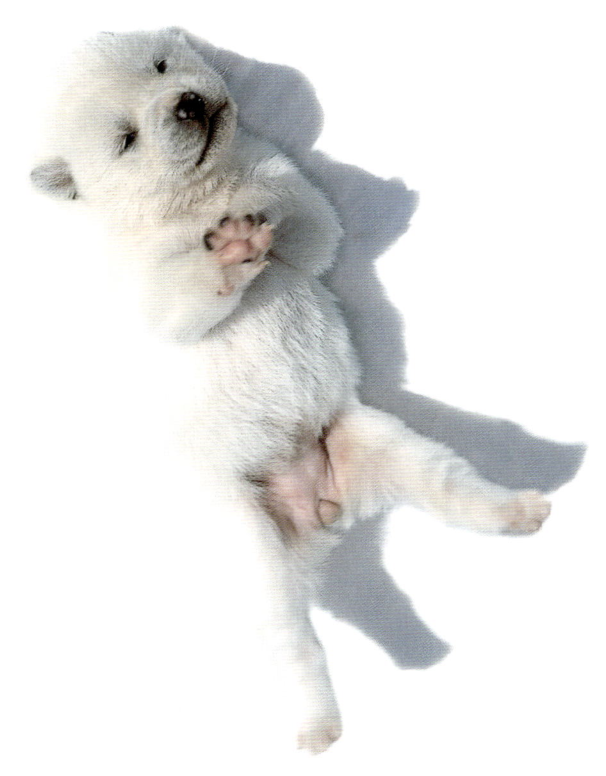

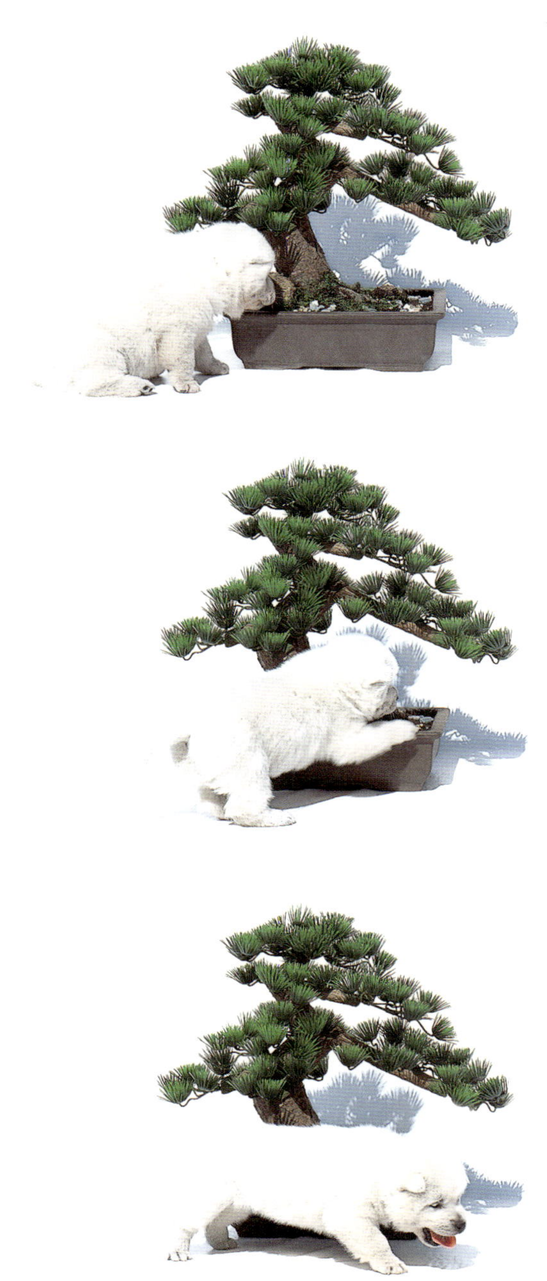

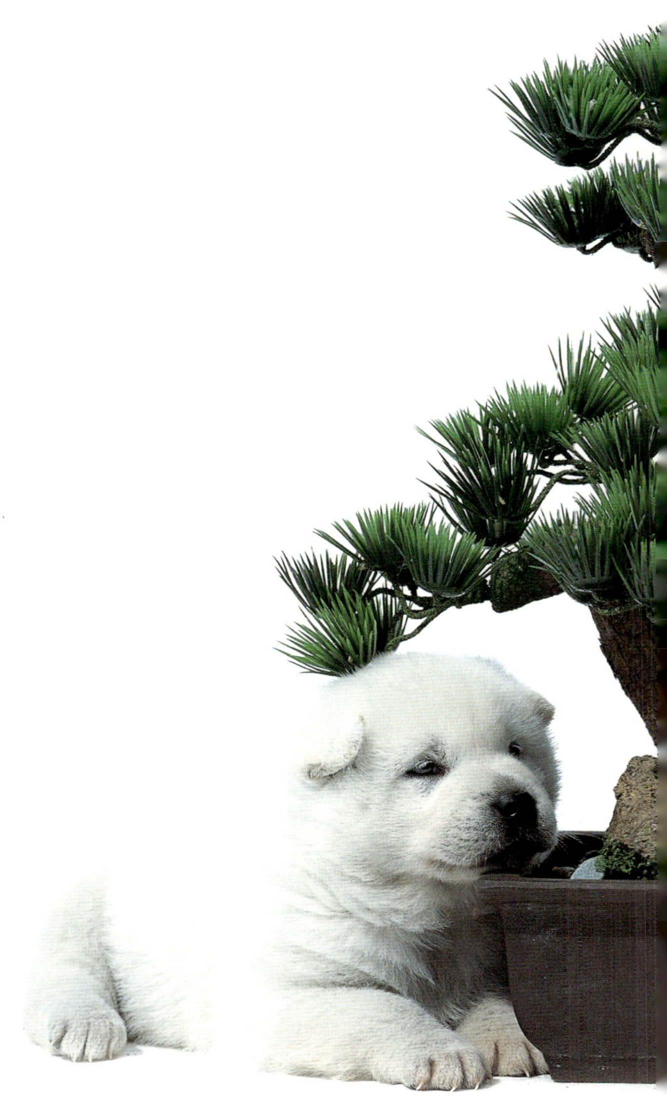

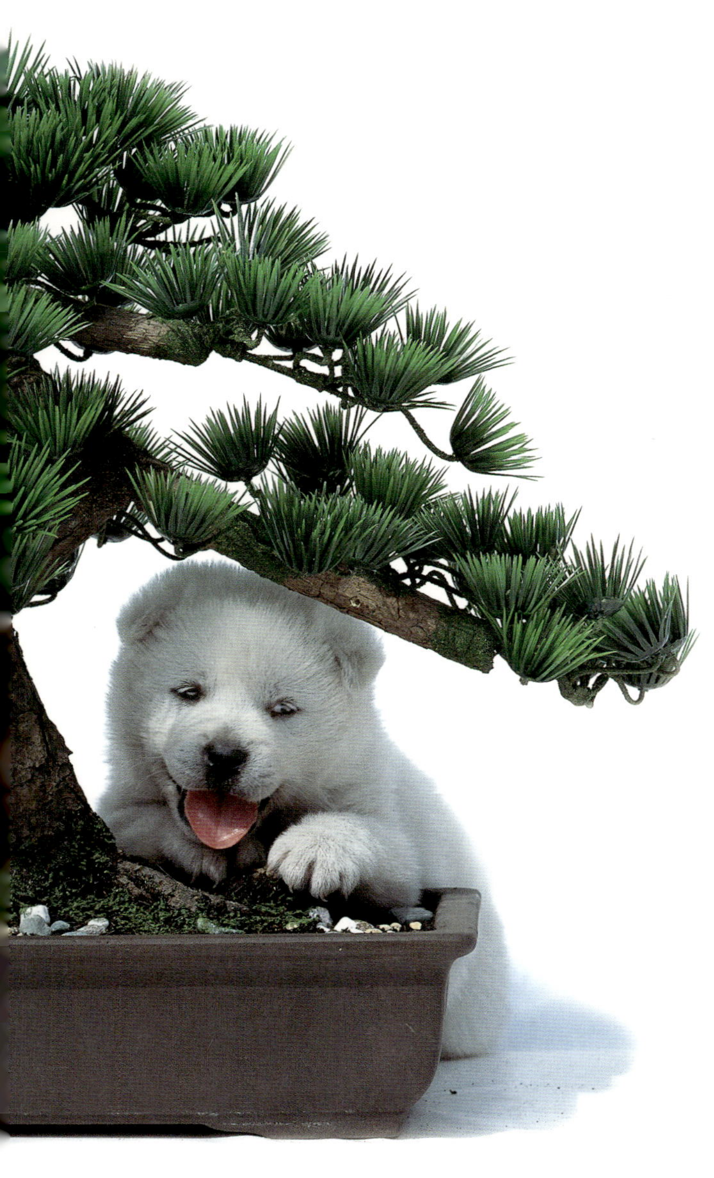

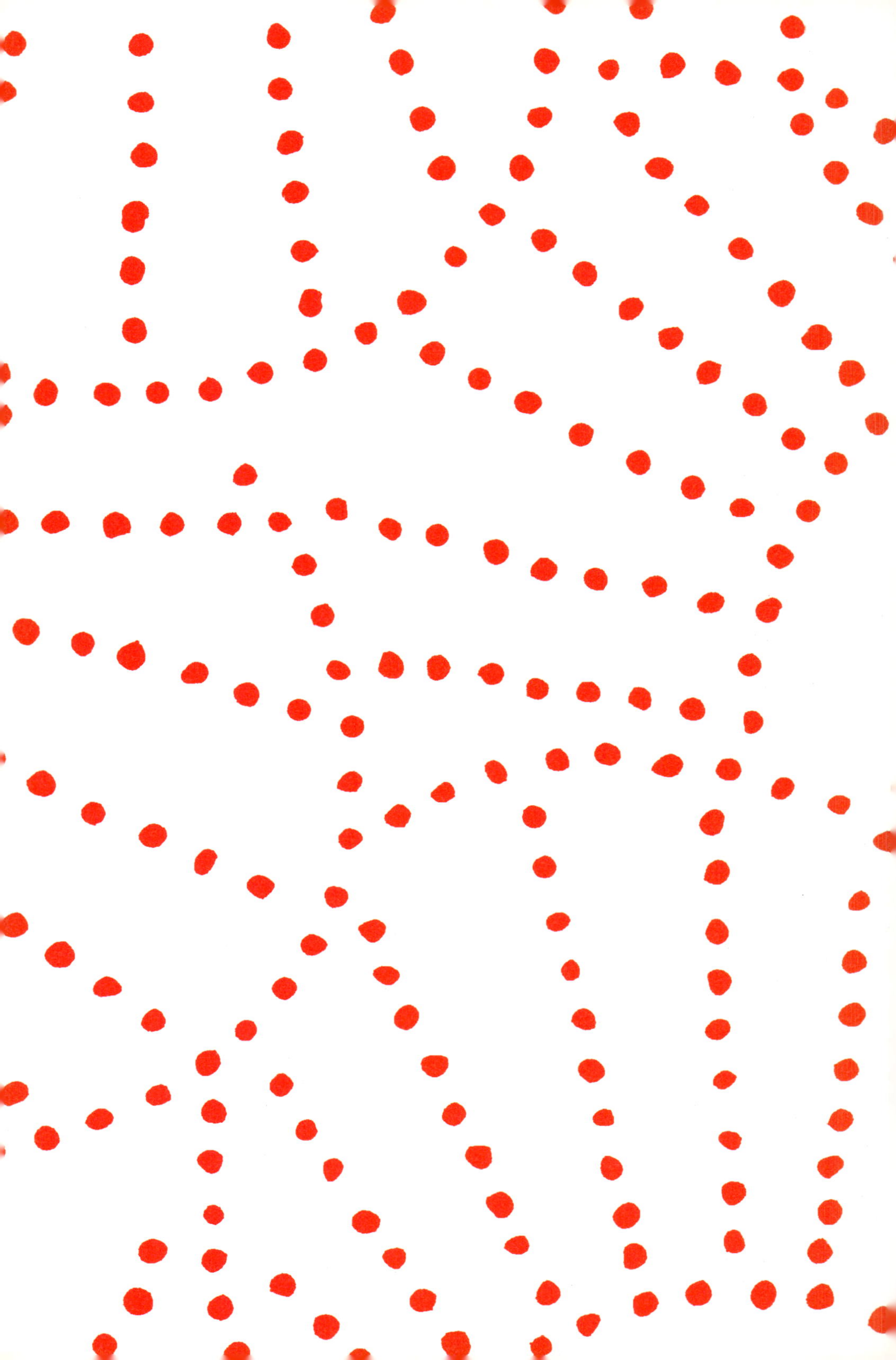

十二支

第十一番

戌

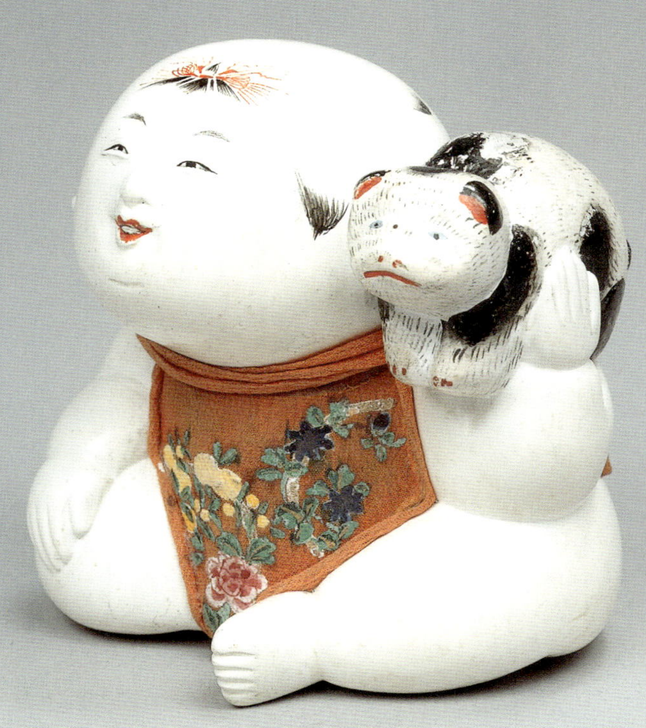

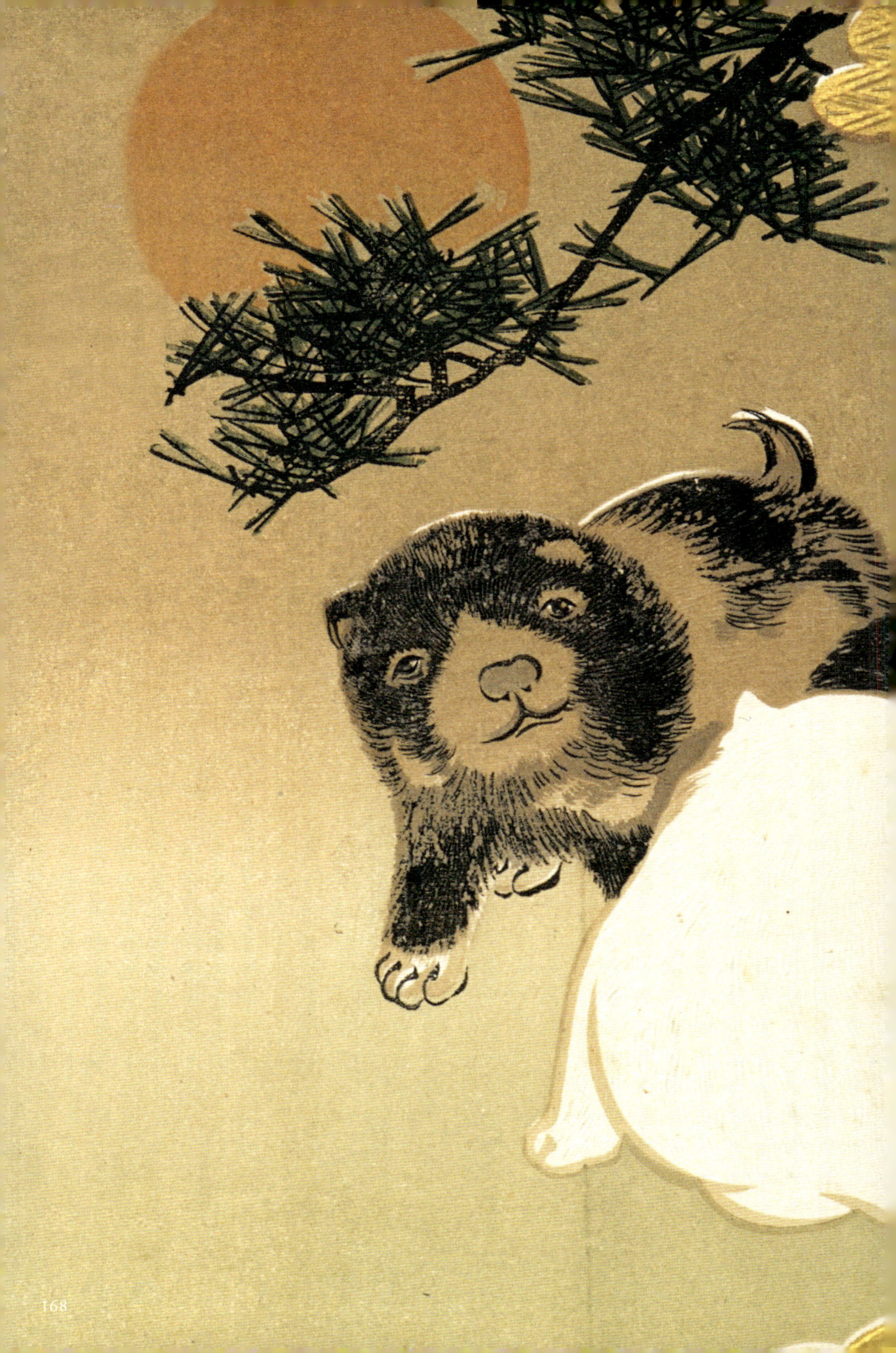

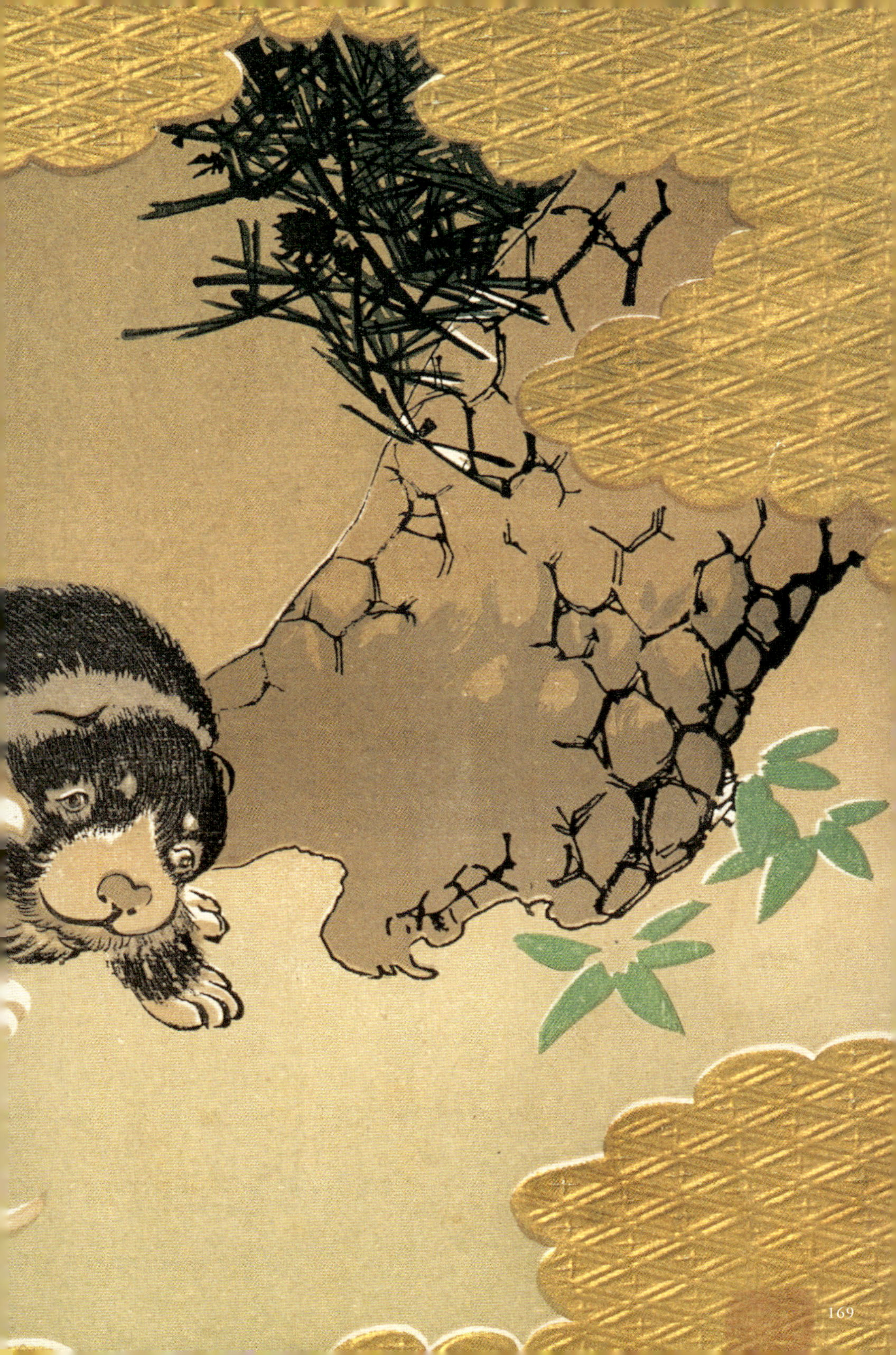

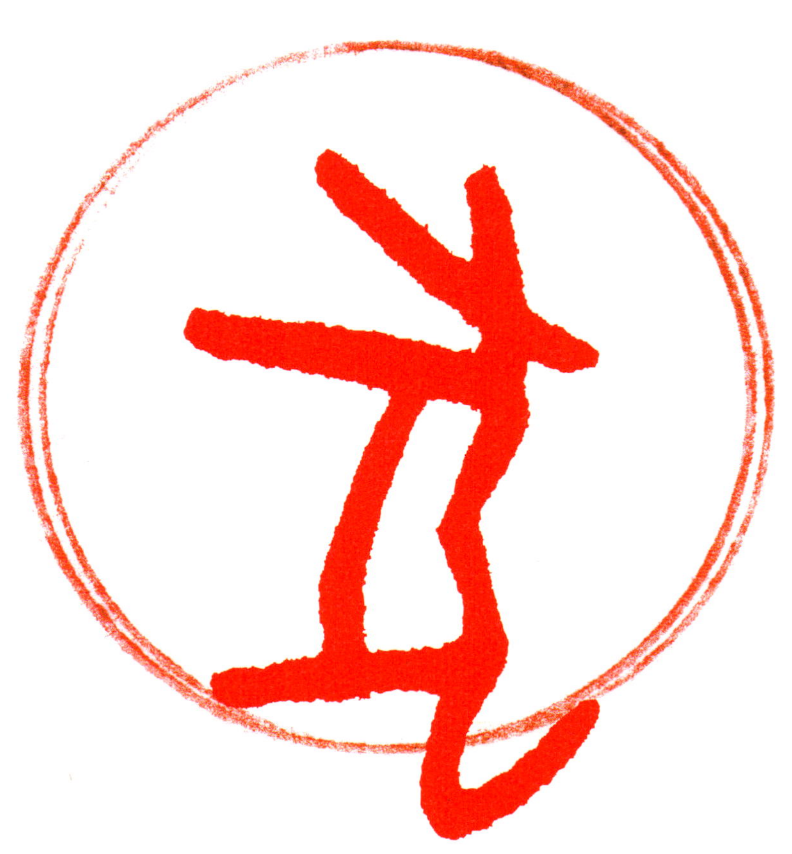

日本犬は、古来から狩猟犬または番犬として

Japanese dogs are domesticated dogs bred since olden times throughout Japan,

全国各地で飼育されてきた家犬である。1934 年

initially for use as either hunting dogs or watchdogs.

（昭和 9 年）に日本犬保存会が定めたスタンダー

The Japanese Dog Standard established in 1934 by the Nihon-ken Hozonkai (NIPPO)

ド（日本犬標準）には、秋田犬、甲斐犬、紀州犬、

mentions the names of six established dog breeds: the Akita Inu, Kai-ken,

柴犬、四国犬、北海道犬の 6 つの在来犬種の

Kishu-ken, Shiba Inu, Shikoku-ken, and Hokkaido-ken,

名が挙げられており、1931 年（昭和 6 年）から

all of which were designated Natural Monuments of Japan

1937 年（昭和 12 年）の間にすべて国の天然

in the period between 1931 and 1937.

記念物に指定された。この他に川上犬、三河犬、

In addition to these the Kawakami-ken, Mikawa-ken, Satsuma-ken, Ryukyu-ken, Tosa Token,

薩摩犬、琉球犬、土佐闘犬、狆、日本スピッツ、

Chin, Japanese Spitz, and Japanese Terrier are also recognized as native Japanese breeds.

日本テリアも日本原産の犬種とされる。その

The breed with the largest number registered is the Shiba Inu.

うち最も登録頭数が多いのが柴犬である。

日本の犬

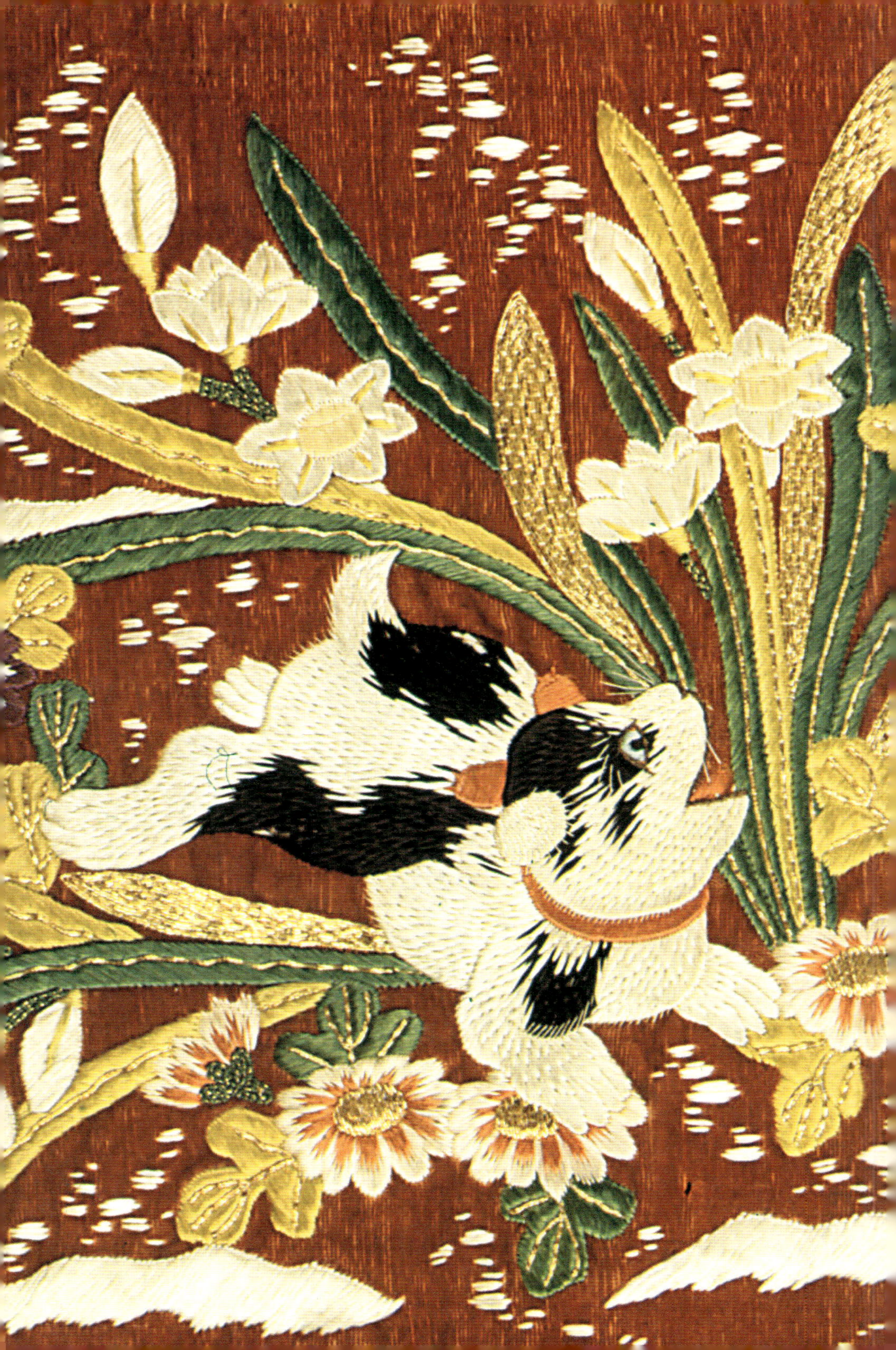

体の大きさによって小型犬、中型犬、大型犬に

Japanese dogs are divided according to the size of their bodies into the categories of small-,

区分され、いずれも共通する魅力として、胸を

medium-, and large-sized dogs, although all share the same appealing characteristics

反って四肢を踏んばり、ぐっとしまったスキの

of standing firmly on all four legs with their chest thrust out and having well-proportioned,

ない体構をしている。筋肉や腱がよく発達し、

solid builds. They have well-developed muscles and tendons and are able to remain agile

疲れを知らずいつまでも敏捷かつ軽快に活動で

and nimble for extended periods of tireless activity. The coat comes in pure, vivid colors

きる。毛色は鮮明でにごりのない赤、黒、胡麻、

including red, black, sesame, and white. The ears are ideally positioned and firmly pricked,

虎、白など。耳はピンと尖ってほどよい位置に

the eyes deep, appealing, and intelligent-looking, and the neck sturdy to support the head

収まっている。瞳は理知的で深く味わいがあり、

in a constant high position, all characteristics that contribute to an impressive overall

たくましい頚が常に頭部を高く支え凛とした

appearance. These builds and characteristics have been maintained with virtually

風情を保っている。これらの体型や特質は、人間

no loss of full-bloodedness and no pandering to human taste.

の好みを加えられず、ほぼ純血を失わずにきた。

Japanese dogs are natural, simple creatures that retain much of their wildness.

野生を残し、自然のままの素朴なものである。

The Japanese Dog

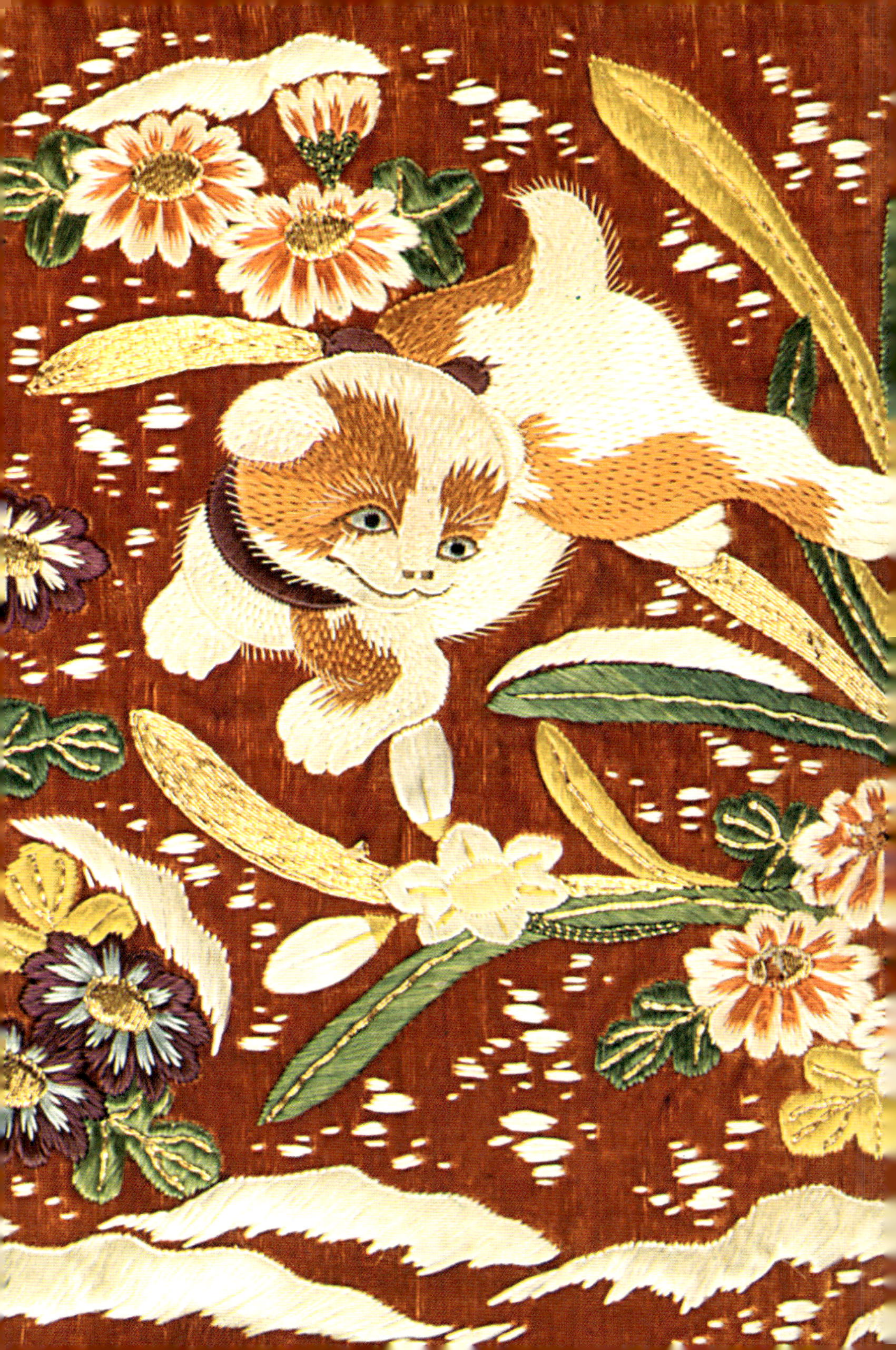

十二支

	第一番	第二番	第三番	第四番	第五番	第六番	第七番	第八番	第九番	第十番	第十一番	第十二番
	子	丑	寅	卯	辰	巳	午	未	申	酉	戌	亥
	ネ	ウシ	トラ	ウ	タツ	ミ	ウマ	ヒツジ	サル	トリ	イヌ	イ
	鼠	牛	虎	兎	竜	蛇	馬	羊	猿	鶏	犬	猪

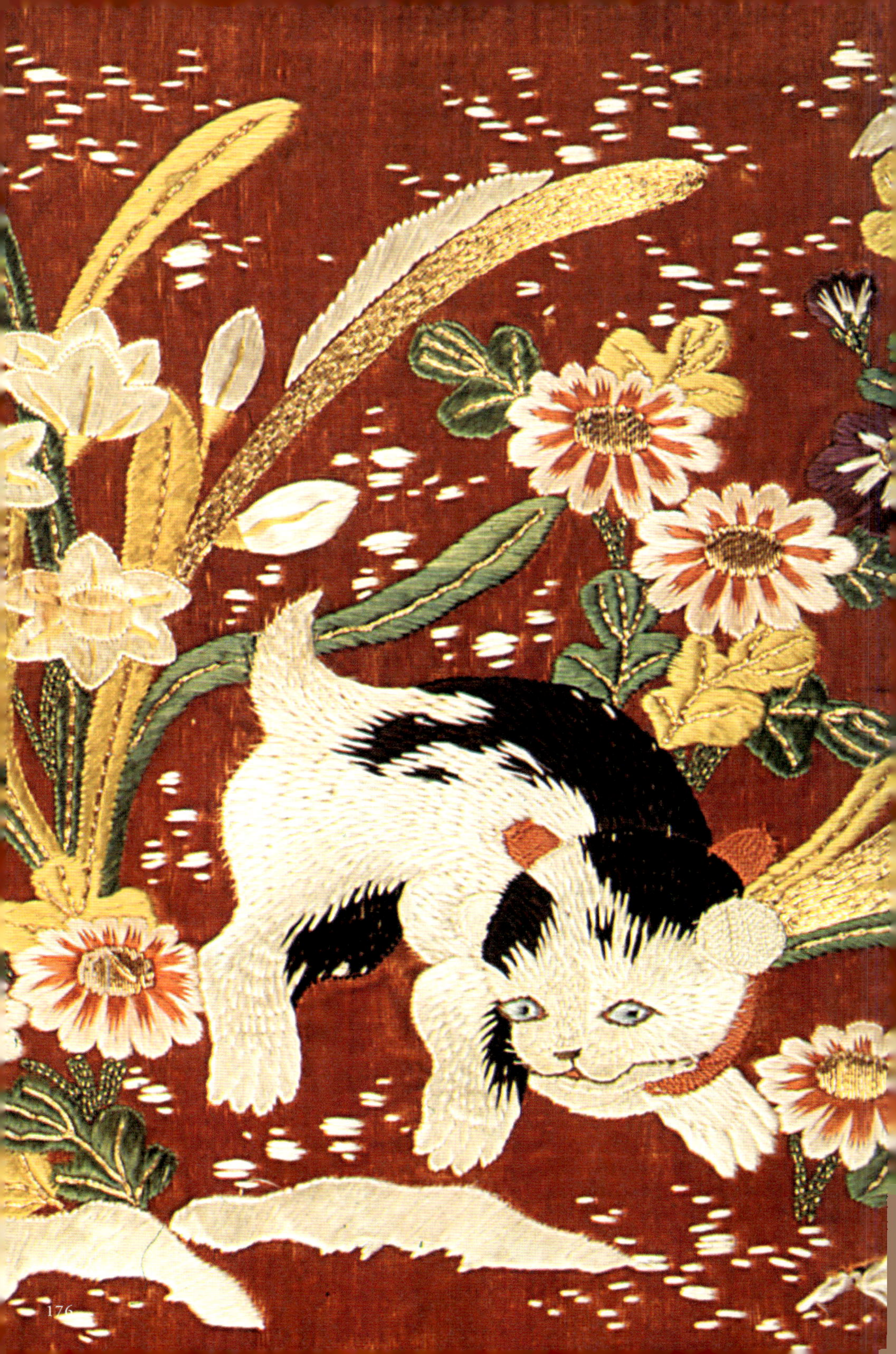

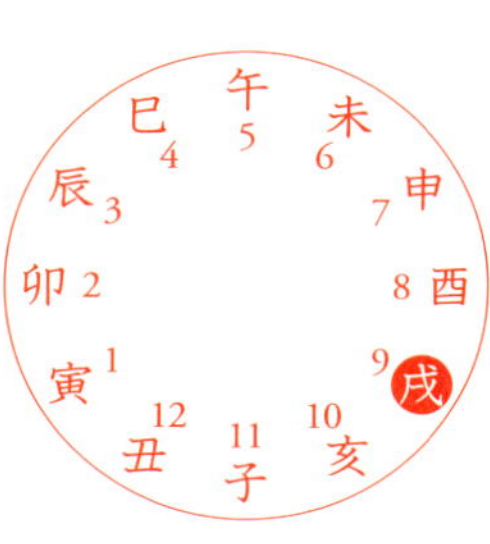

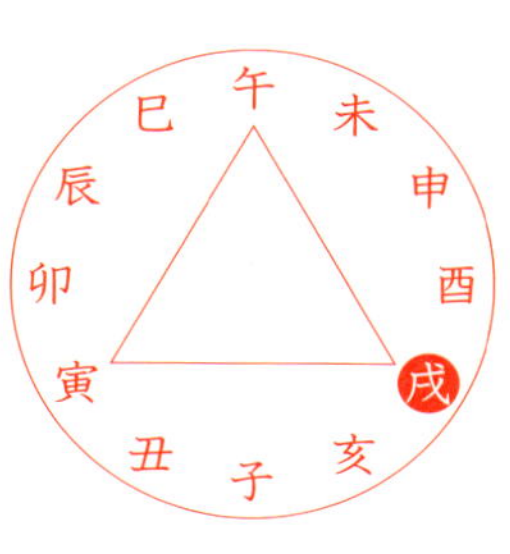

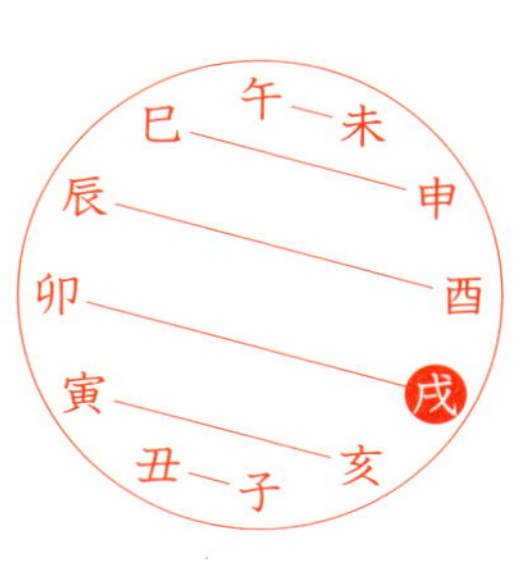

五行の「戌」

第十一位

西北西三〇度の間

九月

午後七時　午後九時まで

季秋　九月寒露　十月立冬の前日まで

三合の「戌」

火気三合

寅……生
午……旺
戌……墓

土気三合

午……生
戌……旺
寅……墓

寅・午・戌の三支は合して「火」と化す

支合の「戌」

子丑……土
亥寅……木
戌卯……火
辰酉……金
巳申……水
午羊……土

戌・卯の三支は合して「火」と化す

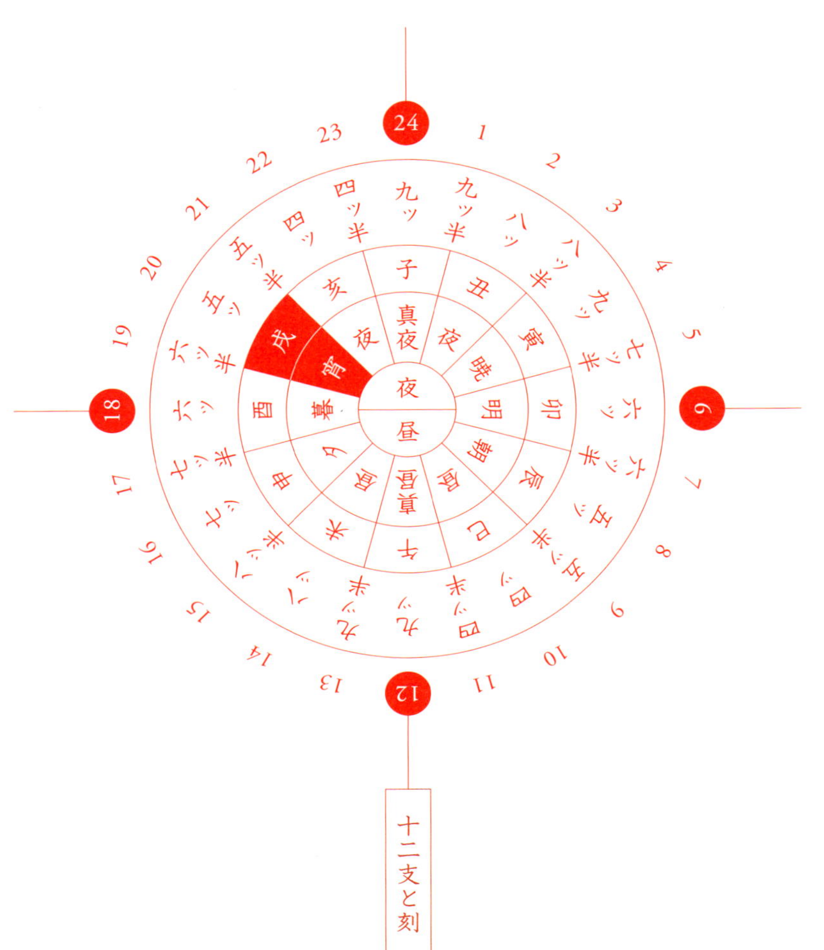

十二支と刻

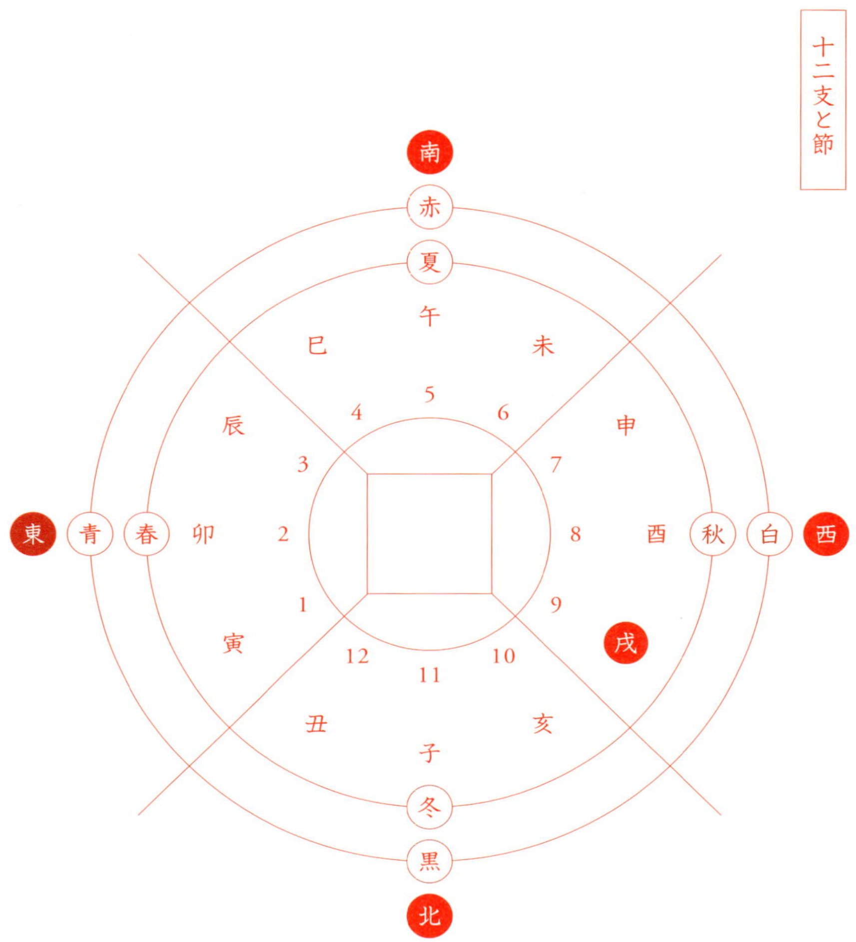

南
赤
夏
午
巳
未
4
5
6
辰
申
3
7
東
青
春
卯
2
8
酉
秋
白
西
1
9
戌
寅
12
10
丑
11
亥
子
冬
黒
北

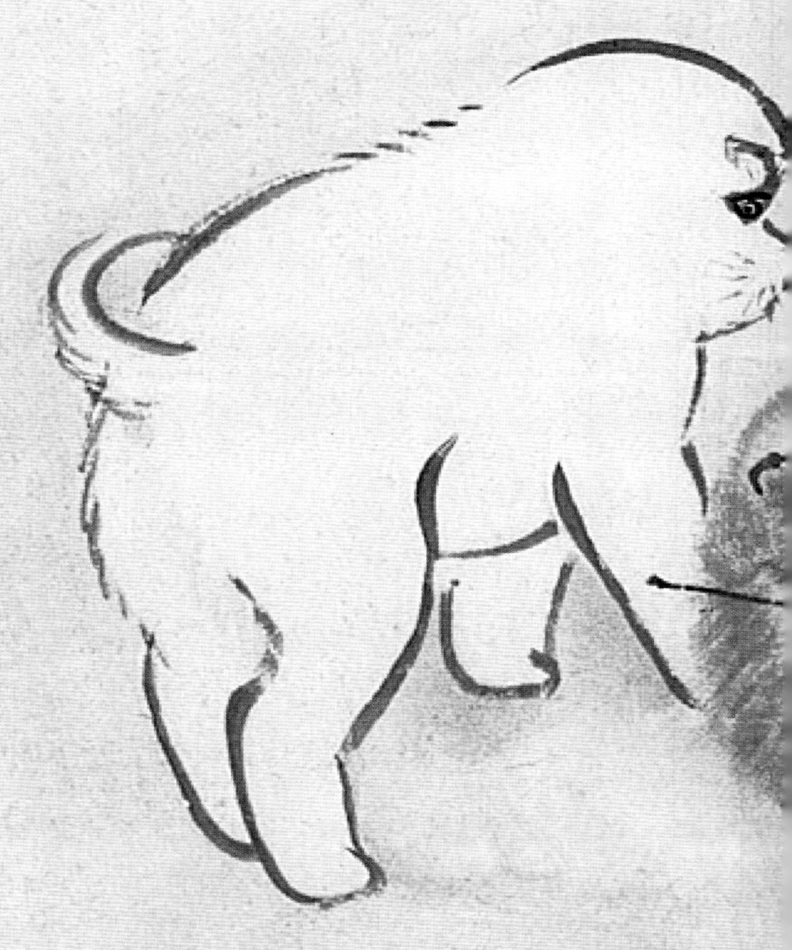

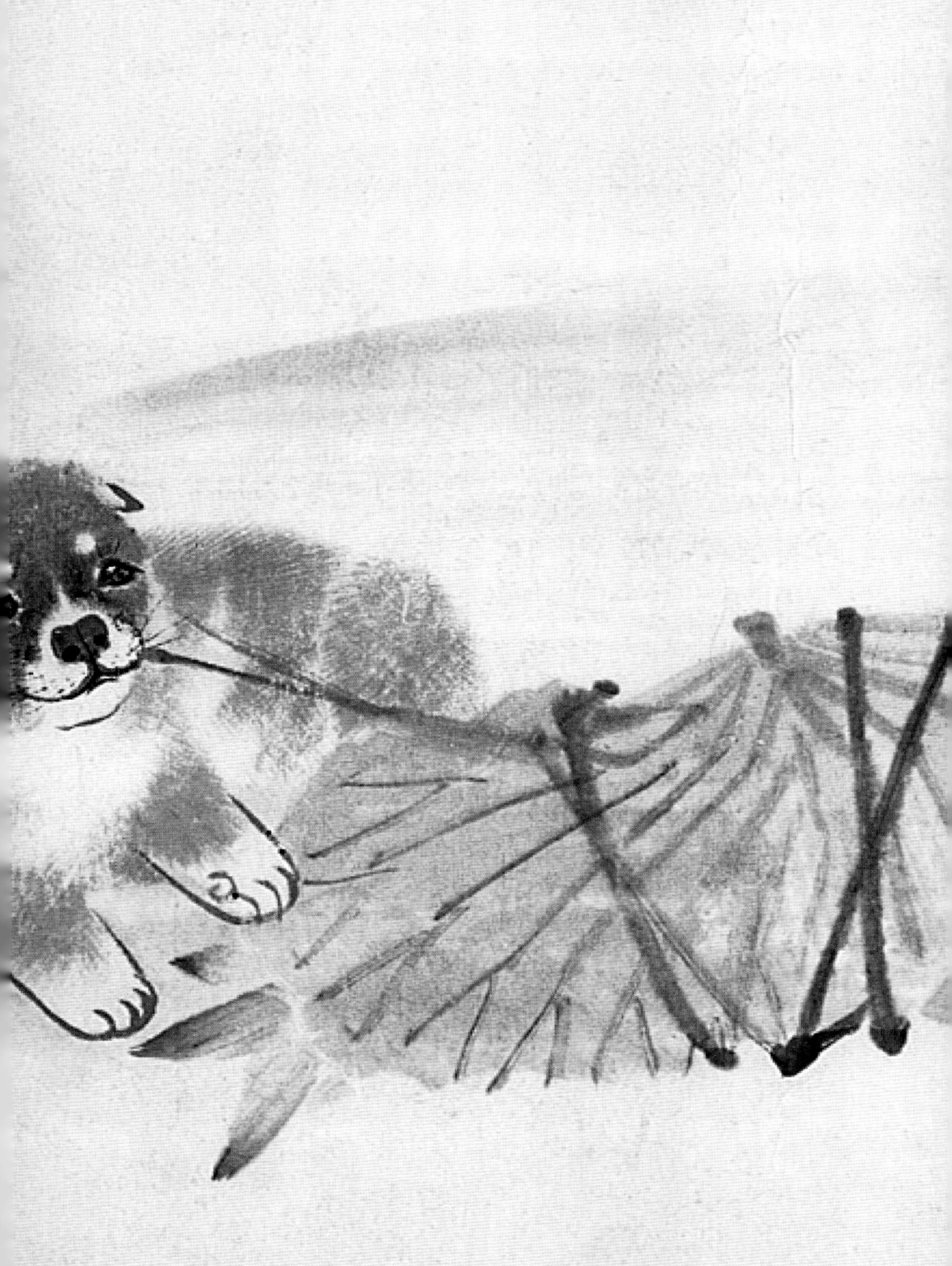

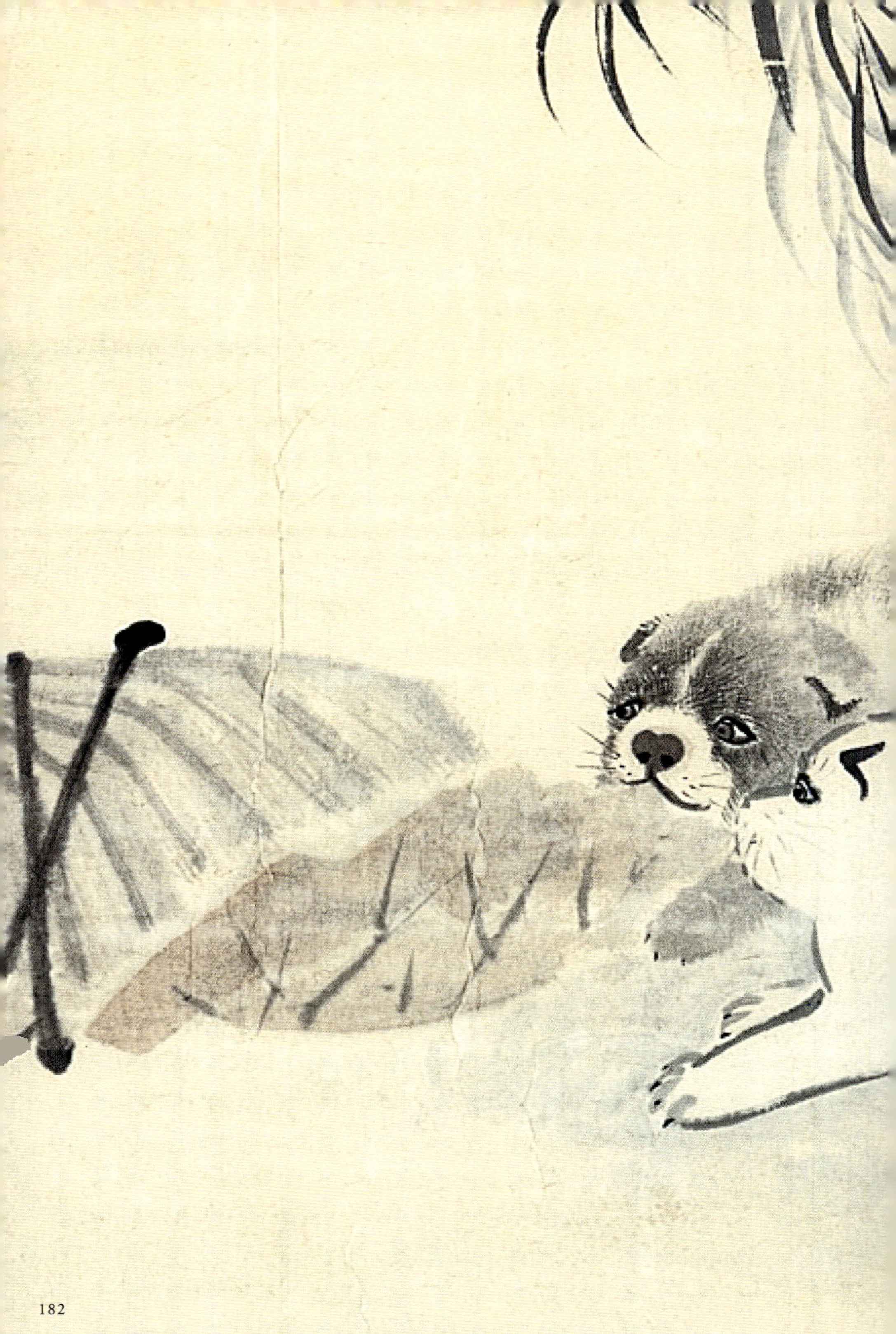

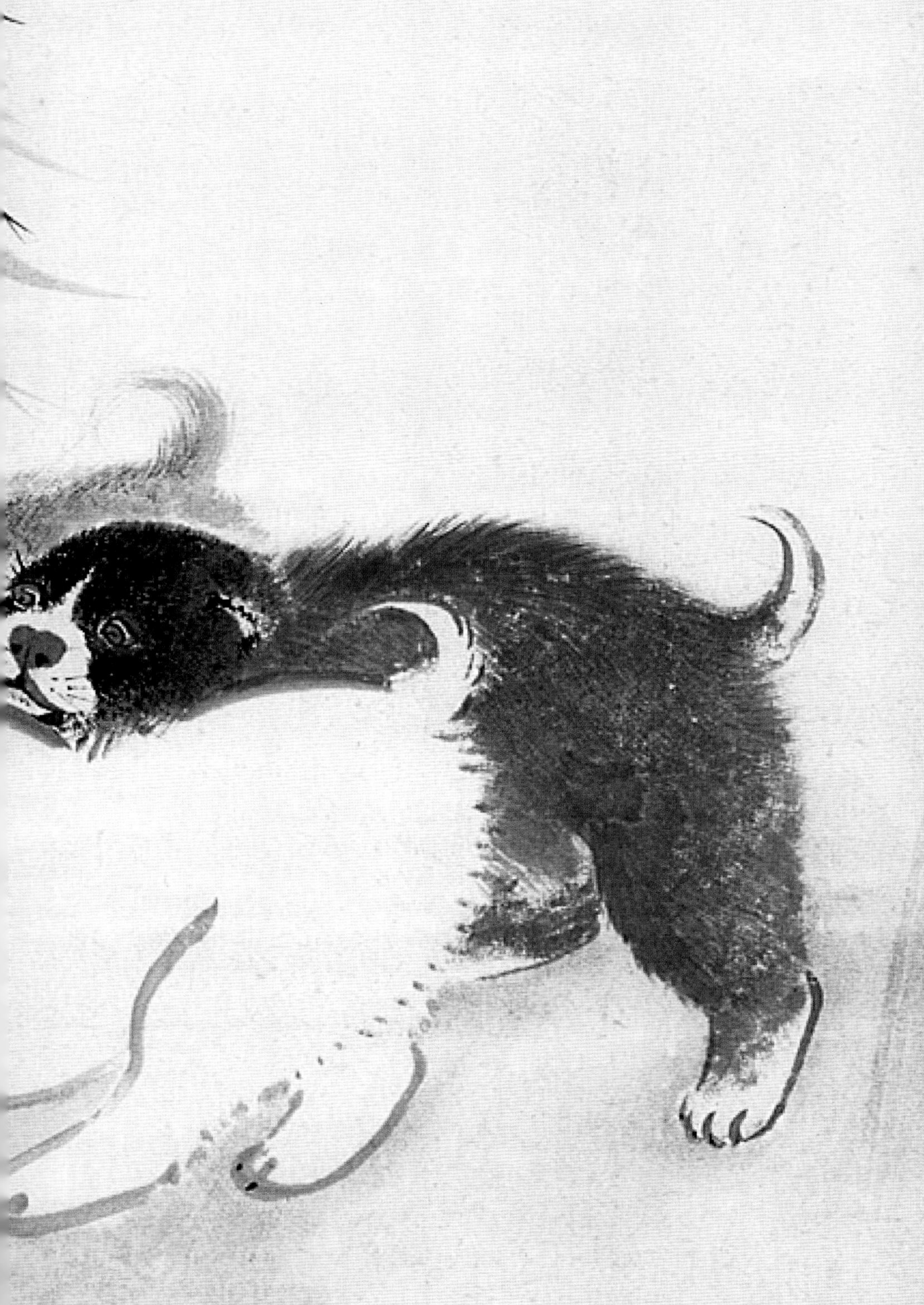

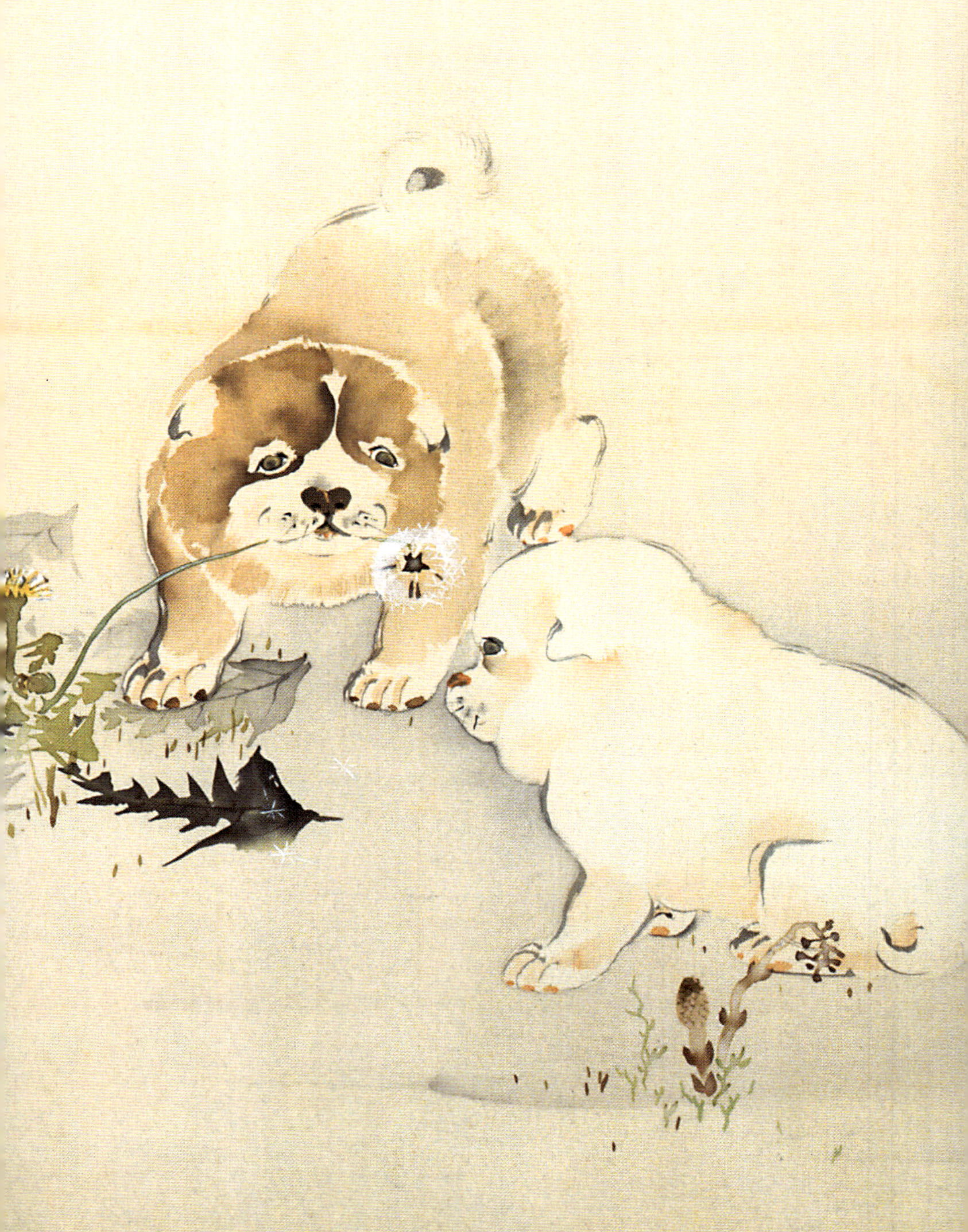

五行	木（き）	火（ひ）	土（つ）	金（か）	水（み）
兄（え）	甲 コウ きのえ	丙 ヘイ ひのえ	戊 ボ つちのえ	庚 コウ かのえ	壬 ジン みずのえ
弟（と）	乙 オツ きのと	丁 サイ ひのと	己 キ つちのと	辛 シン かのと	癸 キ みずのと

十二支　守り本尊

十二支	守り本尊
子	千手観音
丑	虚空蔵菩薩
寅	虚空蔵菩薩
卯	文殊菩薩
辰	普賢菩薩
巳	普賢菩薩
午	勢至菩薩
未	大日如来
申	大日如来
酉	不動明王
戌	阿弥陀如来
亥	阿弥陀如来

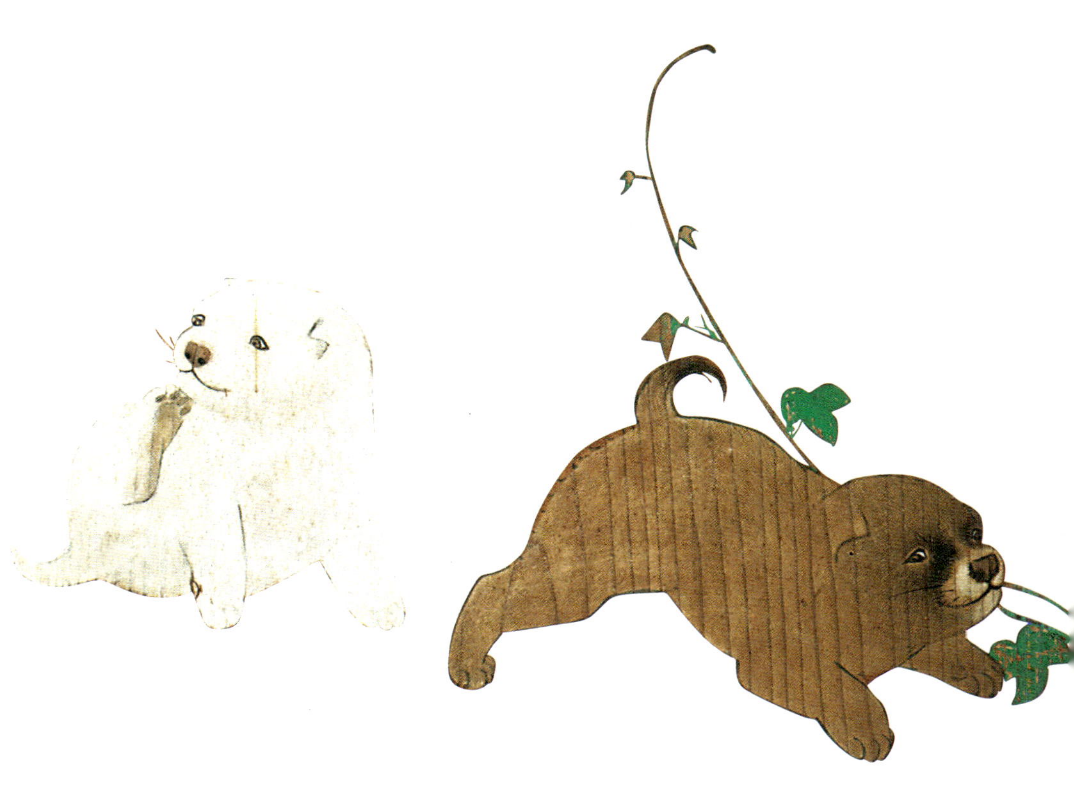

六十一年目に最初の年に戻る。これが還暦。

年	十干十二支	五行	兄弟（えと）の読み
1	甲子	木（き）	きのえね／コウシ・カッシ
2	乙丑	木（き）	きのとうし／イッチュウ
3	丙寅	火（ひ）	ひのえとら／ヘイイン
4	丁卯	火（ひ）	ひのとう／テイボウ
5	戊辰	土（つ）	つちのえたつ／ボシン
6	己巳	土（つ）	つちのとみ／キシ
7	庚午	金（か）	かのえうま／コウゴ
8	辛未	金（か）	かのとひつじ／シンビ・シンミ
9	壬申	水（み）	みずのえさる／ジンシン
10	癸酉	水（み）	みずのとり／キユウ
11	甲戌	木（き）	きのえいぬ／コウジュツ
12	乙亥	木（き）	きのとい／イツガイ
13	丙子	火（ひ）	ひのえね／ヘイシ
14	丁丑	火（ひ）	ひのとうし／テイチュウ
15	戊寅	土（つ）	つちのえとら／ボイン
16	己卯	土（つ）	つちのとう／キボウ
17	庚辰	金（か）	かのえたつ／コウシン
18	辛巳	金（か）	かのとみ／シンシ
19	壬午	水（み）	みずのえうま／ジンゴ
20	癸未	水（み）	みずのとひつじ／キビ・キミ
21	甲申	木（き）	きのえさる／コウシン
22	乙酉	木（き）	きのとり／イツユウ
23	丙戌	火（ひ）	ひのえいぬ／ヘイジュツ
24	丁亥	火（ひ）	ひのとい／テイガイ
25	戊子	土（つ）	つちのえね／ボシ
26	己丑	土（つ）	つちのとうし／キチュウ
27	庚寅	金（か）	かのえとら／コウイン
28	辛卯	金（か）	かのとう／シンボウ
29	壬辰	水（み）	みずのえたつ／ジンシン
30	癸巳	水（み）	みずのとみ／キシ
31	甲午	木（き）	きのえうま／コウゴ
32	乙未	木（き）	きのとひつじ／イツビ・イツミ
33	丙申	火（ひ）	ひのえさる／ヘイシン
34	丁酉	火（ひ）	ひのとり／テイユウ
35	戊戌	土（つ）	つちのえいぬ／ボジュツ
36	己亥	土（つ）	つちのとい／キガイ
37	庚子	金（か）	かのえね／コウシ
38	辛丑	金（か）	かのとうし／シンチュウ
39	壬寅	水（み）	みずのえとら／ジンイン
40	癸卯	水（み）	みずのとう／キボウ
41	甲辰	木（き）	きのえたつ／コウシン
42	乙巳	木（き）	きのとみ／イツシ
43	丙午	火（ひ）	ひのえうま／ヘイゴ
44	丁未	火（ひ）	ひのとひつじ／テイビ・テイミ
45	戊申	土（つ）	つちのえさる／ボシン
46	己酉	土（つ）	つちのとり／キユウ
47	庚戌	金（か）	かのえいぬ／コウジュツ
48	辛亥	金（か）	かのとい／シンガイ
49	壬子	水（み）	みずのえね／ジンシ
50	癸丑	水（み）	みずのとうし／キチュウ
51	甲寅	木（き）	きのえとら／コウイン
52	乙卯	木（き）	きのとう／イツボウ
53	丙辰	火（ひ）	ひのえたつ／ヘイシン
54	丁巳	火（ひ）	ひのとみ／テイシ
55	戊午	土（つ）	つちのえうま／ボゴ
56	己未	土（つ）	つちのとひつじ／キビ・キミ
57	庚申	金（か）	かのえさる／コウシン
58	辛酉	金（か）	かのとり／シンユウ
59	壬戌	水（み）	みずのえいぬ／ジンジュツ
60	癸亥	水（み）	みずのとい／キガイ

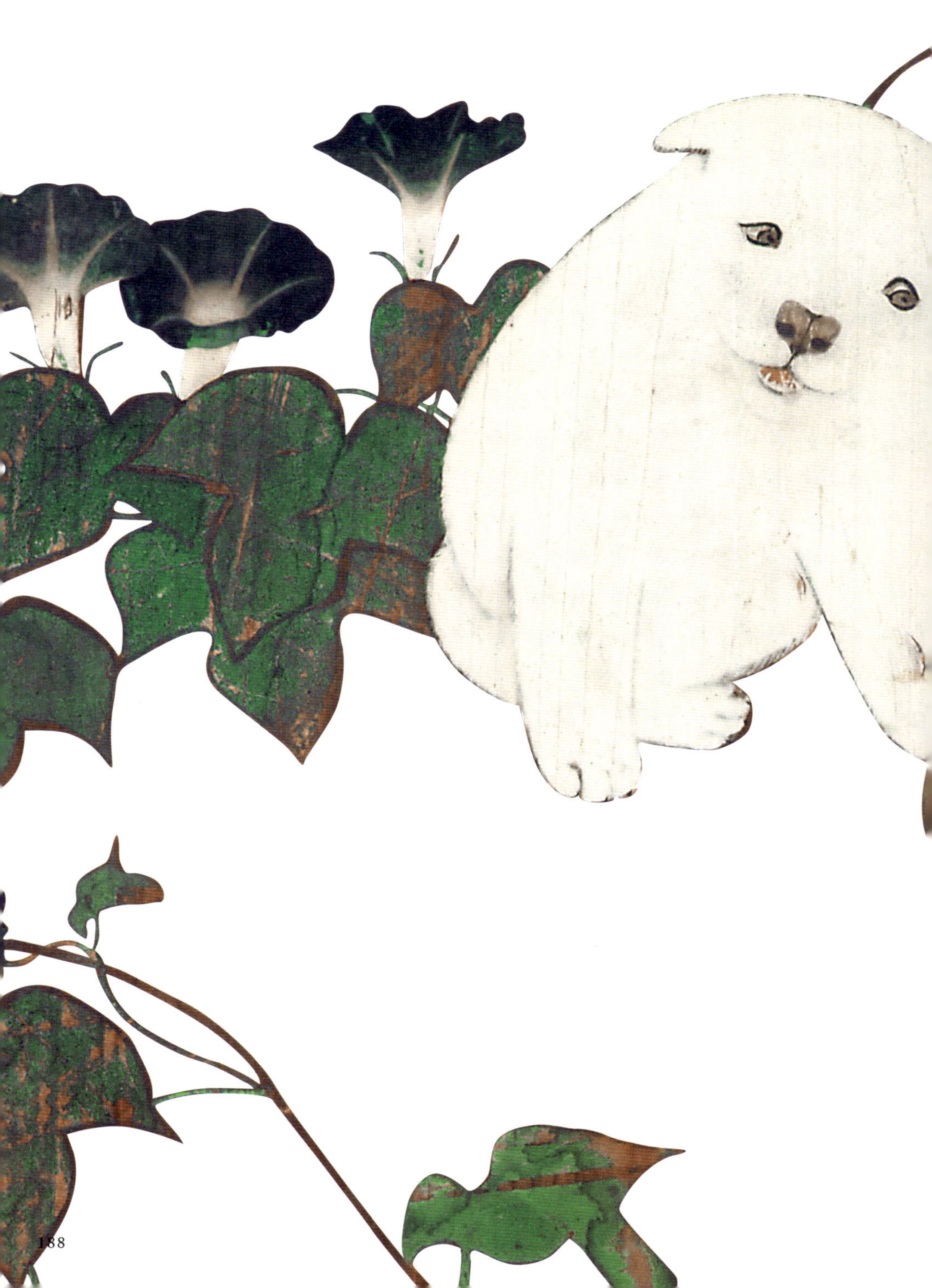

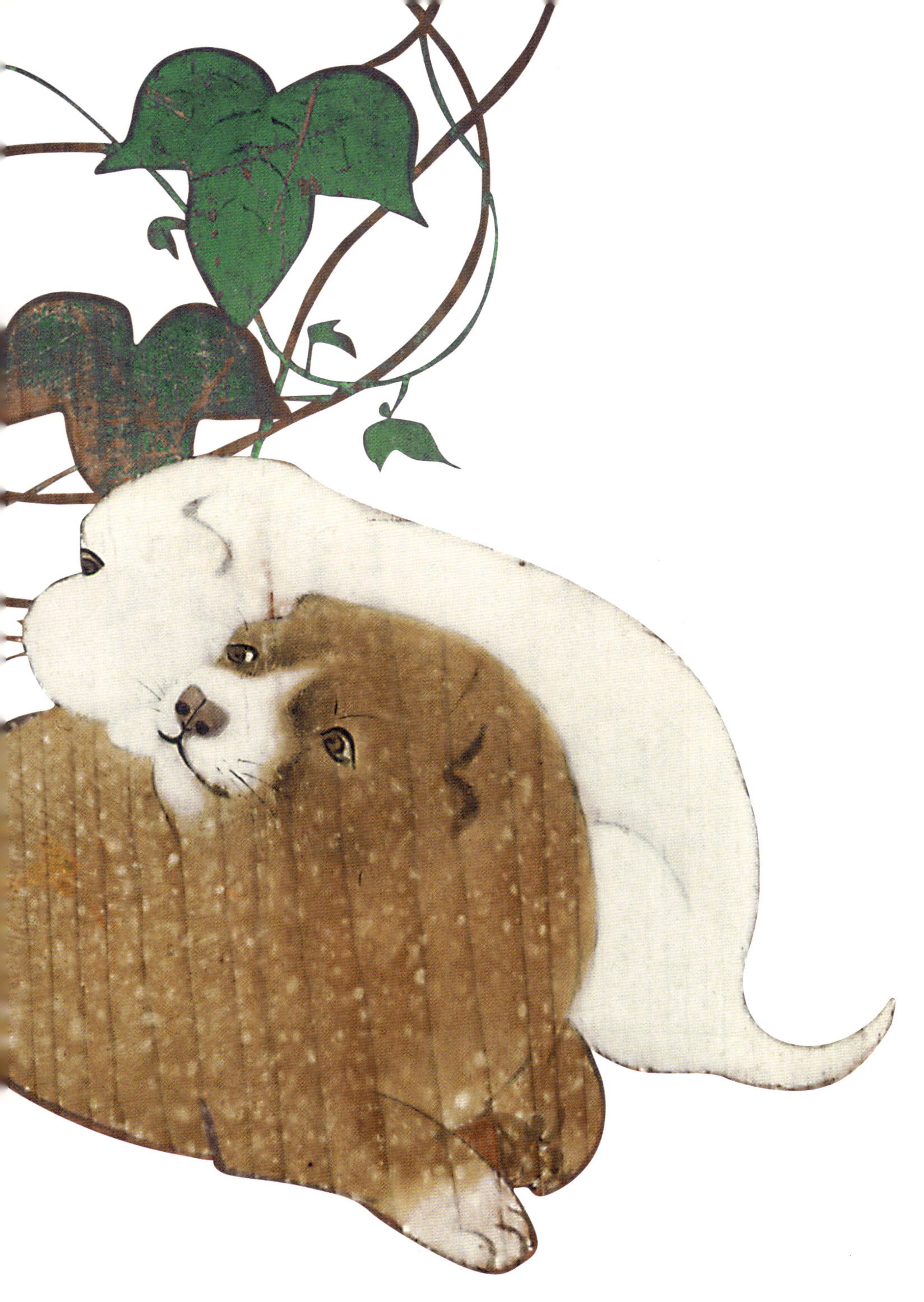

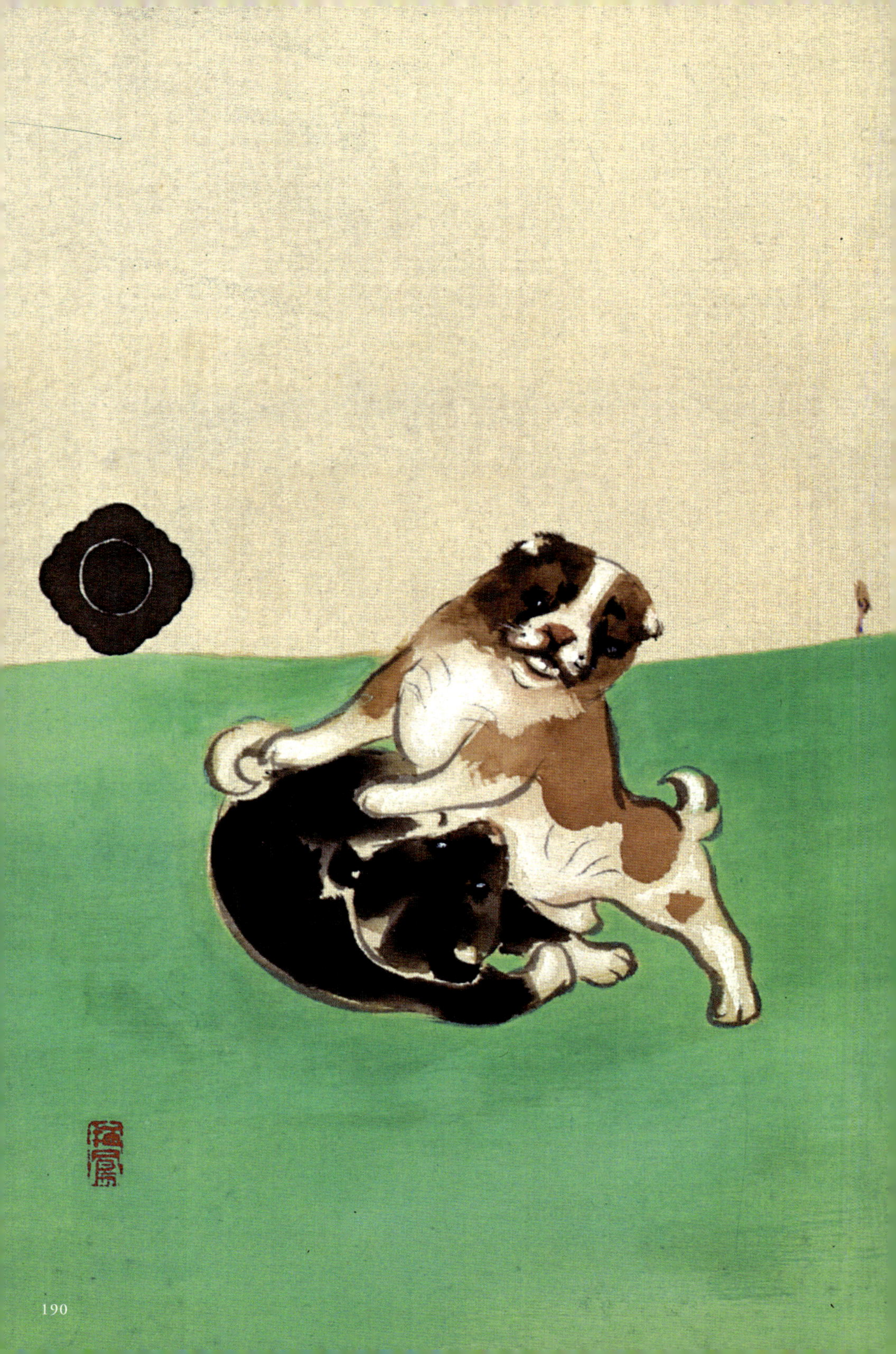

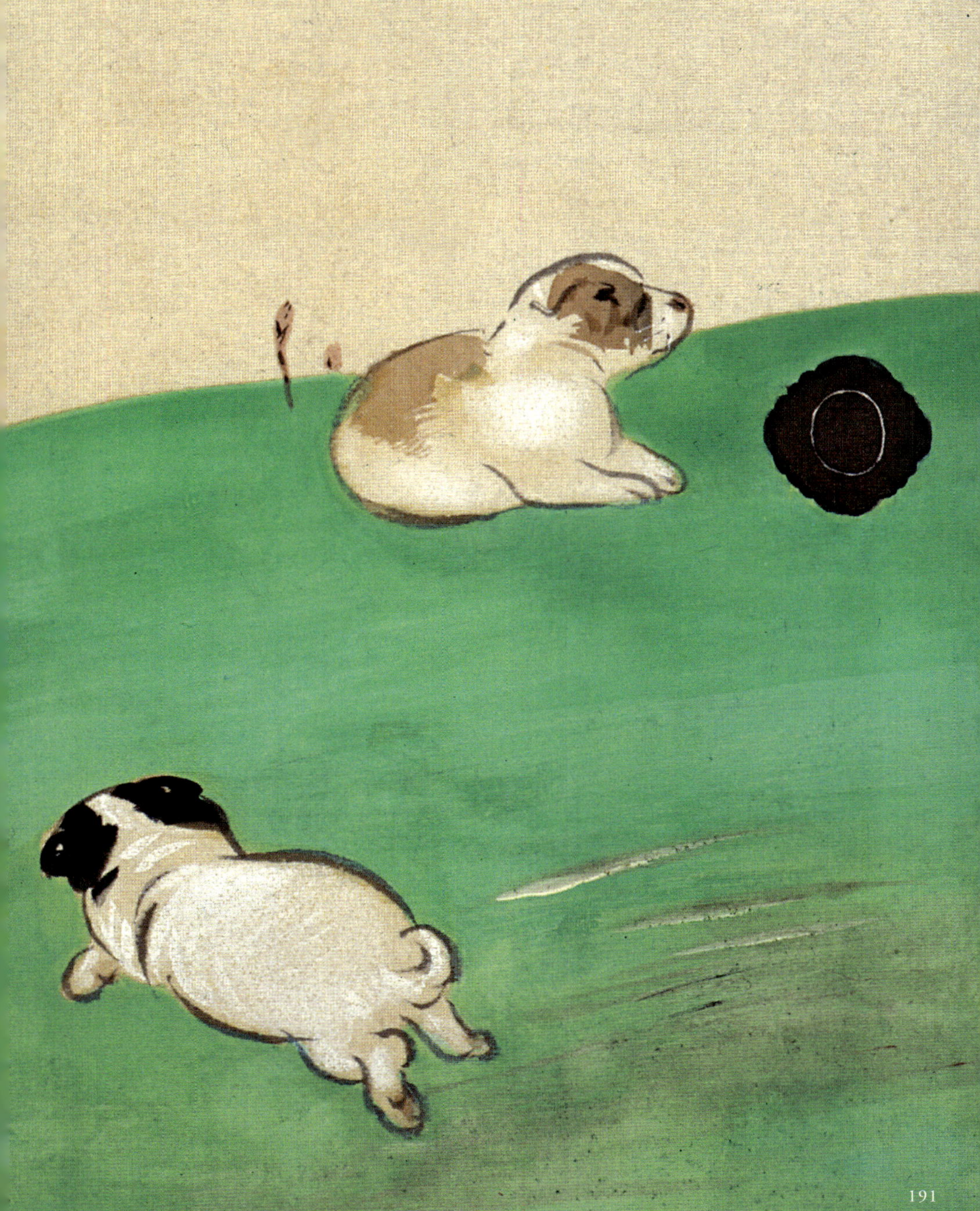

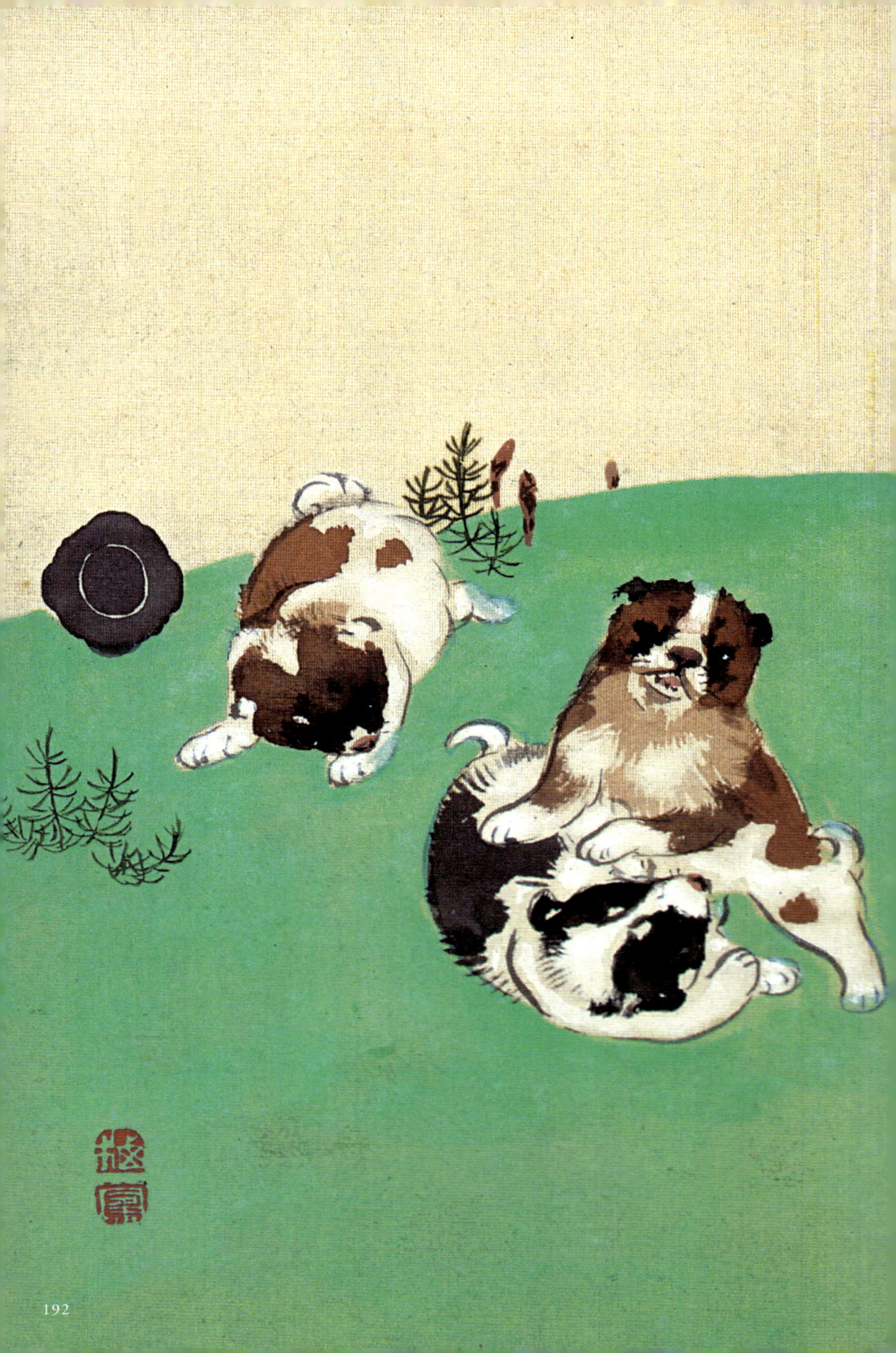

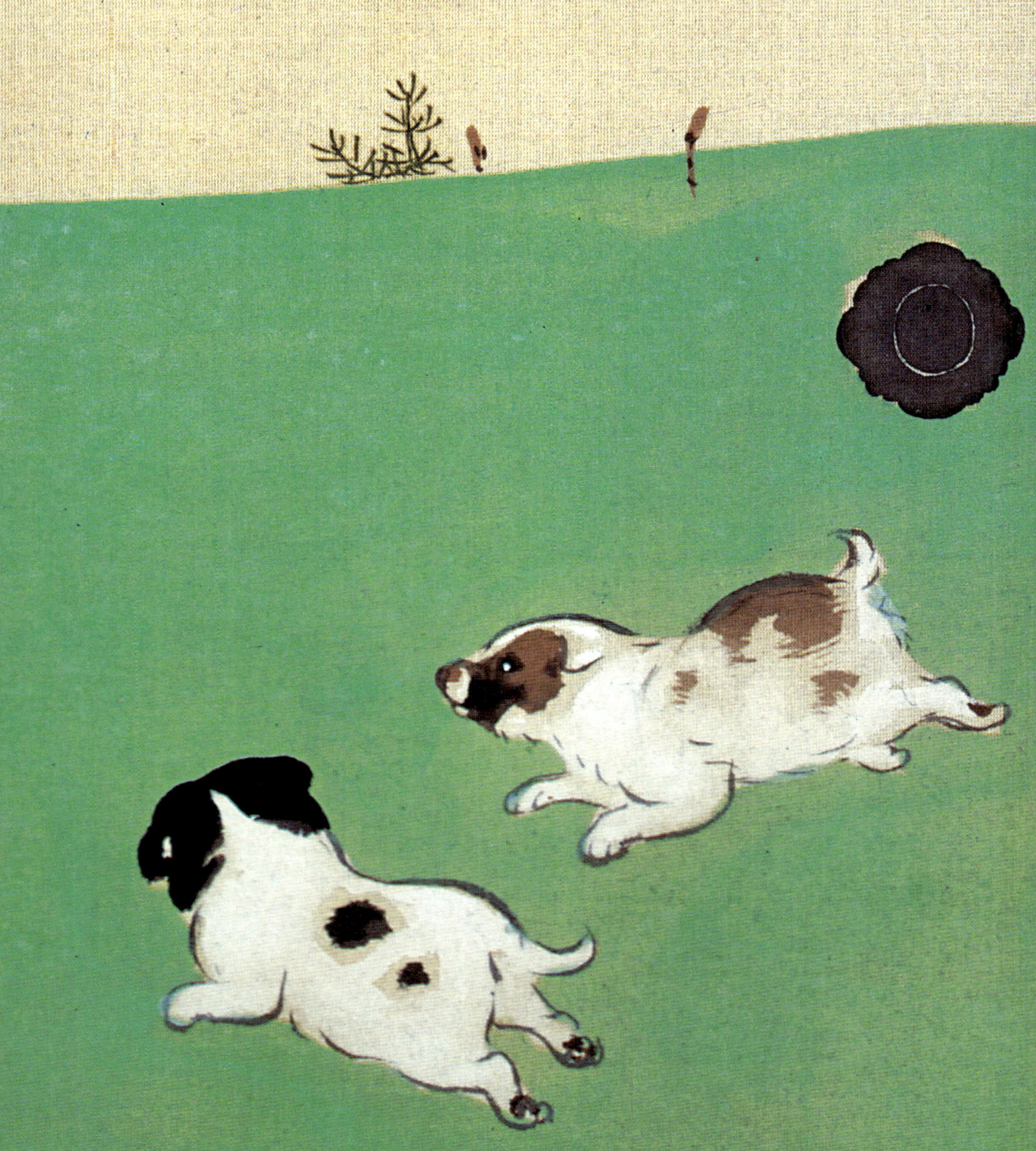

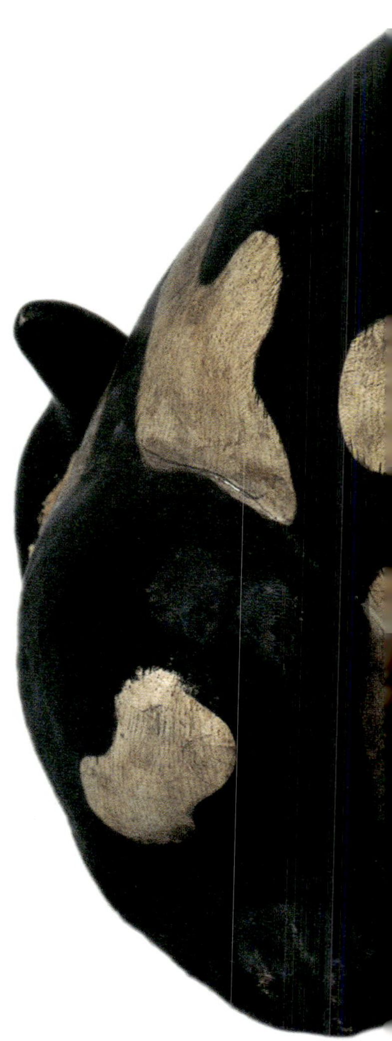

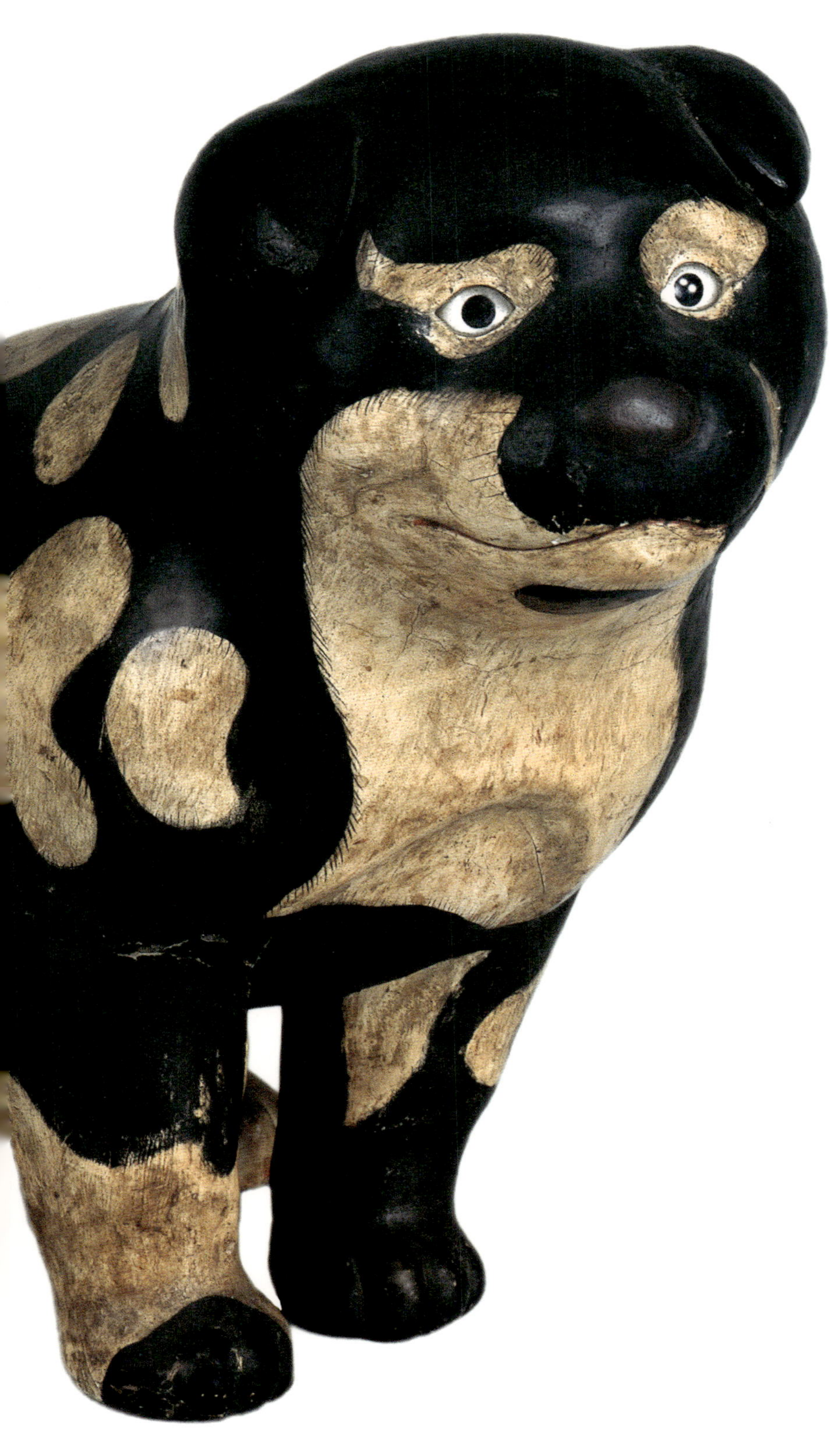

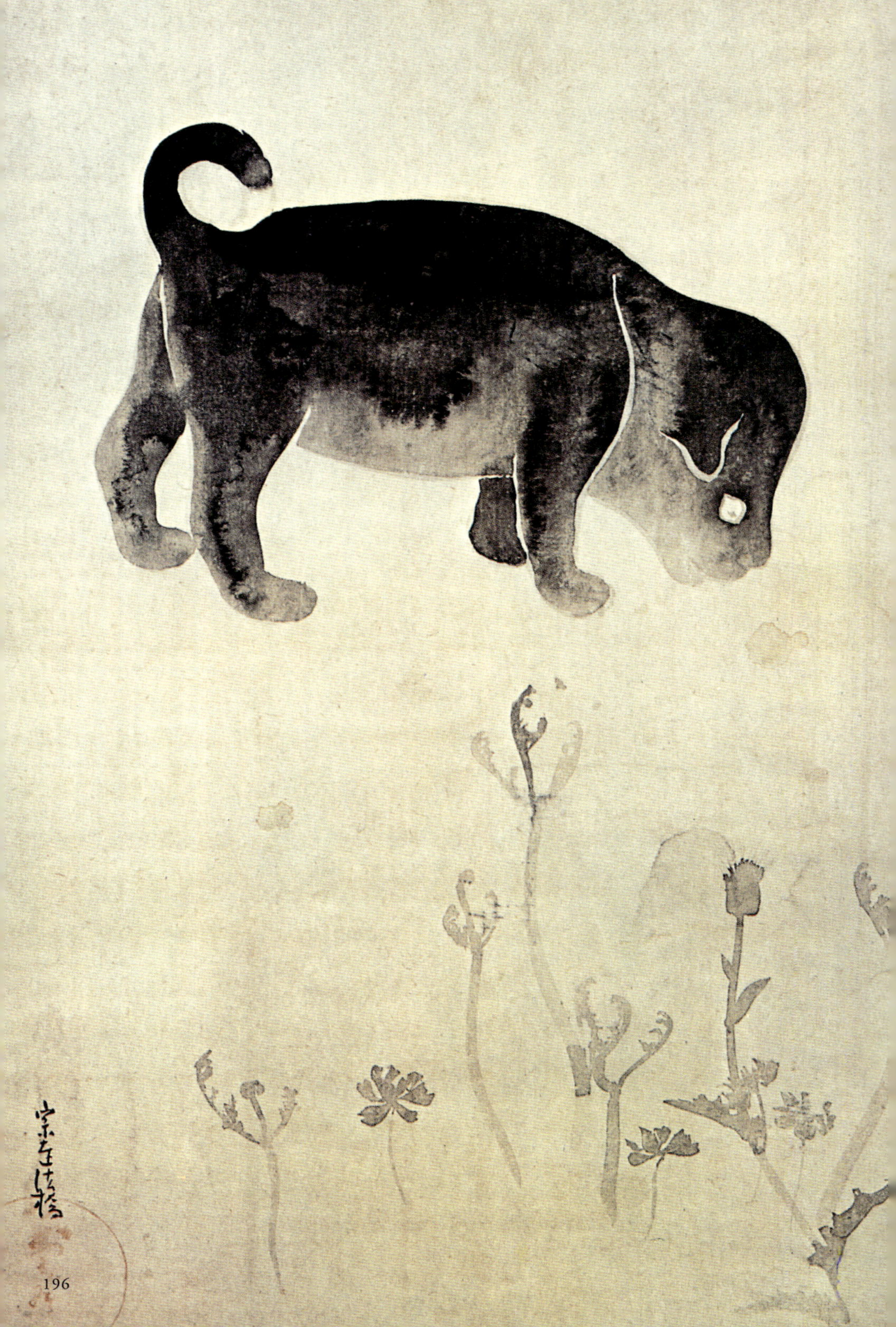

柴犬

Shiba Inu

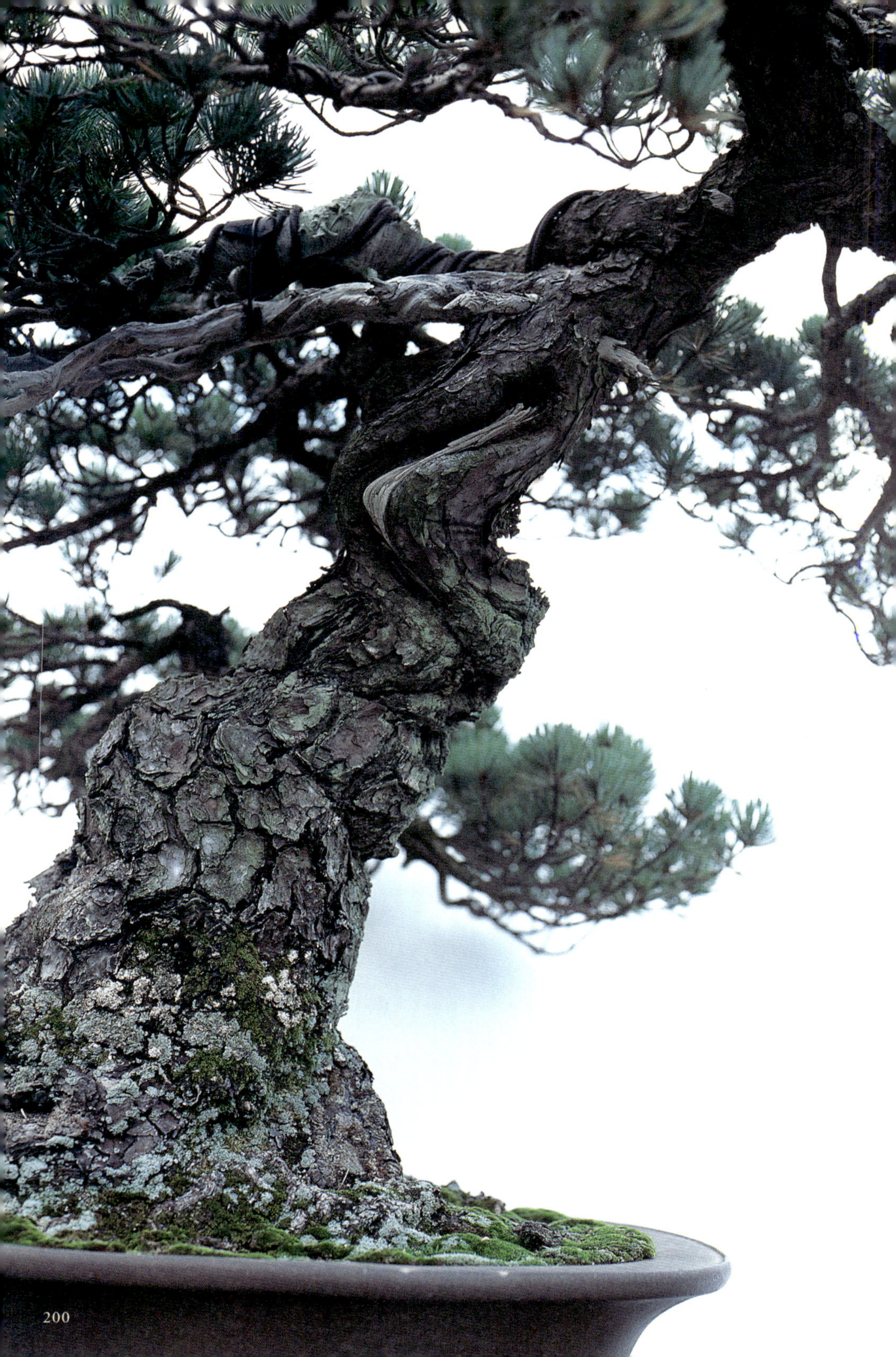

As the name suggests (one of the meanings of
the Japanese word "shiba" is "diminutive"),
the Shiba Inu is the only small dog
among the six Japanese breeds
designated Natural Monument of Japan.
Reputed to be able to read its owner's thoughts
and act accordingly, the Shiba Inu is intelligent,
brave, and loyal, qualities much
admired byits devotees.

シバとは「小さなもの」を意味するが、
この名が示す通り柴犬は
天然記念物に指定される日本犬のうちで
唯一の小型犬である。
飼い主の気持ちを読んで行動するといわれ、
賢く勇敢で忠実な性格が愛されている。
柴犬

しばいぬ

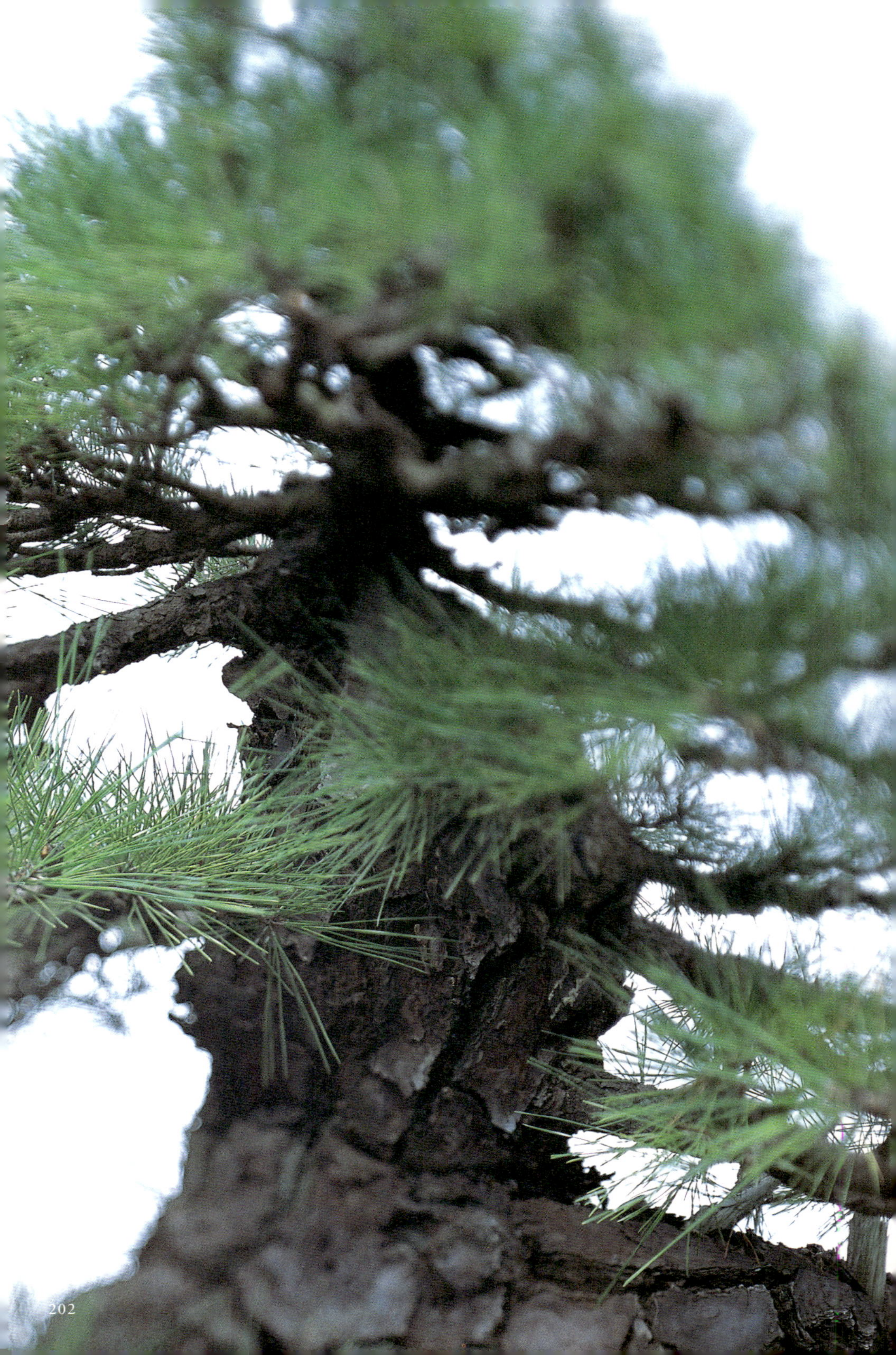

Shiba Inu

It has a solid, well-balanced physique and
well-developed muscles.
Because of its strong constitution and agility,
it was used as a hunting dog for hunting
small animals and birds.
Its ears are triangular in shape,
firmly pricked, and small.
Its coat is short and in most cases red,
although sesame, crimson,
or blackish brown coats are also common.
Shiba Inu generally have a curly tail,
the underside of which is white,
as is the chest and stomach.
Males grow to a height of 39 cm,
and females to 35 cm.
The Shiba Inu was designated
a Natural Monument in 1936.

骨格がしっかりとしていて均整がとれ、
筋肉がよく発達している。
強健な体質と敏捷さから、小動物や鳥の猟犬と
しても使われていた。
耳はピンと立った小さな三角形。
短毛で、毛色は赤が最も多く、他に胡麻、濃赤、
黒褐色もみられる。
尾は巻尾がほとんどで、胸もとや腹と同じく
裏白である。体高は雄39センチ、雌35センチ。
昭和11年、国の天然記念物に指定。

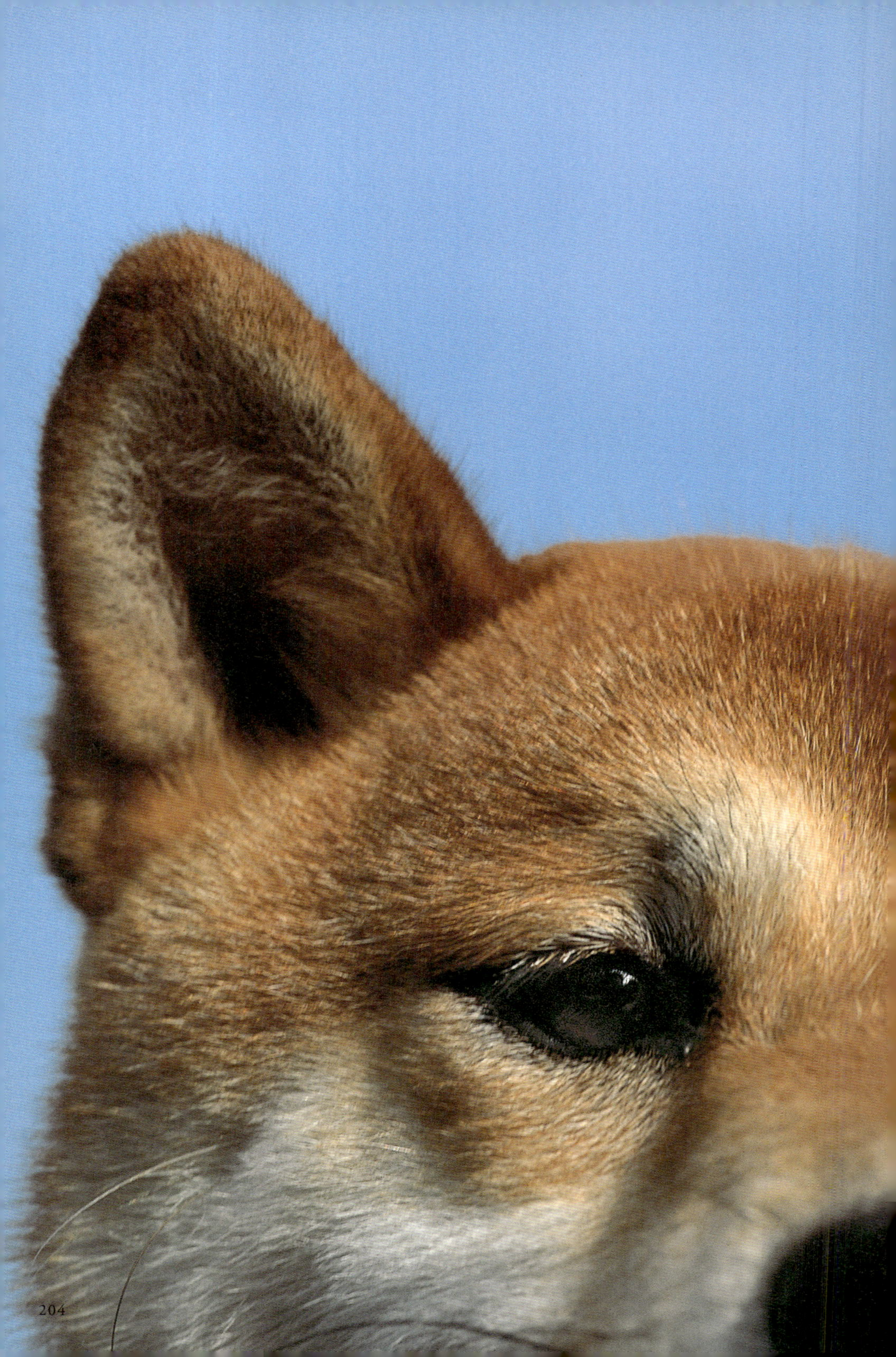

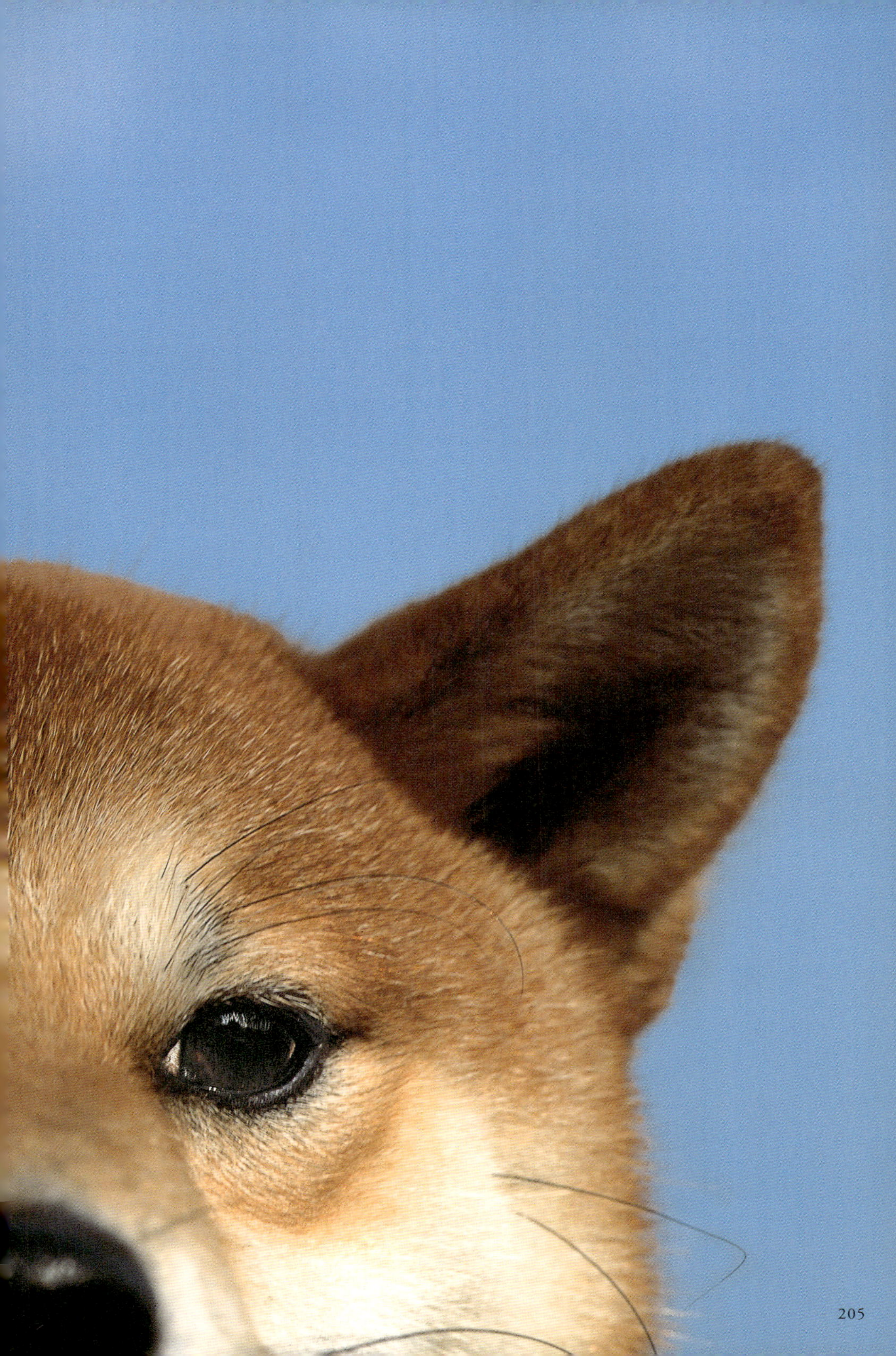

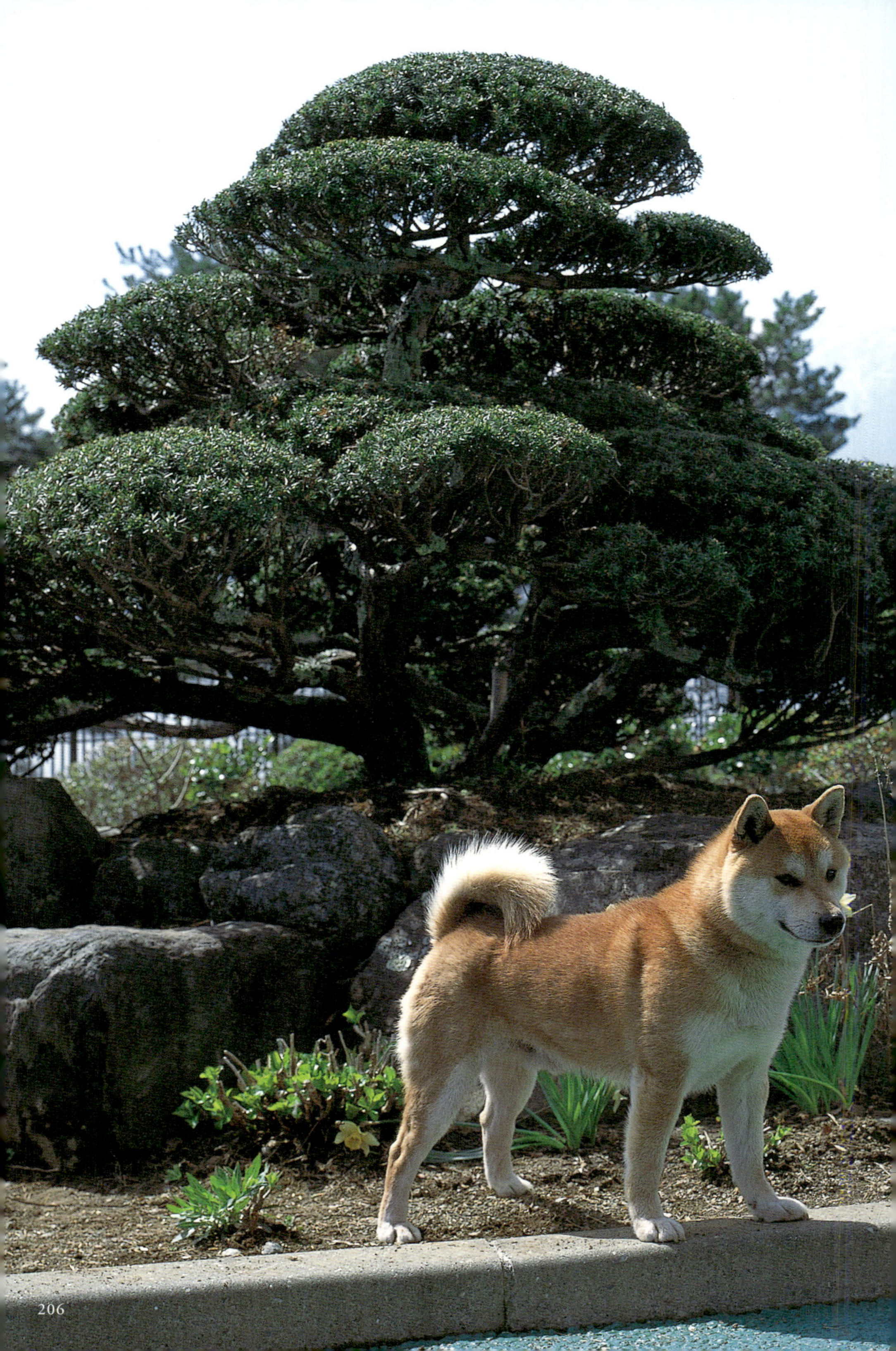

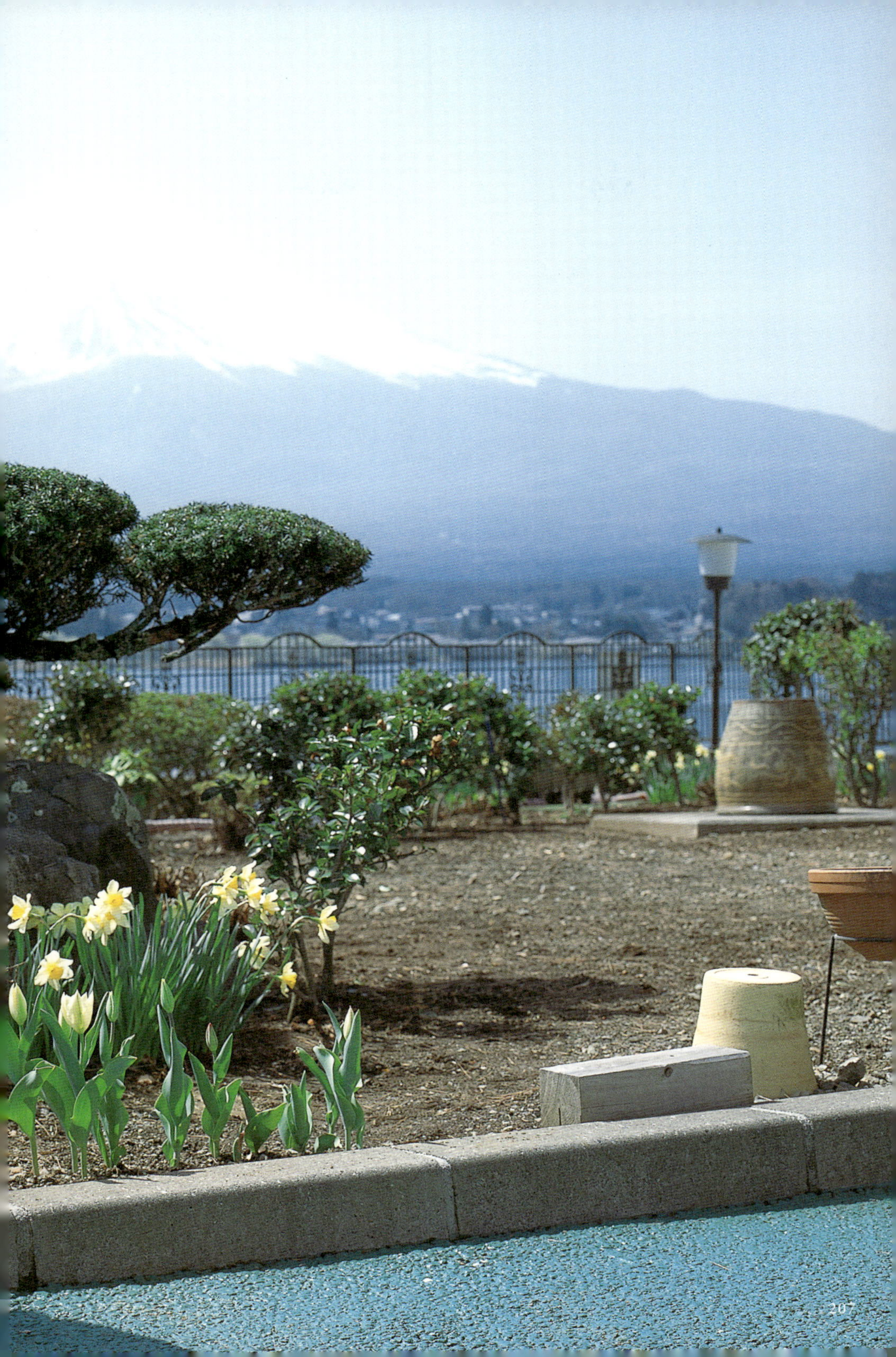

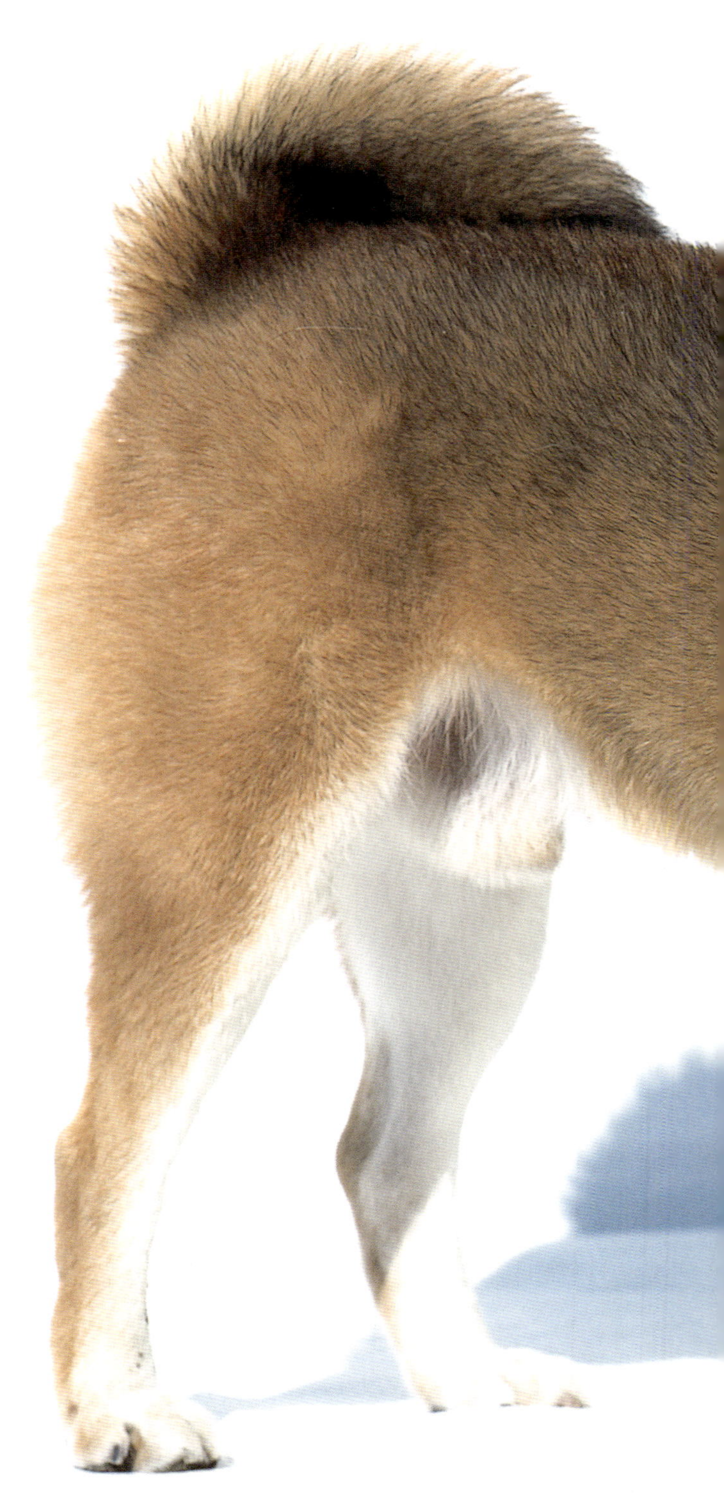

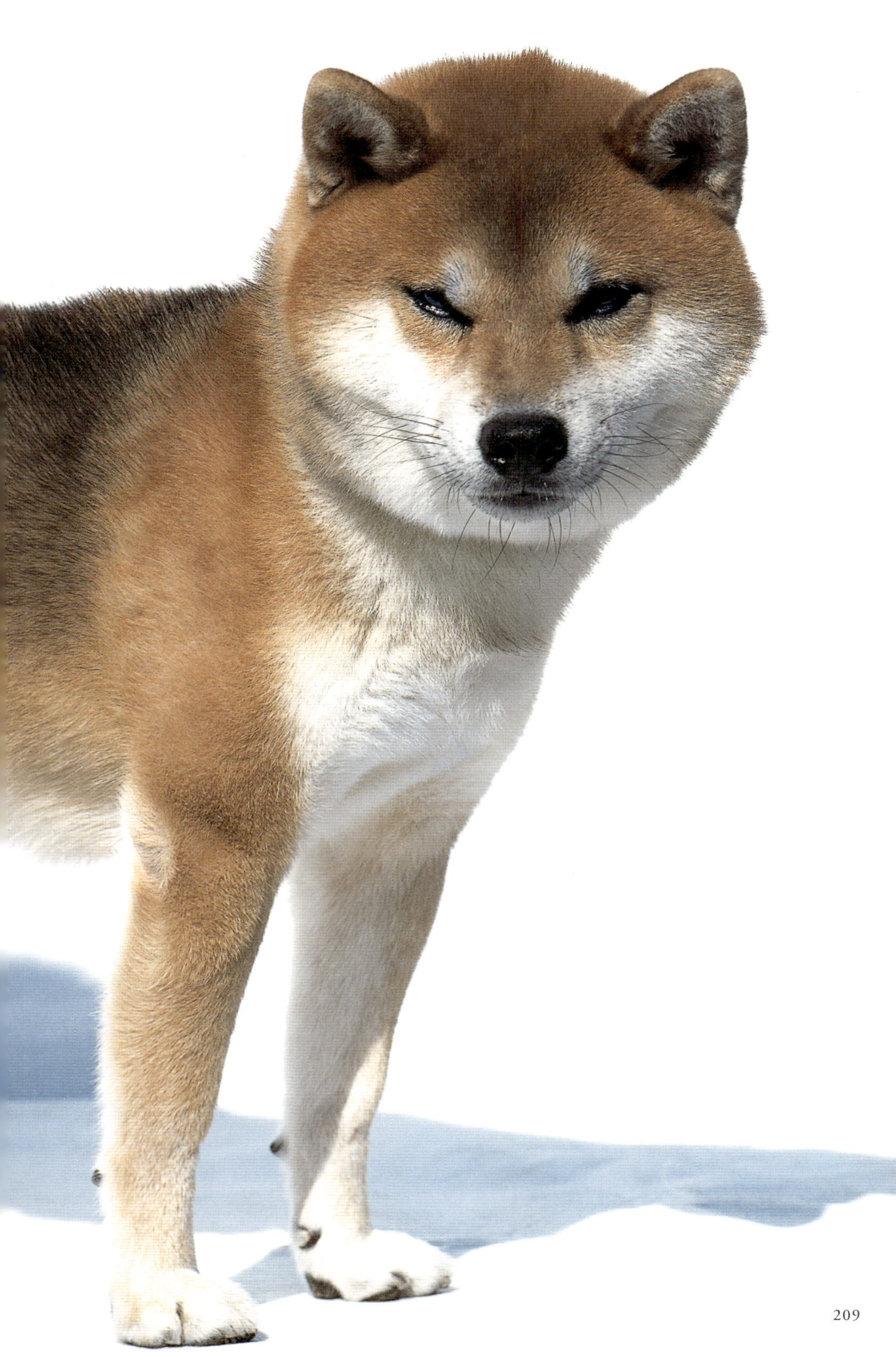

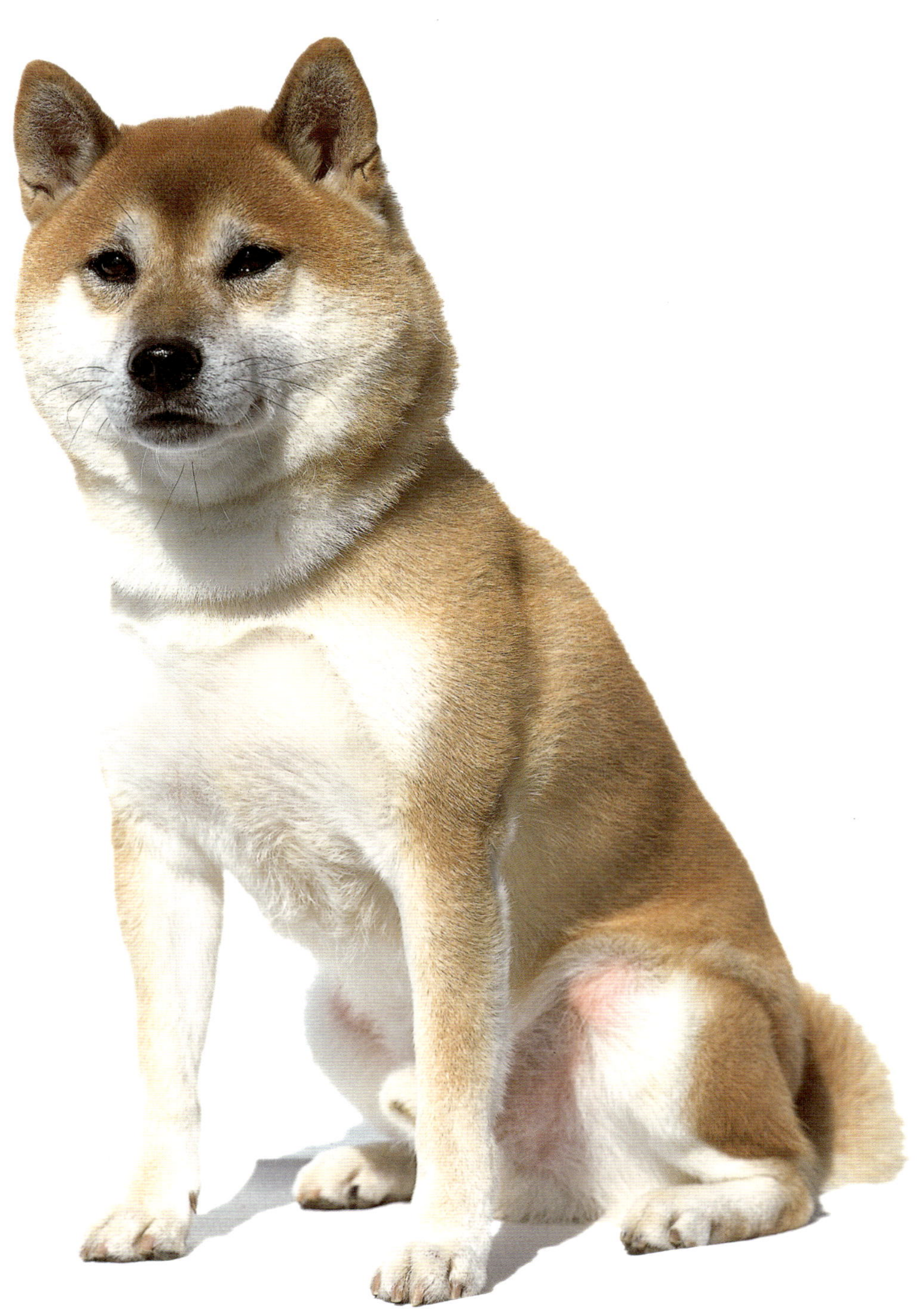

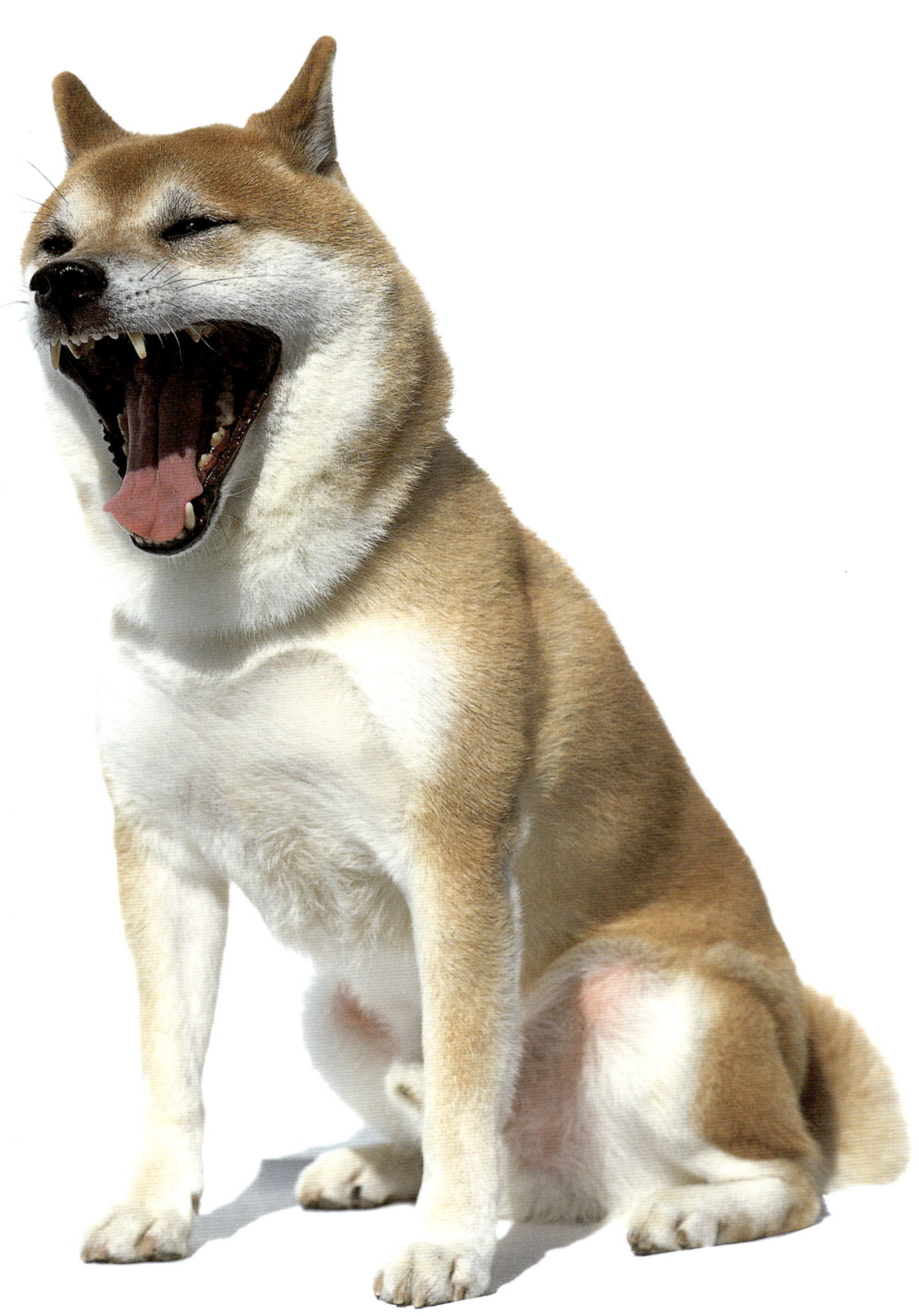

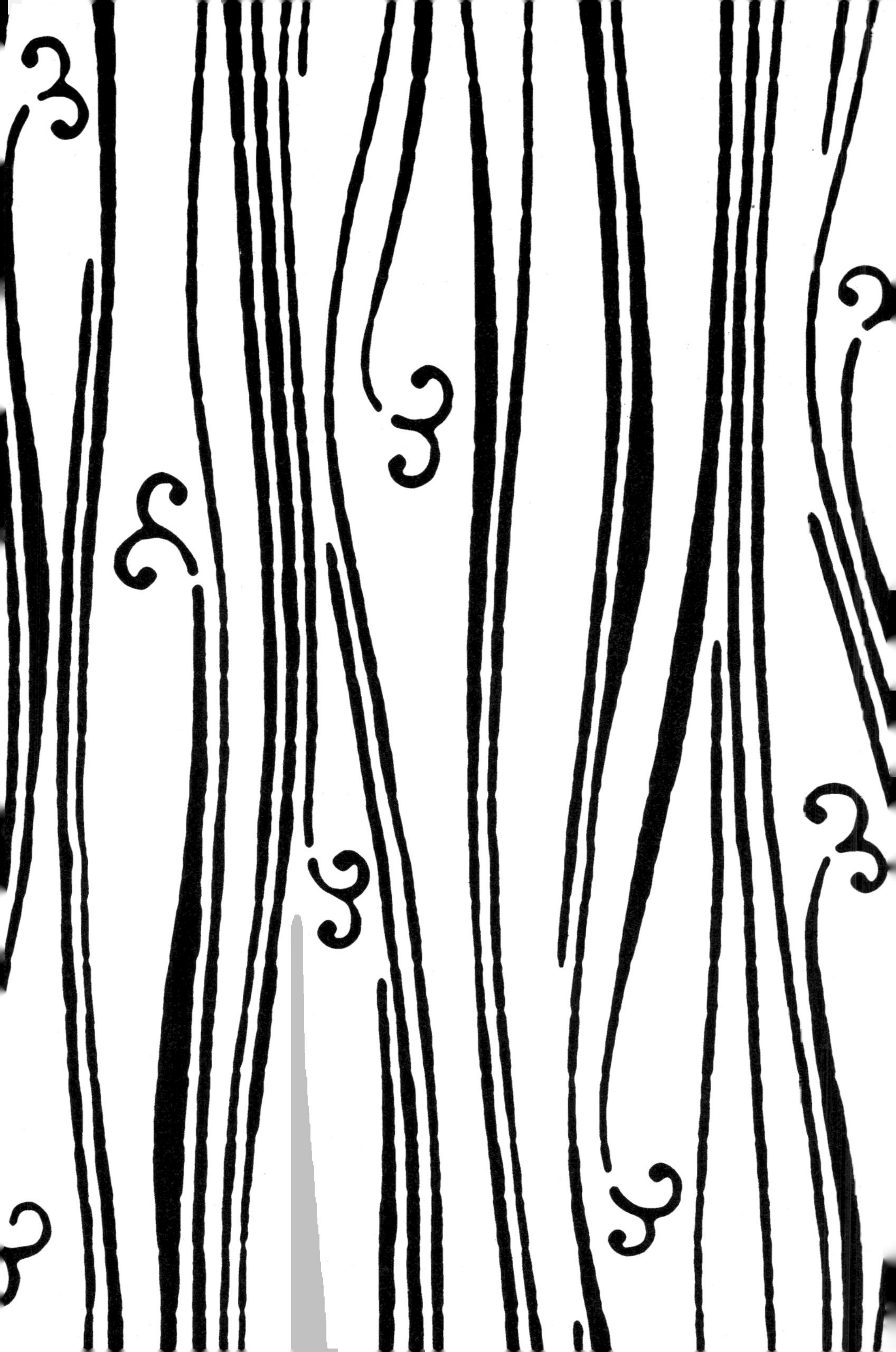

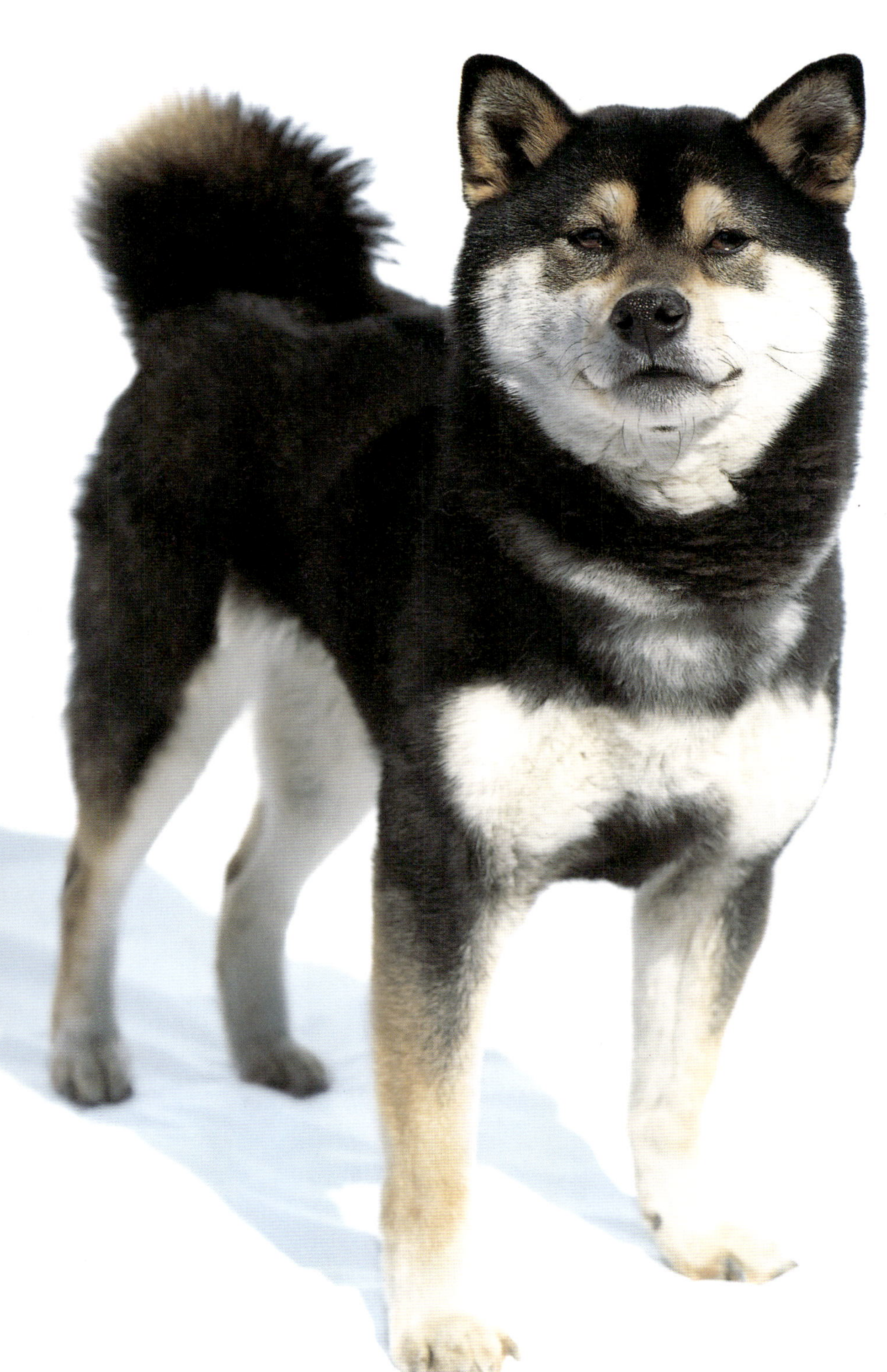

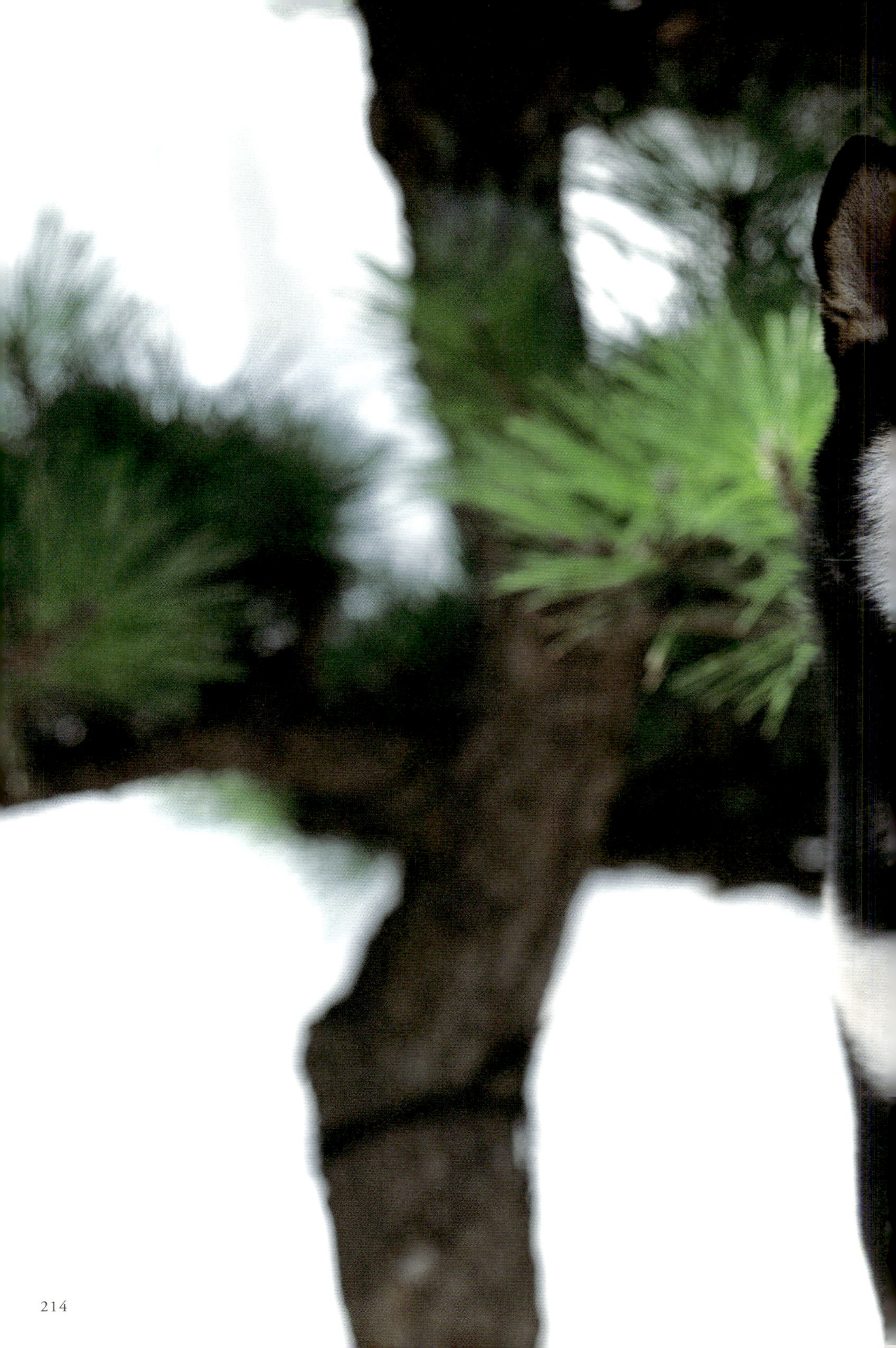

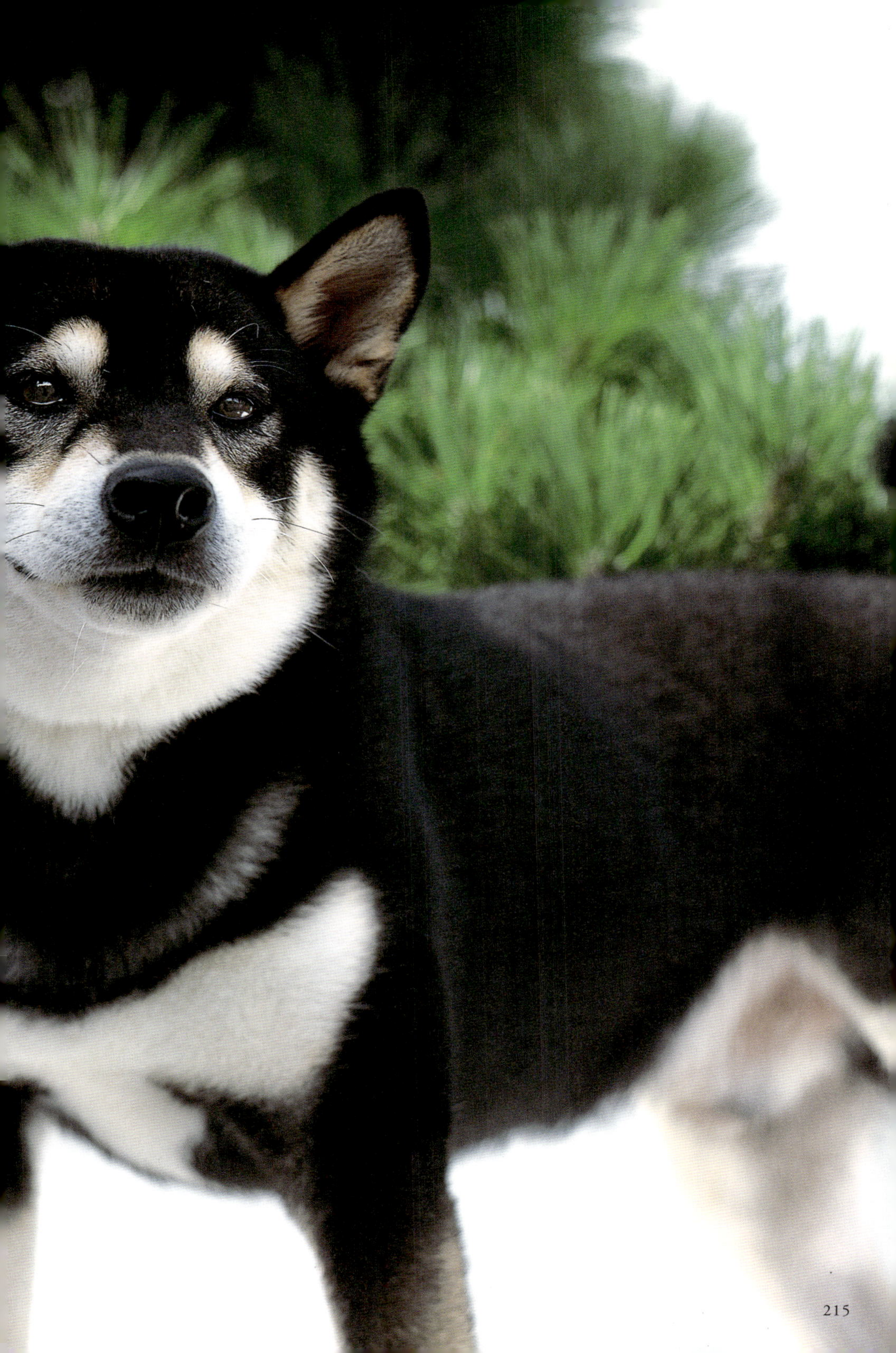

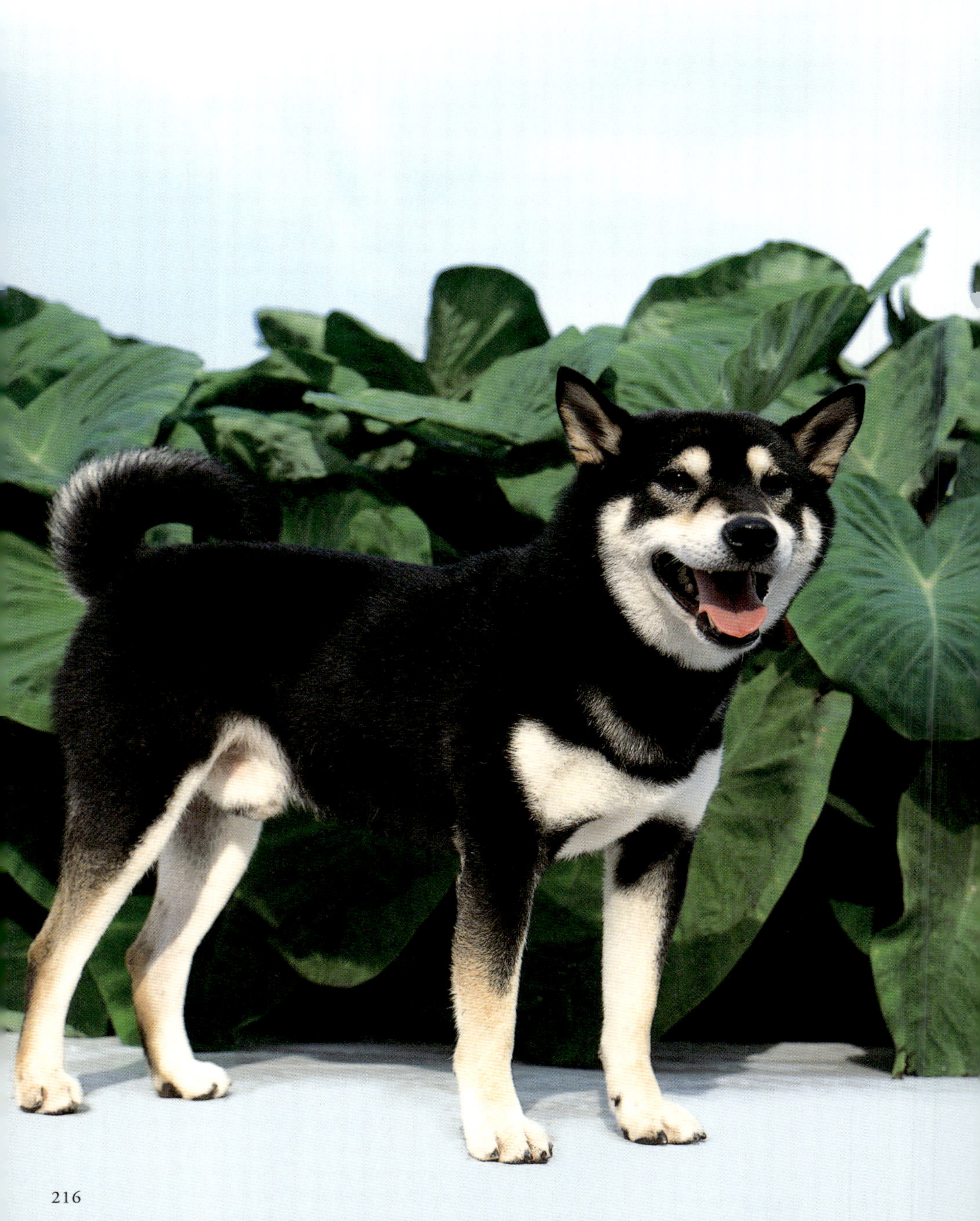

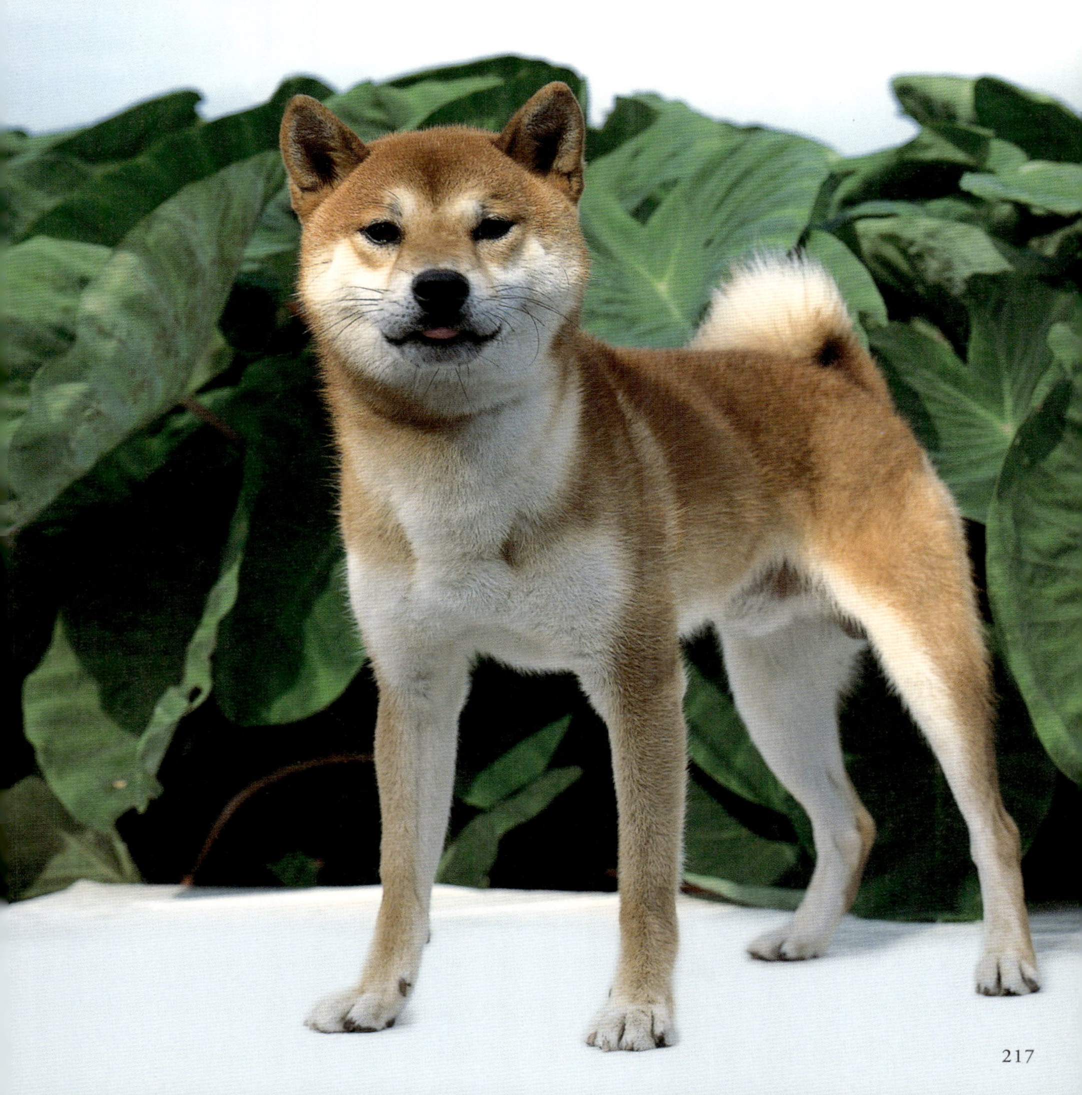

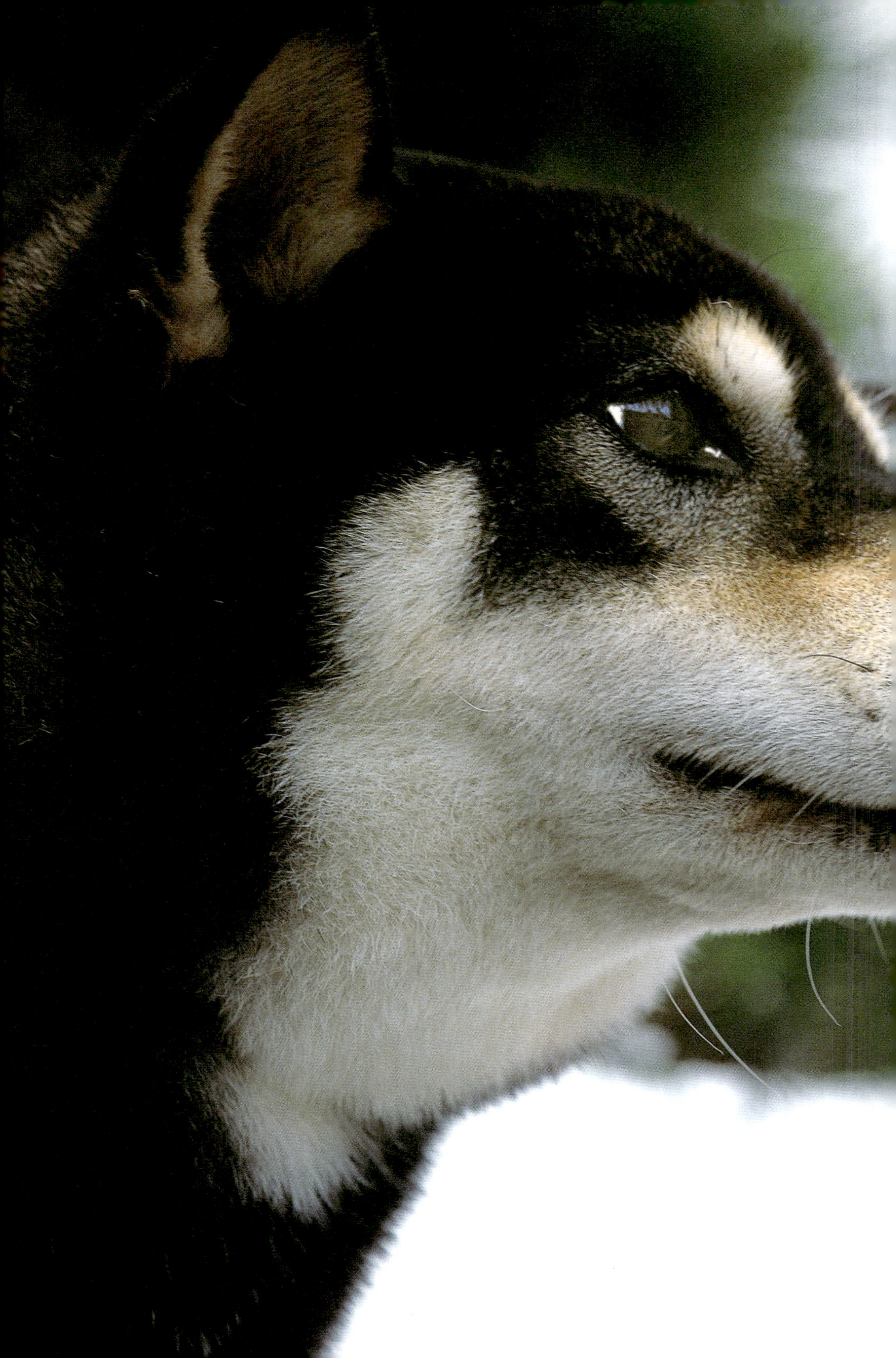

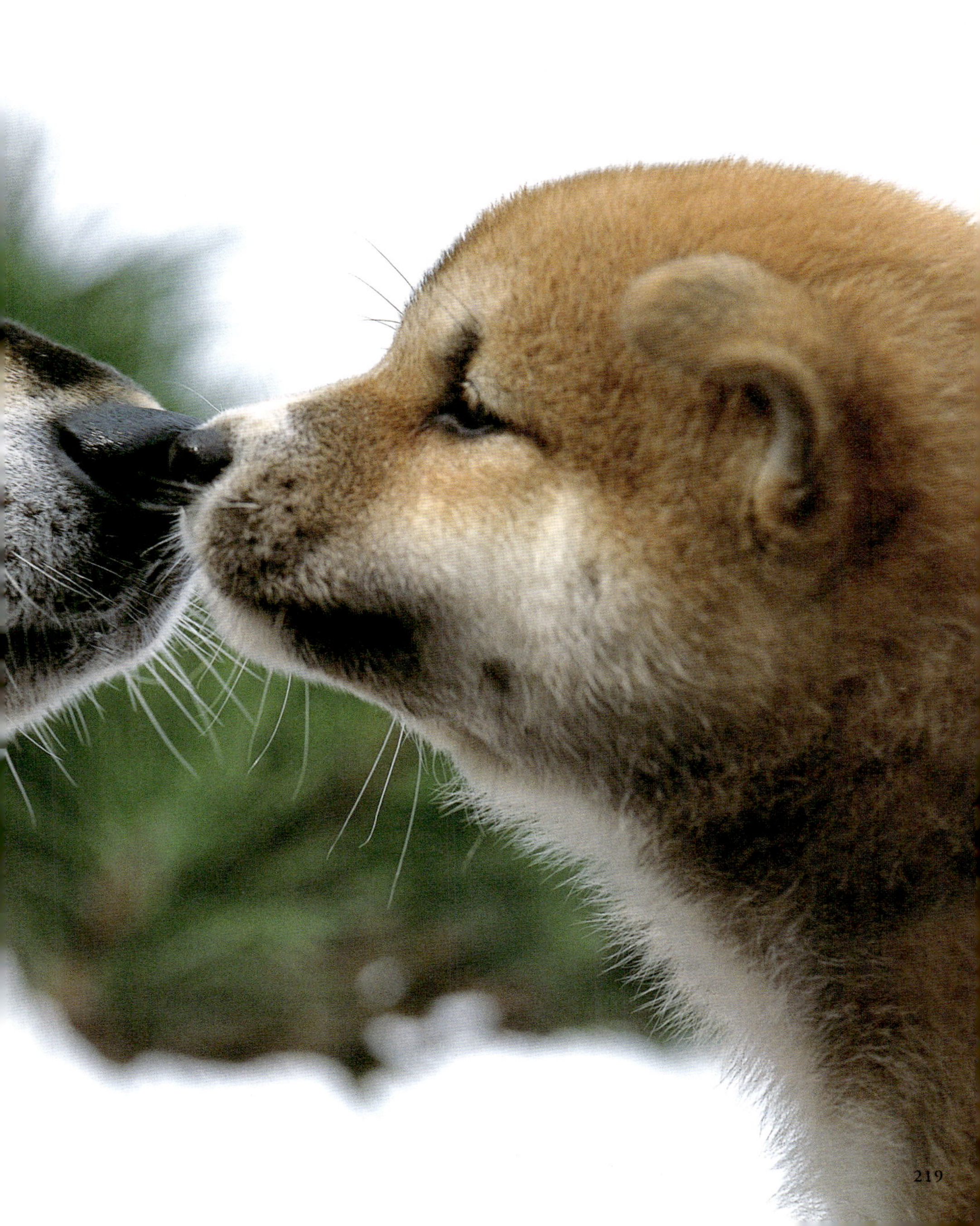

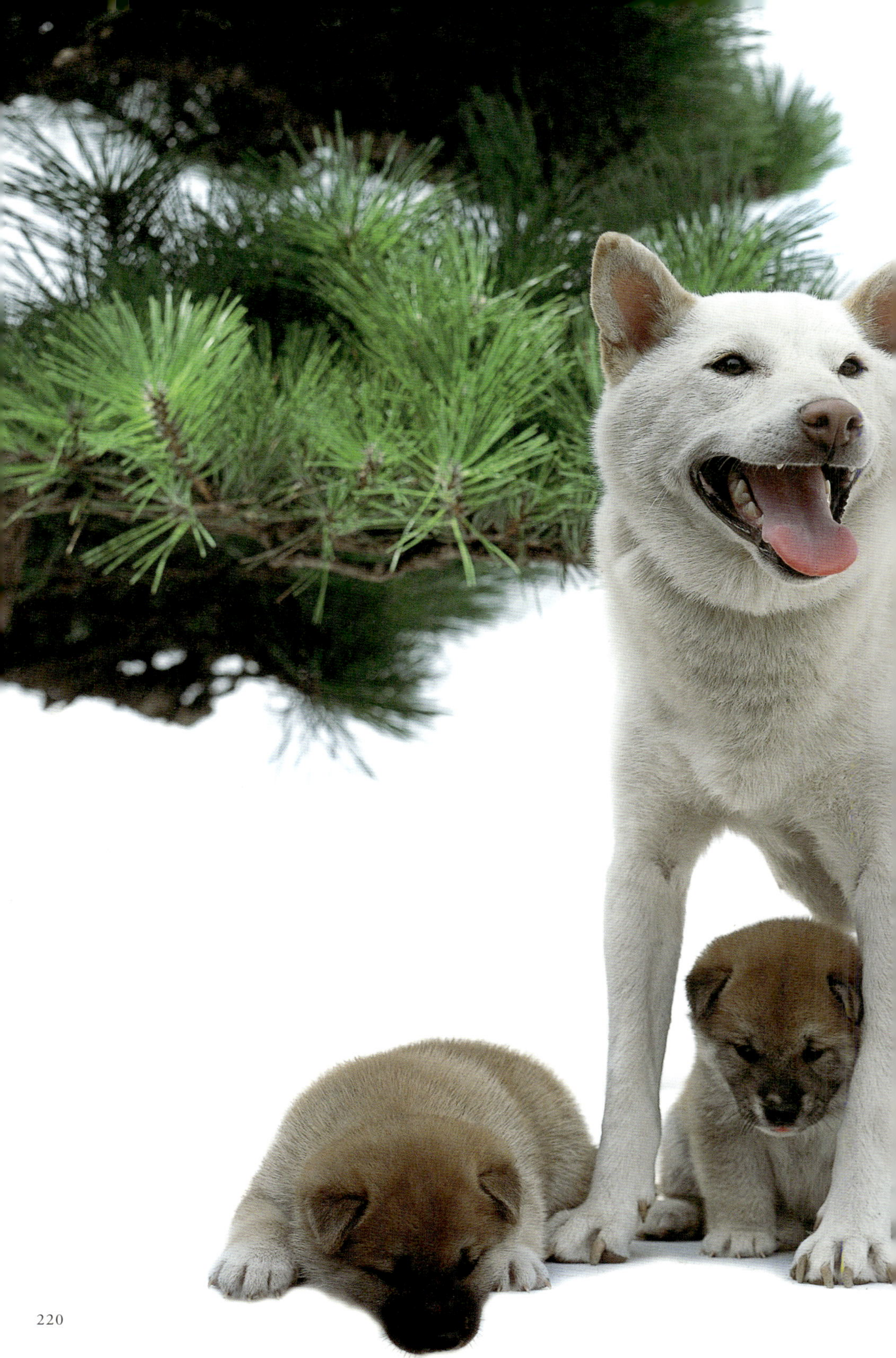

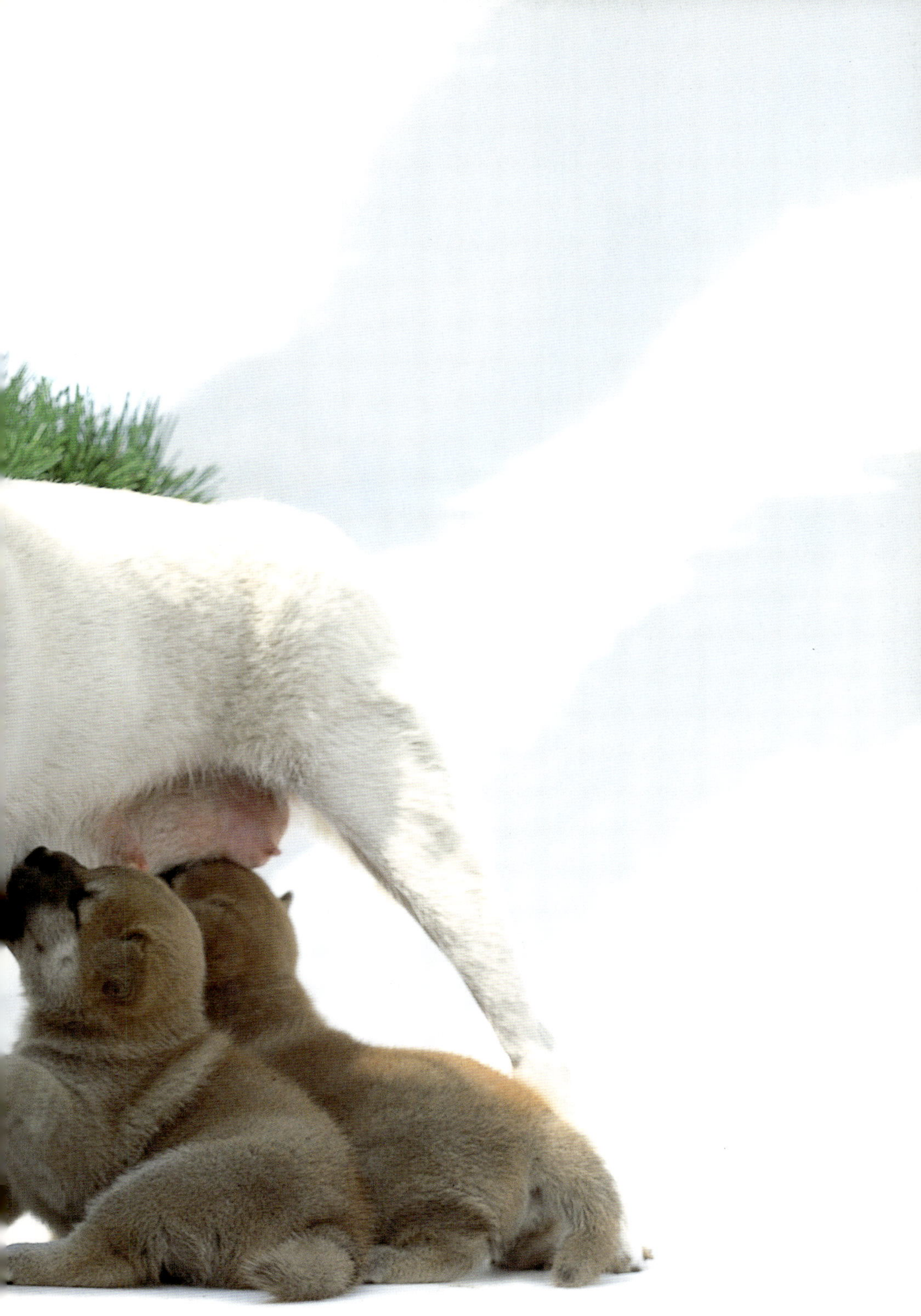

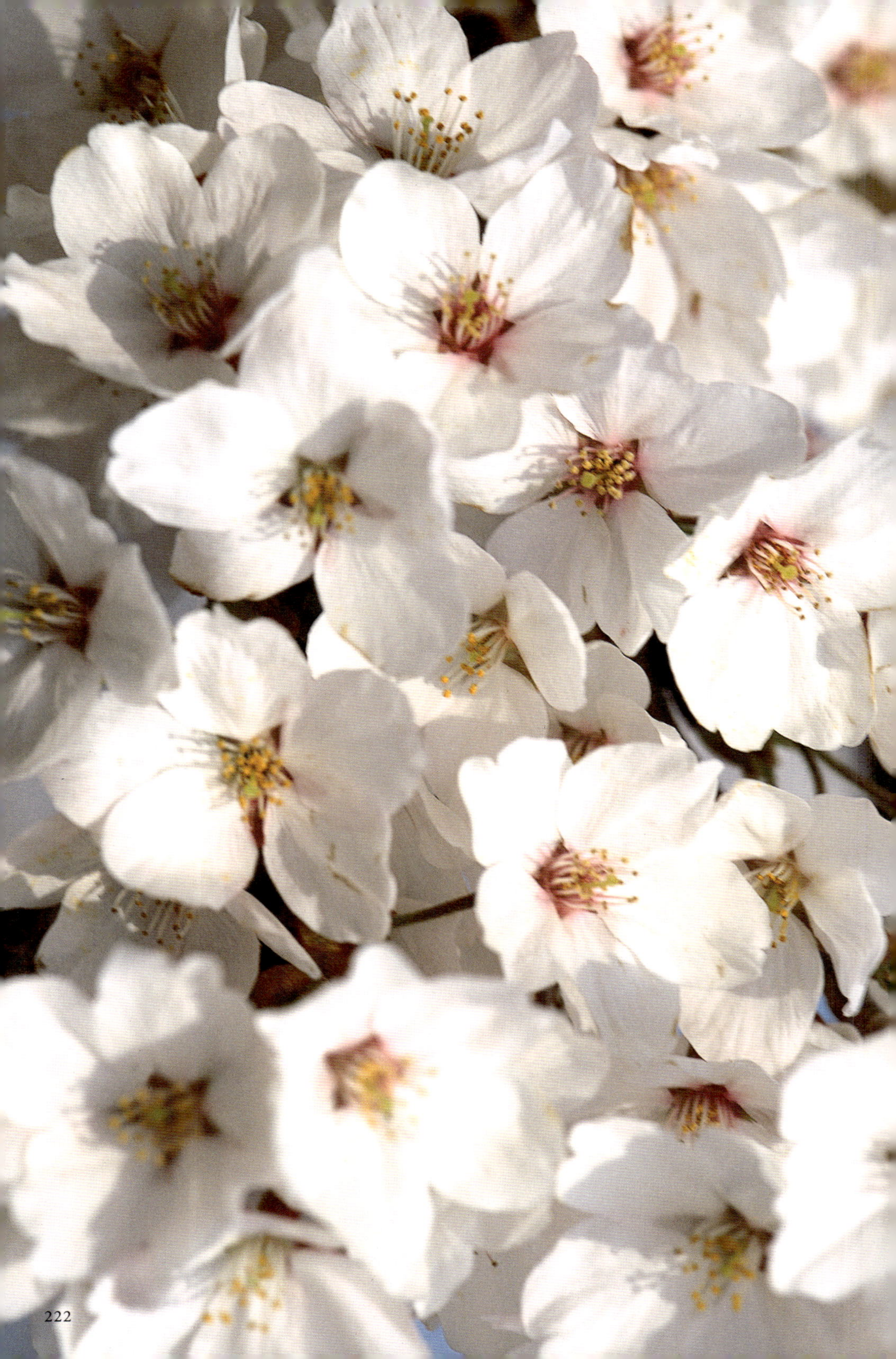

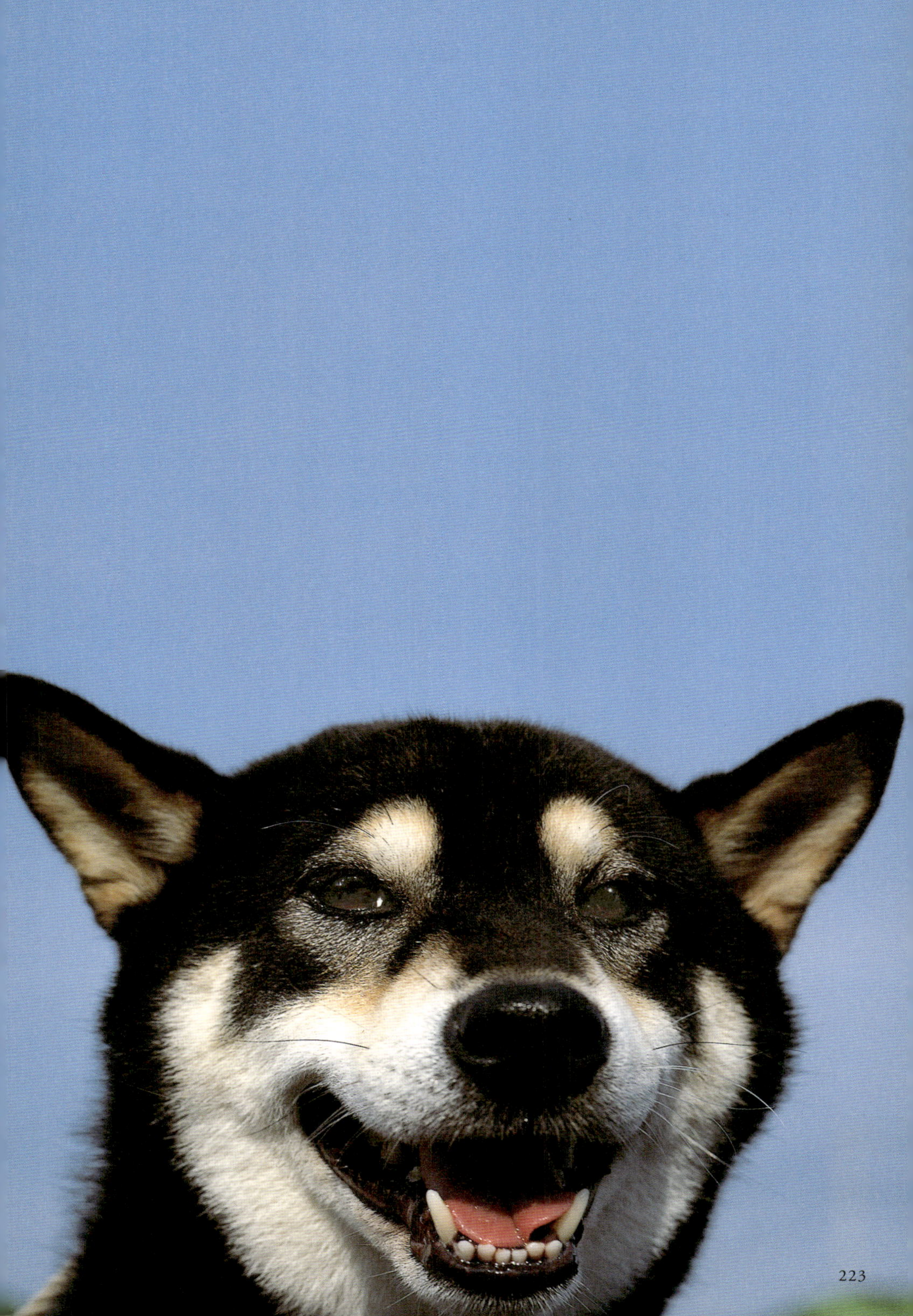

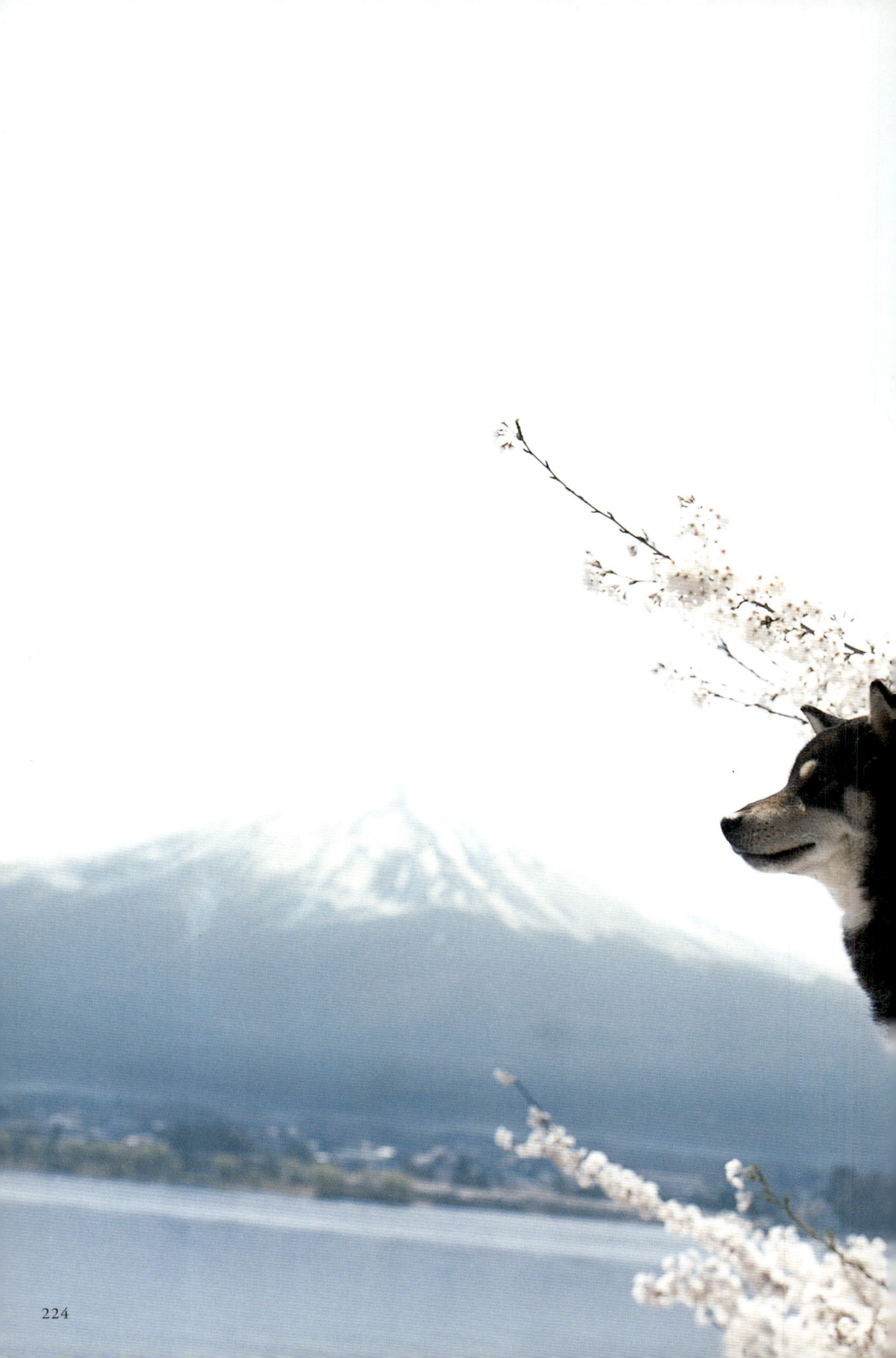

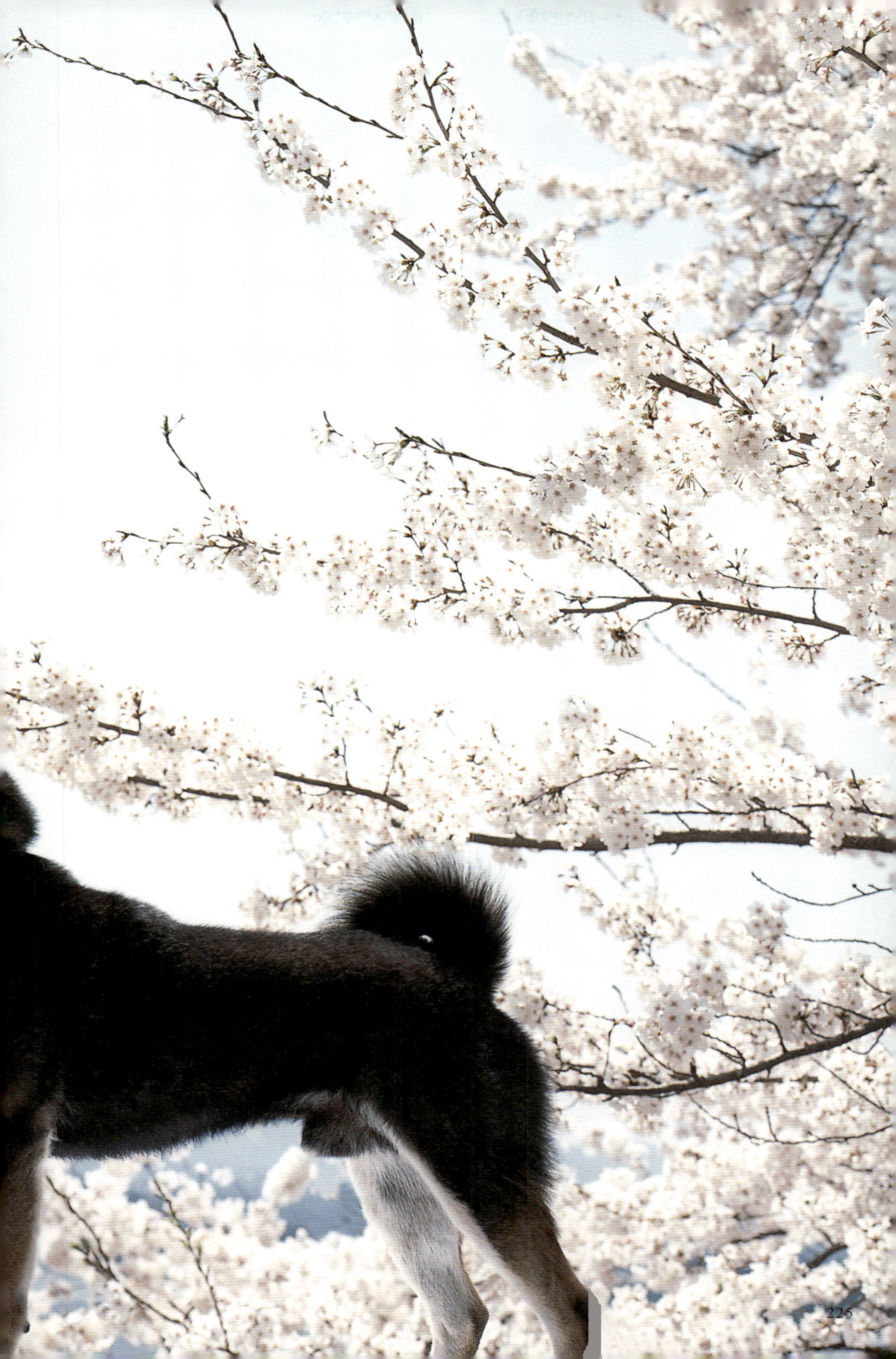

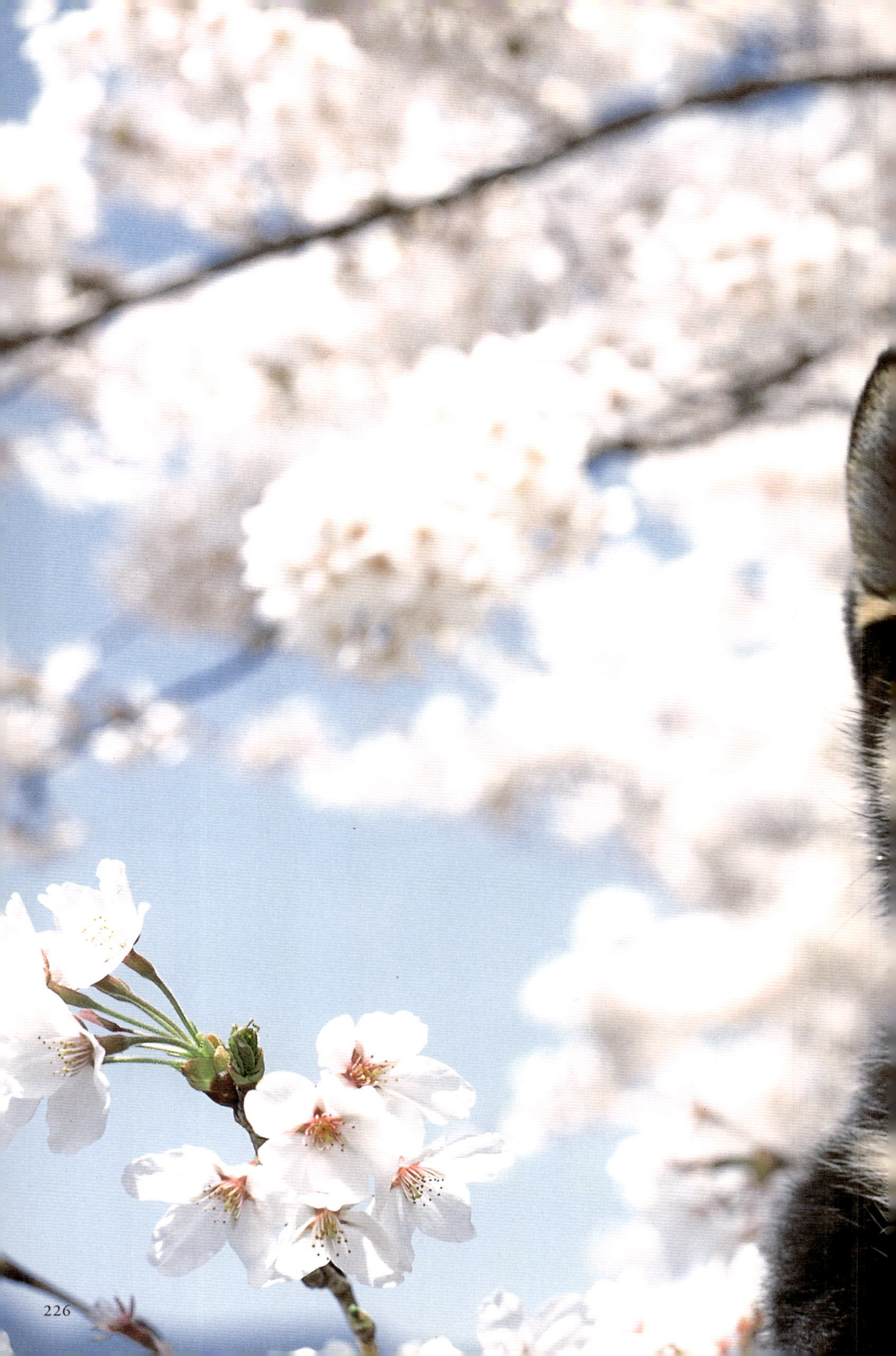

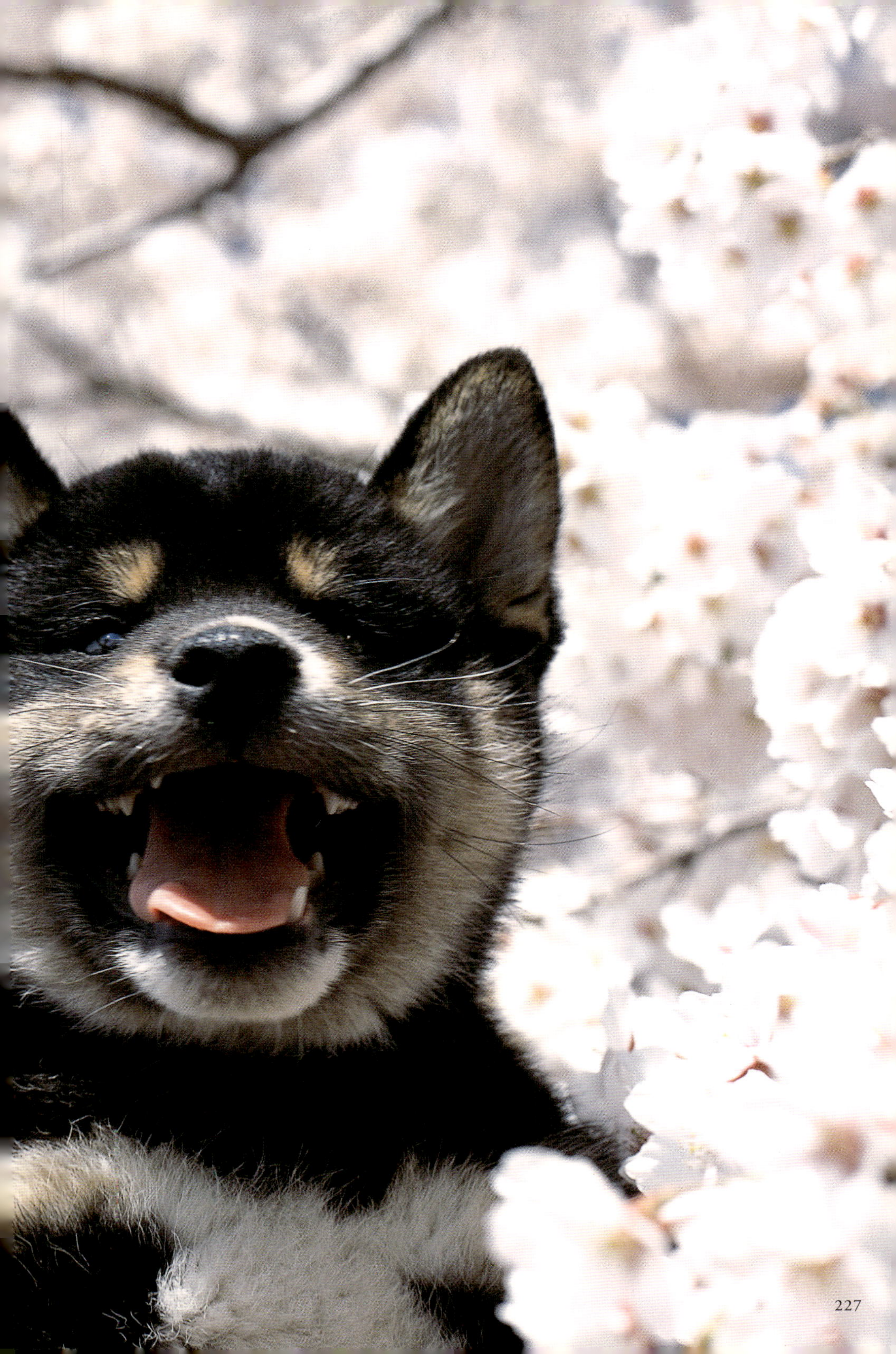

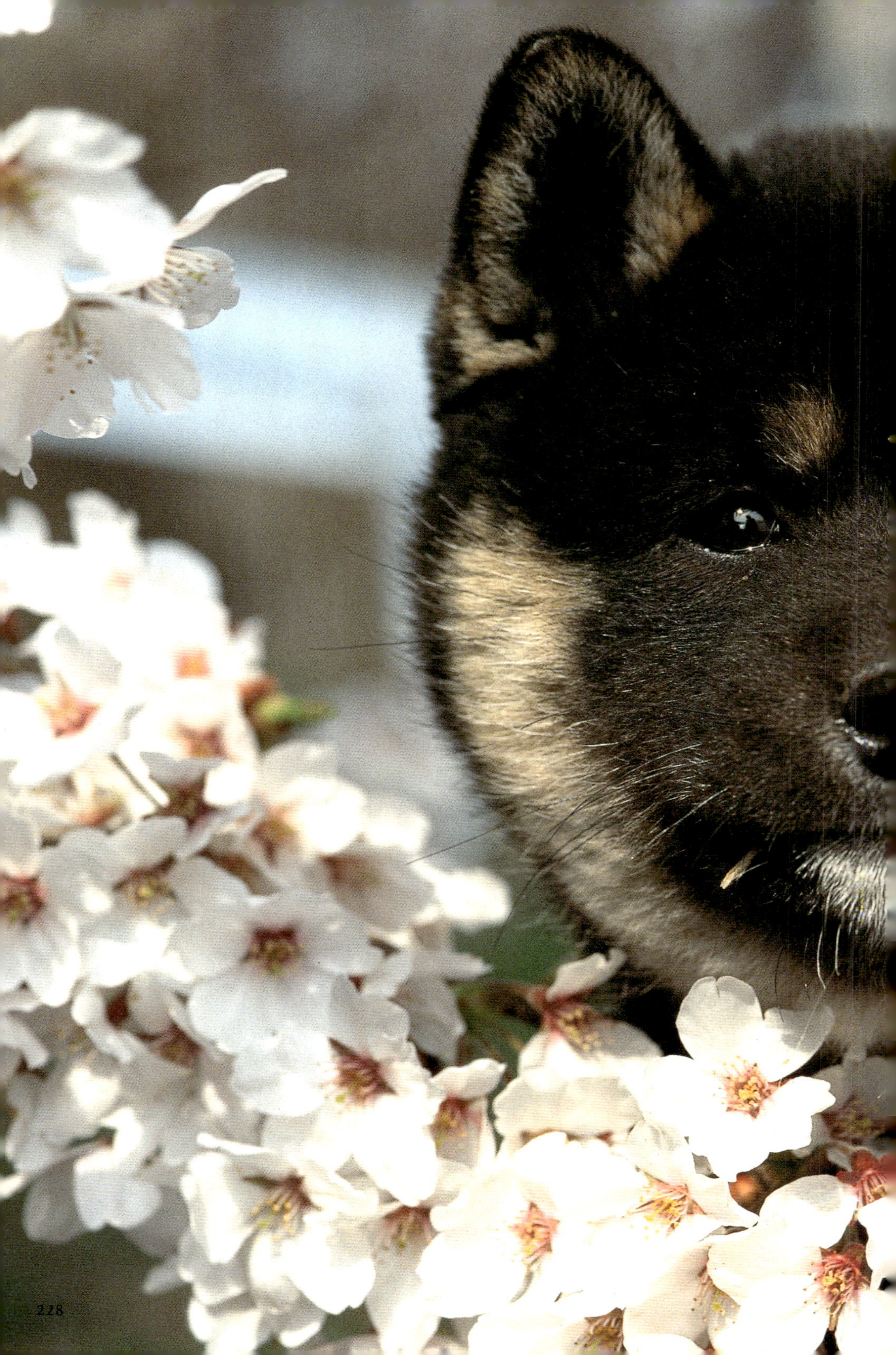

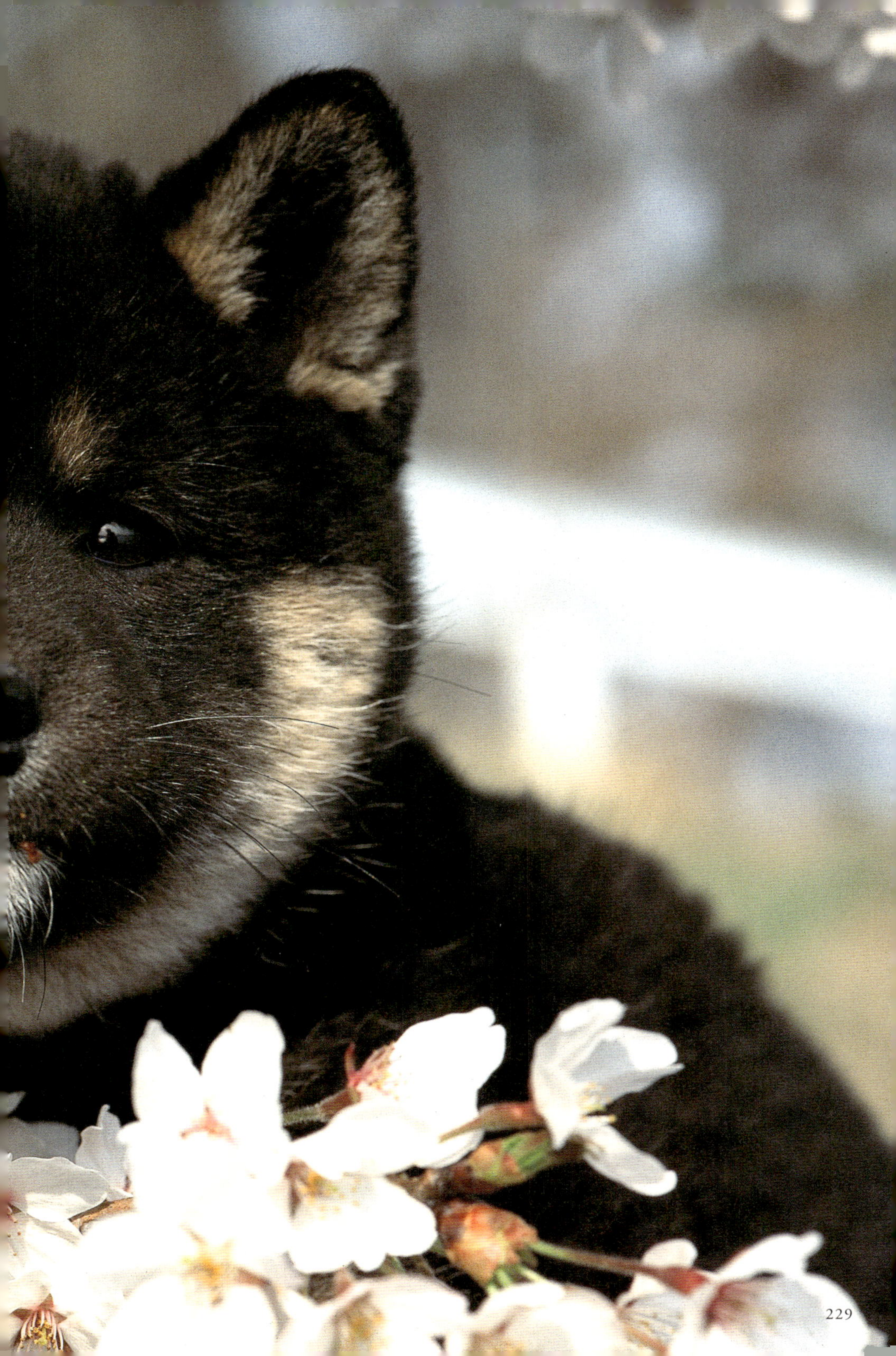

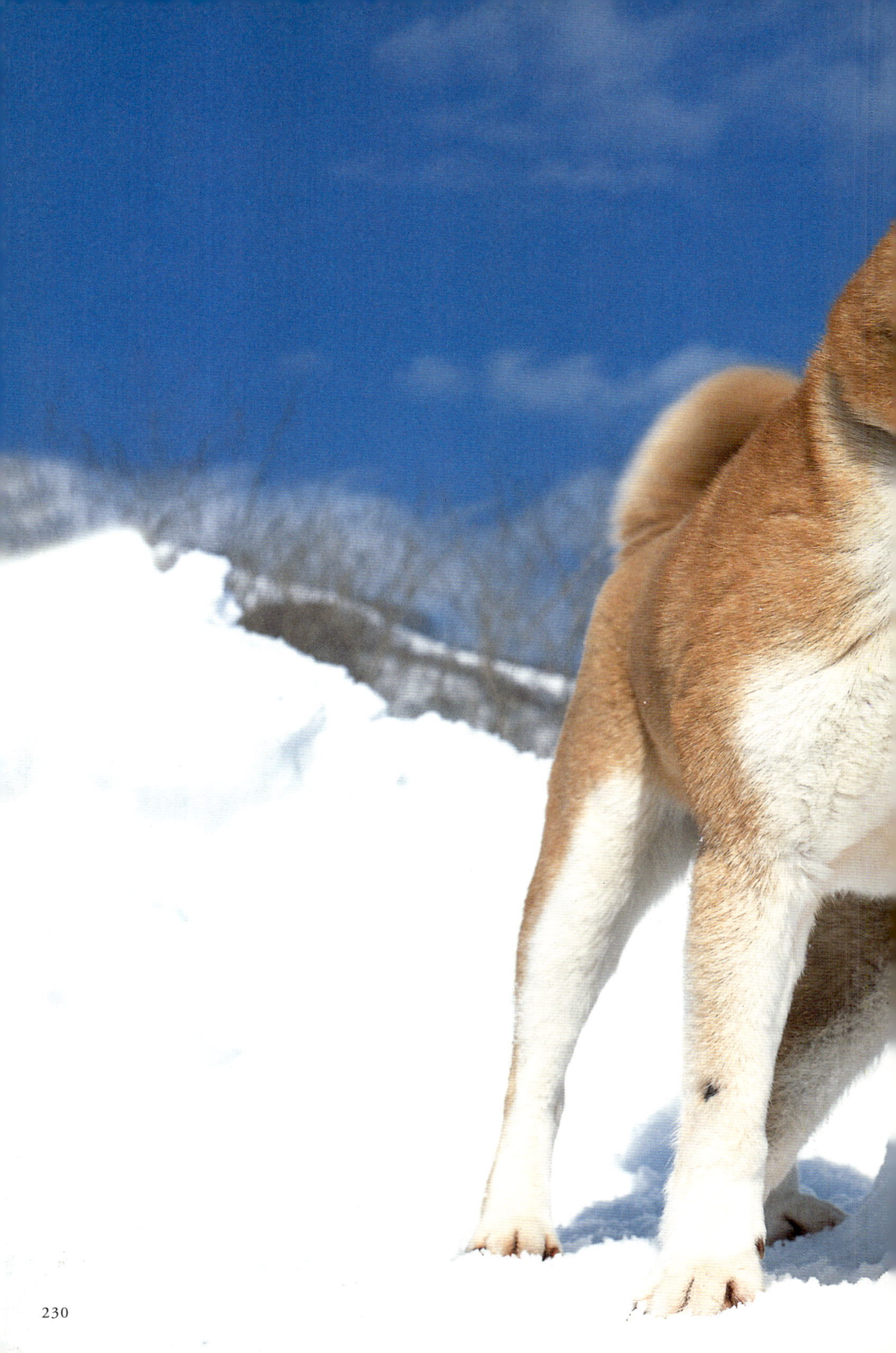

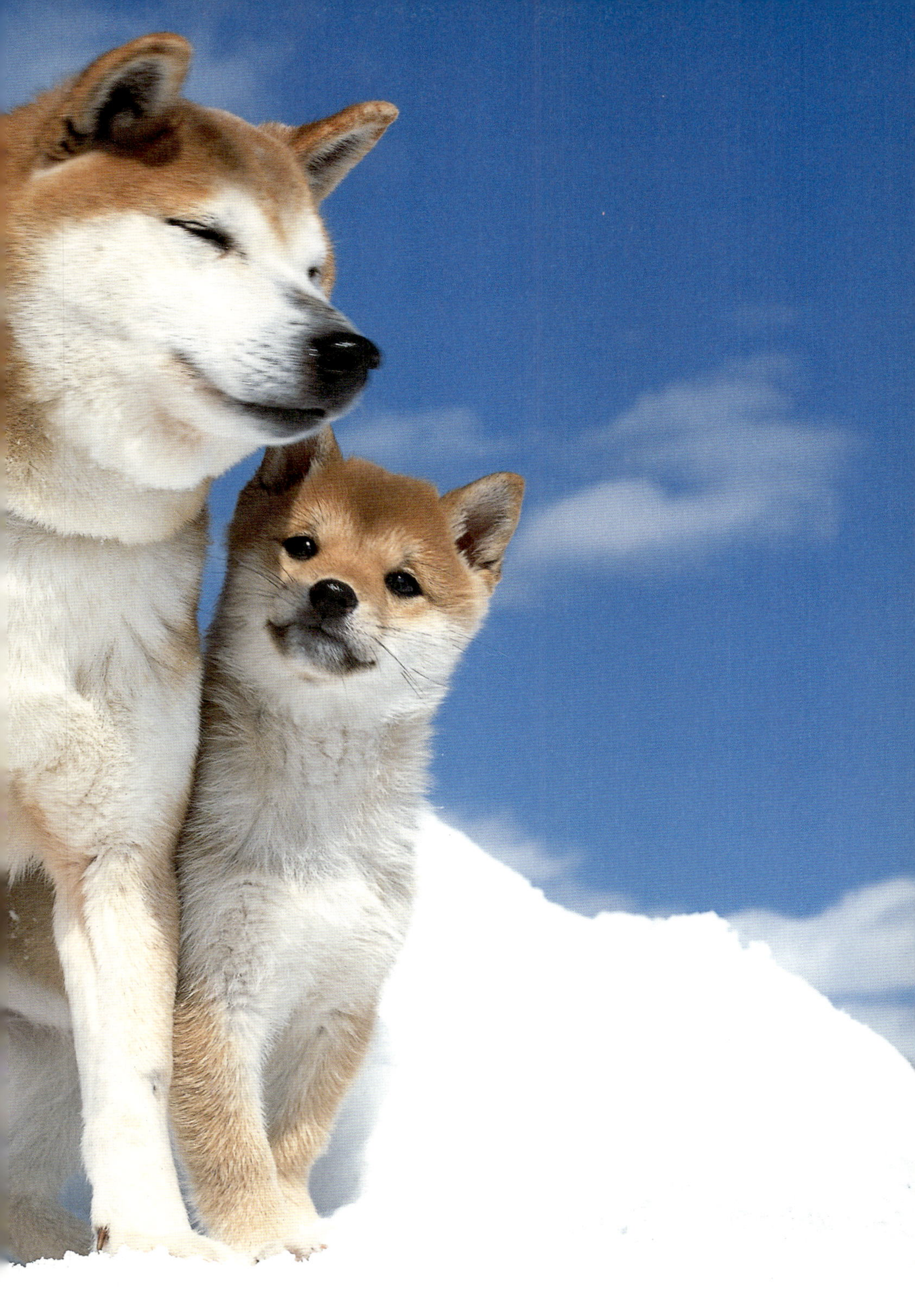

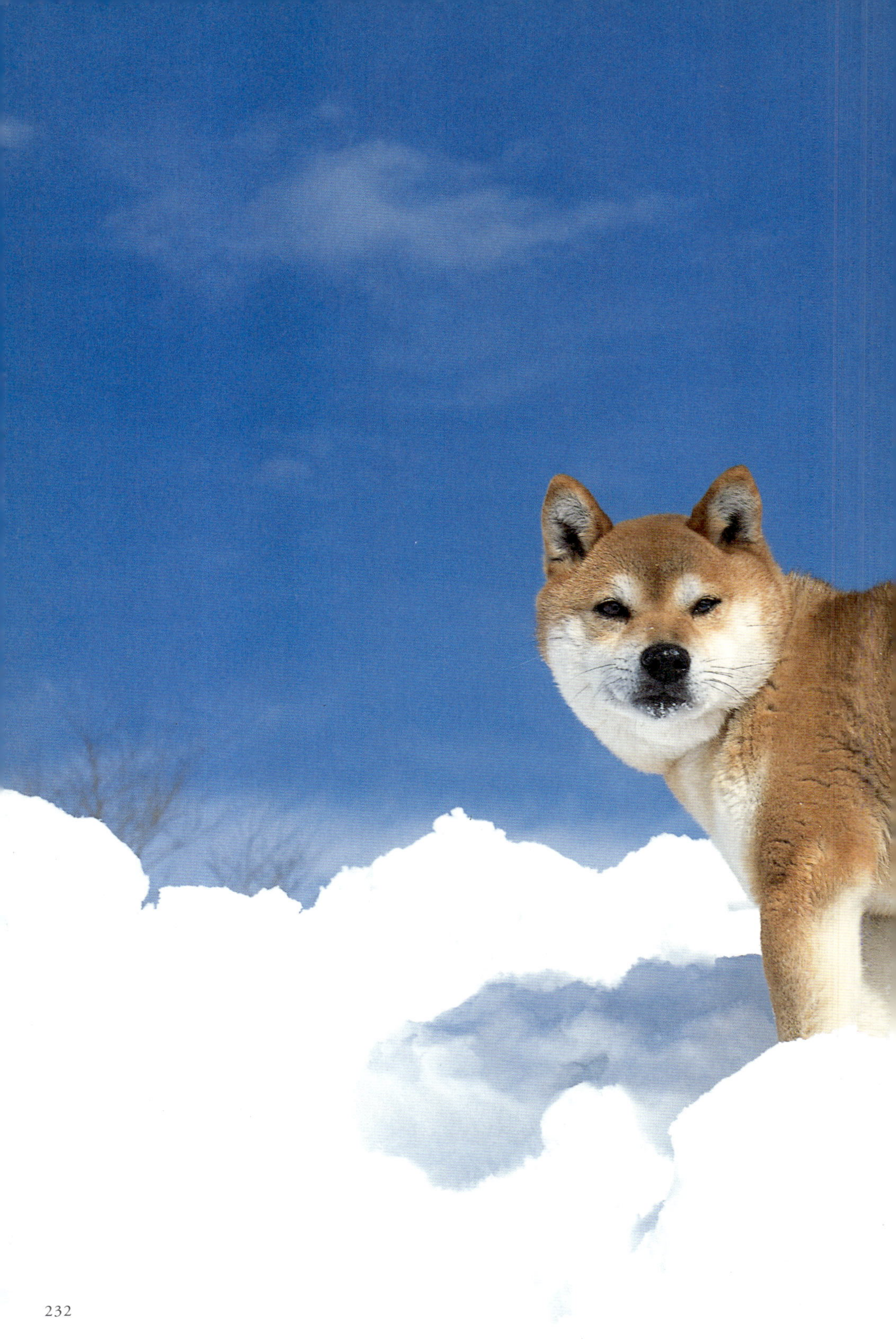

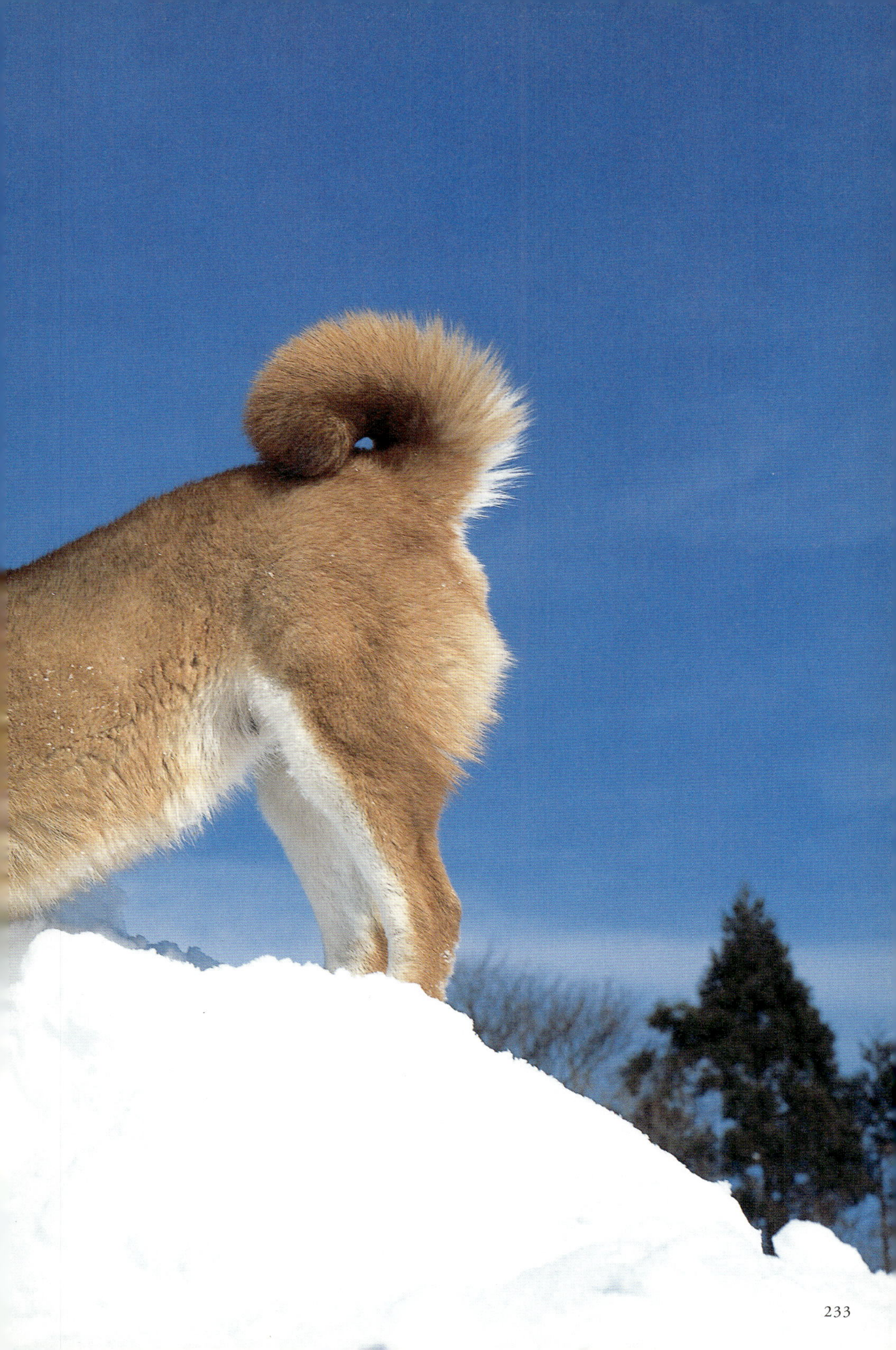

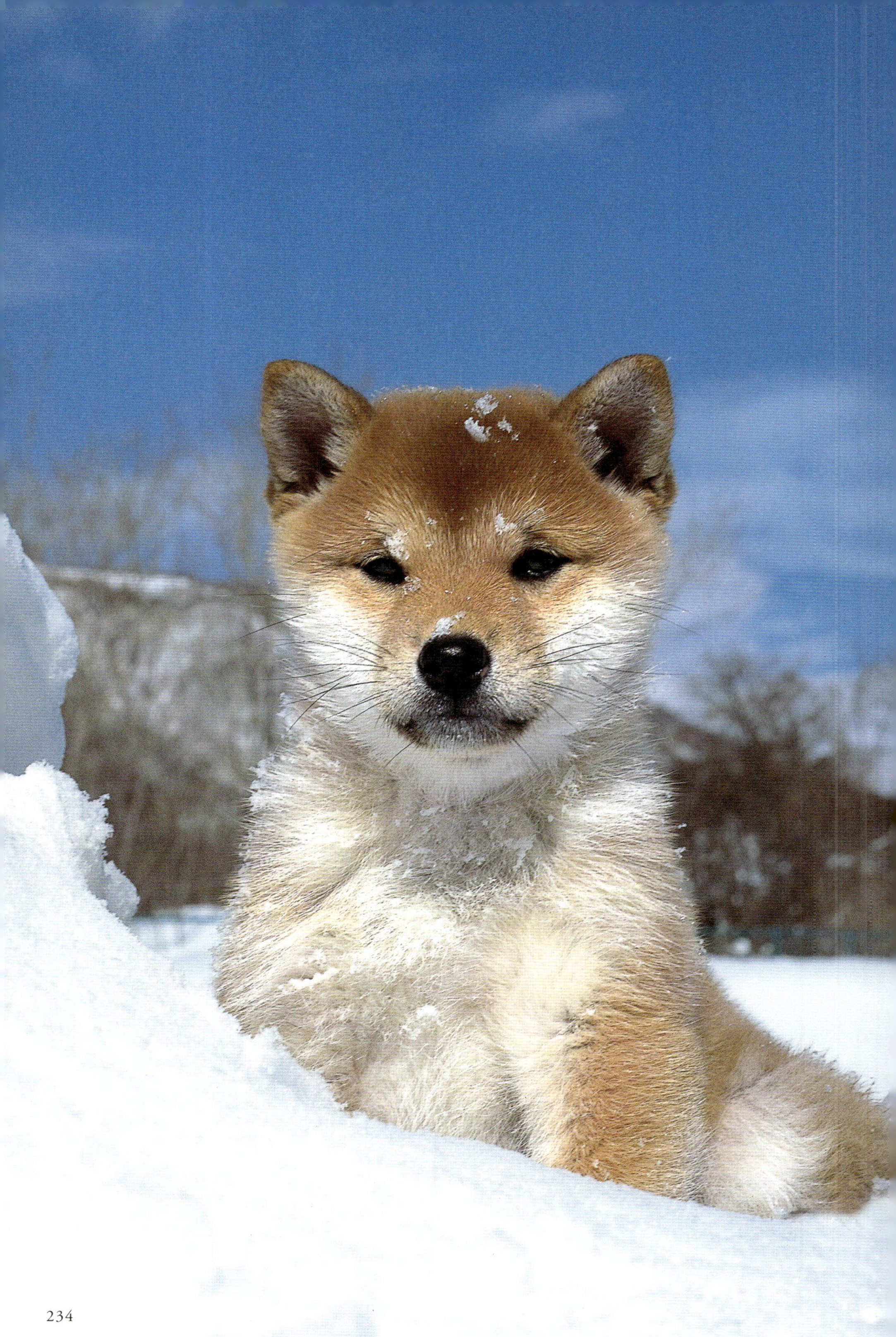

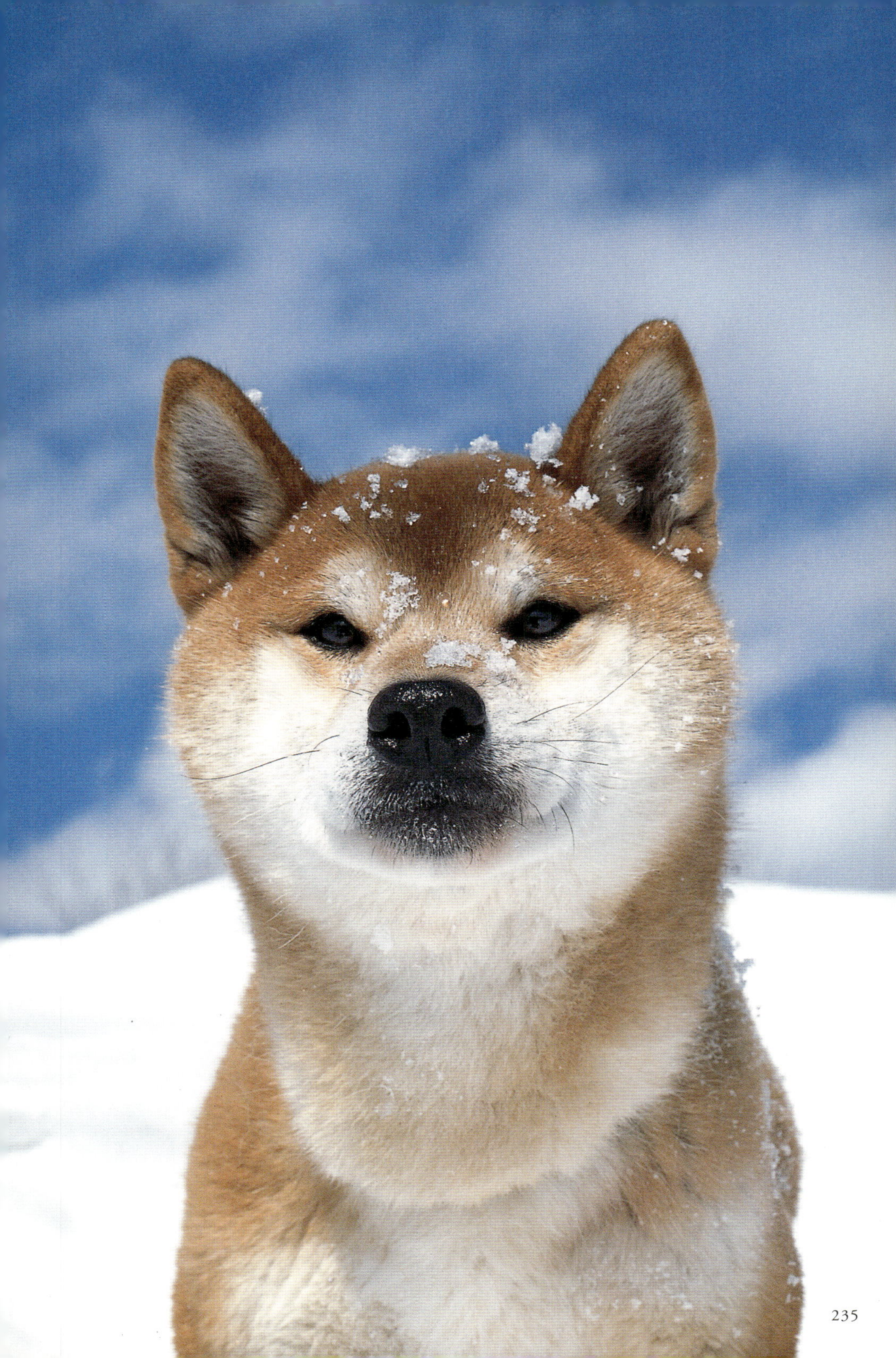

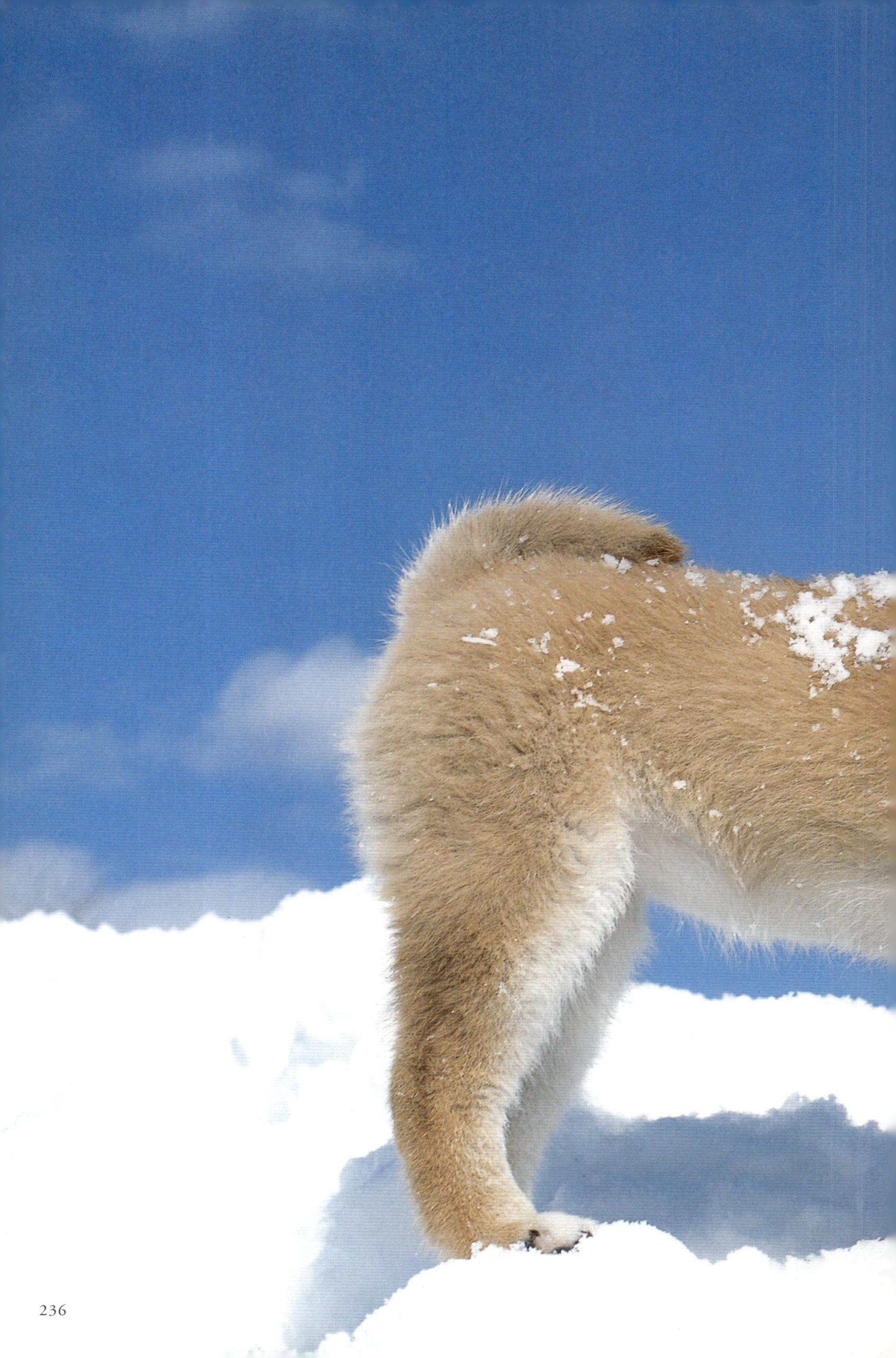

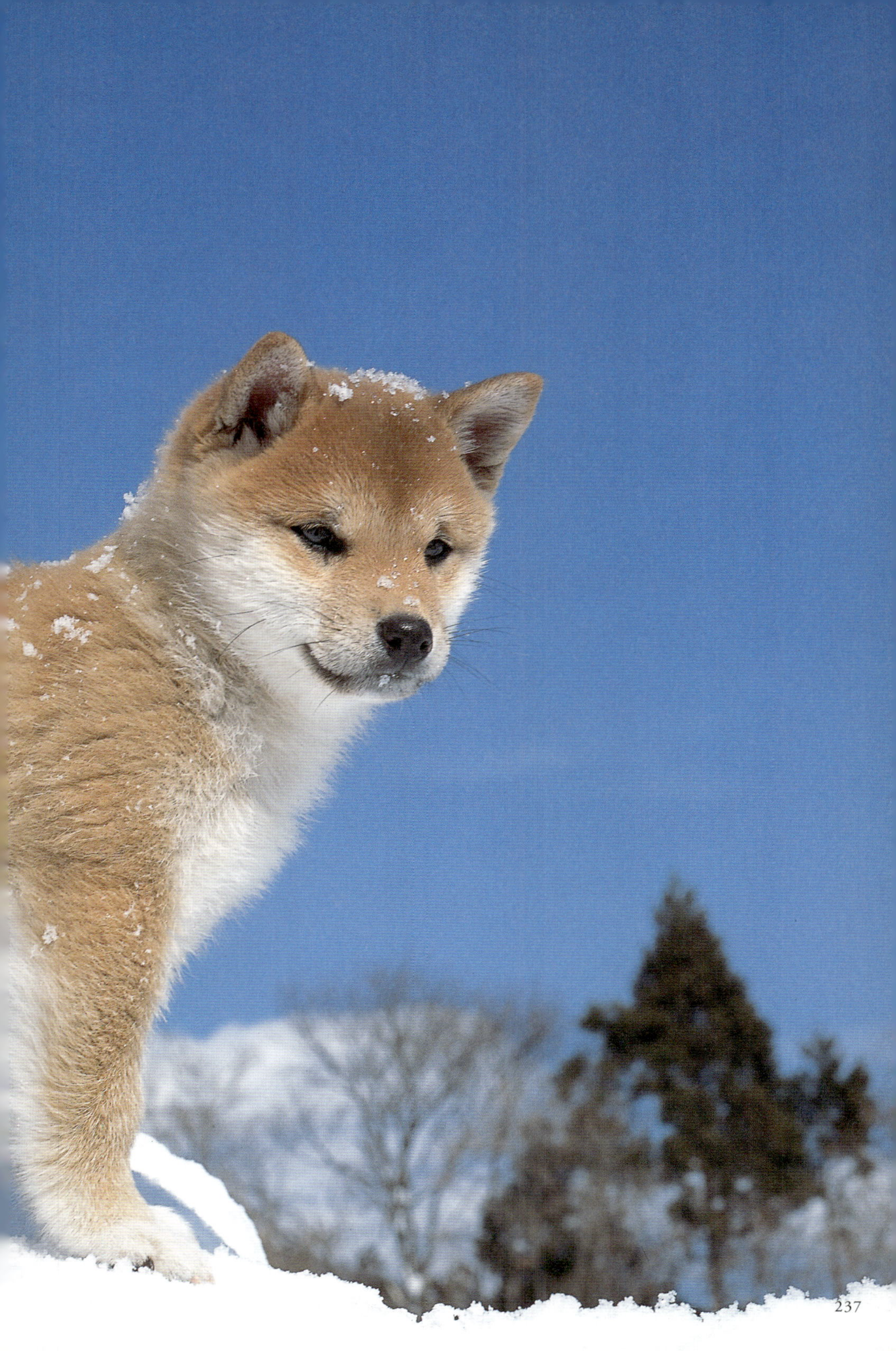

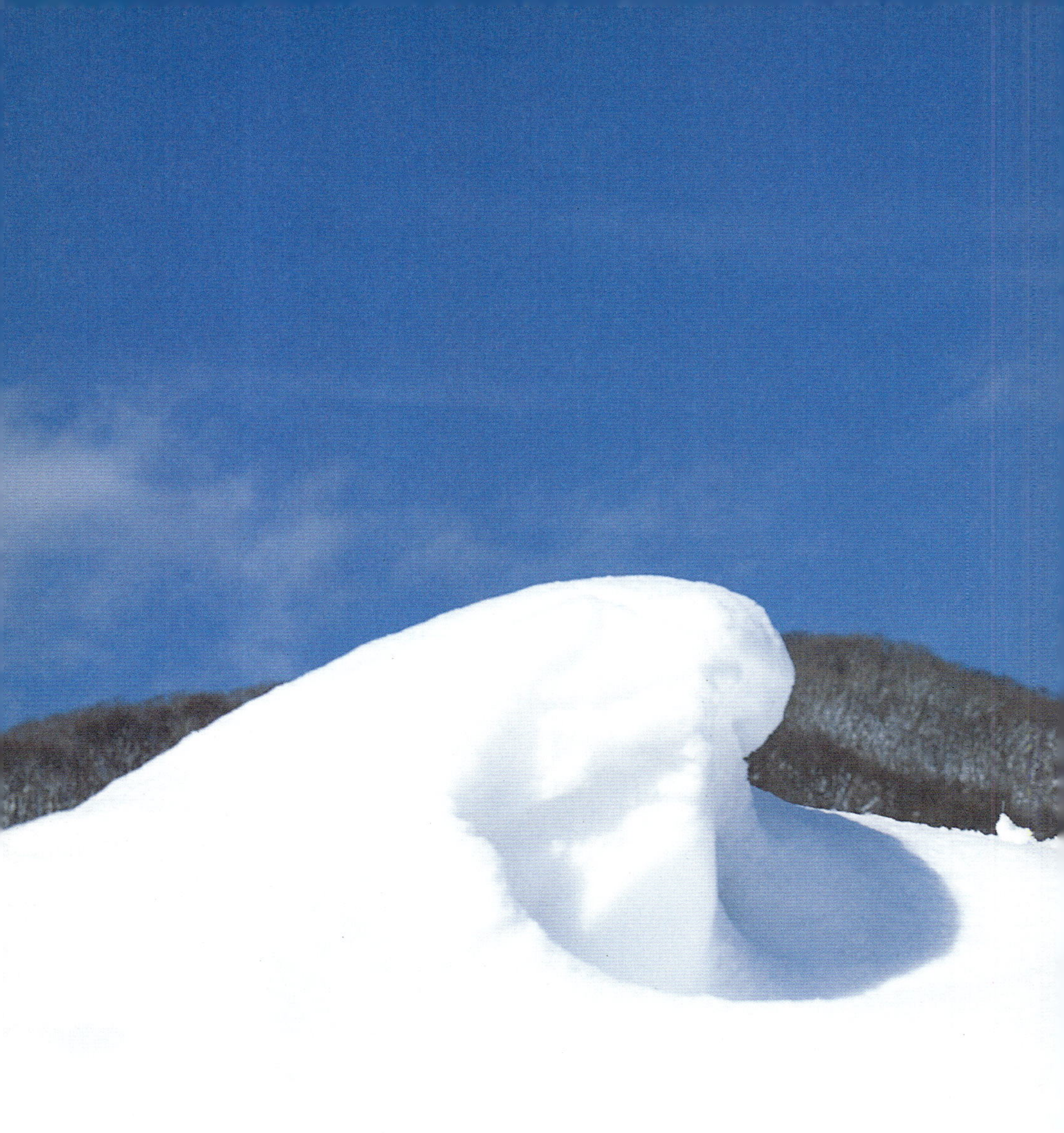

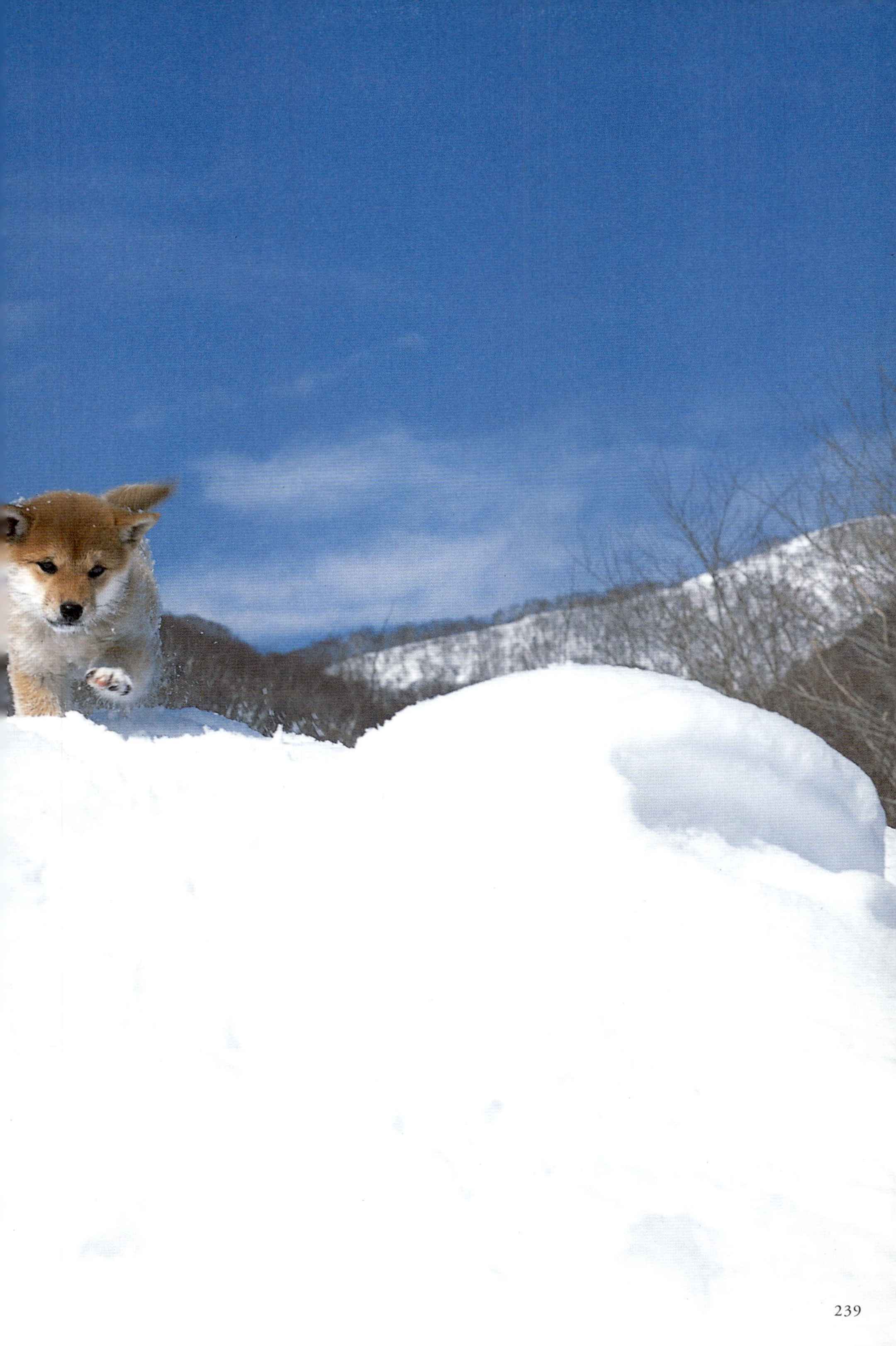

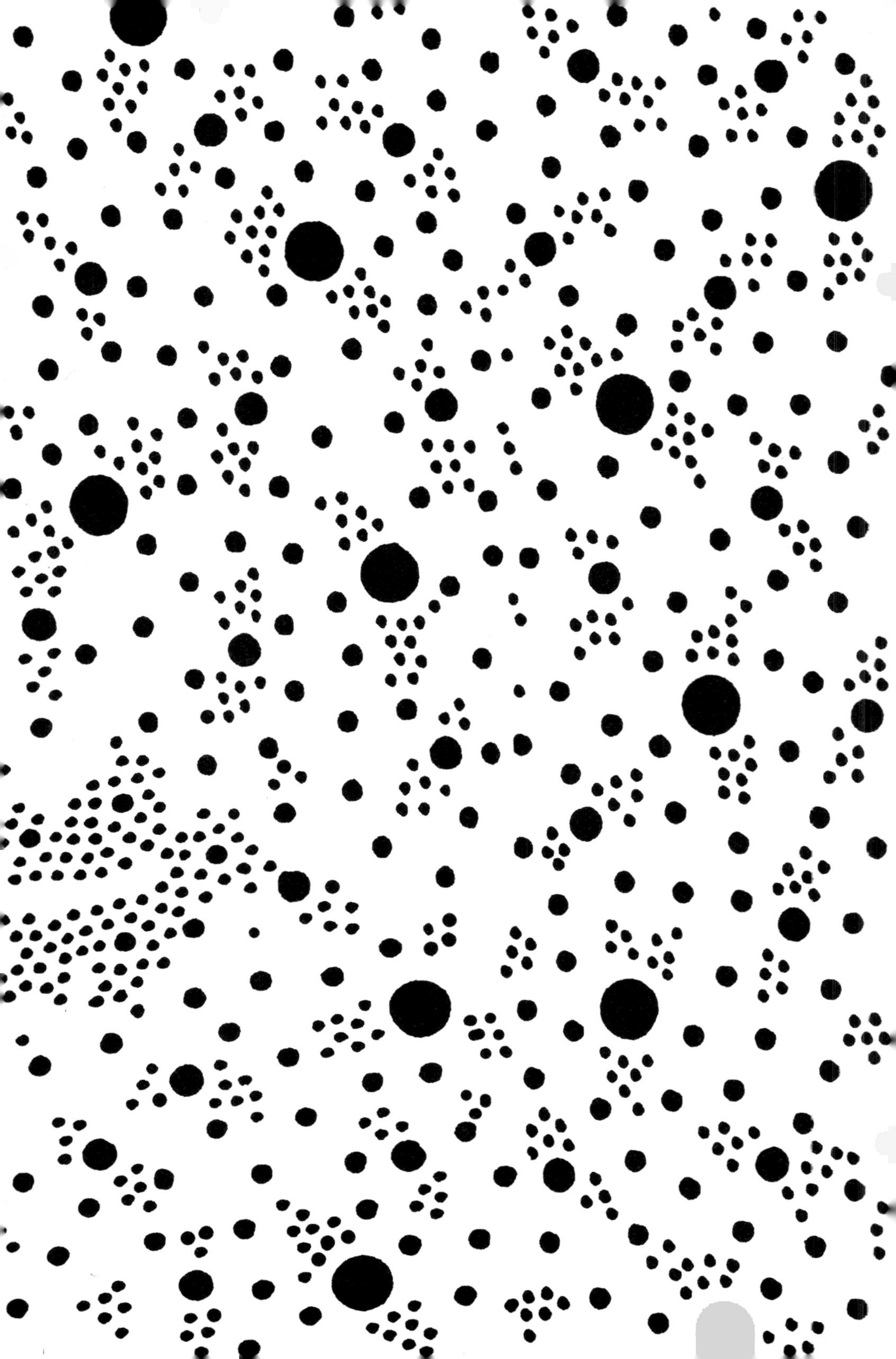

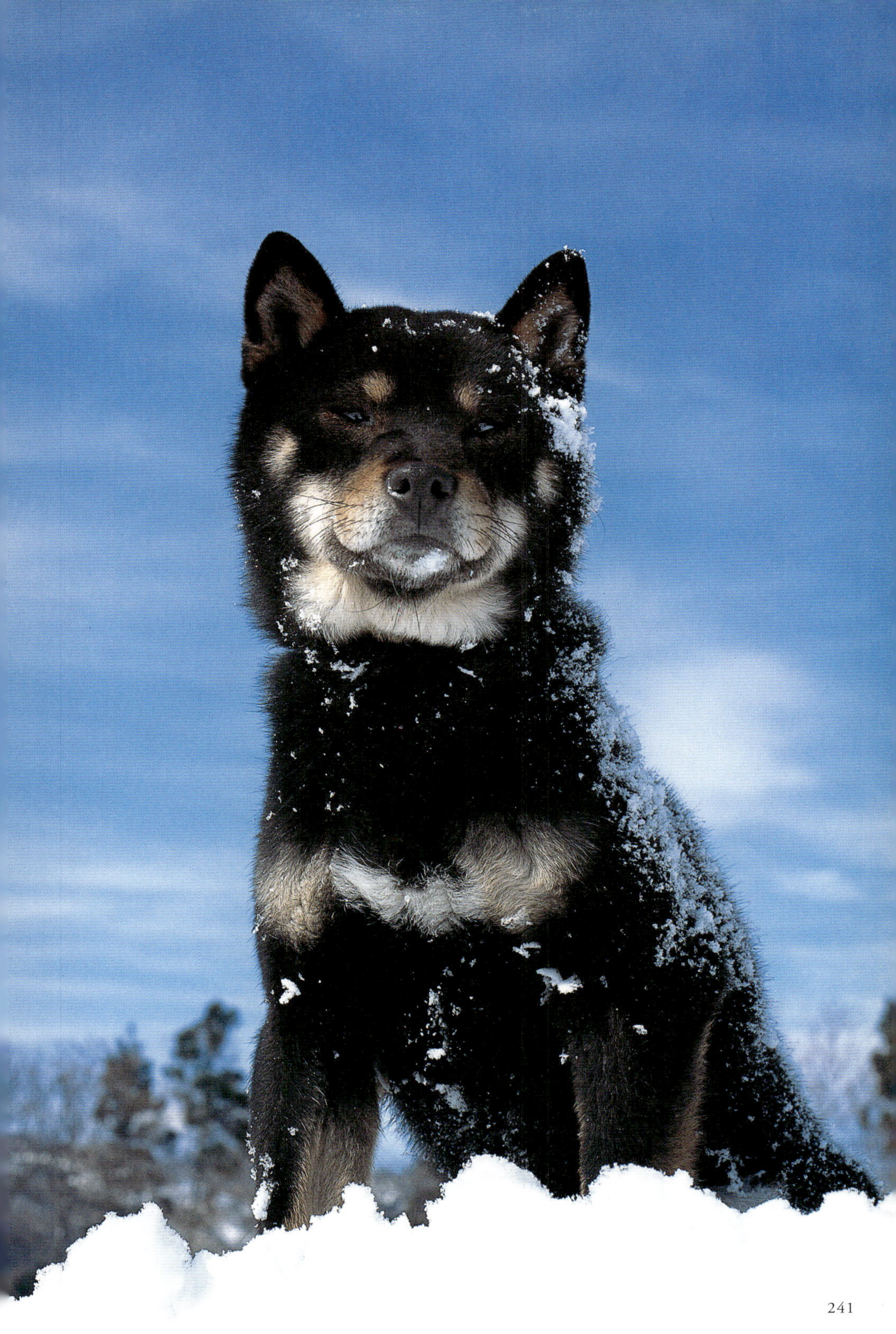

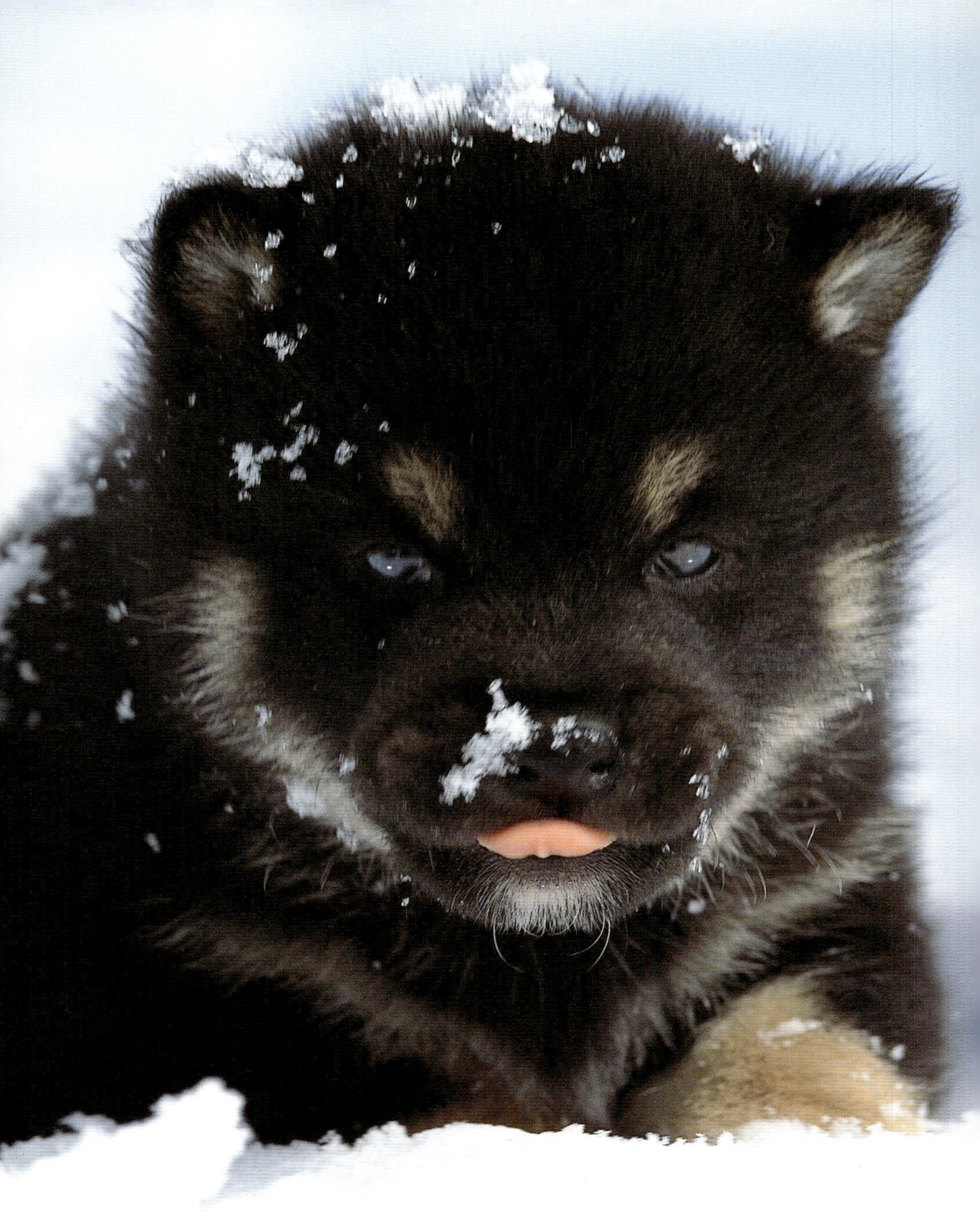

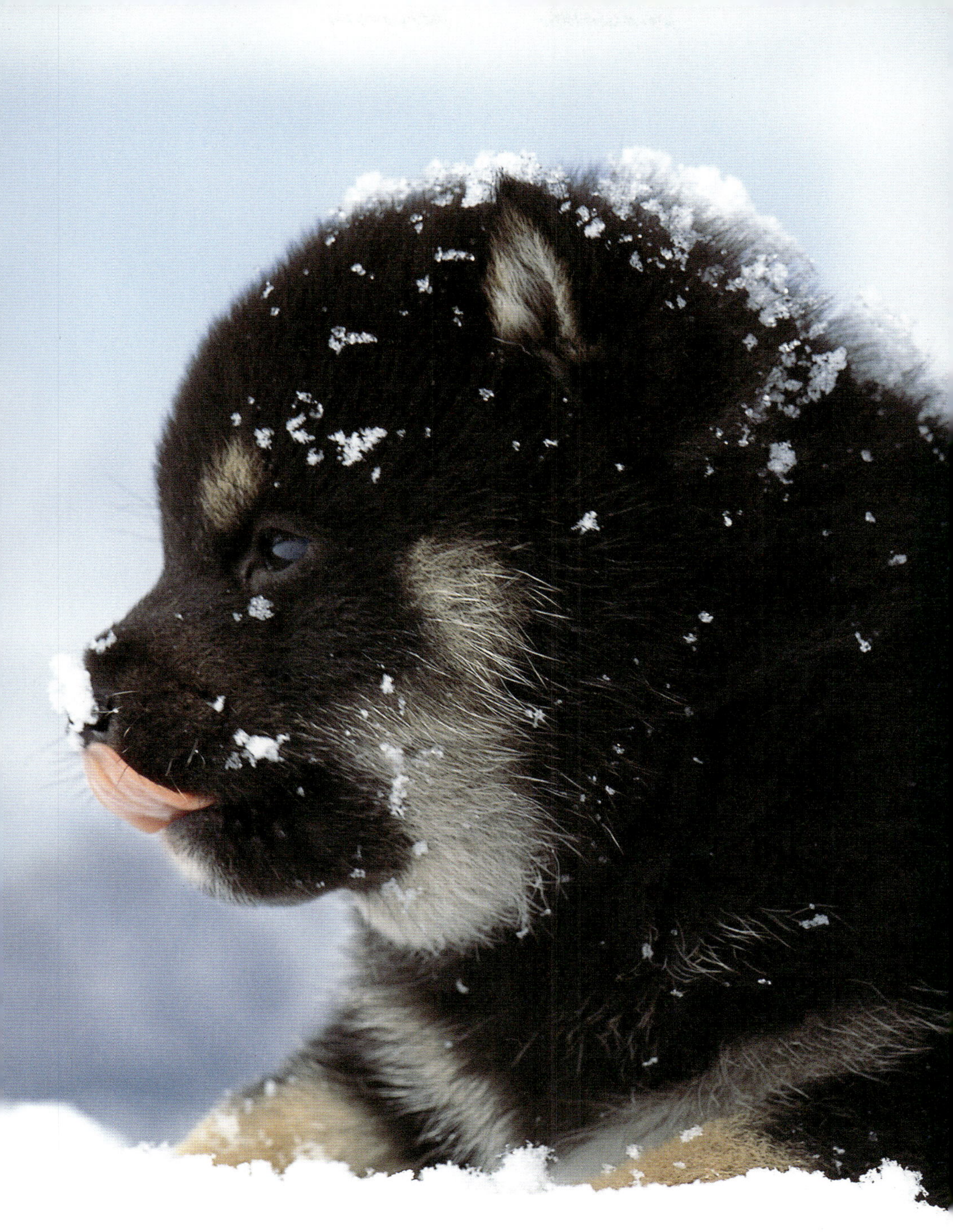

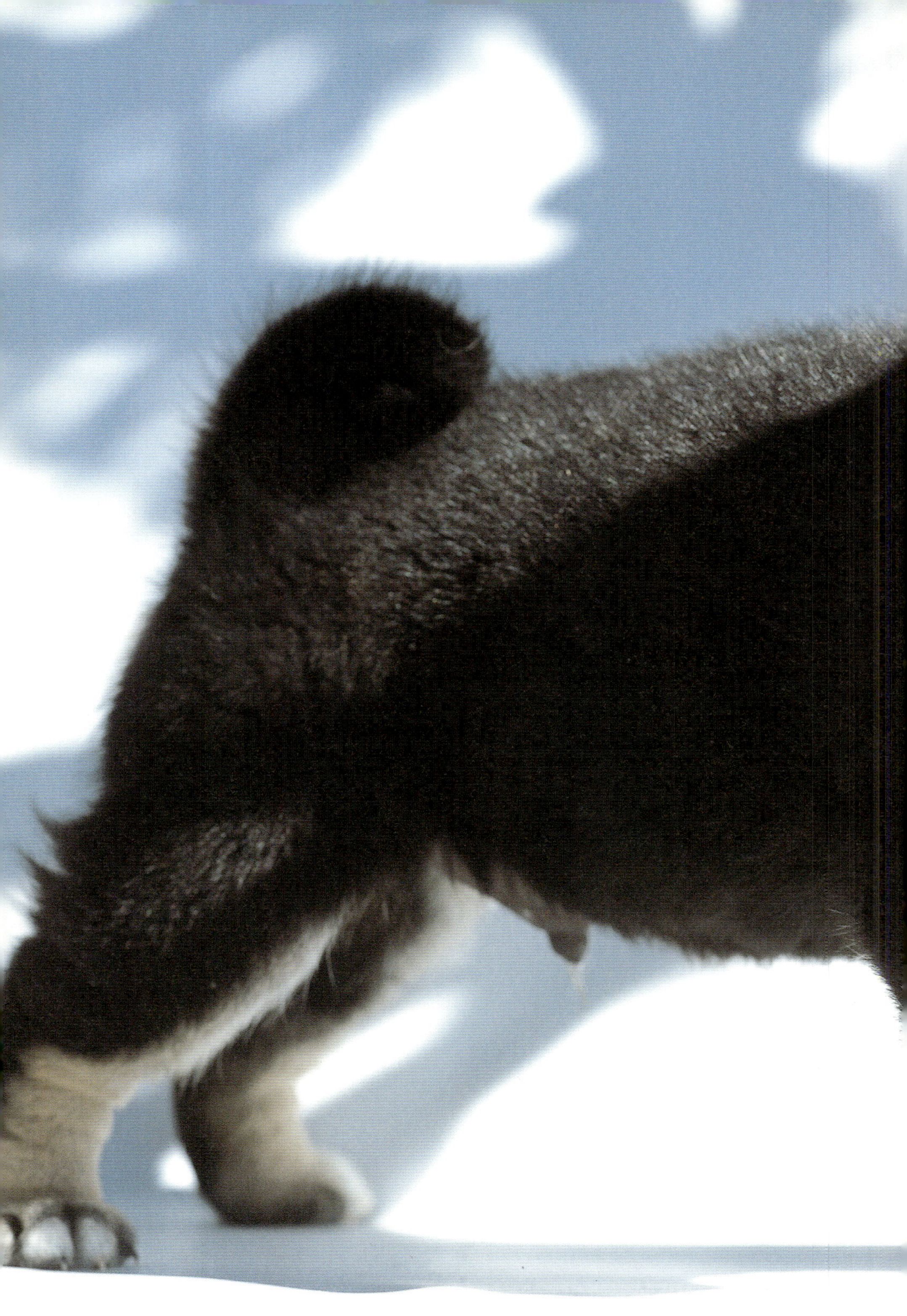

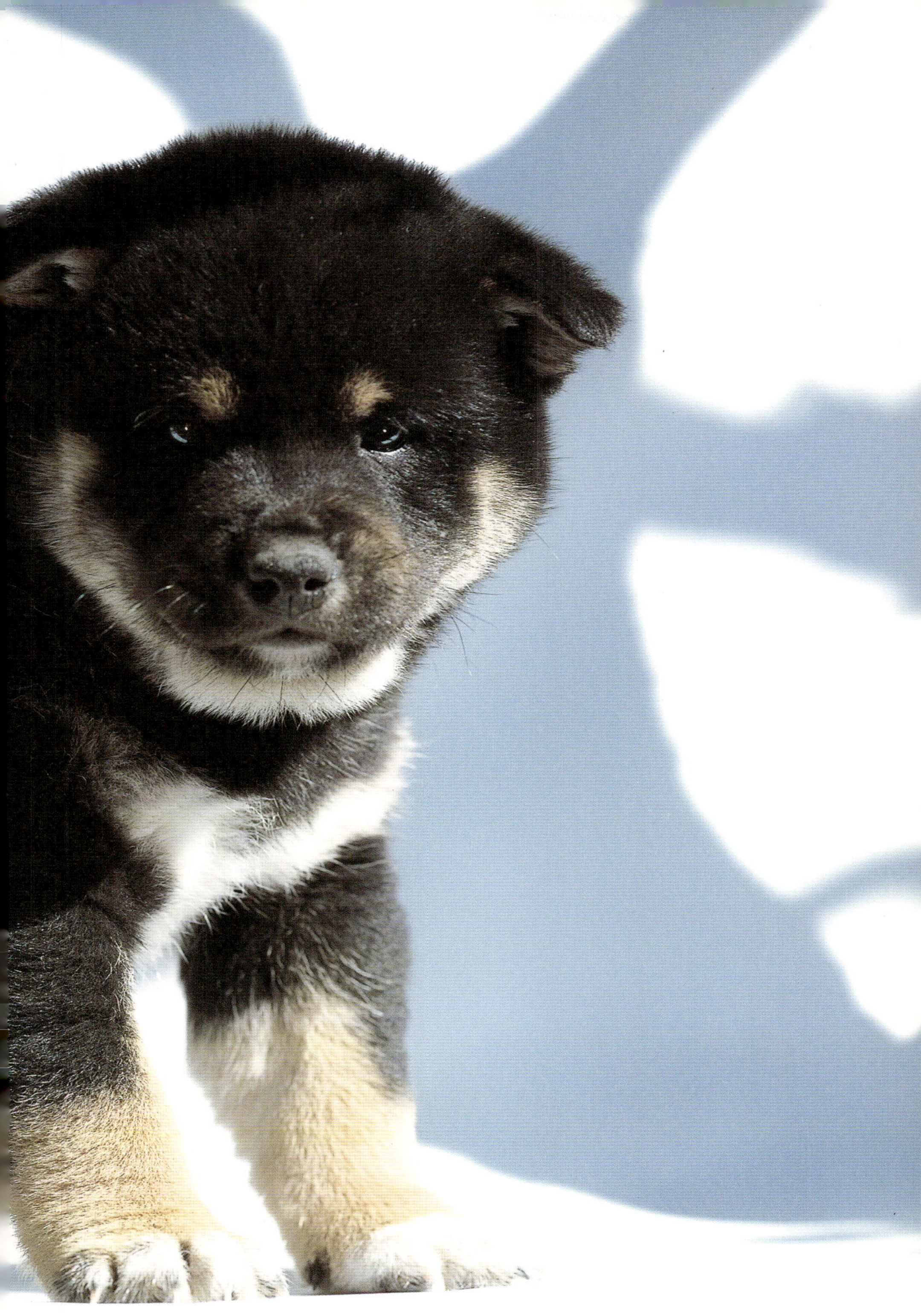

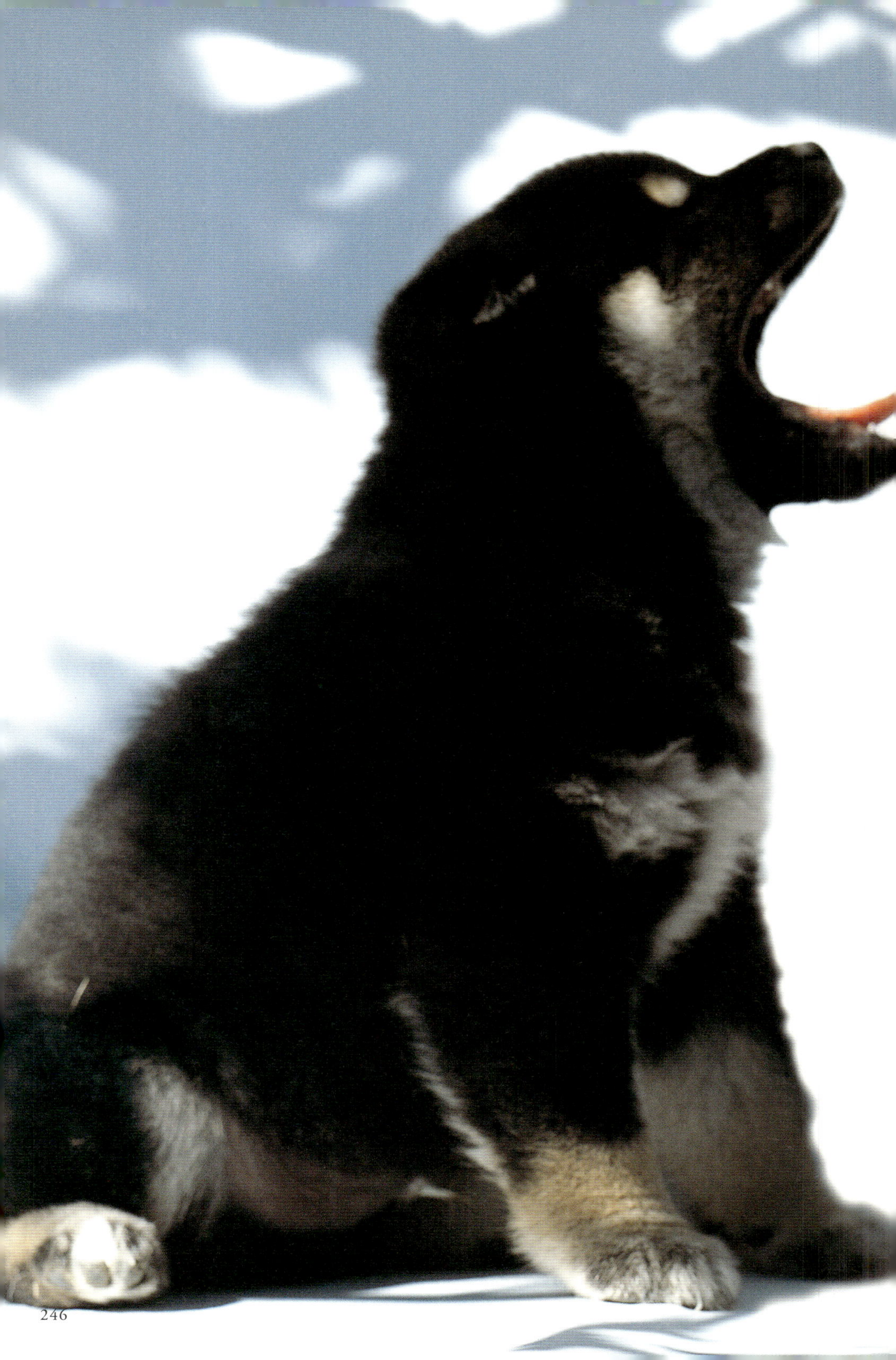

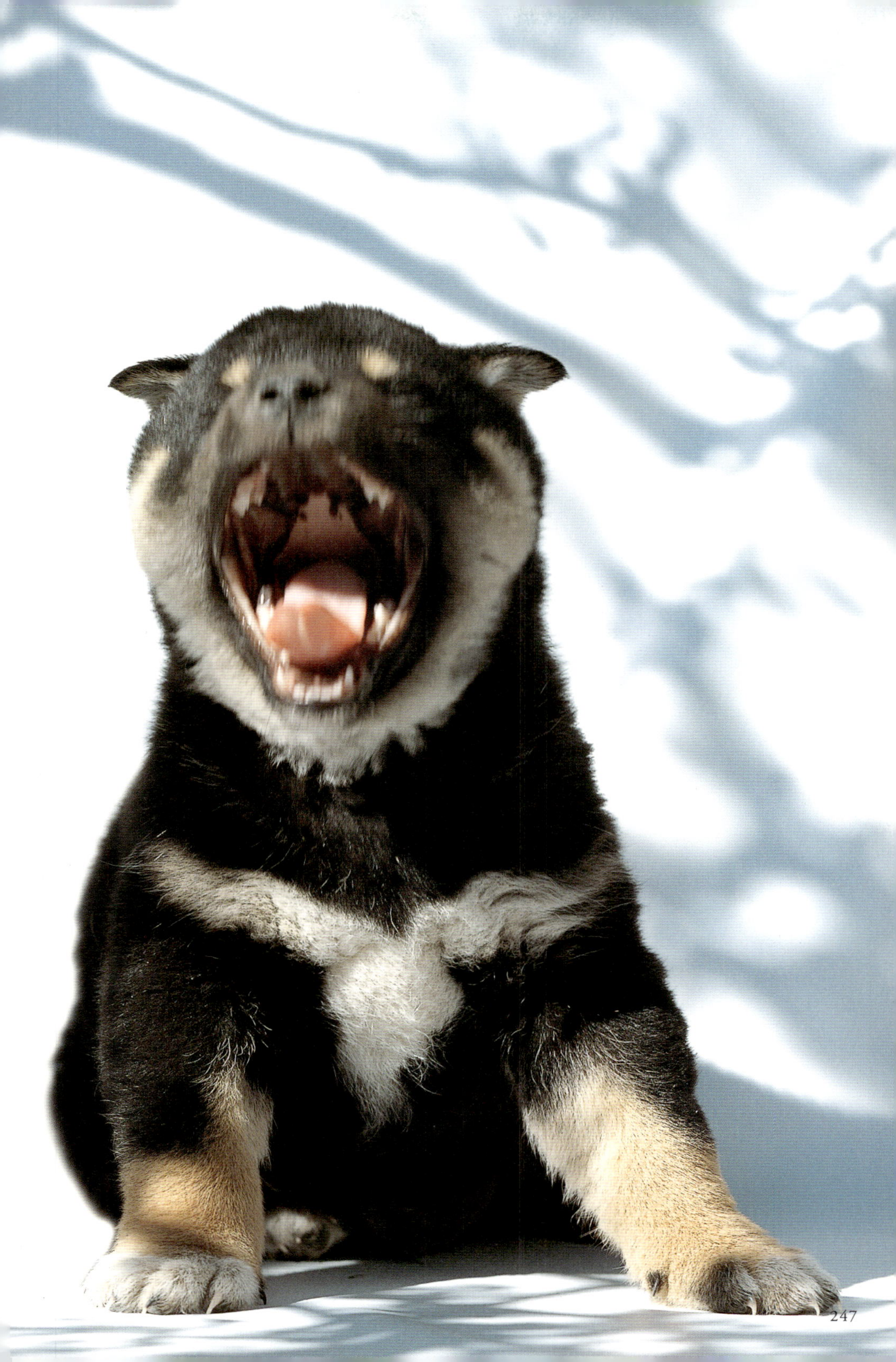

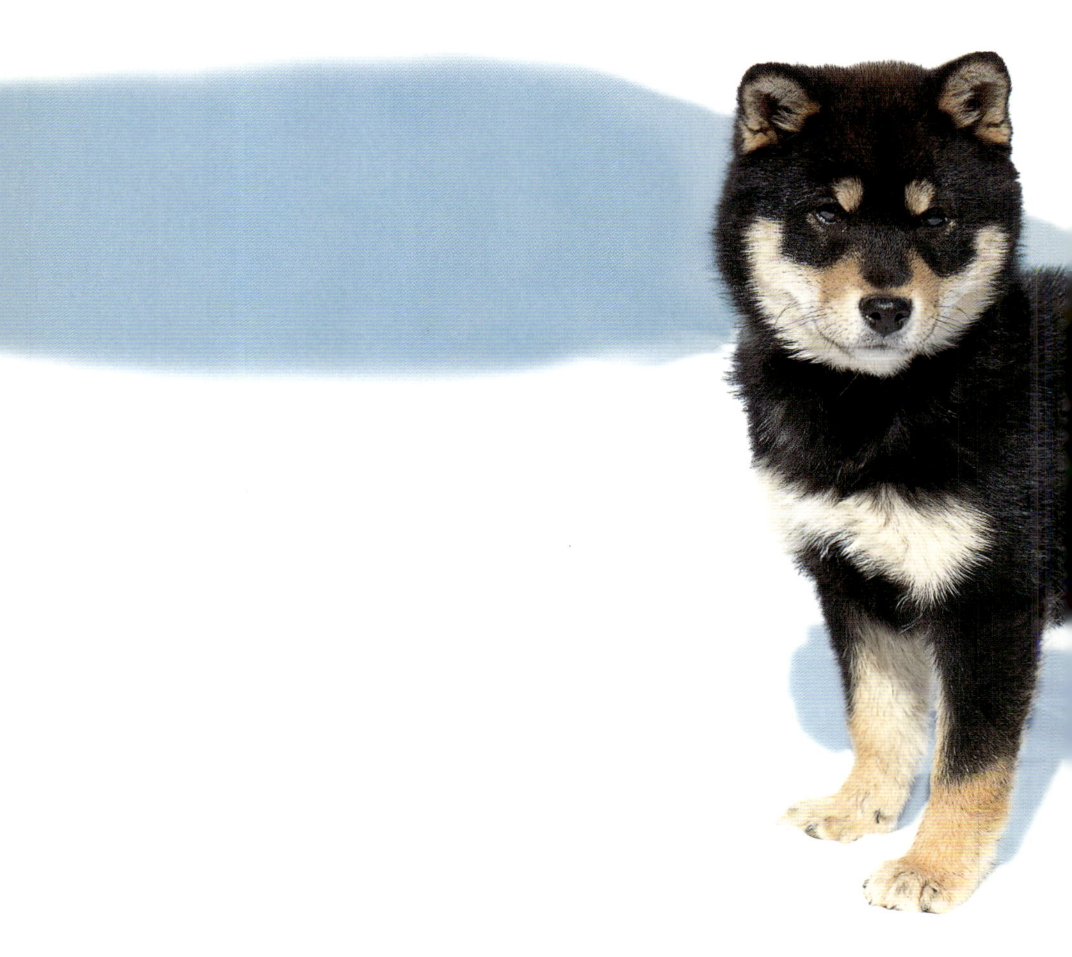

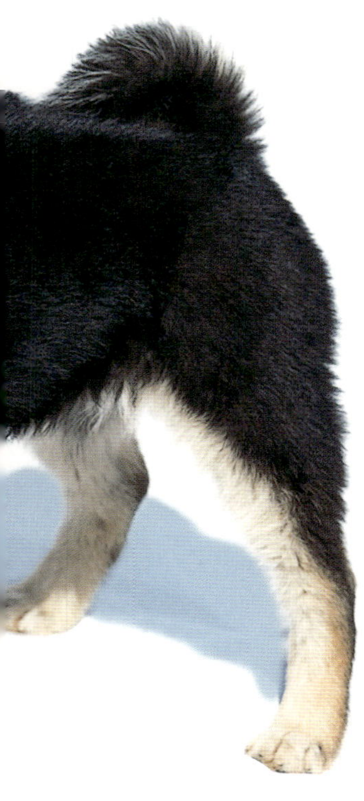

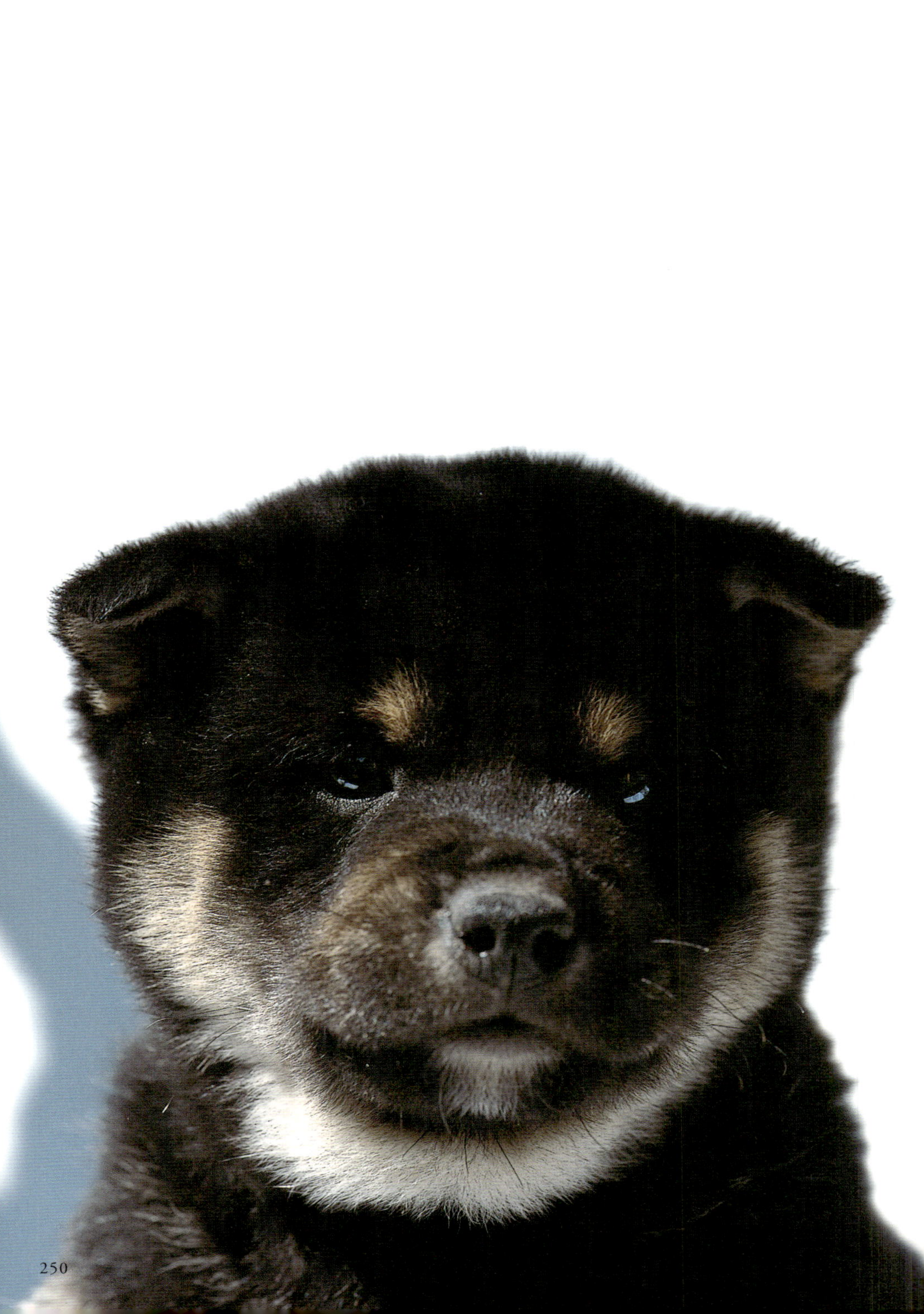

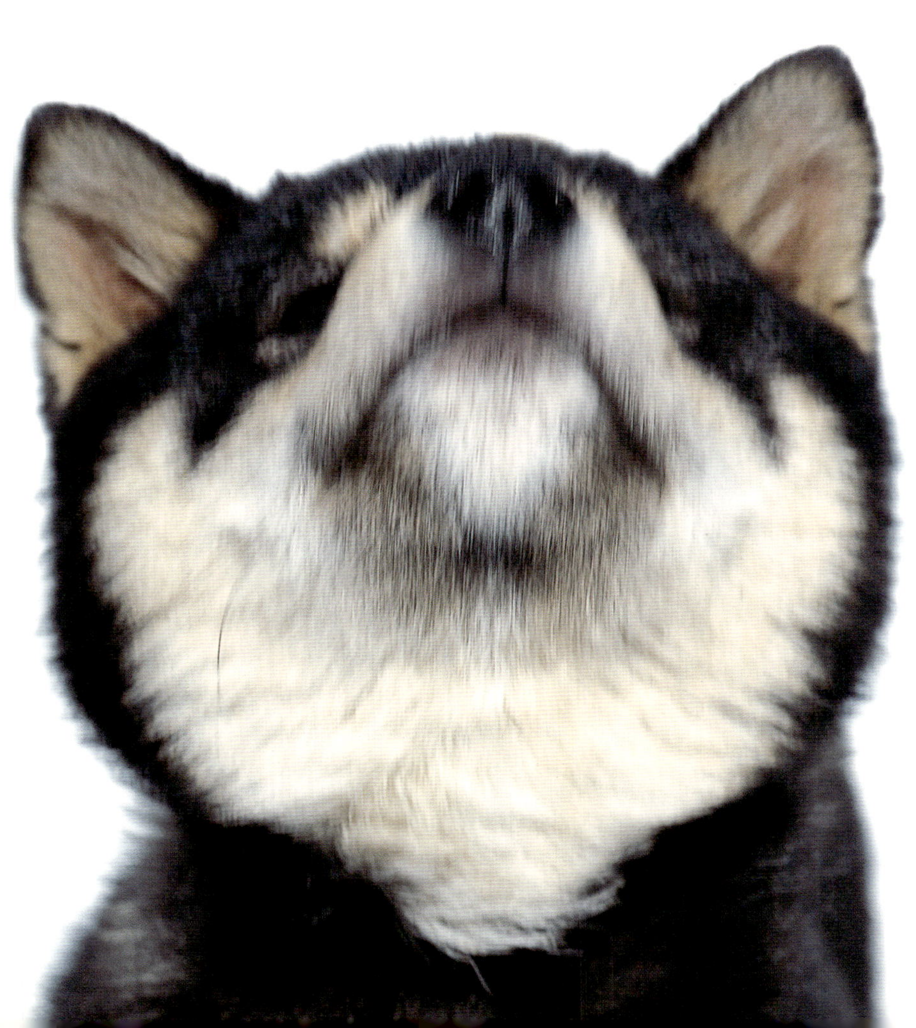

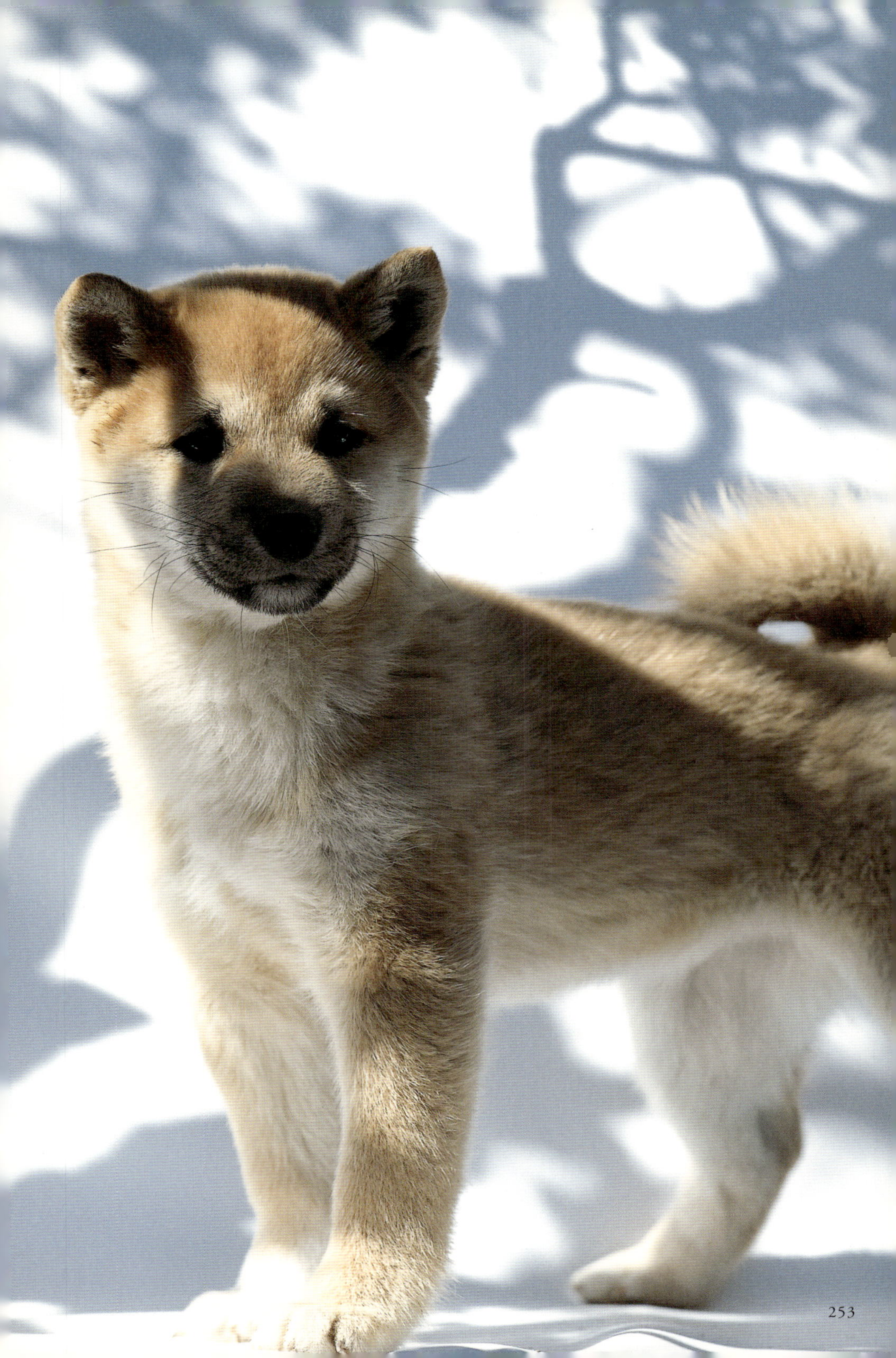

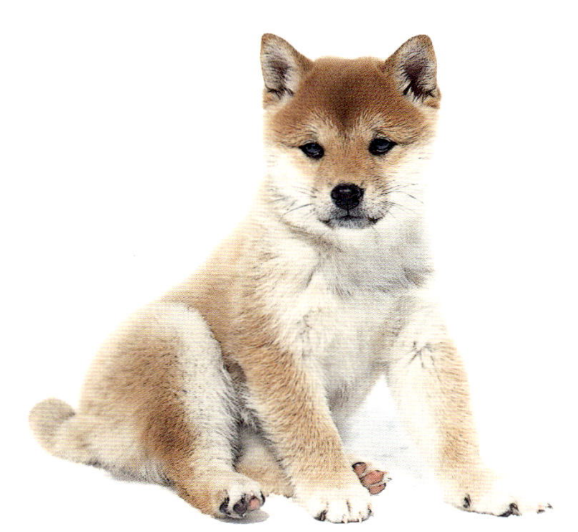

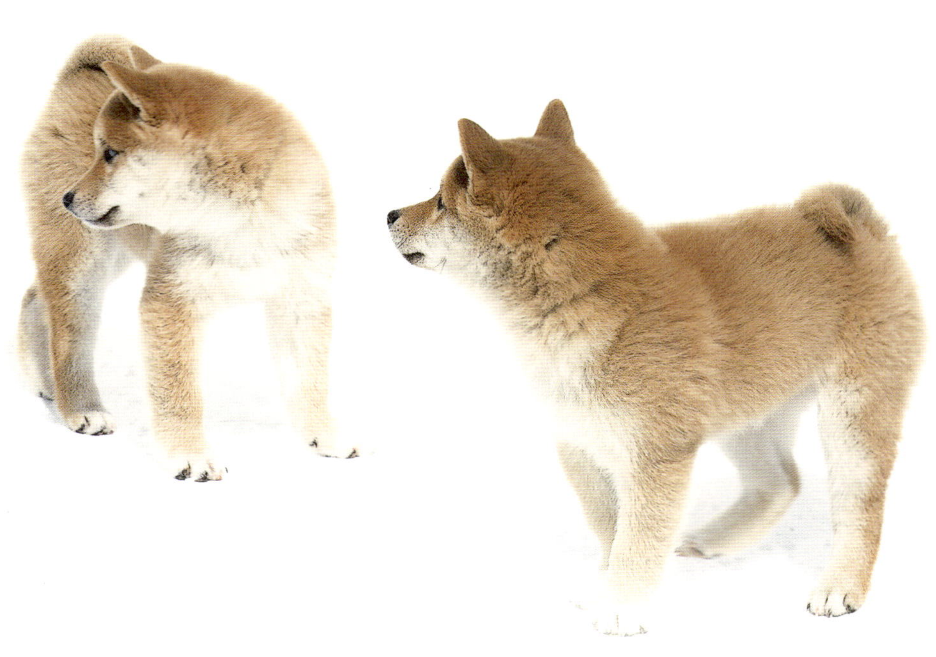

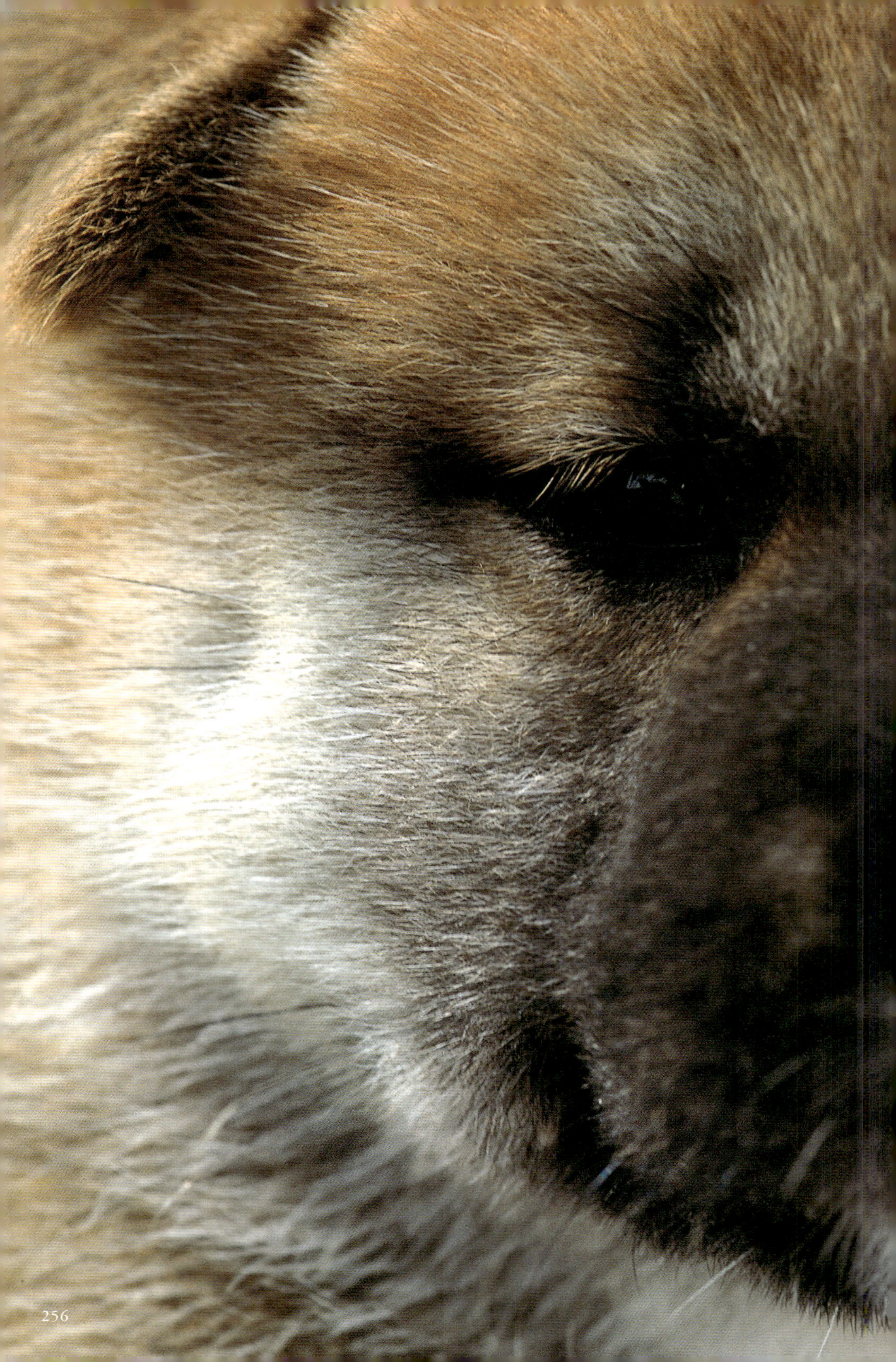

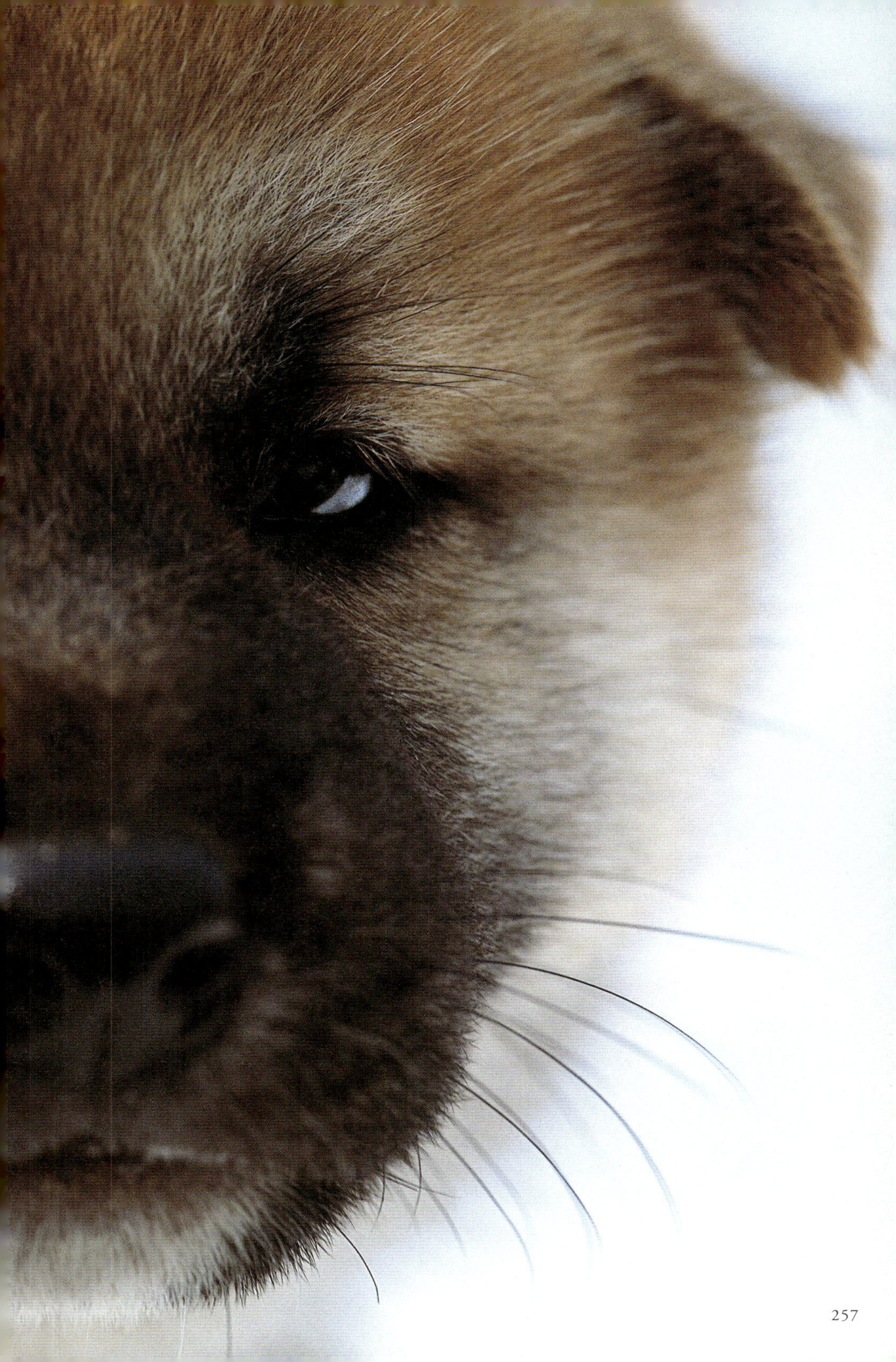

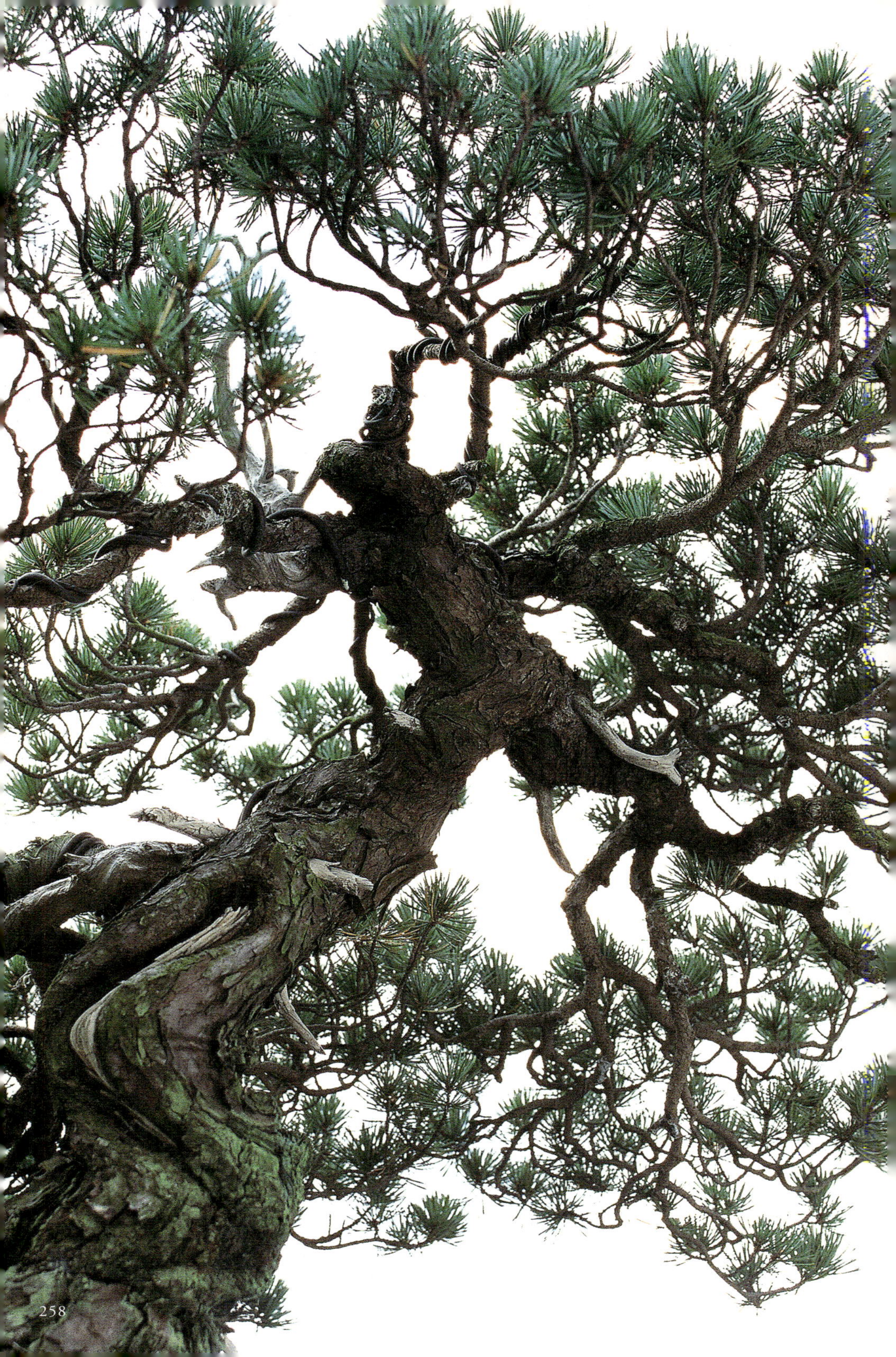

秋
田
犬

Akita Inu

A large dog native to Akita Prefecture.
With its solid build and majestic stature,
the Akita Inu is an impressive breed.
It is obedient and calm,
traits highlighted by the famous episode
involving the dog Hachiko,
who continued waiting outside Tokyo's Shibuya Station
for his owner even after his death.
The Akita Inu has erect ears
and usually a red and white coat,
although some have tawny, sesame,
or even brindled coats.
The tail is always curly and white.
There are few if any colored spots on the tongue.

秋田県を原産とする大型犬。
骨格は頑丈で威風堂々とし、重厚感がある。
温順、沈着で、風格に富む性格は、
東京・渋谷の駅頭で主人を待ち続けた
忠犬ハチ公のエピソードでよく知られている。
立耳で、毛色は赤と白が多いが、虎、淡黄、胡麻もある。
尾はすべて巻き尾で、裏白。
舌斑はほとんどない。
秋田犬

あきたいぬ

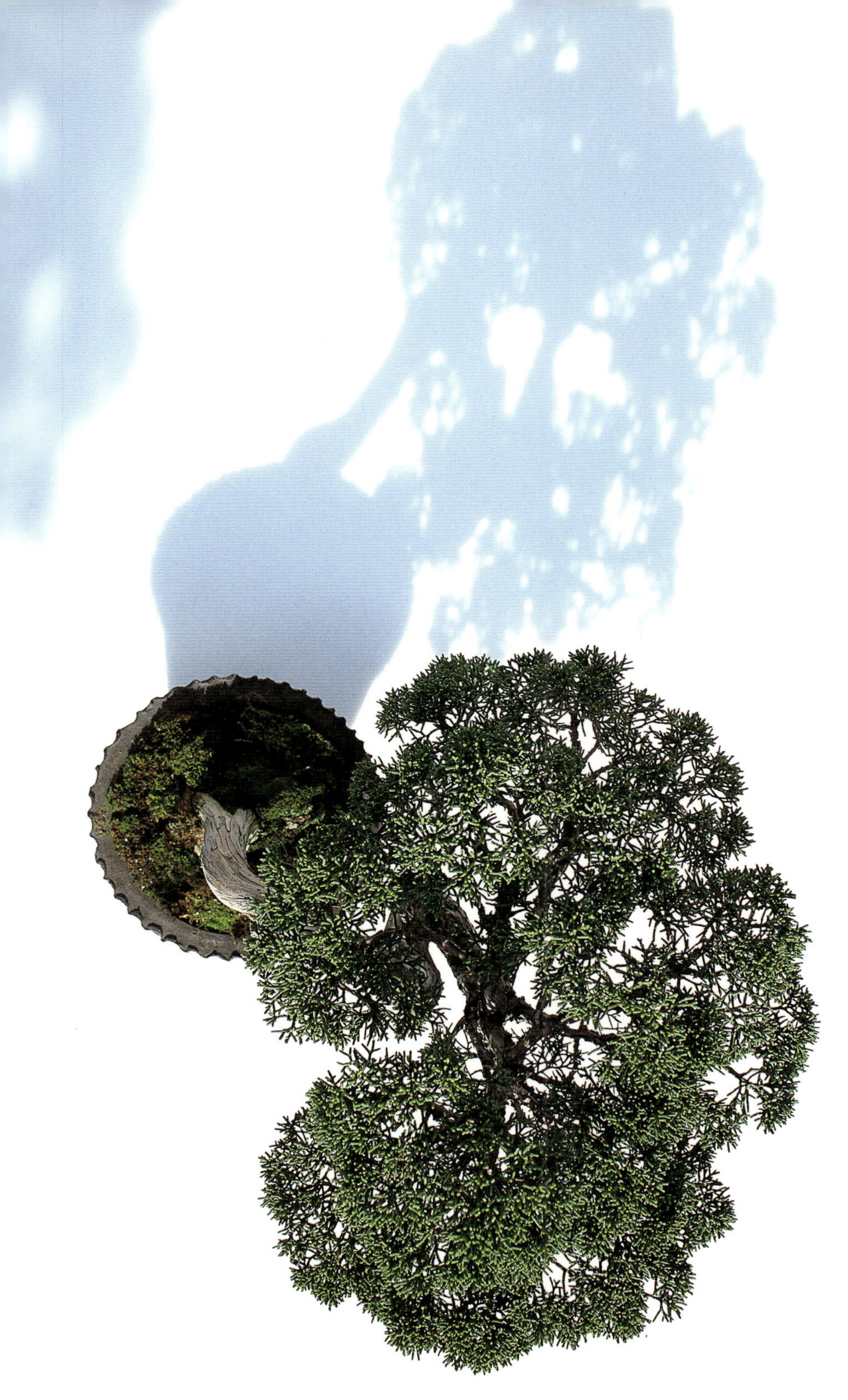

Akita Inu

Descendants of Akita Inu taken back to the U.S.
after the Second World War by American troops in Japan
as part of the occupation forces subsequently
found their way to other countries around the world,
where they are known as American Akita Dogs.
Males grow to a height of 62 cm,
while females grow to 57 cm.
The Akita Inu was designated
a Natural Monument in 1931.

第二次世界大戦後に占領軍兵士の帰国とともに
アメリカに渡った秋田犬の子孫は、
アメリカン・アキタ・ドッグとして
世界各地に広がっている。
体高は雄 62 センチ、雌 57 センチ。
昭和 6 年、国の天然記念物に指定。

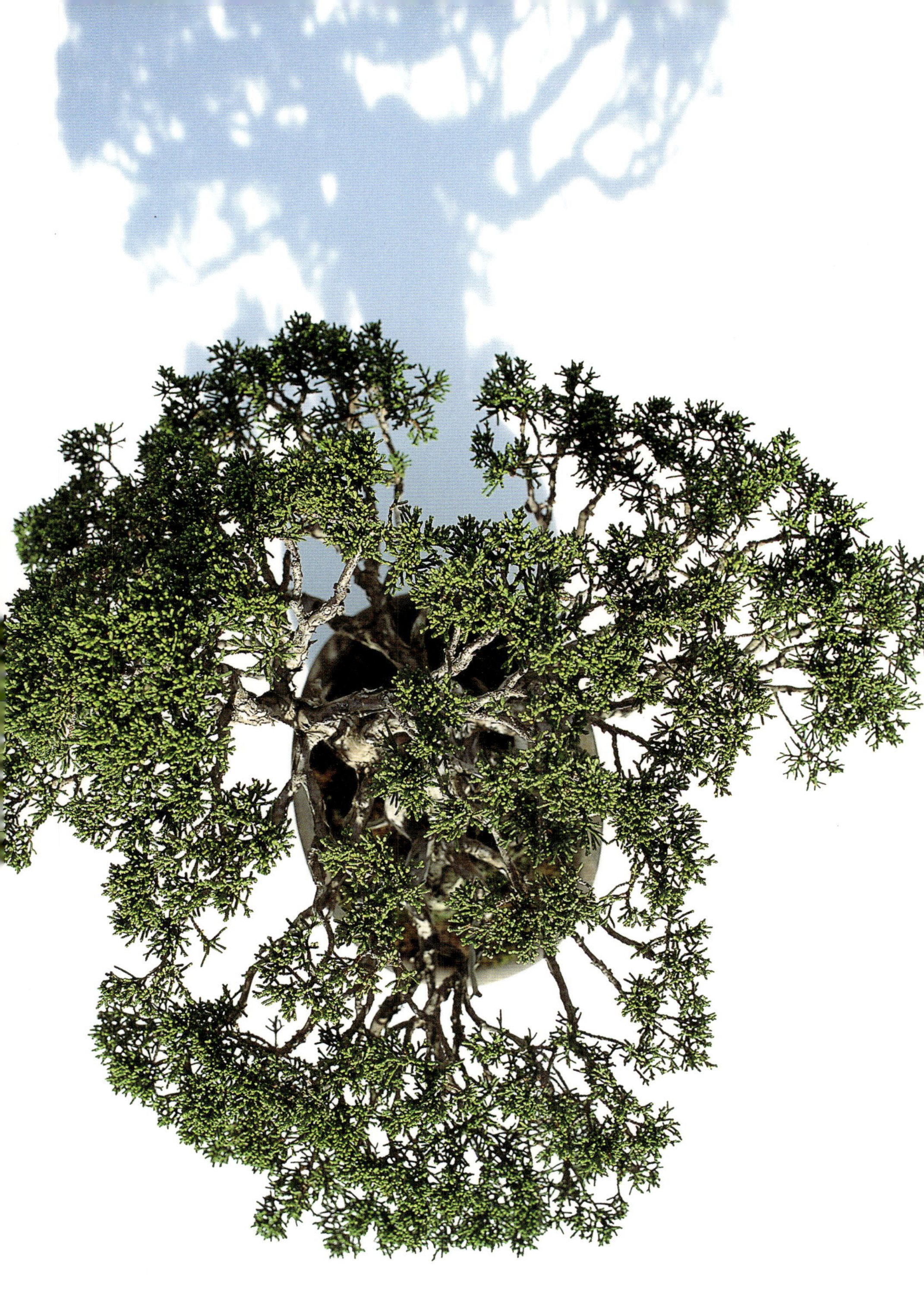

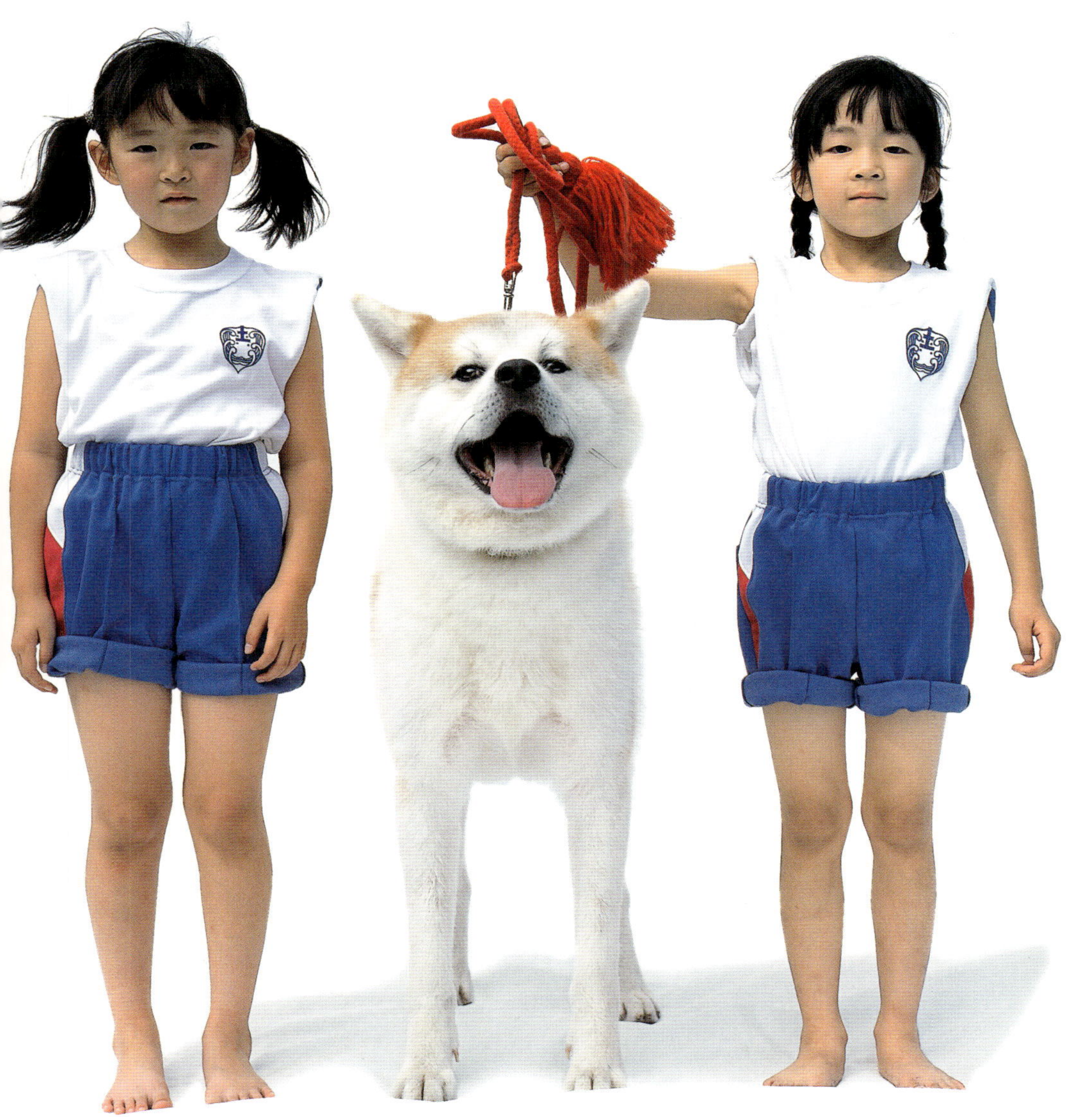

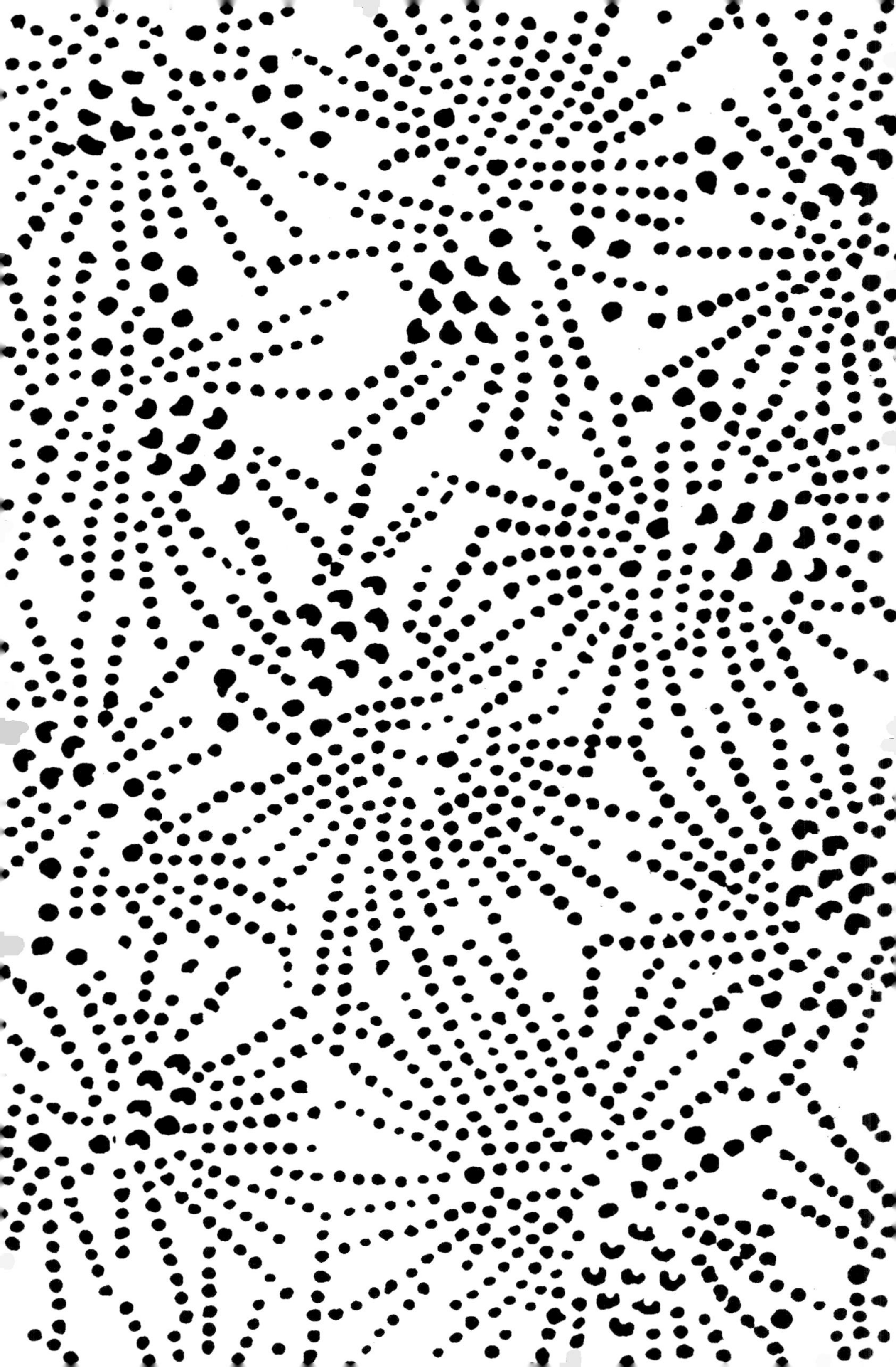

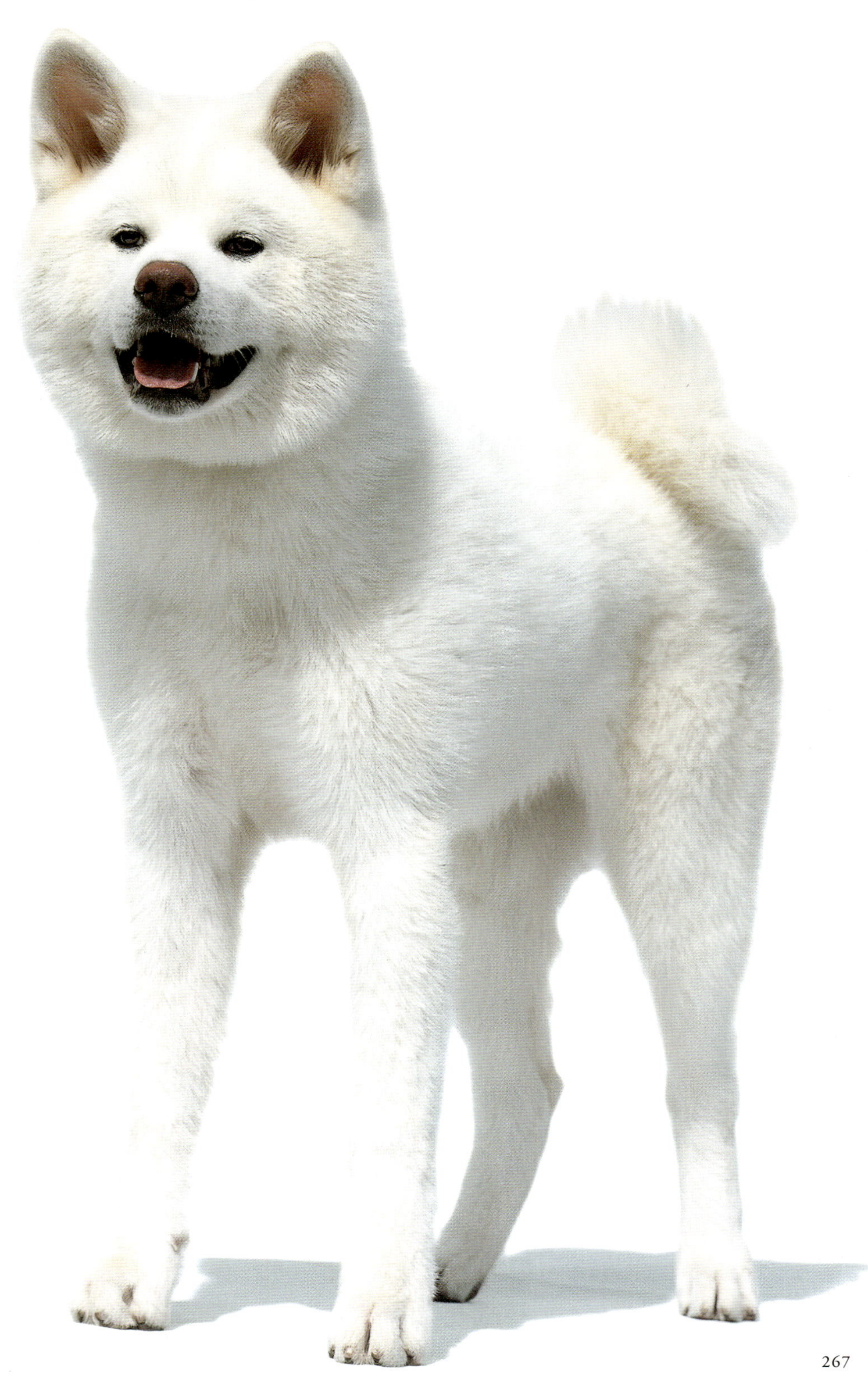

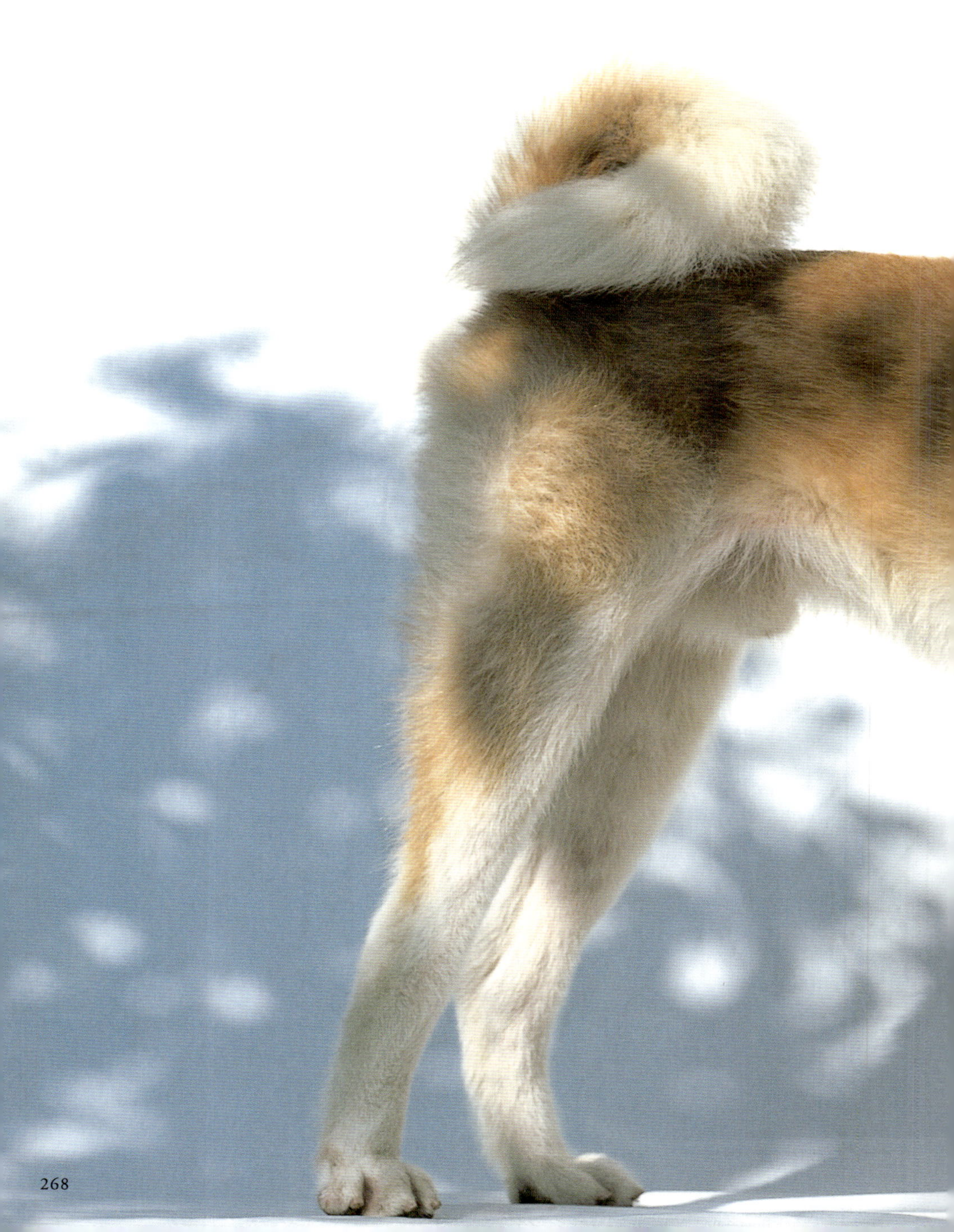

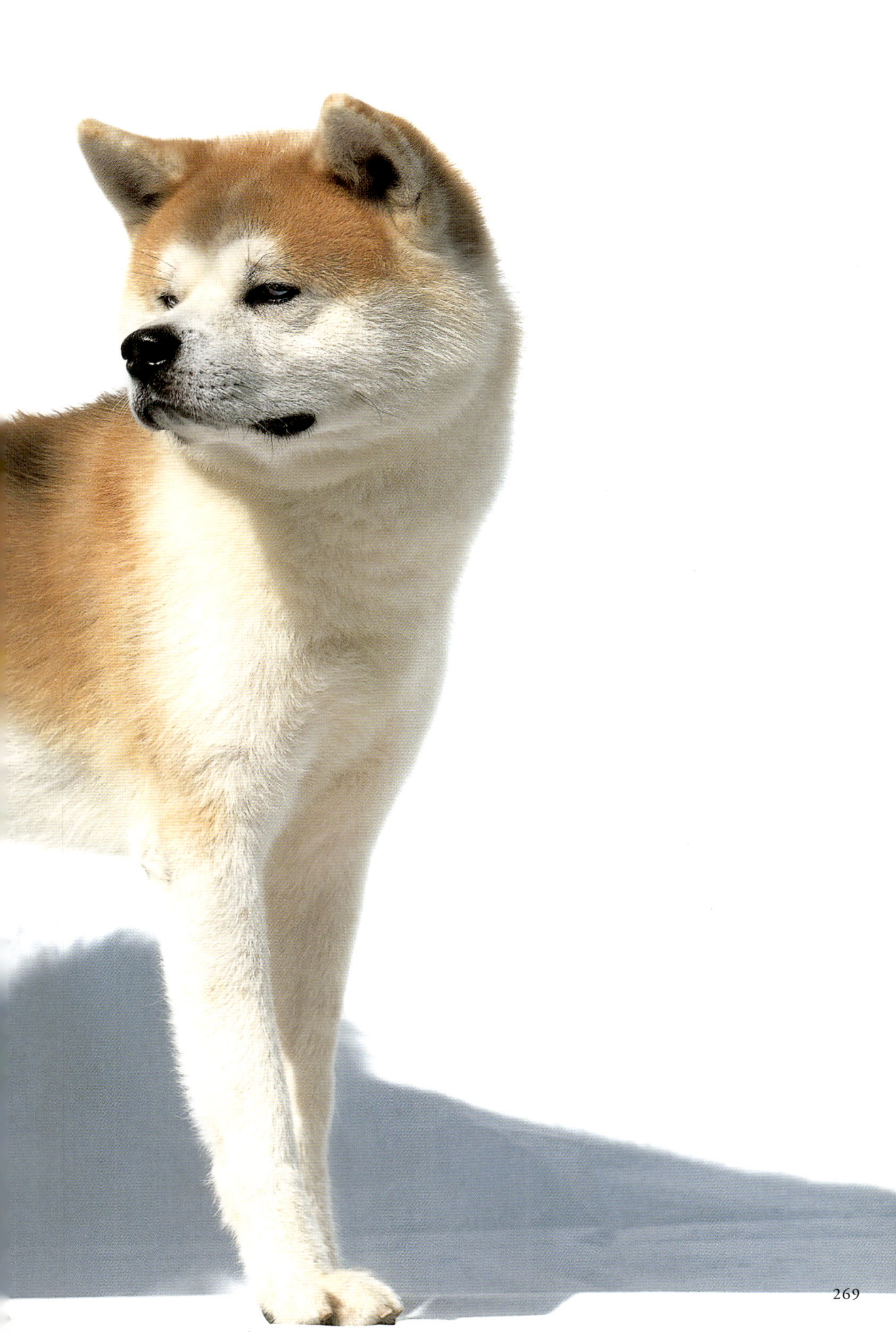

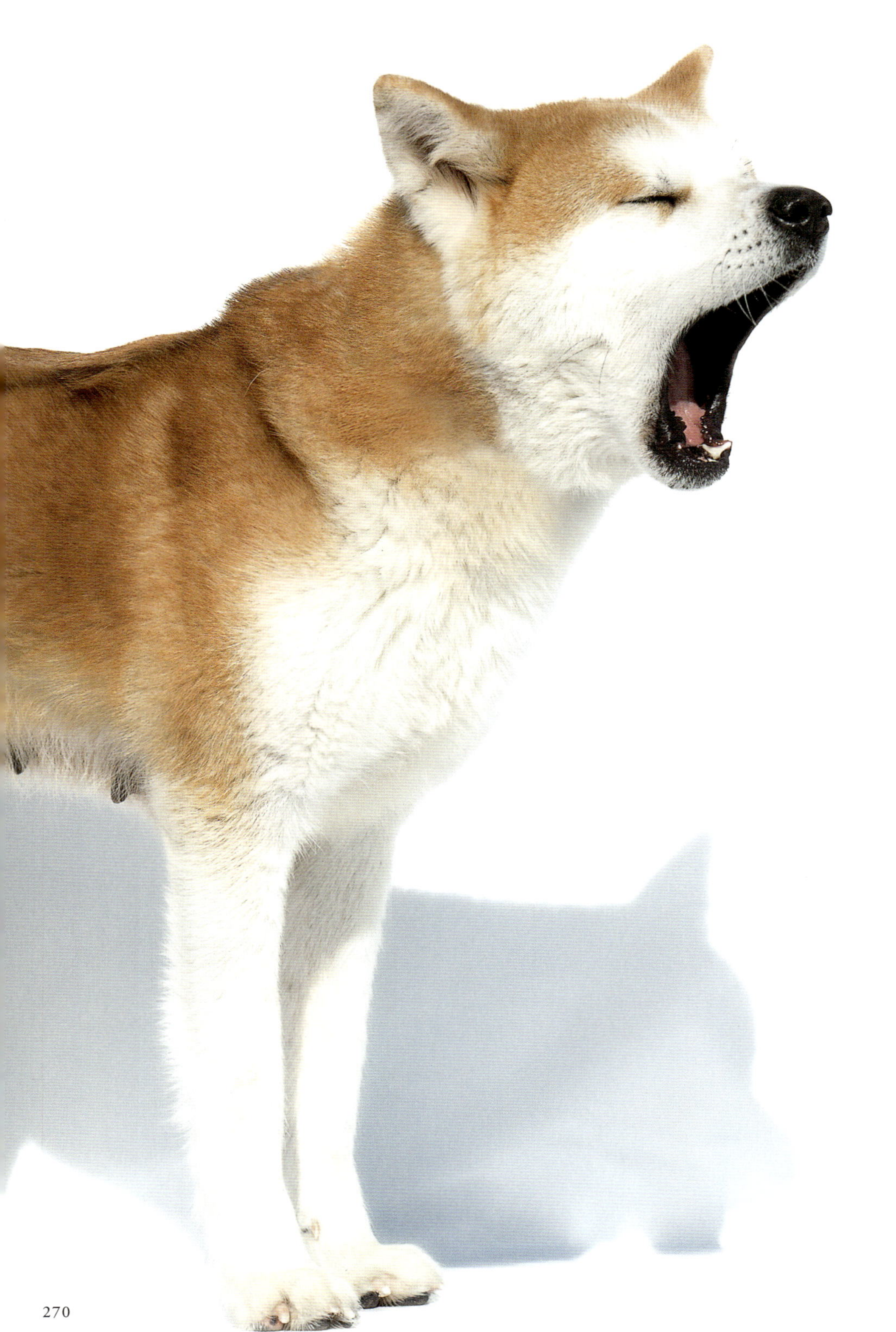

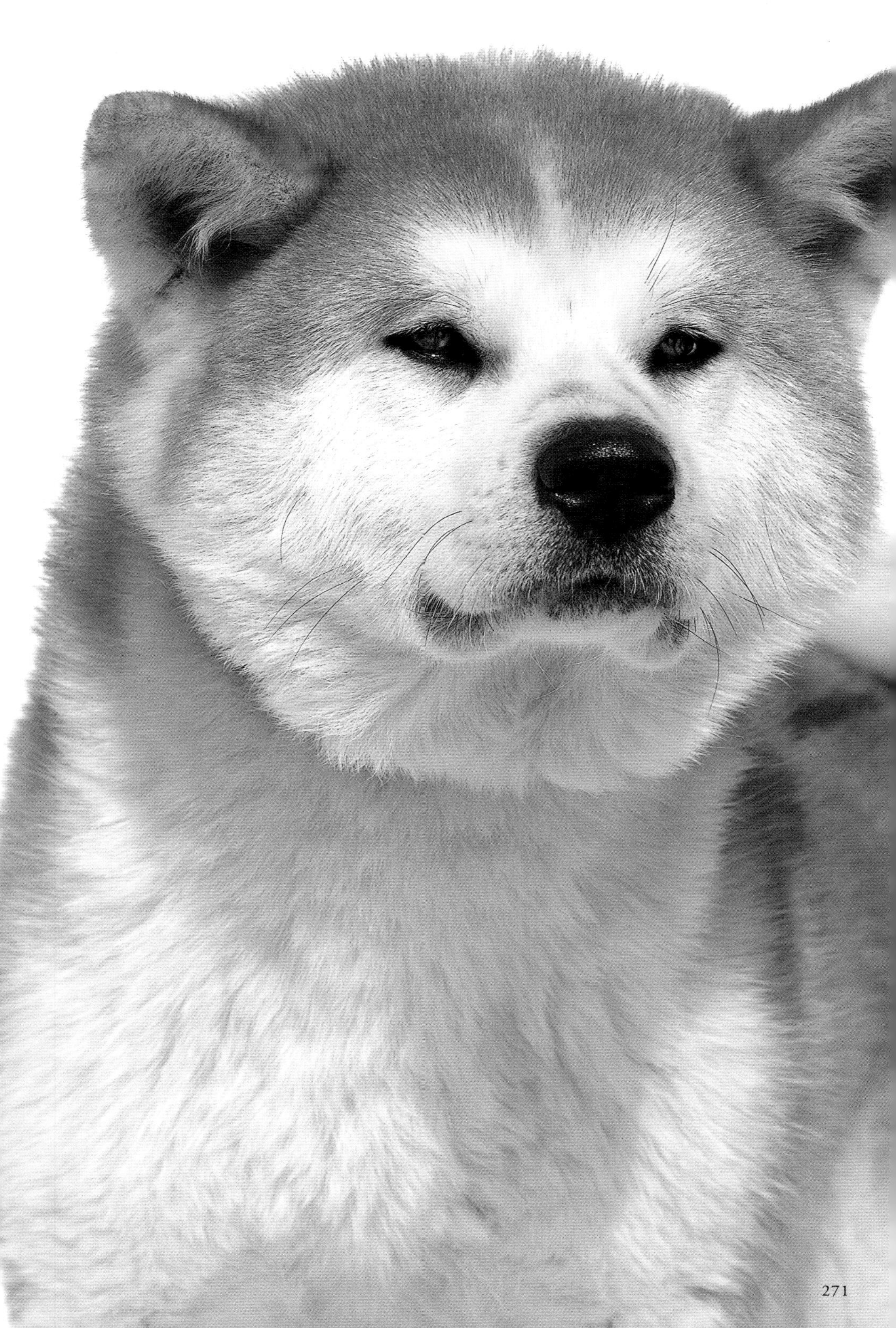

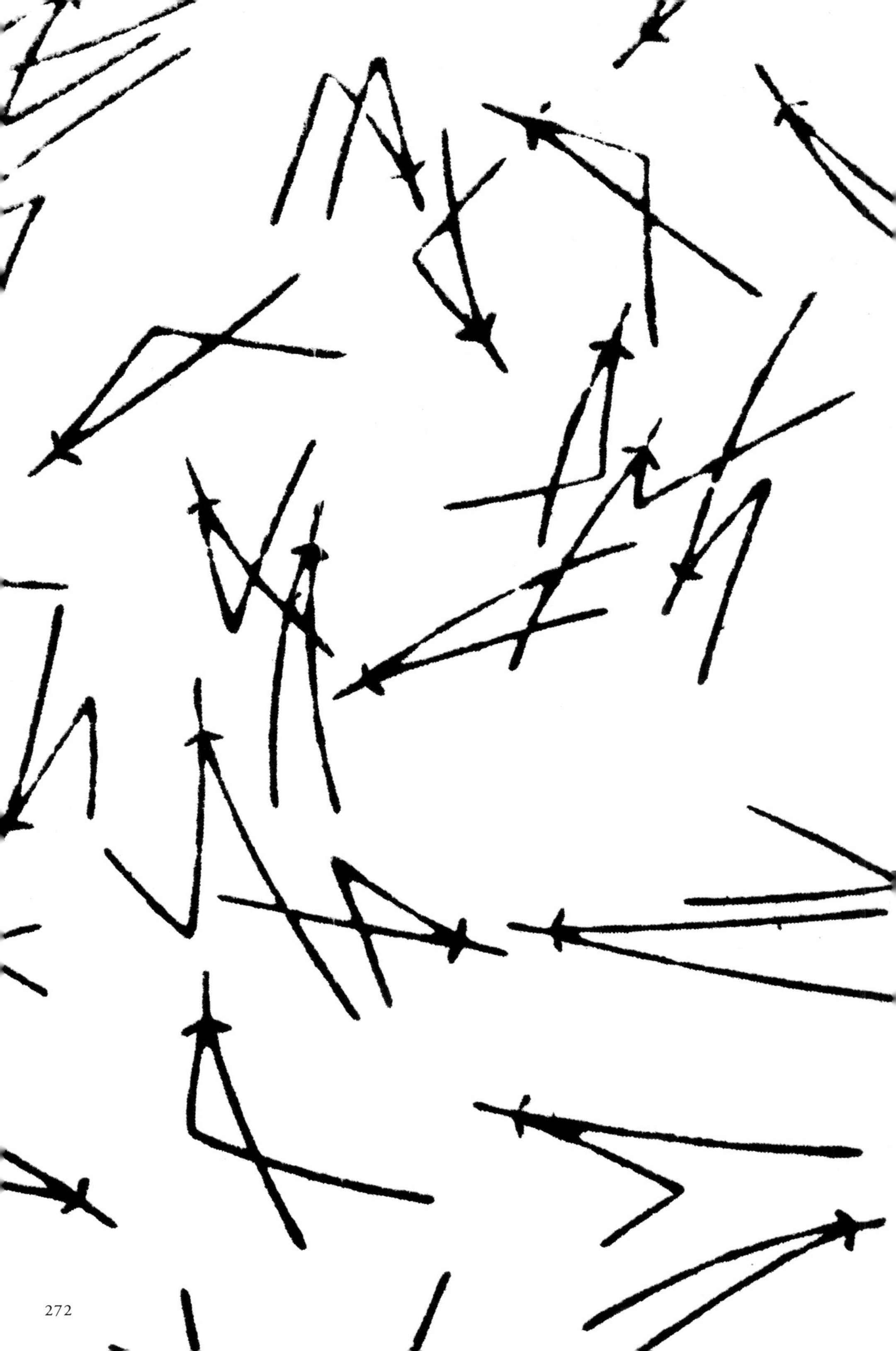

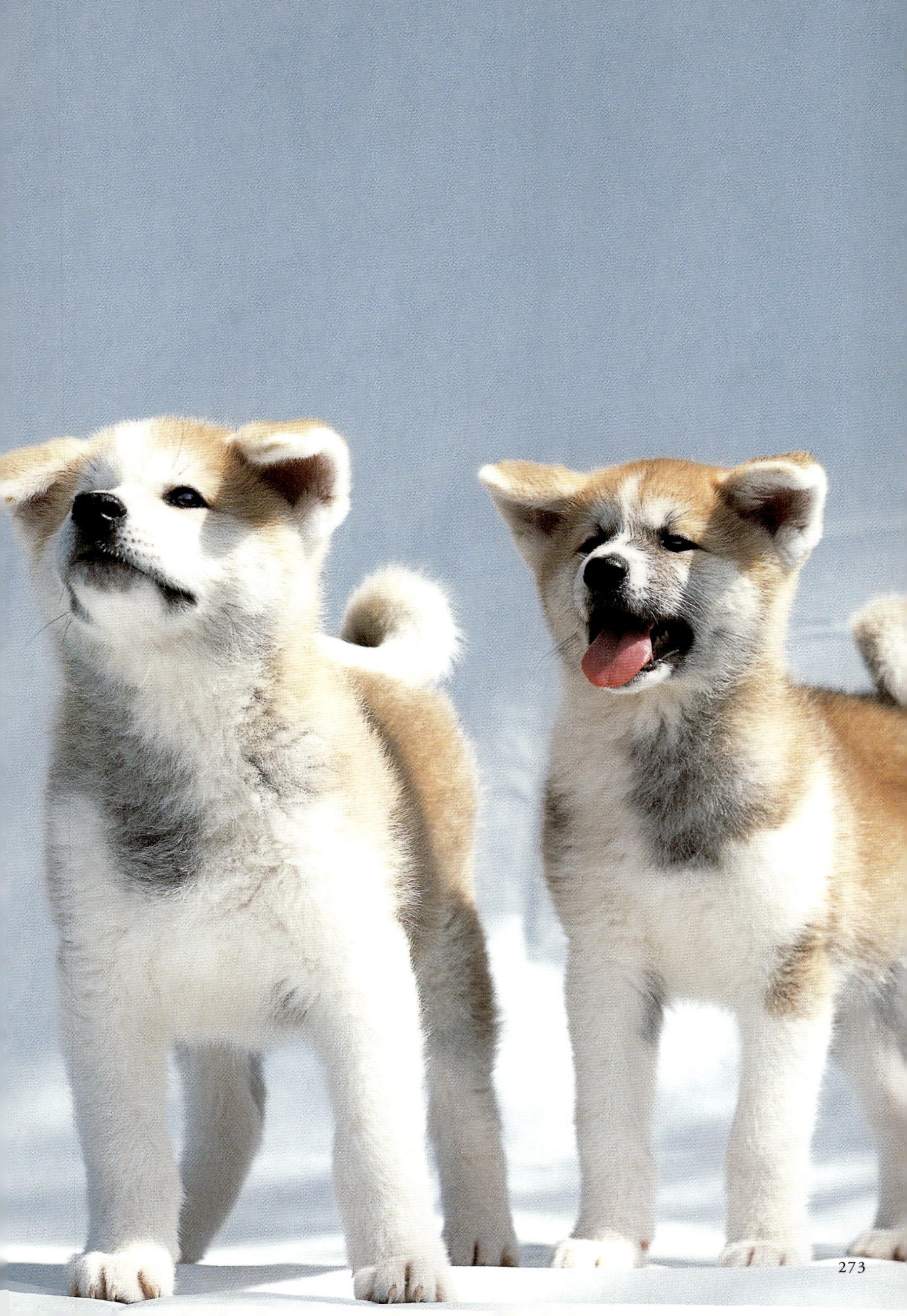

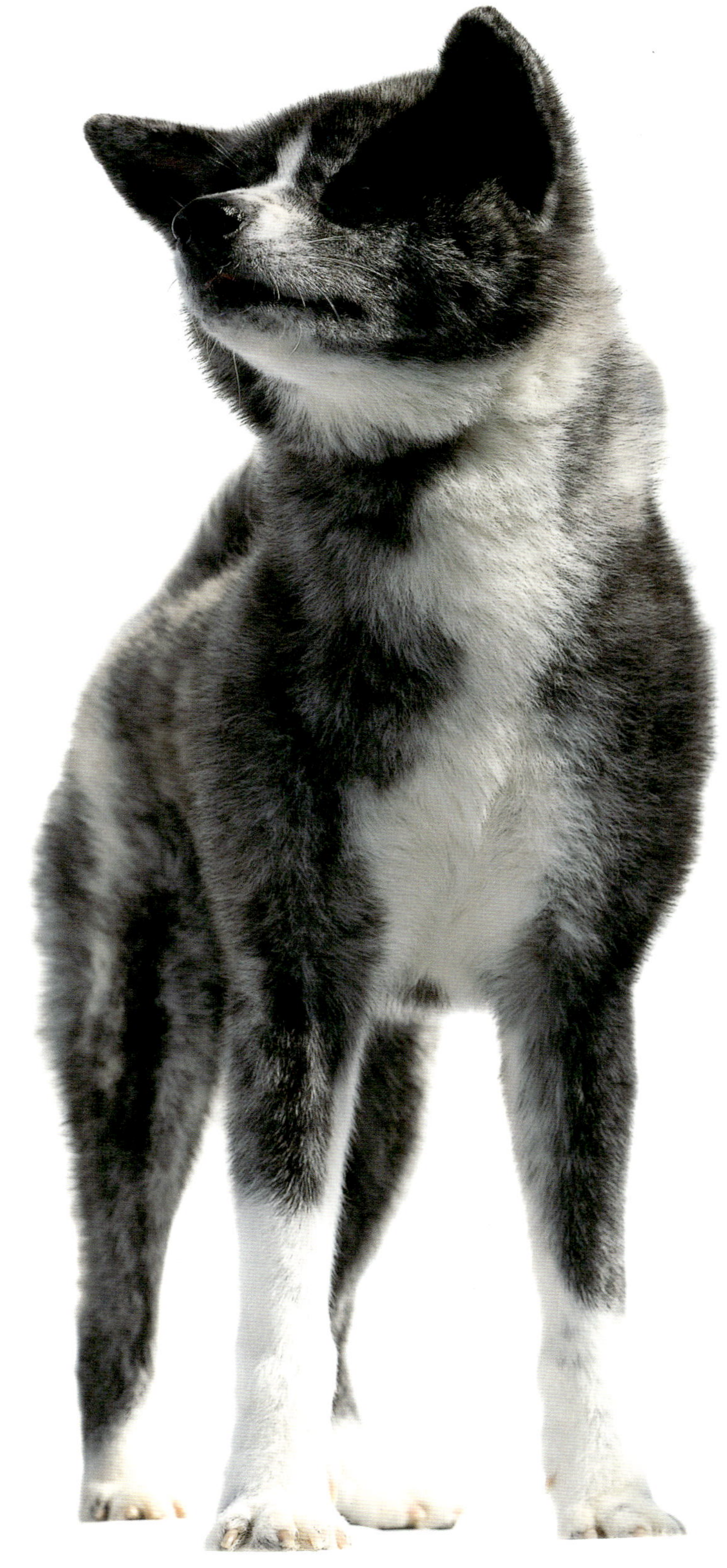

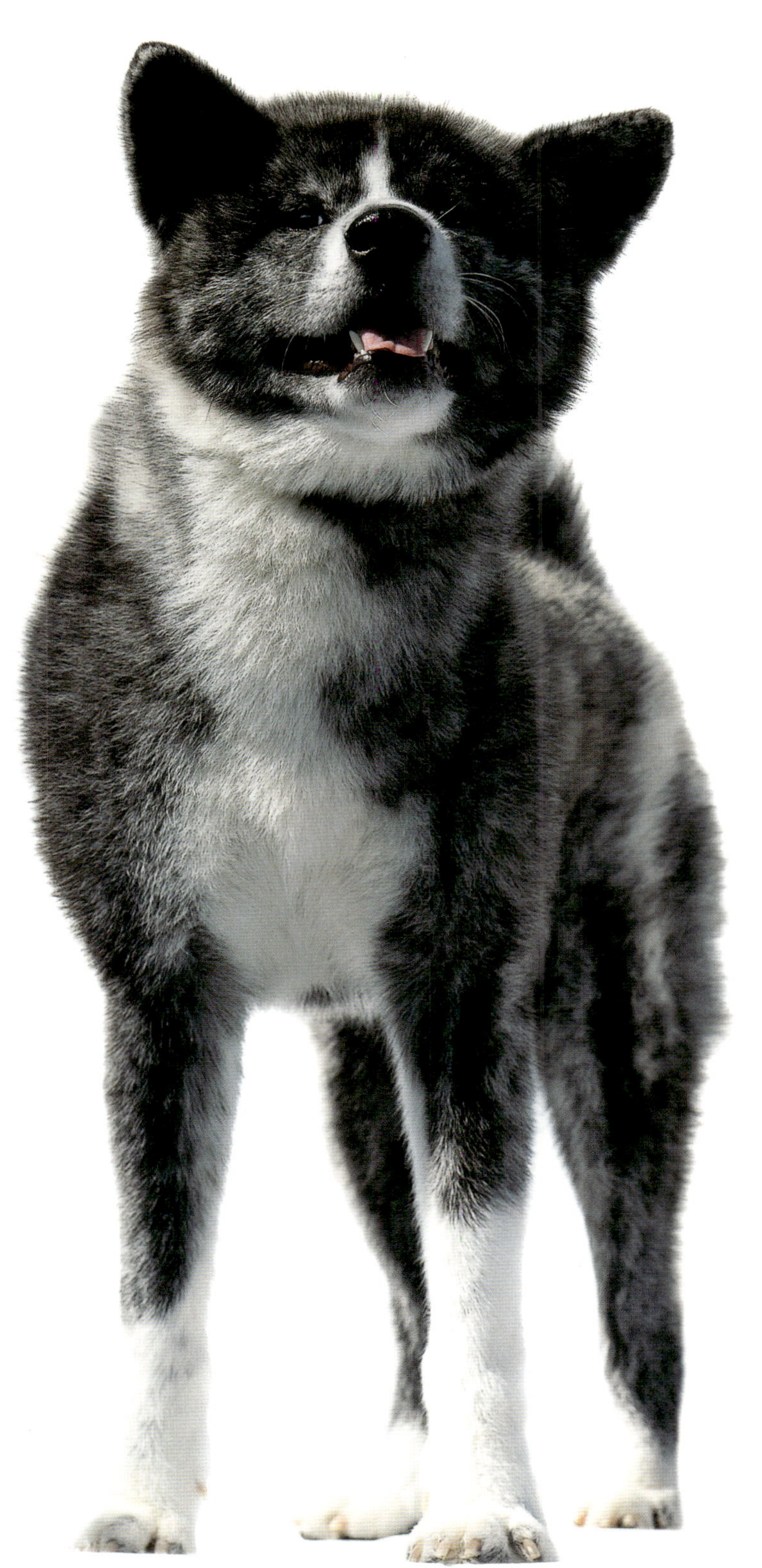

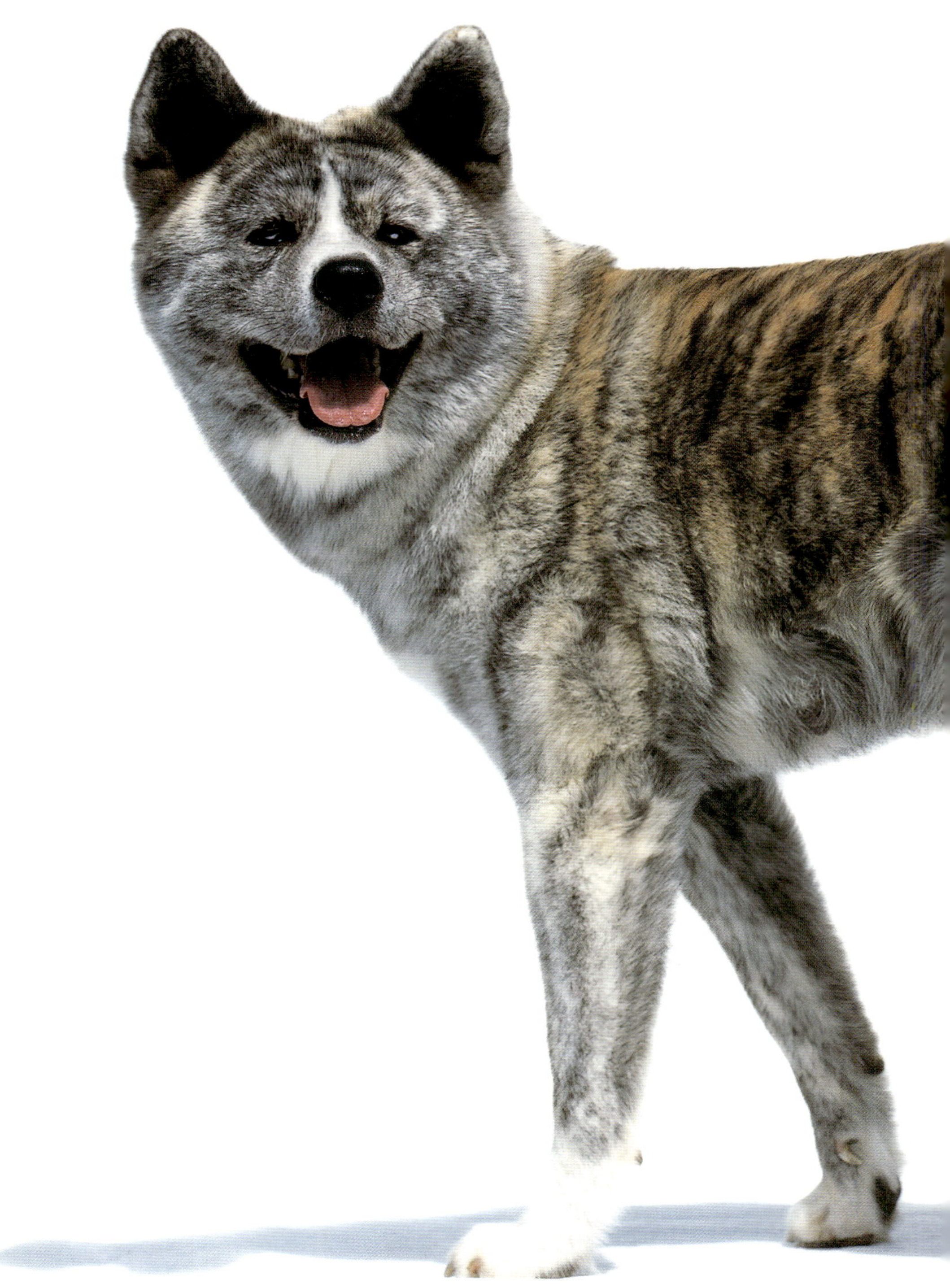

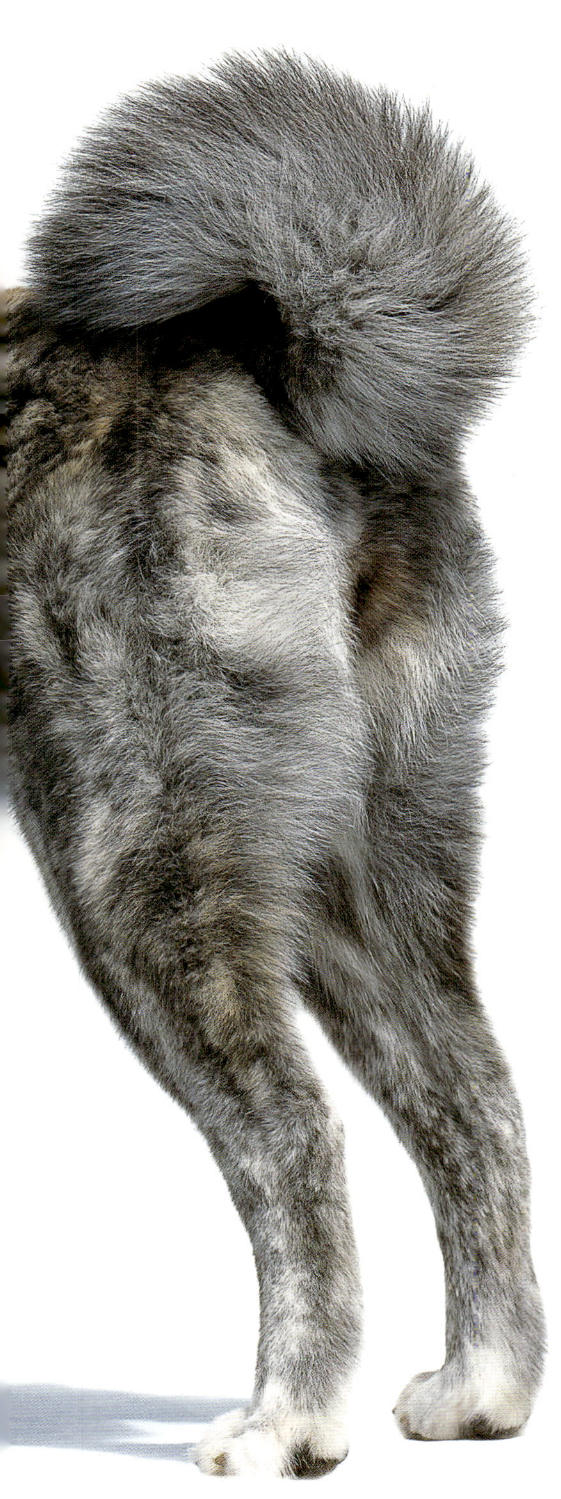

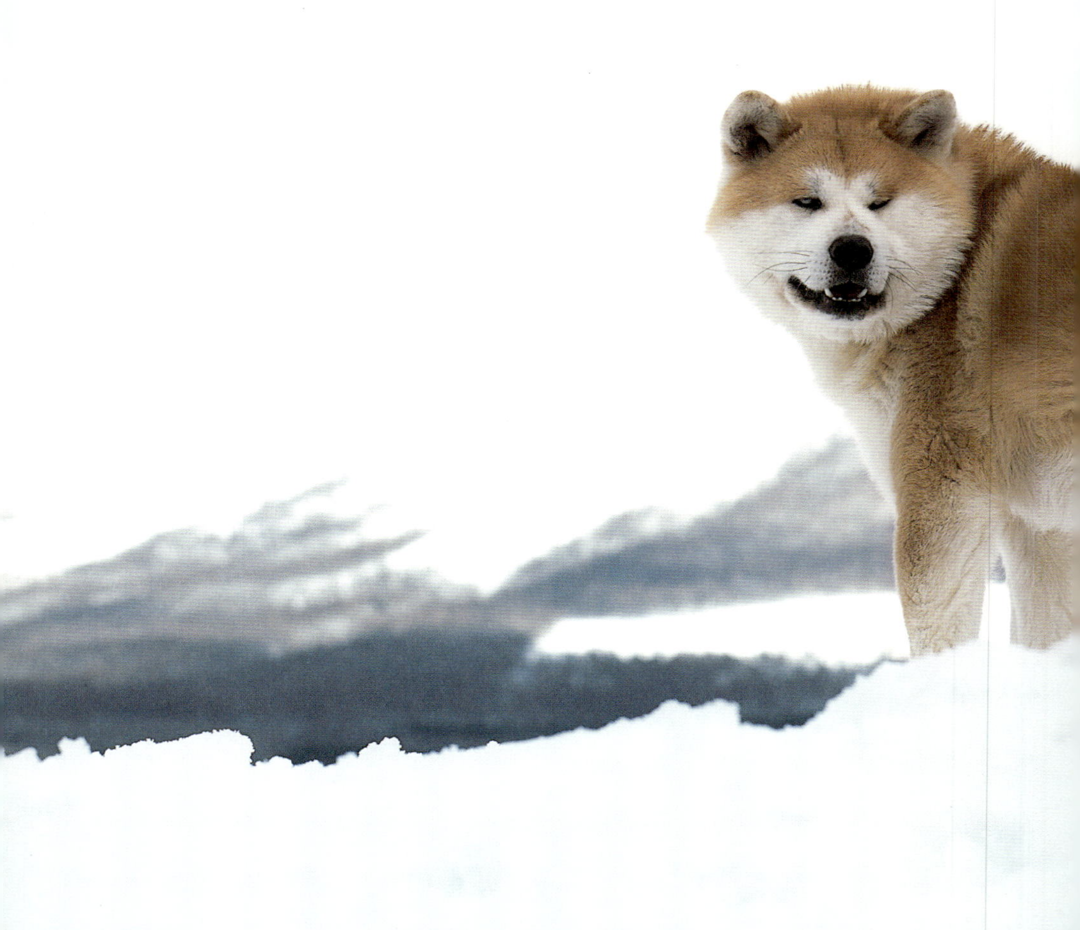

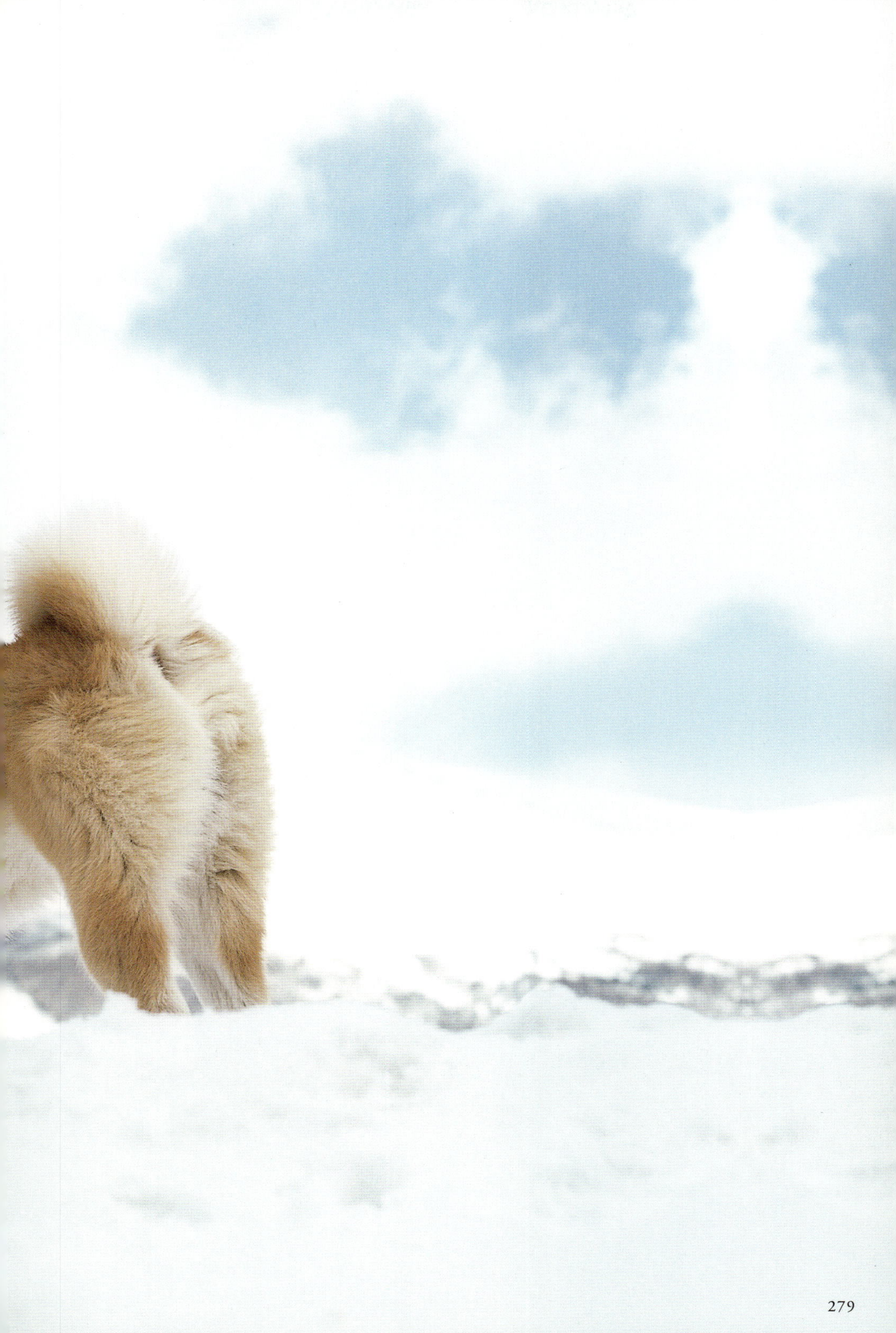

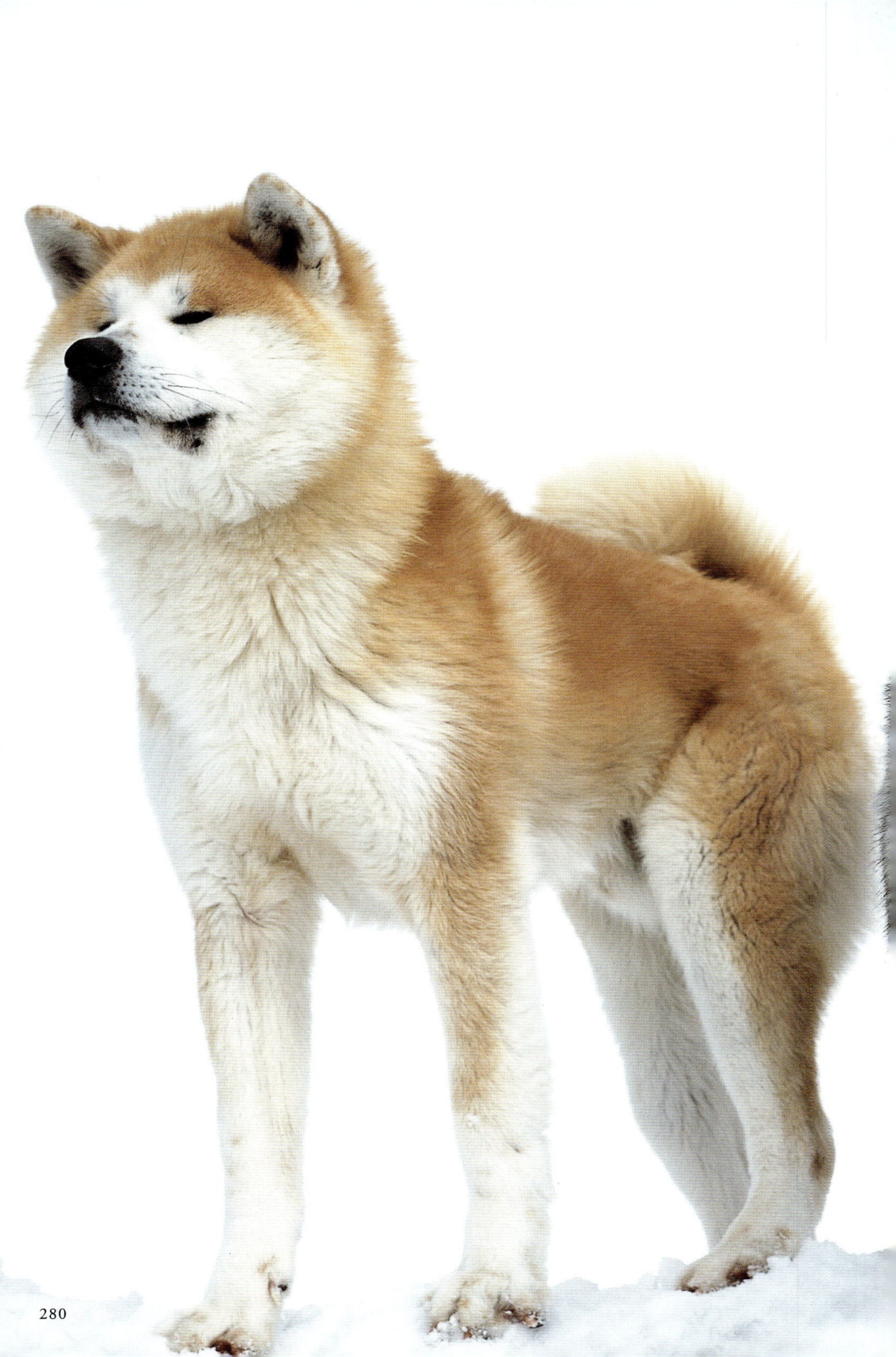

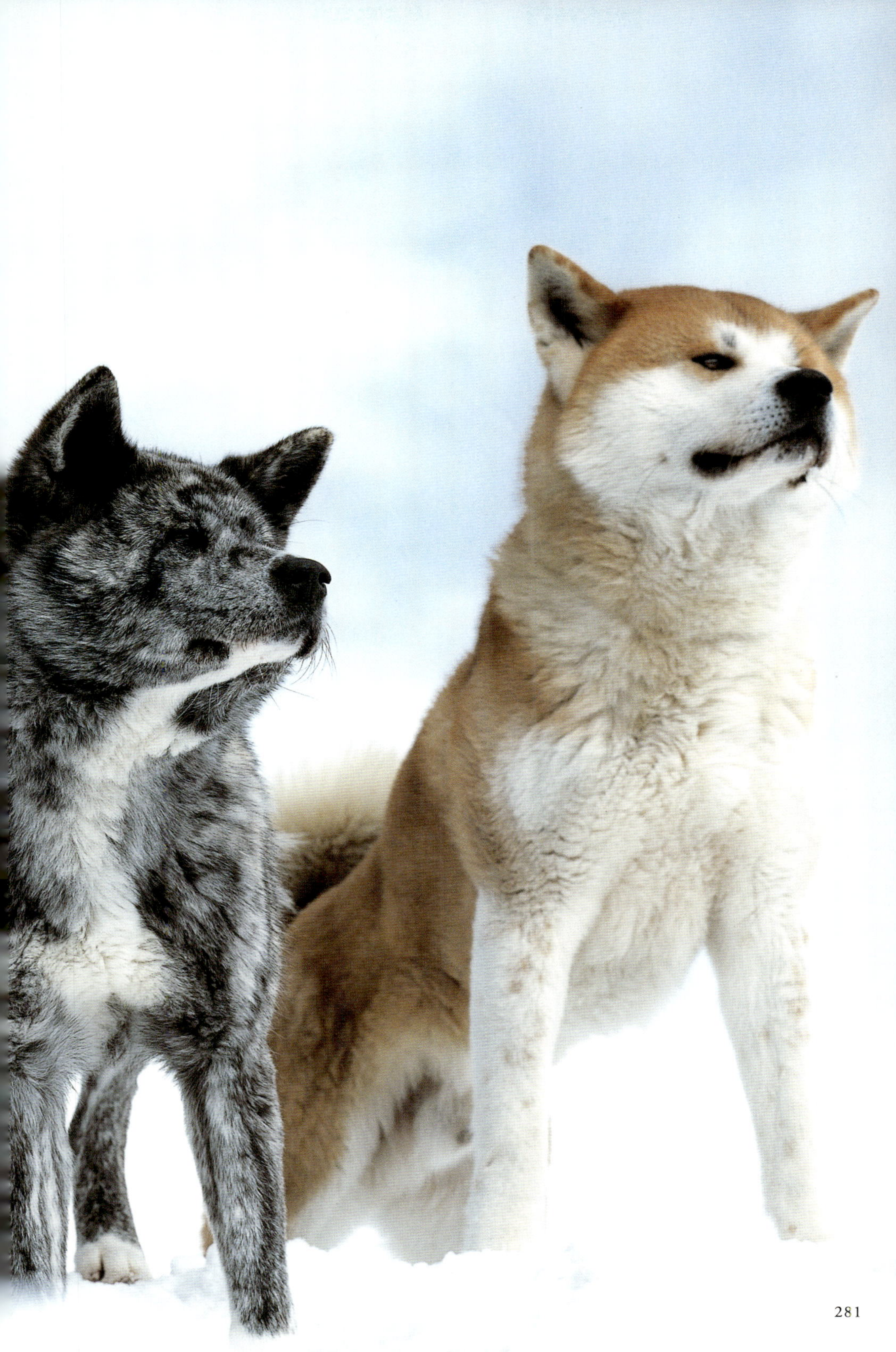

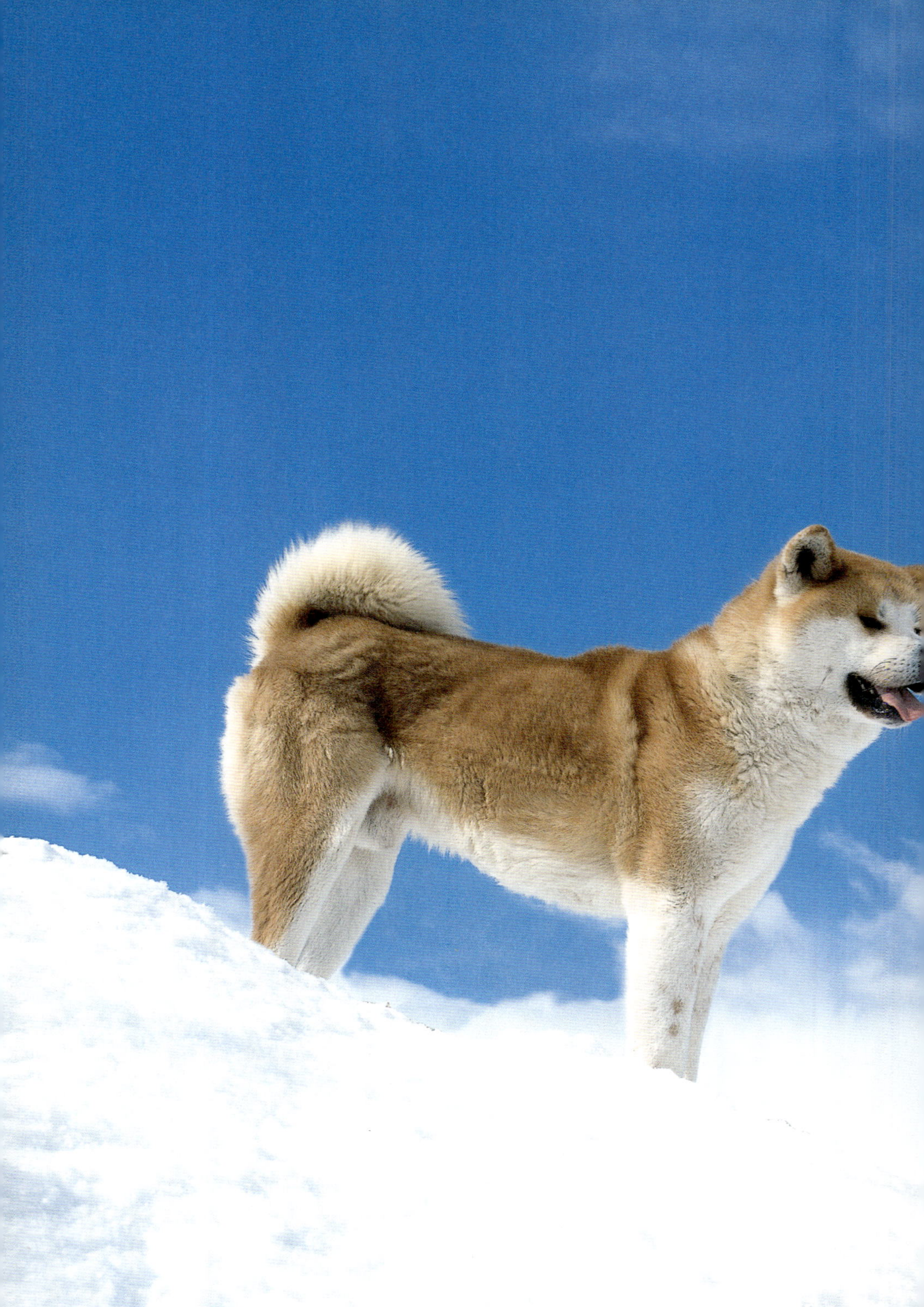

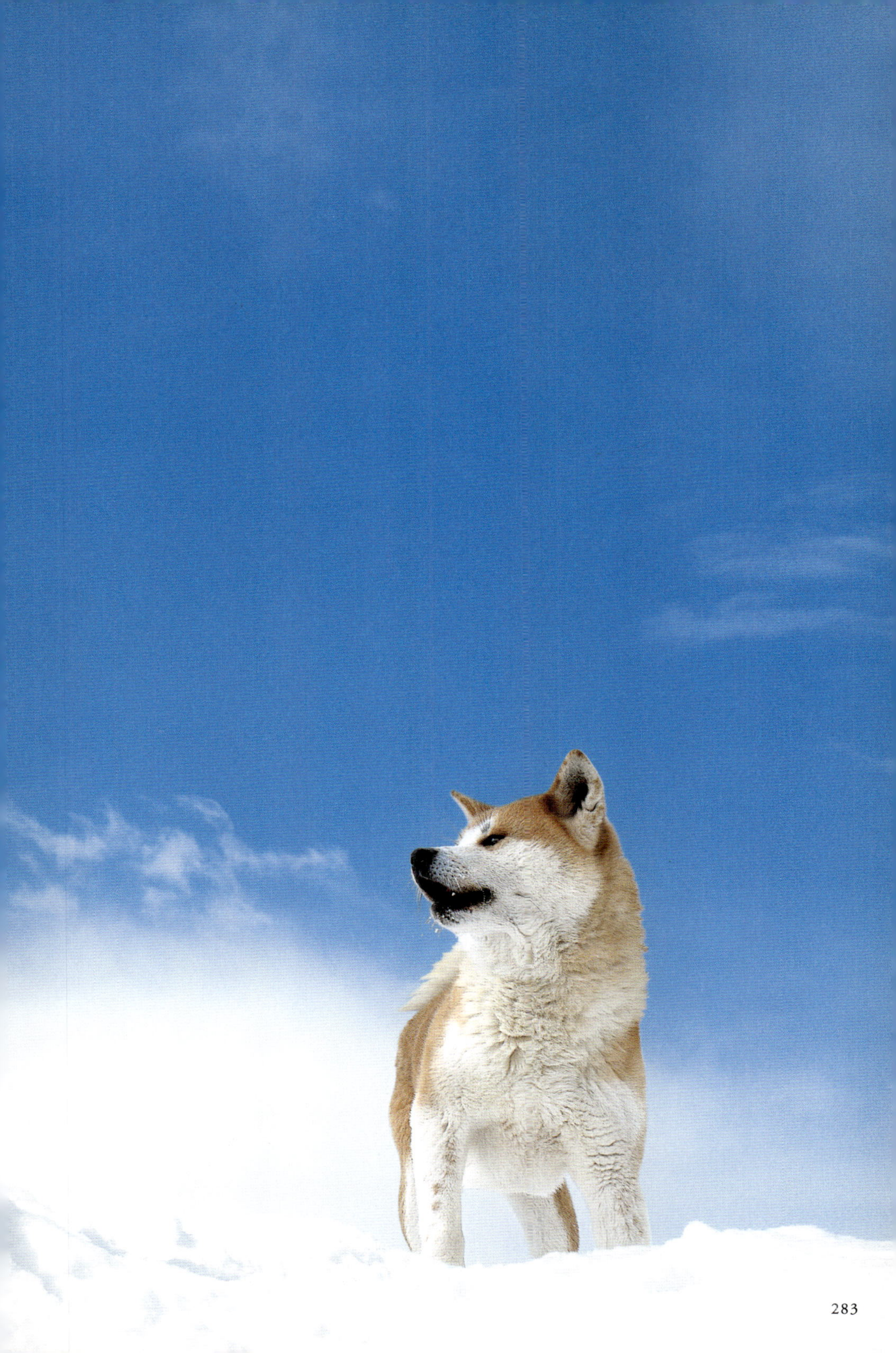

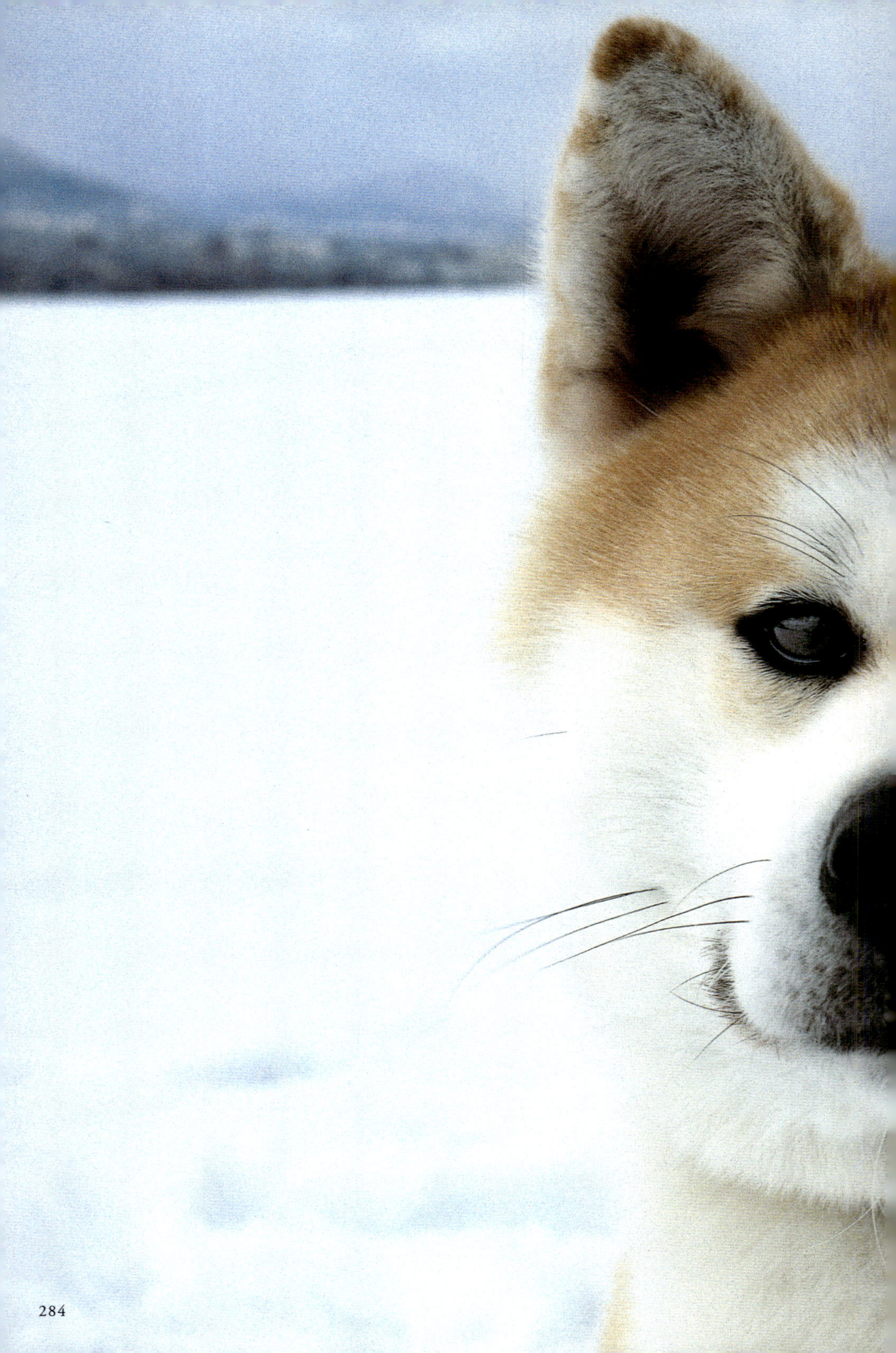

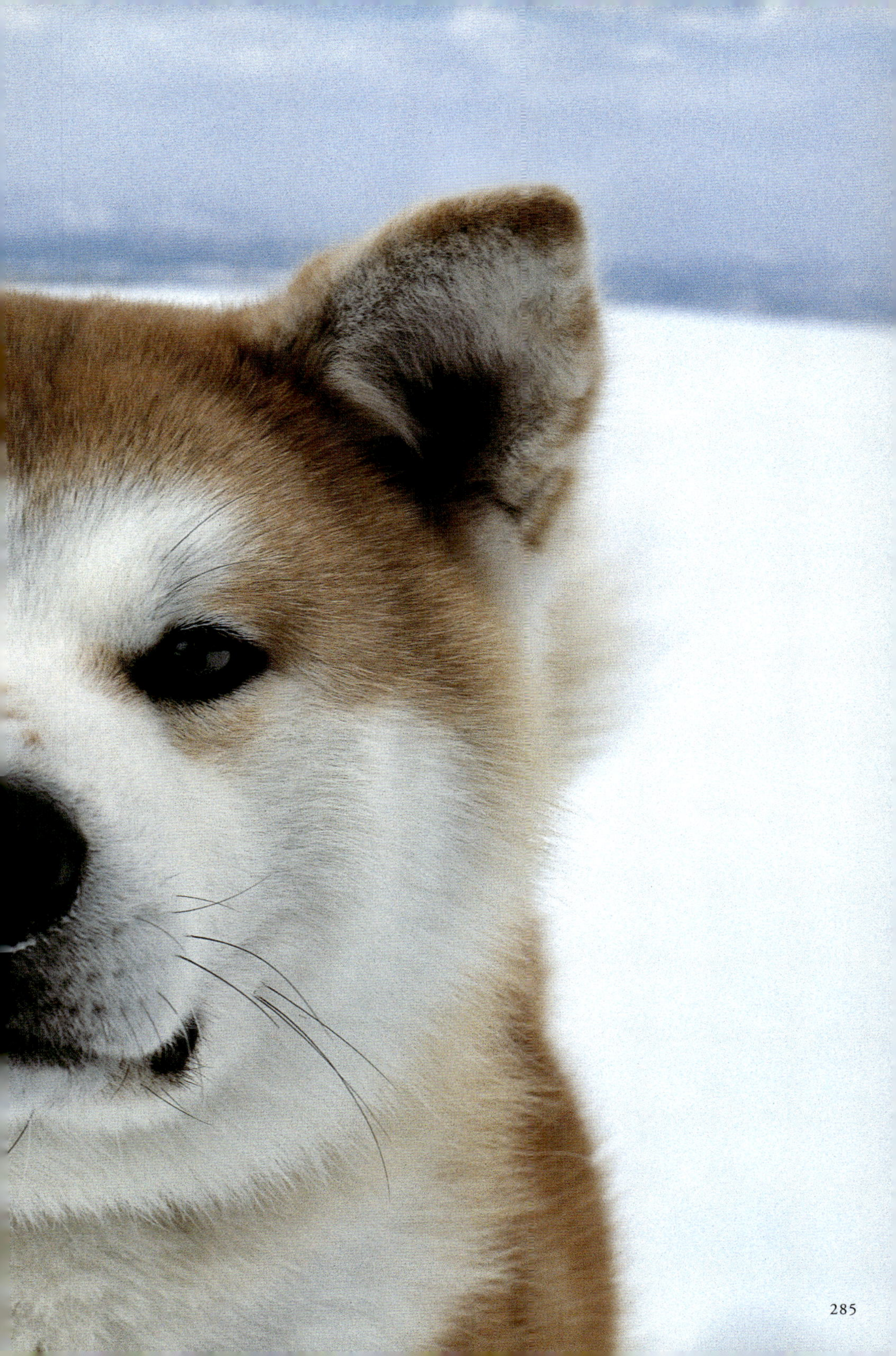

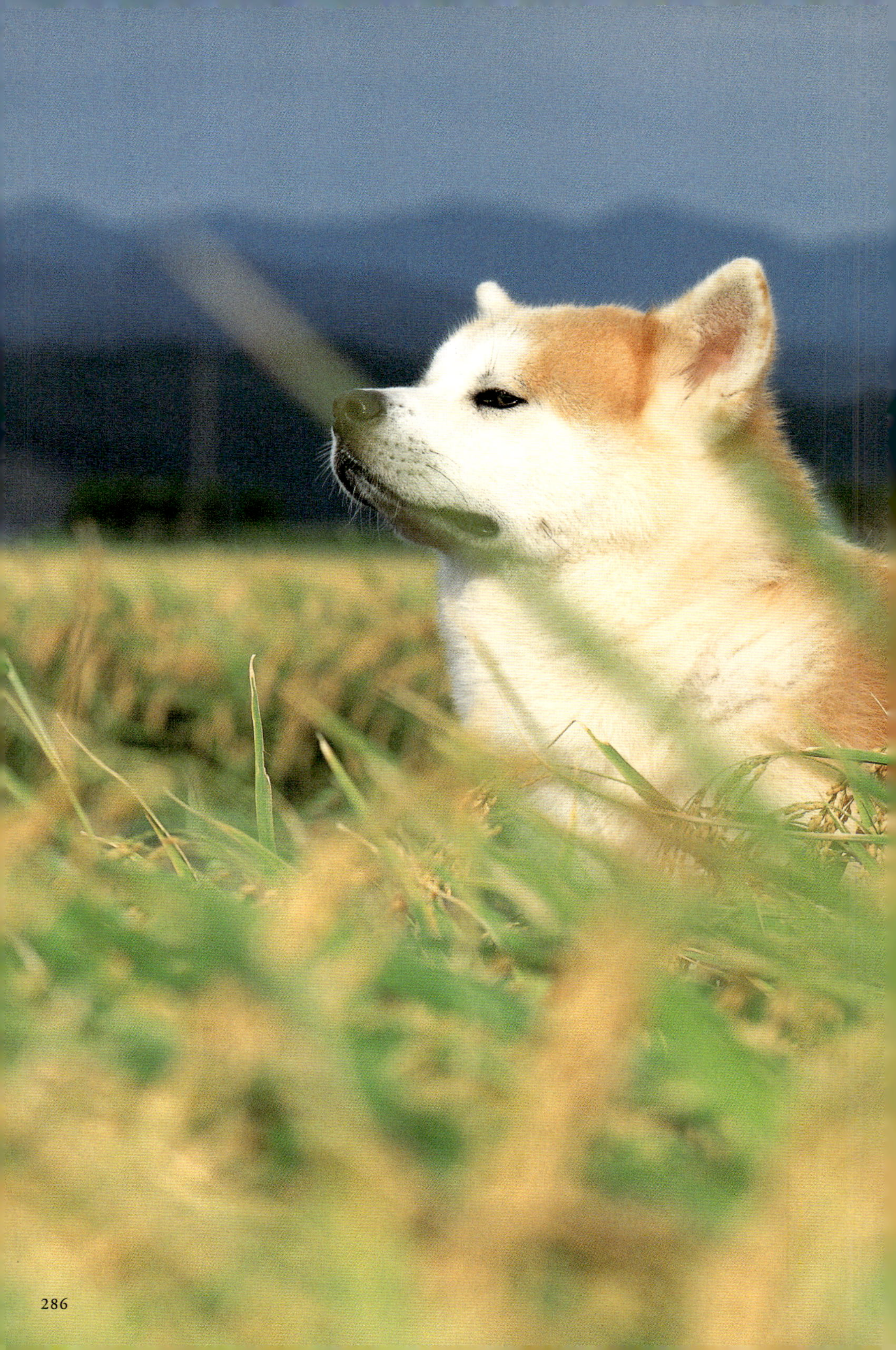

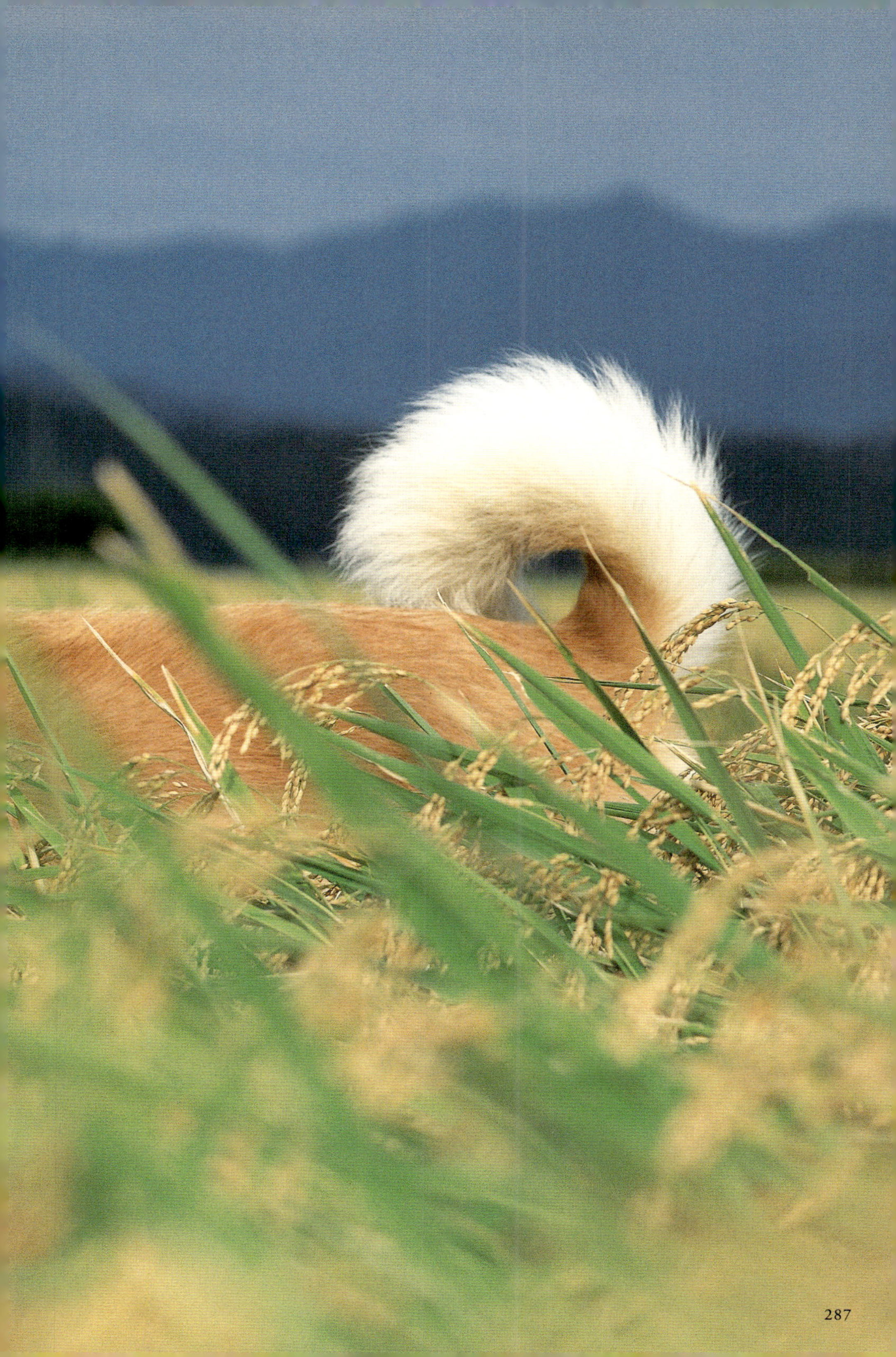

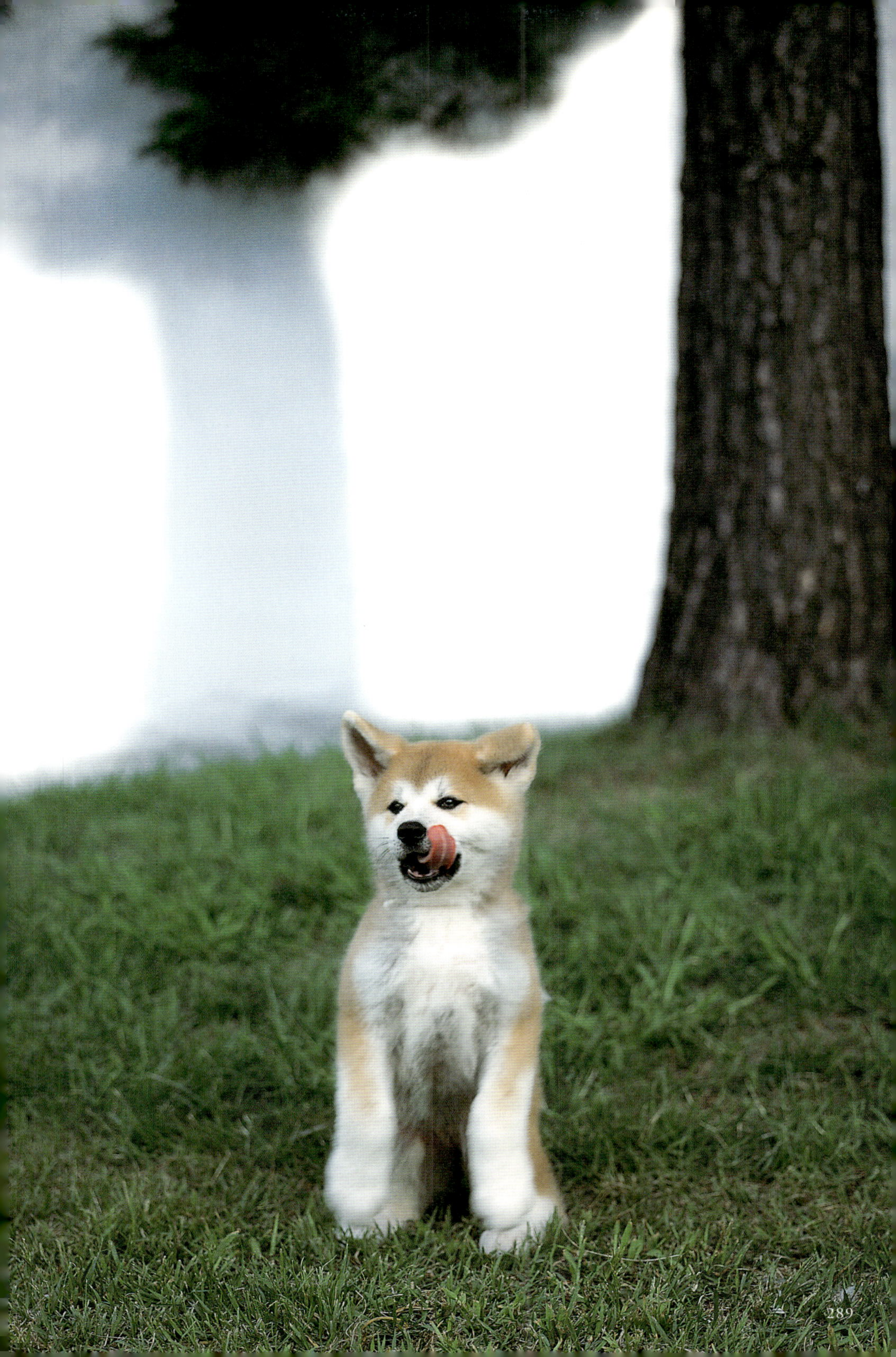

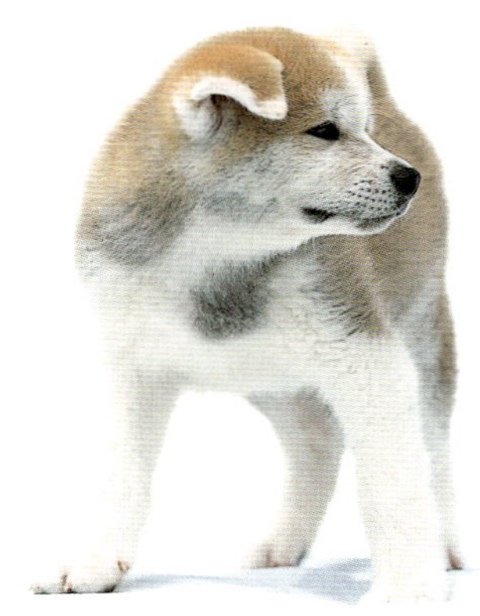

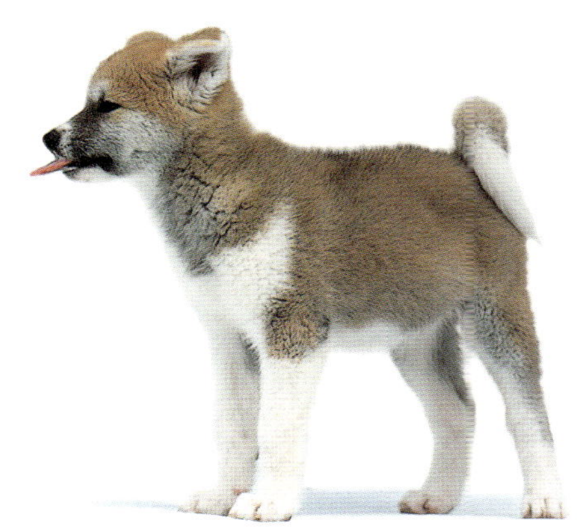

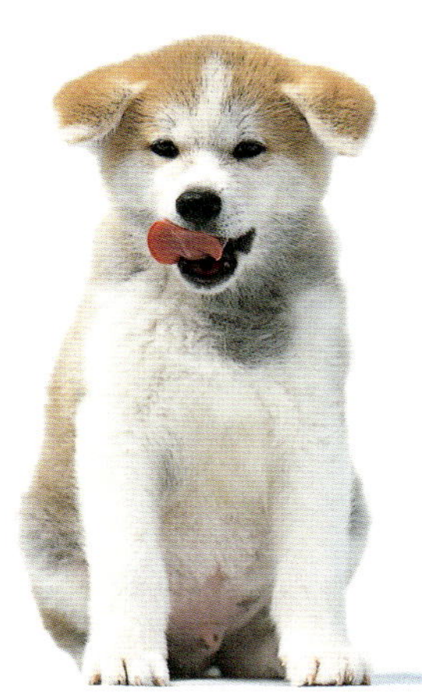

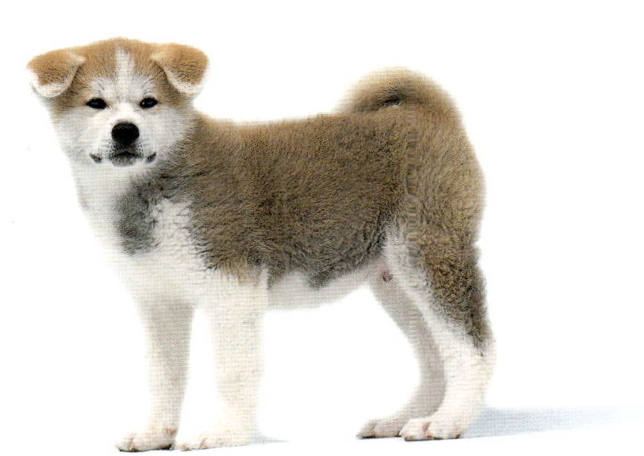

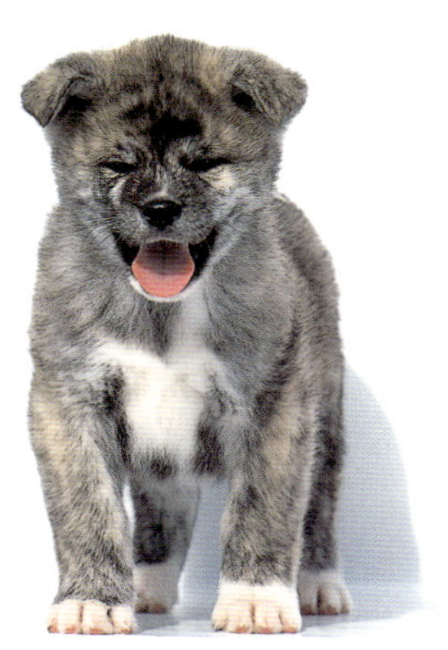

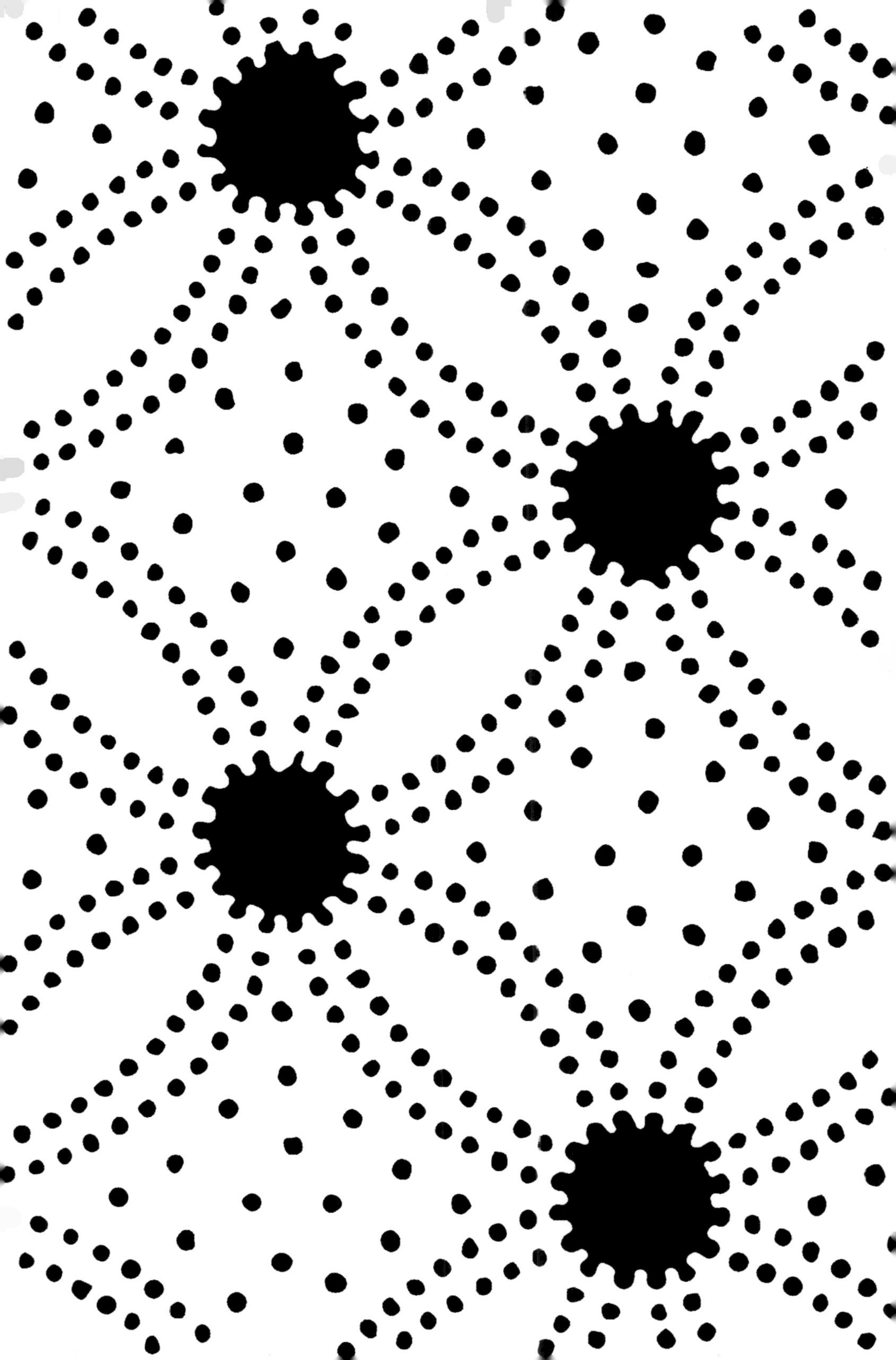

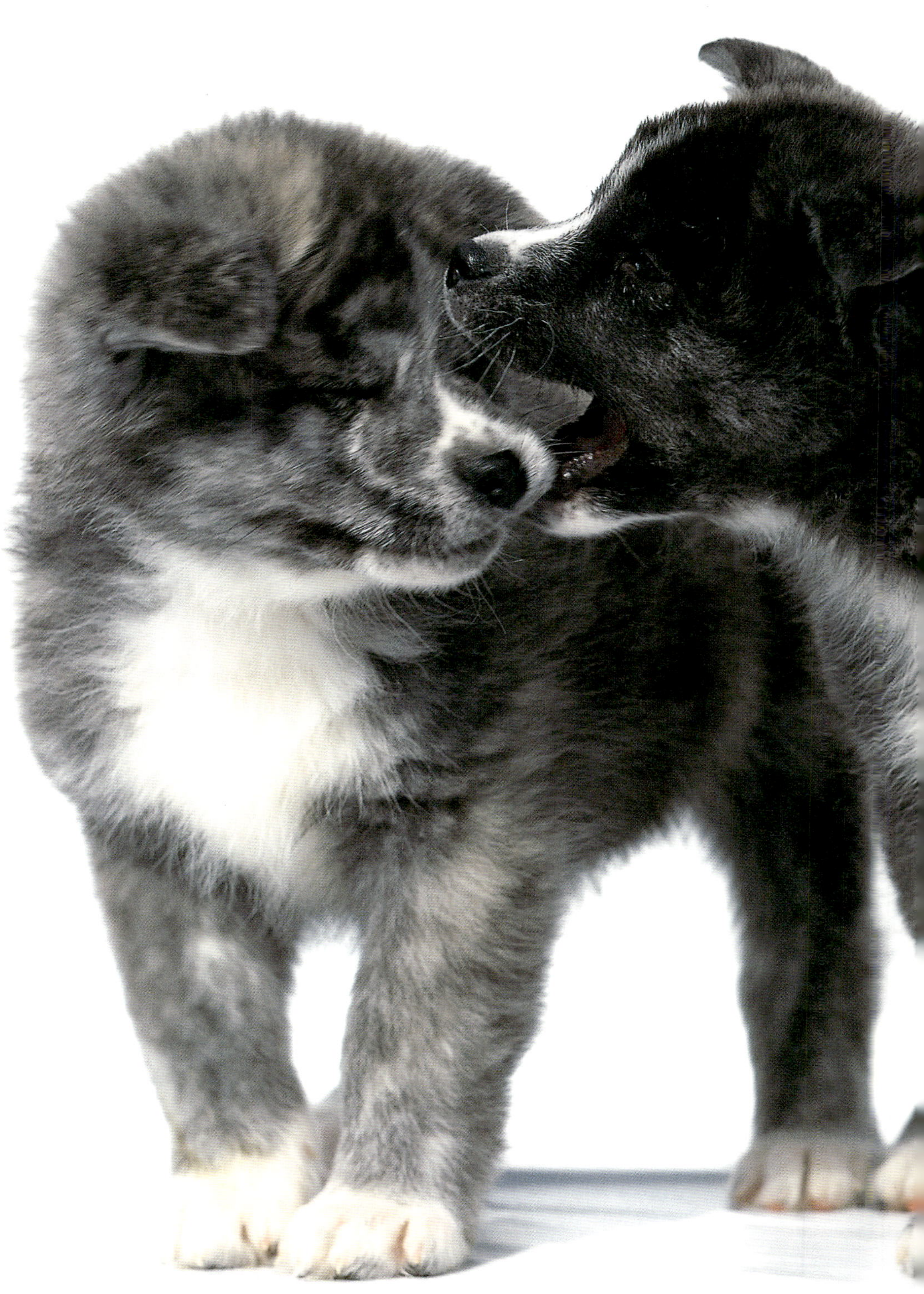

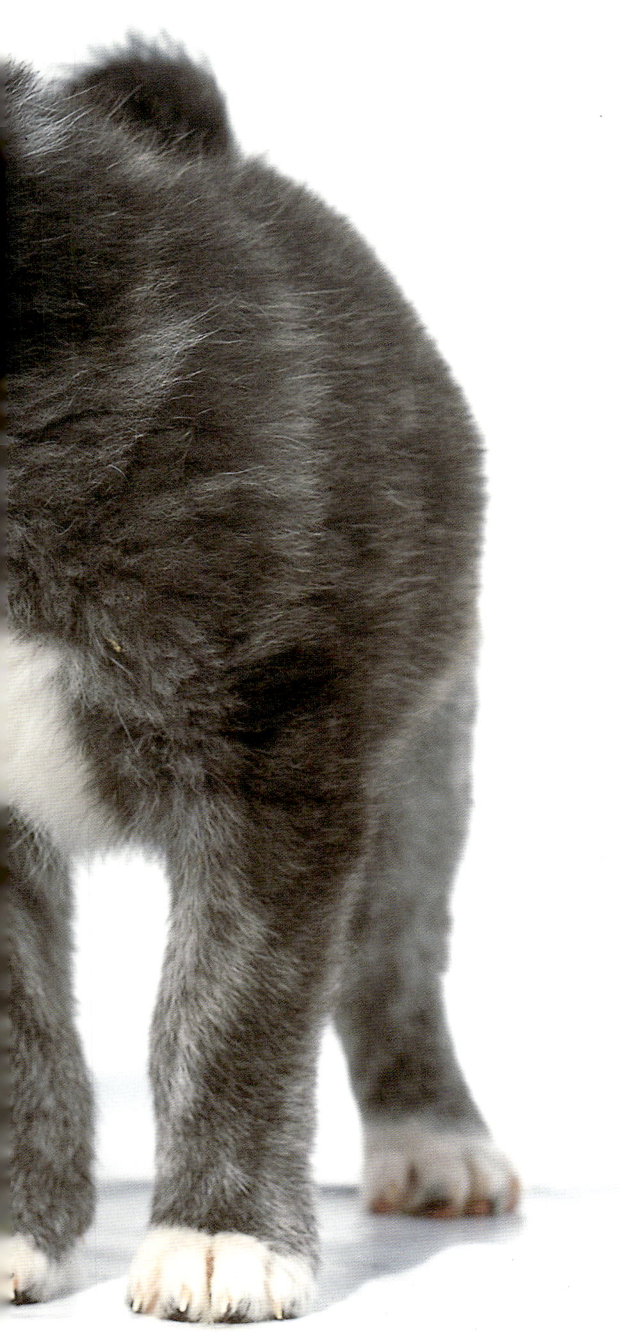

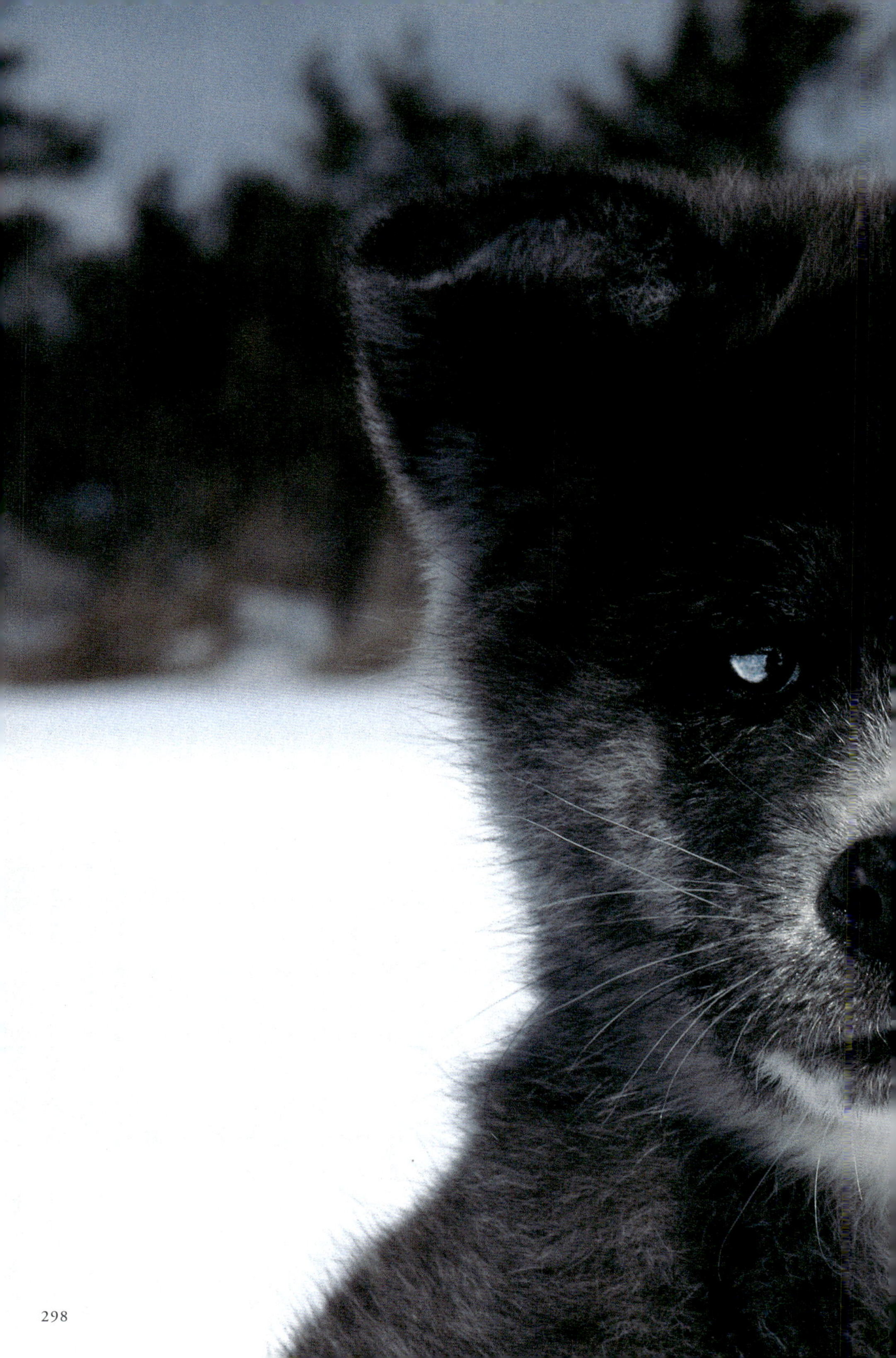

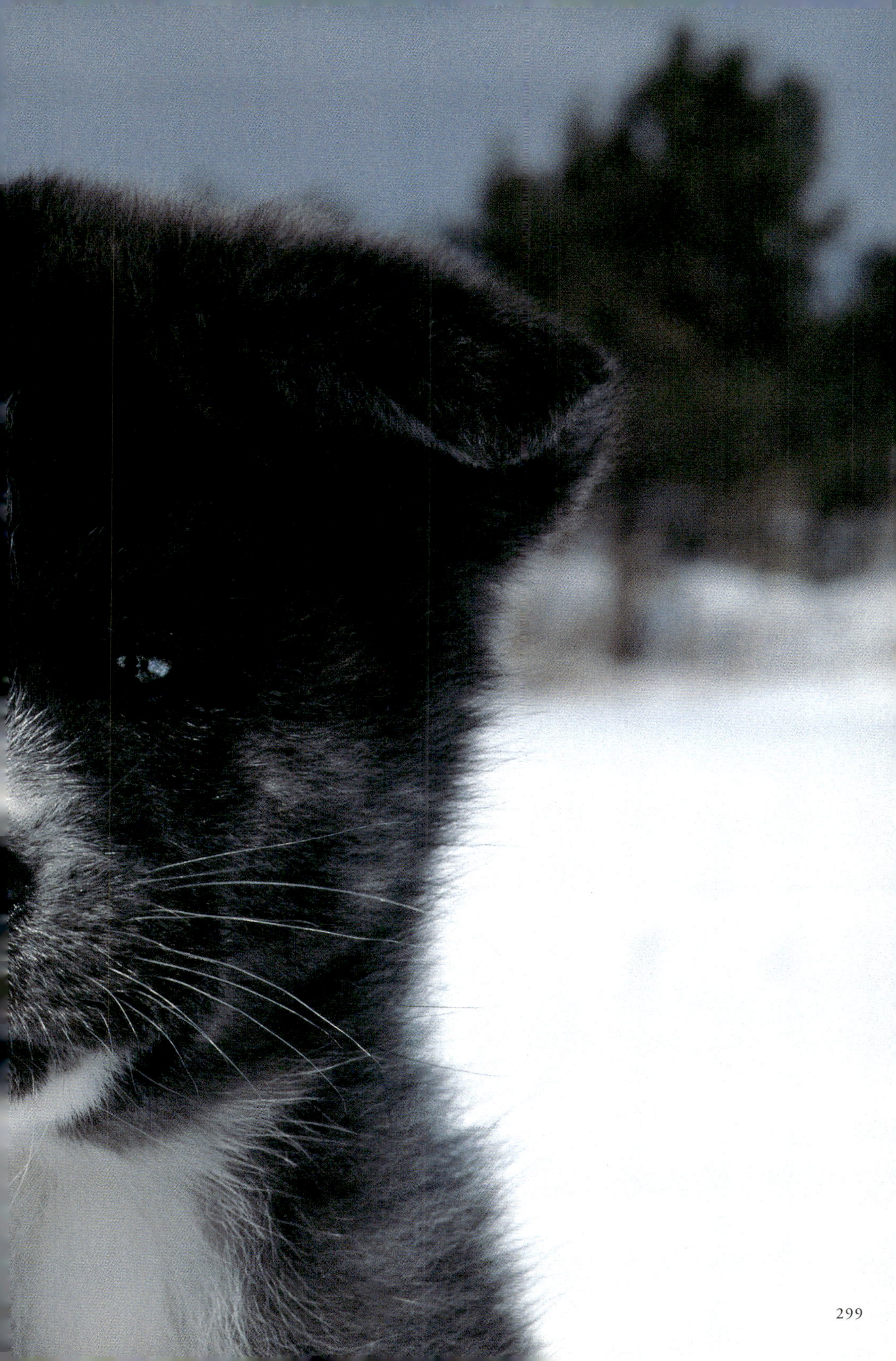

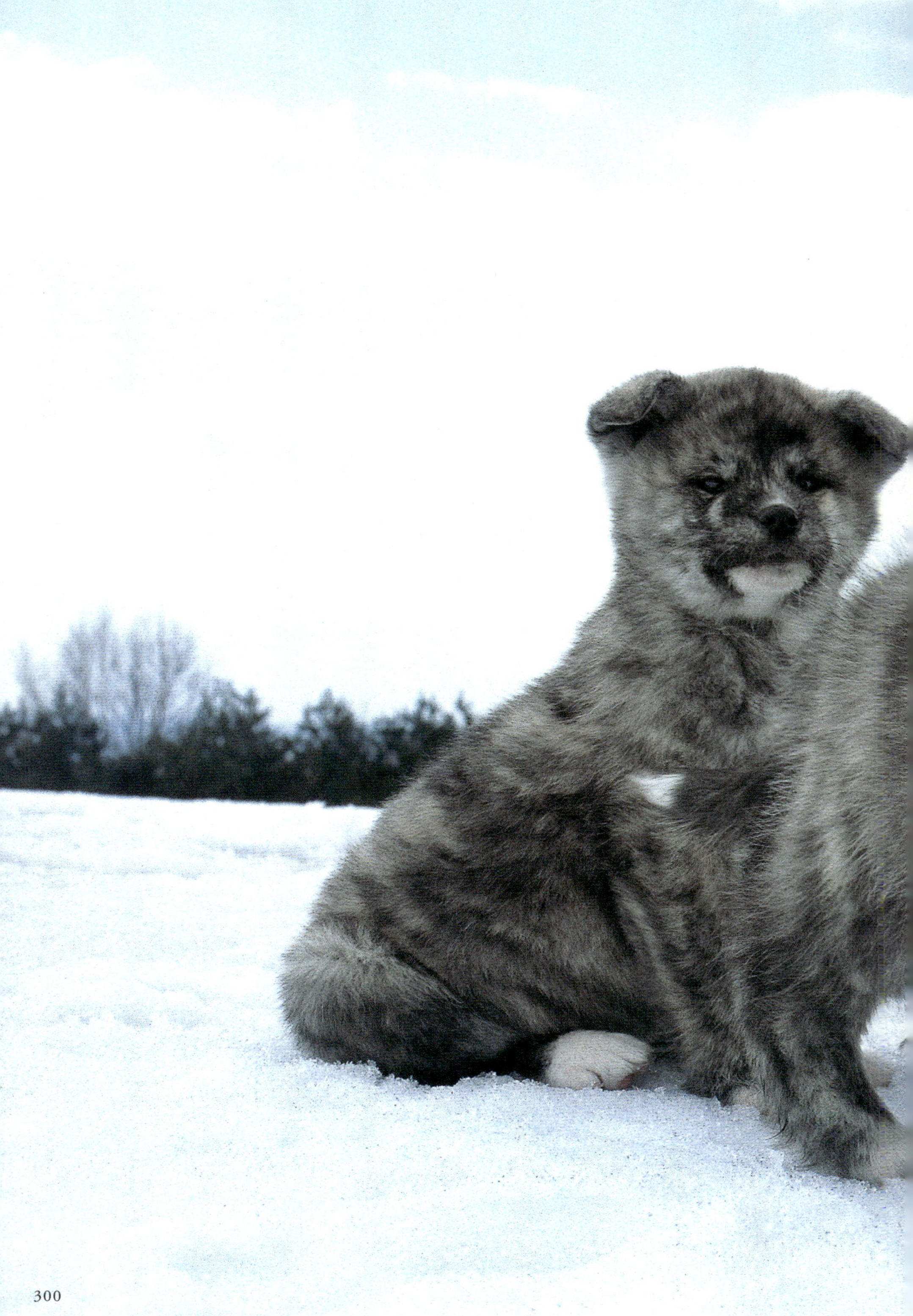

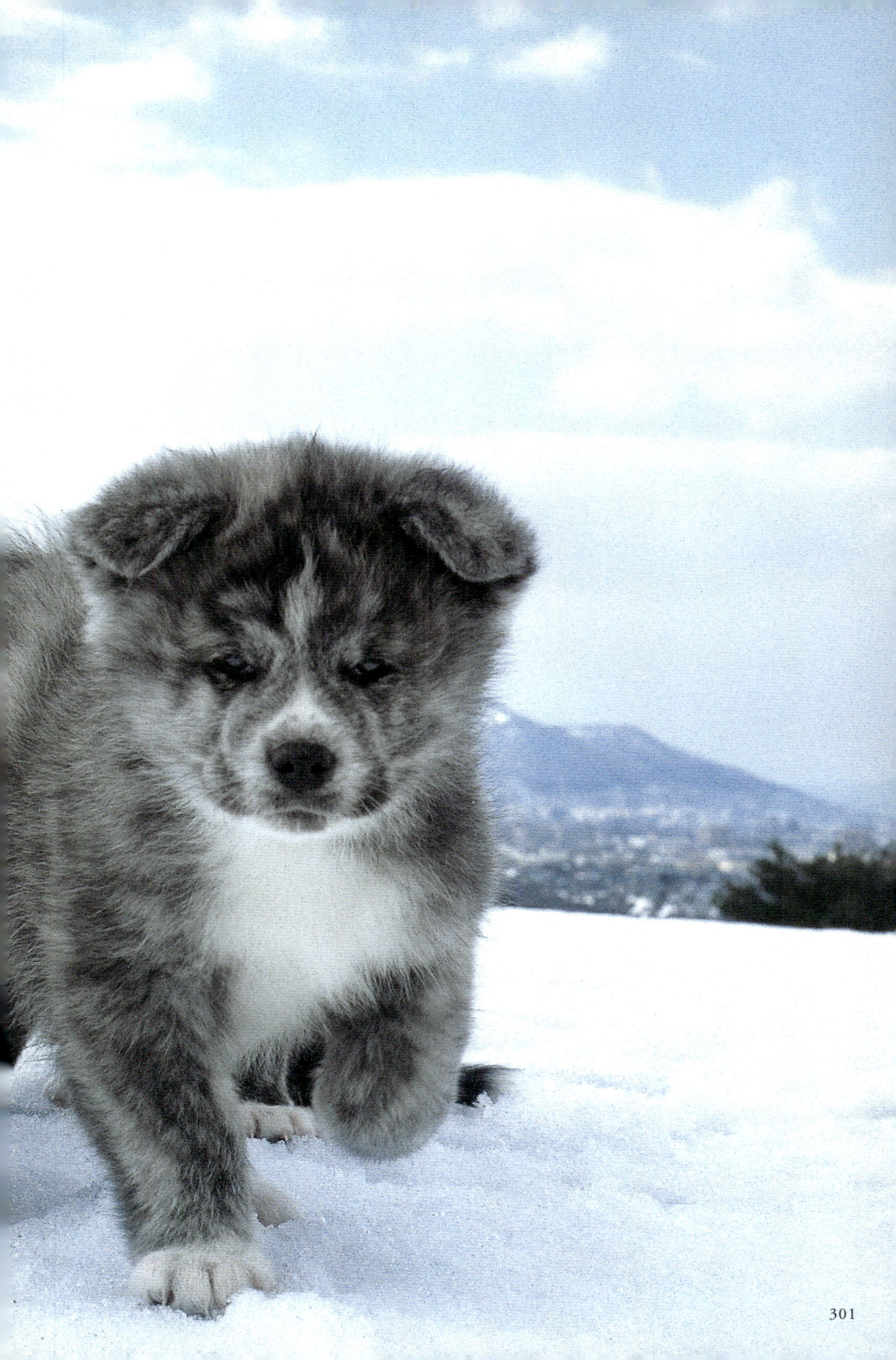

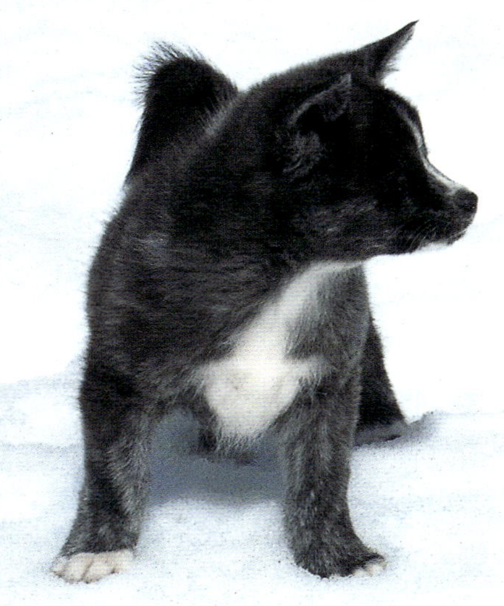

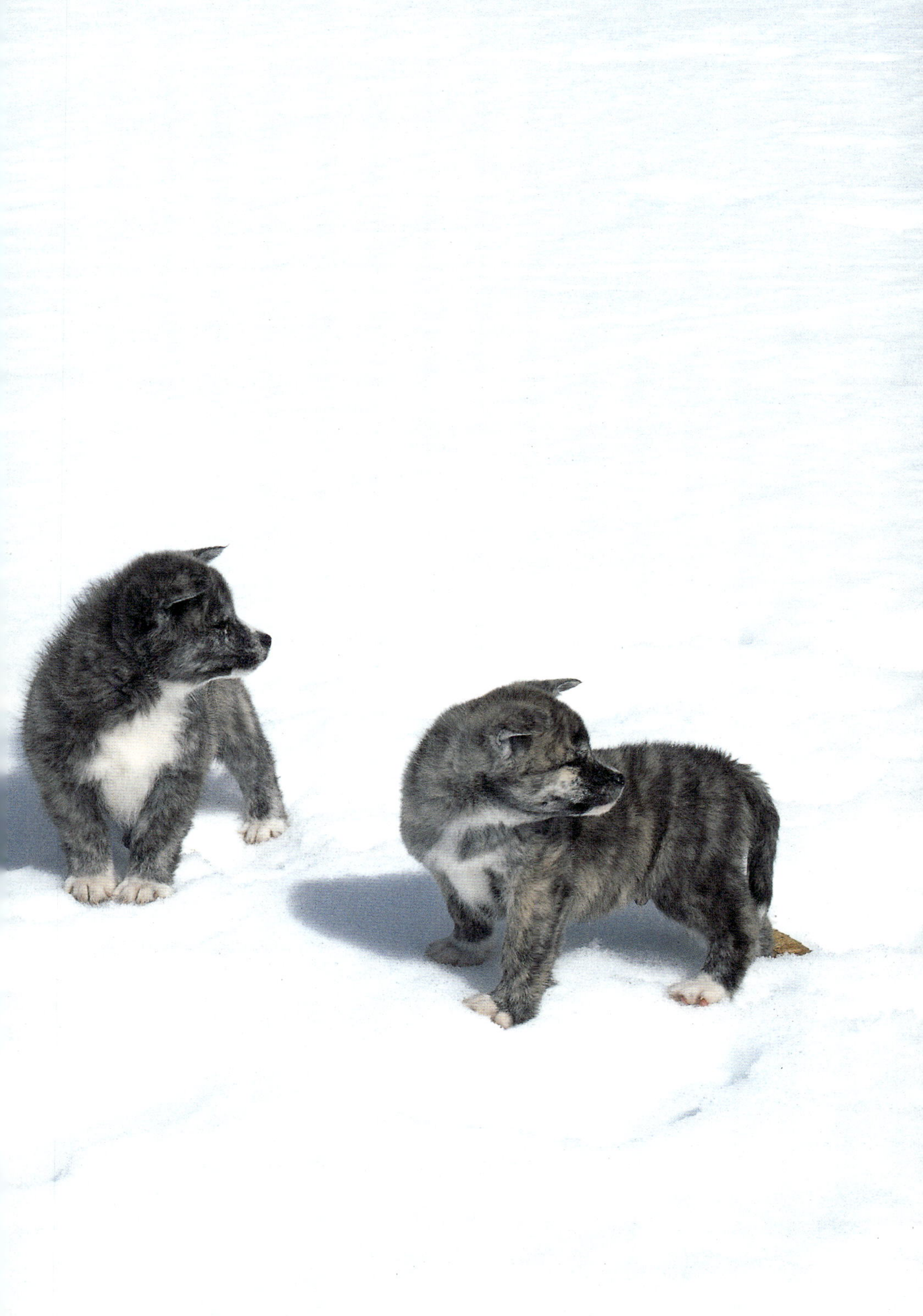

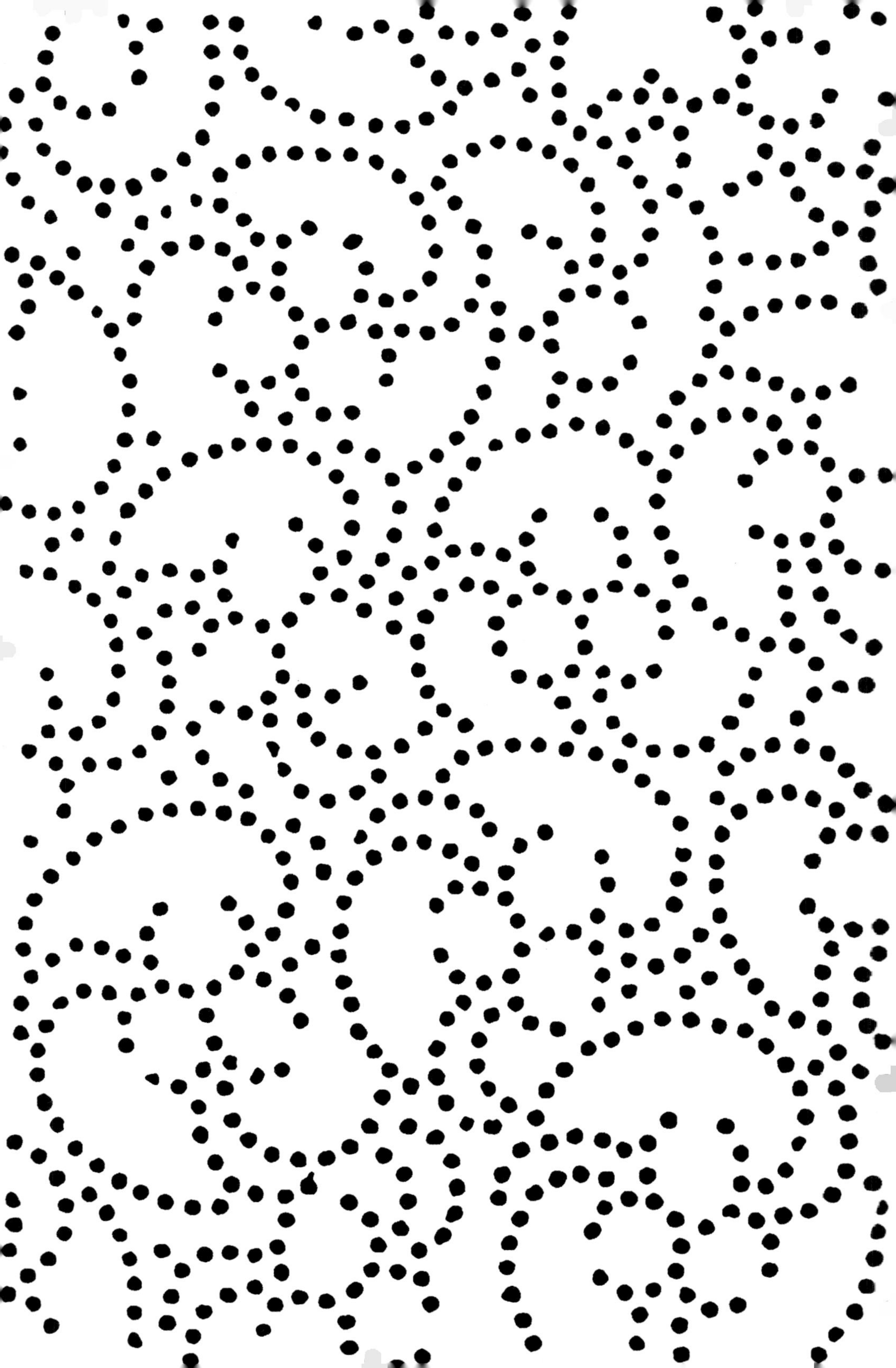

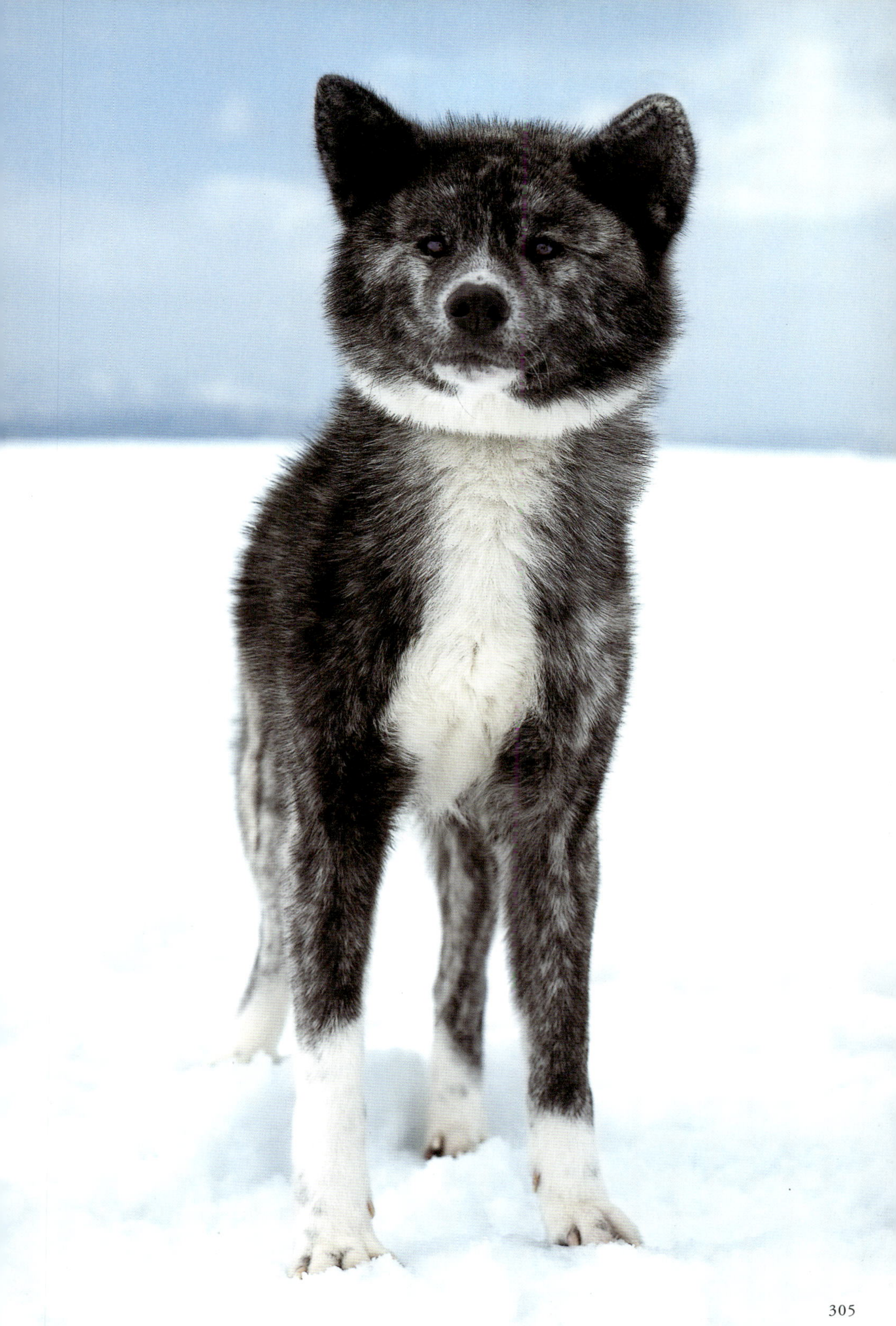

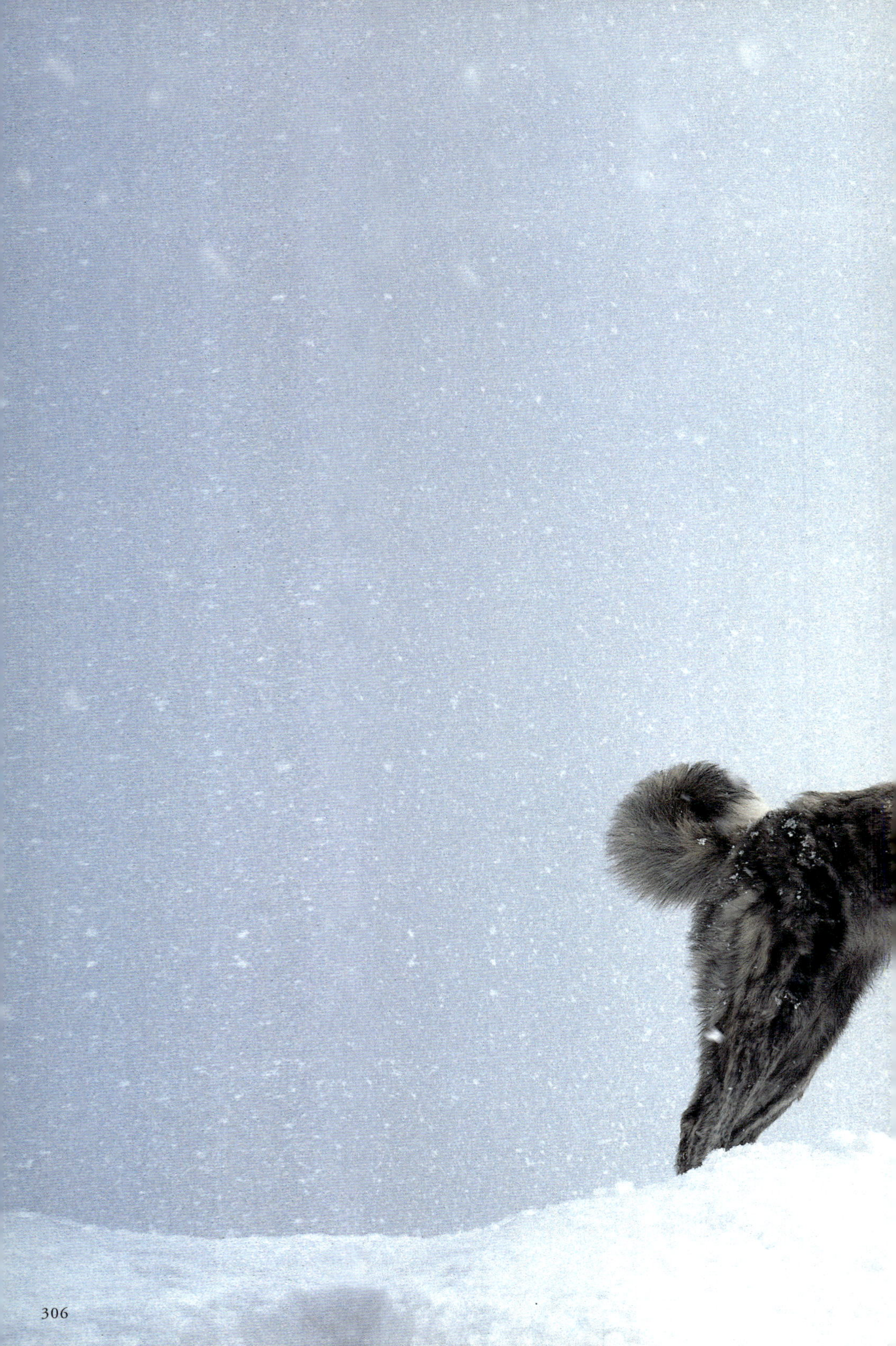

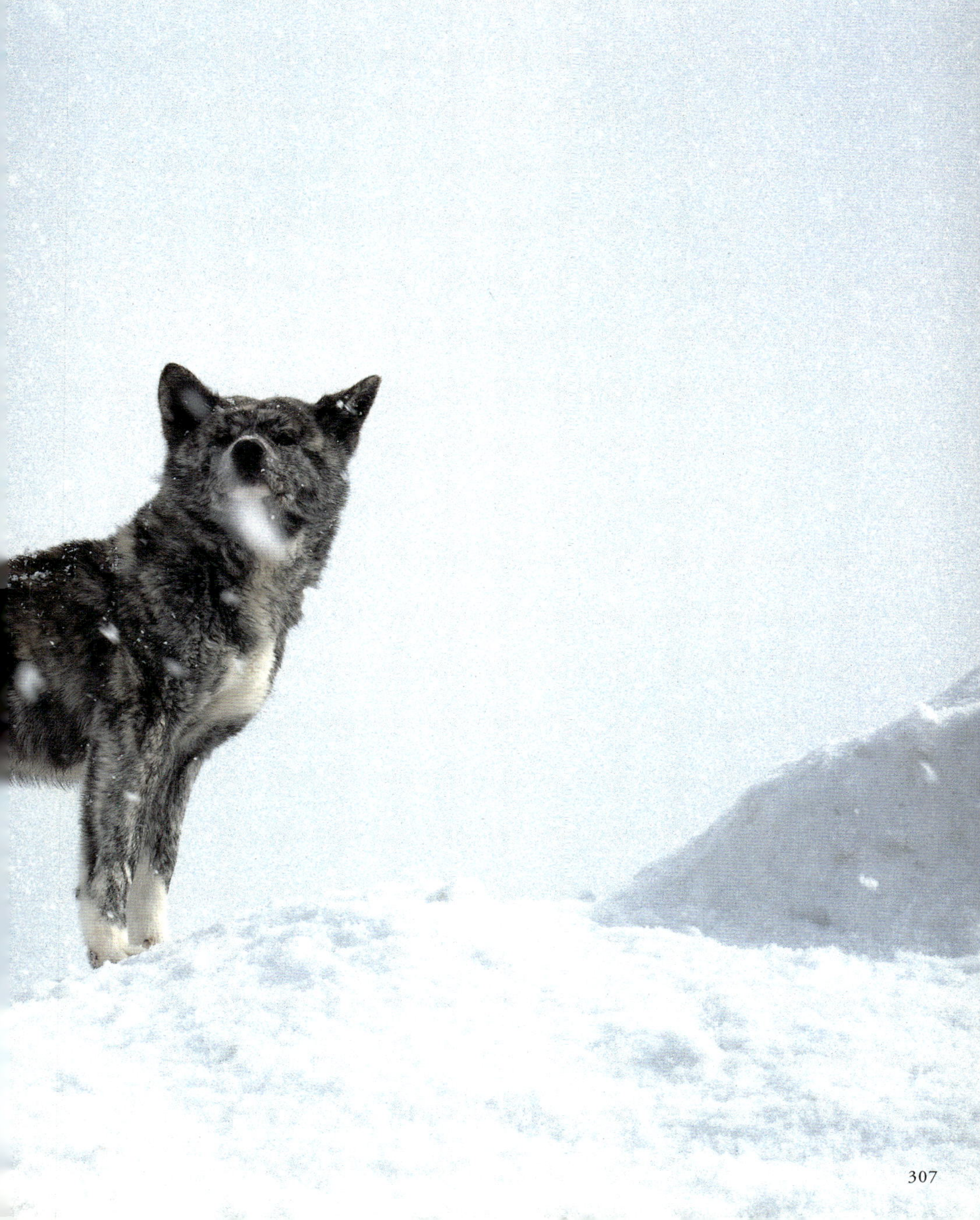

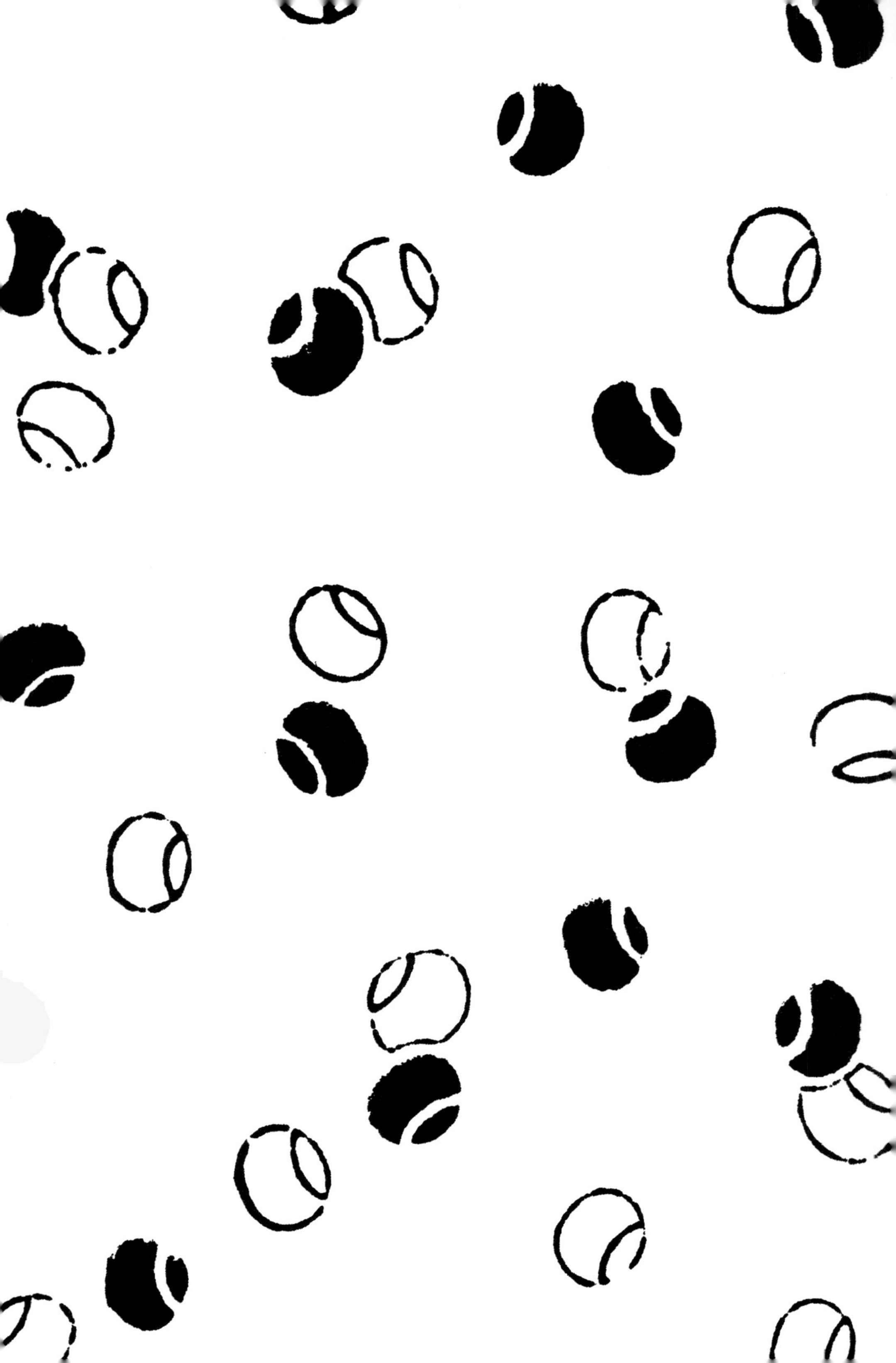

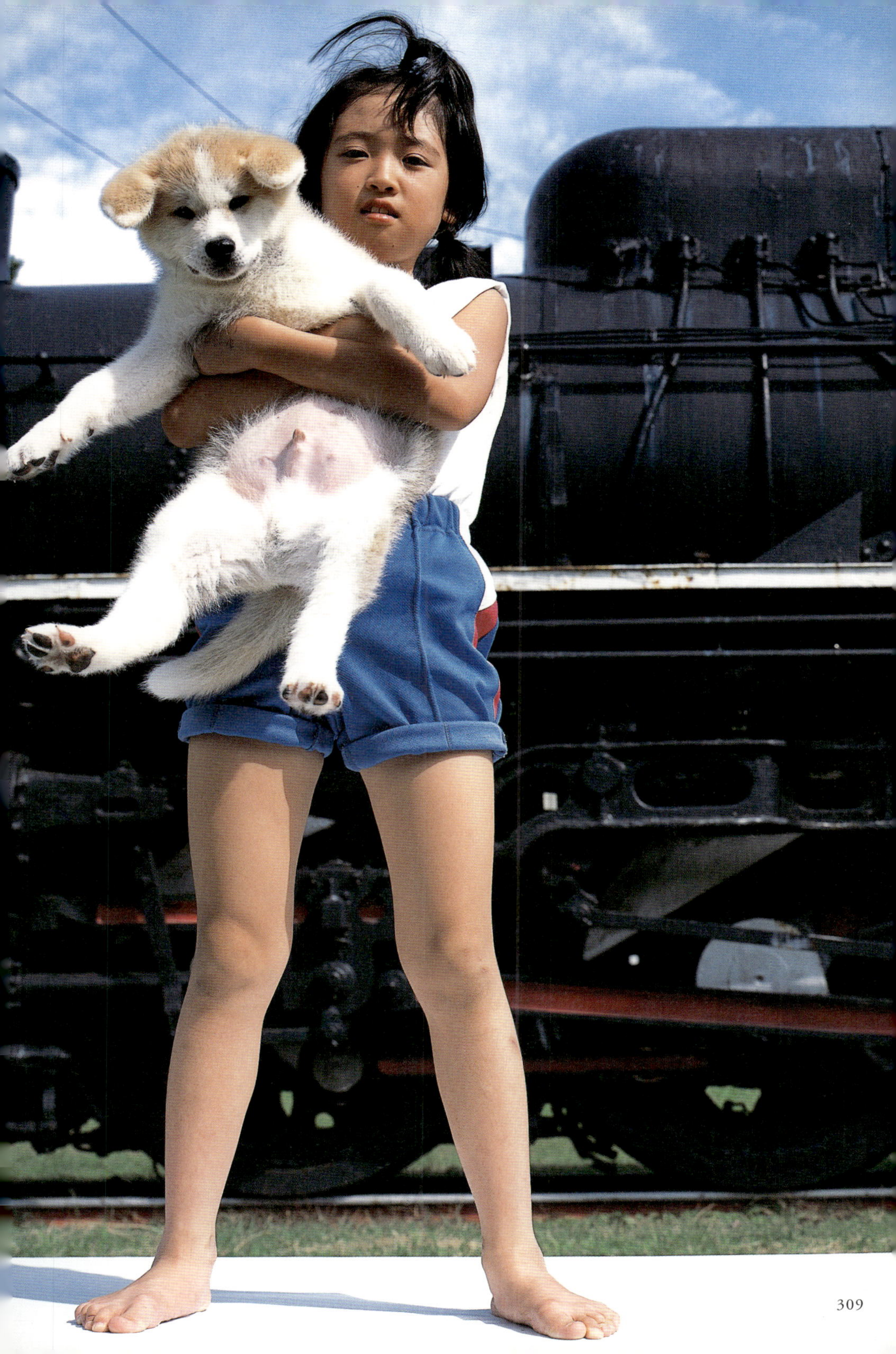

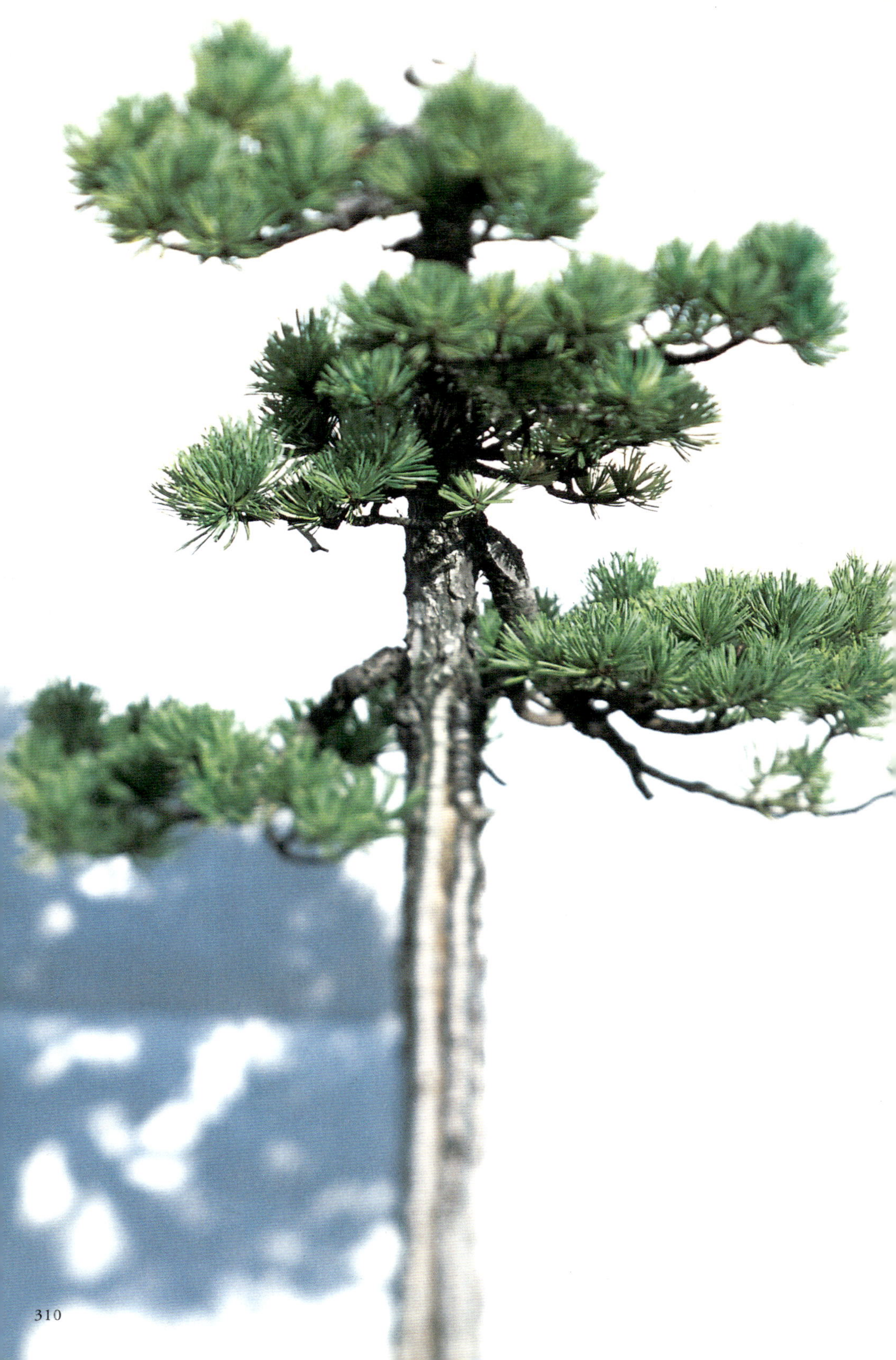

北海道犬

Hokkaido-ken

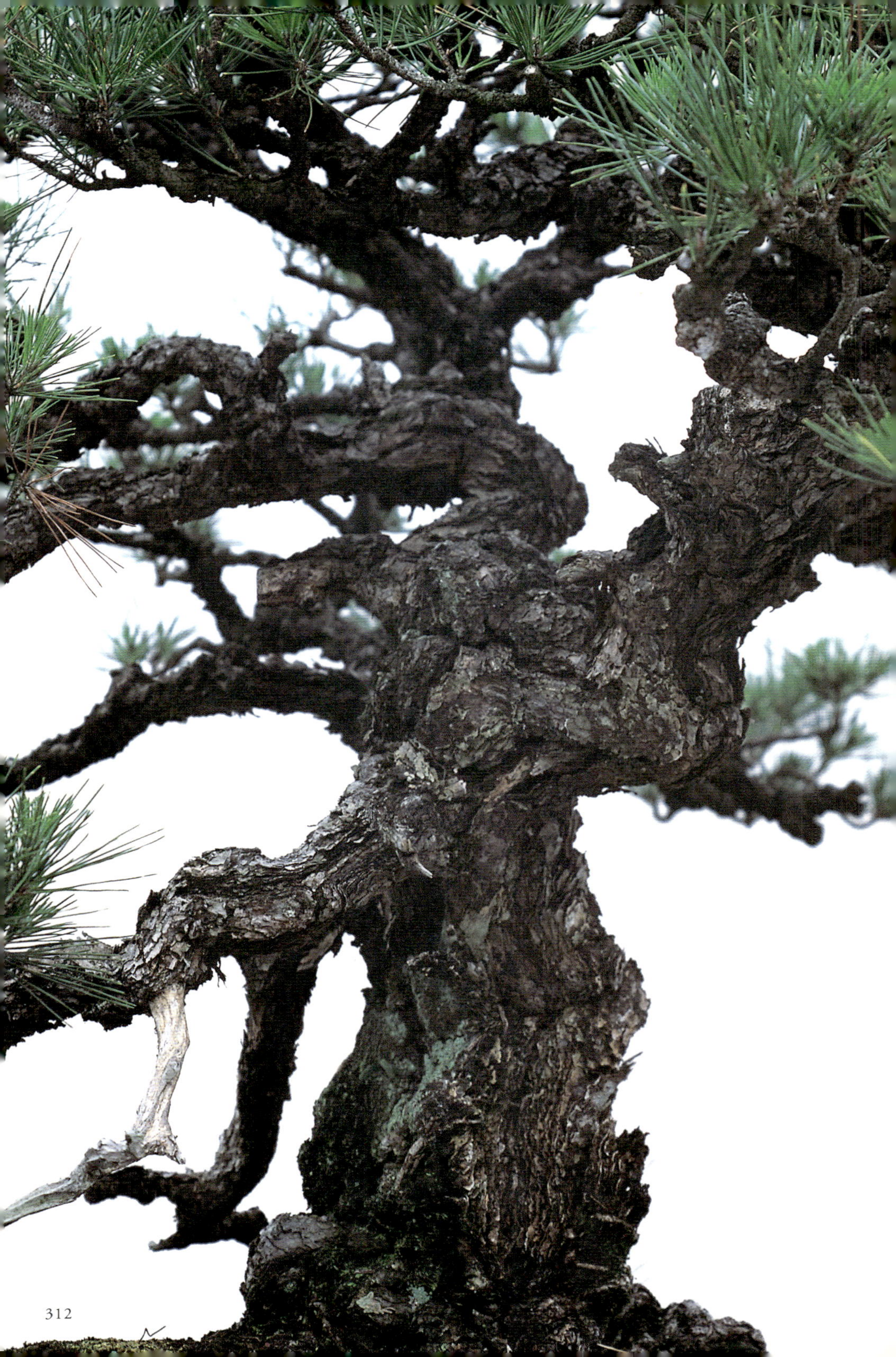

ほっかいどうけん

北海道犬

かつてはアイヌ犬と呼ばれ、北海道先住民族の集落（コタン）で
番犬、またはクマなどの獣猟犬として飼育されてきた。
強靭な筋肉を持ち、厳寒と豪雪に耐える強い体質で
持久力に富んでいる。
一方で、沖縄の琉球犬との共通点も多く指摘され、
血液タンパク質の遺伝子構成からも
非常に近い関係にあることが明らかになっている。
耳は比較的小さく、巻き尾が多い。
毛色は赤を筆頭に、白、胡麻、黒褐などがある。
中型で、体高は雄50センチ、雌45センチ。
昭和12年、国の天然記念物に指定。

Previously known as the Ainu-ken,
the Hokkaido-ken was bred in the villages of
the native inhabitants of the island of Hokkaido
as a guard dog and a hunting dog for
hunting bears and other animals.
The Hokkaido-ken has a muscular physique
and strong constitution that enables
it to survive freezing temperatures and heavy snow,
and is also gifted with strong endurance.
At the same time, it has been pointed out that the
Hokkaido-ken has many similarities
with the Ryukyu-ken of Okinawa, and in fact an analysis
of the genetic makeup of the blood proteins of
both breeds has determined that they are very closely related.
The Hokkaido-ken has relatively small ears and generally a curly tail.
The coat is red on the head and white, sesame,
or blackish brown on the body. It is a medium-sized dog,
with males growing to a height of 50cm, and females to 45 cm.
The Hokkaido-ken was designated a Natural Monument in 1937.

Hokkaido-ken

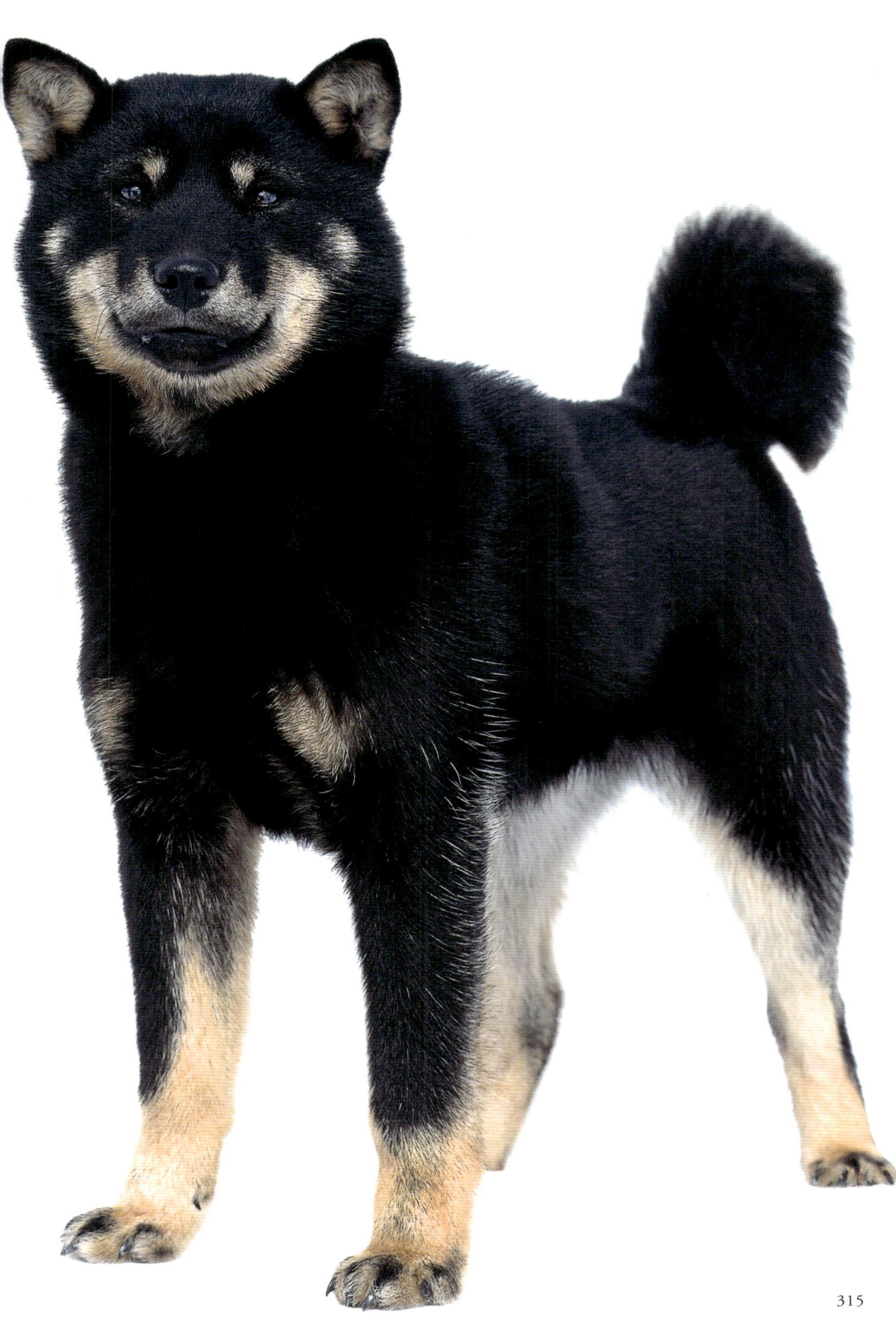

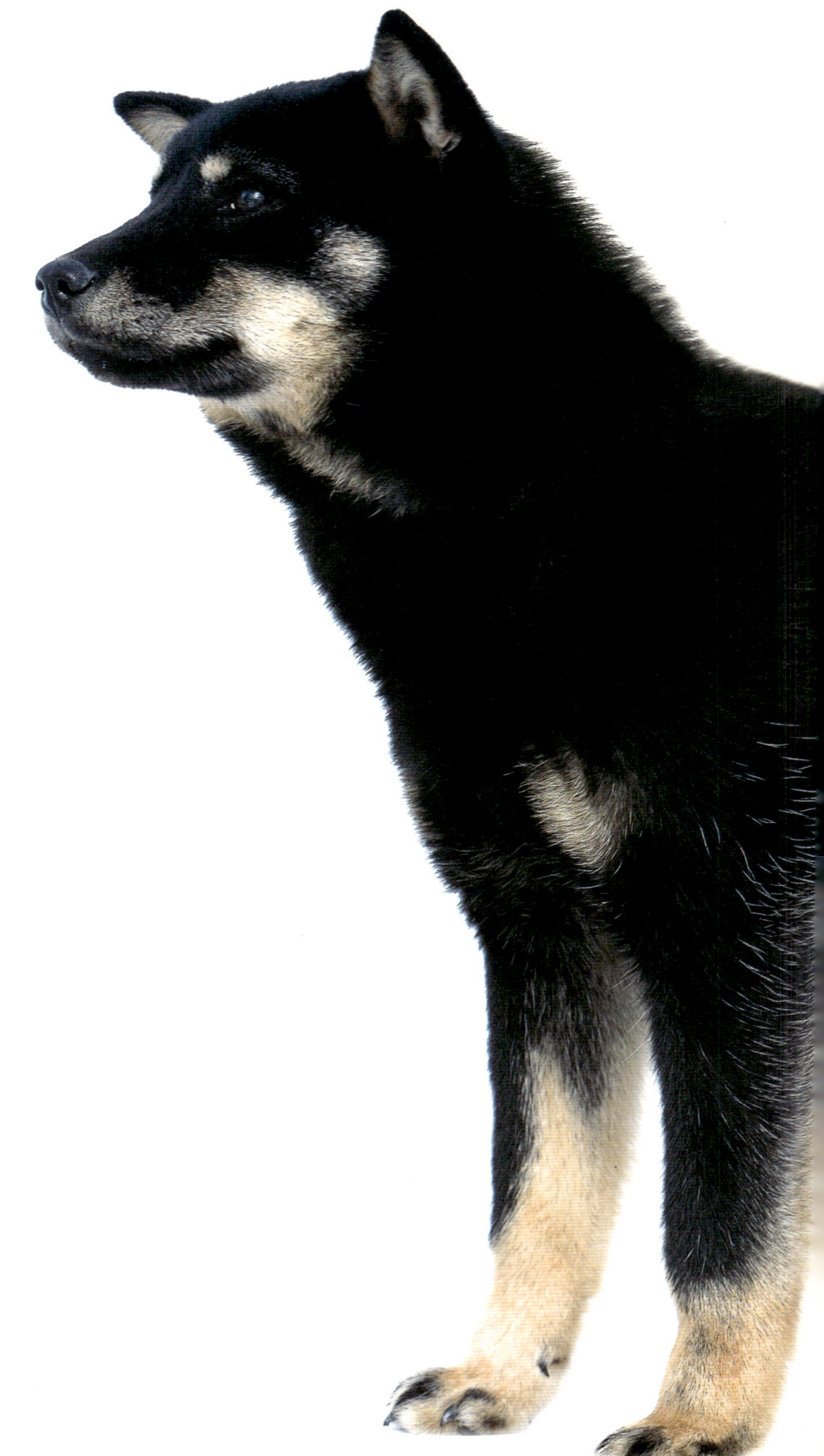

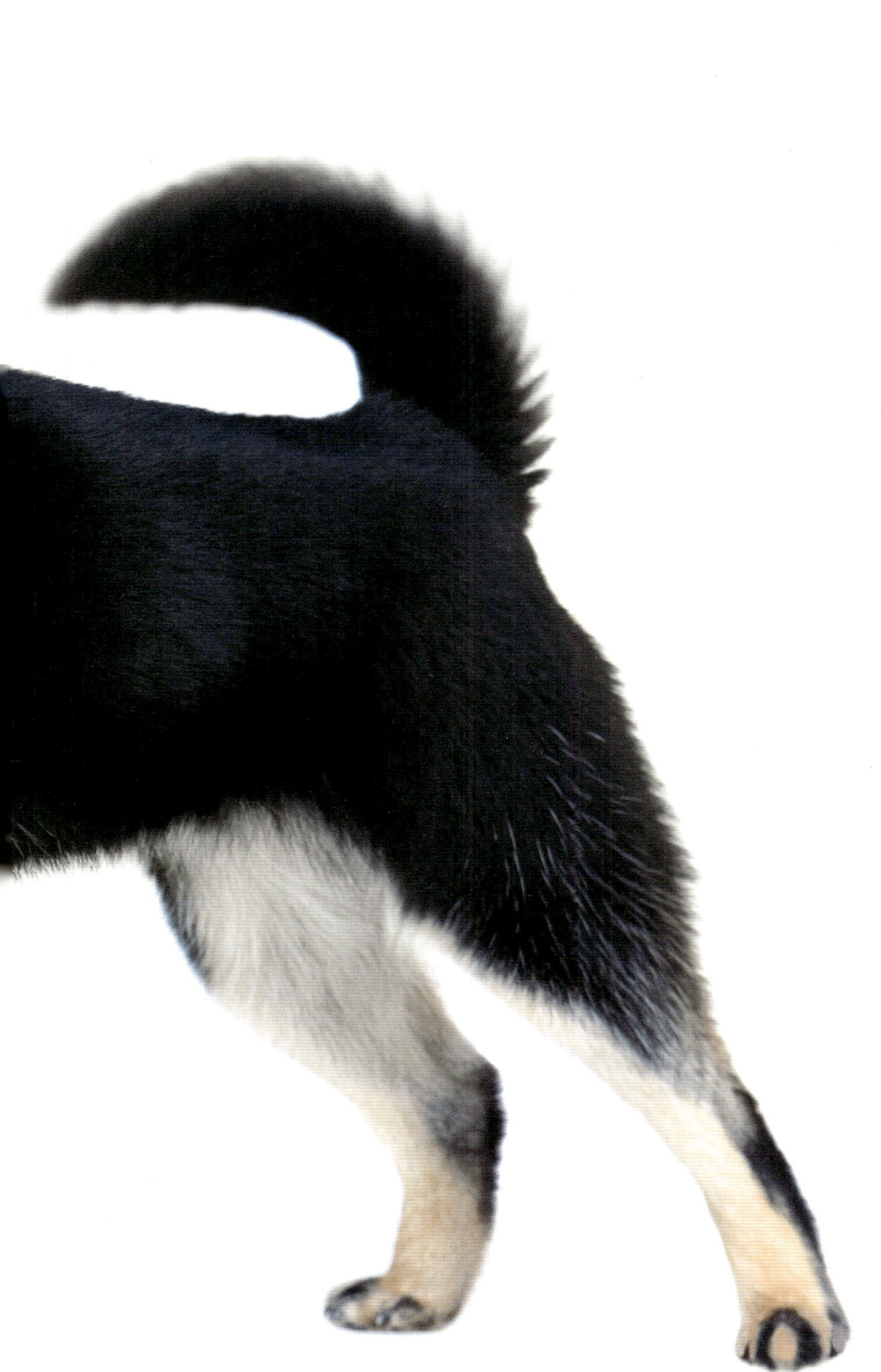

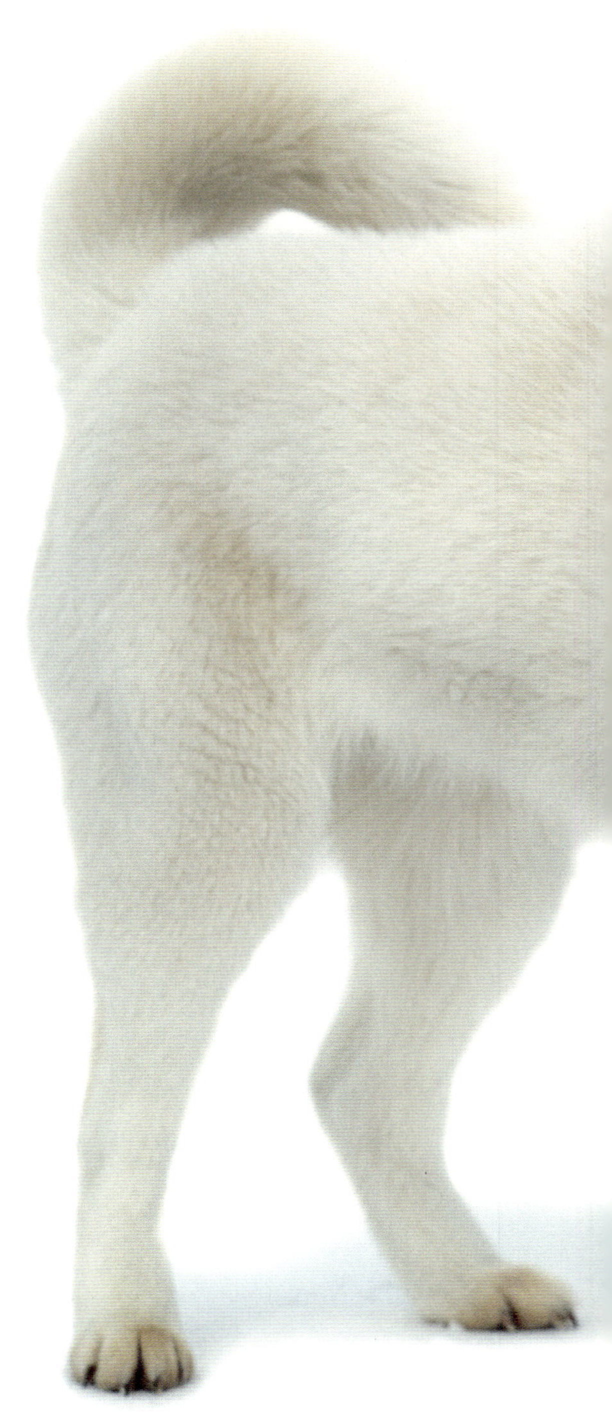

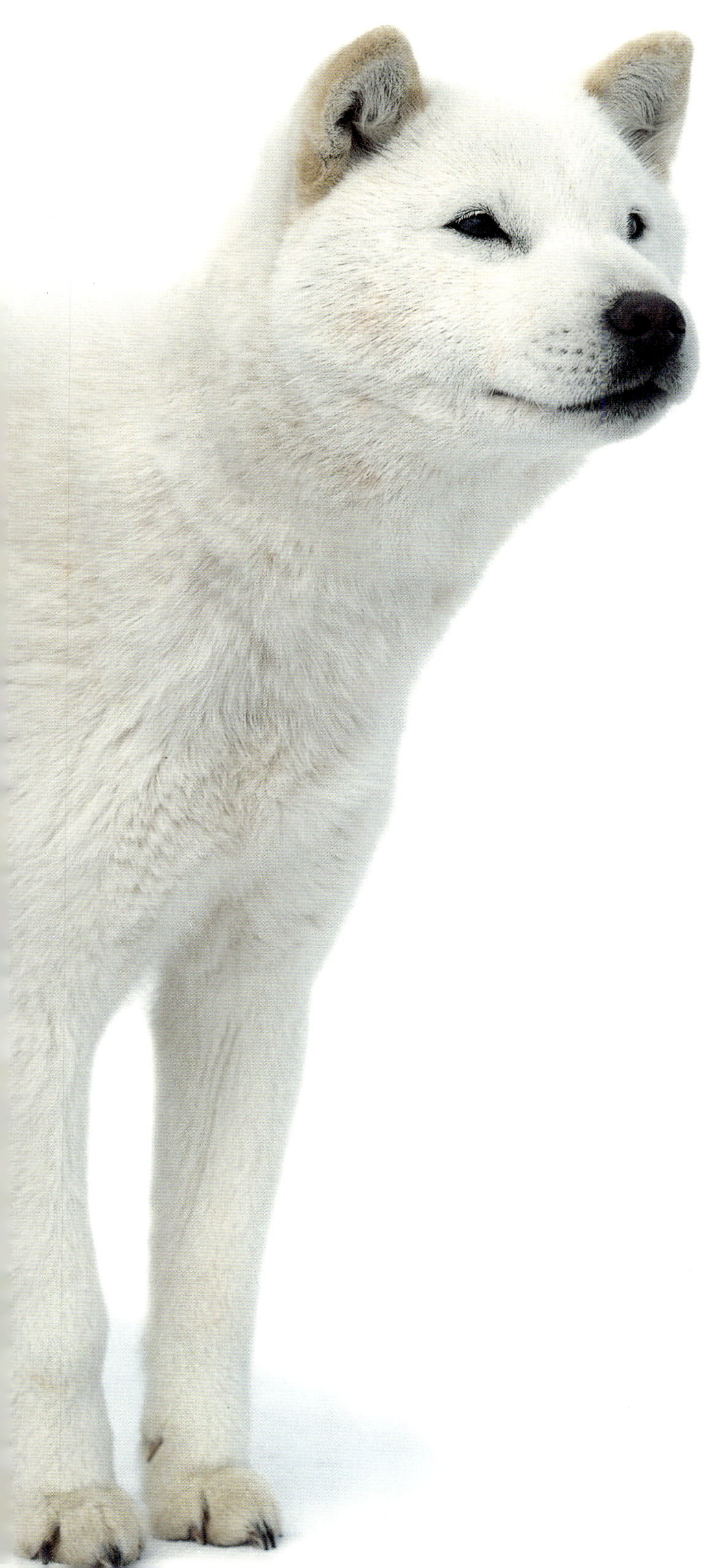

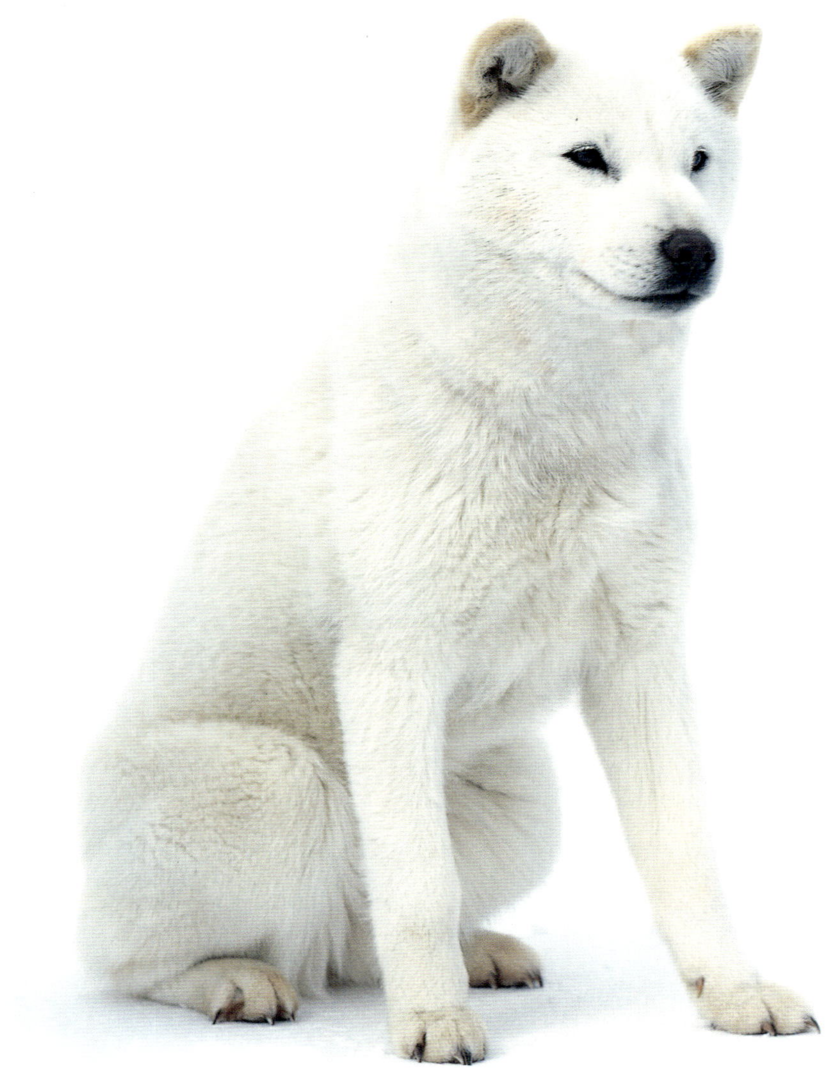

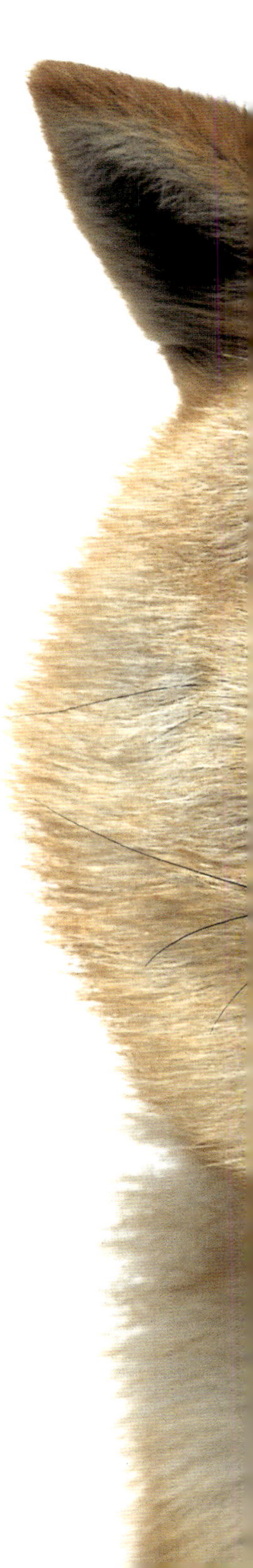

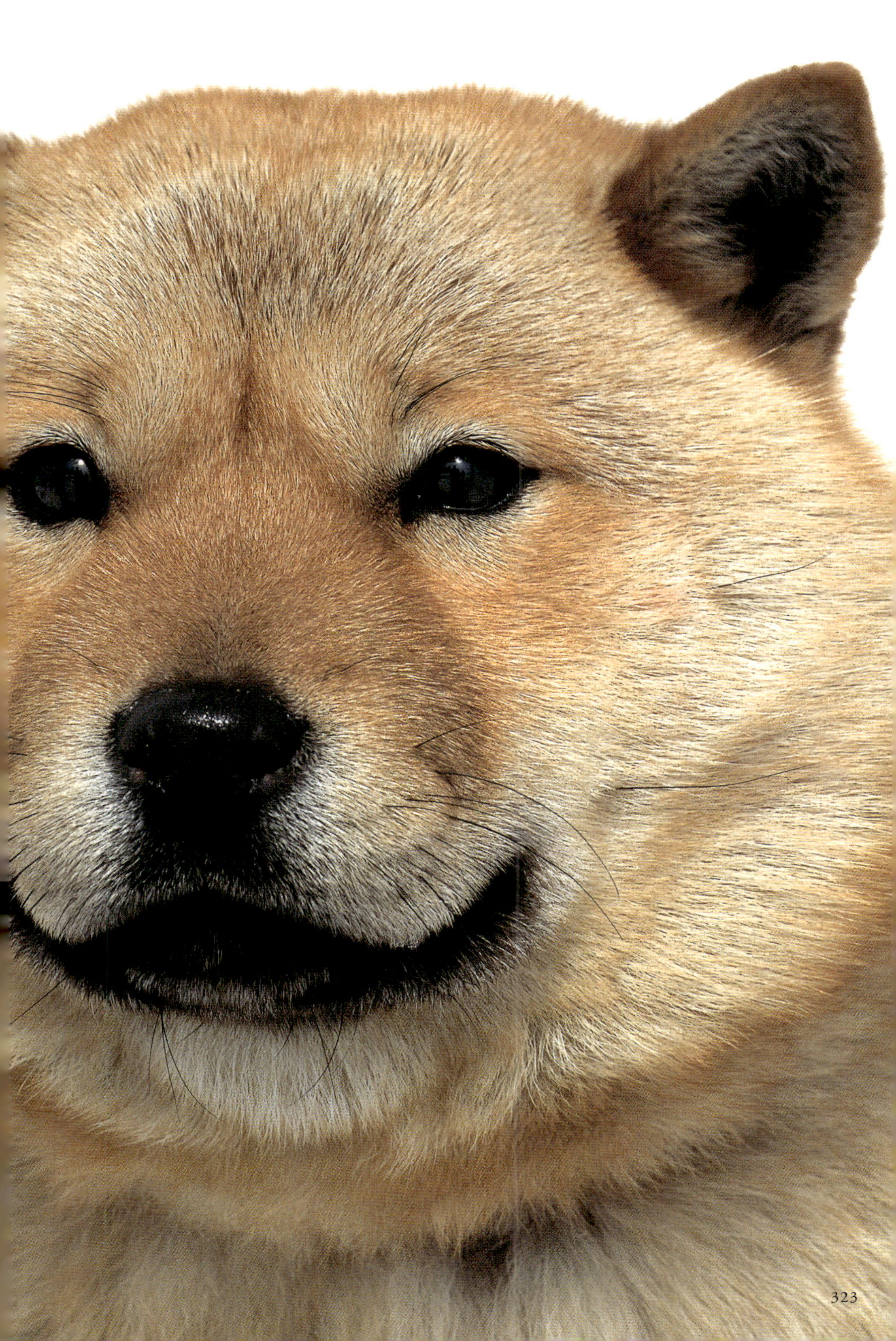

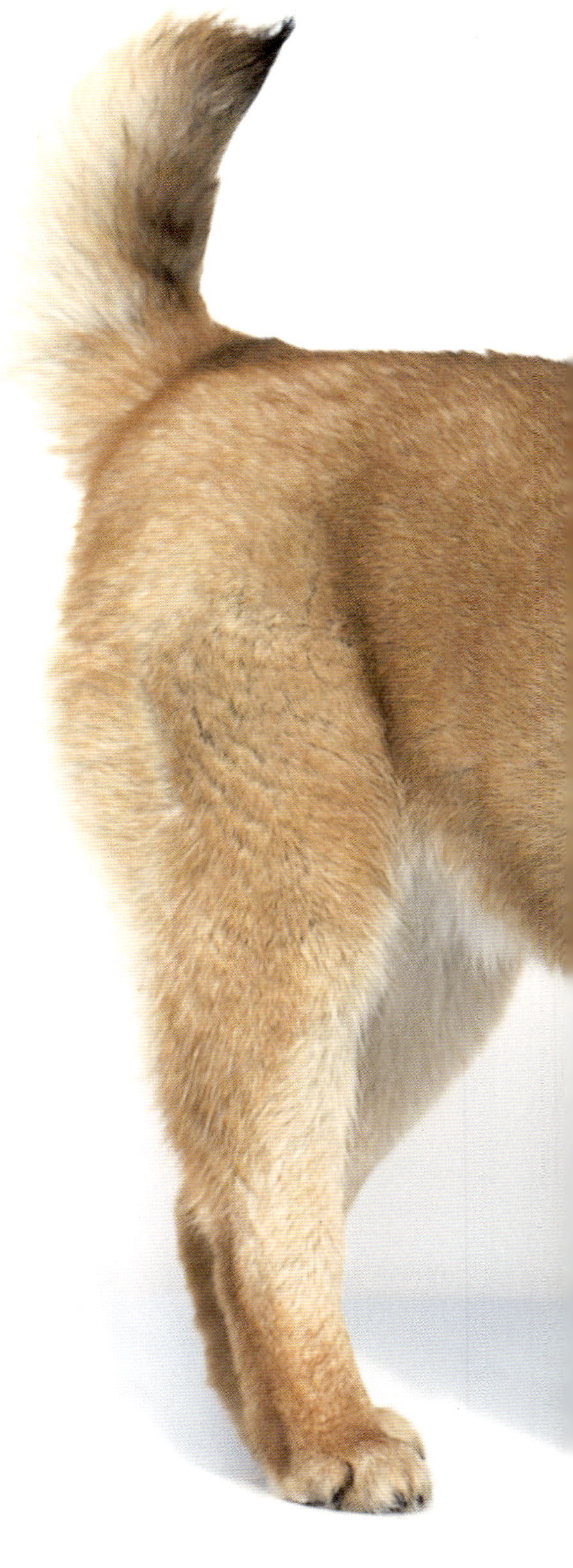

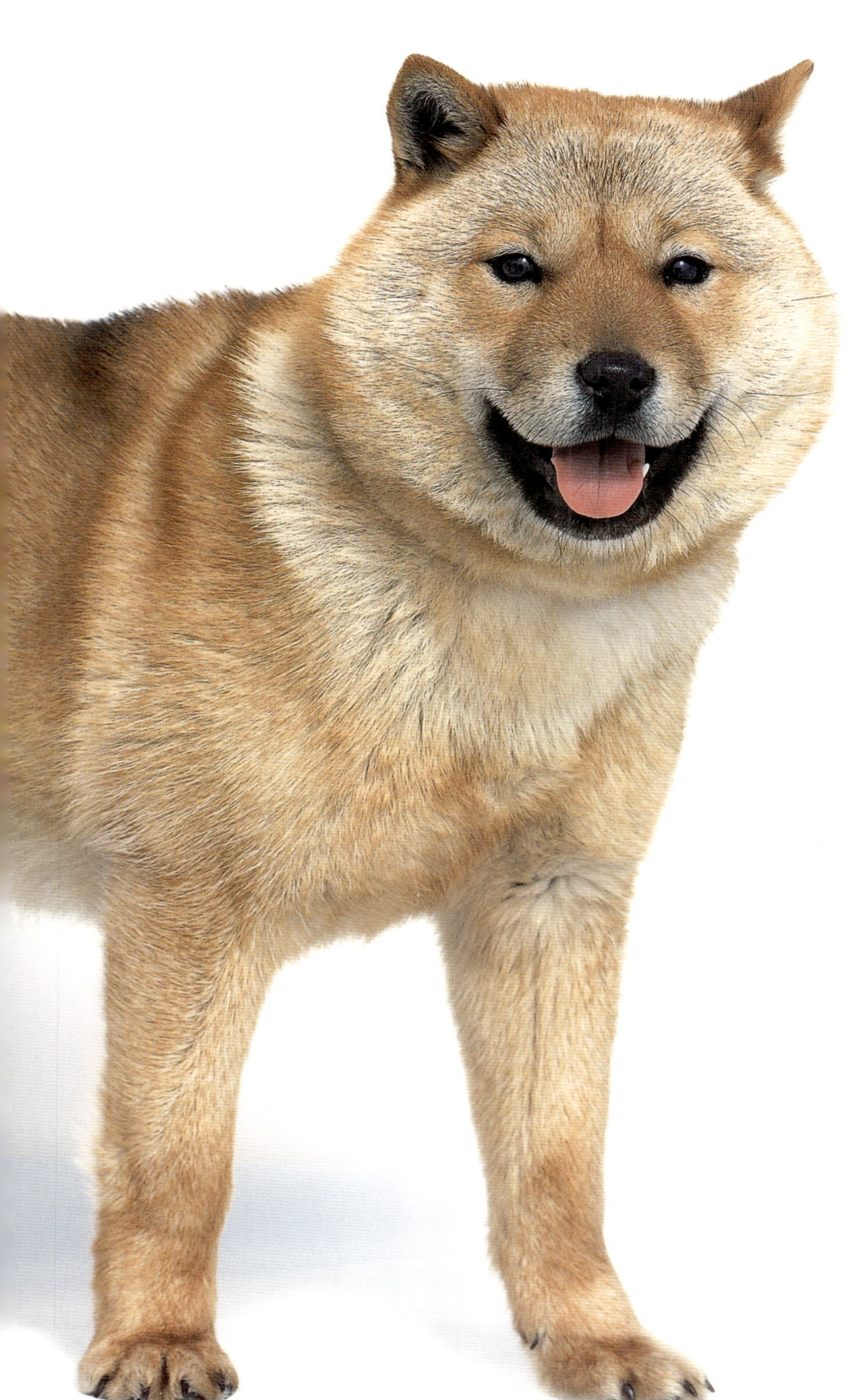

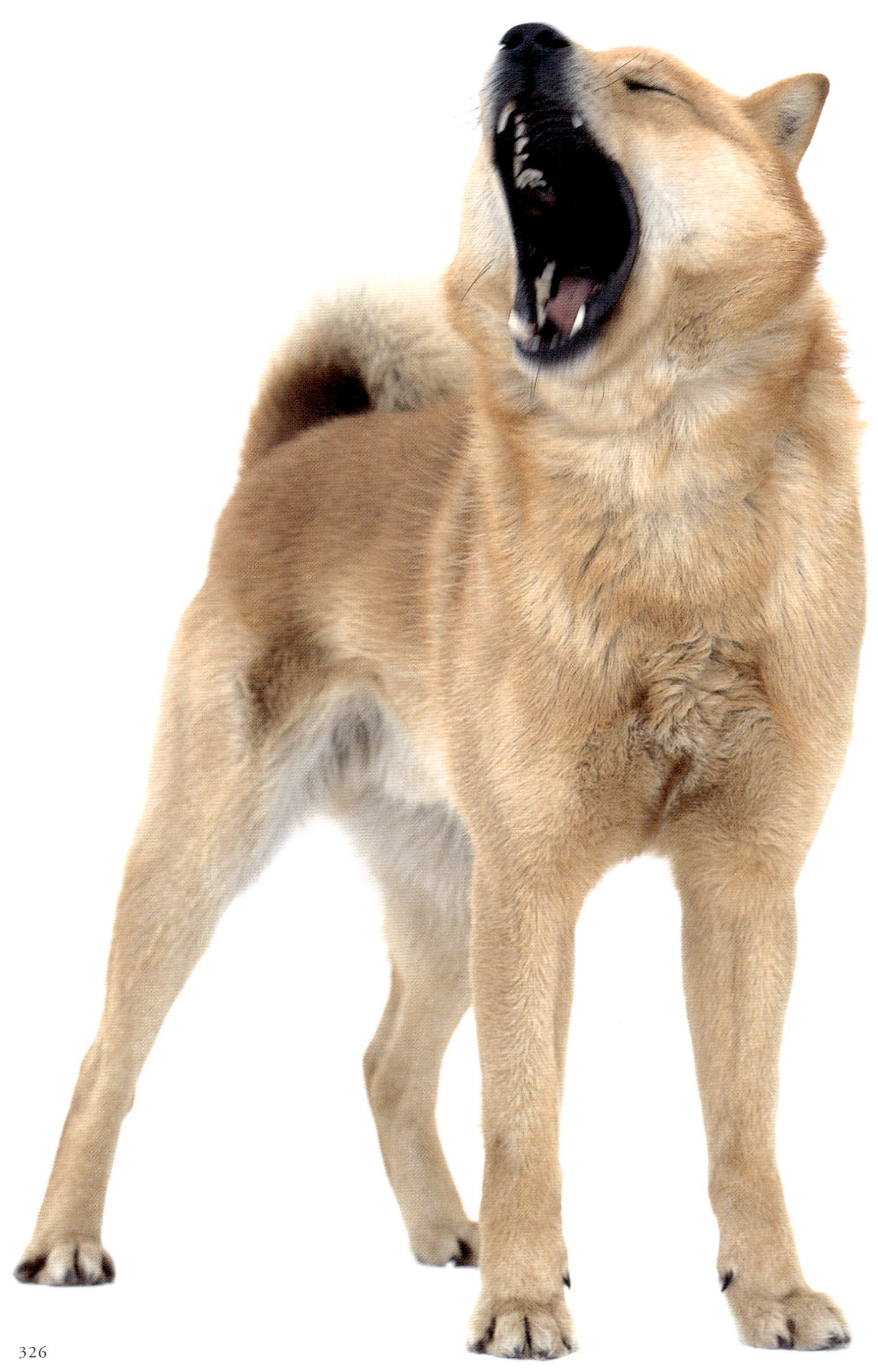

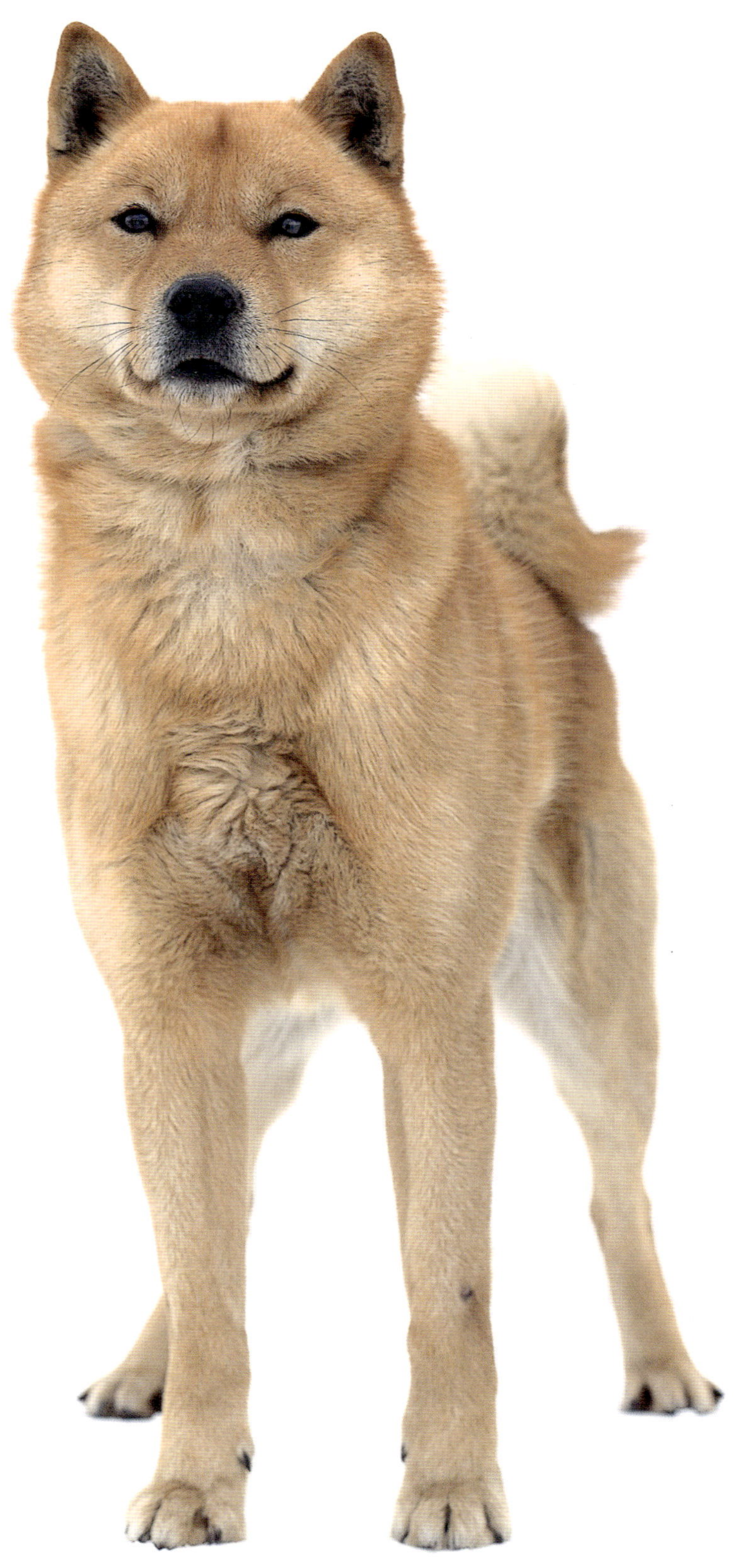

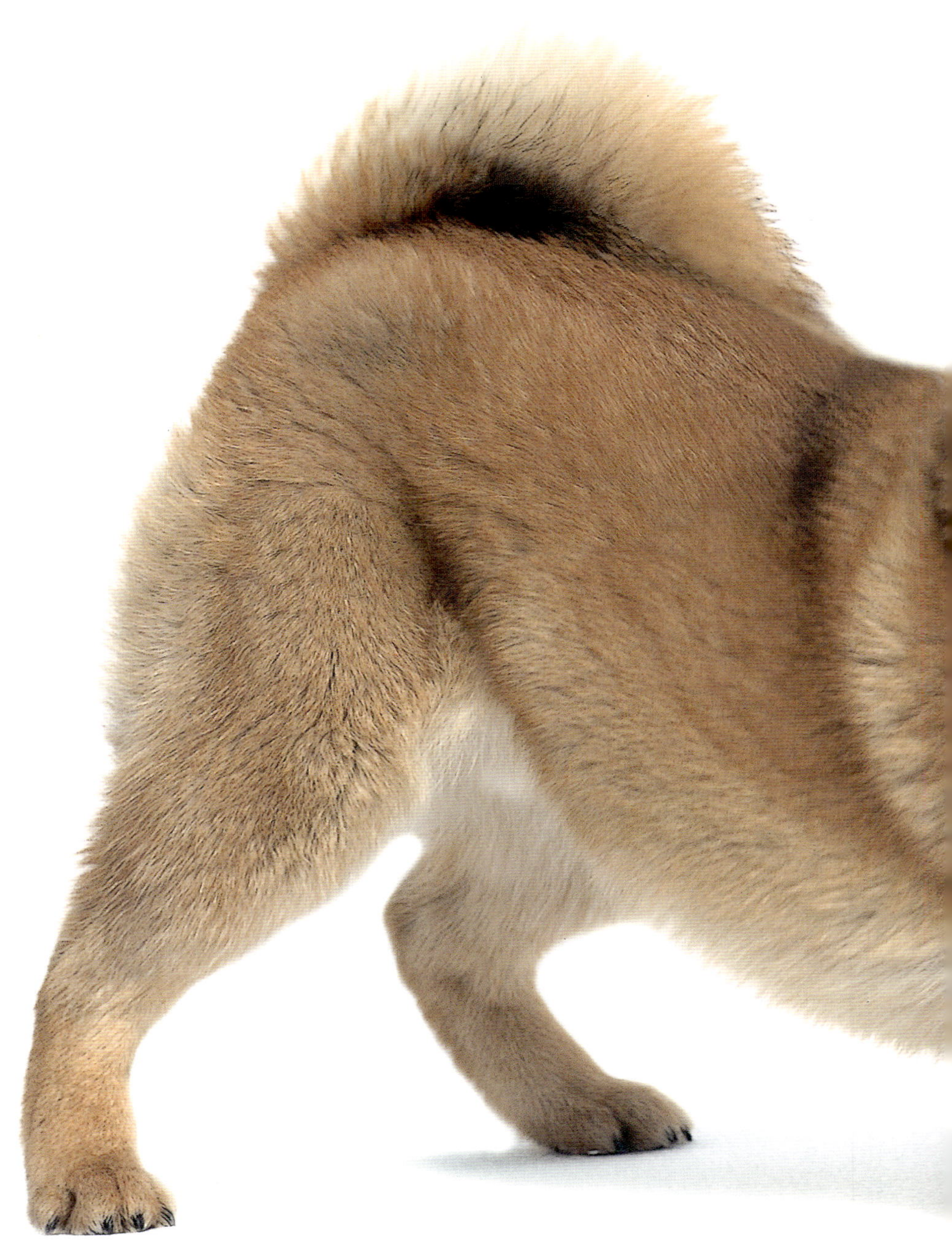

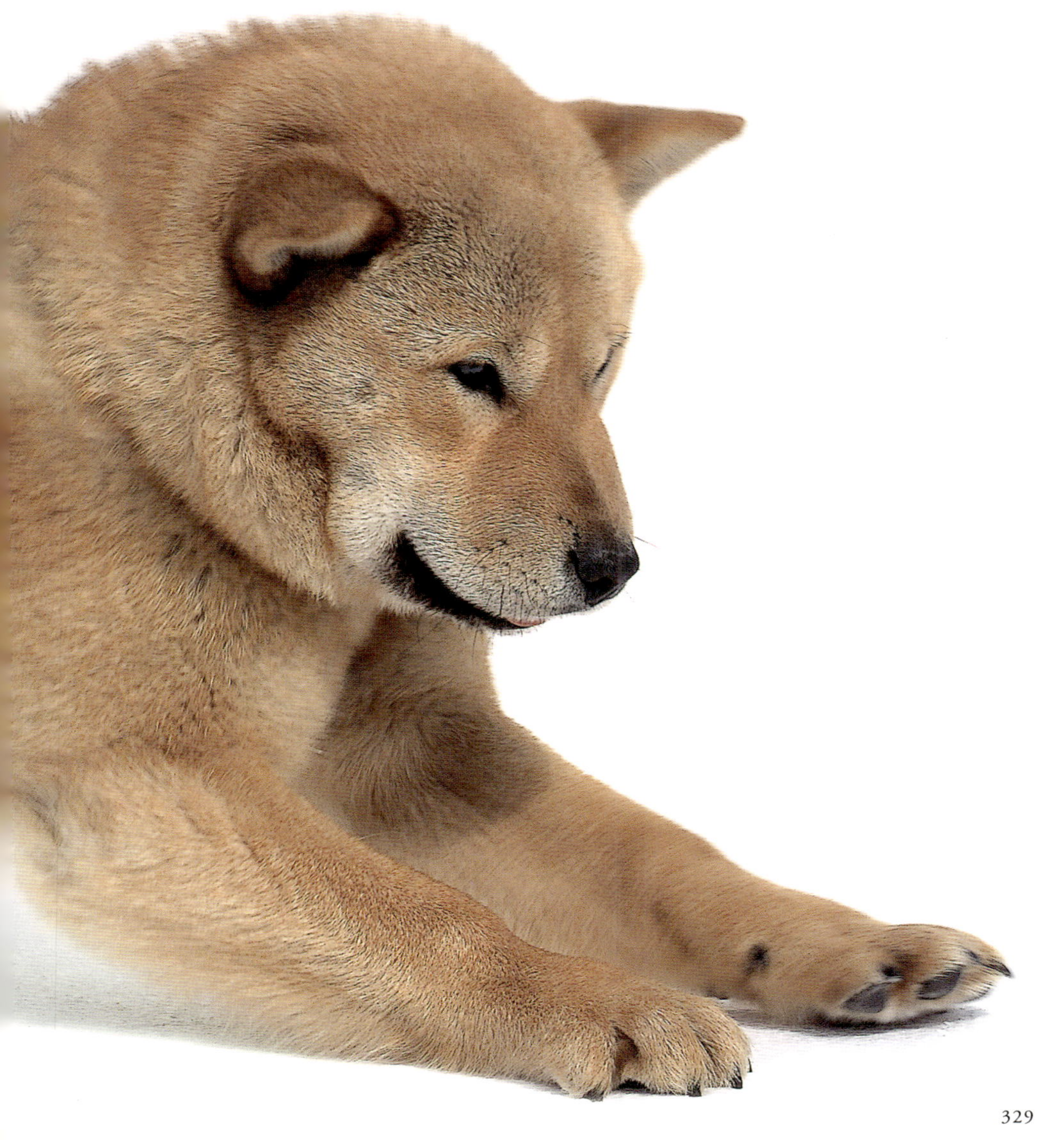

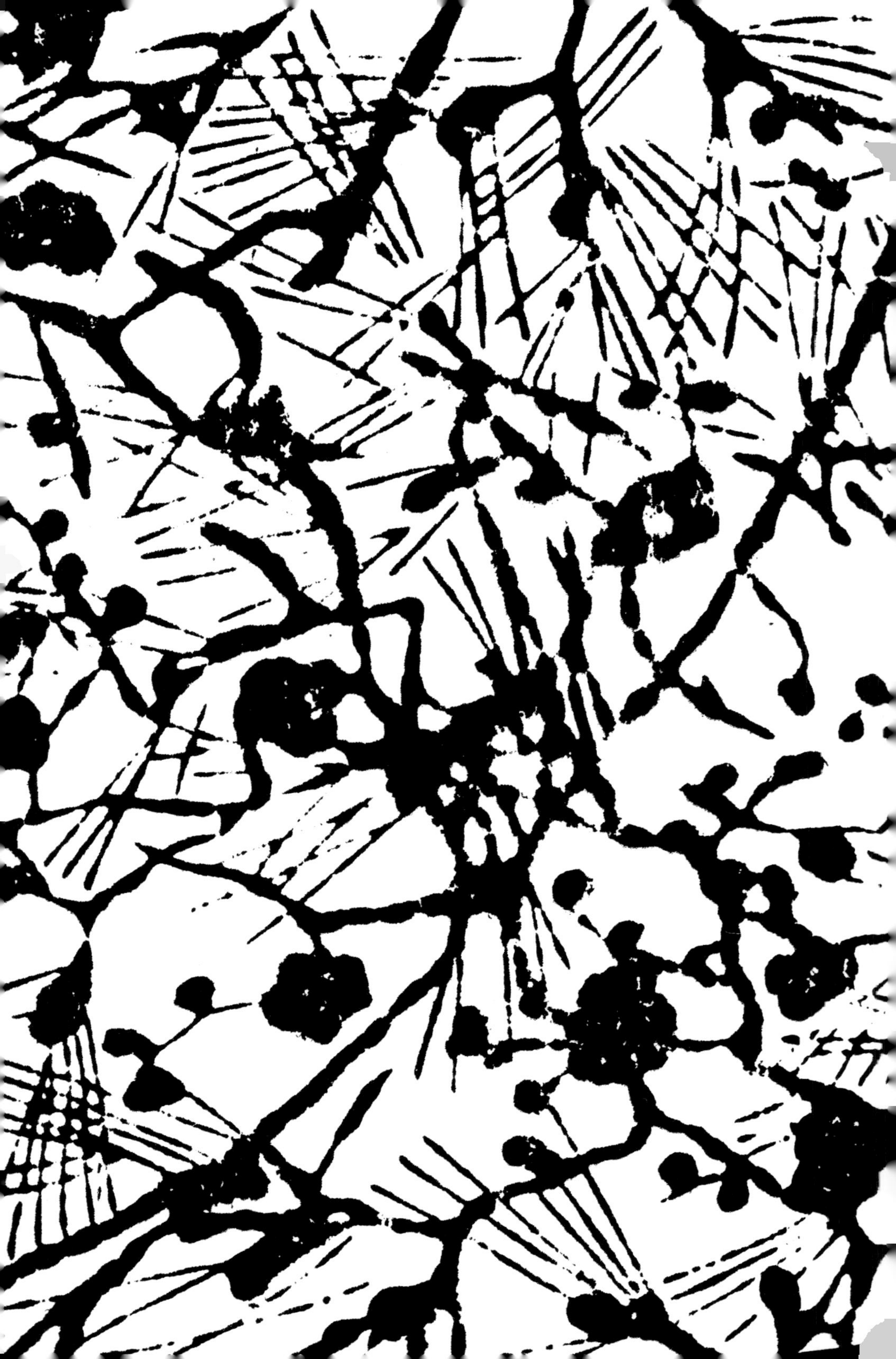

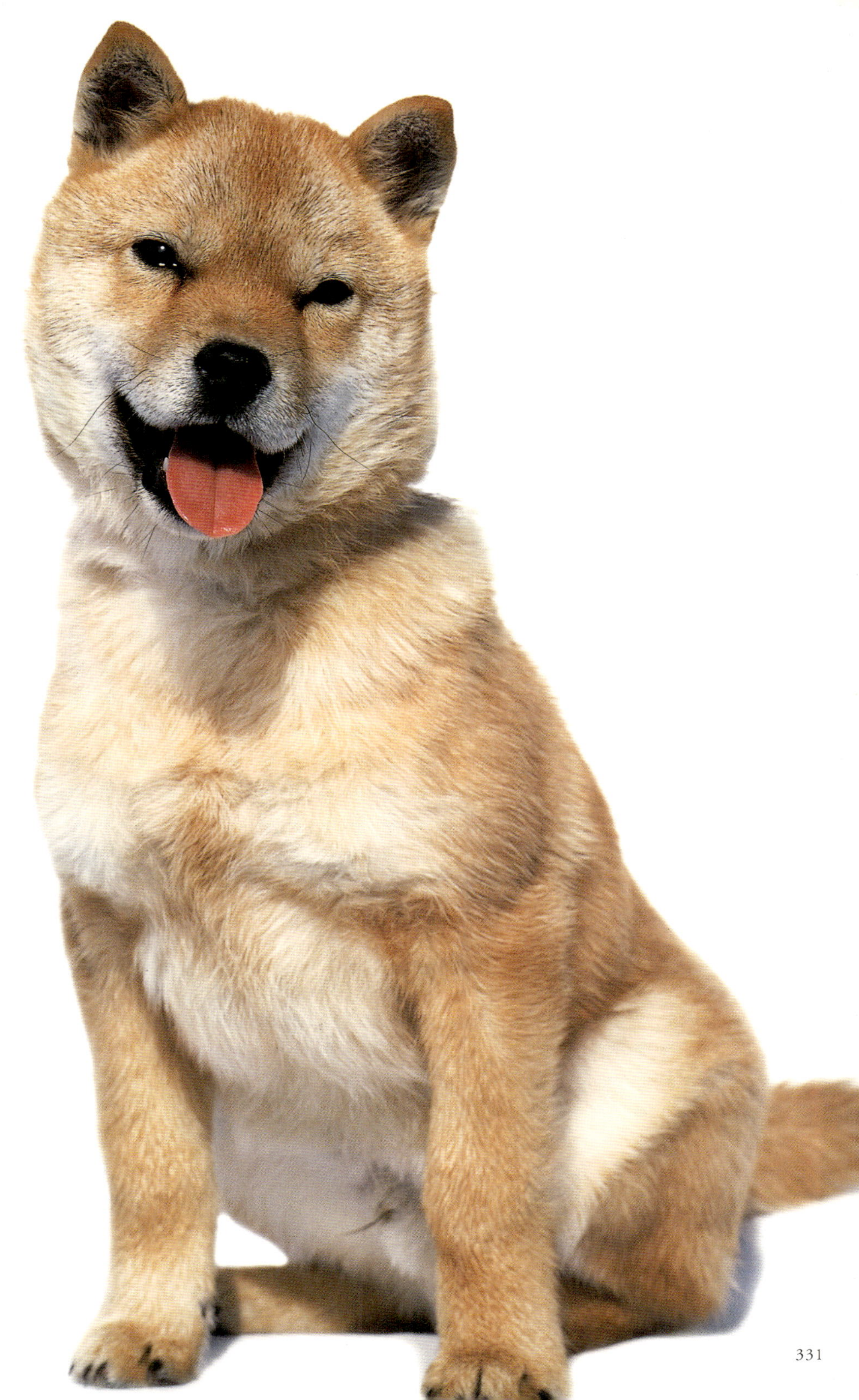

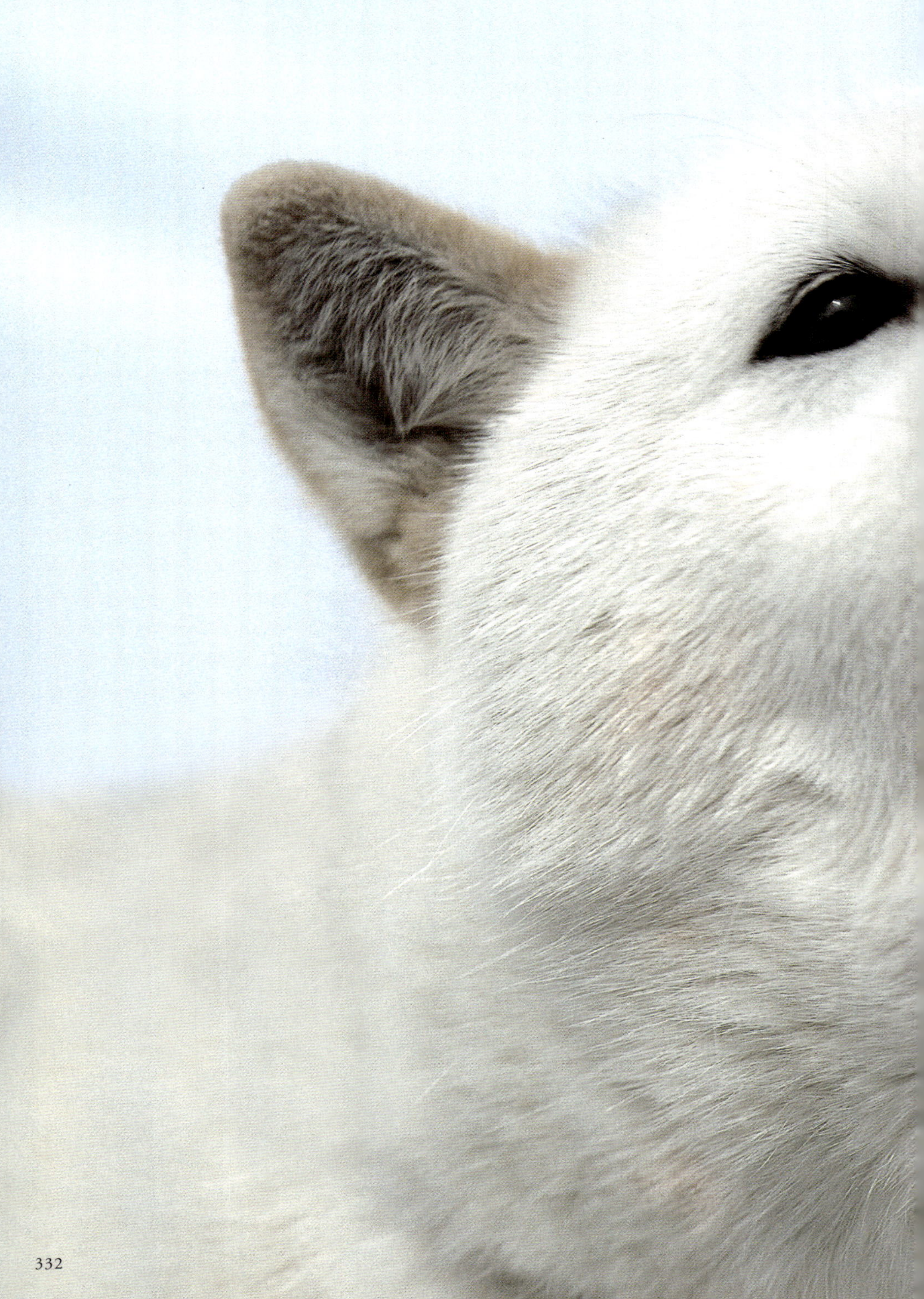

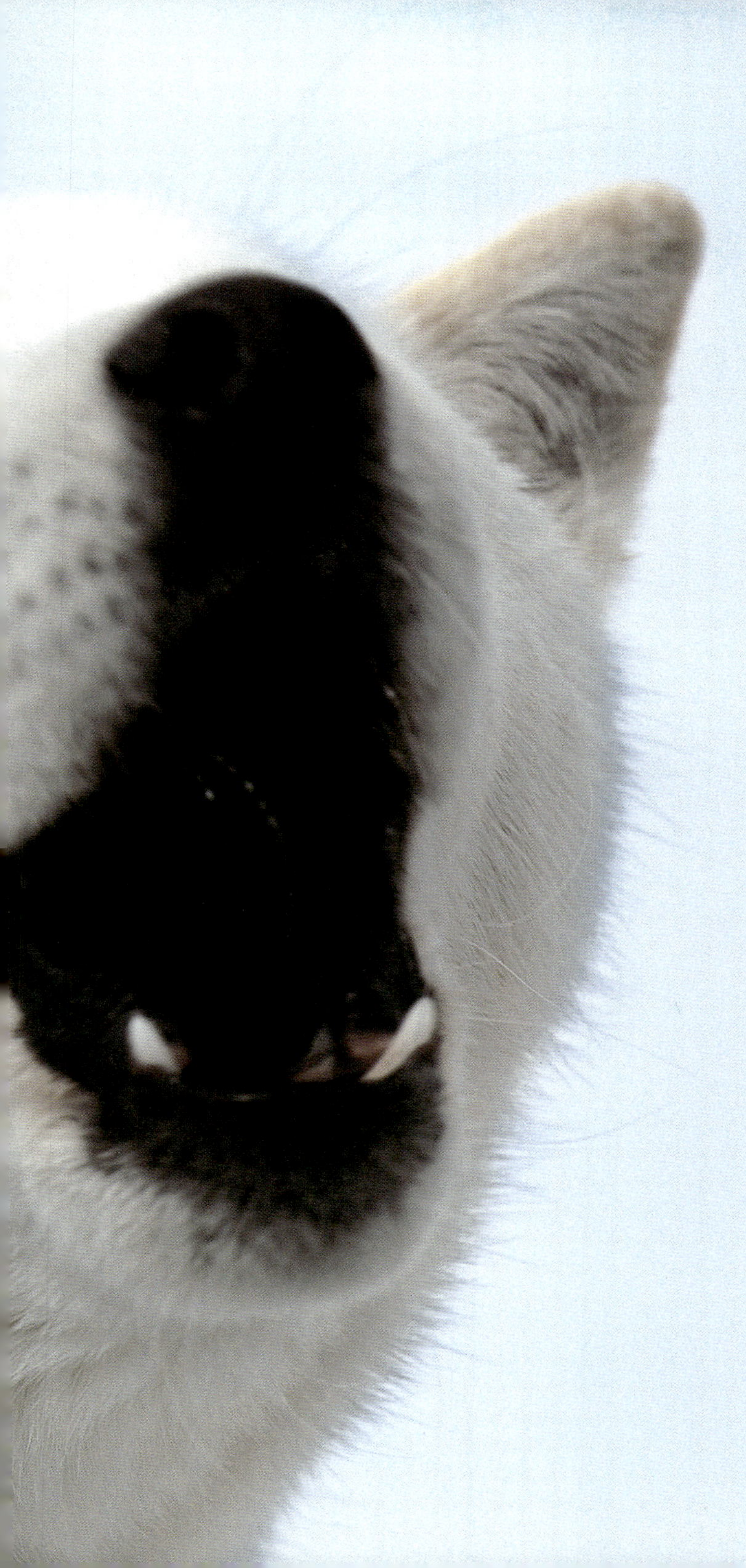

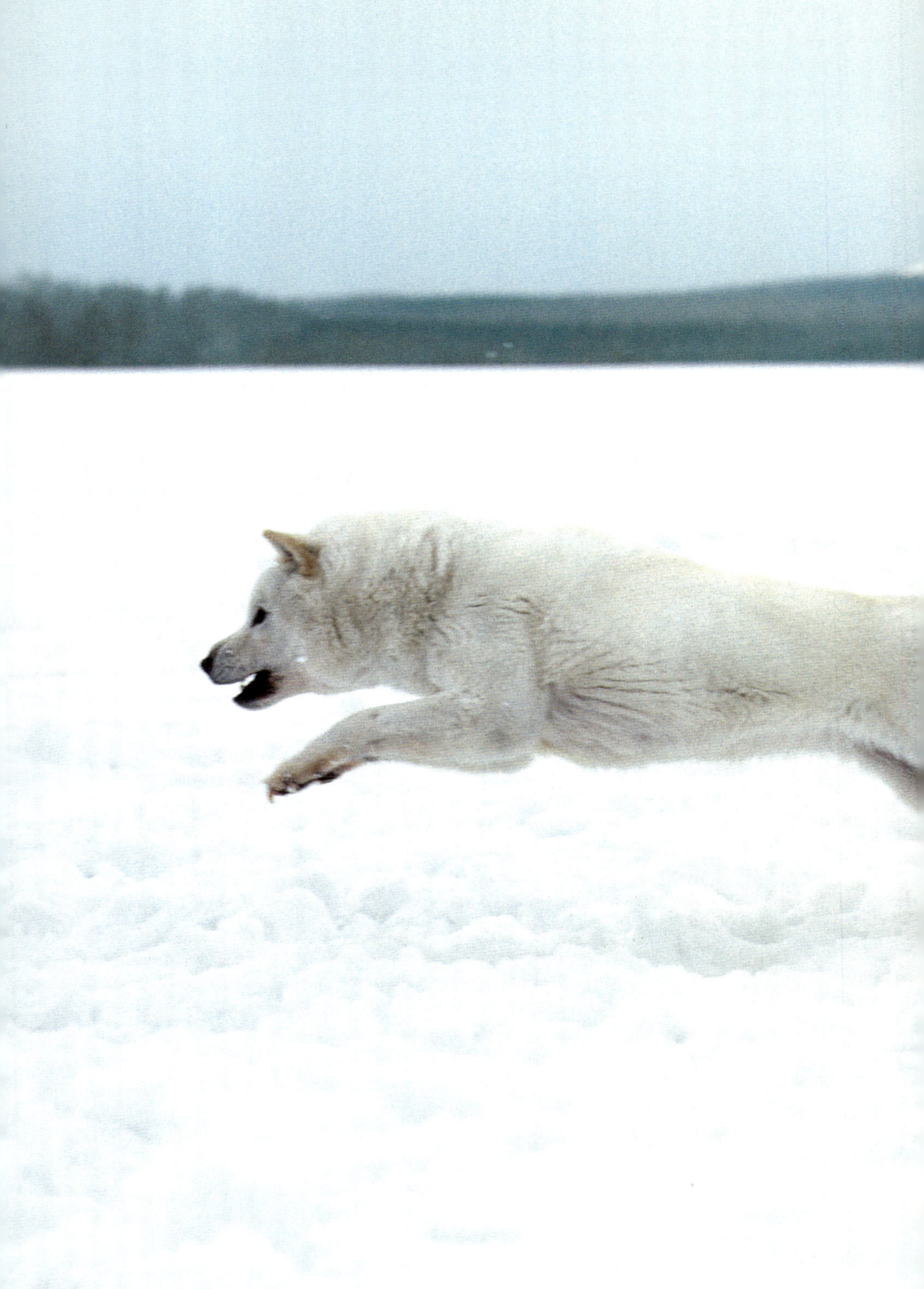

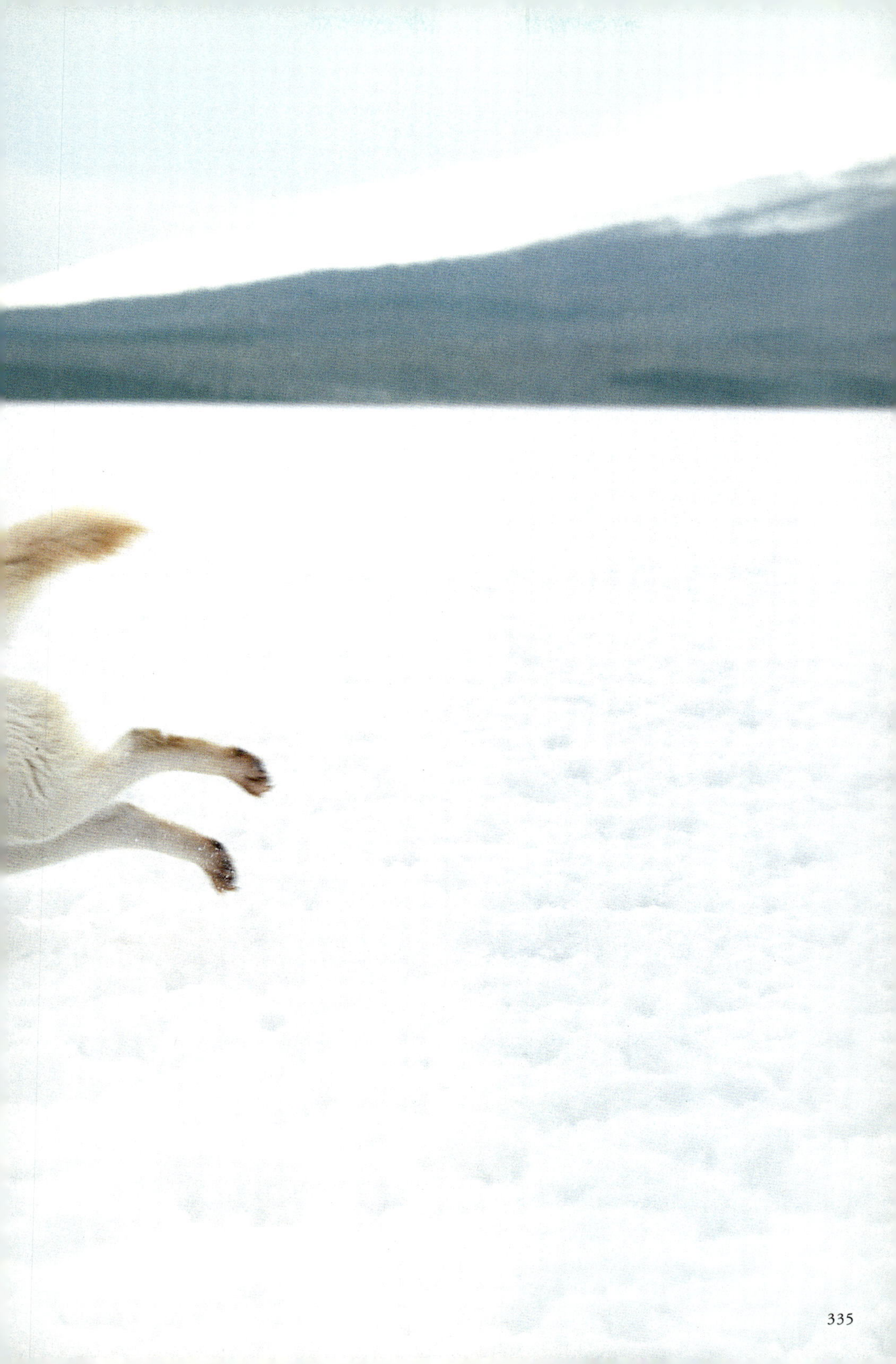

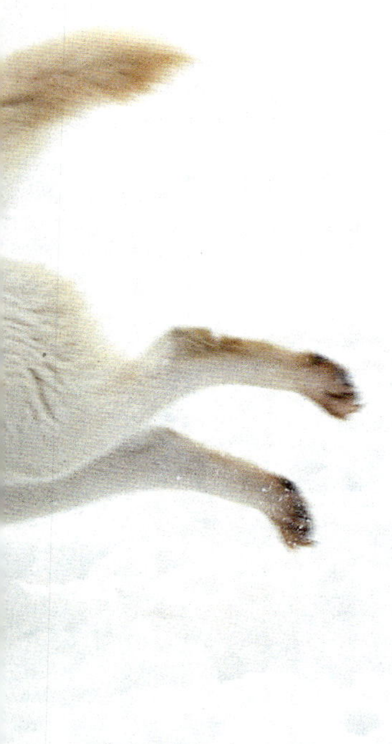

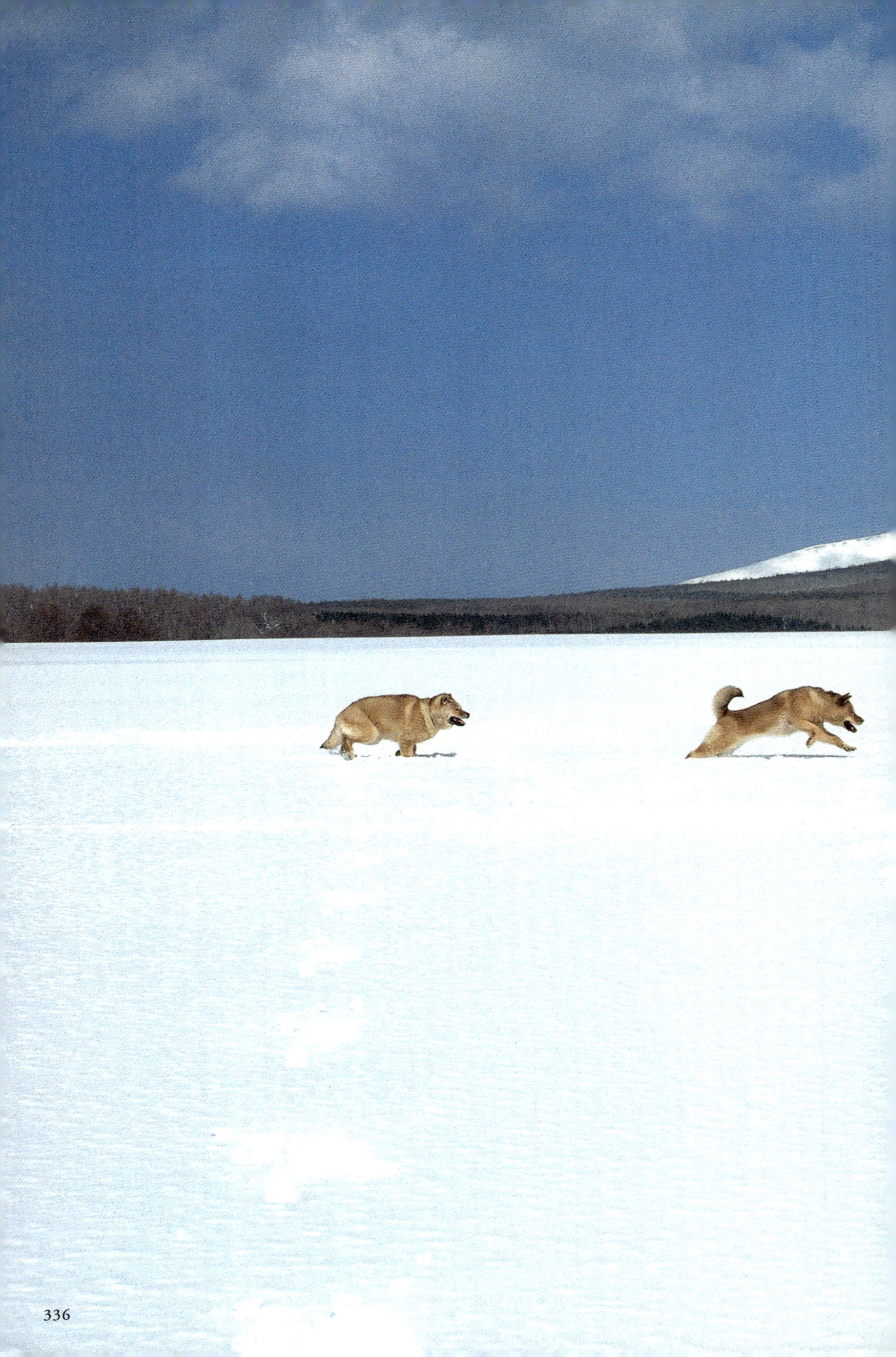

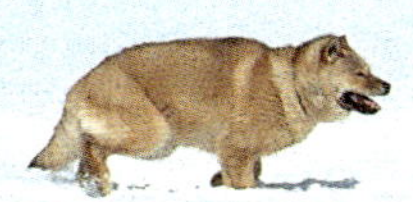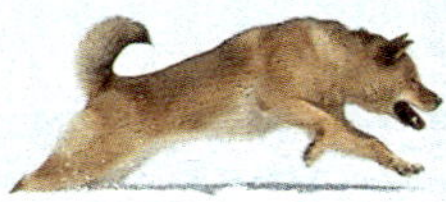

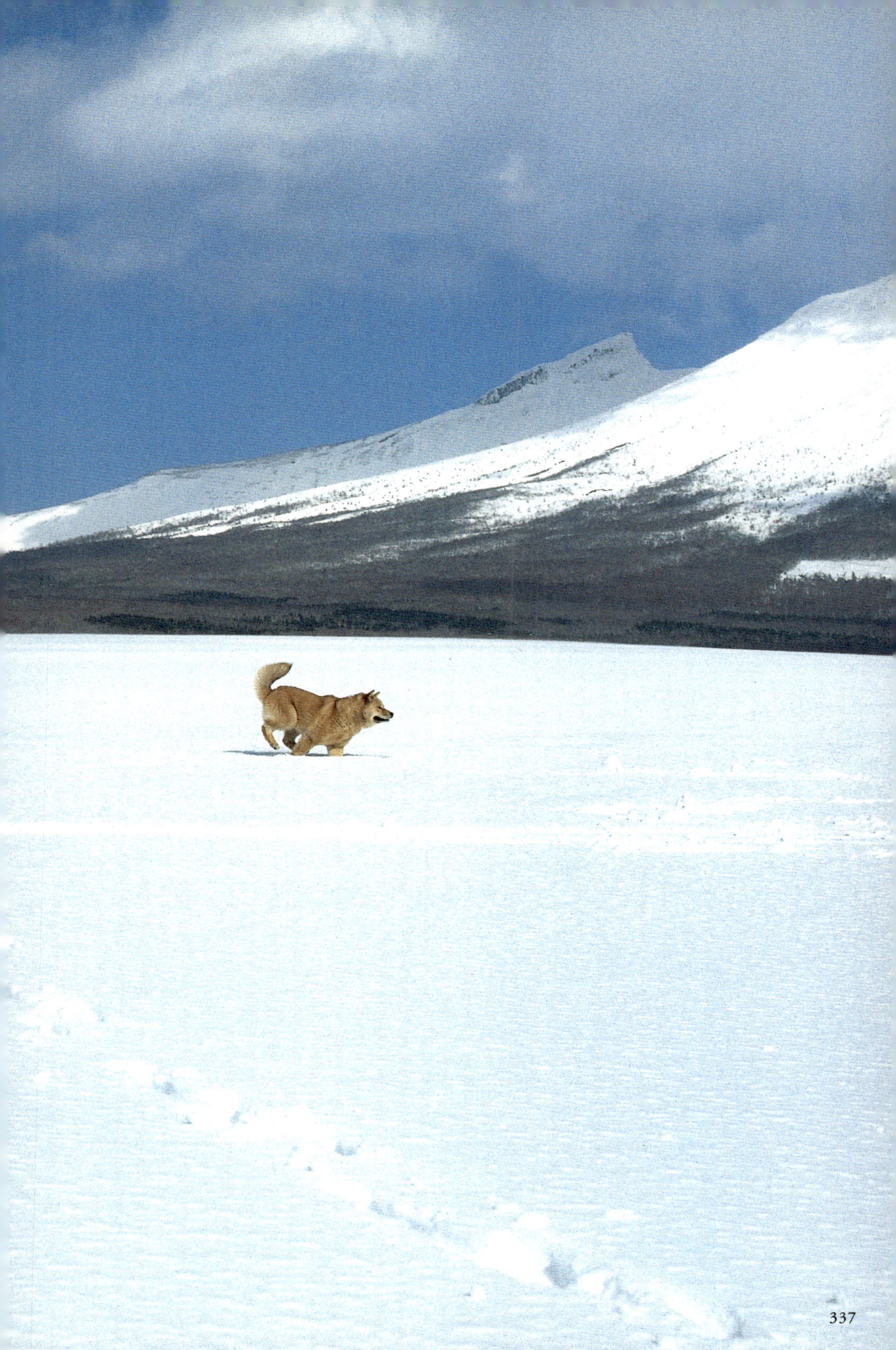

琉球犬

Ryukyu-ken

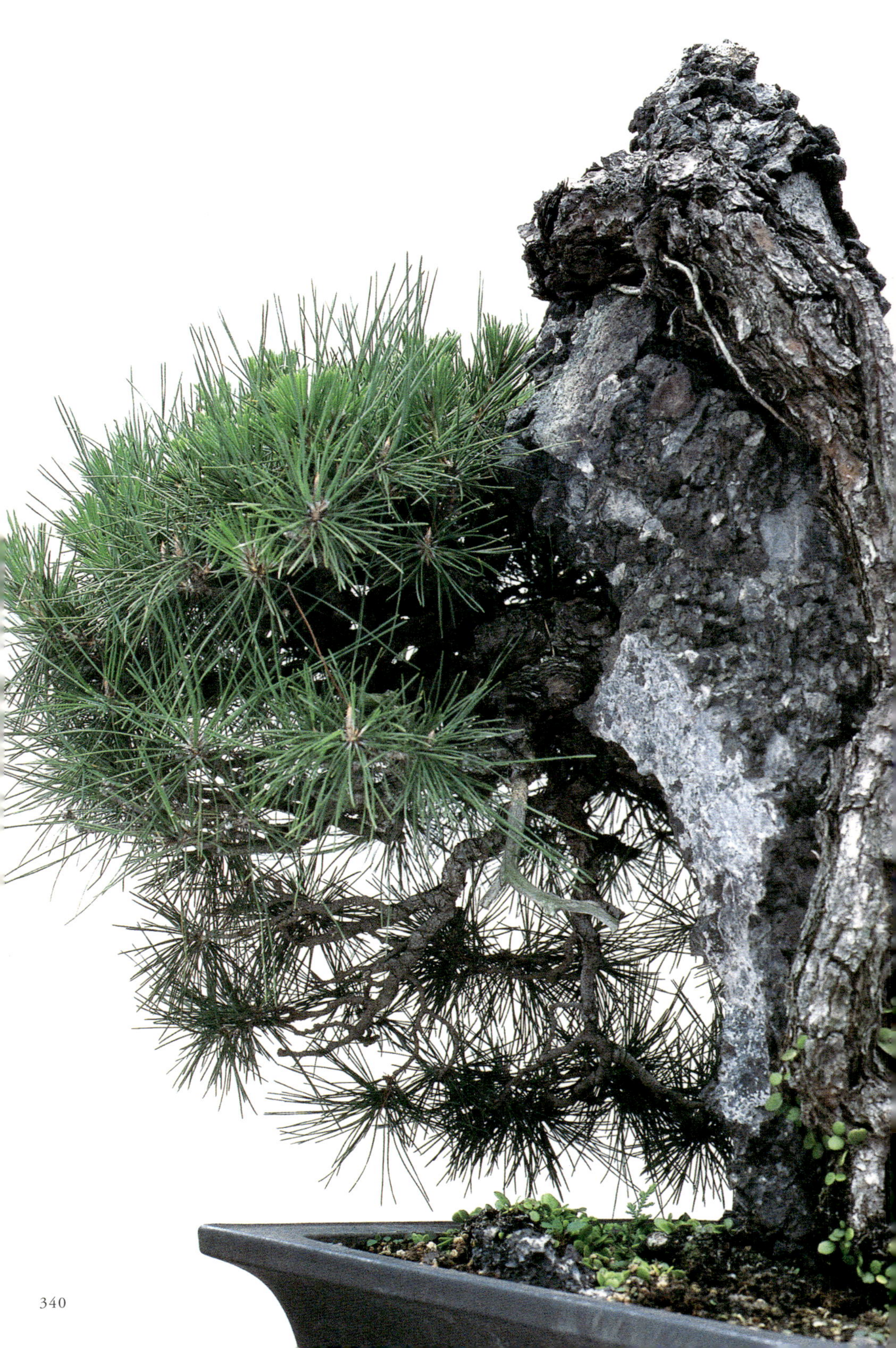

りゅうきゅうけん

琉球犬
沖縄本島北部の山原(やんばる)地方と
八重山(やえやま)地方で飼育されてきた在来犬。
主にイノシシ猟の猟犬として使われてきた。
虎毛模様は「トゥラー（トラ）」、
茶一色のものは「アカイン（赤イヌ）」と方言で呼ばれ、
細かくみると赤、黒、白、胡麻、アイボリーなど
10種類の毛色がでるといわれている。毛は短い。
耳はピンと立ち、左右の間隔が広いのも特徴だ。
胸の幅や厚みが豊富で、前駆の発達が著しく、胴ののびがよい。
性質はおとなしく、飼い主にとても従順である。
中型犬で、体高は山原系雄46センチ、雌43センチ。
八重山系雄50センチ、雌47センチ。

Native to the Yanbaru and Yaeyama regions
in the north of the island of Okinawa.
The Ryukyu-ken has traditionally been used
as a hunting dog mainly for hunting wild boar.
The brindled variety and brown solid-colored variety are referred
to in the local dialect as Tora (tiger) and Akainu (red dog) respectively,
although it is said the Ryukyu-ken can in fact be broken down
into ten varieties according to color,
including red, black, white, sesame, and ivory.
The coat is short.
The ears are firmly pricked, and the wide gap
between the ears is also a distinguishing feature of the breed.
The chest is extremely wide and deep, with the front area noticeably
well developed and the abdomen fully rounded.
The Ryukyu-ken has a docile temperament and is
extremely obedient towards its owner.
It is a medium-sized dog, with males of the Yanbaru variety
growing to a height of 46 cm, and females to 43 cm.
Males of the Yaeyama variety grow to a height of 50 cm,
and females to a height of 47 cm.

Ryukyu-ken

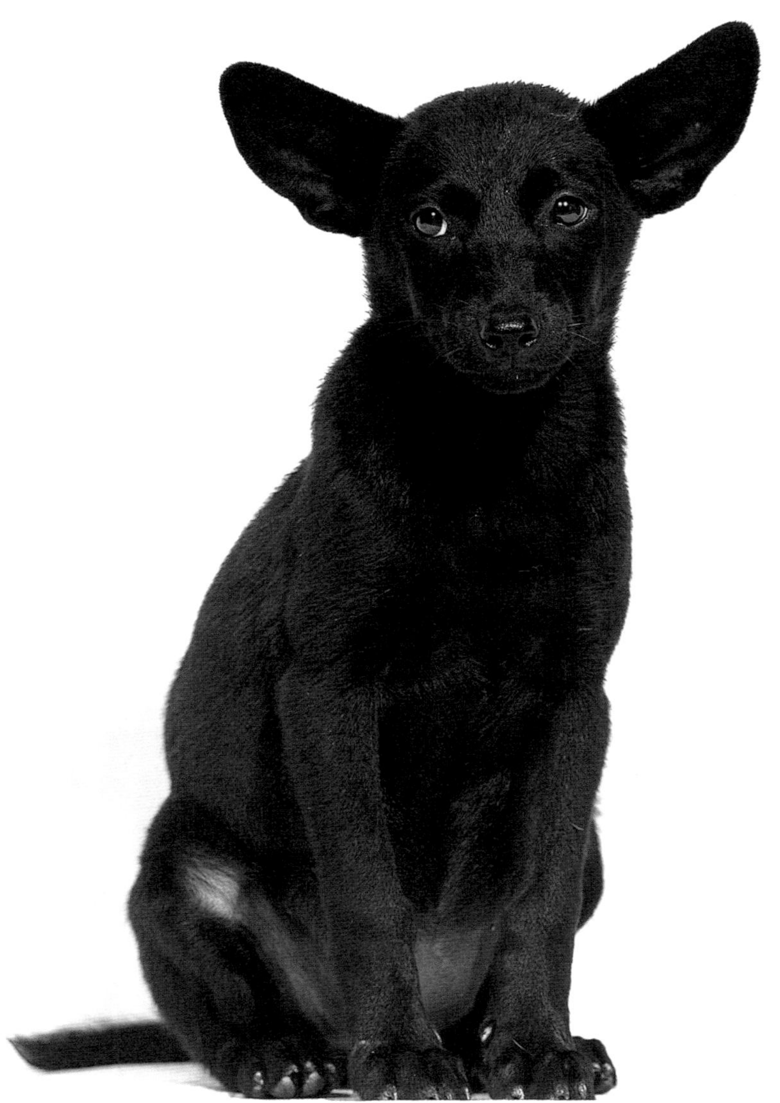

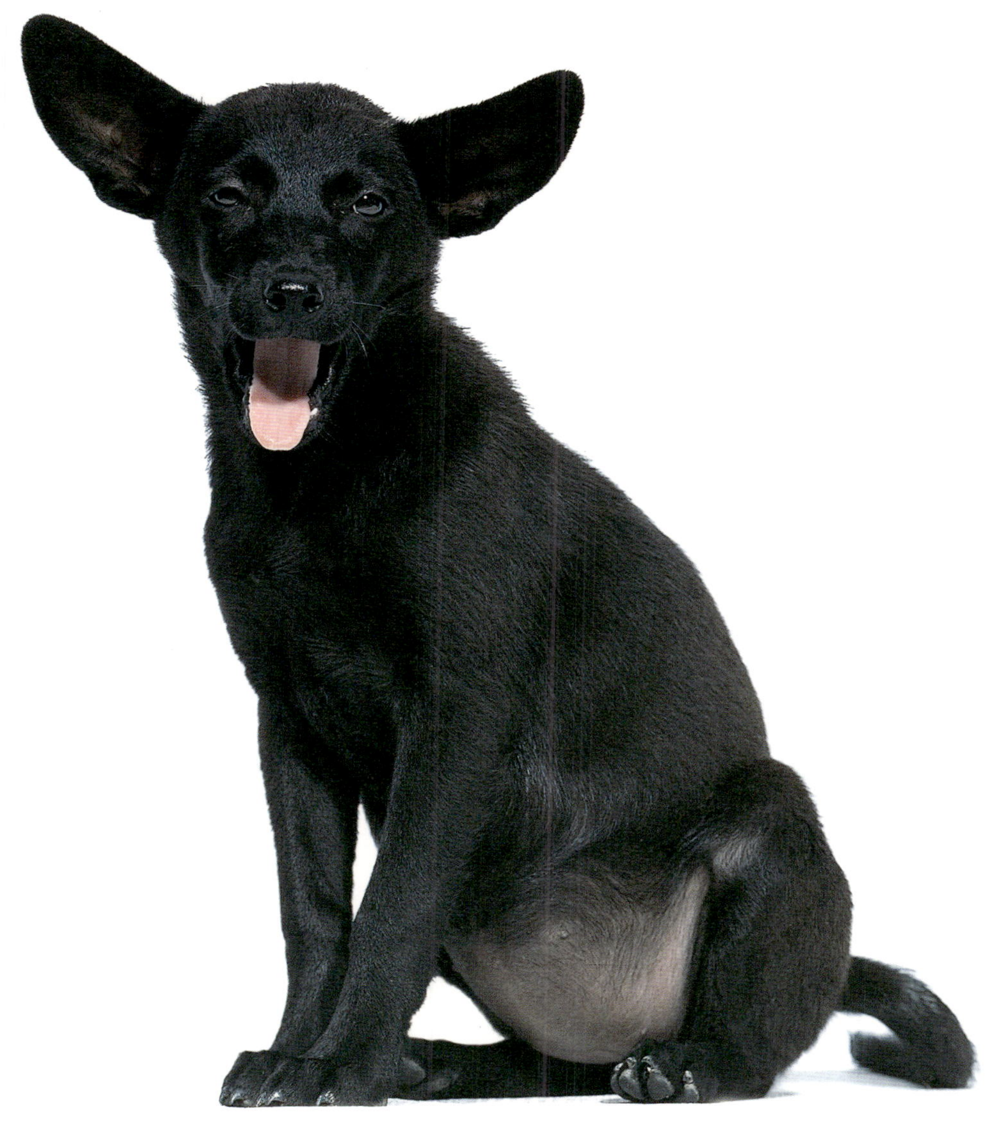

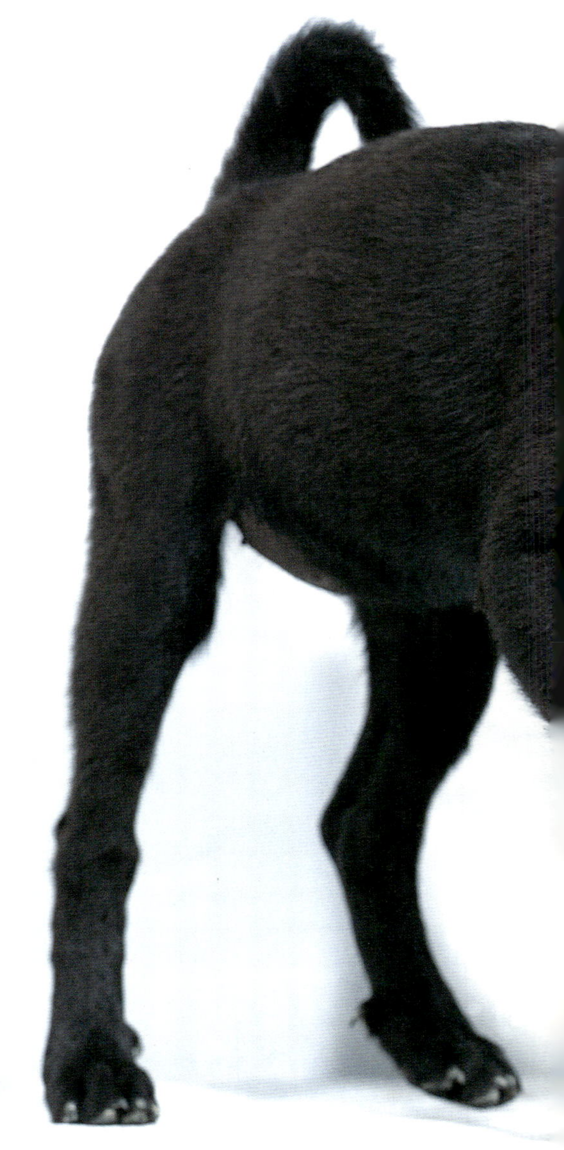

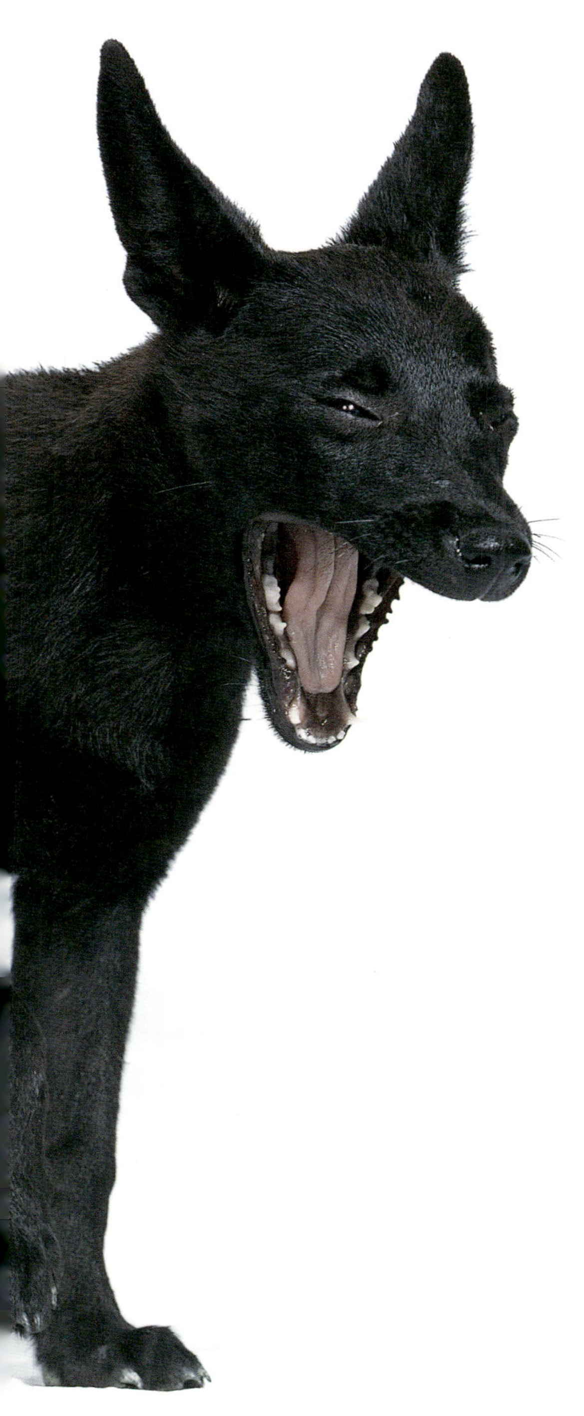

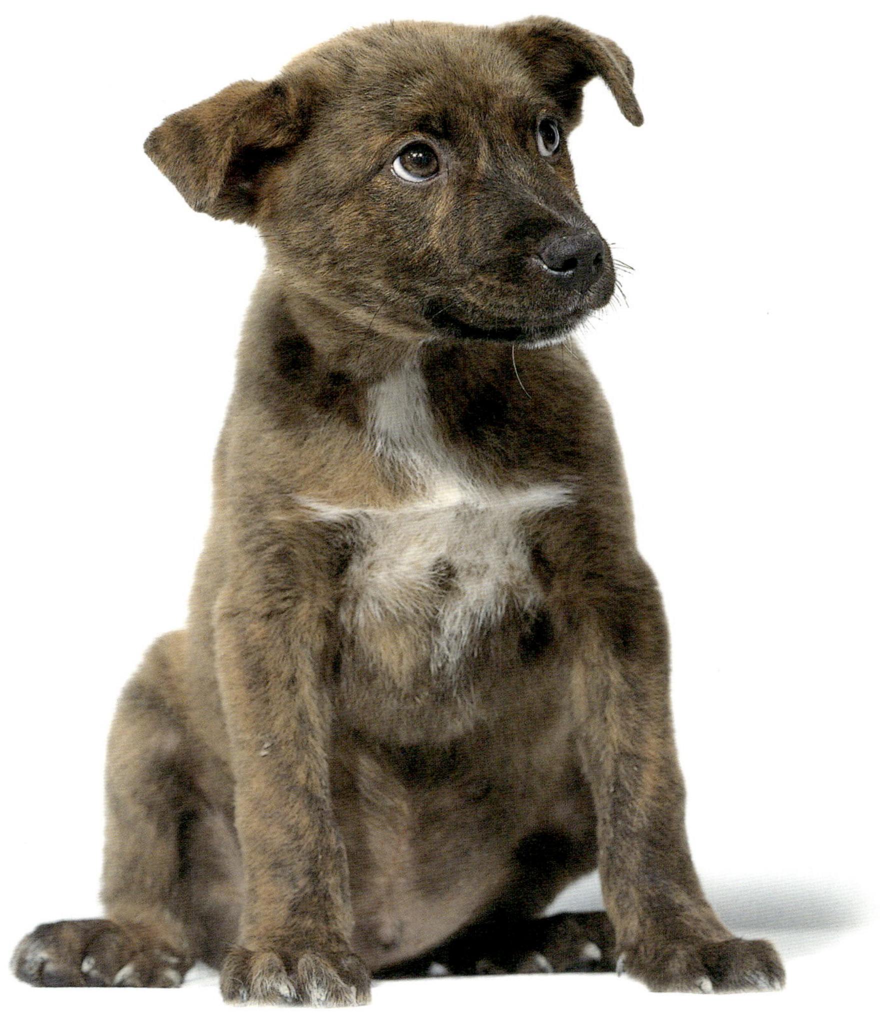

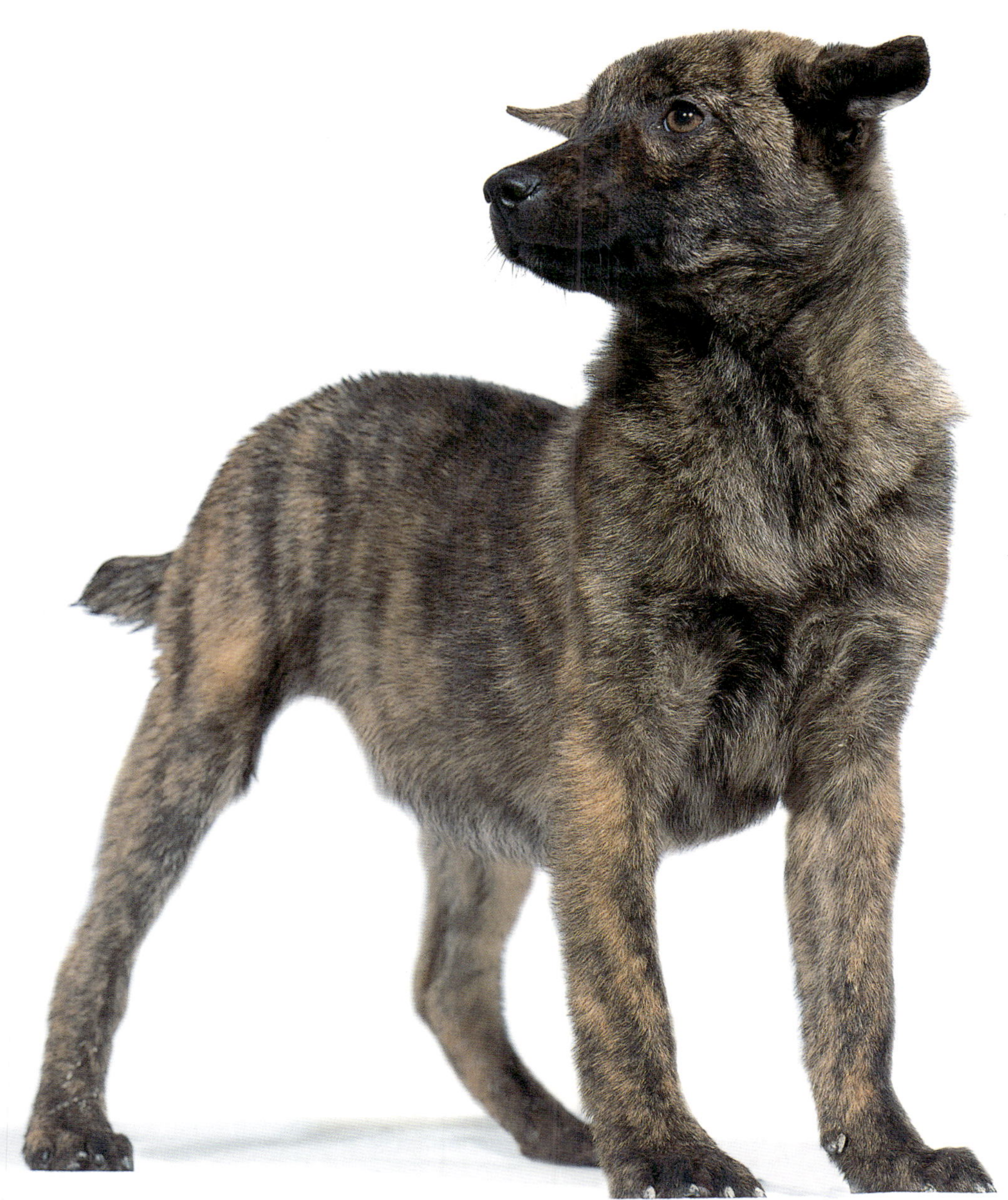

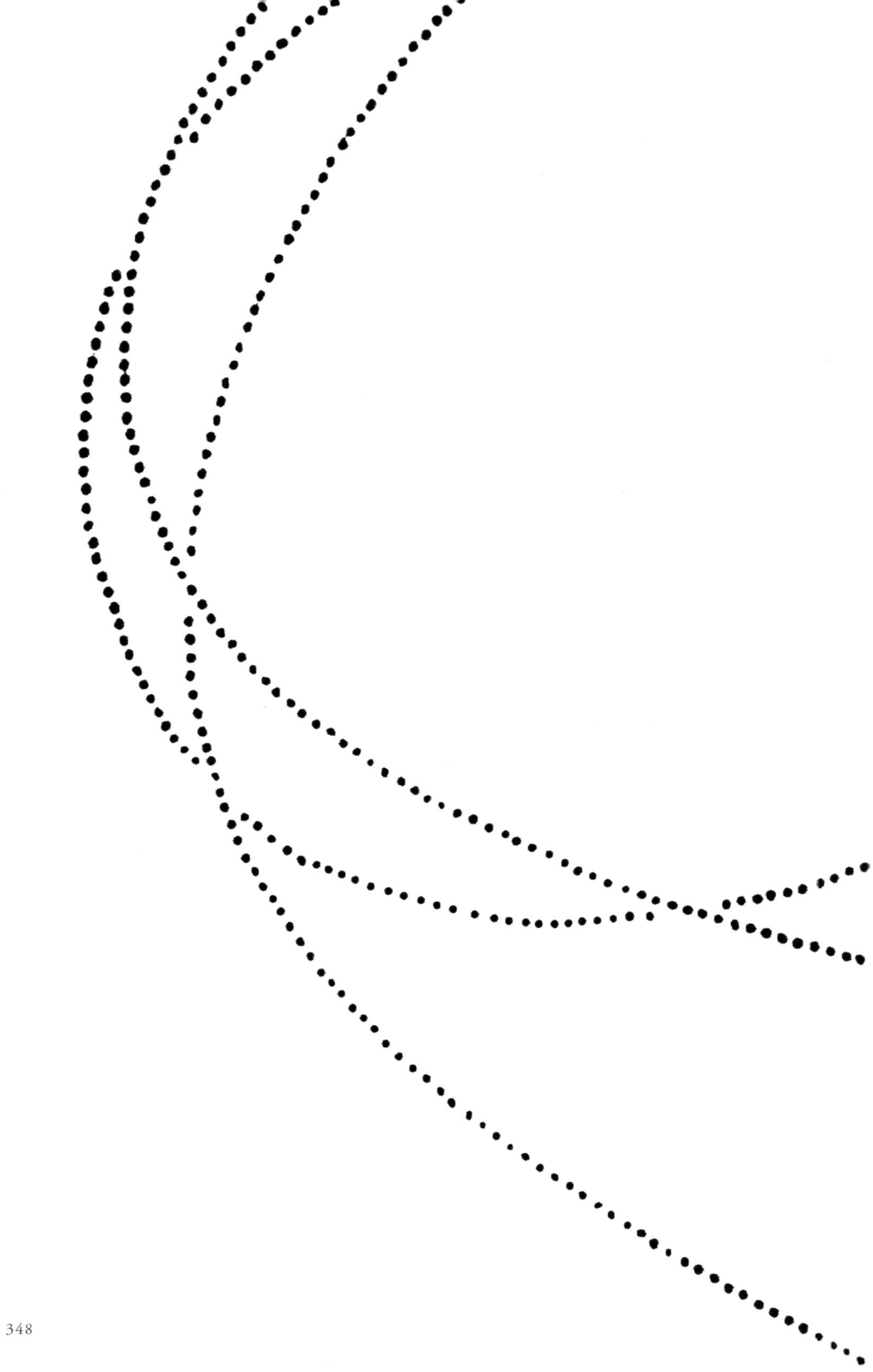

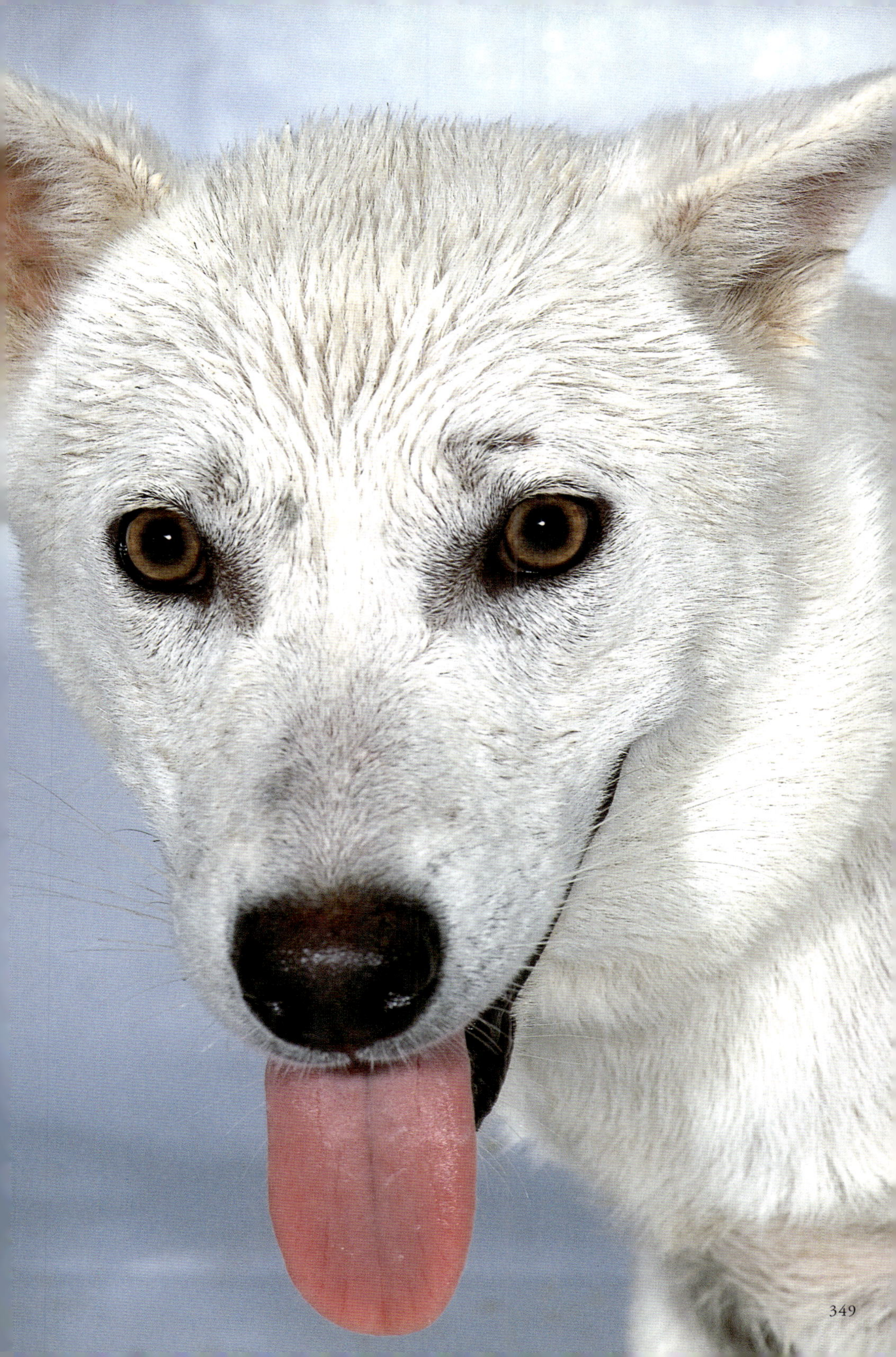

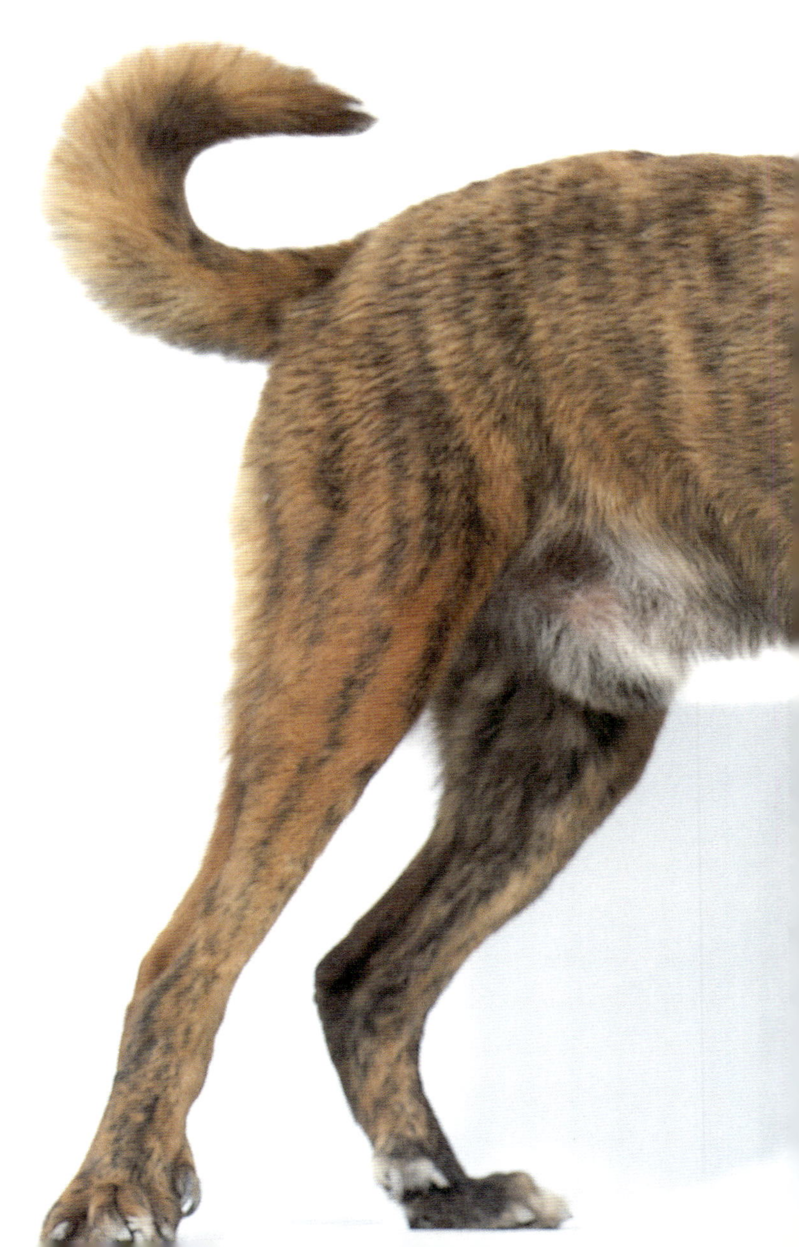

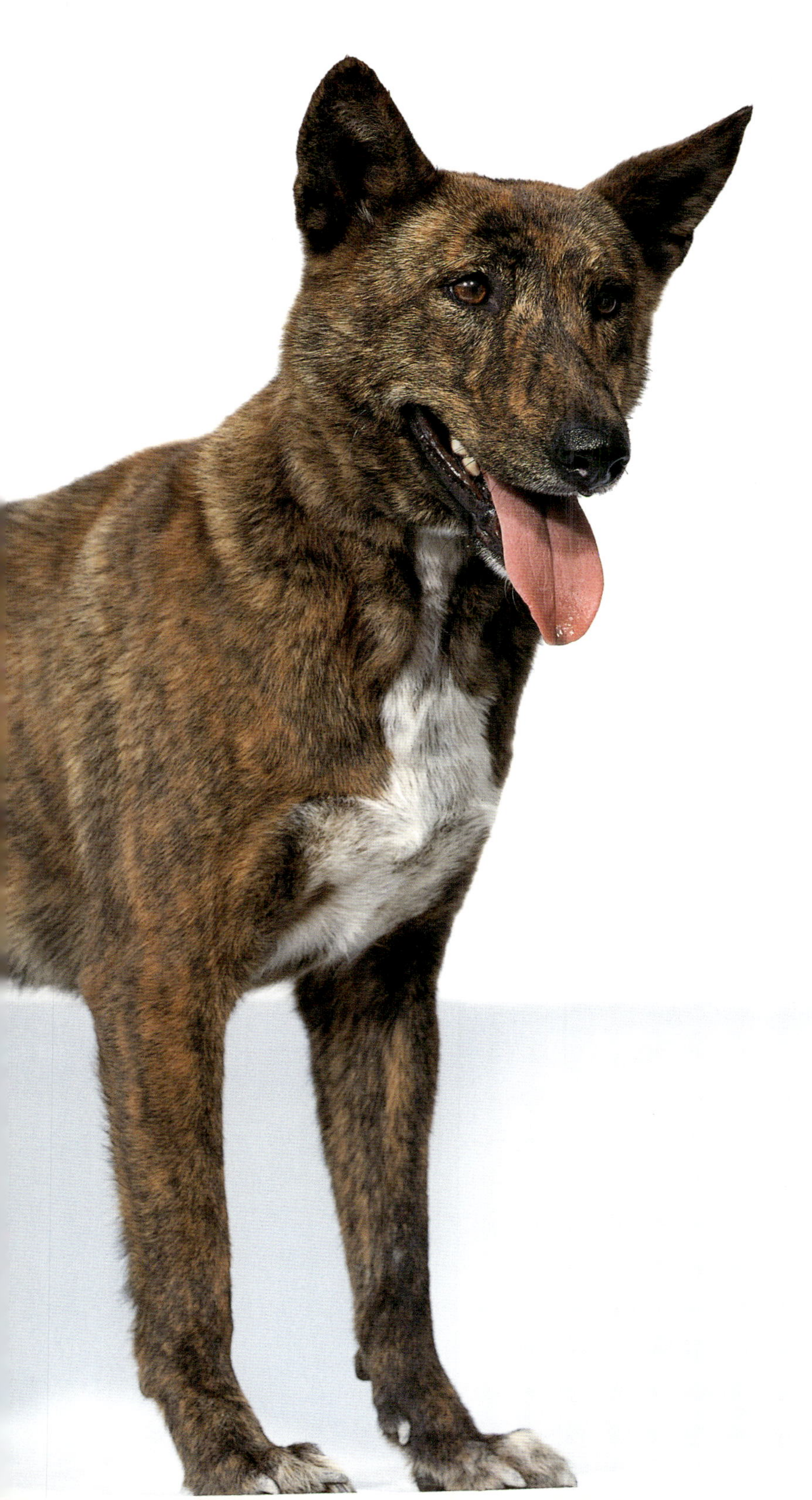

土佐闘犬

Tosa Token

Tosa Token

Also known as Tosa-ken,
the Tosa Token was developed by crossbreeding the indigenous
Tosa-ken (the present-day Shikoku-ken) with Mastiffs,
Bulldogs, Great Danes, and other European breeds
following the promotion by Yodo Yamanouchi
of dog fighting in the Tosa fiefdom (present-day Kochi Prefecture)
in the closing days of the Tokugawa Period.
The Tosa Token took on its current appearance
as a result of this crossbreeding,
and developed into a dog with strong endurance
and patience that will not release its prey once it bites.
As its imposing and robust physique suggests,
the Tosa Token also possesses a calm temperament
and is extremely brave.
It has a short coat that is red in color.
Its tail is thick at the base and tapered, and its ears hanging.
The Tosa Token is a large dog that grows to a height of 60-70 cm
and around 57 kg in weight.

土佐犬とも呼ばれる。
幕末の土佐藩（高知県）では山内容堂によって闘犬が奨励され、
在来の土佐犬（現在の四国犬）に、マスティフ、ブルドッグ、
グレート・デーンなどの洋犬種を交配させた。
これによって土佐犬は現在見るような姿になり、
食いついたら放さない、耐久力と忍耐力に富む犬種となった。
威風堂々として頑健な体躯が示す通り、
性質も沈着大胆かつ勇気に満ちている。
被毛は短く、毛色は赤。
付け根の太い垂れ尾で、耳も垂れている。
大型で体重57キロ前後、体高60〜70センチ。
土佐闘犬

とさとうけん

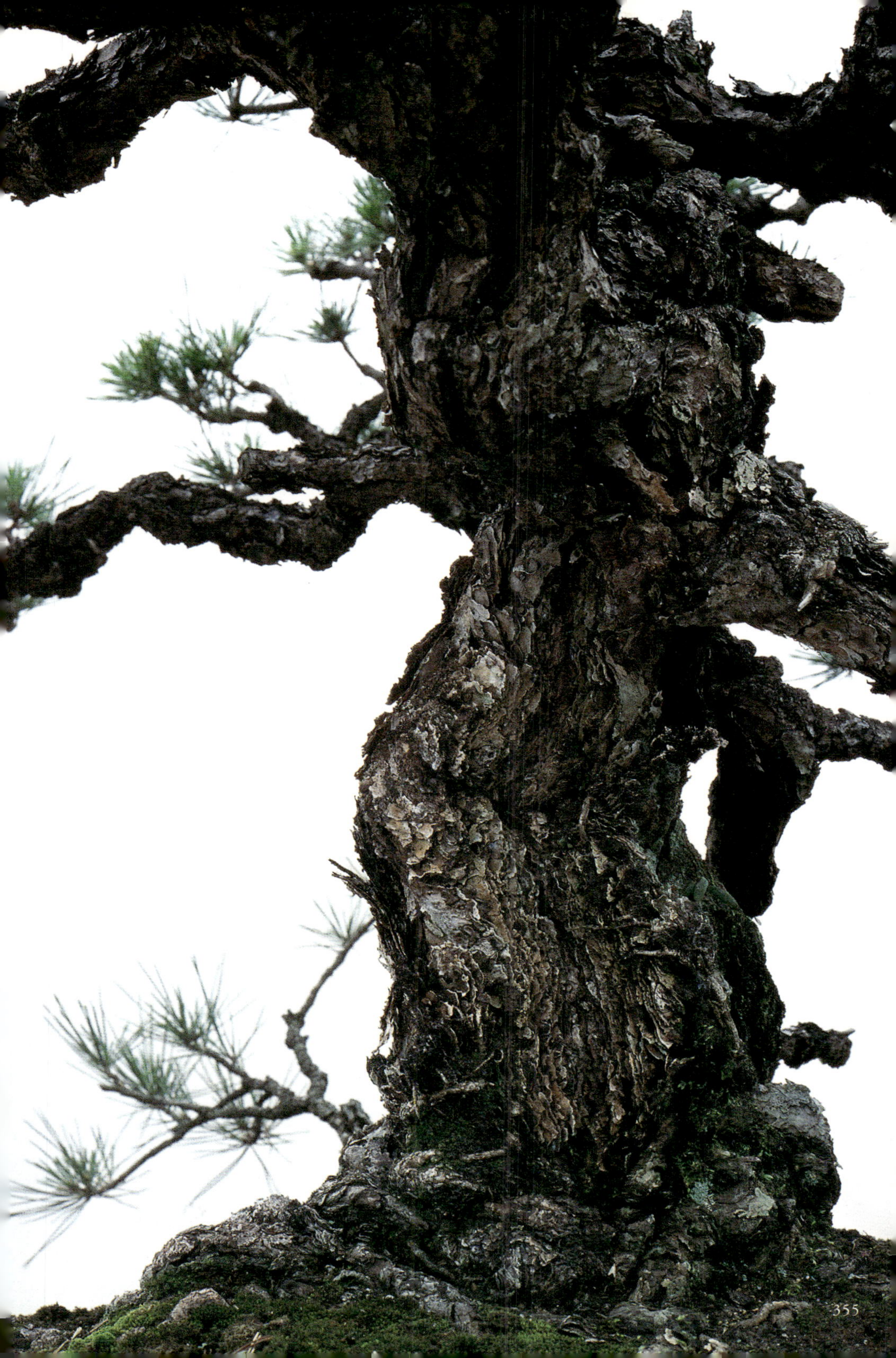

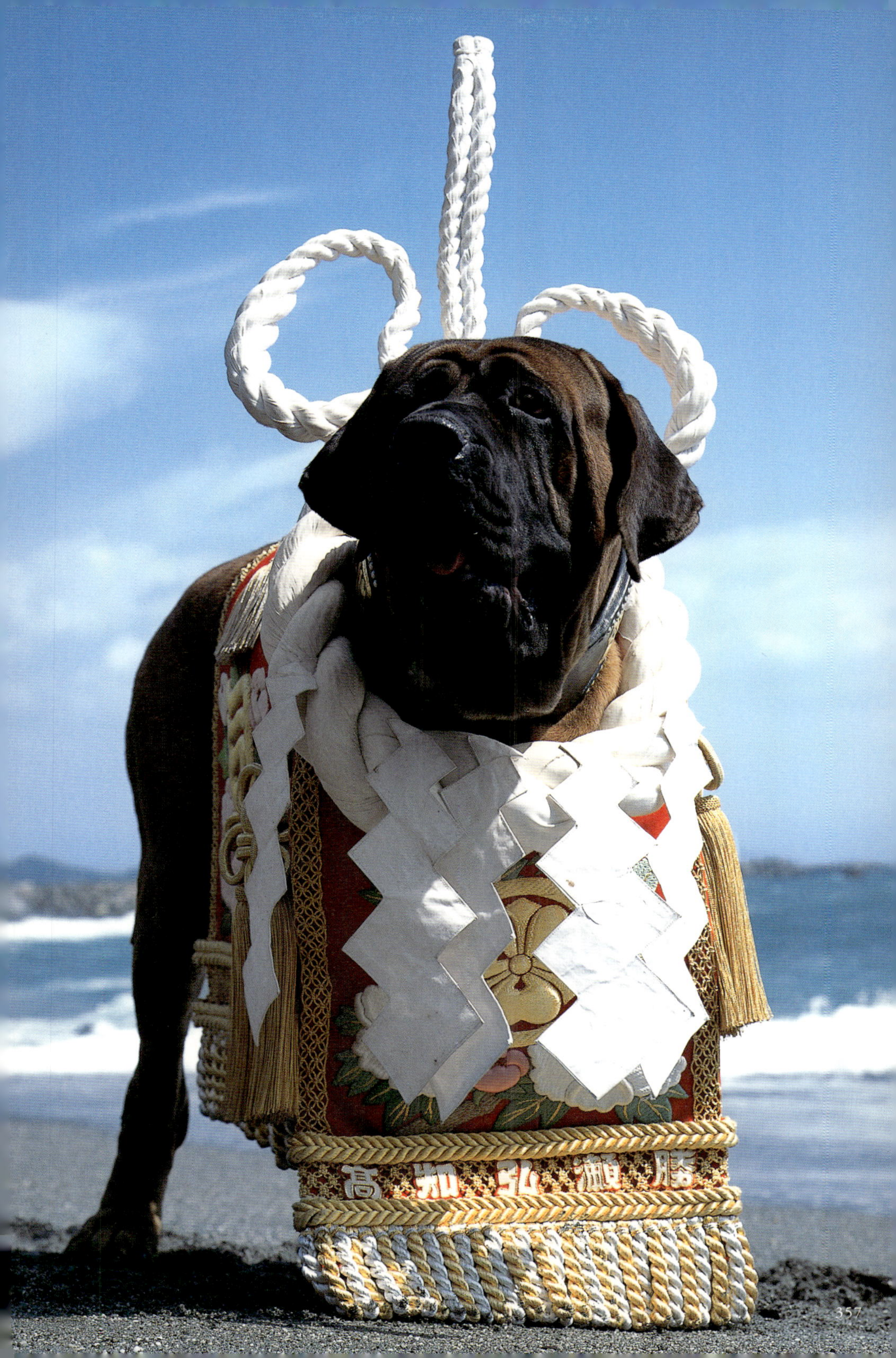

高知　弘瀬　勝

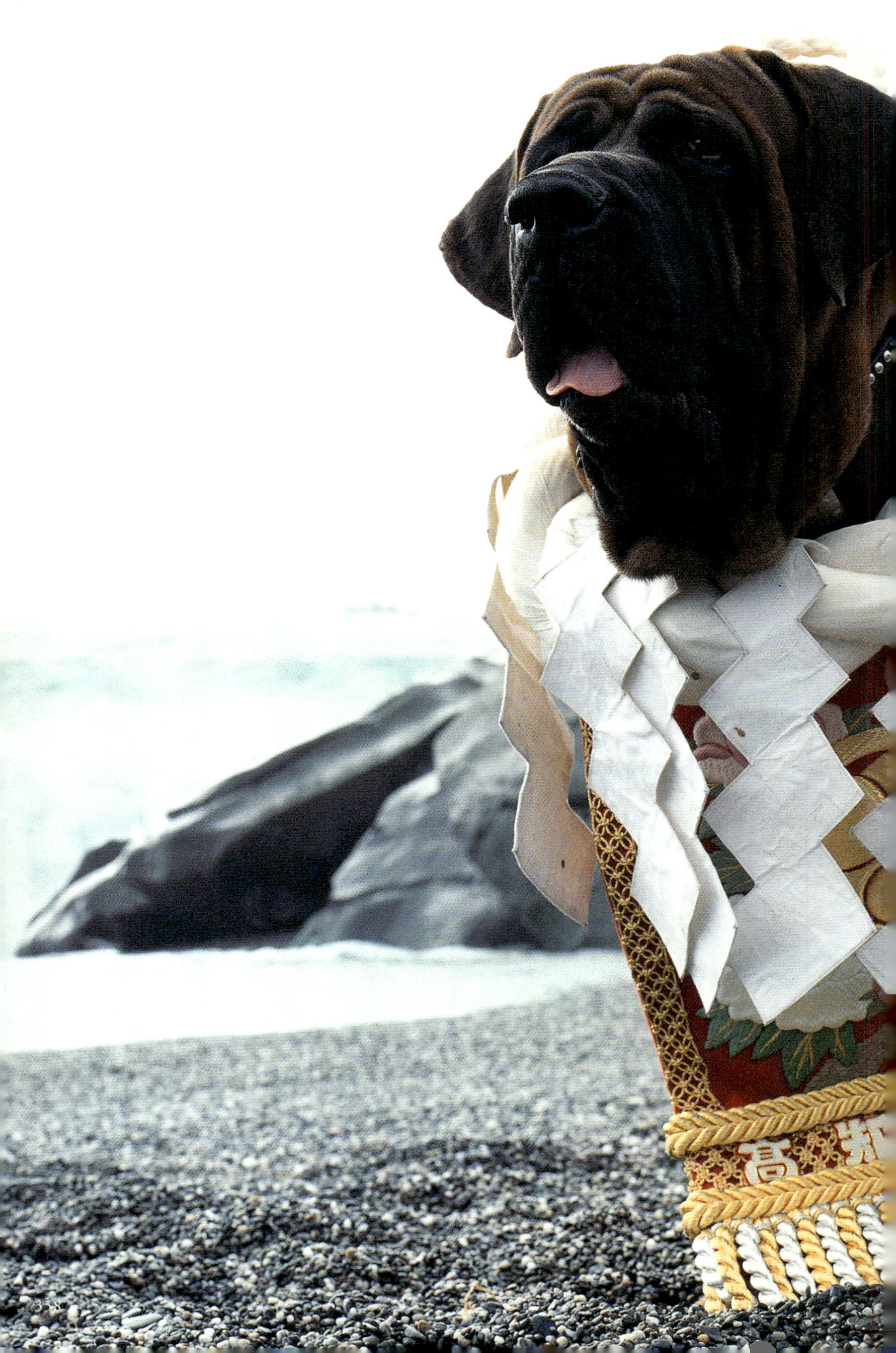

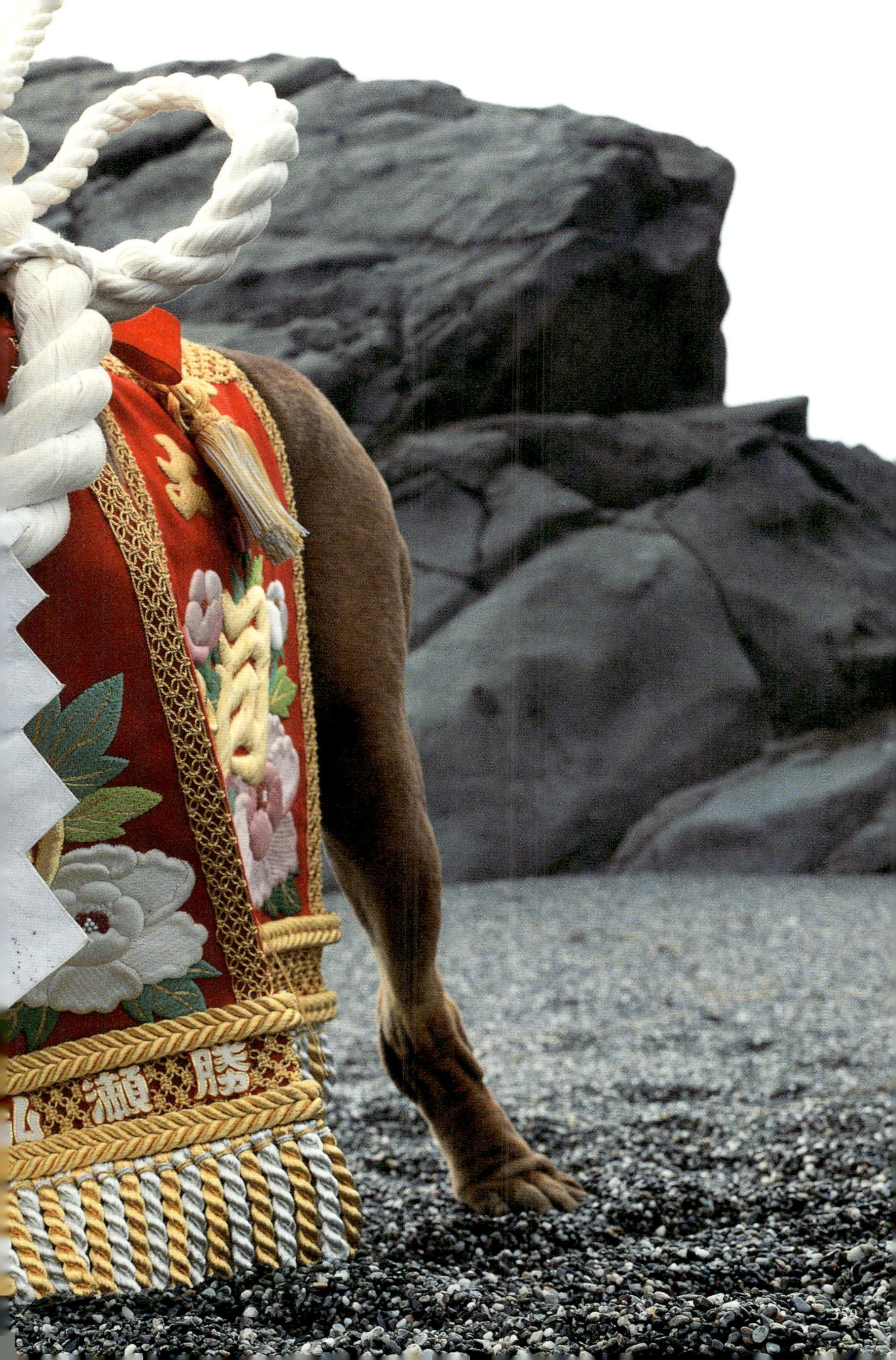
勝瀬

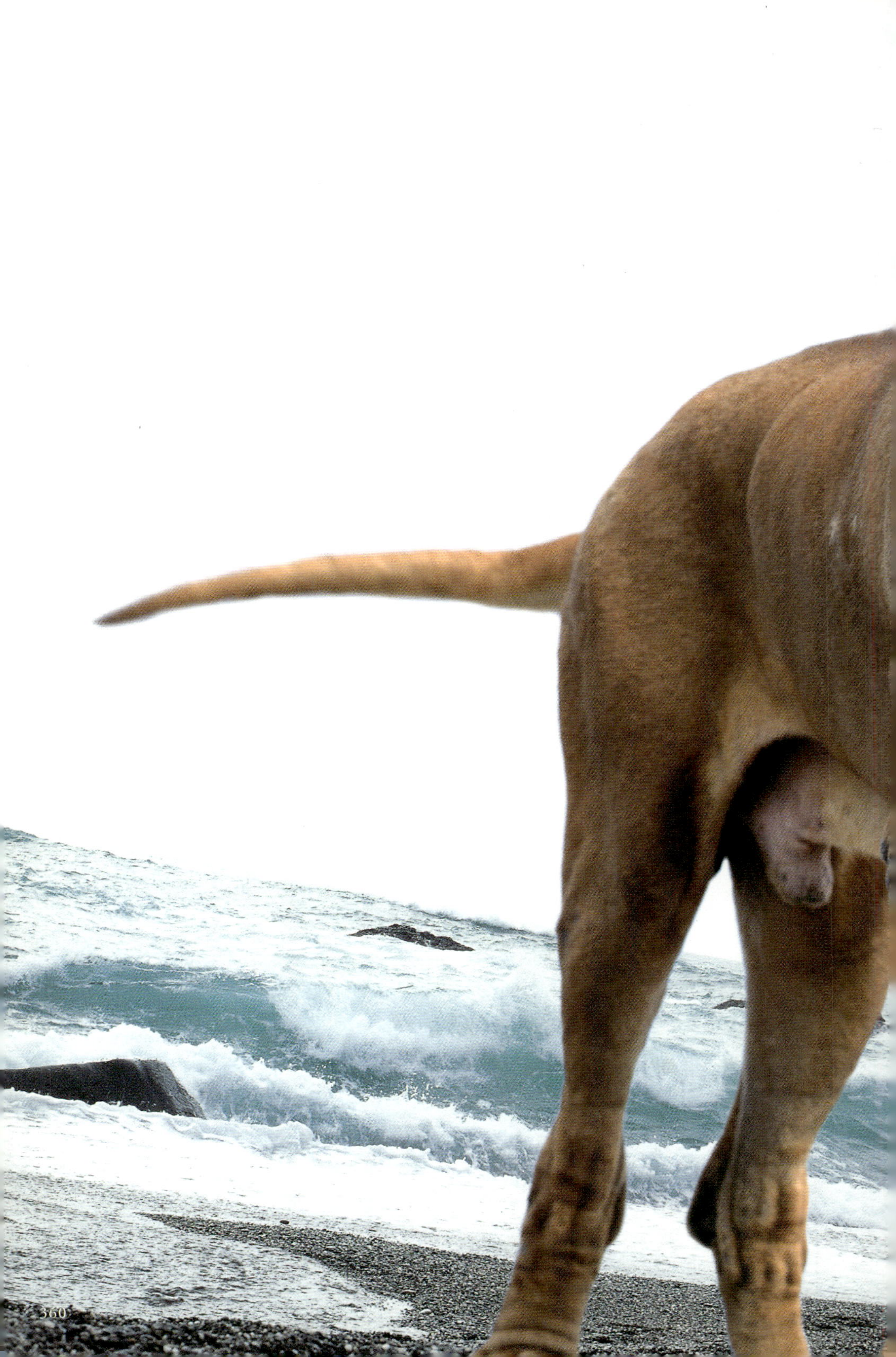

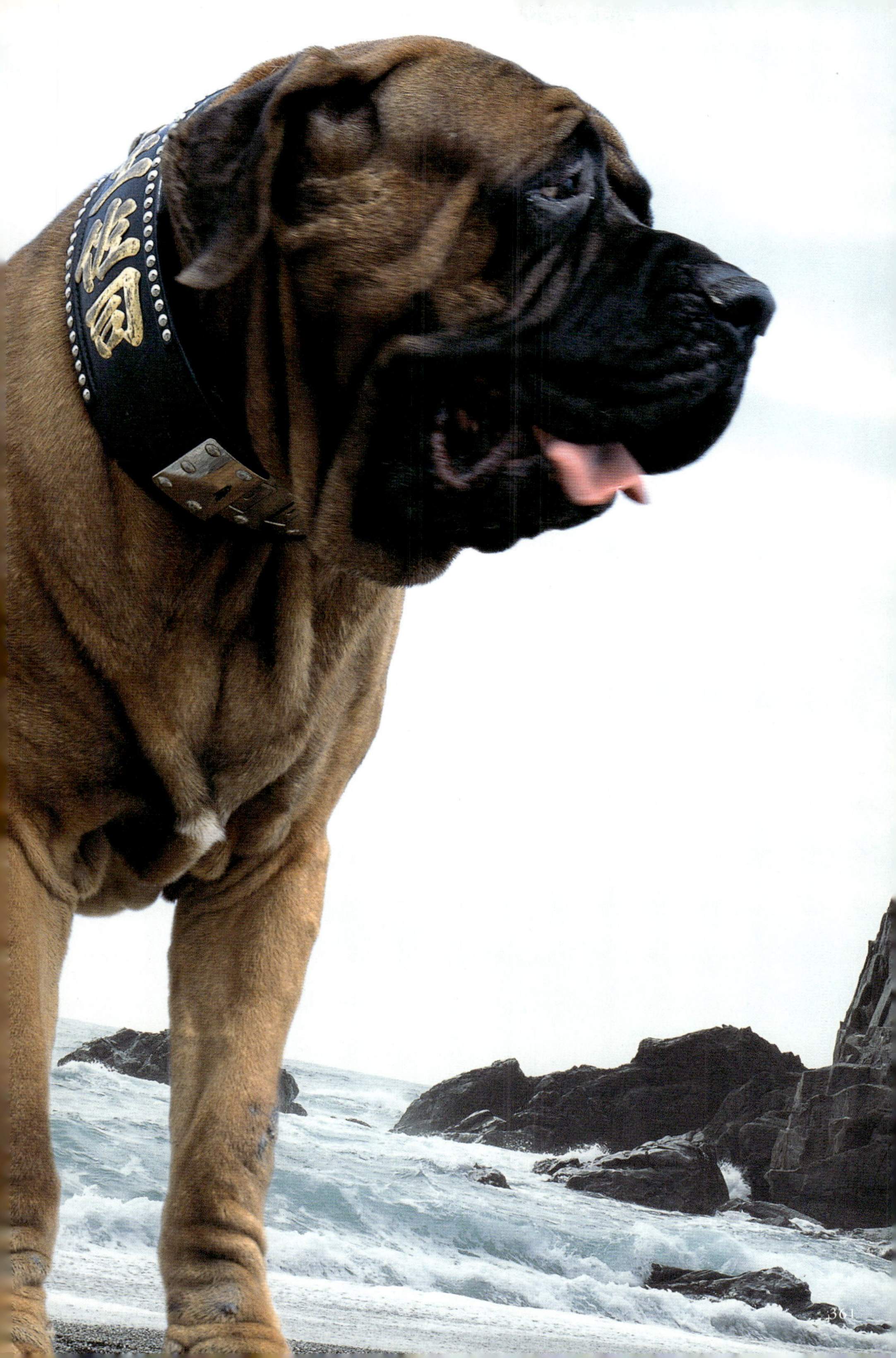

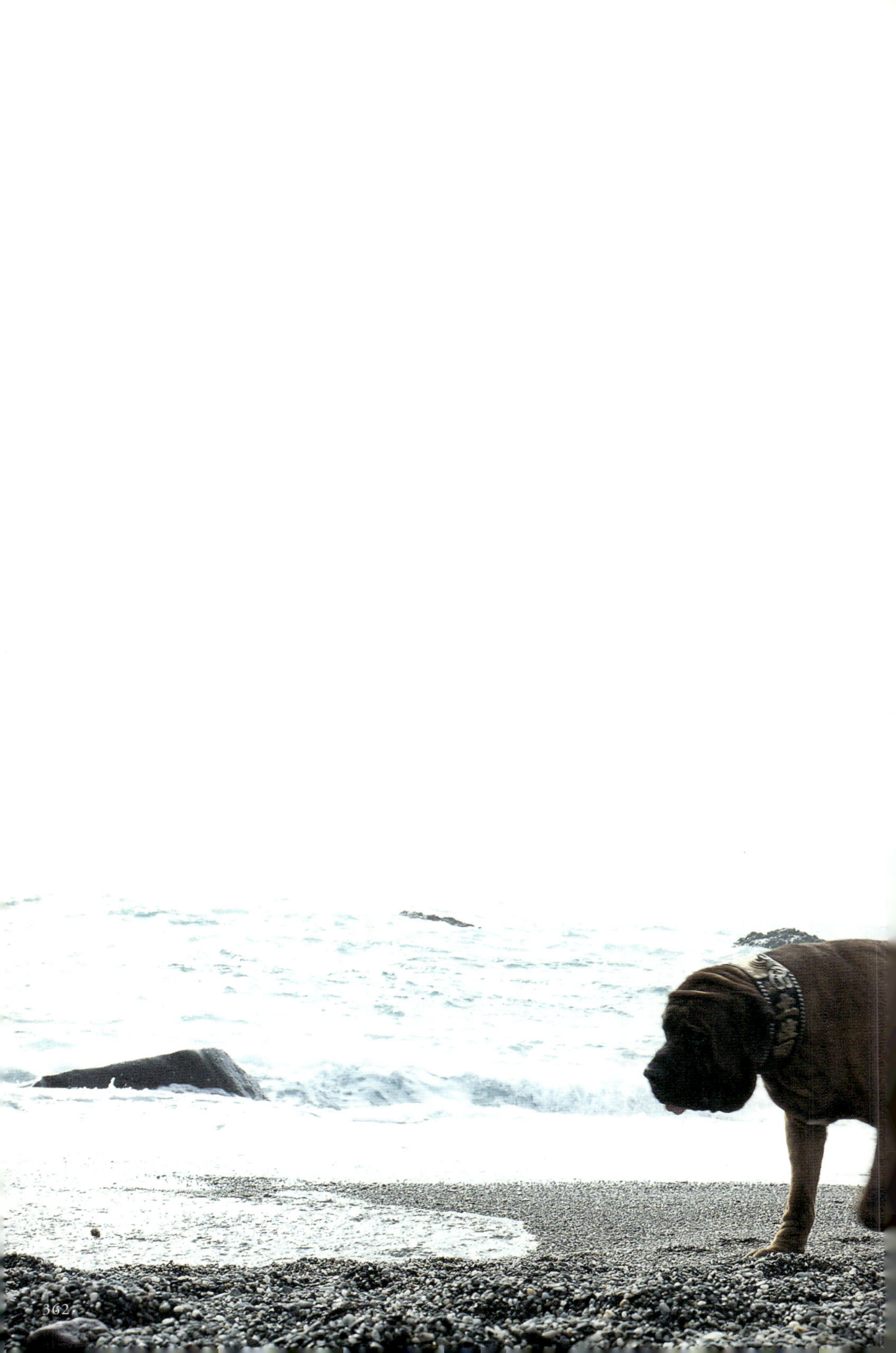

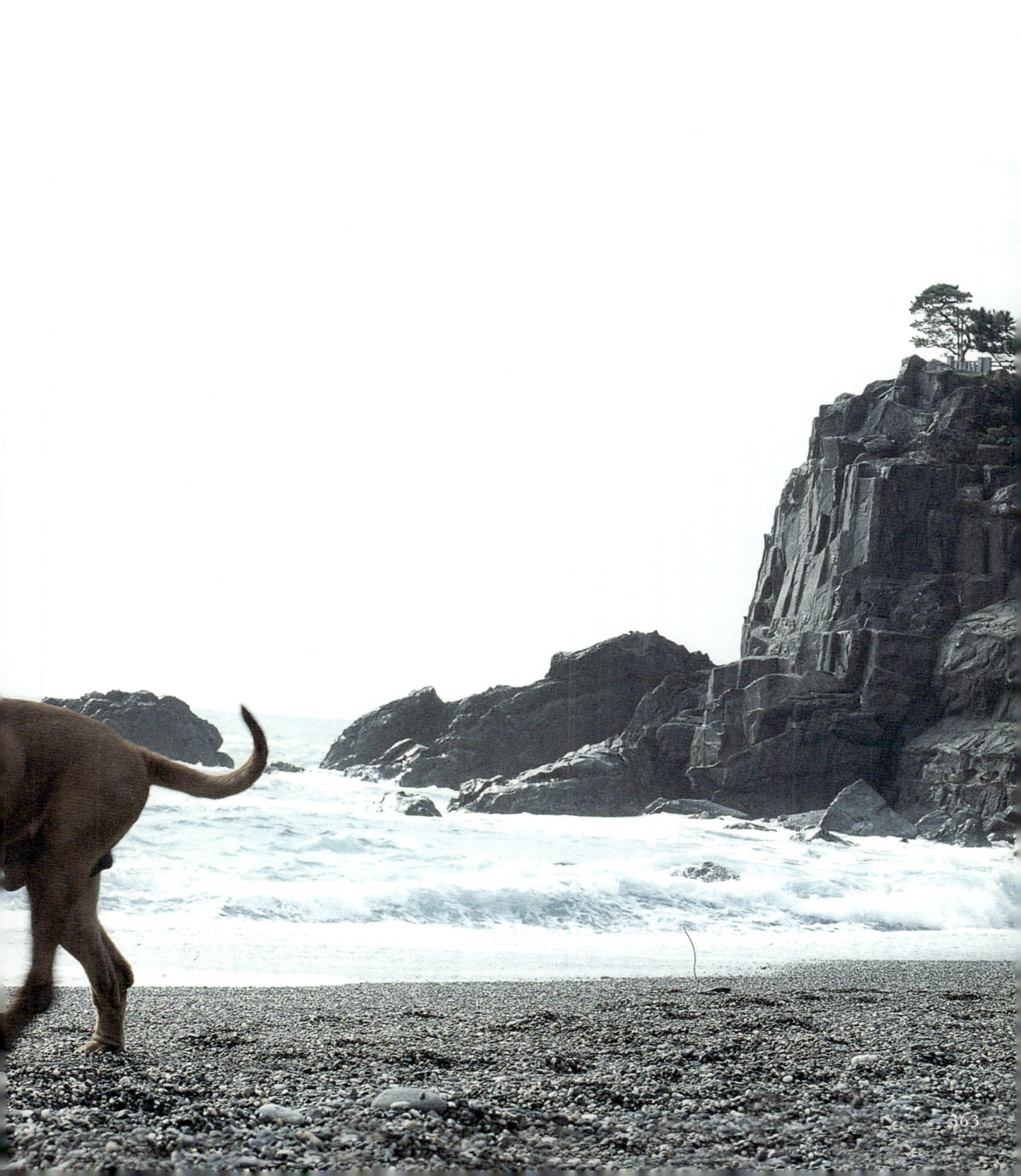

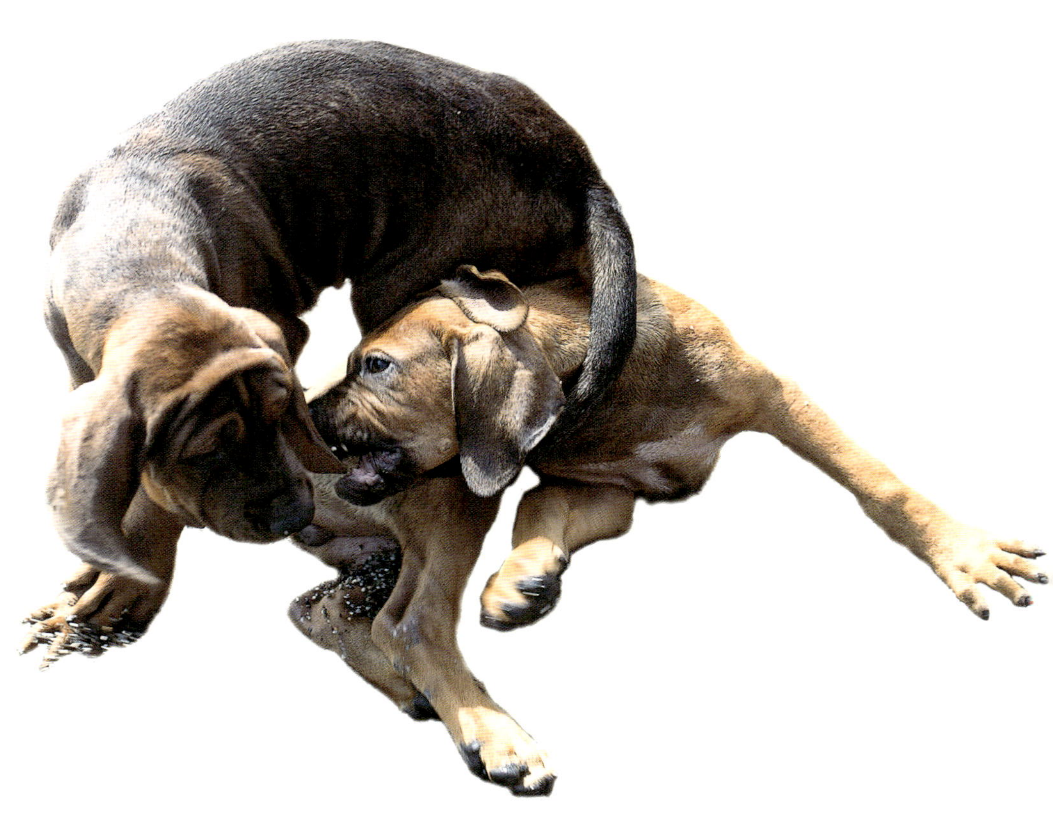

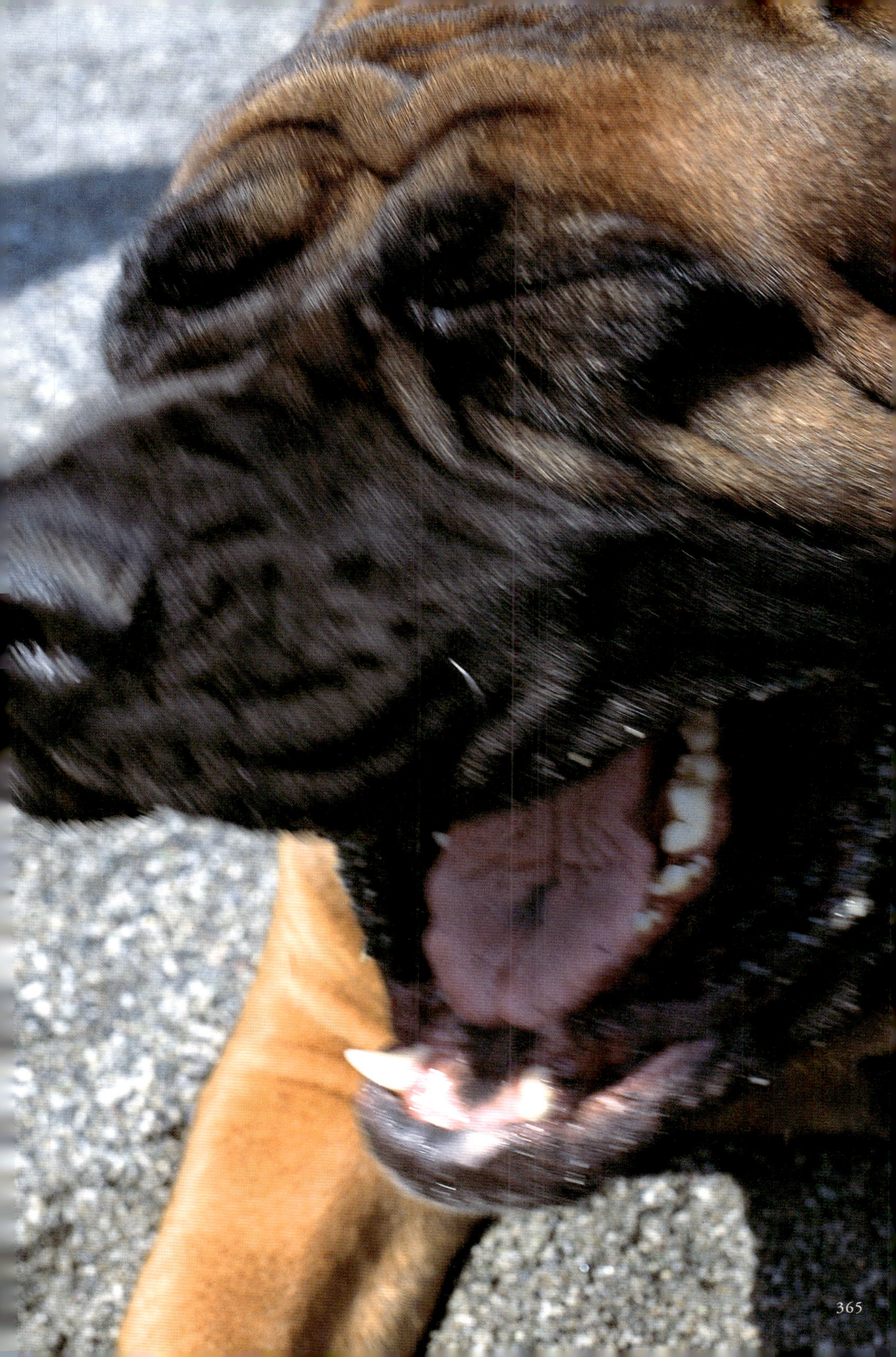

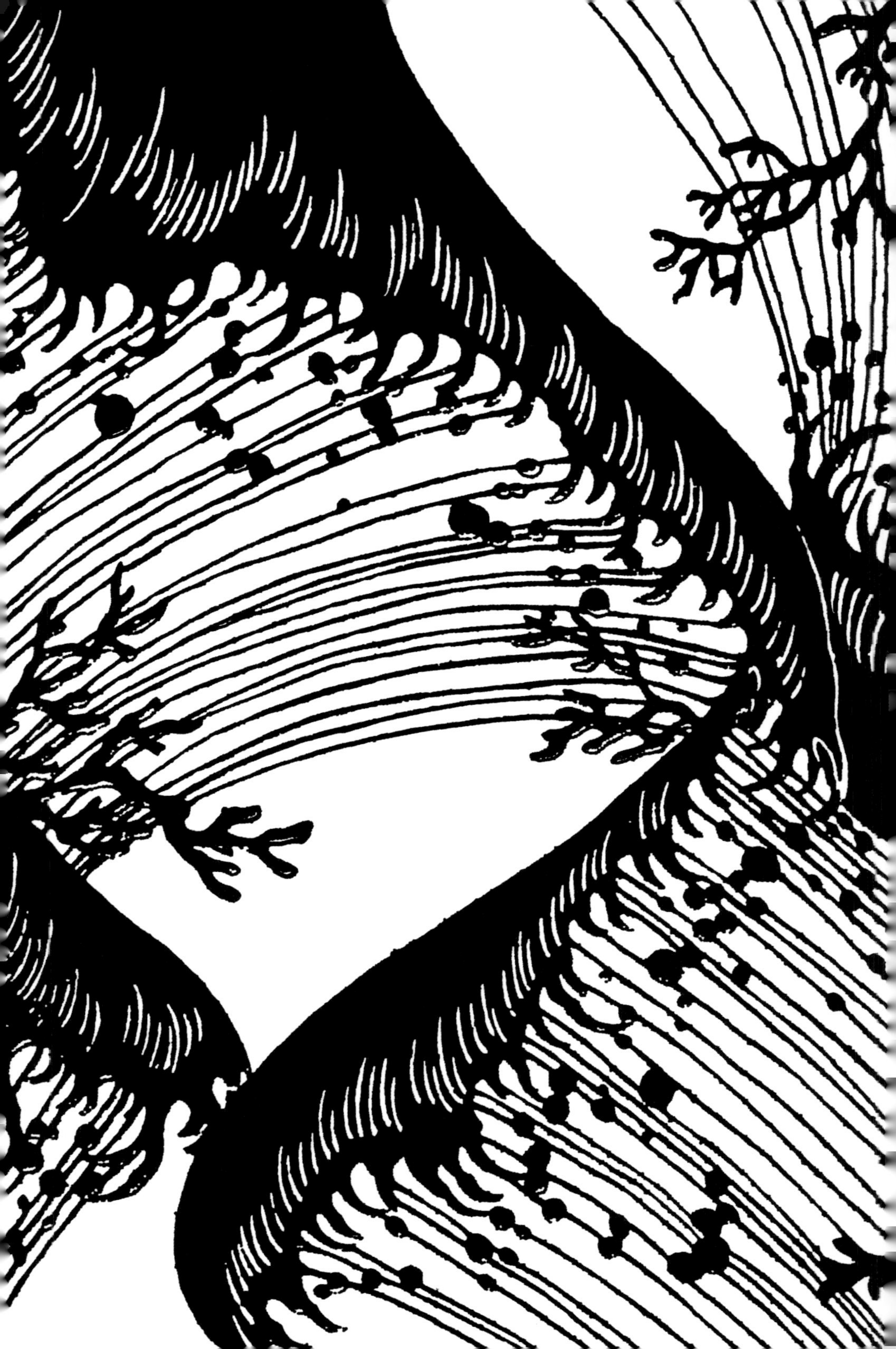

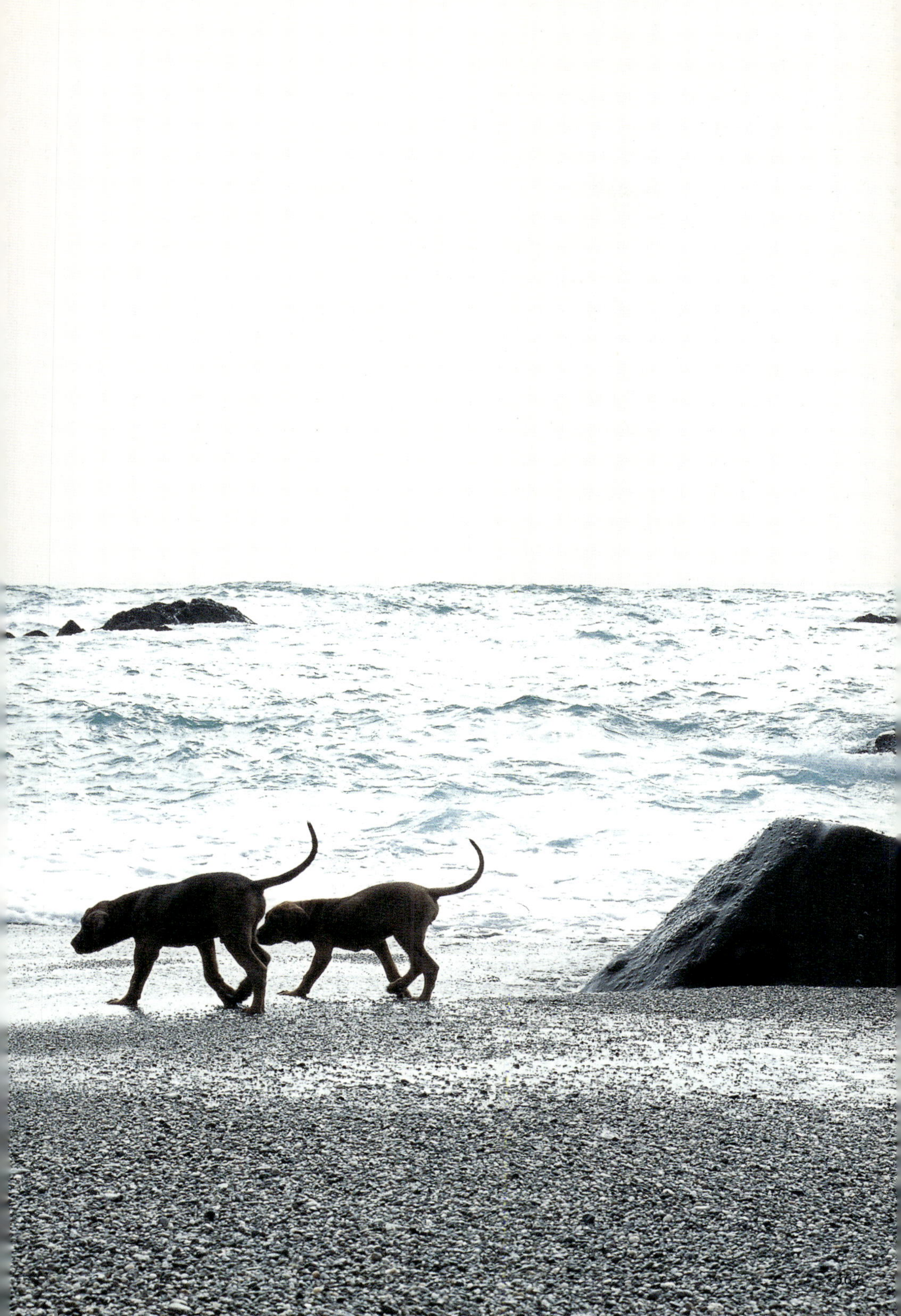

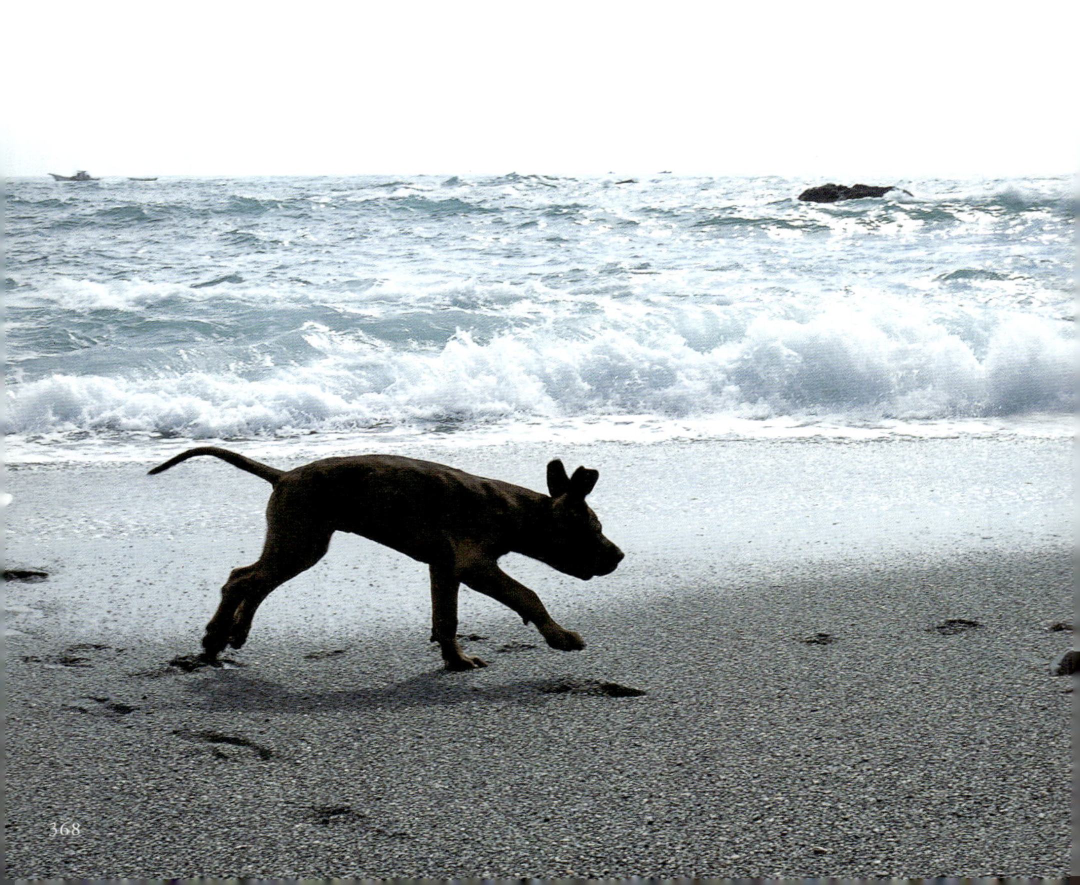

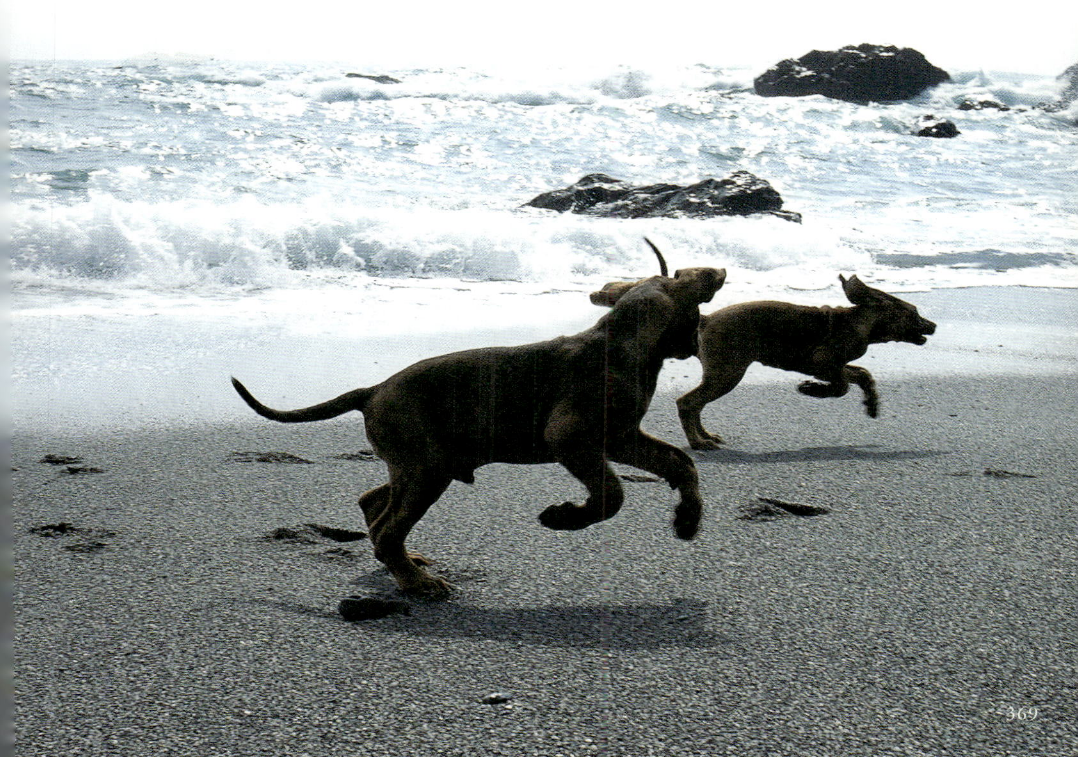

狆・日本スピッツ・日本テリア

Chin
Japanese Spitz
Japanese Terrier

Chin

Native to China.

The Chin is highly prized in Japan,

where it has been bred and established since its introduction

in the Nara Period as a gift to the Imperial Court.

For a variety of reasons, including the fact that it often appears

in bijinga (paintings of courtesans and other beautiful women)

from the Edo Period, it is known that the Chin was bred in the inner palace.

As well, a pair of Chins was presented to Queen Victoria,

well known as a dog-lover,

by Commodore Perry in the closing years of the Tokugawa Period.

Its head is large and its round eyes set wide apart.

It has a silky coat that is white with black or sometimes red patches.

Symmetry of facial markings is preferable.

The Chin is a toy dog that normally grows

to a height of around 28 cm.

中国原産。

奈良時代に宮廷への献上物として導入されて以来、

日本で育種され成立した愛玩犬である。

江戸時代の美人画にしばしば描かれていることからも、

大奥で飼育されていたことが知られている。

また幕末にはアメリカのペリー提督によって、

愛犬家として知られる英国のヴィクトリア女王にも贈られた。

優美で気品に富んだ容姿、

利口で愛嬌のある性質が貴婦人たちに愛されたのだ。

頭が大きく、丸い眼は左右に離れている。

絹糸のような被毛は、白地に黒または赤の斑が見られる。

顔面の斑は左右対称が好ましい。

小型で、体高28センチが標準。

狆

ちん

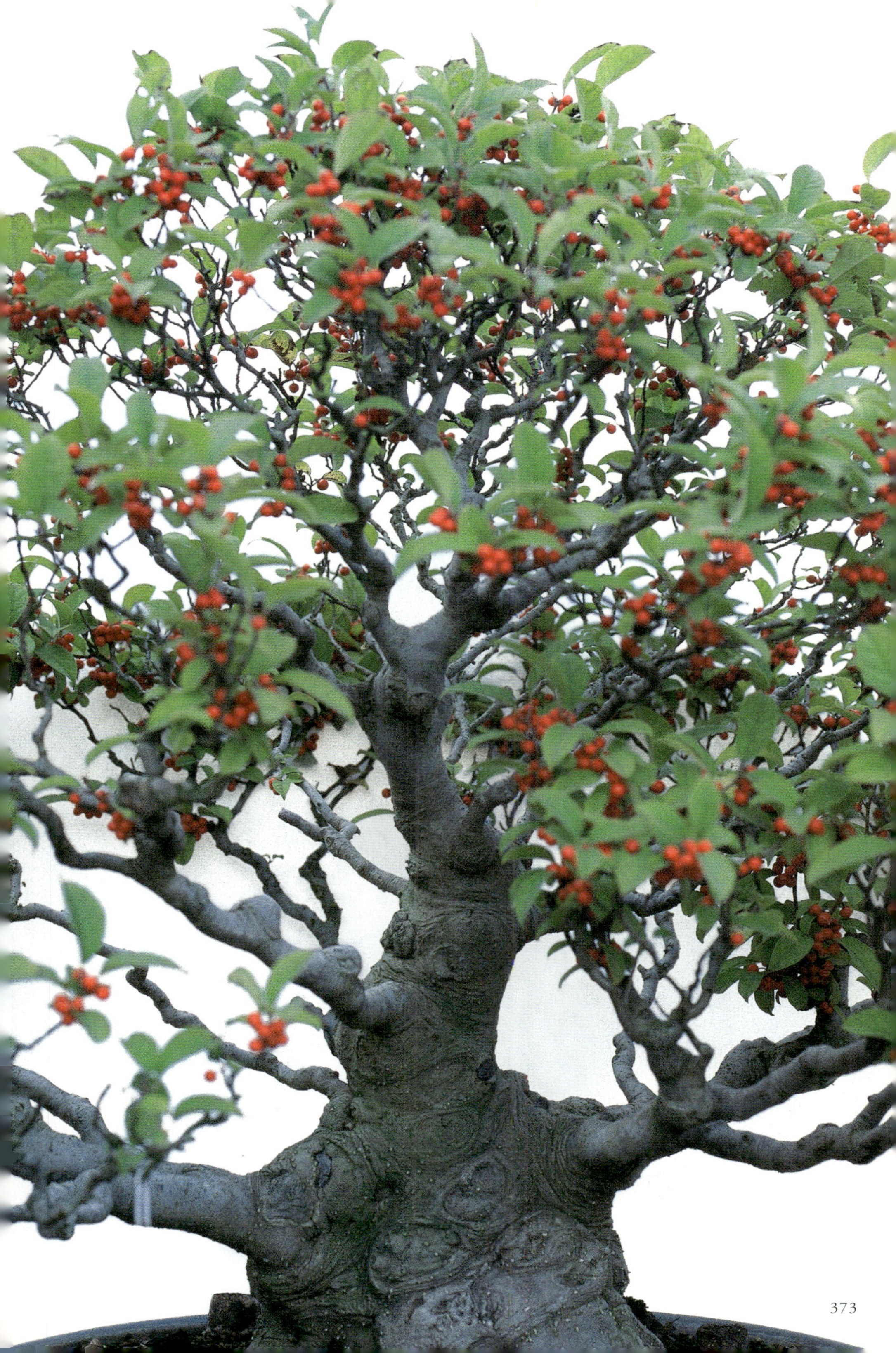

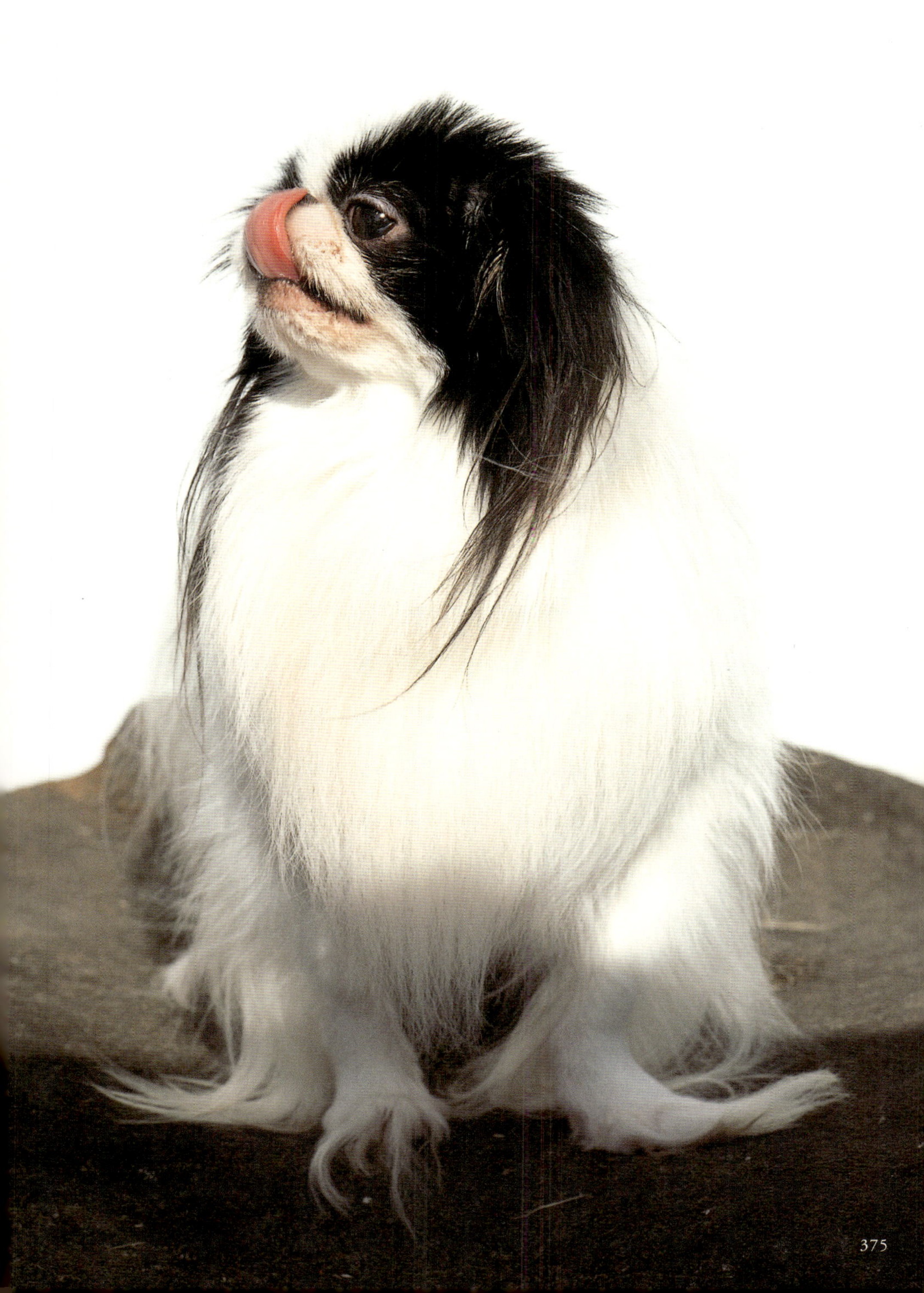

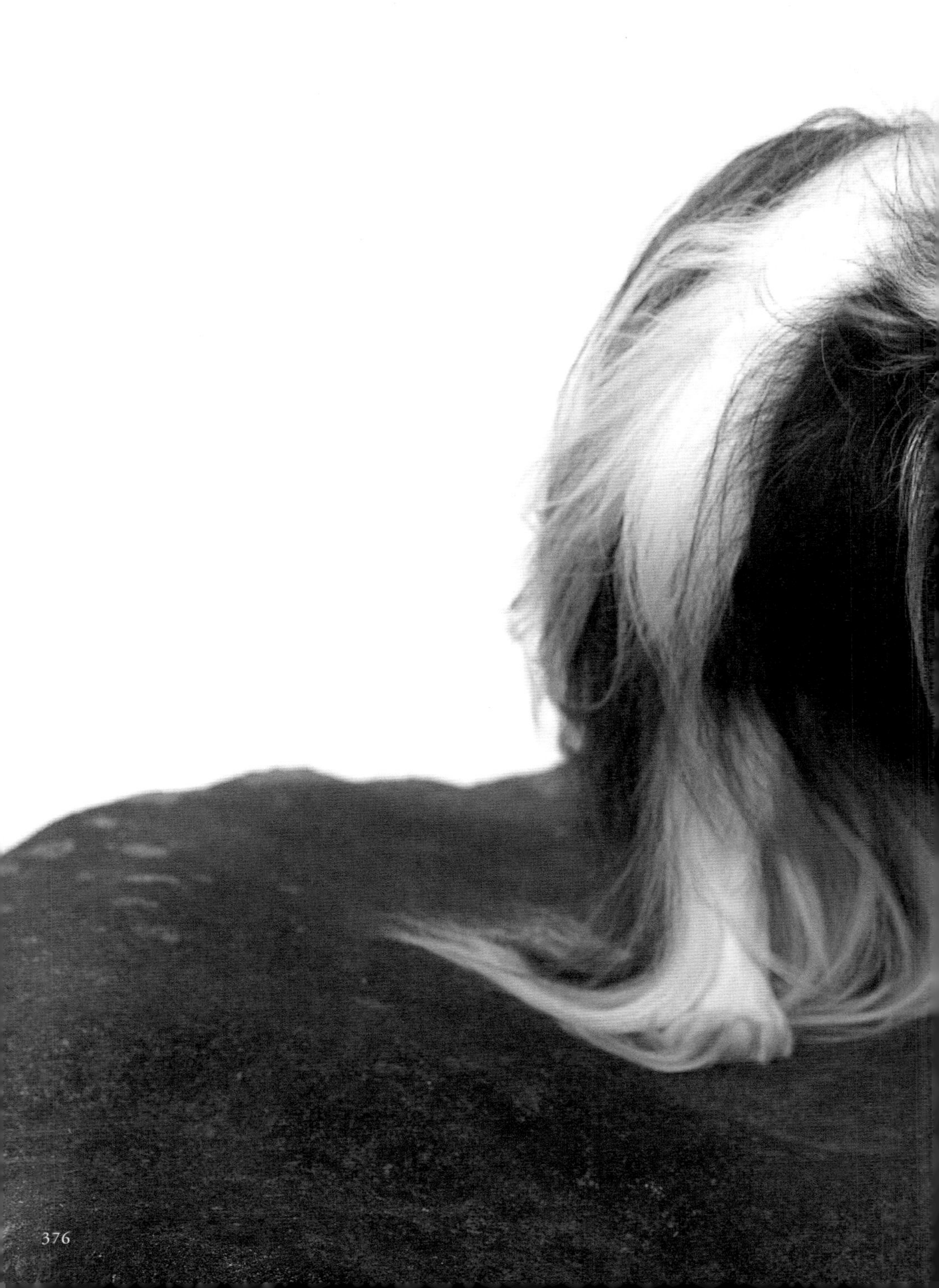

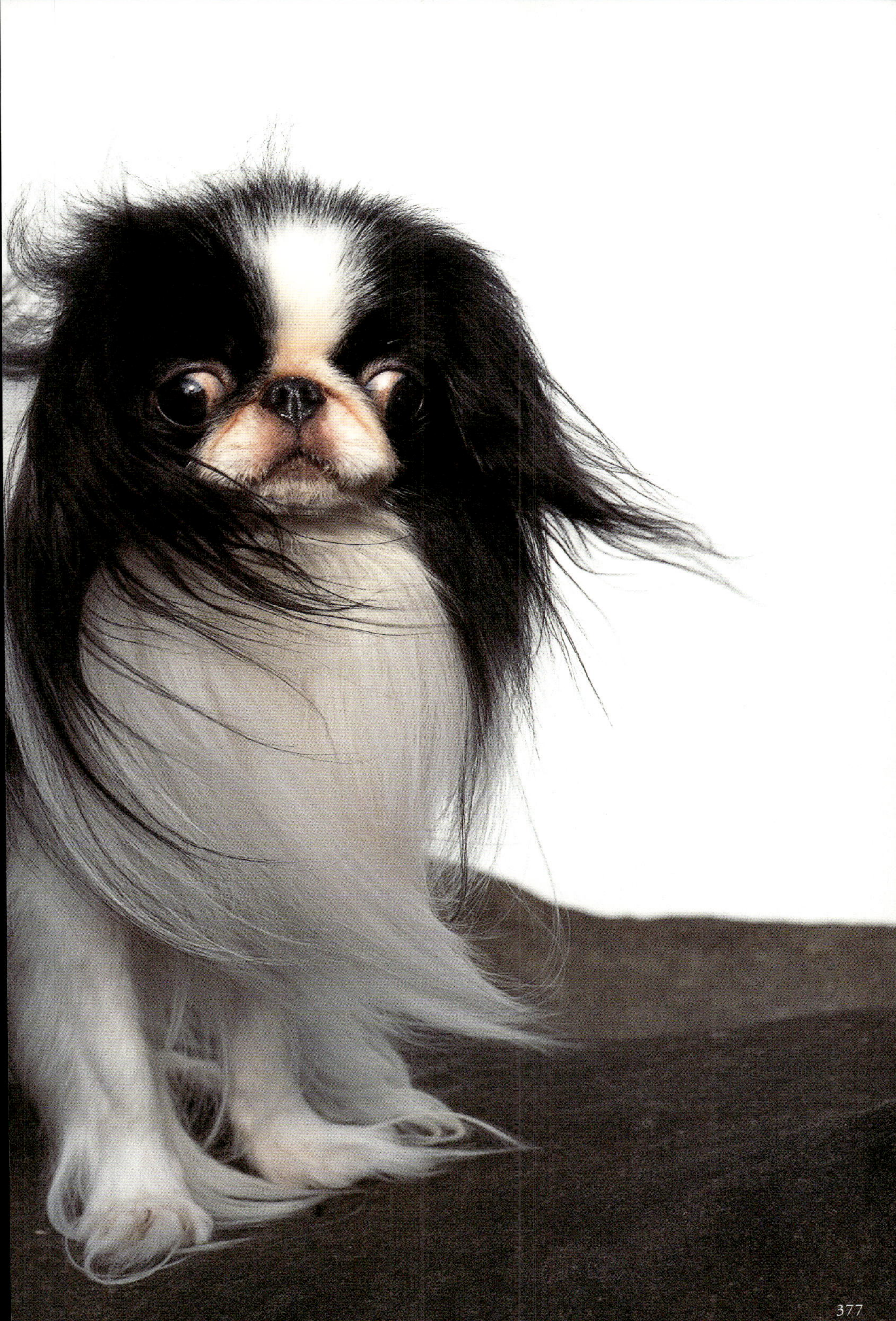

日本スピッツ
カナダやアメリカから輸入された白色のスピッツや
中国から輸入された白色のサモエドをもとにして、
戦後に日本で固定された犬種。
遺伝的には完全な西洋犬である。
ふさふさと豊富な非常に美しい純白の被毛に覆われ、
その体型バランスの良さと相まって
独特の品位と優美さを備えている。
とがった口吻も特徴である。
耳は三角形の立耳で、尾は巻いて背中に背負う。
体質は強固で活動的だ。
親しみやすく、ものおぼえがよい。
体高 30 〜 38 センチ。

A Japanese breed established after World War
II based on white Spitz introduced from Canada
and the U.S. and white Samoyeds introduced from China.
Genetically it is a completely Western breed.
The Japanese Spitz is covered in an extremely beautiful flowing,
pure white coat that,
combined with its well-balanced physique,
lends it a peculiar dignity and grace.
The shrill bark is another distinguishing feature of this breed.
The ears are triangular and pricked,
and the tail is carried curled over the back.
The Japanese Spitz has a determined and lively temperament.
It is friendly and a fast learner.
Grows to a height of 30-38 cm.

Japanese Spitz

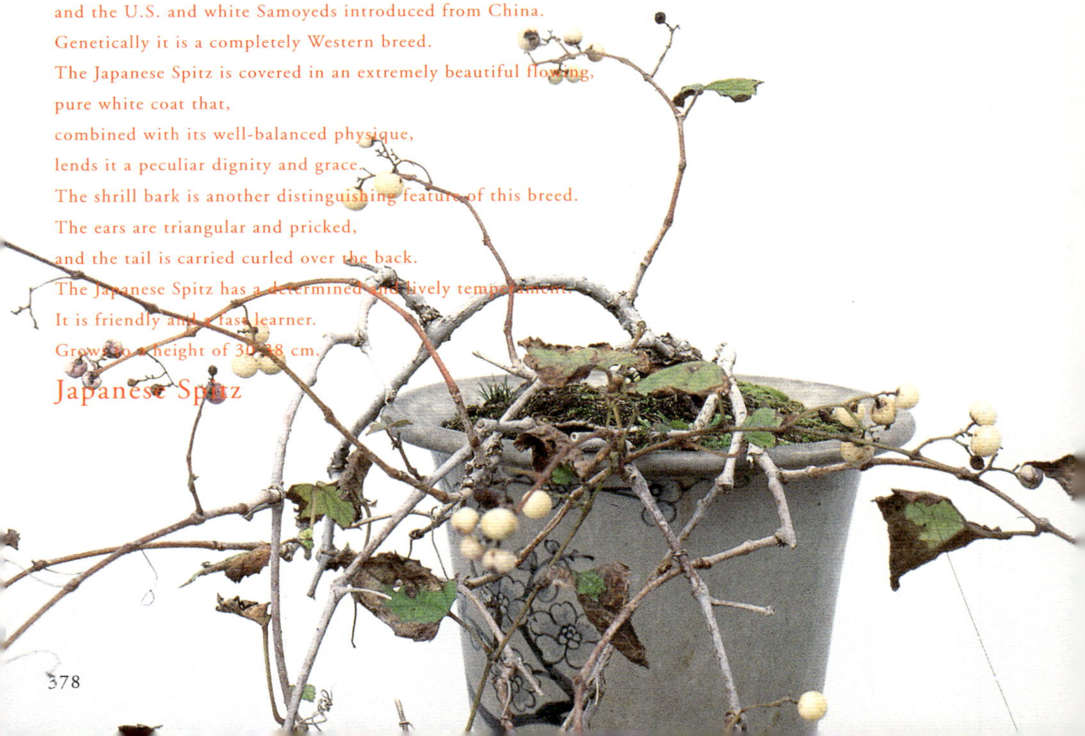

Japanese Terrier

Although genetically a completely Western dog,
the Japanese Terrier is classified as a native of Japan.
The breed developed from Fox Terriers brought to Japan
by Dutch seamen in the early eighteenth century,
which were then crossbred with small local breeds.
The coat is smooth and glossy,
grows to a length of around 2 mm,
and is velvety to the touch.
The Japanese Terrier, which is also known as
the Oyuki Terrier or Mikado Terrier,
was traditionally kept as a lapdog in port cities
such as Kobe and Yokohama.
Its compact, smart appearance and intelligent,
lively temperament are still popular among fanciers.
Its coat is black or red around the head,
and white around the body, sometimes with spots.
It has a thin tail that is traditionally docked.
Grows to a height of 30 cm.

遺伝的には完全な西洋犬だが、日本原産の犬種とされる。
18世紀初めにオランダの船員が持ち込んだ
フォックス・テリアを祖とし、
土着の小型犬を交配し作出された。
滑らかで光沢のある毛は2ミリ程度と短く、
ビロードのような感触。
「お雪テリア」「ミカド・テリア」と呼ばれ、
神戸や横浜などの港町で抱きイヌとして愛されてきた。
小柄でスマートな外貌や、
利発で機敏な性質も好まれている。
毛色は頭部は黒、赤、体は白で斑のあるものもいる。
尾は細く、断尾させる習慣がある。
体高30センチ。
日本テリア

ニホンテリア

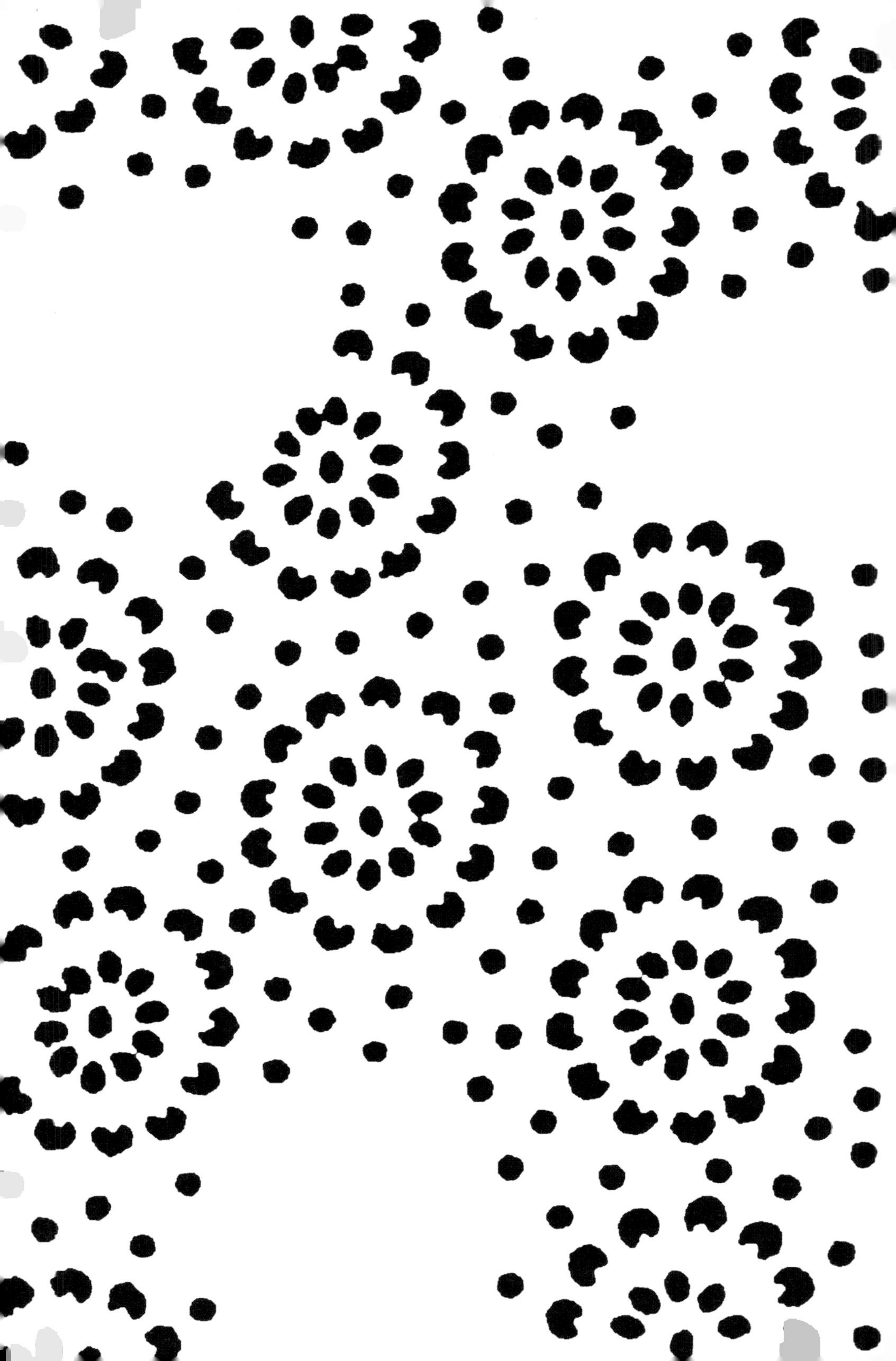

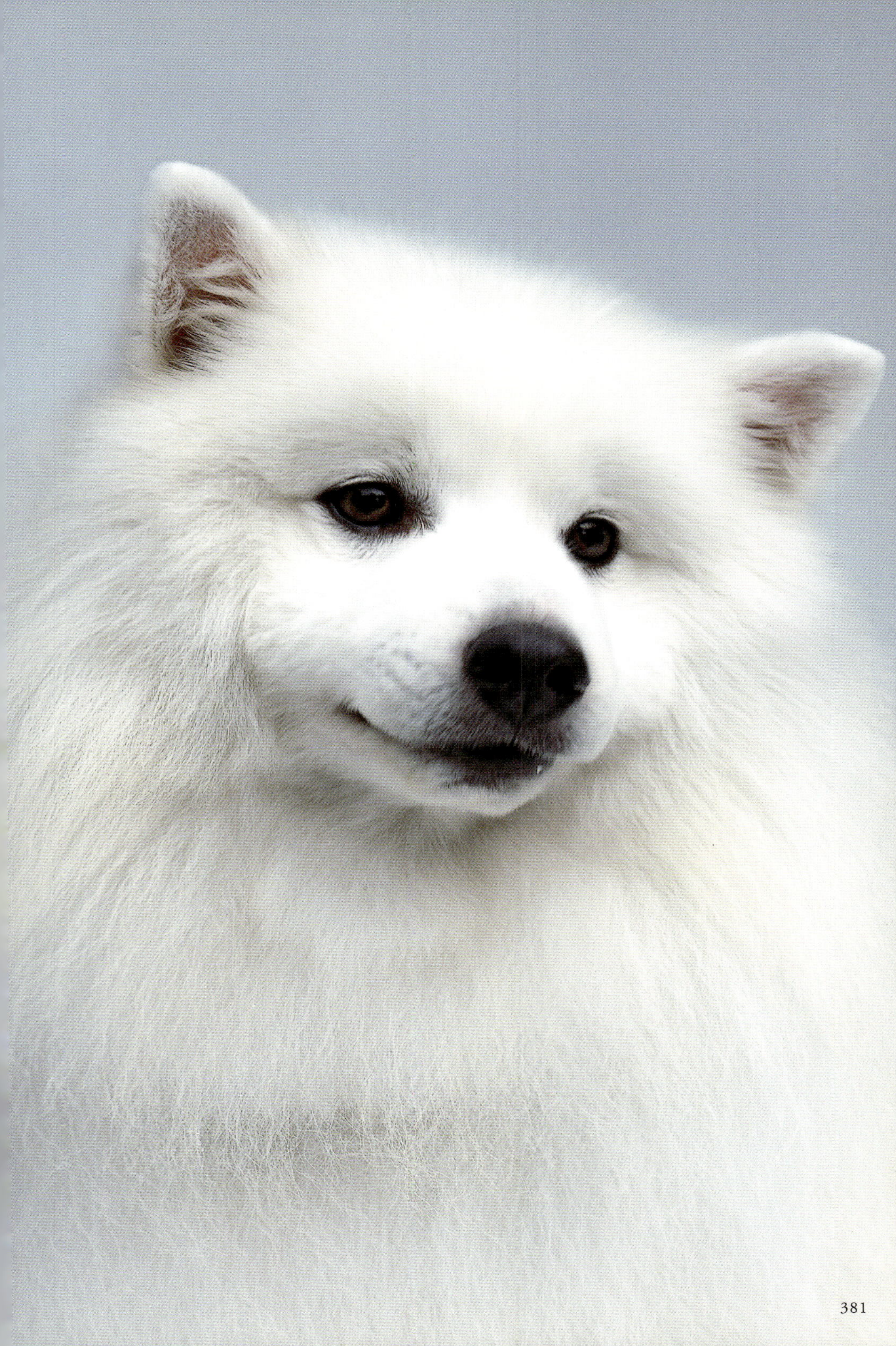

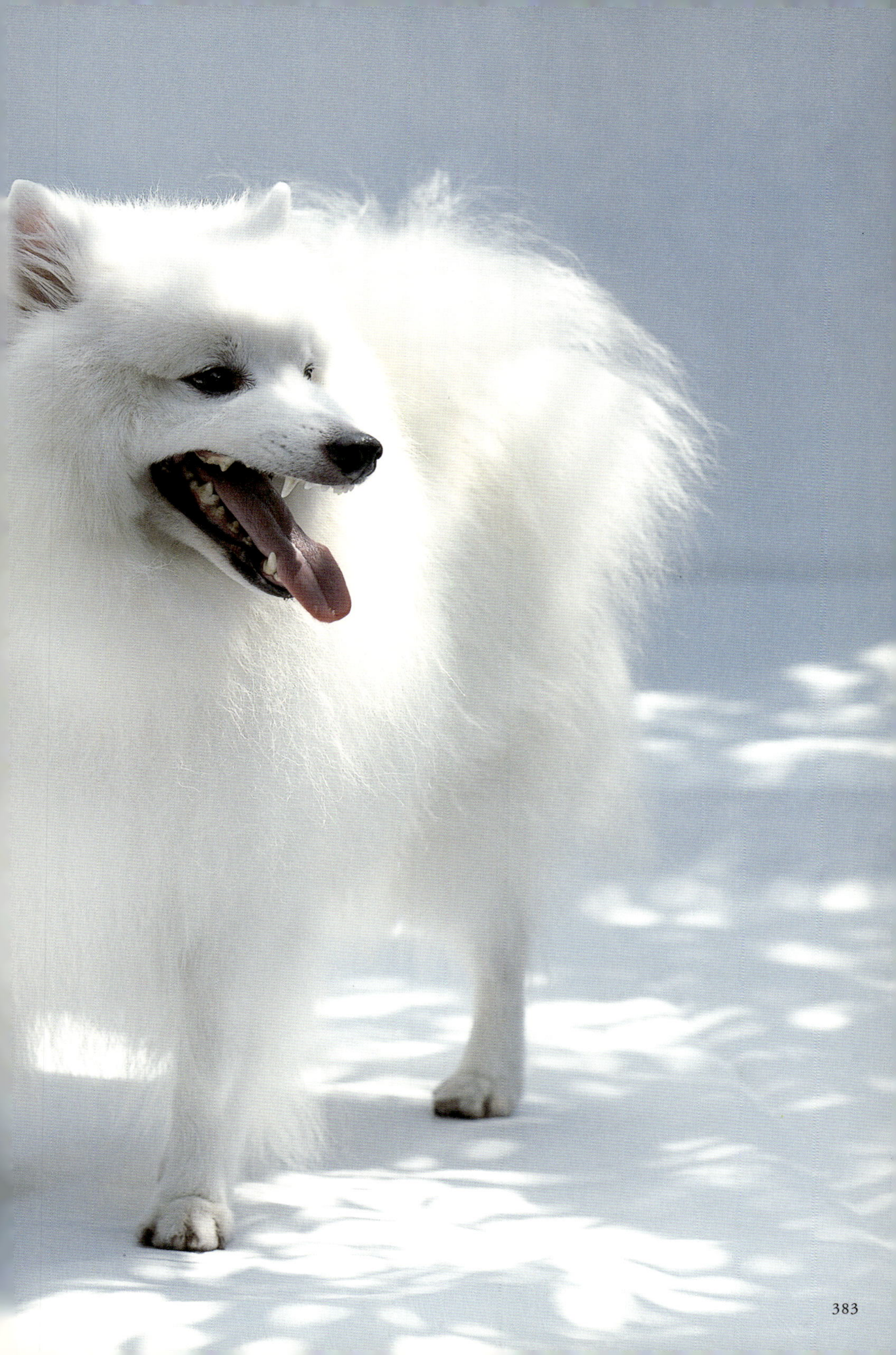

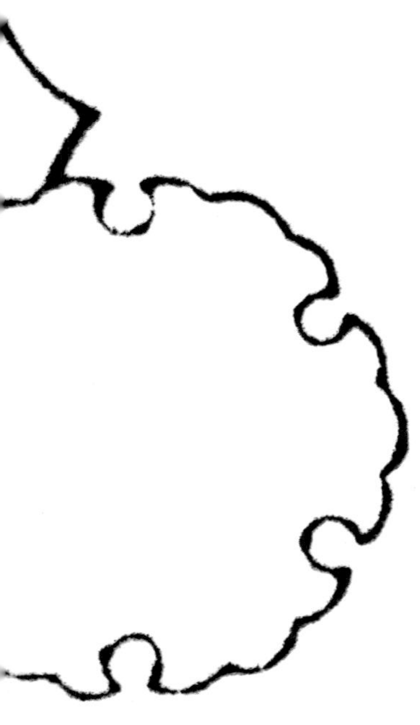

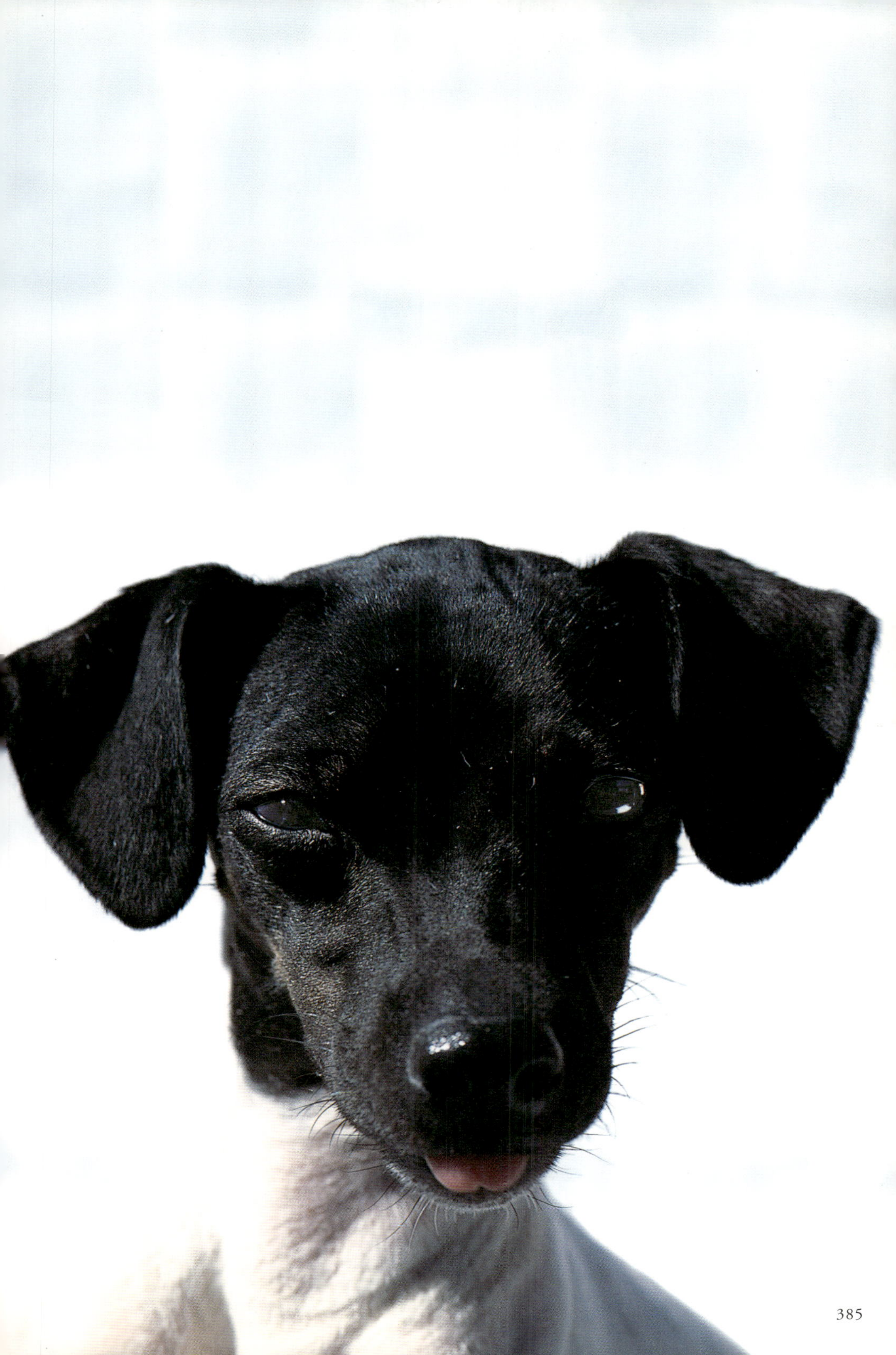

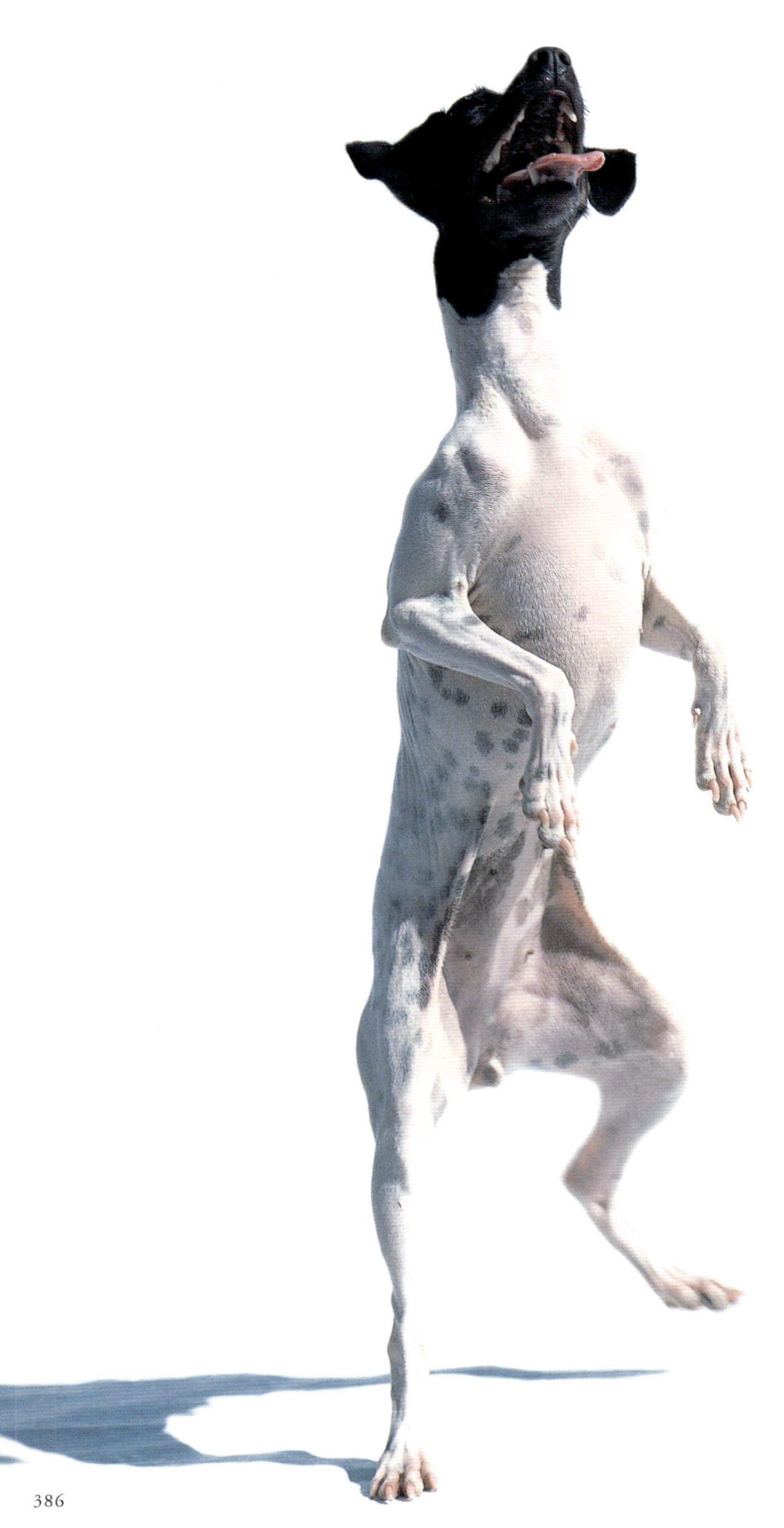

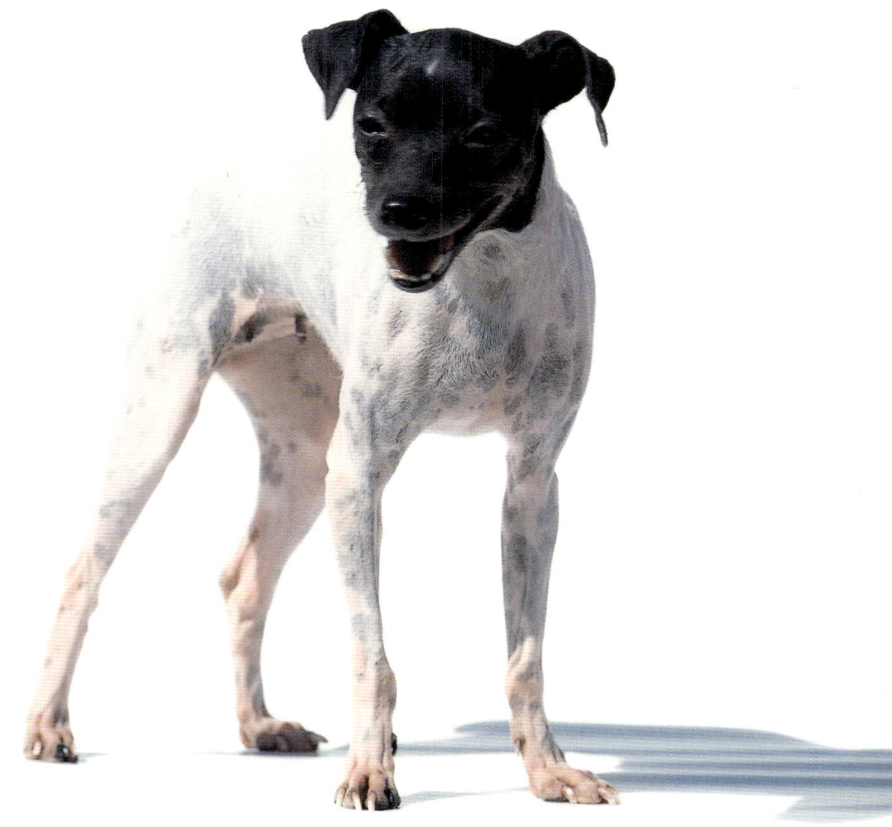

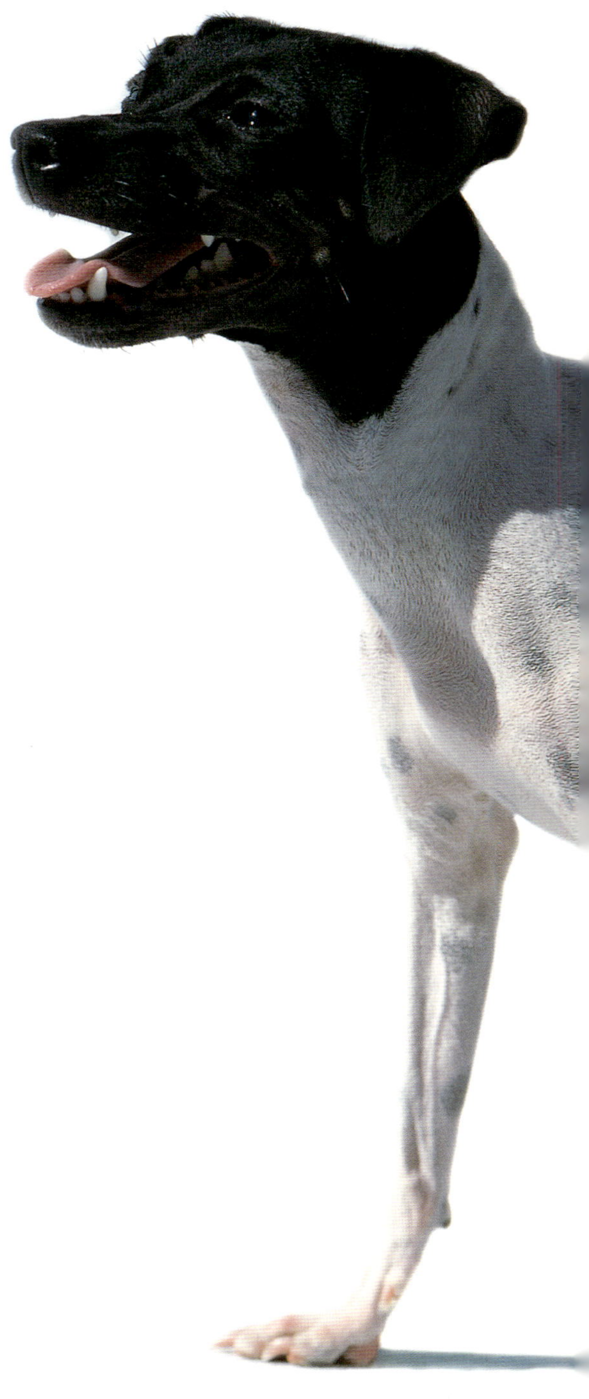

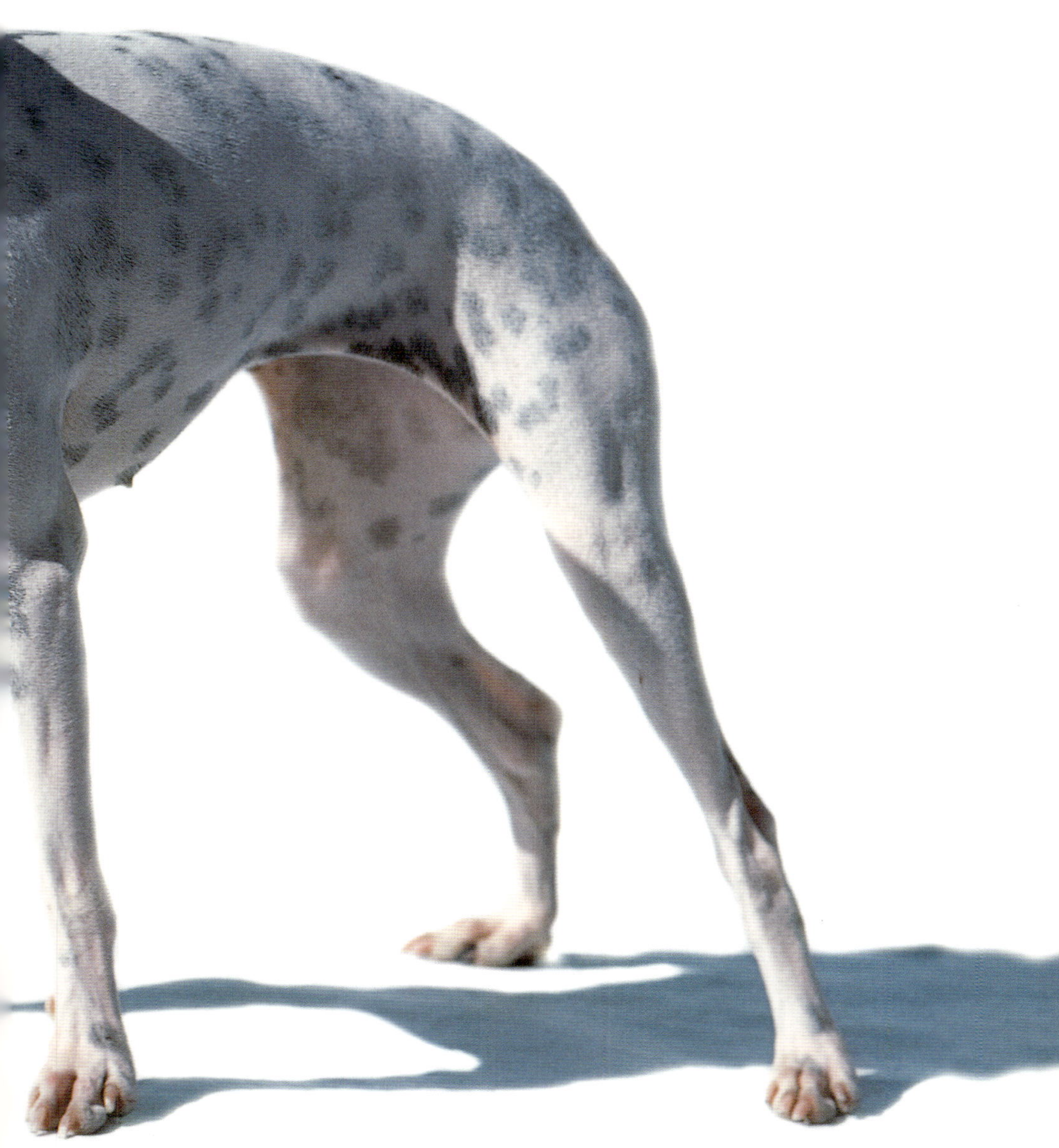

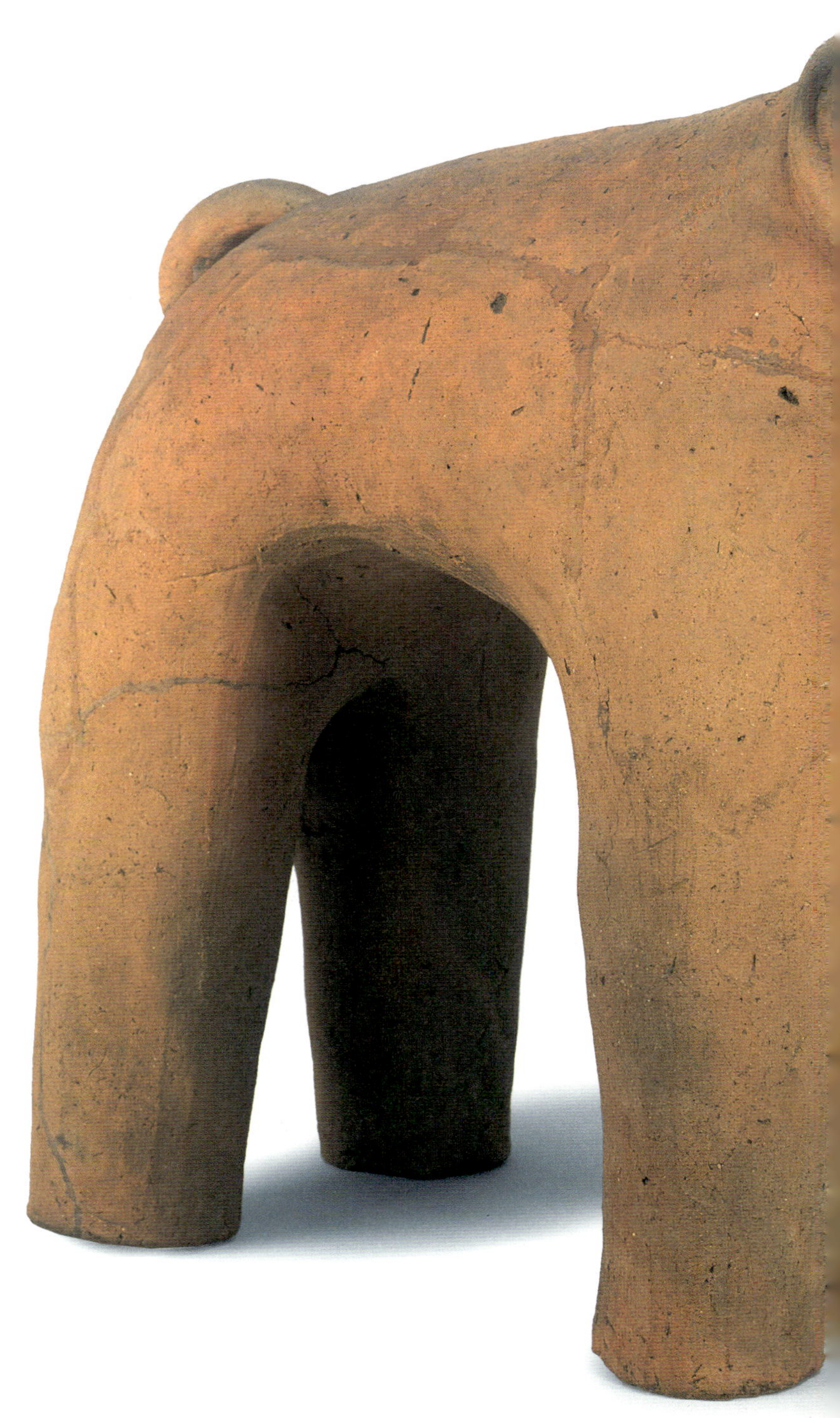

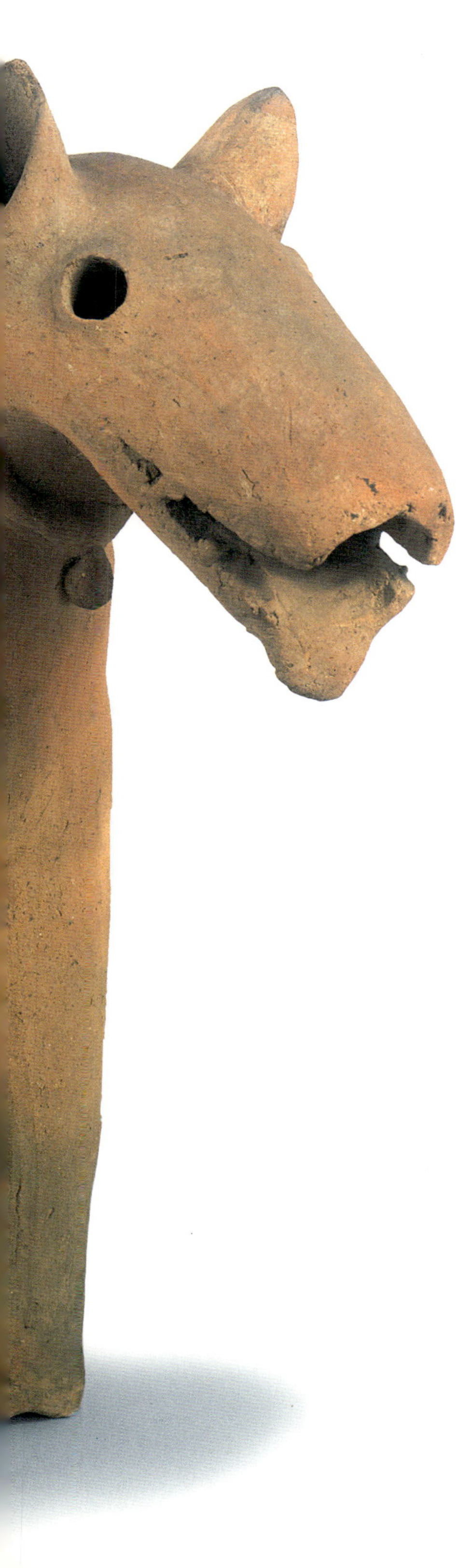

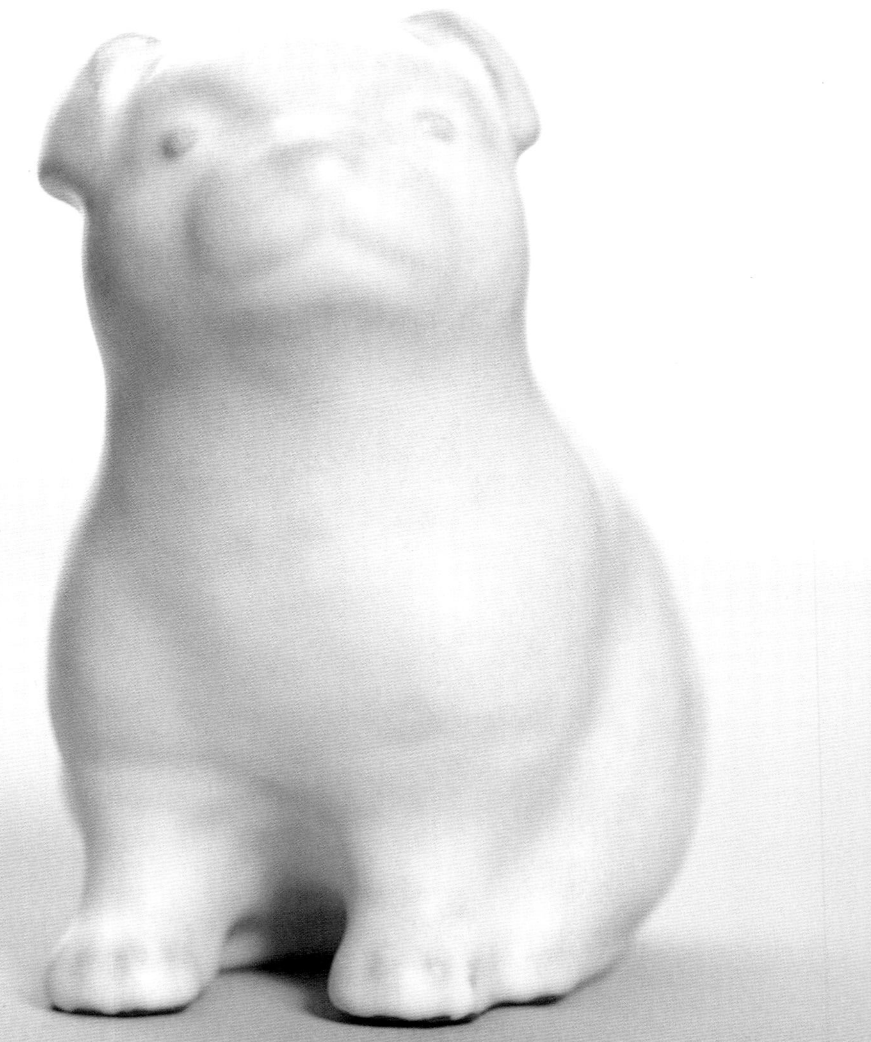

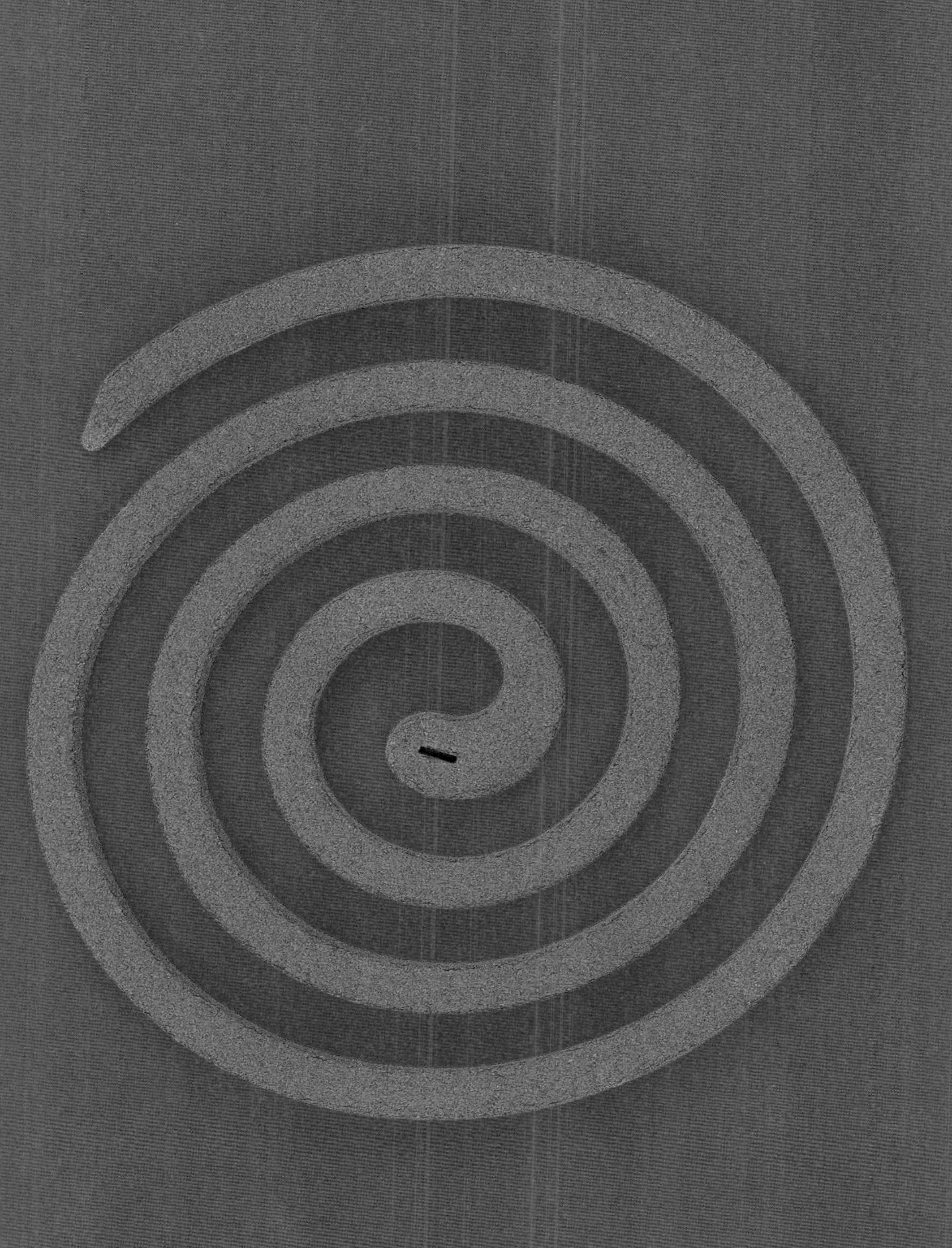

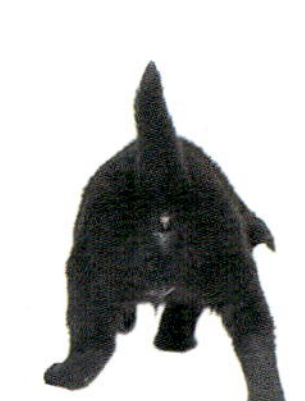

撮影・取材協力

南佐久郡南部森林組合
藤原忠彦
植島幸弘・愛子
野沢 清
秦泉寺宗昭
大杉潔巳
国沢光雄
池田大助
田名和歩
弓削田 忍
花田紀夫
北野雅夫
岩田圭司
小熊哲造
酒井東陽一
加藤英敏
久保敏幸
島崎 泰
田路雅之
水之江隆臣
原田眞太郎
細田吉人
遠藤莞爾
遠藤兵治
山崎良信
寺山良法
工藤照義
柴田孝一
武田幸士
菊地 力
内田千良
新垣義雄
弘瀬隆司
真間 茂
袖山隆男
前田民子
橋本幸彦
(社)日本犬保存会 卯木照邦
(財)高木伝統園芸文化振興財団 高木盆栽美術館

図版協力

14-15, 18-19	高木春山「本草図説」　西尾市岩瀬文庫蔵
167	御所人形「狗子持」　京都国立博物館蔵
168-169	引礼類 小犬　京都国立博物館蔵
172, 174, 176	碇に菖蒲文様 菊に狗児文様掛下帯　東京国立博物館蔵
180-183	円山応挙「柳下狗子図」　大乗寺蔵
184	三島蕉窓「狗子図」　東京国立博物館蔵
186	円山応挙「朝顔狗子杉戸」　東京国立博物館蔵
188-189	円山応挙「朝顔狗図」　東京国立博物館蔵
190-191	竹内栖鳳「皇居造営下絵 土筆に犬図」　東京国立博物館蔵
192-193	竹内栖鳳「皇居造営下絵 土筆に小犬図」　東京国立博物館蔵
194-195	張子の犬(明恵上人遺愛品複製)　(財)紙の博物館蔵
196	俵屋宗達「狗子図」　個人蔵
390-391	埴輪 犬　東京国立博物館蔵

Image: TNM Image Archives　Source: http://TnmArchives.jp/

日本の犬

十二支　第十一番　戌・犬
2005 年 12 月 8 日　初版第 1 刷発行

アートディレクション　高岡一弥
写真　久留幸子

企画編集　高岡一弥
デザイン　山崎恵　加藤剛章
制作進行　小澤研太郎　山本智子（PIE BOOKS）
テキスト進行　深谷恵美
翻訳　パメラ・ミキ
製版　高柳昇（東京印書館）
印刷進行　長澤隆司（東京印書館）

発行者　三芳伸吾
発行所　ピエ・ブックス
〒 170-0005 東京都豊島区南大塚 2-32-4
編集 TEL: 03-5395-4820 FAX: 03-5395-4821
営業 TEL: 03-5395-4811 FAX: 03-5395-4812
e-mail:（編集）editor@piebooks.com/
　　　　（営業）sales@piebooks.com
HP: http://www.piebooks.com

印刷・製本　株式会社 東京印書館
Book and Cover Design © 2005 Kazuya Takaoka
Photographs © 2005 Sachiko Kuru
© Photo Daijyoji/digital file by DNPAC

Published by PIE BOOKS

ISBN4-89444-493-3 C0072
Printed in Japan